OXFORD READINGS IN FEMINISM

FEMINISM AND 'RACE'

PUBLISHED IN THIS SERIES

Feminism and Science
edited by Evelyn Fox Keller and Helen E. Longino

Feminism, the Public and the Private
edited by Joan Landes

Feminism and Politics
edited by Anne Phillips

Feminism and History
edited by Joan Wallach Scott

Feminism and Cultural Studies
edited by Morag Shiach

OXFORD READINGS IN FEMINISM

Feminism and 'Race'

Edited by

Kum-Kum Bhavnani

OXFORD
UNIVERSITY PRESS

Great Clarendon Street, Oxford OX2 6DP

Oxford University Press is a department of the University of Oxford.
It furthers the University's objective of excellence in research, scholarship,
and education by publishing worldwide in

Oxford New York

Auckland Cape Town Dar es Salaam Hong Kong Karachi Kuala Lumpur
Madrid Melbourne Mexico City Nairobi New Delhi Shanghai Taipei Toronto

With offices in

Argentina Austria Brazil Chile Czech Republic France Greece
Guatemala Hungary Italy Japan South Korea Poland Portugal
Singapore Switzerland Thailand Turkey Ukraine Vietnam

Oxford is a registered trade mark of Oxford University Press
in the UK and in certain other countries

Published in the United States
by Oxford University Press Inc., New York

First published 2001

British Library Cataloguing in Publication Data
Data available

Library of Congress Cataloging in Publication Data
Data available

ISBN 978-0-19-878236-0

Typeset in Minion
by RefineCatch Limited, Bungay, Suffolk
Printed in Great Britain
on acid-free paper by
Biddles Ltd., King's Lynn, Norfolk

Acknowledgements

Many people have helped me with this collection. I am grateful to Susan James and Teresa Brennan, along with Tim Barton of Oxford University Press for encouraging me in the early stages of this project. The anonymous reviewers of my proposal helped me to sharpen it and be more selective in the extracts I eventually included. The editors at Oxford University Press showed patience and understanding of what is required in producing such a collection, and, most recently, it was Miranda Vernon and Jo Stanbridge who made sure the volume went to press in a timely manner. The authors of the many important pieces without which this volume could not exist all co-operated with me as I edited their work, and many helped me contact the publishers when necessary. Peter Chua, Dana Collins, John Foran, and Susan James read the Introduction, making incisive comments. Thanks to all of you.

My thinking has been influenced by the writings of, and discussion with Chetan Bhatt, Avtar Brah, Angela Y. Davis, Stuart Hall, Susan James, Gail Lewis, Ann Phoenix, Esther Saraga, and Jane Shallice. Each has engaged with me at different times, have respected me enough to tell me when they disagree with me, and have never presumed to know my what I was thinking. Such intellectual (and personal) engagement has never failed to bring me pleasure. Raj Bhavnani's determination throughout her life, and my sisters' and their families' close support as well as their often irreverent yet respectful attitudes towards scholarly production have invariably helped me place my work in perspective: thank you Anil, Anjuli, Arun, Ashoke, Ian, Manju, Nil, and Reena.

My best friend, life-time companion, lover, and intellectual comrade, John Foran, has always been present for me when proofs had to be checked, bibliographies finalised, and meals ready. Our children, Cerina and Amal, often create turmoil just when I need the most peace, making sure that I never forget their importance to my work. This book is dedicated to the three of them for making me optimistic that it is possible to have a world without inequalities.

Kum-Kum Bhavnani
September 2000

Contents

Part II. Engaging the Debates

Part III. Shifting the Debates

Notes on Contributors

HALEH AFSHAR teaches Politics and Women's Studies at the University of York and Islamic Law at the Faculté Internationale de Droit Comparé at Strasbourg. She was born and raised in Iran where she worked as a journalist and a civil servant before the revolution. She has published extensively, her most recent book is *Women and Globalization* (edited with Stephanie Barrientos, 1999).

BINA AGARWAL is Professor of Economics at the Institute of Economic Growth, New Delhi. Her most recent book, *A Field of One's Own: Gender and Land Rights in South Asia* (1994), was awarded the A.K. Coomaraswamy Book Prize 1996 (Association for Asian Studies, USA), the Edgar Graham Book Prize 1996 (SOAS, University of London, UK), and the K.H. Batheja Award 1995–96 (University of Bombay, India). She is currently working on some theoretical and empirical aspects of gender, environment, and collective action.

M. JACQUI ALEXANDER is the Fuller-Maathai Associate Professor of Gender and Women's Studies at Connecticut College.

PAULA GUNN ALLEN, Emerita Professor UCLA, has won a number of awards for writing and scholarship. Her anthologies of critical studies and American Indian fiction include *Studies in American Indian Literature* (1983) and *Voice of the Turtle: American Indian Literature* (1997). Her other books include *The Sacred Hoop: Recovering the Feminine in American Indian Traditions* (1986) and poetry, including *Life Is A Fatal Disease* (1998).

VALERIE AMOS was appointed a Government Whip in the House of Lords in July 1998. In addition to her role as a Spokesperson on International Development, she also speaks on Social Security and Womens Issues. She was created a life peer in August 1997. She was born in Guyana, studied at the Universities of Warwick, Birmingham, and East Anglia and was awarded an Honorary Professorship at Thames Valley University in 1995 in recognition of her work on equality and social justice.

IEN ANG is Professor of Cultural Studies and Director of the Research Centre in Intercommunal Studies at the University of Western Sydney, Australia. She has published widely on issues of difference and diversity in media and cultural studies. Her forthcoming book is entitled *On Not Speaking Chinese: Living Between Asia and the West.*

GLORIA ANZALDUA has edited *Making Face, Making Soul/Haciendos Caras: Creative and Critical Perspectives by Feminists of Color* (1990) and is the author of *Interviews/Entrevistas* (forthcoming).

KUM-KUM BHAVNANI is Senior Editor of *Meridians* at Smith College and Professor of Sociology and Women's Studies at the University of California at Santa Barbara. She is author of *Talking Politics* (1991) and has guest edited Special Issues of *Feminism* and *Psychology and Signs*. Her current work draws on a cultural studies approach to better comprehend the interconnections of women, feminism, and development in the Third World.

AVTAR BRAH is Director of Social Studies in the Faculty of Continuing Education at Birkbeck College, University of London. She is author of *Cartographies of Diaspora: Contesting Identities* (1996). She is co-editor with Mary Hickman and Mairtin Mac an Ghaill of *Thinking Identities: Ethnicities, Racism and Culture* (1999) and *Global Futures: Migration, Environment and Globalisation* (1999), and with Annie Coombes of *Hybridity and its Discontents: Politics, Science and Culture* (2000).

BARBARA CHRISTIAN was Professor of African American Studies at the University of California, Berkeley. She died 25 June 2000, aged 56. She made a critical contribution to the debates over the relationship between race, class, and gender. She is well known for her book, *Black Women Novelists: The Development of a Tradition* (1980), and for her widely cited article, *The Race for Theory* (1987).

PATRICIA HILL COLLINS is Professor of Sociology and Chair of the Department of African American Studies at the University of Cincinnati. She is author of *Black Feminist Thought: Knowledge, Consciousness, and the Politics of Empowerment* (revised edition 2000) and *Fighting Words: Black Women and the Search for Justice* (1998).

MARGARET COULSON has taught sociology and women's studies in Scotland, the north of England and more recently, in Australia at the University of Wollongong. Challenged and informed by the impacts of 'race' on feminism since the 1970s, she has worked for change and policy developments in tertiary education. Her book, *Approaching Sociology* (1997), co-authored with Carol Riddell, has been translated into Dutch, French, Spanish, and Portuguese.

ANGELA Y. DAVIS is the author of five books, including *Women, Race and Class* (1983), *Women, Culture and Politics* (1989), and *Blue Legacies and Black Feminism: Gertrude 'Ma' Rainey, Bessie Smith and Billie Holiday* (1999). She is Professor of History of Consciousness at University of California, Santa Cruz.

ANN DUCILLE is Chair of African-American Studies at Wesleyan University. She is the author of *The Coupling Convention: Sex, Text, and Tradition in Black Women's* Fiction (1993) and *Skin Trade* (1996).

RUTH FRANKENBERG is the author of *White Women, Race Matters: The Social Construction of Whiteness* (1993). She is editor of *Displacing Whiteness: Essays in Social and Cultural Criticism* (1997). Her ethnography in progress is *Faith as Praxis: Poetics, Politics, Epistemology.*

EVELYNN HAMMONDS is Associate Professor of the History of Science in the Program of Science, Technology, and Society at the Massachusetts Institute of Technology. She is currently completing a new book entitled *The Logic of Difference: A History of 'Race' in Science and Medicine in the United States.*

DONNA HARAWAY is a Professor in the History of Consciousness Department at the University of California at Santa Cruz, where she teaches feminist theory, science studies, and women's studies. She is the author of *Primate Visions: Gender, Race, and Nature in the World of Modern Science* (1989 and 1992); *Simians, Cyborgs, and Women: The Reinvention of Nature* (1991), and *Modest_Witness@Second_Millennium.FemaleMan© Meets OncoMouse™* (1997). Her present project, *Birth of the Kennel: Alpha Bitches Online*, analyzes webs of action in dog-human culture.

BELL HOOKS is the author of *Feminist Theory from Margin to Center* (1984), *Talking Back: Thinking Feminist, Thinking Black* (1984), *Ain't I a Woman: Black Women and Feminism* (1998), *All About Love* (2000) and *Feminism is for Everybody: Passionate Politics* (forthcoming).

LATA MANI has written articles on feminism, colonial historiography, postcolonialism, and the interface of the sacred and secular life. She is the author of *Contentious Traditions: The Debate on Sati in Colonial India* (1999).

MARNIA LAZREG is the author of *Eloquence of Silence: Algerian Women in Question* (1994) and *Making the Transition Work for Women in Europe and Central Asia* (2000).

GERDA LERNER is the author of many books including *Why History Matters* (1997) and *The Creation of Feminist Consciousness: From the Middle Ages to 1870* (1994). She has also edited *Black Women in White America: A Documentary History* (1992).

GAIL LEWIS is Lecturer in Social Policy at the Open University. She was a member of the Brixton Black Women's Group and a founder member of the Organisation of Women of African and Asian Descent (OWAAD), the first national black women organisation in Britain. Her current research interests focus on processes of construction of gendered and racialised difference and how these processes are articulated in past and contemporary social policy. She has recently published *'Race', Gender, Social Welfare: Encounters in a Postcolonial Society* (2000).

AUDRE LORDE is the author of *Sister Outsider: Essays and Speeches* (1984), *I Am Your Sister: Black Women Organizing Across Sexualities* (1986), and *Collected Poems of Audre Lorde* (1997).

MARIANNE H. MARCHAND is Senior Lecturer in the Department of Political Science and member of the Belle Van Zuijlen Institute and the Amsterdam School of Social Science Research at the University of Amsterdam. Recently she published *Gender and Global Restructuring: Sightings, Sites and Resistances* (with Anne Sisson Runyan, 2000). She is also the co-editor of the RIPE Series in *Global Political Economy*.

MARY MAYNARD is Professor in the Department of Social Policy and Social Work at the University of York, UK, where she is also head of the Social Policy Section. She previously lectured in the Department of Sociology and was Director of the Centre for Women's Studies. Her main interests are social and feminist theory, research methodologies, gender and women's studies, ethnicities, and later life. She is writing about feminist methodology and co-directing comparative research on women and ageing.

MARIA MIES is (retired) Professor of Sociology at Fachhochschule Köln in Germany. In 1979 she initiated the programme 'Women and Development' at the Institute of Social Studies in The Hague. She has been active in the feminist and ecology movements since the late sixties and has published a number of articles and books related to these themes.

TRINH T. MINH-HA is a writer, filmmaker, and composer. Her work includes a multi-media installation (in collaboration, *Nothing but Ways,* 1999); seven books, including *Cinema Interval* (1999) and *Drawn from African Dwellings* (with Jean-Paul Bourdier, 1996); and five feature-length films, including *Shoot for the Contents* (1992) and *A Tale of Love* (1996). She is Professor in Women's Studies, Film Studies and Rhetoric at the University of California at Berkeley.

CHANDRA TALPADE MOHANTY is Professor of Women's Studies at Hamilton College and core faculty at the Union Institute Graduate School, Cincinnati. She is co-editor of *Third World Women and the Politics of Feminism* (1991) and *Feminist Genealogies, Colonial Legacies, Democratic Futures* (1997). Her current work focuses on globalization, higher education and anti-racist feminist praxis.

MOLARA OGUNDIPE-LESLIE is the author of *Re-Creating Ourselves: African Women and Critical Transformations* (1994).

AIHWA ONG is Professor of Anthropology in the Department of Anthropology at the University of California, Berkeley.

PRATIBHA PARMAR is an award-winning filmmaker whose films and videos have been shown internationally on television and at film festivals. Her films include *A Place of Rage, Khush, Brimful of Asia, The Righteous Babes,* and *Warrior Marks.* She has written and edited several books including *Warrior Marks: Female Genital Mutilation and the Sexual Blinding of Women,* co-authored with Alice Walker and published in the UK and US.

JANE L. PARPART is Professor of History, Women's Studies and International Development Studies at Dalhousie University. She is also Visiting Professor of Political Science at Stellenbosch University in South Africa. She is a research fellow at the University of Zimbabwe where she is currently carrying out a research project on notions of modernity, progress, and development among the African elite of Bulawayo, Zimbabwe.

ANNIE PHIZACKLEA is author with Carol Walkowitz of *Homeworking Women: Gender, Racism and Class at Work* (1995) and with Robert Miles of *Trades Union Congress, Black Workers and New Commonwealth Immigration, 1954–73* (1997).

ANN PHOENIX is a Senior Lecturer in Psychology at the Open University. Her research interests include motherhood and social identities (including 'those of 'race', ethnicity, and gender). She is author with Barbara Tizard of *Black, White or Mixed Race? Race and Racism in the Lives of Young People of Mixed Parentage* (1993), and editor with Kum-Kum Bhavnani of *Shifting Identities, Shifting Racisms* (1994) and with K. Henwood and C. Griffin of *Standpoints and Differences* (1998).

CHELA SANDOVAL is Associate Professor of Critical Theory for the Department of Chicano Studies at the University of California at Santa Barbara. She is a member of the History of Consciousness School of Cultural Theory, and a participant of the Women of Color Cohort. She is the author of numerous articles including *Theorizing White Consciousness for a Post-Empire World.* Her forthcoming book is entitled *Methodology of the Oppressed.*

VANDANA SHIVA is author of *Staying Alive: Women, Ecology and Development* (1989) and *Stolen Harvest: The Hijacking of the Global Food Supply* (2000). She is also author with Maria Mies of *Ecofeminism* (1993) and editor with Ingunn Moser of *Biopolitics: A Feminist and Ecological Reader on Biotechnology* (1995).

ELIZABETH V. SPELMAN is Professor of Philosophy and the Barbara Richmond 1940 Professor in the Humanities at Smith College. The author of *Inessential Woman: Problems of Exclusion in Feminist Thought* (1989) and *Fruits of Sorrow: Framing Our Attention to Suffering* (1998), she is presently at work on a book about the nature of repair.

LOLA YOUNG is Professor of Cultural Studies at Middlesex University. She has written and broadcast widely on television and radio, on issues of 'race', gender and representation, black British culture, and film. She is the author of *Fear of the Dark: 'Race', Gender and Sexuality in Cinema* (1996). Professor Young is currently Project Director for the National Museum and Archives of Black History and Culture (NMABHC).

NIRA YUVAL-DAVIS is a Professor and Post-Graduate Course Director in Gender and Ethnic Studies at the University of Greenwich, London. She has written extensively on nationalism, racism, fundamentalism, and gender relations theoretically and in relation to Britain and Europe, as well as to Israel/Palestine and other settler societies. Among her books are *Gender and Nation* (1997) and *Women, Citizenship and Difference* (1999).

Introduction

Kum-Kum Bhavnani

A volume such as this invariably omits too much, and can therefore appear incomplete to those who are familiar with the debates and discussions. That is the anxiety with which all editors and teachers live—have I said it all? What was not intended yet could be read into the omissions? The usual response to such questions is that it is rarely possible to say it all—because there is too much to be said. While such a response is reasonable, it still begs the question of why, then, have I decided to include a particular piece or argument rather than another. What are the implications of my selections? In this Introduction, I will focus on these implications, so that the reader may comprehend the rationale for this volume.

The past two decades have seen the incursion of feminist thought into many academic areas. Within the academy—for example in the social sciences, the humanities, law, geography, international studies and the natural sciences—feminist approaches have gained some legitimacy. Simultaneous with these disciplinary advances, the charge of racism has been directed at feminist theory, with the result that feminist work, both scholarship and political action—has had to continuously reshape itself. This has been done to a large extent by engaging with ideas that circulate in relation to identity and the politics of location,[1] by thinking through the implications of difference for feminist work, and by paying close attention to histories of colonization and the ways in which those histories affect present day arguments about post-coloniality and imperialism.

Identity is an area that has influenced feminist scholarship as well as being heavily influenced by this scholarship. From the social psychological approaches to identity—often rooted in experimental work—to the more recent work of Judith Butler, for example, it can be seen that identity is a term that travels across disciplinary boundaries—rather like feminism—and 'captures succinctly the possibilities of unraveling the complexities of the relationship between "structure" and agency'[2] Thus, although identity politics is often decried as an essentialist discourse, it is also the case that work on identity, and the political ramifications of like-identified people coming together, have often prompted European and North American feminist scholarship to shift its focus of interest (e.g. Grewal *et al.* 1988).[3]

Difference, in feminist thought, was initially taken to refer to the difference between women and men. The use of difference to signal racism and ethnocentrism (as well as 'race' and ethnicity)[4] proved to be a further impetus for feminist work to engage issues of representation. In addition, difference has become the pivot through which many feminist scholars have interrogated the fundamental bases of feminist intellectual projects. Yet 'difference' itself is contested, and used in different ways by different analysts. For example, Henrietta Moore points out that 'such is the malleability of the term that almost anything can be subsumed under it' (Moore, 1994, p. 1).[5] For Donna Gabaccia,[6] by contrast, difference starts by examining the experience of migratory women. Her book then moves on to look at the relationship between world development, migration and immigrant life in the United States. In the process, she focuses on the interconnections between varying meanings of difference to see how foreign immigrant women redefine the meaning of American womanhood. Her work also demonstrates that through an attention to gender it is possible to see the differences between how African-Americans and other minorities are viewed in the United States, and that the making of a distinction between African-Americans and 'the rest' also serves to reproduce the powerful delineation between 'race' and ethnicity that structures most writings about 'race' in the United States.

Discussions of colonialism and imperialism have also had a significant impact on contemporary feminist scholarship, as well as being influenced by it. Researchers of these issues have started to recognize that woman is not only an agent and a subject on axes of inequality such as class, sexuality and age, as well as 'race', (see Mani 1998 for such an analysis)[7] but also that the focus of feminist enquiry must, of necessity, be a world-wide focus, and not centred on Europe, North America and Australia/New Zealand.[8] It is also necessary to say that much of this recognition by white feminists was achieved through struggles by women of colour—feminists and others—showing the racism that was, and still is, intrinsic to many parts of the women's movements and feminist scholarship in The North (e.g. Smith).[9] It is also the case that many women from The North—of colour or otherwise—are coming to realize that the anti-colonial struggles and struggles of women in the Third World, are critical for understanding how gender subordination is both reproduced and challenged everywhere.[10] As a result, this dynamic intellectual relationship between analyses of colonialism in the Third World and feminist scholarship has meant that closer attention is being paid by feminist scholars to concepts such as 'diaspora' or a 'politics of location'.[11]

This edited volume draws upon three strands—identity, difference and colonialism—in order to represent the strength as well as the diversity of writings which discuss 'race' and feminism. In this way, readers can see how these two modalities—usually considered to be discrete—have developed a close relationship with each other in the past two decades. To date, there is no one volume that pulls together a range of writings on 'race' and feminism from many differing standpoints and origins. While the relationship between 'race' and feminism is present in some of the chapters in retrospective collections such as those by Lovell[12] and Kauffman,[13] these collections focus on either the USA or Britain, thus avoiding analysis of the way in which writings from both sites have informed, influenced or diverged from each other. Further, it is clear that as feminist work in Third World and Development Studies is drawn upon to a greater extent by feminist scholars in the West, issues which were often thought only to be of relevance to women living in the Third World are now understood to be central for the projects of feminisms.[14]

I have previously written a review of the literature on 'race' and feminism,[15] and here shall summarize some of its main themes:

- a demand for visibility and inclusion for women of colour within feminist writings, with a consequent resolve for explicit acknowledgement and analysis of racial/ethnic difference;
- a teasing out of the historical and representational implications of such analyses with a particular focus on difference;
- most recently, a set of arguments which both suggest new boundaries for feminist studies and insist that, for feminist theorizing to be of value, scholars must engage not only with the agency of women of colour in the West, but also of women in the Third World.

The first category, which has formed the basis of many debates within feminism in the past two decades, has demonstrated powerfully the weaknesses and failings of second wave feminisms. The central point, made in different, yet complementary, ways is that an assumption that woman is a unitary (and, by implication ahistorical) category is misguided at best, and theoretically and politically hazardous at worst. For this latter reason, feminists of colour and women of colour in Europe and North America often wrote angrily at the racism of 'feminist' analyses. The racism they identified was expressed either as an invisibility of women of colour—from analyses of the state, where welfare and immigration policies were rarely critiqued for their racism, from discussions of employment, and from feminist examinations of the family and sexuality—or, as one in which women of colour were seen as epitomizing an issue, be it free and frequent heterosexual liaisons (in the case of women of African origin) or subjection to strict patriarchal/familial codes (in the case of women of South Asian or North African origin). Even when women of colour were considered in mainstream feminist scholarship, it was argued that this inclusion was merely an 'add-on' and did not decentre white women in feminist scholarship and practices, and thus avoided engaging with the tricky question of how feminist endeavours might be transformed as a result of such inclusion. For these reasons, many scholarly writings in the early 1980s directed analyses of women's exploitation and oppression away from a notion of woman as a unitary and Western category, and towards analyses that were more inclusive of all women, while not resorting to tokenistic inclusion of non-white, non-Western women. It is this work that formed the basis of the debates during the late 1970s and 1980s, and the chapters in Section One reflect the range of issues, politics and tone that were used to force open the discussion of racism and ethnocentrism within feminism.

Writings on difference have always informed feminist work, and Audre Lorde's classic 'Age, Race, Class and Sex: Women Redefining Difference'[16] contains ideas that have now become commonplace within these discussions. Her work is important because, in earlier writings, difference was taken to refer to differences between men and women, and it was assumed that 'difference' operated in opposition to the creation of equality between women and men (see Bock and James for a more recent collection that avoids this dichotomy[17]). That debate—on equality and difference—has also shifted, and much of the feminist writing that uses 'race' and ethnicity as a starting point for its understandings of difference (in terms of the state, multi-culturalism, sexuality, the nation and colonialism) argues that 'difference' is a concept that can be worked with, rather than being a concept that divides women from each other.

The emphasis on difference became clearer because women of colour, in writing about racism in relation to women's movements and feminism, often drew on our experience as a starting point to demonstrate why attention to 'race' was a central aspect for feminist analyses. We used our experiences to point to some of the difficulties we had with the prevailing (which we often called 'white') feminist analyses. For example, we wrote about how our families could be a shelter against the racisms directed at people of colour in the First World and not simply a site for the reproduction of patriarchal inequalities, about how immigration laws usually operated to separate us from those families, a separation that seemed to be common for all those who migrated to the First World and yet was rarely discussed as being relevant for feminism, and we wrote, often very angrily, about how the 'sisterhood is global' discourse denied us the space to assert our differences from white women and masked the power inequalities present within women's movements.[18]

The consequence of this simultaneous focus upon experience and difference meant that discussions of difference shifted to a new level, and discussions now focus both on how difference is to be represented and how knowledge about difference is created. Representation, knowledge production and processes of difference are intimately inscribed within and by each other, so that representational questions often converge on visual, literary and historical representations as well as on research practices.[19] Thus, discussions of 'race', ethnicity and racism within feminist scholarship and practice have led to thorough and sensitive analyses of the relationship between difference, representation and knowledge construction, and the chapters in Section Two aim to cover those concerns.

Yet it is evident that feminist work addresses much more than the above. Juliet Mitchell's[20] now classic categorization of women's subordination into the domains of production, reproduction, socialization and sexuality (see Bhavnani, 1997 for an amendment to this categorization) is helpful—and it is clear that attempts to ensure that feminist work does not have white or Western women as its main referent has consequently produced a wider set of issues for feminist analysts and critics. While production, reproduction, socialization and sexuality are still key to developing feminist insights over 25 years after Mitchell introduced them, it has also become evident that such insights simultaneously warrant new ways of thinking about identity, class, the state, colonization, international and global processes and politics. This last, politics and political change—both within and outside the academy—is intrinsic to feminist projects, and, it could be argued, is the source of the present urgency to develop new ways of being, acting and changing.

THE VOLUME

The first section of this collection—The Basis for the Debates—includes extracts that allow a reader to become acquainted with the fundamentals of the arguments. The articles have been selected to reflect a variety of analytic styles and tones. Some of the arguments appear extremely familiar. However, it is worth noting that at the time when they first appeared in academically respectable arenas, their publication was experienced by many of us as a relief, because although they drew upon feminist thinking, they simultaneously presented powerful and systematic arguments as to why the projects of feminism were failing.[21] We were not alone, and started to realize that our work at conferences such as the UK Socialist Feminist Conference held in Manchester in 1979, attended by close to 1000 women, when a few hundred were expected,[22] was beginning to lead to some change.

In the first chapter, Valerie Amos and Pratibha Parmar develop the work of Hazel Carby[23] to argue that feminism as understood and experienced by many black women[24] was an imperialist project, while bell hooks' chapter demonstrates the ways in which the underlying discourses of what is claimed to be feminist theorizing reproduces racist notions of black women. These points still have resonance 15 years later. The historical work that underlay these arguments—for example by Gerda Lerner and Angela Davis—demonstrates the extent of the difficulty of challenging the hegemony of white/Western feminist thought, particularly with regard to historical framings of what is meant by 'woman', and who counted as a 'real' feminist. Paula Gunn Allen urgently reminded all feminists that the causes and politics of both black and white feminists often excluded indigenous women, a reminder that is as telling now as it was when it was first published.

In the same period, Kum-Kum Bhavnani and Margaret Coulson argued that socialist feminists needed to do as much work on theorizing patriarchies as liberal, cultural and radical feminists, while Elizabeth Spelman's argument about the 'ampersand problem' in feminist work dovetailed with a key point in the Bhavnani and Coulson argument about the need for feminist scholarship and politics to be transformed if charges of racism were to be taken seriously by feminist academics. At the same time, yet in a different vein, Audre Lorde insisted that feminist methods of analysis and resistance should not replicate prevailing modes of thought and practice, an insistence exemplified in the extract from Gloria Anzaldua's 1987 book. Finally, Aihwa Ong, writing from the USA as a woman of colour, firmly reminded feminist scholars that 'the non-feminist Other is not so much patriarchy as the non-Western woman'[25]—in other words, she argued that feminist scholarship, while claiming to be oppositional to mainstream academic enterprise, had fallen prey to a colonial, hegemonic world view in which women in the Third World are constructed as fixed in 'sexualities and natural capacities'.[26]

To summarize, the articles included in the first section demonstrated that the invisibility of women in white feminist analyses, showed how such an invisibility was synonymous with exclusion, and therefore showed how that exclusion reproduced racist and ethnocentric ideas within feminist work, both inside and outside the academy. While some have suggested otherwise, it is also evident from the writings of these feminists that they refused to define all white feminism as being monolithic—that is, most of the writers in this section differentiated between different types of feminisms, and between different types of white women. Thus, in these extracts, one can already see the beginnings of subsequent discussions on how to theorize and act upon the intersections of feminist thinking with other axes of inequality such as 'race', class and sexuality.

The second section—Engaging the Debates—starts by demonstrating how the interconnections between feminist work and 'race' (among others) could be conceptualized through reflecting on difference. The overall argument by Mary Maynard is that if a serious analysis of the concept of difference were to be conducted, it would permit feminist thinking to develop in an innovative manner, rather than remain in the impasse in which it currently finds itself. Other ways of engaging the debates were achieved through the writings of Molara Ogundipe-Leslie who showed how the concept of the 'African woman' was at best an unhelpful notion, while Donna Haraway also engages with difference through an examination of the study of primatology. The Haraway extract demonstrates the importance of nuancing many approaches to the study of society—human or primate—and she achieves this by reflecting simultaneously on identity and difference in her discussions. Her argument touches on issues of representation by discussing the representations of those who study primate behaviour, and it is a concern with how identities are represented, that is also discussed by Trinh T. Minh-ha. Trinh considers identity in the context of displacement and marginalization and suggests that a hyphenated identity is one means of signalling the means by which these conditions come to be firmly embedded in public memory. Similar issues are taken up in the chapter by Lola Young on cultural criticism and the cinema, but with a preference for drawing upon psychoanalytic insights—a key trope in some feminist approaches to difference.

Patricia Hill Collins also engages debates about 'race' and feminism by suggesting that an epistemological shift is needed within feminist thought, and argues for an African-centred feminist epistemology. While it has been argued that this argument runs counter to the anti-essentialist tenor of many feminist writings in this period, and merely reproduces a monolithic notion of the 'African woman', others have found her work to be helpful in developing an intellectual identity for African-American women. Ann Phoenix also engages with epistemological issues through her discussions of research practices, and her thoughtful insights into the relationship between the researcher and researched have given many social scientists pause for thought. This focus on the construction of knowledge is continued within the humanities by Barbara Christian in her chapter on historical novels by African-American women. Her argument, like her now classic piece on the 'race for theory', shows how and why the writings by black women about slavery have taken the forms they have, and it is evident that her contribution to the debates has influenced Ann duCille. duCille also focuses on African-American women's writings—but in her case she reflects on the delicacy of the tensions and relationships that are negotiated in the current surge in literary representations of African-American women, and thus opens up possibilities for reflecting on how critique and change affect each other.

Marnia Lazreg and Chela Sandoval, self-defined feminists, engage with difference as politics—Lazreg through her analysis of the relationship between identity politics and feminist practices in relation to women and religion in Algeria, while Sandoval turns her gaze to US Third World women (for which read US-based women of colour) who, she argues, demonstrate an 'oppositional consciousness'[27] in their construction of feminisms.

Thus, it can be seen that feminist scholars whose work focused on 'race'/ethnicity in the late 1980s and up to the mid-1990s explicitly engaged with the debates laid out in the first section by seeing the issues through the lens of difference—and by calling for more detailed work on the intersections of 'race' with other axes of inequality—not just gender, but also class and sexuality. However, some of the work on difference and representation seems to be talking past other discussions of difference. For example, Molara Ogundipe Leslie and Patricia Hill Collins approach questions of difference and representation rather differently, even though both focus on the epistemological implications of their critiques for feminist thought. Equally, although both Barbara Christian and Ann du Cille engage with representation, sharing similar anxieties about African-American women's writings, they approach the issue of what constitutes 'black feminism' in the United States in ways that are clearly distinct. In a similar vein, the commentaries of Young and Trinh reflect the wide variety of approaches that feminists have taken, and continue to take, in discussions of representation. Thus, difference and representation have been central to critiques of hegemonic feminist thought, and this has led to some critics arguing that an emphasis on representation has meant that many socialist feminist and Marxist feminist insights on the state have been sidestepped and forgotten.

The final section of the book—Shifting the Debates—demonstrates that when feminism is conceptualized as having 'race' and ethnicity inscribed within itself, a utopian idea it must be admitted but valuable none the less, it becomes possible to address issues that are not only diverse but appropriately complicated. Continuing to use Juliet Mitchell's work, this section is organized around pieces which look at production, reproduction, socialization and sexuality in ways that Mitchell perhaps never imagined when she wrote *Women's Estate* in 1971. Gail Lewis, writing in the mid-1980s, looks anew at issues of production by carefully detailing the ways in which the state has regulated black women's employment in Britain while Annie Phizacklea examines the same issue through her assessment of the implications of migration for women. In their powerful critique of strategies of population control, Vandana Shiva and Maria Mies not only re-examine reproduction, but, in so doing, discuss the role of the state in regulating women's lives. Haleh Afshar and Nira Yuval Davis, writing about women, religion and feminisms, focus on the socialization of women, and the ways in which women use religious heritage to develop public concern about the plight of women and on the ways in which Muslim women in Iran may be creating new feminisms. Finally, Evelyn Hammonds' discussion of her personal, political and intellectual relationship to queer theory and black lesbianism provides a new way of reflecting on sexuality and 'race'. These articles, as well as the ones that follow them, draw upon work from many geographical locations including the Third World, for it is becoming increasingly evident that the engagement of feminism with 'race' demands that attention be paid to writing, scholarship and action across the globe.

While Juliet Mitchell's typology is still helpful, it clearly needs further development given the dramatic shifts in conceptions of global, political, economic, cultural, social and ideological. Thus, Bina Agarwal takes issue with ecofeminism by showing that some of the arguments it employs, plausible and tempting as they may be, are incomplete or inaccurate. Both Ang and Brah challenge simplistic notions of an all-inclusive feminism—Ang by revealing the links between multicultural approaches to feminism and nationalist ideology, Brah by taking us through the reasons why discussions of difference have often been so disparate and apparently unconnected. Ruth Frankenberg and Lata Mani show us how a politics of location is implicated in what is defined as colonialism, and Jacqui Alexander and Chandra Mohanty take such an argument to its logical conclusion by specifying the links between 'race' and feminism in the First World, and between those arguments and Third World feminisms in general. Their notion of a feminist democracy is intriguing, focusing as it does on the role of the state in creating possibilities and obstacles for women's liberation. Finally, the chapter by Parpart and Marchand examines how feminist work on development is informed by contemporary debates on post-modernism, and argues that 'an approach to development that accepts and understands difference and the power of discourse . . . can empower women in the South to articulate their own needs and agendas'.[28]

A final word on the pieces I have selected. Feminism has successfully legitimated the use of autobiographical insights in scholarly work and the pieces in this collection are no exception. Some are straightforwardly autobiographical, while others draw upon personal history to make a general scholarly point. The articles also span a number of disciplinary areas. This is the nature of the beast—writings on 'race' and feminism demand a rethinking of single disciplinary endeavours such as history, philosophy sociology and literary criticism, and also require multi- or trans-disciplinary analyses. In order to provide a narrative of the scholarship on feminism and 'race', and to allow readers to assess the complexities of the arguments contained within it, it is necessary to include writings that address issues within one discipline as well as to include writings that span disciplines, issues and styles. It might have been possible simply to summarize some of the debates through the judicious use of review articles and chapters. Yet, all too often, such reviews, by their very nature, cannot adequately convey the passion and sometimes anger that motivated the authors to write. I have deliberately rejected the 'review' strategy so that readers may see the wide range of tone as well as range of styles that have shaped the debates. My goal has been to include articles—some of which I do not agree with—that will allow the reader both to see how much has shifted during the past two decades, and to see how much more needs changing. The arguments in the chapters also demonstrate the differences and disagreements that exist among these contributors: that is, there is not a unified or unitary perspective that informs discussions of feminism and 'race'. In this way, I trust the volume will provide some insights into the politics, history and theory of how second wave feminisms have negotiated 'race', as well as indicating the direction being taken by these debates at the end of the twentieth century.

August 1999

Notes

1. Henrietta Moore, *A Passion for Difference: Essays in Anthropology and Gender* (Bloomington: Indiana University Press, 1994).
2. Bhavnani and Phoenix, 'Editorial Introduction: Shifting Identities Shifting Racisms', *Feminism and Psychology* (Special Issue), 4 (1994), 6.
3. Shabnum Grewal, Jackie Kay, Liliane Landor, Gail Lewis and Pratibha Parmar (eds.), *Charting the Journey. Writings by Black and Third World Women* (London: Sheba Feminist Publishers, 1988), 6. George Lipsitz's marvellous book, *The Possessiveness Investment in Whiteness: How White People Profit from Identity Politics* (Philadephia: Temple University Press), is one aspect of identities that are not discussed in this Introduction, mainly because although his work is stunning in its breadth and analysis, it is not one that draws explicitly on feminist scholarship.
4. I write 'race' with quotation marks to signal that the concept has no validity for human biology yet has a powerful presence in human societies.
5. Moore, *A Passion for Difference*, 1.
6. Donna Gabbaccia, *From the Other Side: Women, Gender and Immigrant Life in the U.S. 1820–1990* (Bloomington: Indiana University Press, 1994).
7. Lata Mani, *Contentious Traditions: The Debate on Sati in Colonial India* (Berkeley: University of California Press, 1998).
8. Rochelau in Dianne Rochelau, Barbara Thomas-Slayter and Esther Wangari (eds.), *Feminist Political Ecology: Global Issues and Local Experiences* (London and New York: Routledge, 1996); Saskia Wieringa Wieringa, *Subversive Women: Women's Movements in Africa, Asia, Latin America and the Caribbean* (London: Zed Books, 1995).
9. B. Smith, 'Racism and Women's Studies', in Gloria T. Hull, Patricia Bell Scott

and Barbara Smith (eds.), *All the Women are White, All the Blacks are Men, But Some of Us Are Brave* (New York: Feminist Press, 1982), 48–51.

10. Chandra Talpade Mohanty, 'Under Western Eyes: Feminist Scholarship and Colonial Discourses', *Feminist Review*, 30 (Autumn, 1988), 61–89; Uma Narayan, *Disclosing Cultures: Identities, Traditions and Third World Feminism* (London and New York: Routledge). I use 'Third World' to refer to regions in Africa, Asia (excluding Japan), the Middle East and Latin America.
11. Avtar Brah, 'Difference, Diversity, Differentiation', in Avtar Brah (ed.), *Cartographies of Diaspora: Contesting Identities* (London: Routledge, 1996), 95–127; Sharmeen Islam, 'Towards a Global Network of Asian Lesbians', in Rakesh Ratti (ed.), *A Lotus of Another Colour* (Boston: Alyson Publications, 1993), 41–6.
12. Terry Lovell (ed.), *British Feminist Thought* (Oxford: Basil Blackwell, 1990).
13. Linda Kauffman (ed.), *American Feminist Thought at Century's End* (Cambridge: Basil Blackwell, 1993).
14. Rigoberta Menchu, *I, Rigoberta Menchu: An Indian Woman in Guatemala* (London and New York: Verso, 1984).
15. Bhavnani, 'Women's Studies and its Interconnections with "Race", Ethnicity and Sexuality', in Diane Richardson and Victoria Robinson (eds.), *Introducing Women's Studies The Second Edition* (London: Macmillan Press, 1997) and *Thinking Feminist* (New York: New York University Press, 1997).
16. Audre Lorde, 'Age, Race, Class and Sex: Women Redefining Difference', in Audre Lorde (ed.), *Sister Outsider* (Freedom, CA: The Crossing Press, 1984), 123.
17. G. Bock and Susan James (eds.), *Beyond Equality and Difference* (London: Routledge, 1992).
18. See Julia Sudbury, *'Other Kinds of Dreams': Black Women's Organisations and the Politics of Transformation* (London and New York: Routledge, 1998), for an overview of these arguments in the UK from the 1970s to the 1990s and the autonomous black women's organizations that developed as a result.
19. For example, Reina Lewis, *Gendering Orientalism: Race, Femininity and Representation* (London: Routledge, 1996).
20. Juliet Mitchell, *Women's Estate* (London: Penguin, 1971).
21. Although not included, in the two years before the publication of Carby's chapter mentioned earlier, feminists of colour had been making similar points—in a much more piecemeal manner—at women's liberation and socialist feminist conferences, as well as through the production of anthologies such as: Gloria Anzaldua and Cherie Moraga (eds.), *This Bridge Called My Back* (Watertown, MA: Persephone Press, 1981) and Hull, *But Some of Us Are Brave*.
22. Kum-Kum Bhavnani and Pratibha Parmar, 'Racism and the Women's Movement'. Discussion Paper for Workshop on Women Against Racism and Fascism. *Socialist Feminist Conference 1979* (Manchester: Mimeo, 1979).
23. Hazel Carby's piece, 'White women Listen! Black Feminism and the Boundaries of Sisterhood', in Centre for Contemporary Cultural Studies, *The Empire Strikes Back: Race and Racism in 70s Britain* (London: Hutchison, 1982), could not be included in this collection because she is in the process of producing a volume of her own writings.
24. Black was used in Britain as a political term to denote the common experi-

ences of racism directed at non-white peoples. I say 'was' for it is evident to me that the term is not so popular in the late 1990s. The phrase most frequently used in the USA is 'people of colour', for there, black refers specifically to African-Americans.

25. Aihwa Ong, 'Colonialism and Modernity: Feminist Re-presentations of Women in Non-Western Societies', *Inscriptions*, Nos 3/4 (Santa Cruz: University of California Santa Cruz, 1988), 80.
26. Ong, 'Colonialism and Modernity', 81.
27. Chela Sandoval, 'U.S. Third World Feminism: The Theory and Method of Oppositional Consciousness in the Postmodern World', *Genders*, 10 (Spring 1991).
28. Marianne H. Marchand and Jane L. Parpart, 'Exploding the Canon', in *Feminism/Postmodernism/Development* (London and New York: Routledge, 1995), 19.

Part I. The Basis for the Debates

Challenging Imperial Feminism

Valerie Amos and Pratibha Parmar*

Our task here is to begin to identify the ways in which a particular tradition, white Eurocentric and Western, has sought to establish itself as the only legitimate feminism in current political practice. [. . .] The growth of the Black feminist movement in Britain in the last decade has forced the question of the centrality of Black women's oppression and exploitation onto the political and theoretical agendas. The political energy of Black women who have organized at the grassroots within our communities against the myriad of issues engendered by the racism of the British state has inspired and pointed to the urgent need to challenge many of the theoretical conceptualizations and descriptions of Black and Third World women existing within white feminist literature.

[. . .] It is our aim in this article to critically examine some of the key theoretical concepts in white feminist literature, and discuss their relevance or otherwise for a discussion and development of Black feminist theory.

It would be naive of us to suggest in any way that the white women's movement is a monolithic structure or organization, indeed we recognize that it is a variety of groups with a diversity of interests and perspectives.

However, our concern here is to show that white, mainstream feminist theory, be it from the socialist feminist or radical feminist perspective, does not speak to the experiences of Black women and where it attempts to do so it is often from a racist perspective and reasoning.

[. . .] Our starting point then is the oppressive nature of the women's movement in Britain both in terms of its practice and the theories which have sought to explain the nature of women's oppression and

* From Valerie Amos and Pratibha Parmar, 'Challenging Imperial Feminism', *Feminist Review: Many Voices, One Chant* No. 17 (Taylor & Francis, 1984), 3–19, reprinted by permission of the publisher.

legitimize the political practices which have developed out of those analyses. In describing the women's movement as oppressive we refer to the experiences of Black and working class women of the movement and the inability of feminist theory to speak to their experience in any meaningful way.[1]

In arguing that most contemporary feminist theory does not begin to adequately account for the experience of Black women we also have to acknowledge that it is not a simple question of their absence, consequently the task is not one of rendering their visibility.

On the contrary we will have to argue that the process of accounting for their historical and contemporary position does, in itself, challenge the use of some of the central categories and assumptions of recent mainstream feminist thought.[2] This work has already begun; Black women are not only making history but rewriting it.

The publication in recent years of a number of books by Black feminists in the US marks the beginning of a systematic documentation of Black women's individual and collective histories. Dominant among these are the rediscovery of ourselves; our place in the Black movement; the boundaries of our sisterhood with white feminists.[3]

These are important areas for us Black women, for our experience is the shared experience of Black people but it is also the shared experience of women within different class contexts. Our political responses have been and will continue to be shaped by that duality, the range of political options available to us will depend on the social context in which we experience that dualism. To date, the majority of work available by Black women addresses itself to the situation in the USA or to the situation in the Third World countries from which our ancestors are drawn. Although comparisons can be made between Britain and the USA and although it is important to draw on the histories of the communities and countries of the Third World which have contributed to our world view, it is important that Black women in Britain locate their experiences within the context of what is happening to Black people here.

There is little recognition in the women's movement of the ways in which the gains made by white women have been and still are at the expense of Black women. Historically white women's sexuality has been constructed in oppositional terms to that of Black women[4] and it is to this history that white women refer as their starting point, it is with this history that they seek to come to terms but in an uncritical way—the engagement with it is essentially selective. The 'herstory' which white women use to trace the roots of women's oppression or to justify some form of political practice is an imperial history rooted in the prejudices of colonial and neo-colonial periods, a 'herstory' which suffers the same form of historical amnesia of white male historians, by ignoring the fundamental ways in which white women have benefited from the oppression of Black people. [. . .]

Thus the perception white middle-class feminists have of what they need liberating from has little or no relevance to the day to day experience of the majority of Black women in Britain and the ways in which they determine the political choices which have to be made. Nowhere is this more apparent than in the oppositional terms in which women's liberation and Black people's liberation has been and still is posed and [. . .] this line of reasoning was not only limited to the USA; the movement for female emancipation in Britain was closely linked to theories of racial superiority and Empire.

It would appear that although feminists and indeed Marxists invoke the spectre of history/herstory at will in an attempt to locate the articulation of class and gender oppression, at the point at which that very history is called into question and challenges the bases of their analyses there is a curious kind of amnesia. The past is invoked at will, but differentially, to make sense of the range of political options open to socialists and feminists.[5]

Few white feminists in Britain and elsewhere have elevated the question of racism to the level of primacy, within their practical political activities or in their intellectual work. The women's movement has unquestioningly been premised on a celebration of 'sisterhood' with its implicit assumption that women *qua* women have a necessary basis for unity and solidarity; a sentiment reflected in academic feminist writings which is inevitably influenced by the women's movement and incorporates some of its assumptions.

While one tendency has been for Black women to have either remained invisible within feminist scholarship or to have been treated purely as women without any significance attached to our colour and race, another tendency has been the idealization and culturalism of anthropological works. Often we have appeared in cross cultural studies which under the guise of feminist and progressive anthropology, renders us as 'subjects' for 'interesting' and 'exotic' comparison. [. . .] By adopting the research methods and frameworks of white male academics much academic feminist writing fails to challenge their assumptions, repeats their racial chauvinism and is consequently of less use to us.

One such assumption is that pre-capitalist economies equal

backwardness in both a cultural and ideological sense and in fact are responsible for the continued oppression of women in these societies. It is further implied that it is only when Third World women enter into capitalist relations that they will have any hope of liberation:

> There can be little doubt that on balance the position of women in imperialist, i.e. advanced capitalist societies is, for all its implications more advanced than in the less developed capitalist and non capitalist societies. In this sense the changes brought by imperialism to Third World societies may, in some circumstances have been historically progressive.[6]

The above analysis falsely assumes that imperialism necessarily brings capitalist relations and is parallel to the resurgence of development theories in neo-marxist literature that argue that imperialism is progressive for 'underdeveloped' nations.[7]

Furthermore, when Black and Third World women are being told that imperialism is good for us, it should be of no great surprise to anyone when we reject a feminism which uses Western social and economic systems to judge and make pronouncements about how Third World women can become emancipated. Feminist theories which examine our cultural practices as 'feudal residues' or label us 'traditional', also portray us as politically immature women who need to be versed and schooled in the ethos of Western feminism. They need to be continually challenged, exposed for their racism and denied any legitimacy as authentic feminists.

STRENGTH IN DIFFERENCES

The failure of the academic feminists to recognize difference as a crucial strength is a failure to reach beyond the first patriarchal lesson. Divide and conquer in our world must become define and empower.[8]

Many white feminists' failure to acknowledge the differences between themselves and Black and Third World women has contributed to the predominantly Eurocentric and ethnocentric theories of women's oppression. Recently, some white feminist academics have attempted to deal with the question of differences but again this has raised many problems and often perpetuated white feminist supremacy.

[. . .] Historically, it was not the movement who turned to these women but Black women themselves who instigated the debates on our differences. For instance in America, many Black women were involved in the women's movement from its beginnings, and they struggled to bring home the following to their Black sisters who were pessimistic about the viability of joint political work with white feminists:

> The real political and economic advances acquired by women of colour involved in the women's movement more than made up for the very real problems and personal contradictions evident among certain petty bourgeois white women's 'leaders'.[9]

Black women were also raising the issue of feminism and feminist demands within the Black movement and such questions were continually raised in the civil rights movement well before Black women were engaging in debate within the predominantly white women's movement in the 1960s. [. . .] We now turn to look at three critical areas in which Black women's experience is very different from that of white women: the family, sexuality and the women's peace movement. Each of these areas, in very different ways points to the 'imperial' nature of feminist thought and practice.

FAMILY

To date socialist feminist theory has sought to harness what is perceived as two strands of women's oppression—class oppression and patriarchal oppression—the one being viewed as the economic basis of relationships, the other, the social or ideological. Attempts have been made to locate patriarchal relations within the social relations of reproduction and these analyses have sought to link the modes of production and reproduction in an attempt to define women's position in a capitalist, patriarchal society. Indeed the complexities of that relationship have been discussed at length but no workable synthesis of the concepts of gender and class has emerged. Patriarchy cannot be viewed only in terms of its relationship to capital and capitalist relations but neither is it merely an analytical tool which explains the oppression of women by men within a range of different economic systems.

It is important to go back to the classic definition of patriarchy[10] which also encompassed the oppression of younger men by the father. Patriarchy is about gender oppression but it is also about power relations which are not always gender specific. The film *Padre Padroni* amply demonstrates this. A definition of patriarchal relations which looks only at the power of men over women without placing that in a wider political and economic framework has serious consequences for the way in which relationships within the Black community are viewed. Relationships within the Black community are structured by racism and it is a denial of racism and its relationship to patriarchy to posit patriarchal relations as if they were non-contradictory. We would argue that the arguments of radical feminists who see patriarchy as the primary determining feature of women's oppression ignores totally the inapplicability of such a concept in analysing the complex of relations obtaining in the Black communities both historically and at present.[11]

The family, rightly, has been the object of much debate in the women's movement and has been cited as one of the principal sites of women's oppression—women's role in reproducing the labour force, their supposed dependence on men and the construction of a female identity through notions of domesticity and motherhood have all been challenged. Indeed within that questioning there have been attempts to elevate domestic labour to the same level of analysis as the Marxist analysis of the mode of production and the relations between capital and labour. The family and its role in the construction of a consensual ideology remains central to discussions of feminism. We would question however the ways in which white academics, particularly sociologists and anthropologists, have sought to define the role of Black women in the family.

Much work has already been done which shows the ways in which sociology, especially the sociology of 'ethnicity', pathologizes and problematizes the Black communities in Britain. Our concern here is the impact the above analyses have had on Euro-American contemporary feminist thought, particularly socialist feminists. Although it is true to say that some of these feminists have distanced themselves from the crude stereotyping common in such analyses, some stereotypes do stick and they are invariably linked to colonial and historical interpretations of the Black woman's role. The image is of the passive Asian woman subject to oppressive practices within the Asian family with an emphasis on wanting to 'help' Asian women liberate themselves from their role. Or there is the strong, dominant Afro-Caribbean woman, the head of the household who despite her 'strength' is exploited by the 'sexism' which is seen as being a strong feature in relationships between Afro-Caribbean men and women. So although the crude translation of theories of ethnicity which have become part and parcel of the nation's common sense image of Black people[12] may not be accepted by many white feminists, they are influenced by the ideas and nowhere is this more apparent than in debates about the family, where there has certainly been a failure to challenge particular pathological ideas about the Black family. There is little or no engagement by white feminists with the contradictions which constitute and shape our role as women in a family context, as sisters, aunts or daughters. For both Black and white women, it is a critical issue which has to be addressed, but in this area of struggle it is Black women who have sought to look critically at the family, its strengths and weaknesses, its advantages and disadvantages, its importance for certain women in class and race terms and all this in the broader context of state harassment and oppression of Black people. [. . .]

White feminists have fallen into the trap of measuring the Black female experience against their own, labelling it as in some way lacking, then looking for ways in which it might be possible to harness the Black women's experience to their own. Comparisons are made with our countries of origin which are said to fundamentally exploit Black women. The hysteria in the Western women's movement surrounding issues like arranged marriages, purdah, female headed households, is often beyond the Black woman's comprehension—being tied to so-called feminist notions of what constitutes good or bad practice in our communities in Britain or the Third World.

In rejecting such analyses we would hope to locate the Black family more firmly in the historical experiences of Black people—not in the romantic idealized forms popular with some social anthropologists, and not merely as a tool of analysis. There are serious questions about who has written that history and in what form, questions which have to be addressed before we as Black people use that history as an additional element of our analysis. Black women cannot just throw away their experiences of living in certain types of household organization; they want to use that experience to transform familial relationships. Stereotypes about the Black family have been used by the state to justify particular forms of oppression. The issue of fostering and adoption of Black kids is current: Black families are seen as being 'unfit' for fostering and adoption. Racist immigration legislation has had the effect of separating family members, particularly of the Asian community, but no longer is that legislation made legitimate just by appeals to racist ideologies contained in notions of 'swamping'. Attempts have actually been made by some feminists to justify such legislative practices on the basis of protecting Asian girls from the 'horrors' of the arranged marriage system. White feminists beware—your unquestioning and racist assumptions about the Black family, your critical but uninformed approach to 'Black culture' has found root and in fact informs state practice.

SEXUALITY

Sexuality has been and continues to be a central issue of discussion and debate within the white women's movement, and much political energy has been spent on understanding and questioning sexuality and sexual oppression:

> . . . feminism has thrown up enormous challenges in the whole field of sexuality. We have challenged the 'rights' of men to women's bodies; the compulsory nature of heterosexuality; the stigma and invisibility of lesbianism; the primacy of the nuclear family; rigid gender roles—patriarchal definitions of what is 'natural'; the violence of rape; the exploitation of pornography; sexist imagery and symbolism. Even the importance and priority given to sexual relationships have been questioned.[13]

While such debates rage virulently amongst white feminists, many Black women have rightly felt that we do not have the 'luxury' of engaging in them in the context of the intense racism of the British state. But the fact that Black women have been peripheral to these debates that have taken place within the women's movement, does not mean that we have not always thought about and discussed these issues with each other. The ways in which we have discussed and prioritized issues around sexuality have differed markedly from white women. [. . .]

As we have increasingly grown confident in our feminism, some of us have begun to look at the area of sexuality in ways that are relevant to us as Black women. The absence of publicly overt debates on and around sexuality by Black women does not mean that such discussions have not been taking place. As illustrated in Brixton Black women's group's analysis of the demise of the Organization of Women of Asian and African Descent (OWAAD), this was and continues to be one area which has been recognized as an essential element of Black feminist practice and theory. [. . .]

More specifically when challenging heterosexuality as the norm many Black lesbians have had to face the profound homophobia of both Blacks and whites. As Barbara Smith comments when talking about the American situation:

> Implicit in our communities' attitudes towards Black lesbians is the notion that they have transgressed both sexual and racial norms. Despite all the forces with which we must contend, Black women have a strong tradition of sexual self determination.[14]

Black women's continued challenges to the question of forced sterilization and the use of the contraceptive drug Depo Provera has meant that such campaigns as the National Abortion Campaign have been forced to reassess the relevance of their single issue focus for the majority of working class, Black women, and to change the orientation of their campaigns and actions. [. . .]

It is worthwhile at this point to look back at history and highlight the fact that some of the unquestioned assumptions inherent in contemporary feminist demands have remained the same as those of the nineteenth and early twentieth-century feminists who in the main were pro-imperialist. One strand of early feminism in Britain has its roots in the radical liberal and social purity campaign work of Josephine Butler who drew on religious rhetoric with its notions of purity and impurity, virtue and vice and linked her analysis to aspects of contemporary theories of evolution. Christabel Pankhurst, a leading light at the time, echoed her agreement with the growing eugenic lobby when she said, 'sex powers are given . . . as a trust to be used not for . . . immorality and debauchery, but . . . reverently and in a union based on love for the purpose of carrying on the *race*'.[15]

While the growth of the birth control movement and birth control information and clinics in the 1920s and 1930s is to be recognized as a crucial gain for women in the fight for control over their own bodies, the grounds on which such a movement gained respectability was not on a woman's right to self-determination but on the grounds of eugenics and health. Marie Stopes was a committed eugenist, and the name of her organization—the Society for Constructive Birth Control and Racial Progress—clearly stated her racialist position. The class interest of many such women was revealed when such woman's organizations as the National Society for Equal Citizenship and 'The Woman's Co-operative Guild' supported campaigns to legalize sterilization in the 1930s for certain groups of 'unfit' persons, i.e. working class women.

Many suffragists campaigned around slogans such as 'votes for women, chastity for men' and created new spaces for women but their compliance with the development of an ideology of women as mothers and reproducers of the race highlighted their interest in upholding white supremacy.

At the beginning of the nineteenth century a healthy and growing population was seen as a national resource and neo-Malthusians alongside eugenists recommended contraception not only as an artificial check on population but also as a means of selective limitation of population growth to prevent the 'deterioration' of the 'race' and decline as an imperial nation through the proliferation of those they regarded as 'unfit' (to breed). It must however be said that there was a small section of women who attempted to counter the Eugenicist movement, such as Stella Brown.

In 1958 Charles Kingsley argued that over-population was impossible 'in a country that has the greatest colonial empire that the world has ever seen', and he believed that it was 'a duty, one of the noblest of duties to help the increase of the English race as much as possible'.[16] Women were being defined as the breeders of the race, bearing and rearing the next generation of soldiers and workers of the imperial race. Within this context developed a new definition of women's role and the pressures which led to the formation of an ideology of motherhood:

> In many cases the terms in which reforms to do with marriage, child rearing and bearing were proposed also involved reference to the nation, the empire, or the race . . .[17]

White feminists have attacked this for its oppressiveness to them but not on the grounds of race and anti-imperialism.

Such a development of an ideology of women as mothers duty bound to reproduce for the race went alongside the development of an imagery of them as vulnerable creatures who needed protection not only at home but also in the colonies.

There are historical counterparts of contemporary white male use of the image of vulnerable and defenceless white women being raped and mugged by Black men, images which are reinforced by racist ideologies of black sexuality. Also in responding to the use of physical violence to control white women's sexuality white feminists have singularly failed to see how physical violence to control the sexuality of Black men is a feature of our history (e.g. lynching). This has implications for analyses and campaigning around sexual violence.

Historically, there are many instances of how white women's vulnerability to physical violence from men has been used to bring in oppressive legislation which justified an extension of police and state powers, with oppressive results for both men and women in countries under colonial rule. For instance in 1926 a White Women's Protection Ordinance was passed in Papua (New Guinea), then under British rule, which introduced the death penalty for the crime of rape or attempted rape of any European female. The 'Black Peril', or the fear that 'native men', who were seen as endowed with 'strong sex instincts' particularly for white women, were going around in their hordes raping white women, was the background to this severe legislation. In fact there was little proof that this was happening.

Not only were there double standards for white men, who, far from being penalized for having sexual relationships with local Black women, were in fact encouraged to 'satisfy' their 'natural' desires; but furthermore Black women's experiences and vulnerability to male violence was judged to be of little consequence.

> Doubtless there are native women who set the highest value on their chastity, but they are the exception and *the rape of an ordinary native women does not present any element of comparison with the rape of a respectable white woman* even where the offence upon the latter is committed by one of her own race and colour.[18]

The racist ideology that black and immigrant men are the chief perpetrators of violent crimes against women permeates not only the racist media fed regularly by police 'revelations' of 'racial' crime statistics as in 1982 but also sections of the white women's liberation movement as illustrated by their actions and sometimes their inaction.

For example, the compliance of many white feminists with the racist media and the police is shown in their silence when public hysteria is periodically whipped up through images of white women as innocent victims of black rapists and muggers. When white feminists have called for safer streets, and curfew of men at nights they have not distanced themselves from the link that exists in common sense racist thinking between street crime and Black people. Again, when women marched through Black inner city areas to 'Reclaim the Night' they played into the hands of the racist media and the fascist organizations, some of whom immediately formed vigilante groups patrolling the streets 'protecting' innocent white women by beating up black men. Therefore we would agree that 'any talk of male violence that does not emphatically reject the idea that race or colour is relevant automatically reinforces these racist images'.[19]

Black women's sexuality has been used in various oppressive ways throughout imperialist history. For instance, during slavery women were forced to breed a slave labour force, raped, assaulted and experimented on; practices that still continue today under 'scientific' and sophisticated guises.

For Asian women, one such historical example of control over them was in the form of the Contagious Diseases Act passed in India in 1868. Throughout the nineteenth century the British military in India was only concerned with maintaining an efficient and 'healthy' army who had 'natural' sexual desires which needed to be fulfilled. Prostitution was encouraged and local Indian women were either taken on as 'mistresses' or regularly visited in the brothels both within and outside of the cantonments. Such practices were so widespread that venereal disease increased rapidly. What the Act did was call for compulsory registration of brothels and prostitutes and periodic medical examinations and compulsory treatment of such 'diseases'. The soldiers were not required to do this. This is just one example of state regulation of prostitutes which was a result of imperialist policies which required the maintenance of huge and 'healthy' armies.[20]

In identifying the institution of the family as a source of oppression for women, white feminists have again revealed their cultural and racial myopia, because for Asian women in particular, the British state through its immigration legislation has done all it can to destroy the Asian family by separating husbands from wives, wives from husbands and parents from children.

But while many Black feminists would agree that the ideology of mother/wife roles is oppressive to women and that marriage only serves to reinforce and institutionalize that oppression, in a political climate where the state is demanding proof of the 'genuine' nature of 'arranged marriages' as a blatant attack on Asian culture, and Asian people's right to enter this country, we demand the right to choose and struggle around the issue of family oppression ourselves, within our communities without state intervention, and without white feminists making judgments as to the oppressive nature of arranged marriages.

Many white feminists have argued that as feminists they find it very difficult to accept arranged marriages which they see as reactionary. Our argument is that it is not up to them to accept or reject arranged marriages but up to us to challenge, accept or reform, depending on our various perspectives, on our own terms and in our own culturally specific ways.

NUCLEAR POWER ON THE NORTH LONDON LINE

With the setting up of the Greenham Common Women's Peace camp in 1981, world attention has focused on the women's peace movement in Britain. Thousands of women have identified the threat of a nuclear war as a priority issue to organize around. While some feminists have sought to distance themselves from women peace activists who have fallen into the trap of elevating the feminine nature of women with its stress on mothering and nurturing, finding its organized manifestation in groups such as the Families against the Bomb and Babies against the Bomb, other problems remain.[21]

The women's peace movement is and continues to remain largely white and middle-class because yet again their actions and demands have excluded any understanding of or sensitivity to Black and Third World women's situations.

Black women's political priorities have not been to organize around the siting of American cruise missiles at Greenham or to focus on the disarmament campaigns. This has been inevitable given the implicit and often explicit nationalist sentiments of its campaigns as much as the overall framework within which they have addressed these questions. The patriotic cries of 'We want to protect our country' which extend both to the mixed left anti-nuclear groups as much as sections of the women's peace movement is not one with which many Black people seek to or want to identify with, particularly when we know that we are not recognized or accepted as legitimate and equal inhabitants of this island and are continuously fighting for our right to be here. The parochial concerns of the Campaign for Nuclear Disarmament (CND) and the women's peace movement are manifest in their unwillingness to take up any international issues. Why, for instance, are they not exposing, campaigning and mobilizing against Britain's role in illegal mining of uranium in Namibia for fuel for its Trident submarines? Why are connections not being made with people in the Pacific who are fighting for land rights? Why is there continued silence and inaction on the war going on in Britain's own 'backyard', Northern Ireland? Why is it that some white women who have sought to involve Black women in their peace campaigns at Greenham can only include them by asking them to service them yet again and play the role of caterers?

It is inevitable that such questions and issues do not feature on the agendas of either the women's peace movement or the CND, because both these movements are imbued with the uncritical acceptance of the concept of 'the nation', in particular the 'British nation'. Their failure to distance themselves or be critical of anti-Americanism prevalent in public opinion which supports nuclear arms but opposes American nuclear arms is a result of their deep-seated and entrenched patriotism. In Britain, there is not a single social or political institution that has not been fundamentally affected by the ideology of Empire and its corollary of British superiority. [. . .]

The slogan 'Yanks out' and 'Yankees go home' has been widely adopted by many women peace activists and is an illustration of racism arising out of a confusion of collapsing the American state with individual Americans. An example of such a tactic is an incident witnessed recently when a group of white, middle-class women began to shout and chant 'Yanks out' and 'Yankee go home' at a Black American soldier walking through the train carriage they were sitting in. To some of the Black women present this was reminiscent of 'Blacks go home' and 'wogs out'. When confronted with the racism of their action one woman justified their actions by saying that in an individual situation, such confrontations are necessary and legitimate. Necessary and legitimate to whom? [. . .]

Internationally, while Black and Third World women are fighting daily battles for survival, for food, land and water, western white women's cries of anguish for concern about preserving the standards of life for their children and preserving the planet for future generations sound hollow. Whose standards of life are they fighting to preserve?—white, middle-class standards undoubtedly. Recently, Madhu Kishwar, an Indian feminist, came to speak to the Women For Life on Earth and she stressed that what is needed is a realization that:

> A movement for disarmament begins with a movement against the use of guns, the everyday weapons. Here (in Britain) you may have a fear of a nuclear holocaust and death and destruction—in India millions die of water pollution—that is a more deadly weapon for women in India. I think it is very important that nuclear piles be made targets for political action, but we have to begin with confronting the guns and the dandas (sticks) that is disarmament for us.[22]

[. . .] In saying that as Black women we have sought not to prioritize our political energies on organizing around 'peace' and disarmament, does not in any way mean we do not consider these as crucial political issues.

Indeed, the arms race is fundamentally political and the complexities of the new cold war and the increasing drive for American global supremacy are crucial questions of importance which concern us all. But, it is only when Western peace activists, be they male or female, begin to broaden the parameters of their campaigns and integrate an international perspective within their frameworks, will there be a radical shift away from the predominantly white composition of these movements.

CONCLUSION

For us the way forward lies in defining a feminism which is significantly different to the dominant trends in the women's liberation movement. We have sought to define the boundaries of our sisterhood with white feminists and in so doing have been critical not only of their theories but also of their practice. True feminist theory and practice entails an understanding of imperialism and a critical engagement with challenging racism—elements which the current women's movement significantly lacks, but which are intrinsic to Black feminism. We are creating our own forms and content. As Black women we have to look at our history and at our experiences at the hands of a racist British state. We have to look at the crucial question of how we organize in order that we address ourselves to the totality of our oppression. For us there is no choice. We cannot simply prioritize one aspect of our oppression to the exclusion of others, as the realities of our day to day lives make it imperative for us to consider the simultaneous nature of our oppression and exploitation. Only a synthesis of class, race, gender and sexuality can lead us forward, as these form the matrix of Black women's lives.

Black feminism as a distinct body of theory and practice is in the process of development and debate both here in Britain and internationally and has begun to make significant contribution to other movements of liberation, as well as challenging the oppression and exploitation of Black women.

Notes

1. Some attempts have been made to look at both racism and feminism. For example, Jenny Bourne in her essay 'Towards an Anti-Racist Feminism', *Race and Class*, 25 (Summer 1983), 1–22, attempts to locate anti-racist practice within a (white) feminist context. However, Jenny Bourne's essay fails

adequately to address contemporary debates within feminism and ignores the contribution of black feminists to the broader debate around issues of racism, feminism, class and sexuality.

2. Hazel Carby, 'White Women Listen! Black Feminism and the Boundaries of Sisterhood', in Centre for Contemporary Cultural Studies (eds.), *The Empire Strikes Back: Race and Racism in 70s Britain* (London: Hutchison, 1982).
3. Gail Lewis and Pratibha Parmar, 'Review Essay of American Black Feminist Literature', *Race and Class*, 25 (Autumn 1983).
4. Angela Davis, *Women, Race and Class* (London: The Women's Press, 1982); Veronica Ware, 'Imperialism, Racism and Violence Against Women', *Emergency*, 1 (Winter 1983/4).
5. There have been a range of debates around socialism and feminism which have ignored the issue of race. See for example, Sheila Rowbotham, Lynne Segal and Hilary Wainwright, *Beyond the Fragments: Feminism and the Making of Socialism* (London: Merlin, 1979), and Lydia Sargent (ed.), *The Unhappy Marriage of Marxism and Feminism* (London: Pluto, 1981), which has only one essay on 'The Incompatible *Menage à Trois*'.
6. Maxine Molyneux, 'Socialist Societies Old and New: Progress Towards Women's Emancipation', *Feminist Review*, 8 (1981), 1–34.
7. Bill Warren, *Imperialism, Pioneer of Capitalism* (London: New Left Books, 1980); for critique see A. Sivanandan, 'Capitalism, Highest Stage of Imperialism. Warren and the Third World', *Race and Class*, 24 (1982).
8. Audre Lorde (ed.), *Sister Outsider* (Freedom, CA: The Crossing Press, 1984).
9. Manning Marabel, *How Capitalism Underdeveloped Black America* (New York: Southend Press, 1983).
10. See Michèle Barrett, *Women's Oppression Today, Problems in Marxist Feminist Analysis* (London: Verso, 1980).
11. See Christine Delphy, *The Main Enemy: a Materialist Analysis of Women's Oppression* (London: Women's Research and Resources Centre Publications, 1977).
12. See Errol Lawrence, 'Just Plain Common Sense: the "Roots" of Racism', in Centre for Contemporary Cultural Studies (eds.), *The Empire Strikes Back*, 47–94.
13. Sue Cartledge and Joanna Ryan, *Sex and Love, New Thoughts on Old Contradictions* (London: The Women's Press, 1983).
14. Gloria T. Hull, Patricia Bell Scott and Barbara Smith (eds.), *All the Women are White, All the Blacks are Men, But Some of Us Are Brave* (New York: Feminist Press, 1982).
15. Lucy Bland, 'Purity, Motherhood, Pleasure or Threat', in Cartledge and Ryan, *Sex and Love.* Emphasis added.
16. Anna Davin, 'Imperialism and Motherhood', *History Workshop Journal*, 5 (Spring 1978).
17. Ibid.
18. Ware, 'Imperialism, Racism and Violence Against Women'.
19. Ibid.
20. Kenneth Ballhatchett, *Race, Sex and Class Under the Raj: Imperial Attitudes and Policies 1793–1905* (London: Weidenfeld and Nicolson, 1980).
21. Radical Feminist Papers, *Breaching the Peace, Collection of Radical Feminist Papers* (London: Onlywomen Press, 1984).
22. Madhu Kishwar, Interview, *Outwrite*, 22 (February 1984).

Black Women: Shaping Feminist Theory

bell hooks*

Feminism in the United States has never emerged from the women who are most victimized by sexist oppression; women who are daily beaten down, mentally, physically and spiritually—women who are powerless to change their condition in life. They are a silent majority. A mark of their victimization is that they accept their lot in life without visible question, without organized protest, without collective anger or rage. Betty Friedan's *The Feminine Mystique* is still heralded as having paved the way for contemporary feminist movement—it was written as if these women did not exist. Friedan's famous phrase, 'the problem that has no name', often quoted to describe the condition of women in this society, actually referred to the plight of a select group of college-educated, middle- and upper-class, married white women—housewives bored with leisure, with the home, with children, with buying products, who wanted more out of life. [. . .] She made her plight and the plight of white women like herself synonymous with a condition affecting all American women. In so doing, she deflected attention away from her classism, her racism, her sexist attitudes towards the masses of American women. In the context of her book, Friedan makes clear that the women she saw as victimized by sexism were college-educated, white women who were compelled by sexist conditioning to remain in the home. [. . .] Specific problems and dilemmas of leisure-class white housewives were real concerns that merited consideration and change but they were not the pressing political concerns of masses of women. Masses of women were concerned about economic survival, ethnic and racial discrimination, etc. [. . .] It remains a useful discussion of the impact of sexist discrimination on a select group of women. Examined from a different perspective, it can

* From bell hooks, 'Black Women: Shaping Feminist Theory', in *Feminist Theory from Margin to Centre* (South End Press, 1984), 1–15, reprinted by permission of the publisher.

also be seen as a case study of narcissism, insensitivity, sentimentality and self-indulgence which reaches its peak when Friedan, in a chapter titled 'Progressive Dehumanization', makes a comparison between the psychological effects of isolation on white housewives and the impact of confinement on the self-concept of prisoners in Nazi concentration camps.[1]

[. . .] Like Friedan before them, white women who dominate feminist discourse today rarely question whether or not their perspective on women's reality is true to the lived experiences of women as a collective group. Nor are they aware of the extent to which their perspectives reflect race and class biases, although there has been a greater awareness of biases in recent years. Racism abounds in the writings of white feminists, reinforcing white supremacy and negating the possibility that women will bond politically across ethnic and racial boundaries. Past feminist refusal to draw attention to and attack racial hierarchies suppressed the link between race and class. Yet class structure in American society has been shaped by the racial politic of white supremacy; it is only by analyzing racism and its function in capitalist society that a thorough understanding of class relationships can emerge. Class struggle is inextricably bound to the struggle to end racism.

[. . .] White women who dominate feminist discourse, who for the most part make and articulate feminist theory, have little or no understanding of white supremacy as a racial politic, of the psychological impact of class, of their political status within a racist, sexist, capitalist state. [. . .]

There is much evidence substantiating the reality that race and class identity creates differences in quality of life, social status and lifestyle that take precedence over the common experience women share—differences which are rarely transcended. [. . .]

A central tenet of modern feminist thought has been the assertion that 'all women are oppressed'. This assertion implies that women share a common lot, that factors like class, race, religion, sexual preference, etc. do not create a diversity of experience that determines the extent to which sexism will be an oppressive force in the lives of individual women. Sexism as a system of domination is institutionalized but it has never determined in an absolute way the fate of all women in this society. *Being oppressed means the absence of choices.* It is the primary point of contact between the oppressed and the oppressor. Many women in this society do have choices (as inadequate as they are) therefore exploitation and discrimination are words that more accurately describe the lot of women collectively in the United States. [. . .] There are oppressed women in the United States, and it is both appropriate and necessary that we speak against such oppression. [. . .] However, feminist emphasis on 'common oppression' in the United States was less a strategy for politicization than an appropriation by conservative and liberal women of a radical political vocabulary that masked the extent to which they shaped the movement so that it addressed and promoted their class interests. [. . .]

Initially, radical participants in the women's movement demanded that women penetrate that isolation and create a space for contact. Anthologies like *Liberation Now, Women's Liberation: Blueprint for the Future, Class and Feminism, Radical Feminism* and *Sisterhood Is Powerful*, all published in the early 1970s, contain articles that attempted to address a wide audience of women, an audience that was not exclusively white, middle-class, college-educated, and adult (many have articles on teenagers). [. . .] Women who were not opposed to patriarchy, capitalism, classism or racism labeled themselves 'feminist'. Their expectations were varied. Privileged women wanted social equality with men of their class; some women wanted equal pay for equal work; others wanted an alternative lifestyle. Many of these legitimate concerns were easily co-opted by the ruling capitalist patriarchy. [. . .]

Feminists in the United States are aware of the contradictions. Carol Ehrlich makes the point in her essay, 'The Unhappy Marriage of Marxism and Feminism: Can It Be Saved?', that 'feminism seems more and more to have taken on a blind, safe, nonrevolutionary outlook' as 'feminist radicalism loses ground to bourgeois feminism', stressing that 'we cannot let this continue'.[2] [. . .]

It is no accident that feminist struggle has been so easily co-opted to serve the interests of conservative and liberal feminists since feminism in the United States has so far been a bourgeois ideology. [. . .] The ideology of 'competitive, atomistic liberal individualism' has permeated feminist thought to such an extent that it undermines the potential radicalism of feminist struggle. The usurpation of feminism by bourgeois women to support their class interests has been to a very grave extent justified by feminist theory as it has so far been conceived. (For example, the ideology of 'common oppression'.) Any movement to resist the co-optation of feminist struggle must begin by introducing a different feminist perspective—a new theory—one that is not informed by the ideology of liberal individualism.

The exclusionary practices of women who dominate feminist discourse have made it practically impossible for new and varied theories to emerge. Feminism has its party line and women who feel a need for a different strategy, a different foundation, often find themselves ostracized and silenced. [. . .] Non-white women who feel affirmed within the current structure of feminist movement (even though they may form autonomous groups) seem to also feel that their definitions of the party line, whether on the issue of black feminism or on other issues, is the only legitimate discourse. Rather than encourage a diversity of voices, critical dialogue and controversy, they, like some white women, seek to stifle dissent. As activists and writers whose work is widely known, they act as if they are best able to judge whether other women's voices should be heard. [. . .]

We resist hegemonic dominance of feminist thought by insisting that it is a theory in the making, that we must necessarily criticize, question, re-examine and explore new possibilities. My persistent critique has been informed by my status as a member of an oppressed group, experience of sexist exploitation and discrimination, and the sense that prevailing feminist analysis has not been the force shaping my feminist consciousness. This is true for many women. There are white women who had never considered resisting male dominance until the feminist movement created an awareness that they could and should. My awareness of feminist struggle was stimulated by social circumstances. Growing up in a Southern, black, father-dominated, working class household, I experienced (as did my mother, my sisters and my brother) varying degrees of patriarchal tyranny and it made me angry—it made us all angry. Anger led me to question the politics of male dominance and enabled me to resist sexist socialization. Frequently, white feminists act as if black women did not know sexist oppression existed until they voiced feminist sentiment. [. . .]

These black women observed white feminists focus on male tyranny and women's oppression as if it were a 'new' revelation and felt such a focus had little impact on their lives. To them it was just another indication of the privileged living conditions of middle- and upper-class white women that they would need a theory to inform them that they were 'oppressed'. The implication being that people who are truly oppressed know it even though they may not be engaged in organized resistance or are unable to articulate in written form the nature of their oppression. These black women saw nothing liberatory in party line analyses of women's oppression. Neither the fact that black women have not organized collectively in huge numbers around the issues of 'feminism' (many of us do not know or use the term) nor the fact that we have not had access to the machinery of power that would allow us to share our analyses or theories about gender with the American public negate its presence in our lives or place us in a position of dependency in relationship to those white and non-white feminists who address a larger audience.

The understanding I had by age thirteen of patriarchal politics created in me expectations of the feminist movement that were quite different from those of young, middle-class, white women. When I entered my first women's studies class at Stanford University in the early 1970s, white women were revelling in the joy of being together—to them it was an important, momentous occasion. I had not known a life where women had not been together, where women had not helped, protected and loved one another deeply. I had not known white women who were ignorant of the impact of race and class on their social status and consciousness. (Southern white women often have a more realistic perspective on racism and classism than white women in other areas of the United States.) I did not feel sympathetic to white peers who maintained that I could not expect them to have knowledge of or understand the life experiences of black women. Despite my background (living in racially segregated communities) I knew about the lives of white women, and certainly no white women lived in our neighborhood, attended our schools or worked in our homes.

[. . .] Frequently, college-educated black women (even those from poor and working-class backgrounds) were dismissed as mere imitators. Our presence in movement activities did not count, as white women were convinced that 'real' blackness meant speaking the patois of poor black people being uneducated, streetwise and a variety of other stereotypes. If we dared to criticize the movement or to assume responsibility for reshaping feminist ideas and introducing new ideas, our voices were tuned out, dismissed, silenced. We could be heard only if our statements echoed the sentiments of the dominant discourse.

Attempts by white feminists to silence black women are rarely written about. [. . .] Often the white women who are busy publishing papers and books on 'unlearning racism' remain patronizing and condescending when they relate to black women. This is not surprising given that frequently their discourse is aimed solely in the direction of a white audience and the focus solely on changing attitudes rather than addressing racism in a historical and political context. They make us the 'objects' of their privileged discourse on race. As 'objects', we remain unequals, inferiors. Even though they may be sincerely concerned about racism, their methodology suggests they are not yet free of the type of paternalism endemic to white supremacist ideology. Some of these women place themselves in the position of 'authorities' who must mediate communication between racist white women (naturally they see themselves as having come to terms with their racism) and angry black women whom they believe are incapable of rational discourse. Of course, the system of racism, classism and educational elitism remain intact if they are to maintain their authoritative positions. [. . .]

Racist stereotypes of the strong, superhuman black woman are operative myths in the minds of many white women, allowing them to ignore the extent to which black women are likely to be victimized in this society and the role white women may play in the maintenance and perpetuation of that victimization. In Lillian Hellman's autobiographical work *Pentimento*, she writes, 'All my life, beginning at birth, I have taken orders from black women, wanting them and resenting them, being superstitious the few times I disobeyed.'[3] The black women Hellman describes worked in her household as family servants and their status was never that of an equal. Even as a child, she was always in the dominant position as they questioned, advised or guided her; they were free to exercise these rights because she or another white authority figure allowed it. Hellman places power in the hands of these black women rather than acknowledge her own power over them; hence she mystifies the true nature of their relationship. By projecting onto black women a mythical power and strength, white women both promote a false image of themselves as powerless, passive victims and deflect attention away from their aggressiveness, their power (however limited in a white supremacist, male-dominated state), their willingness to dominate and control others. These unacknowledged aspects of the social status of many white women prevent them from transcending racism and limit the scope of their understanding of women's overall social status in the United States. [. . .]

As a group, black women are in an unusual position in this society, for not only are we collectively at the bottom of the occupational ladder, but our overall social status is lower than that of any other group. Occupying such a position, we bear the brunt of sexist, racist and classist oppression. At the same time, we are the group that has not been socialized to assume the role of exploiter/oppressor in that we are allowed no institutionalized 'other' that we can exploit or oppress. (Children do not represent an institutionalized other even though they may be oppressed by parents.) White women and black men have it both ways. They can act as oppressor or be oppressed. Black men may be victimized by racism, but sexism allows them to act as exploiters and oppressors of women. White women may be victimized by sexism, but racism enables them to act as exploiters and oppressors of black people. Both groups have led liberation movements that favor their interests and support the continued oppression of other groups. Black male sexism has undermined struggles to eradicate racism just as white female racism undermines feminist struggle. As long as these two groups or any group defines liberation as gaining social equality with ruling-class white men, they have a vested interest in the continued exploitation and oppression of others.

Black women with no institutionalized 'other' that we may discriminate against, exploit or oppress often have a lived experience that directly challenges the prevailing classist, sexist, racist social structure and its concomitant ideology. This lived experience may shape our consciousness in such a way that our world view differs from those who have a degree of privilege (however relative within the existing system). It is essential for continued feminist struggle that black women recognize the special vantage point our marginality gives us and make use of this perspective to criticize the dominant racist, classist, sexist hegemony as well as to envision and create a counter-hegemony. I am suggesting that we have a central role to play in the making of feminist theory and a contribution to offer that is unique and valuable. The formation of a liberatory feminist theory and praxis is a collective responsibility, one that must be shared. Though I criticize aspects of the feminist movement as we have known it so far, a critique which is sometimes harsh and unrelenting, I do so not in an attempt to diminish feminist struggle but to enrich, to share in the work of making a liberatory ideology and a liberatory movement.

Notes

1. Betty Friedan, *The Feminine Mystique* (New York: W. W. Norton Co., 1963).
2. Carol Ehrlich, 'The Unhappy Marriage of Marxism and Feminism: Can it be Saved?', in Lydia Sargent (ed.), *Women and Revolution* (Boston: South End Press, 1981).
3. Lillian Hellman, *Pentimento* (Boston, MA: Little Brown, 1973).

3 Angry Women are Building: Issues and Struggles Facing American Indian Women Today

Paula Gunn Allen*

The central issue that confronts American Indian women throughout the hemisphere is survival, *literal survival*, both on a cultural and biological level. According to the 1980 census, population of American Indians is just over one million. This figure, which is disputed by some American Indians, is probably a fair estimate, and it carries certain implications.

Some researchers put our pre-contact population at more than 45 million, while others put it at around 20 million. The US government long put it at 450,000—a comforting if imaginary figure, though at one point it was put at around 270,000. If our current population is around one million; if, as some researchers estimate, around 25 percent of Indian women and 10 percent of Indian men in the United States have been sterilized without informed consent; if our average life expectancy is, as the best-informed research presently says, 55 years; if our infant mortality rate continues at well above national standards; if our average unemployment for all segments of our population—male, female, young, adult and middle-aged—is between 60 and 90 percent; if the US government continues its policy of termination, relocation, removal and assimilation along with the destruction of wilderness, reservation land and its resources, and severe curtailment of hunting, fishing, timber harvesting and water-use rights—then existing tribes are facing the threat of extinction which for several hundred tribal groups has already become fact in the past 500 years.

In this nation of more than 200 million, the Indian people constitute less than one-half of 1 percent of the population. In a nation that

* From Paula Gunn Allen, 'Angry Women are Building: Issues and Struggles Facing American Indian Women Today', in *The Sacred Hoop* by Paula Gunn Allen (Beacon Press, Boston, 1986, 1992), 189–93, copyright © Paula Gunn Allen 1986, 1992, reprinted by permission of the publisher.

offers refuge, sympathy and billions of dollars in aid from federal and private sources in the form of food to the hungry, medicine to the sick, and comfort to the dying, the indigenous subject population goes hungry, homeless, impoverished, cut out of the American deal, new, old and in between. Americans are daily made aware of the world-wide slaughter of native peoples such as the Cambodians, the Palestinians, the Armenians, the Jews—who constitute only a few groups faced with genocide in this century. We are horrified by South African apartheid and the removal of millions of indigenous African black natives to what is there called 'homelands'—but this is simply a replay of nineteenth-century US government removal of American Indians to reservations. Nor do many even notice the parallel or fight South African apartheid by demanding an end to its counterpart within the borders of the United States. The American Indian people are in a situation comparable to the imminent genocide in many parts of the world today. The plight of our people north and south of us is no better; to the south it is considerably worse. Consciously or unconsciously, deliberately, as a matter of national policy, or accidentally as a matter of 'fate', *every single government*, right, left or centrist in the Western hemisphere is consciously or subconsciously dedicated to the extinction of those tribal people who live within its borders.

Within this geopolitical charnel house, American Indian women struggle on every front for the survival of our children, our people, our self-respect, our value systems and our way of life. The past 500 years testify to our skill at waging this struggle: for all the varied weapons of extinction pointed at our heads, we endure.

We survive war and conquest; we survive colonization, acculturation, assimilation; we survive beating, rape, starvation, mutilation, sterilization, abandonment, neglect, death of our children, our loved ones, destruction of our land, our homes, our past and our future. We survive, and we do more than just survive. We bond, we care, we fight, we teach, we nurse, we bear, we feed, we earn, we laugh, we love, we hang in there, no matter what.

Of course, some, many of us, just give up. Many are alcoholics, many are addicts. Many abandon the children, the old ones. Many commit suicide. Many become violent, go insane. Many go 'white' and are never seen or heard from again. But enough hold on to their traditions and their ways so that even after almost 500 brutal years, we endure. And we even write songs and poems, make paintings and drawings that say 'We walk in beauty. Let us continue'.

Currently our struggles are on two fronts: physical survival and cultural survival. For women this means fighting alcoholism and drug abuse (our own and that of our husbands, lovers, parents, children);[1] poverty; affluence—a destroyer of people who are not traditionally socialized to deal with large sums of money; rape, incest, battering by Indian men; assaults on fertility and other health matters by the Indian Health Service and the Public Health Service; high infant mortality due to substandard medical care, nutrition and health information; poor educational opportunities or education that takes us away from our traditions, language and communities; suicide, homicide or similar expressions of self-hatred; lack of economic opportunities; substandard housing; sometimes violent and always virulent racist attitudes and behaviors directed against us by an entertainment and educational system that wants only one thing from Indians: our silence, our invisibility and our collective death.

A headline in the *Navajo Times* in the fall of 1979 reported that rape was the number one crime on the Navajo reservation. In a professional mental health journal of the Indian Health Services, Phyllis Old Dog Cross reported that incest and rape are common among Indian women seeking services and that their incidence is increasing. 'It is believed that at least 80 percent of the Native Women seen at the regional psychiatric service center (five state area) have experienced some sort of sexual assault.'[2] Among the forms of abuse being suffered by Native American women, Old Dog Cross cites a recent phenomenon, something called 'training'. This form of gang rape is 'a punitive act of a group of males who band together and get even or take revenge on a selected woman'.[3]

These and other cases of violence against women are powerful evidence that the status of women within the tribes has suffered grievous decline since contact, and the decline has increased in intensity in recent years. The amount of violence against women, alcoholism, and violence, abuse, and neglect by women against their children and their aged relatives have all increased. These social ills were virtually unheard of among most tribes fifty years ago, popular American opinion to the contrary. As Old Dog Cross remarks:

> Rapid, unstable and irrational change was required of the Indian people if they were to survive. Incredible loss of all that had meaning was the norm. Inhuman treatment, murder, death, and punishment was a typical experience for all the tribal groups and some didn't survive.
>
> The dominant society devoted its efforts to the attempt to change the Indian into a white-Indian. No inhuman pressure to effect this change was

overlooked. These pressures included starvation, incarceration and enforced education. Religious and healing customs were banished.

In spite of the years of oppression, the Indian and the Indian spirit survived. Not, however, without adverse effect. One of the major effects was the loss of cultured values and the concomitant loss of personal identity . . . The Indian was taught to be ashamed of being Indian and to emulate the non-Indian. In short, 'white was right.' For the Indian male, the only route to be successful, to be good, to be right, and to have an identity was to be as much like the white man as he could.[4]

Often it is said that the increase of violence against women is a result of various sociological factors such as oppression, racism, poverty, hopelessness, emasculation of men and loss of male self-esteem as their own place within traditional society has been systematically destroyed by increasing urbanization, industrialization and institutionalization, but seldom do we notice that for the past forty to fifty years, American popular media have depicted American Indian men as bloodthirsty savages devoted to treating women cruelly. While traditional Indian men seldom did any such thing—and in fact among most tribes abuse of women was simply unthinkable, as was abuse of children or the aged—the lie about 'usual' male Indian behavior seems to have taken root and now bears its brutal and bitter fruit.

Image casting and image control constitute the central process that American Indian women must come to terms with, for on that control rests our sense of self, our claim to a past and to a future that we define and that we build. Images of Indians in media and educational materials profoundly influence how we act, how we relate to the world and to each other, and how we value ourselves. They also determine to a large extent how our men act toward us, toward our children and toward each other. The popular American media image of Indian people as savages with no conscience, no compassion, and no sense of the value of human life and human dignity was hardly true of the tribes—however true it was of the invaders. But as Adolf Hitler noted a little over fifty years ago, if you tell a lie big enough and often enough, it will be believed. Evidently, while Americans and people all over the world have been led into a deep and unquestioned belief that American Indians are cruel savages, a number of American Indian men have been equally deluded into internalizing that image and acting on it. Media images, literary images and artistic images, particularly those embedded in popular culture, must be changed before Indian women will see much relief from the violence that destroys so many lives.

To survive culturally, American Indian women must often fight the United States government, the tribal governments, women and men of their tribe or their urban community who are virulently misogynist or who are threatened by attempts to change the images foisted on us over the centuries by Whites. The colonizers' revisions of our lives, values and histories have devastated us at the most critical level of all—that of our own minds, our own sense of who we are.

Many women express strong opposition to those who would alter our life supports, steal our tribal lands, colonize our cultures and cultural expressions, and revise our very identities. We must strive to maintain tribal status; we must make certain that the tribes continue to be legally recognized entities, sovereign nations within the larger United States, and we must wage this struggle in many ways—political, educational, literary, artistic, individual and communal. We are doing all we can: as mothers and grandmothers; as family members and tribal members; as professionals, workers, artists, shamans, leaders, chiefs, speakers, writers and organizers, we daily demonstrate that we have no intention of disappearing, of being silent, or of quietly acquiescing in our extinction.

Notes

1. It is likely, say some researchers, that fetal alcohol syndrome (FAS), which is serious among many Indian groups, will be so serious among the White Mountain Apache and the Pine Ridge Sioux that if present trends continue, by the year 2000 some people estimate that almost one-half of all children born on those reservations will in some way be affected by FAS. (Michael Dorris, Native American Studies, Dartmouth College, private conversation. Dorris has done extensive research into the syndrome as it affects native populations in the United States as well as in New Zealand.)
2. Phyllis Old Dog Cross, 'Sexual Abuse, a New Threat to the Native American Woman: An Overview', *Listening Post: A Periodical of the Mental Health Programs of Indian Health Services*, 6, (April 1982), 18.
3. Ibid., 18.
4. Ibid., 20.

Black Women in White America

Gerda Lerner*

Until the very recent past, black people in America have been denied their history. The discovery of Black history, and its legitimization and acceptance into the body of American history, is progressing at this very time and has already immensely enriched our knowledge of our national past. Black history is beginning to serve whites as an antidote to centuries of racist indoctrination by providing essential knowledge without which a more truly democratic, non-racist society cannot be built. Black history is serving Blacks in a somewhat different sense by arousing pride in a legitimate past, enhancing self-respect and providing heroes and leaders with whom black people can identify.

American women have also been denied their history, but this denial has not yet been as widely recognized. History, in the past largely written by white male historians, has simply failed to ask those questions which would elicit information about the female contribution, the female point of view. Women as a group have been denied knowledge of their legitimate past and have been profoundly affected individually by having to see the world through male eyes. Seeing women cast only in subordinate and inferior positions throughout history and seldom, if ever, learning about female heroines or women of achievement, American girls are conditioned to limit their own life goals and self-esteem. Black women have been doubly victimized by scholarly neglect and racist assumptions. Belonging as they do to two groups which have traditionally been treated as inferiors by American society—Blacks and women—they have been doubly invisible. Their records lie buried, unread, infrequently noticed and even more seldom interpreted. Their names and their achievements are known to only a few specialists. The papers of outstanding figures such as Mary

* From Gerda Lerner, 'Preface' from *Black Women in White America* by Gerda Lerner (Pantheon Books, a division of Random House, Inc, 1972), xvii–xxv, copyright © Gerda Lerner 1972, reprinted by permission of the publisher.

McLeod Bethune, Charlotte Hawkins Brown and Nannie Burroughs are scattered in various libraries, have never been edited nor even partially published. There have been few biographies of black women of the past, fewer monographs, no scholarly interpretative works. The organizational records of black women's organizations are equally scattered, unclassified and unused. [. . .]

Having said this, something must be said about the role of the white historian. White scholars, by their culturally conditioned racist assumptions, bear a heavy responsibility for having neglected and distorted the black past. One can expect the present generation of white historians, who are challenged on all sides, to rectify these omissions and distortions in their work, and to do so with a more modest approach to the limitations of their own findings and interpretations than they have done in the past. [. . .] I do not believe that recognizing the existence of large cultural subdivisions means succumbing to separatism, cultural nationalism and a narrow particularistic vision. There is a place for universalistic interpretations of that which is common to all humanity, and there is a place for that which is particular to one group, to one special entity. We accept that there is a world history and a history of France or of India which are not the same, but which fit into similar categories. [. . .]

Certainly, historians who are members of the culture, or subculture, about which they write will bring a special quality to their material. Their understanding and interpretation is apt to be different from that of an outsider. On the other hand, scholars from outside a culture have frequently had a more challenging vision than those closely involved in and bound by their own culture. Both angles of vision are complementary in arriving at the truth about the past and in finding out 'what actually happened'. The interpretation of the black past as made by Blacks must be different from that of whites. This does not mean that it can or should only be made by Blacks. It should be made by both groups, and in the clash of opinions, in debate, in the juxtaposition of different interpretations, a richer and fuller and more solidly based history will emerge. [. . .]

The historiography of this subject imposes limitations of a different kind. In the writing of history or the compiling of documents, the modern historian is dependent on the availability of sources. The kinds of sources collected depend to a large extent on the predilections, interests, prejudices and values of the collectors, archivists and historians of an earlier day. 'We have the record of kings and gentlemen ad nauseam and in stupid detail', Dr W. E. B. DuBois wrote twenty years ago,

> but of the common run of human beings . . . the world has saved all too little of authentic record and tried to forget or ignore even the little saved. With regard to Negroes in America . . . came also the attempt, conscious or unconscious, to excuse the shame of slavery by stressing natural inferiority which would render it impossible for Negroes to make, much less leave, any record of revolt or struggle, any human reaction to utter degradation.[1]

The historical sources available reflect the indifferent attention given to women in history. Collected sources predominantly concern middle-class educated women and their activities. The historian relying on such sources can easily fall into an unintended distortion. While this holds true for all women, when one seeks out information concerning black women the distortion becomes compounded. [. . .] Black history collections, which abound in source material concerning 'anonymous people', have failed to pay attention to black women, except for a handful of 'leaders'.

It was possible to find primary documents pertaining to women in slavery because abolitionists as well as defenders of the slave system collected evidence, including primary sources, pertaining to life under slavery. No comparable interest was manifested by contemporaries or historians in the living conditions of tenant farmers and rural Blacks. What descriptions exist are secondary and frequently biased in that they see Blacks only as passive victims of poverty, discrimination, exploitation and abuse. The great migration to the cities, the transition from rural to urban life, the experience of industrialization as it applied to Blacks, were not generally preserved through primary documents. [. . .]

Future interpreters of the history of black women may benefit from approaching this subject not only as a part of Black history in general, but, as is done in this anthology, as part of the history of women in general. A great many facile generalizations about black matriarchy, the black family, black women, black morality are currently circulated without much scholarly evidence and without much basis in careful research. The historian must recognize the complexity, multiplicity and differentiation of this subject. [. . .]

Black women have always been more conscious of and more handicapped by race oppression than by sex oppression. They have been subject to all the restrictions against Blacks and to those against women. In no area of life have they ever been permitted to attain higher levels of status than white women. Additionally, ever since slavery, they have been sexually exploited by white men through rape or enforced sexual services. These sexual mores, which are characteristic of the relationship of colonizers to the women of the conquered group, function not only symbolically but actually to fasten the badge of inferiority onto the enslaved group. The black man was degraded by being deprived of the power and right to protect his women from white men. The black woman was directly degraded by the sexual attack and, more profoundly, by being deprived of a strong black man on whom she could rely for protection. This slavery pattern was carried into the postslavery period and has only in this century begun to yield to the greater strength and militancy of the black community.

Black women have had an ambiguous role in relation to white society. Because they were women, white society has considered them more docile, less of a threat than black men. It has 'rewarded' them by allowing—or forcing—black women into service in the white family. Black women, ever since slavery, have nursed and raised white children, attended white people in sickness and kept white homes running smoothly. Their intimate contact with white people has made them interpreters and intermediaries of the white culture in the black home. At the same time, they have struggled in partnership with their men to keep the black family together and to allow the black community to survive. This dual and often conflicting role has imposed great tensions on black women and has given them unusual strength.

The question of black 'matriarchy' is commonly misunderstood. The very term is deceptive, for 'matriarchy' implies the exercise of power by women, and black women have been the most powerless group in our entire society. [. . .]

But the status of black women can be viewed from two different viewpoints: one, as members of the larger society; two, within their own group. When they are considered as Blacks among Blacks, they have higher status within their own group than do white women in white society. This paradox is the direct result of the special relationship of white society to black women: because the lowest-status, lowest-paid jobs in white society are reserved for black women, they often can find work even when black men cannot. In fact, one can say quite definitely that white society has economically pitted black women against black men. For black women, this has meant that they are trained from childhood to become workers, and expect to be financially self-supporting for most of their lives. [. . .] The financially independent and often better-educated black woman has higher status within her family than some men, although there are many black families with husbands holding steady jobs which follow the usual middle-class family pattern. The greater equality in relations between black men and black women, which are perceived and expressed by many black authors in their writings, may well be due more to the embattled situation of the black family and the constant stress and danger with which it is faced in a hostile world than to any other factor. Certainly it has made a decisive difference in the way the black woman perceives herself and sees her role in society. This alone can adequately explain the resistance most black women feel toward the rhetoric and concepts of the Women's Liberation movement. [. . .]

The black woman's aim throughout her history in America has been for the survival of her family and of her race. While she has for many long periods been forced to socialize her children to a pretended acceptance of discriminatory patterns, she also has managed to imbue them with race pride and a desire for full equality. This dual role has resulted in the unusual resilience and flexibility of black women and in their oft-repeated stance of dignified passive resistance to oppression. Black women, speaking with many voices and expressing many individual opinions, have been nearly unanimous in their insistence that their own emancipation cannot be separated from the emancipation of their men. Their liberation depends on the liberation of the race and the improvement of the life of the black community. [. . .]

Note

1. W. E. B. DuBois, Preface to Herbert Aptheker (ed.), *A Documentary History of The Negro People in the United States* (New York: Citadel Press, 1951), p. v.

5 Rape, Racism and the Myth of the Black Rapist

Angela Y. Davis*

Some of the most flagrant symptoms of social deterioration are acknowledged as serious problems only when they have assumed such epidemic proportions that they appear to defy solution. Rape is a case in point. In the United States today, it is one of the fastest-growing violent crimes.[1] [. . .]

In the United States and other capitalist countries, rape laws as a rule were framed originally for the protection of men of the upper classes, whose daughters and wives might be assaulted. What happens to working-class women has usually been of little concern to the courts; as a result, remarkably few white men have been prosecuted for the sexual violence they have inflicted on these women. [. . .] The rape charge has been indiscriminately aimed at Black men, the guilty and innocent alike. Thus, of the 455 men executed between 1930 and 1967 on the basis of rape convictions, 405 of them were Black.[2]

In the history of the United States, the fraudulent rape charge stands out as one of the most formidable artifices invented by racism. The myth of the Black rapist has been methodically conjured up whenever recurrent waves of violence and terror against the Black community have required convincing justifications. If Black women have been conspicuously absent from the ranks of the contemporary anti-rape movement, it may be due, in part, to that movement's indifferent posture toward the frame-up rape charge as an incitement to racist aggression. [. . .]

That Black women have not joined the anti-rape movement *en masse* does not, therefore, mean that they oppose anti-rape measures in general. Before the end of the nineteenth century pioneering Black club women conducted one of the very first organized public

* From Angela Davis, 'Rape, Racism and the Myth of the Black Rapist' from *Women, Race and Class* by Angela Davis (Random House, 1981), 172–201, copyright © Angela Davis 1981, reprinted by permission of the publisher.

protests against sexual abuse. Their eighty-year-old tradition of organized struggle against rape reflects the extensive and exaggerated ways Black women have suffered the threat of sexual violence. One of racism's salient historical features has always been the assumption that white men—especially those who wield economic power—possess an incontestable right of access to Black women's bodies.

Slavery relied as much on routine sexual abuse as it relied on the whip and the lash. [. . .] In other words, the right claimed by slaveowners and their agents over the bodies of female slaves was a direct expression of their presumed property rights over Black people as a whole. The license to rape emanated from and facilitated the ruthless economic domination that was the gruesome hallmark of slavery.[3]

The pattern of institutionalized sexual abuse of Black women became so powerful that it managed to survive the abolition of slavery. Group rape, perpetrated by the Ku Klux Klan and other terrorist organizations of the post-Civil War period, became an uncamouflaged political weapon in the drive to thwart the movement for Black equality. [. . .]

Racism has always drawn strength from its ability to encourage sexual coercion. While Black women and their sisters of color have been the main targets of these racist-inspired attacks, white women have suffered as well. For once white men were persuaded that they could commit sexual assaults against Black women with impunity, their conduct toward women of their own race could not have remained unmarred. Racism has always served as a provocation to rape, and white women in the United States have necessarily suffered the ricochet fire of these attacks. This is one of the many ways in which racism nourishes sexism, causing white women to be indirectly victimized by the special oppression aimed at their sisters of color.

The experience of the Vietnam War furnished a further example of the extent to which racism could function as a provocation to rape. Because it was drummed into the heads of US soldiers that they were fighting an inferior race, they could be taught that raping Vietnamese women was a necessary military duty. [. . .]

It is a painful irony that some anti-rape theorists, who ignore the part played by racism in instigating rape, do not hesitate to argue that men of color are especially prone to commit sexual violence against women. In her very impressive study of rape, Susan Brownmiller claims that Black men's historical oppression has placed many of the 'legitimate' expressions of male supremacy beyond their reach. They must resort, as a result, to acts of open sexual violence. In her portrayal of 'ghetto inhabitants', Brownmiller insists that

> (c)orporate executive dining rooms and climbs up Mount Everest are not usually accessible to those who form the subculture of violence. Access to a female body—through force—is within their ken.[4]

When Brownmiller's book *Against Our Will: Men, Women and Rape* was published, it was effusively praised in some circles. *Time* magazine, which selected her as one of its women of the year in 1976, described the book as ' . . . the most rigorous and provocative piece of scholarship that has yet emerged from the feminist movement'.[5] In other circles, however, the book has been severely criticized for its part in the resuscitation of the old racist myth of the Black rapist.

It cannot be denied that Brownmiller's book is a pioneering scholarly contribution to the contemporary literature on rape. Yet many of her arguments are unfortunately pervaded with racist ideas. Characteristic of that perspective is her reinterpretation of the 1953 lynching of fourteen-year-old Emmett Till. After this young boy had whistled at a white women in Mississippi, his maimed body was found at the bottom of the Tallahatchie River. 'Till's action', said Brownmiller, 'was more than a kid's brash prank'.[6]

> Emmett Till was going to show his black buddies that he, and by inference, *they* could get a white woman and Carolyn Bryant was the nearest convenient object. In concrete terms, the accessibility of *all* white women was on review . . . And what of the wolf whistle, Till's 'gesture of adolescent bravado?' . . . The whistle was no small tweet of hubba-hubba or melodious approval for a well-turned ankle . . . It was a deliberate insult just short of physical assault, a last reminder to Carolyn Bryant that this black boy, Till, had in mind to possess her.[7]

While Brownmiller deplores the sadistic punishment inflicted on Emmett Till, the Black youth emerges, none the less, as a guilty sexist—almost as guilty as his white racist murderers. After all, she argues, both Till and his murderers were exclusively concerned about their rights of possession over women. [. . .]

Diana Russell's *Politics of Rape* unfortunately reinforces the current notion that the typical rapist is a man of color—or, if he is white, a poor or working-class man. Subtitled *The Victims' Perspective*, her book is based on a series of interviews with rape victims in the San Francisco Bay Area. Of the twenty-two cases she describes, twelve—i.e., more than half—involve women who have been raped by Black,

Chicano or Native American Indian men. It is revealing that only 26 percent of the original ninety-five interviews she conducted involved men of color.[8] If this dubious process of selection is not enough to evoke deep suspicions of racism, consider the advice she offers to white women:

> . . . (I)f some black men see rape of white women as an act of revenge or as a justifiable expression of hostility toward whites, I think it is equally realistic for white women to be less trusting of black men than many of them are.[9]

Brownmiller, MacKellar and Russell are assuredly more subtle than earlier ideologues of racism. But their conclusions tragically beg comparison with the ideas of such scholarly apologists of racism as Winfield Collins, who published in 1918 a book entitled *The Truth About Lynching and the Negro in the South* (In Which the Author Pleads that the South Be Made Safe for the White Race):

> Two of the Negro's most prominent characteristics are the utter lack of chastity and complete ignorance of veracity. The Negro's sexual laxity, considered so immoral or even criminal in the white man's civilization, may have been all but a virtue in the habitat of his origin. There, nature developed in him intense sexual passions to offset his high death rate.[10]

Collins resorts to pseudo-biological arguments, while Brownmiller, Russell and MacKellar invoke environmental explanations, but in the final analysis they all assert that Black men are motivated in especially powerful ways to commit sexual violence against women.

One of the earliest theoretical works associated with the contemporary feminist movement that dealt with the subject of rape and race was Shulamith Firestone's *The Dialectic of Sex: The Case For Feminist Revolution.* Racism in general, so Firestone claims, is actually an extension of sexism. Invoking the biblical notion that ' . . . the races are no more than the various parents and siblings of the Family of Man',[11] she develops a construct defining the white man as father, the white woman as wife and mother, and Black people as the children. Transposing Freud's theory of the Oedipus complex into racial terms, Firestone implies that Black men harbor an uncontrollable desire for sexual relations with white women. They want to kill the father and sleep with the mother.[12] Moreover, in order to 'be a man', the Black man must

> . . . untie himself from his bond with the white female, relating to her if at all only in a degrading way. In addition, due to his virulent hatred and jealousy of her Possessor, the white man, he may lust after her as a thing to be conquered in order to revenge himself on the white man.[13]

Like Brownmiller, MacKellar and Russell, Firestone succumbs to the old racist sophistry of blaming the victim. Whether innocently or consciously, their pronouncements have facilitated the resurrection of the timeworn myth of the Black rapist. Their historical myopia further prevents them from comprehending that the portrayal of Black men as rapists reinforces racism's open invitation to white men to avail themselves sexually of Black women's bodies. The fictional image of the Black man as rapist has always strengthened its inseparable companion: the image of the Black woman as chronically promiscuous. For once the notion is accepted that Black men harbor irresistible and animal-like sexual urges, the entire race is invested with bestiality. If Black men have their eyes on white women as sexual objects, then Black women must certainly welcome the sexual attentions of white men. Viewed as 'loose women' and whores, Black women's cries of rape would necessarily lack legitimacy. [. . .]

Calvin Hernton unfortunately succumbs to similar falsehood about Black women. In the study *Sex and Racism*, he insists that ' . . . the Negro woman during slavery began to develop a depreciatory concept of herself, not only as a female but as a human being as well'.[14] According to Hernton's analysis, '(A)fter experiencing the ceaseless sexual immorality of the white South',

> . . . the Negro woman became 'promiscuous and loose,' and could be 'had for the taking'. Indeed, she came to look upon herself as the South viewed and treated her, for she had no other morality by which to shape her womanhood.[15]

Hernton's analysis never penetrates the ideological veil which has resulted in the minimizing of the sexual outrages constantly committed against Black women. He falls into the trap of blaming the victim for the savage punishment she was historically forced to endure.

Throughout the history of this country, Black women have manifested a collective consciousness of their sexual victimization. They have also understood that they could not adequately resist the sexual abuses they suffered without simultaneously attacking the fraudulent rape charge as a pretext for lynching. The reliance on rape as an instrument of white-supremacist terror predates by several centuries the institution of lynching. During slavery, the lynching of Black people did not occur extensively—for the simple reason that slaveowners were reluctant to destroy their valuable property. Flogging, yes, but lynching, no. Together with flogging, rape was a terribly efficient method of keeping Black women and men alike in check. It was a routine arm of repression.

Lynchings did occur before the Civil War—but they were aimed more often at white abolitionists, who had no cash value on the market. According to William Lloyd Garrison's *Liberator* over 300 white people were lynched over the two decades following 1836.[16] [. . .]

With the emancipation of the slaves, Black people no longer possessed a market value for the former slaveholders, and ' . . . the lynching industry was revolutionized'.[17] When Ida B. Wells researched her first pamphlet against lynching, published in 1895 under the title *A Red Record*, she calculated that over 10,000 lynchings had taken place between 1865 and 1895. [. . .]

In connection with these lynchings and their countless barbarities, the myth of the Black rapist was conjured up. It could only acquire its terrible powers of persuasion within the irrational world of racist ideology. However irrational the myth may be, it was not a spontaneous aberration. On the contrary, the myth of the Black rapist was a distinctly political invention. As Frederick Douglass points out, Black men were not indiscriminately labeled as rapists during slavery. Throughout the entire Civil War, in fact, not a single Black man was publicly accused of raping a white woman.[18] If Black men possessed an animalistic urge to rape, argued Douglass, this alleged rape instinct would have certainly been activated when white women were left unprotected by their men who were fighting in the Confederate Army.

In the immediate aftermath of the Civil War, the menacing specter of the Black rapist had not yet appeared on the historical scene. But lynchings, reserved during slavery for the white abolitionists, were proving to be a valuable political weapon. Before lynching could be consolidated as a popularly accepted institution, however, its savagery and its horrors had to be convincingly justified. These were the circumstances which spawned the myth of the Black rapist—for the rape charge turned out to be the most powerful of several attempts to justify the lynching of Black people. The institution of lynching, in turn, complemented by the continued rape of Black women, became an essential ingredient of the postwar strategy of racist terror. In this way the brutal exploitation of Black labor was guaranteed, and after the betrayal of Reconstruction, the political domination of the Black people as a whole was assured.

During the first great wave of lynchings, propaganda urging the defense of white womanhood from Black men's irrepressible rape instincts was conspicuous for its absence. [. . .] Lynching was undisguised counterinsurgency, a guarantee that Black people would not be able to achieve their goals of citizenship and economic equality. [. . .] Lynchings were represented as a necessary measure to prevent Black supremacy over white people—in other words, to reaffirm white supremacy.[19]

After the betrayal of Reconstruction and the accompanying disfranchisement of Black people, the specter of Black political supremacy as a pretext for lynching became outmoded. Still, as the postwar economic structure took shape, solidifying the superexploitation of Black labor, the number of lynchings continued to rise. This was the historical juncture when the cry of rape emerged as the major justification for lynching. Frederick Douglass' explanation of the political motives underlying the creation of the mythical Black rapist is a brilliant analysis of the way ideology transforms to meet new historical conditions.

> The times have changed and the Negro's accusers have found it necessary to change with them. They have been compelled to invent a new charge to suit the times. The old charges are no longer valid. Upon them the good opinion of the North and of mankind cannot be secured. Honest men no longer believe that there is any ground to apprehend Negro supremacy. Times and events have swept away these old refuges of lies. They were once powerful. They did their work in their day and did it with terrible energy and effect, but they are now cast aside as useless. The lie has lost its ability to deceive. The altered circumstances have made necessary a sterner, stronger and more effective justification of Southern barbarism, and hence we have, according to my theory, to look into the face of a more shocking and blasting charge than either Negro supremacy or Negro insurrection.[20]

This more shocking and blasting charge, of course, was rape. [. . .] Although the majority of lynchings did not even involve the accusation of sexual assault, the racist cry of rape became a popular explanation which was far more effective than either of the two previous attempts to justify mob attacks on Black people. In a society where male supremacy was all-pervasive, men who were motivated by their duty to defend their women could be excused of any excesses they might commit. That their motive was sublime was ample justification for the resulting barbarities. As Senator Ben Tillman of South Carolina told his Washington colleagues at the beginning of this century,

> (w)hen stern and sad-faced white men put to death a creature in human form who has deflowered a white woman, they have avenged the greatest wrong, the blackest crime . . .[21]

Such crimes, he said, caused civilized men to '. . . revert to the original savage type whose impulses under such circumstances have always been to "kill, kill, kill" '.[22]

The repercussions of this new myth were enormous. Not only was opposition to individual lynchings stifled—for who would dare to defend a rapist?—white support for the cause of Black equality in general began to wane. By the end of the nineteenth century the largest mass organization of white women—the Women's Christian Temperance Union—was headed by a woman who publicly vilified Black men for their alleged attacks on white women. What is more, Frances Willard went so far as to characterize Black men as especially prone to alcoholism, which in turn exacerbated their instinctual urge to rape. [. . .]

What was the reality behind this terribly powerful myth of the Black rapist? To be sure, there were some examples of Black men raping white women. But the number of actual rapes which occurred was minutely disproportionate to the allegations implied by the myth. As already indicated, during the entire Civil War, there was not a single reported case of a white woman suffering rape at the hands of a slave. While virtually all the Southern white men were on the battlefront, never once was the cry of rape raised. Frederick Douglass argues that the leveling of the rape charge against Black men as a whole was not credible for the simple reason that it implied a radical and instantaneous change in the mental and moral character of Black people.

> History does not present an example of a transformation in the character of any class of men so extreme, so unnatural and so complete as is implied in this charge. The change is too great and the period for it too brief[23]

[. . .] Although their arguments were disputed by the facts, most apologists for lynching claimed that only white men's obligation to defend their women could motivate them to commit such savage attacks on Black men. [. . .]

The colonization of the Southern economy by capitalists from the North gave lynching its most vigorous impulse. If Black people, by means of terror and violence, could remain the most brutally exploited group within the swelling ranks of the working class, the capitalists could enjoy a double advantage. Extra profits would result from the superexploitation of Black labor, and white workers' hostilities toward their employers would be defused. White workers who assented to lynching necessarily assumed a posture of racial solidarity with the white men who were really their oppressors. This was a critical moment in the popularization of racist ideology.

If Black people had simply accepted a status of economic and political inferiority, the mob murders would probably have subsided. But because vast numbers of ex-slaves refused to discard their dreams of progress, more than 10,000 lynchings occurred during the three decades following the war.[24] Whoever challenged the racial hierarchy was marked a potential victim of the mob. The endless roster of the dead came to include every sort of insurgent—from the owners of successful Black businesses and workers pressing for higher wages to those who refused to be called 'boy' and the defiant women who resisted white men's sexual abuses. Yet public opinion had been captured, and it was taken for granted that lynching was a just response to the barbarous sexual crimes against white womanhood. And an important question remained unasked: What about the numerous women who were lynched—and sometimes raped before they were killed by the mob. Ida B. Wells refers to

> . . . the horrible case of the woman in San Antonio, Texas, who had been boxed up in a barrel with nails driven through the sides and rolled down a hill until she was dead.[25]

[. . .] Given the central role played by the fictional Black rapist in the shaping of post-slavery racism, it is, at best, irresponsible theorizing to represent Black men as the most frequent authors of sexual violence. At worst, it is an aggression against Black people as a whole, for the mythical rapist implies the mythical whore. Perceiving the rape charge as an attack against the entire Black community, Black women were quick to assume the leadership of the anti-lynching movement. Ida B. Wells-Barnett was the moving force behind a crusade against lynching which was destined to span many decades. In 1892 three acquaintances of this Black newspaperwoman were lynched in Memphis, Tennessee. They were murdered by a racist mob because the store they opened in a Black neighborhood was successfully competing with a white-owned store. Ida B. Wells hastened to speak out against this lynching in the pages of her newspaper, *The Free Speech*. During her trip to New York three months later, the offices of her paper were burned to the ground. Threatened with lynching herself, she decided to remain in the East and to '. . . tell the world for the first time the true story of Negro lynchings, which were becoming more numerous and horrible'.[26]

Wells' articles in the *New York Age* motivated Black women to organize a support campaign on her behalf, which eventually led to the establishment of Black women's clubs.[54] [. . .] During her trips abroad, an important solidarity movement was organized in Britain, which had a marked impact on US public opinion. This vicious editorial was published after Wells' 1904 trip to England:

Immediately following the day of Miss Wells' return to the United States, a Negro man assaulted a white woman in New York City 'for the purposes of lust and plunder.' . . . The circumstances of his fiendish crime may serve to convince the mulatress missionary that the promulgation in New York just now of her theory of Negro outrages is, to say the least, inopportune.[27]

Mary Church Terrell, the first president of the National Association of Colored Women, was another outstanding Black woman leader who was devoted to the fight against lynching. In 1904 she answered Thomas Nelson Page's virulent article on 'The Lynching of Negroes—Its Cause and Prevention'. In the *North American Review*, where Page's article had appeared, she published an essay entitled 'Lynching From a Negro's Point of View'. With compelling logic, Terrell systematically refuted Page's justification of lynching as an understandable response to alleged sexual assaults on white women.[28]

Thirty years after Ida B. Wells had initiated the anti-lynching campaign, an organization called the Anti-Lynching Crusaders was founded. Established in 1922 under the auspices of the NAACP and headed by Mary Talbert, its purpose was to create an integrated women's movement against lynching.

What will Mary B. Talbert do next? What next will the colored American women do under her leadership? An organization has been effected by colored women to get ONE MILLION WOMEN of all kinds and colors united by December, 1922 against lynching.

Look out, Mr. Lyncher!

This class of women generally get what they go after.[29]

This was not the first time Black women had reached out to their white sisters. They were struggling in the tradition of such historical giants as Sojourner Truth and Frances E. W. Harper. Ida B. Wells had personally appealed to white women, as had her contemporary, Mary Church Terrell. And Black clubwomen had collectively attempted to persuade the white women's club movement to direct some of their energies toward the anti-lynching campaign.

White women did not respond to these appeals *en masse* until the Association of Southern Women for the Prevention of Lynching was founded in 1930 under the leadership of Jessie Daniel Ames.[30] The

Association set out to repudiate the claim that lynching was necessary for the protection of Southern womanhood:

> The program of the Southern women has been directed to exposing the falsity of the claim that lynching is necessary to their protection and to emphasize the real danger of lynching to all the values of home and religion.[31]

[. . .] Jessie Daniel Ames and her co-founders of the Association of Southern Women for the Prevention of Lynching resolved in 1930 to recruit the masses of Southern white women into the campaign to defeat the racist mobs bent on killing Black people. Eventually they obtained over 40,000 signatures to the Association's pledge:

> We declare lynching is an indefensible crime, destructive of all principles of government, hateful and hostile to every ideal of religion and humanity, debasing and degrading to every person involved . . .[32] [. . .]

These courageous white women encountered opposition, hostility and even physical threats on their lives. Their contributions were invaluable within the overall anti-lynching crusade. [. . .] Yet the Association of Southern Women for the Prevention of Lynching was a movement that was 40 years late in coming. For four decades or more, Black women had been leading the anti-lynching campaign, and for just about as long, they had appealed to their white sisters to join them. [. . .]

While the Association of Southern Women for the Prevention of Lynching was a belated response to their Black sisters' appeals, these women's far-reaching achievements dramatically illustrate white women's special place in the struggle against racism. When Mary Talbert and her Anti-Lynching Crusaders reached out to white women, they felt that white women could more readily identify with the Black cause by virtue of their own oppression as women. Besides, lynching itself, as a terrifying tool of racism, also served to strengthen male dominance.

> Economic dependence, contacts with none save 'polite, refined, womanly' pursuits, mental activities in no other field than home life—all these man-imposed restrictions have borne more heavily upon women in the South and have been maintained more rigidly, than in any other part of the country.[33]

Throughout the anti-lynching crusade, the critics of the racist manipulation of the rape charge did not intend to excuse those individual Black men who actually committed the crime of sexual assault. [. . .]

The resurgence of racism during the mid-1970s has been accompanied by a resurrection of the myth of the Black rapist. Unfortunately, this myth has sometimes been legitimized by white women associated with the battle against rape. Consider, for example, Susan Brownmiller's concluding passage of the chapter of her book entitled 'A Question of Race':

> Today the incidence of actual rape combined with the looming spectre of the rapist in the mind's eye, and in particular the mythified spectre of the black man as rapist to which the black man in the name of his manhood now contributes, must be understood as a control mechanism against the freedom, mobility and aspirations of all women, white and black. The crossroads of racism and sexism had to be a violent meeting place. There is no use pretending it doesn't exist.[34]

Brownmiller [. . .] seems as if she wants to intentionally conjure up in her readers' imaginations armies of Black men, their penises erect, charging full speed ahead toward the most conveniently placed white women. [. . .]

In pretending to defend the cause of all women, she sometimes boxes herself into the position of defending the particular cause of *white* women, regardless of its implications. Her examination of the Scottsboro Nine case is a revealing example. As Brownmiller herself points out, these nine young men, charged and convicted of rape, spent long years of their lives in prison because two white women perjured themselves on the witness stand. Yet she has nothing but contempt for the Black men and their defense movement—and her sympathy for the two white women is glaring.

> The left fought hard for its symbols of racial injustice, making bewildered heroes out of a handful of pathetic, semi-literate fellows caught in the jaws of Southern jurisprudence who only wanted to beat the rap.[35]

On the other hand, the two white women, whose false testimony sent the Scottsboro Nine to prison, were

> . . . corraled by a posse of white men who already believed a rape had taken place. Confused and fearful, they fell into line.[36]

No one can deny that the women were manipulated by Alabama racists. However, it is wrong to portray the women as innocent pawns, absolved of the responsibility of having collaborated with the forces of racism. In choosing to take sides with white women, regardless of the circumstances, Brownmiller herself capitulates to racism. Her failure to alert white women about the urgency of combining a fierce challenge to racism with the necessary battle against sexism is an important plus for the forces of racism today.

The myth of the Black rapist continues to carry out the insidious work of racist ideology. It must bear a good portion of the responsibility for the failure of most anti-rape theorists to seek the identity of the enormous numbers of anonymous rapists who remain unreported, untried and unconvicted. [. . .]

But why are there so many anonymous rapists in the first place? Might not this anonymity be a privilege enjoyed by men whose status protects them from prosecution? Although white men who are employers, executives, politicians, doctors, professors, etc., have been known to 'take advantage' of women they consider their social inferiors, their sexual misdeeds seldom come to light in court. Is it not therefore quite probable that these men of the capitalist and middle classes account for a significant proportion of the unreported rapes? Many of these unreported rapes undoubtedly involve Black women as victims: their historical experience proves that racist ideology implies an open invitation to rape. As the basis of the license to rape Black women during slavery was the slaveholders' economic power, so the class structure of capitalist society also harbors an incentive to rape. It seems, in fact, that men of the capitalist class and their middle-class partners are immune to prosecution because they commit their sexual assaults with the same unchallenged authority that legitimizes their daily assaults on the labor and dignity of working people.

The existence of widespread sexual harassment on the job has never been much of a secret. It is precisely on the job, indeed, that women—especially when they are not unionized—are most vulnerable. Having already established their economic domination over their female subordinates, employers, managers and foremen may attempt to assert this authority in sexual terms. That working-class women are more intensely exploited than their men adds to their vulnerability to sexual abuse, while sexual coercion simultaneously reinforces their vulnerability to economic exploitation. [. . .]

The class structure of capitalism encourages men who wield power in the economic and political realm to become routine agents of sexual exploitation. [. . .] It is not a mere coincidence that as the incidence of rape has risen, the position of women workers has visibly worsened. So severe are women's economic losses that their wages in relationship to men are lower than they were a decade ago. The proliferation of sexual violence is the brutal face of a generalized intensification of the sexism which necessarily accompanies this economic assault.

Following a pattern established by racism, the attack on women mirrors the deteriorating situation of workers of color and the rising influence of racism in the judicial system, the educational institutions and in the government's posture of studied neglect toward Black people and other people of color. The most dramatic sign of the dangerous resurgence of racism is the new visibility of the Ku Klux Klan and the related epidemic of violent assaults on Blacks, Chicanos, Puerto Ricans and Native Americans. [. . .]

Given the complexity of the social context of rape today, any attempt to treat it as an isolated phenomenon is bound to founder. [. . .] The struggle against racism must be an ongoing theme of the anti-rape movement, which must not only defend women of color, but the many victims of the racist manipulation of the rape charge as well. The crisis dimensions of sexual violence constitute one of the facets of a deep and ongoing crisis of capitalism. [. . .] The anti-rape movement and its important current activities—ranging from emotional and legal aid to self-defence and educational campaigns—must be situated in a strategic context which envisages the ultimate defeat of monopoly capitalism.

Notes

1. Nancy Gager and Cathleen Schurr, *Sexual Assault: Confronting Rape in America* (New York: Grosset and Dunlap, 1976), 1.
2. Michael Meltsner, *Cruel and Unusual: The Supreme Court and Capital Punishment* (New York: Random House, 1973), 75.
3. See Angela Y. Davis, *Women, Race and Class* (New York: Random House, 1981), ch. 1.
4. Susan Brownmiller, *Against Our Will: Men, Women and Rape* (New York: Simon and Schuster, 1975), 194.
5. 'A Dozen Who Made a Difference,' *Time*, Vol. 107 (January 5, 1976), p. 20.
6. Brownmiller, *Against Our Will*, 247.
7. Ibid.
8. Diana Russell, *The Politics of Rape: The Victim's Perspective* (New York: Stein and Day, 1975).
9. Ibid., 163.
10. Winfield H. Collins, *The Truth About Lynching and the Negro in the South* (In Which the Author Pleads that the South Be Made Safe for the White Race) (New York: Neale Publishing Co., 1918), 94–5.
11. Shulamith Firestone, *The Dialectic of Sex: The Case for Feminist Revolution* (New York: Bantam Books, 1971), 108.
12. Ibid., 108ff.

13. Ibid., 110.
14. Calvin Hernton, *Sex and Racism in America* (New York: Grove Press, 1965), 125.
15. Ibid., 124.
16. Walter White, *Rope and Faggot: A Biography of Judge Lynch* (New York, Alped A. Knof, Inc, 1929), 91.
17. Ibid., 94.
18. Frederick Douglass, 'The Lesson of the Hour' (pamphlet published in 1894). Reprinted under the title 'Why is the Negro Lynched' in Foner, *The Life and Writings of Frederick Douglass*, Vol. 4, 498–9.
19. Ibid.
20. Ibid., 502.
21. Cager and Schurr, *Sexual Assault*, 163.
22. Ibid.
23. Foner, *The Life and Writings of Frederick Douglass*, Vol. 4, 499.
24. Wells-Barnett, *On Lynching*, 8.
25. Ida B. Wells-Barnett, *Crusade for Justice: the Autobiography of Ida B. Wells*, ed. Alfred M. Duster (Chicago: University of Chicago Press, 1970), 149
26. Wells, *Crusade for Justice*, 63.
27. Wells, *Crusade for Justice*, 218.
28. Lerner, *Black Women in White America* (New York: Pantheon), 205–11.
29. Ibid., 215.
30. See Jessie Daniel Ames, *The Changing Character of Lynching, 1931–1941*
31. Ibid., 19.
32. Ames, *Changing Character*, 64.
33. White, *Rope and Faggot*, 159.
34. Brownmiller, *Against Our Will*, 255.
35. Ibid., 237.
36. Ibid., 233.

6 Transforming Socialist-Feminism: The Challenge of Racism

Kum-Kum Bhavnani and Margaret Coulson*

Feminism is the political theory and practice that struggles to free *all* women: women of colour, working class women, poor women, disabled women, lesbians, old women—as well as white economically privileged, heterosexual women.

(Smith, 1982)[1]

[. . .] Through struggle, in heated arguments and in writings, black women have been trying to shift socialist-feminist politics. In their 1985 article, Michèle Barrett and Mary McIntosh[2] have provided one response to these initiatives. The two of us are anxious to take seriously this attempt by white feminists to take up the challenge of the charge of racism which has been made against white feminist analysis. [. . .]

Our own contribution arises out of our reactions to and discussion of their article. We also want to take up some of the arguments raised in 'Many Voices, One Chant', a special issue of *Feminist Review*[3] produced by black women about black struggles. That issue was itself situated in a recent history, which includes the setting up of the Organization of Women of Asian and African Descent, the struggles around Imperial Typewriters, Trico and Grunwicks, as well as the development of Women Against Racism and Fascism groups, the autumn 1980 Socialist-Feminist Conference on anti-imperialism and anti-racism and more recent developments. We see the challenge of the charge of racism as having the potential to motivate a different kind of socialist-feminism. [. . .]

We'd like to thank all those with whom we've discussed these ideas and especially Ruth Frankenberg, Margo Gorman, Lata Mani, Sarah Pyett, Esther Saraga, Andy Shallice and Claudette Williams.

* From Kum-Kum Bhavnani and Margaret Coulson: 'Transforming Socialist Feminism: the Challenge of Racism' from *Feminist Review* No. 23 (Taylor & Francis, 1986), 81–92, reprinted by permission of the publisher.

THE RISK OF ENTERING THIS DEBATE

In our conversations, both with each other and with others, we have tried to identify some of the problems of entering into these discussions, given the tensions that are involved. This means recognizing that black women and white women have different histories and different relationships to present struggles, in Britain and internationally. White women who enter these debates must acknowledge the material basis of their power in relation to black people, both women and men. It is also necessary to acknowledge the complexities of this power relationship—as between white women and black men, where white women may be privileged, oppressed or both.

In contributing to these discussions white women cannot avoid the legacy of racism within feminism. This legacy has a long history which includes the dominance of eugenicism in both the early and more recent birth control movements, the eager acceptance by the majority of the suffragettes of imperialistic nationalism, and at best, the failure of anti-rape campaigns to challenge racist stereotypes of the sexuality of black men. Not only have these generally not taken up racism as an issue, nor seen how their campaigns against male violence are complicated in the context of racism, but by their actions they have reaffirmed racist ideas by marching through black areas and calling for greater policing.

However, we do not subscribe to a politics based on essentialism. We also feel that there are times when black and white political activists have to work together and in this article we are attempting to do that. [. . .] We write this as a political and theoretical piece. We hope that the discussions and actions which may result will contribute to a process which will shift socialist-feminism out of its present rut (sometimes known as its crisis!).

There have been important moments in contemporary socialist-feminism: in the development of analyses of women's work, waged and unwaged, in women's relation to men, to the working class and to capital, and in debates with radical feminists about sexuality. One important commitment of recent socialist-feminism has been to confront the 'masculinist' assumptions which have distorted socialist theory and practice and to transform socialism into something which can more fully represent the struggles and aspirations of women. [. . .] This socialist-feminism must, itself, be open to being transformed under the impetus of black struggles. But it is still hard to find instances where this has happened.

ONE FEMININITY OR MANY?

[. . .] While Sojourner Truth's 'ain't I a woman?'[4] speech has been widely quoted in the women's movement . . . what sense has been made of them? Apart from intended racialism, lack of information has been used as an excuse for leaving black women out of analyses, or black women have been defined as problems, or black women have been exoticized. [. . .] It seems to us that black women are merely being added on and the need to transform the whole analysis is not realized.

[. . .] The racism of the women's movement in Britain can be seen clearly from the following example. Reclaim the Night marches, held in the mid to late 70s, often went through black areas whilst demanding that the streets be made safe for women, sometimes with an accompanying slogan for 'better' policing. Despite the arguments and protests of black women then, and since, Reclaim the Night marches (for example, one held in Cambridge in 1984) often still carry slogans for 'better' policing. Not only is it racist to march through black areas with demands for safer streets for women (which women?), but also, to understate it, we don't know of many black women who see police protection as any way of doing this. Racism operates in a way which places different women in different relationships to structures of power and authority in society. [. . .]

The problem with the concept of gender is that it is rooted in an apparently simple and 'real' material base of biological difference between women and men. But what is constructed on that base is not one femininity in relation to one masculinity, but several. It is not only that there are differences between different groups of women but that these differences are often also conflicts of interest. Whilst it can be difficult, socialist-feminism has to recognize these conflicts and tackle them politically.

THE STATE DEALS WITH DIFFERENT WOMEN DIFFERENTLY

For socialist-feminists, one way into these issues is through an examination of the state and the ways in which it deals differently with different groups of women. Struggles, campaigns, analyses by black people, especially women, against the immigration laws have focused political attention on the significance of these laws in revealing the state's projects in relation to black people. Since the 1940s, immigration and nationality legislation have become central instruments of state racism, irrespective of the political party in government. The state has become obsessively concerned with the entry of black labour into the UK and, in consequence, with the control of black people already here.[5] The main assumption has been that black men enter the labour market, or threaten it, while the extraction of surplus value from black women through their participation in that labour market has often been ignored. This is in spite of the extensive involvement of black women in paid employment.[6] This assumption has been expressed in the sexism of immigration controls. For example, until recently there was some provision for black men to be joined by their fiancées but much tighter controls on women wanting to bring their fiancés into the UK. Appeals against this inequality were upheld in 1985 by the European Court of Human Rights on the grounds of sex discrimination. The British government responded by amending regulations further to tighten the controls on entry of all fiancé(e)s. This contrasts with an earlier decision, included in the 1981 Nationality Act, which allowed some (mainly white) women for the first time to pass on citizenship to their children born abroad. In the first case, the state abandoned its sexism in the negative sense that it reduced the rights of women and men to the same and worse level, and simultaneously consolidated its racism. In the second case, it also proclaimed commitment to sex equality and improved the rights of mainly white women, but further consolidated its racism.[7] Thus under the rhetoric of creating 'equality' between women and men, the state develops further racist practices. While the two of us would not claim to have any easy answers, it is this type of conflict of interests which all of us as socialist-feminists need to confront.

RACISM OR ETHNOCENTRISM?

[. . .] To us, the central problem for socialist-feminist theory is racism, of which ethnocentrism may be a consequence. As far as we can see, the role of the state and international capital in creating and perpetuating inequalities between black people and white people is lost through the use of a term such as ethnocentrism. Further, the word and indeed the concept seem to imply that the problem is one of cultural bias, supported by ignorance. It then follows that, if more sociological information is presented, the problem can be overcome. We are arguing, however, that to consider racism as the central issue involves a fundamental and radical *transformation* of socialist-feminism.

[. . .] We think that if we are to change the conceptual framework we have to begin by asking different questions. When we try to understand the condition of women we ask, what is it that oppresses women? What shapes the lives and identities of women? What shapes the lives and identities of black women? One way into the last question is through an examination of the political dynamic. If we consider what issues black people have been struggling over during the past five or ten years in Britain, we see that these struggles have revolved around challenging racism, specifically in relation to the state: over deportation and anti-deportation campaigns, and the police. From asking these questions and reviewing these struggles we are drawn to the need for fresh analysis of the relationship between the state and 'the family' and of how this differs for black and white people. This may lead us to an analysis, and some understanding, that the state may have different strategies for each group. [. . .]

RACISM, THE STATE AND BLACK HOUSEHOLDS

We begin from a recognition that not all family/household forms and ideologies are equal within Britain, nor are they dealt with as equally valid by the state. For example, the state's practices in terms of the ideology of family unity are pretty contradictory in relation to black people. As a consequence of immigration controls and practices, many black families are split up either permanently or for a large number of years. The state shows no respect for the principles of family unity in these cases. [. . .] But the state claims to desire 'family unity' for black families in other circumstances. For example, if a marriage of black people born overseas comes to an end, with one partner perhaps moving to their country of origin, the state attempts to remove/deport the rest of the family/household, using the argument that family unity must be upheld. For black people the British state's commitment to 'family unity' is strongest where such unity is outside the United Kingdom.[8]

To look at this more analytically we can examine the state's relation to black people through the notion of black labour as surplus labour. We are referring to the argument that capital has an interest in maintaining black labour as surplus labour. By this we mean that such labour is seen as temporary, easily expendable, easily replaceable and in excess of demand. Because of Britain's colonial relationship with the continent of Africa, the Indian sub-continent and the Caribbean, in the 1940s and early 1950s there was *some* rhetoric about colonial subjects coming to work in the 'mother country'. In this limited sense black people were initially viewed as potential settlers, although no social provision was made for such settlers in terms of housing or other human needs. Thus black workers appeared to add to existing pressure on already scarce social resources in poor urban areas. In Sivanandan's analysis,[9] while the economic gain from black workers went to capital, the social costs were borne by labour, but capital and labour were united by racism. Internal and external political pressures including the influence of EEC policy on immigration control led to the rapid development of Britain's racist immigration controls through the 1960s and 1970s, through which black settlers effectively became redefined as migrant labour. Thus, employed black labour in the countries of the white capitalist world retains a temporary status. [. . .]

In the contemporary situation of high and increasing unemployment in Britain, and the changing international division of labour, immigration controls were and are constantly being tightened against black people, and particularly against black men. The patriarchal assumptions of the British state as built into immigration laws must be situated in this dynamic of state racism. [. . .]

The state's relationship to black people is also marked out by ideas and practices which associate black people with crime, deviance and disorder. These ideas and practices are then used to 'justify' particularly heavy and coercive policing. We are not able to present the range of arguments about this here, but we want to signal that policing and 'law and order' are also major means by which the state perpetuates and legitimates its violence against black people. Stuart Hall *et al.*, Paul Gilroy and Errol Lawrence are examples of writers who have presented analyses on these issues.[10]

That many white socialist-feminists ignore racialist attacks on black households is not new. However, in doing so, they also ignore that harassment and racialist attacks from white women and white men, and sometimes white families, can impel a solidarity within black households. Whatever inequalities exist in such households, they are clearly also sites of support for their members. In saying this we are recognizing that black women may have significant issues to face within black households. Struggles over sexuality and against domestic violence, for example, have been important issues for all feminists, including black feminists, and have involved confronting assumptions about domestic relationships. But at the same time the black family is a source of support in the context of harassment and attacks from white people.

[. . .] It is such issues which produce contradictory sets of relationships between black women, white women, black households, the state, and the predominantly white women's movement.

[. . .] To carry this discussion further requires a fuller analysis of the relationship between 'the family' upheld by the state, in dominant ideology and social practice, and black families, within the overall context of a racist society.

IN CONCLUSION

We do not wish to summarize our article here—rather we want to tease out some implications of our arguments and to raise further questions. The first point we would wish to make is that through arguing that an analysis of racism must be central to socialist-feminism, we do not claim to be presenting 'an answer'. We would, however, see that an analysis which we all, as socialist-feminists, need to develop is based on the idea of a racially structured, patriarchal capitalism (excuse the mouthful). This leads us to examine how 'race', class and gender are structured in relation to one another. How do they combine with and/or cut across one another? How does racism divide gender identity and experience? How is gender experienced through racism? How is class shaped by gender and 'race'? To take these questions on does require a fundamental redrawing of the conceptual categories of socialist-feminism, and it may help us to develop a more adequate politics. [. . .]

As we have tried to show, one consequence of not understanding the centrality of racism and its challenge is that socialist-feminism becomes distanced from the political dynamic. [. . .] The importance of this is in relation to political action. Many feminists employed as academics and teachers have been struggling within their educational institutions for greater equality of opportunities for women through challenging conditions of service, employment practices, gendered segregation in jobs and education, and so on. Rarely do these same women, if white, challenge the racism of such institutions with the same clarity and energy. Indeed, sometimes they see anti-racism as competing with anti-sexism for resources and support—for example, in recruitment of staff or students—thus operating on an assumption that anti-sexism concerns white women and anti-racism concerns black people.

The final point of our conclusion is to repeat that an assumption of automatic sisterhood from white women towards black women is ill-founded. Sisterhood can only be nurtured and developed when white women acknowledge the complex power relationships between white women and white men in relation to black women and black men. [. . .] The attempt to try and transform socialist-feminism is not a worthy cause but a political necessity. As Barbara Smith says:

> White women don't work on racism to do a favour for someone else, solely to benefit Third World women. You have to comprehend how racism distorts and lessens your own lives as white women—that racism affects your chances for survival, too, and that it is very definitely your issue. Until you understand this, no fundamental change will come about.[11]

Notes

1. B. Smith, 'Racism and Women's Studies', in Gloria T. Hull, Patricia Bell Scott and Barbara Smith (eds.), *All the Women are White, All the Blacks are Men, But Some of Us Are Brave* (New York: Feminist Press, 1982).
2. M. Barrett and M. McIntosh, 'Ethnocentrism and Socialist-Feminist Theory', *Feminist Review* 20 (1985).
3. V. Amos, G. Lewis, A. Mama and P. Parmar (eds.), 'Many Voices, One Chant: Black Feminist Perspectives', *Feminist Review*, 17 (1984).
4. Quoted in Hazel Carby, 'White women Listen! Black Feminism and the Boundaries of Sisterhood', in Centre for Contemporary Cultural Studies, *The Empire Strikes Back: Race and Racism in 70s Britain* (London: Hutchinson, 1982), 214.
5. The internal controls and checks on black people have been written about in a

number of pamphlets and books. For example, Manchester Law Centre, *From Ill Treatment to No Treatment: The New Health Regulations: Black People and Internal Controls* (Manchester: Manchester Law Centre, 1982); and Paul Gordon, *Passport Raids and Checks: Internal Immigration Controls* (The Runnymede Trust, 1981).

6. The participation of black women in paid employment has been noted and commented on by a number of people, such as Pratibha Parmar, 'Gender, Race and Class: Asian Women in Resistance', in Centre for Contemporary Cultural Studies, *The Empire Strikes Back*.
7. For a detailed discussion of these issues, see J. Bhabha, F. Klug and S. Shutter (eds.), *Worlds Apart: Women Under Immigration Law* (London: Pluto Press for the Women, Immigration and Nationality Group, 1985).
8. This is commented on by the writers and editors of Bhabha, *Worlds Apart*, 100–1.
9. A. Sivanandan, 'Race, Class and the State: The Black Experience in Britain', *Race and Class*, 17 (1976).
10. Stuart Hall *et al.*, *Policing the Crisis* (London: Hutchinson, 1978); Paul Gilroy, 'The Myth of Black Criminality', in M. Eve and D. Musson (eds.), *Socialist Register 1982* (London: Merlin Press, 1982); Errol Lawrence, 'Just Plain Common Sense: The "Roots" of Racism', in Centre for Contemporary Cultural Studies, *The Empire Strikes Back*.
11. Smith, 'Racism and Women's Studies'.

Gender & Race: The Ampersand Problem in Feminist Thought

Elizabeth V. Spelman*

You don't really want Black folks, you are just looking for yourself with a little color to it.

Bernice Johnson Reagon

[. . .] It is not easy to think about gender, race and class in ways that don't obscure or underplay their effects on one another. The crucial question is how the links between them are conceived. So, for example, we see that de Beauvoir tends to talk about comparisons between sex and race, or between sex and class, or between sex and culture; she describes what she takes to be comparisons between sexism and racism, between sexism and classism, between sexism and anti-Semitism. In the work of Chodorow and others influenced by her, we observe a readiness to look for links between sexism and other forms of oppression depicted as distinct from sexism. In both examples, we find an additive analysis of the various elements of identity and of various forms of oppression: there's sex *and* race *and* class; there's sexism *and* racism *and* classism. In both examples, attempts to bring in elements of identity other than gender, to bring in kinds of oppression other than sexism, still have the effect of obscuring the racial and class identity of those described as 'women', still make it hard to see how women not of a particular race and class can be included in the description.

In this chapter we shall examine in more detail how additive analyses of identity and of oppression can work against an understanding of the relations between gender and other elements of identity, between sexism and other forms of oppression. In particular we will see how

* From Elizabeth V. Spelman, 'Gender Race: The Ampersand Problem in Feminist Thought' from *Inessential Women* by Elizabeth V. Spelman (Beacon Press, 1988), 114–132, copyright © Elizabeth V. Spelman 1988, reprinted by permission of the publisher.

some very interesting and important attempts to link sexism and racism themselves reflect and perpetuate racism. [. . .]

As has often been pointed out, what have been called the first and second waves of the women's movement in the United States followed closely on the heels of women's involvement in the nineteenth-century abolitionist movement and the twentieth-century civil rights movement. In both centuries, challenges to North American racism served as an impetus to, and model for, the feminist attack on sexist institutions, practices, and ideology. But this is not to say that all anti-racists were anti-sexists, or that all anti-sexists were anti-racists. Indeed, many abolitionists of the nineteenth century and civil rights workers of the twentieth did not take sexism seriously, and we continue to learn about the sad, bitter, and confusing history of women who in fighting hard for feminist ends did not take racism seriously.[1]

Recent feminist theory has not totally ignored white racism, though white feminists have paid much less attention to it than have Black feminists. Much of feminist theory has reflected and contributed to what Adrienne Rich has called 'white solipsism': the tendency 'to think, imagine, and speak as if whiteness described the world'.[2] White solipsism is 'not the consciously held belief that one race is inherently superior to all others, but a tunnel-vision which simply does not see nonwhite experience or existence as precious or significant, unless in spasmodic, impotent guilt-reflexes, which have little or no long-term, continuing momentum or political usefulness'.[3]

In this chapter I shall focus on what I take to be instances and sustaining sources of this tendency in recent theoretical works by, or of interest to, feminists. In particular, I examine certain ways of comparing sexism and racism in the United States, as well as habits of thought about the source of women's oppression and the possibility of our liberation. I hope that exposing some of the symptoms of white solipsism—especially in places where we might least expect to find them—will help to eliminate tunnel vision and to widen the descriptive and explanatory scope of feminist theory. Perhaps we might hasten the day when it will no longer be necessary for anyone to have to say, as Audre Lorde has, 'How difficult and time-consuming it is to have to reinvent the pencil every time you want to send a message.'[4]

I shall not explicitly be examining class and classism, though at a number of points I suggest ways in which considerations of class and classism affect the topic at hand. Many of the questions I raise about comparisons between sexism and racism could also be raised about comparison between sexism and classism or racism and classism.

I

It is perhaps inevitable that comparisons of sexism and racism include, and often culminate in, questions about which form of oppression is more 'fundamental'.[5] [. . .] To begin, I will examine some recent claims that sexism is more fundamental than racism, a highly ambiguous argument. In many instances the evidence offered in support turns out to refute the claim; and this way of comparing sexism and racism often presupposes the nonexistence of Black women, insofar as neither the description of sexism nor that of racism seems to apply to them. This is a bitter irony indeed, since Black women are the victims of both sexism and racism.

We need to ask first what 'more fundamental' means in a comparison of racism and sexism. It has meant or might mean several different though related things:[6]

It is harder to eradicate sexism than it is to eradicate racism.

There might be sexism without racism but not racism without sexism: any social and political changes that eradicate sexism will eradicate racism, but social and political changes that eradicate racism will not eradicate sexism.

Sexism is the first form of oppression learned by children.

Sexism predates racism.

Sexism is the cause of racism.

Sexism is used to justify racism.

Sexism is the model for racism.

[. . .] For example, in *Sexual Politics*, Kate Millett seems to hold that sexism is more fundamental than racism in three senses: it is 'sturdier' than racism and so presumably is harder to eradicate; it has a more 'pervasive ideology' than racism, and so those who are not racists may nevertheless embrace sexist beliefs; and it provides our culture's 'most fundamental concept of power'.[7] But as Margaret Simons has pointed out, Millett ignores the fact that Black women and other women of color do not usually describe their own lives as ones in which they experience sexism as more fundamental than racism.[8] There is indeed something very peculiar about the evidence Millett offers on behalf of her view that sexism is the more endemic oppression.

On the one hand, she states that everywhere men have power over women. On the other hand, she notes with interest that some observers have described as an effect of racism that Black men do not have such power over Black women, and that only when racism is eradicated will Black men assume their proper position of superiority. She goes on to argue that 'the military, industry, technology, universities, science, political office, and finance—in short, every avenue of power within the society, including the coercive force of the police, is entirely in male hands'.[9] But surely that is white male supremacy. Since when did Black males have such institutionally based power, in what Millett calls 'our culture'? She thus correctly describes as sexist the hope that Black men could assume their 'proper authority' over Black women, but her claim about the pervasiveness of sexism is belied by her reference to the lack of authority of Black males.

There is no doubt that Millett is right to view as sexist the hope that racial equity will be established when Black males have authority over Black females, but it also is correct to describe as racist the hope—not uncommonly found in feminist arguments—that sexual equity will be established when women can be presidents or heads of business. That is no guarantee that they will not be running racist countries and corporations. As Elizabeth F. Hood said: 'Many white women define liberation as the access to those thrones traditionally occupied by white men—positions in the kingdoms which support racism.'[10] Of course, one might insist that any truly anti-sexist vision also is an anti-racist vision, for it requires the elimination of all forms of oppression against all women, white or Black.[11] But, similarly, it can be said that any truly anti-racist vision would have to be anti-sexist, for it requires the elimination of all forms of oppression against all Blacks and other people of color, women or men. [. . .]

II

If Millett's account tends to ignore facts about the status of Black men, other similar accounts ignore the existence of Black women. In the process of comparing racism and sexism, Richard Wasserstrom describes the ways in which women and Blacks have been stereotypically conceived of as less fully developed than white men: In the United

States, 'men and women are taught to see men as independent, capable, and powerful; men and women are taught to see women as dependent, limited in abilities, and passive.'[12] But who is taught to see Black men as 'independent, capable, and powerful', and by whom are they taught? Are Black men taught that? Black women? White men? White women? Similarly, who is taught to see Black women as 'dependent, limited in abilities, and passive'? If this stereotype is so prevalent, why then have Black women had to defend themselves against the images of matriarch and whore?

Wasserstrom continues:

> As is true for race, it is also a significant social fact that to be a female is to be an entity or creature viewed as different from the standard, fully developed person who is male as well as white. But to be female, as opposed to being black, is not to be conceived of as simply a creature of less worth. That is one important thing that differentiates sexism from racism: the ideology of sex, as opposed to the ideology of race, is a good deal more complex and confusing. Women are both put on a pedestal and deemed not fully developed persons.[13]

He leaves no room for the Black woman. For a Black woman cannot be 'female, as opposed to being Black'; she is female *and* Black. Since Wasserstrom's argument proceeds from the assumption that one is either female or Black, it cannot be an argument that applies to Black women. Moreover, we cannot generate a composite image of the Black women from Wasserstrom's argument, since the description of women as being put on a pedestal, or being dependent, never generally applied to Black women in the United States and was never meant to apply to them.

Wasserstrom's argument about the priority of sexism over racism has an odd result, which stems from the erasure of Black women in his analysis. He wishes to claim that in this society sex is a more fundamental fact about people than race. Yet his description of women does not apply to the Black woman, which implies that being Black is a more fundamental fact about her than being a woman and hence that her sex is not a more fundamental fact about her than her race. I am not saying that Wasserstrom actually believes this is true, but that paradoxically the terms of his theory force him into that position. If the terms of one's theory require that a person is either female or Black, clearly there is no room to describe someone who is both. [. . .]

III

[. . .] It is highly misleading to say, without further explanation, that Black women experience 'sexism and racism.' For to say merely that suggests that Black women experience one form of oppression, as Blacks (the same thing Black men experience) and that they experience another form of oppression, as women (the same thing white women experience). [. . .] Thus, as noted earlier, it will not do to say that women are oppressed by the image of the 'feminine' woman as fair, delicate, and in need of support and protection by men. [. . .] More specifically, as Angela Davis reminds us, 'the alleged benefits of the ideology of femininity did not accrue' to the Black female slave—she was expected to toil in the fields for just as long and hard as the Black male was.[14]

Reflection on the experience of Black women also shows that it is not as if one form of oppression is merely piled upon another. As Barbara Smith has remarked, the effect of multiple oppression 'is not merely arithmetic'.[15] This additive method informs Gerda Lerner's analysis of the oppression of Black women under slavery: 'Their work and duties were the same as that of the men, while childbearing and rearing fell upon them as an added burden.'[16] But as Angela Davis has pointed out, the mother/housewife role (even the words seem inappropriate) doesn't have the same meaning for women who experience racism as it does for those who are not so oppressed:

> In the infinite anguish of ministering to the needs of the men and children around her (who were not necessarily members of her immediate family), she was performing the only labor of the slave community which could not be directly and immediately claimed by the oppressor.[17]

The meaning and the oppressive nature of the 'housewife' role has to be understood in relation to the roles against which it is contrasted. The work of mate/mother/nurturer has a different meaning depending on whether it is contrasted to work that has high social value and ensures economic independence or to labor that is forced, degrading and unpaid. All of these factors are left out in a simple additive analysis. How one form of oppression is experienced is influenced by and influences how another form is experienced. An additive analysis treats the oppression of a Black woman in a society that is racist as well as sexist as if it were a further burden when, in fact, it is a different burden. As the work of Davis, among others, shows, to ignore the difference is to deny the particular reality of the Black woman's experience.

[. . .] Racism is sometimes seen as something that is both derivative from sexism and in the service of it: racism keeps women from uniting in alliance against sexism. This view has been articulated by Mary Daly in *Beyond God the Father*. According to Daly, sexism is the 'root and paradigm' of other forms of oppression such as racism. Racism is a 'deformity *within* patriarchy . . . It is most unlikely that racism will be eradicated as long as sexism prevails.'[18]

Daly's theory relies on an additive analysis, and we can see again why such an analysis fails to describe adequately Black women's experience. Daly's analysis makes it look simply as if both Black women and white women experience sexism, while Black women also experience racism. Black women, Daly says, must come to see what they have in common with white women—shared sexist oppression—and see that they are all 'pawns in the racial struggle, which is basically not the struggle that will set them free as women'.[19] But insofar as she is oppressed by racism in a sexist context and sexism in a racist context, the Black woman's struggle cannot be compartmentalized into two struggles—one as a Black and one as a woman. Indeed, it is difficult to imagine why a Black woman would think of her struggles this way except in the face of demands by white women or by Black men that she do so. This way of speaking about her struggle is required by a theory that insists not only that sexism and racism are distinct but that one might be eradicated before the other. [. . .]

Daly's line of thought also promotes the idea that, were it not for racism, there would be no important differences between Black and white women. Since, according to her view, sexism is the fundamental form of oppression and racism works in its service, the only significant differences between Black and white women are differences that men (Daly doesn't say whether she means white men or Black men or both) have created and that are the source of antagonism between women. What is really crucial about us is our sex; racial distinctions are one of the many products of sexism, of patriarchy's attempt to keep women from uniting. According to Daly, then, it is through our shared sexual identity that we are oppressed together; it is through our shared sexual identity that we shall be liberated together.

This view not only ignores the role women play in racism and classism, but it seems to deny the positive aspects of racial identities. It ignores the fact that being Black is a source of pride, as well as an occasion for being oppressed. It suggests that once racism is eliminated, Black women no longer need be concerned about or interested in their Blackness—as if the only reason for paying attention to one's

Blackness is that it is the source of pain and sorrow and agony. The assumption that there is nothing positive about having a Black history and identity is racism pure and simple. Recall the lines of Nikki Giovanni:

> and I really hope no white person ever has cause
> to write about me
> because they never understand Black love is
> Black wealth and they'll
> probably talk about my hard childhood
> and never understand that
> all the while I was quite happy.[20]

[. . .] I think it is helpful too in this connection to remember the opening lines of Pat Parker's 'For the white person who wants to know how to be my friend':

> The first thing you do is to forget that i'm Black.
> Second, you must never forget that i'm Black.[21]

[. . .] In sum, according to an additive analysis of sexism and racism, all women are oppressed by sexism; some women are further oppressed by racism. Such an analysis distorts Black women's experiences of oppression by failing to note important differences between the contexts in which Black women and white women experience sexism. The additive analysis also suggests that a woman's racial identity can be 'subtracted' from her combined sexual and racial identity: 'We are all women.'

IV

In the rest of the chapter I will explore how some ways of conceiving women's oppression and liberation contribute to the white solipsism of feminist theory.

As I have argued in detail elsewhere, feminist theorists as politically diverse as Simone de Beauvoir, Betty Friedan, and Shulamith Firestone have described the conditions of women's liberation in terms that suggest that the identification of woman with her body has been the source of our oppression, and hence that the source of our liberation lies in sundering that connection.[22] For example, de Beauvoir introduces *The Second Sex* with the comment that woman has been regarded as 'womb'; and she later observes that woman is thought of as planted firmly in the world of 'immanence', that is, the physical world of nature, her life defined by the dictates of her 'biologic fate'.[23] In contrast, men live in the world of 'transcendence', actively using their minds to create 'values, mores, religions'.[24] Theirs is the world of culture as opposed to the world of nature. Among Friedan's central messages is that women should be allowed and encouraged to be 'culturally' as well as 'biologically' creative, because the former activities, in contrast to childbearing and rearing, are 'mental' and are of 'highest value to society'—'mastering the secrets of atoms, or the stars, composing symphonies, pioneering a new concept in government or society'.[25]

This view comes out especially clearly in Firestone's work. According to her, the biological difference between women and men is at the root of women's oppression. It is women's body—in particular, our body's capacity to bear children—that makes, or makes possible, the oppression of women by men. Hence we must disassociate ourselves from our bodies—most radically—by making it possible, or even necessary, to conceive and bear children outside the womb, and by otherwise generally disassociating our lives from the thankless tasks associated with the body.[26]

In predicating women's liberation on a disassociation from our bodies, Firestone oddly enough joins the chorus of male voices that has told us over the centuries about the disappointments entailed in being embodied creatures. What might be called 'somatophobia' (fear of and disdain for the body) is part of a centuries-long tradition in Western culture. [. . .]

Somatophobia . . . is a force that contributes to white solipsism in feminist thought, in at least three related ways. First, insofar as feminists ignore, or indeed accept, negative views of the body in prescriptions for women's liberation, we will also ignore an important element in racist thinking. For the superiority of men to women (or, as we have seen, of some men to some women) is not the only hierarchical relationship that has been linked to the superiority of the mind to the body. Certain kinds, or 'races', of people have been held to be more body-like than others, and this has meant that they are perceived as more animal-like and less god-like. For example, in *The White Man's Burden*, Winthrop Jordan describes ways in which white Englishmen portrayed black Africans as beastly, dirty, highly sexual beings.[27] [. . .]

We need to examine and understand somatophobia and look for it in our own thinking, for the idea that the work of the body and for the body has no part in real human dignity has been part of racist as well as sexist ideology. That is, oppressive stereotypes of 'inferior races' and of women (notice that even in order to make the point in this way, we leave up in the air the question of how we shall refer to those who belong to both categories) have typically involved images of their lives as determined by basic bodily functions (sex, reproduction, appetite, secretions and excretions) and as given over to attending to the bodily functions of others (feeding, washing, cleaning, doing the 'dirty work'). Superior groups, we have been told from Plato on down, have better things to do with their lives. It certainly does not follow from the presence of somatophobia in a person's writings that she or he is a racist or a sexist. But disdain for the body historically has been symptomatic of sexist and racist (as well as classist) attitudes.

[. . .] Finally, if one thinks—as de Beauvoir, Friedan, and Firestone do—that the liberation of women requires abstracting the notion of woman from the notion of woman's body, then one might logically think that the liberation of Blacks requires abstracting the notion of a Black person from the notion of a black body. Since the body, or at least certain of its aspects, may be thought to be the culprit, the solution may seem to be: Keep the person and leave the occasion for oppression behind. Keep the woman, somehow, but leave behind her woman's body; keep the Black person but leave the Blackness behind. [. . .]

Once the concept of woman is divorced from the concept of woman's body, conceptual room is made for the idea of a woman who is no particular historical woman—she has no color, no accent, no particular characteristics that require having a body. She is somehow all and only woman; that is her only identifying feature. And so it will seem inappropriate or beside the point to think of women in terms of any physical characteristics, especially if their oppression has been rationalized by reference to those characteristics.

None of this is to say that the historical and cultural identity of being Black or white is the same thing as, or is reducible to, the physical feature of having black or white skin. Historical and cultural identity is not constituted by having a body with particular identifying features, but it cannot be comprehended without such features and the significance attached to them.

V

Adrienne Rich was perhaps the first well-known contemporary white feminist to have noted 'white solipsism' in feminist theorizing and activity. I think it is no coincidence that she also noticed and attended to the strong strain of somatophobia in feminist theory. [. . .] Rich refuses to throw out the baby with the bathwater: she sees that the historical negative connection between woman and body (in particular, between woman and womb) can be broken in more than one way. [. . .] She insists that the negative connection between woman and body be broken along other lines. She asks us to think about whether what she calls 'flesh-loathing' is the only attitude it is possible to have toward our bodies. Just as she explicitly distinguishes between motherhood as experience and motherhood as institution, so she implicitly asks us to distinguish between embodiment as experience and embodiment as institution. Flesh-loathing is part of the well-entrenched beliefs, habits and practices epitomized in the treatment of pregnancy as a disease. But we need not experience our flesh, our body, as loathsome.

I think it is not a psychological or historical accident that having examined the way women view their bodies, Rich also focused on the failure of white women to see Black women's experiences as different from their own. For looking at embodiment is one way (though not the only one) of coming to recognize and understand the particularity of experience. Without bodies we could not have personal histories. Nor could we be identified as woman or man, Black or white. This is not to say that reference to publicly observable bodily characteristics settles the question of whether someone is woman or man, Black or white; nor is it to say that being woman or man, Black or white, just means having certain bodily characteristics (that is one reason some Blacks want to capitalize the term; 'Black' refers to a cultural identity, not simply a skin color). [. . .] Women's oppression has been linked to the meanings assigned to having a woman's body by male oppressors. Blacks' oppression has been linked to the meanings assigned to having a black body by white oppressors. (Note how insidiously this way of speaking once again leaves unmentioned the situation for Black women.) We cannot hope to understand the meaning of a person's experiences, including her experiences of oppression, without first thinking of her as embodied, and second thinking about the particular meanings assigned to that embodiment. If, because of somatophobia, we think and write as if we are not embodied, or as if we would be better off if we were not embodied, we are likely to ignore the ways in which different forms of embodiment are correlated with different kinds of experience.

[. . .] Other feminists have reflected on the meaning of embodiment and recognized the connection between flesh-loathing and woman-hatred, but they have only considered it far enough to try to divorce the concept of woman from the concept of the flesh. In effect, they have insisted that having different bodies does not or need not mean men and women are any different as humans; and having said that, they imply that having different colored bodies does not mean that Black women and white women are any different. Such statements are fine if interpreted to mean that the differences between woman and man, Black and white, should not be used against Black women and white women and Black men. But not paying attention to embodiment and to the cultural meanings assigned to different forms of it is to encourage sexblindness and colorblindness. [. . .]

SUMMARY

I have been discussing the ways in which some aspects of feminist theory exhibit what Adrienne Rich has called 'white solipsism.' In particular, I have been examining ways in which some prominent claims about the relation between sexism and racism ignore the realities of racism. I have also suggested that there are ways of thinking about women's oppression and about women's liberation that reflect and encourage white solipsism, but that thinking differently about women and about sexism might lead to thinking differently about Blackness and about racism.

First, we have to continue to reexamine the traditions which reinforce sexism and racism. Though feminist theory has recognized the connection between somatophobia and misogyny/gynephobia, it has tended to challenge the misogyny without challenging the somatophobia, and without fully appreciating the connection between somatophobia and racism.

Second, we have to keep a cautious eye on discussions of racism versus sexism. They keep us from seeing ways in which what sexism means and how it works is modulated by racism, and ways in which what racism means is modulated by sexism. Most important, discussions of sexism versus racism tend to proceed as if Black women—to take one example—do not exist. None of this is to say that sexism and racism are thoroughly and in every context indistinguishable. [. . .] As long as Black women and other women of color are at the bottom of the economic heap (which clearly we cannot fully understand in the absence of a class analysis), and as long as our descriptions of sexism and racism themselves reveal racist and sexist perspectives, it seems both empirically and conceptually premature to make grand claims about whether sexism or racism is 'more fundamental'. For many reasons, then, it seems wise to proceed very cautiously in this inquiry.

Third, it is crucial to sustain a lively regard for the variety of women's experiences. On the one hand, what unifies women and justifies us in talking about the oppression of women is the overwhelming evidence of the worldwide and historical subordination of women to men. On the other, while it may be possible for us to speak about women in a general way, it also is inevitable that any statement we make about women in some particular place at some particular time is bound to suffer from ethnocentrism if we try to claim for it more generality than it has. [. . .] In Toni Morrison's *The Bluest Eye*, the causes and consequences of Pecola's longing to have blue eyes are surely quite different from the causes and consequences of a white girl with brown eyes having a similar desire.[28] More to the point, the consequences of *not* having blue eyes are quite different for the two. Similarly, the family may be the locus of oppression for white middle-class women, but to claim that it is the locus of oppression for all women is to ignore the fact that for Blacks in America the family has been a source of resistance against white oppression.[29]

In short, the claim that all women are oppressed is fully compatible with, and needs to be explicated in terms of, the many varieties of oppression that different populations of women have been subject to. After all, why should oppressors settle for uniform kinds of oppression, when to oppress their victims in many different ways—consciously or unconsciously—makes it more likely that the oppressed groups will not perceive it to be in their interest to work together?

Finally, it is crucial not to see Blackness only as the occasion for oppression—any more than one sees being a woman only as the occasion for oppression. No one ought to expect the forms of our liberation to be any less various than the forms of our oppression. We need to be at least as generous in imagining what women's liberation will be like as our oppressors have been in devising what women's oppression has been.

Notes

1. See Eleanor Flexner, *Century of Struggle* (New York: Atheneum, 1972), especially chapter 13, on the inhospitality of white women's organizations to Black women, as well as Aileen S. Kraditor's *The Ideas of the Woman Suffrage Movement, 1890–1920* (Garden City, NY: Doubleday, 1971). See also Ellen Carol DuBois, *Feminism and Suffrage: the Emergence of an Independent Women's Movement in America, 1848–1869* (Ithaca: Cornell University Press, 1978); Sara Evans, *Personal Politics* (New York: Vintage, 1979), on sexism in the civil rights movement; Dorothy Sterling, *Black Foremothers* (Old Westbury, NY: Feminist Press, 1979), 147, on Alice Paul's refusal to grant Mary Church Terrell's request that Paul endorse enforcement of the Nineteenth Amendment for all women; Angela Davis, *Women, Race, and Class* (New York: Random House, 1981); Bettina Aptheker, *Women's Legacy: Essays on Race, Sex, and Class in American History* (Amherst: University of Massachusetts Press, 1982); Paula Giddings, *When and Where I Enter: The Impact of Black Women on Race and Sex in America* (New York: Morrow, 1984).
2. Adrienne Rich, 'Disloyal to Civilization: Feminism, Racism, Gynephobia', in her *On Lies, Secrets, and Silence* (New York: Norton, 1979), 299 and *passim*. In the philosophical literature, solipsism is the view according to which it is only one's self that is knowable, or it is only one's self that constitutes the world. Strictly speaking, of course, Rich's use of the phrase 'white solipsism' is at odds with the idea of there being only the self, insofar as it implies that there are other white people; but she is drawing from the idea of there being only one perspective on the world—not that of one person, but of one 'race'.
3. Ibid., 306.
4. Audre Lorde, 'Man Child: A Black Lesbian Feminist's Response', *Conditions* 4 (1979), 35. My comments about racism apply to the racism directed against Black people in the United States. I do not claim that all my arguments apply to the racism experienced by other people of color.
5. See Margaret A. Simons, 'Racism and Feminism: A Schism in the Sisterhood', *Feminist Studies* 5 (1979), 384–401.
6. A somewhat similar list appears in Alison M. Jaggar and Paula Rothenberg's introduction to part 2 of *Feminist Frameworks*, 2nd edn. (New York: McGraw-Hill, 1984), p. 86.
7. Kate Millett, *Sexual Politics* (New York: Ballantine, 1969), 33–4.
8. Simons, 'Racism and Feminism'.
9. Millett, *Sexual Politics*, 33–4.
10. Elizabeth F. Hood, 'Black Women, White Women: Separate Paths to Liberation', *Black Scholar*, (April 1978), 47.
11. See Elizabeth V. Spelman, *Inessential Woman: Problems of Exclusion in Feminist Thought* (Boston: Beacon Press, 1988), ch. 2.
12. Richard A. Wasserstrom, 'Racism and Sexism', in Sharon Bishop and Marjorie Weinzweig (eds.) *Philosophy and Women* (Belmont, Cal: Wadsworth, 1979), 8.

Reprinted from 'Racism, Sexism, and Preferential Treatment: An Approach to the Topics', *UCLA Law Review* (February 1977), 581–615.

13. Ibid.
14. Angela Y. Davis, 'Reflections on the Black Woman's Role in the Community of Slaves', *Black Scholar* 3 (1971), 7.
15. Barbara Smith, 'Notes For Yet Another Paper on Black Feminism, or Will the Real Enemy Please Stand Up', *Conditions* 5 (1979), 123–32. See also 'The Combahee River Collective Statement', Zillah Eisenstein (ed.), *Capitalist Patriarchy and the Case for Socialist Feminism* (New York: Monthly Review Press, 1979), 362–72.
16. Gerda Lerner, (ed.) *Black Woman in White America* (New York: Vintage, 1973), 15.
17. Davis, 'Reflections on the Black Woman's Role', 7. Davis revises this slightly in *Women, Race and Class.*
18. Mary Daly, *Beyond God the Father* (Boston: Beacon Press, 1975), 56–7.
19. Ibid.
20. Nikki Giovanni, 'Nikki Rosa', in Toni Cade (ed.) *The Black Woman* (New York: New American Library, 1980), 16.
21. Pat Parker, *Womanslaughter* (Oakland: Diana Press, 1978), 13.
22. Spelman, 'Woman as Body'.
23. Simone de Beauvoir, *The Second Sex*, transl. ed. H. M. Parshley (New York: Bantam, 1961).
24. Ibid., 119.
25. Betty Friedan, *The Feminine Mystique* (New York: W. W. Norton Co., 1963), 247–77.
26. Firestone, *The Dialectic of Sex* (New York: Bantam, 1970), ch. 10
27. Winthrop P. Jordan, *The White Man's Burden* (New York: Oxford University Press, 1974), ch. 1.
28. Toni Morrison, *The Bluest Eye* (New York: Pocketbooks, 1972).
29. See, for example, Carol Stack, *All Our Kin* (New York: Harper and Row, 1974).

The Master's Tools Will Never Dismantle the Master's House

Audre Lorde*

I agreed to take part in a New York University Institute for the Humanities conference a year ago, with the understanding that I would be commenting upon papers dealing with the role of difference within the lives of American women: difference of race, sexuality, class and age. The absence of these considerations weakens any feminist discussion of the personal and the political.

It is a particular academic arrogance to assume any discussion of feminist theory without examining our many differences, and without a significant input from poor women, Black and Third World women and lesbians. And yet, I stand here as a Black lesbian feminist, having been invited to comment within the only panel at this conference where the input of Black feminists and lesbians is represented. What this says about the vision of this conference is sad, in a country where racism, sexism and homophobia are inseparable. To read this program is to assume that lesbian and Black women have nothing to say about existentialism, the erotic, women's culture and silence, developing feminist theory, or heterosexuality and power. And what does it mean in personal and political terms when even the two Black women who did present here were literally found at the last hour? What does it mean when the tools of a racist patriarchy are used to examine the fruits of that same patriarchy? It means that only the most narrow perimeters of change are possible and allowable.

The absence of any consideration of lesbian consciousness or the consciousness of Third World women leaves a serious gap within this conference and within the papers presented here. For example, in a

Comments at 'The Personal and the Political Panel' Second Sex Conference, New York, September 29, 1979.

* From Audre Lorde, 'The Master's Tools Will Never Dismantle the Master's House' from *Sister Outsider* (The Crossing Press, 1984), 110–13, copyright © 1984, reprinted by permission of the publisher.

paper on material relationships between women, I was conscious of an either/or model of nurturing which totally dismissed my knowledge as a Black lesbian. In this paper there was no examination of mutuality between women, no systems of shared support, no interdependence as exists between lesbians and women-identified women. Yet it is only in the patriarchal model of nurturance that women 'who attempt to emancipate themselves pay perhaps too high a price for the results', as this paper states.

For women, the need and desire to nurture each other is not pathological but redemptive, and it is within that knowledge that our real power is rediscovered. It is this real connection which is so feared by a patriarchal world. Only within a patriarchal structure is maternity the only social power open to women.

Interdependency between women is the way to a freedom which allows the *I* to *be*, not in order to be used, but in order to be creative. This is a difference between the passive *be* and the active *being*.

Advocating the mere tolerance of difference between women is the grossest reformism. It is a total denial of the creative function of difference in our lives. Difference must be not merely tolerated, but seen as a fund of necessary polarities between which our creativity can spark like a dialectic. Only then does the necessity for interdependency become unthreatening. Only within that interdependency of different strengths, acknowledged and equal, can the power to seek new ways of being in the world generate, as well as the courage and sustenance to act where there are no charters.

Within the interdependence of mutual (nondominant) differences lies that security which enables us to descend into the chaos of knowledge and return with true visions of our future, along with the concomitant power to effect those changes which can bring that future into being. Difference is that raw and powerful connection from which our personal power is forged.

As women, we have been taught either to ignore our differences, or to view them as causes for separation and suspicion rather than as forces for change. Without community there is no liberation, only the most vulnerable and temporary armistice between an individual and her oppression. But community must not mean a shedding of our differences, nor the pathetic pretense that these differences do not exist.

Those of us who stand outside the circle of this society's definition of acceptable women; those of us who have been forged in the crucibles of difference—those of us who are poor, who are lesbians, who are Black, who are older—know that *survival is not an academic skill.* It is learning how to stand alone, unpopular and sometimes reviled, and how to make common cause with those others identified as outside the structures in order to define and seek a world in which we can all flourish. It is learning how to take our differences and make them strengths. *For the master's tools will never dismantle the master's house.* They may allow us temporarily to beat him at his own game, but they will never enable us to bring about genuine change. And this fact is only threatening to those women who still define the master's house as their only source of support.

Poor women and women of color know there is a difference between the daily manifestations of marital slavery and prostitution because it is our daughters who line 42nd Street. If white American feminist theory need not deal with the differences between us, and the resulting difference in our oppressions, then how do you deal with the fact that the women who clean your houses and tend your children while you attend conferences on feminist theory are, for the most part, poor women and women of color? What is the theory behind racist feminism?

In a world of possibility for us all, our personal visions help lay the groundwork for political action. The failure of academic feminists to recognize difference as a crucial strength is a failure to reach beyond the first patriarchal lesson. In our world, divide and conquer must become define and empower.

Why weren't other women of color found to participate in this conference? Why were two phone calls to me considered a consultation? Am I the only possible source of names of Black feminists? And although the Black panelist's paper ends on an important and powerful connection of love between women, what about interracial cooperation between feminists who don't love each other?

In academic feminist circles, the answer to these questions is often, 'We did not know who to ask.' But that is the same evasion of responsibility, the same cop-out, that keeps Black women's art out of women's exhibitions, Black women's work out of most feminist publications except for the occasional 'Special Third World Women's Issue', and Black women's texts off your reading lists. But as Adrienne Rich pointed out in a recent talk, white feminists have educated themselves about such an enormous amount over the past ten years, how come you haven't also educated yourselves about Black women and the differences between us—white and Black—when it is key to our survival as a movement?

Women of today are still being called upon to stretch across the gap of male ignorance and to educate men as to our existence and our needs. This is an old and primary tool of all oppressors to keep the oppressed occupied with the master's concerns. Now we hear that it is the task of women of color to educate white women—in the face of tremendous resistance—as to our existence, our differences, our relative roles in our joint survival. This is a diversion of energies and a tragic repetition of racist patriarchal thought.

Simone de Beauvoir once said: 'It is in the knowledge of the genuine conditions of our lives that we must draw our strength to live and our reasons for acting.'[1]

Racism and homophobia are real conditions of all our lives in this place and time. I urge each one of us here to reach down into that deep place of knowledge inside herself and touch that terror and loathing of any difference that lives there. See whose face it wears. Then the personal as the political can begin to illuminate all our choices.

Note

1. Simone de Beauvoir, *The Second Sex*, transl. ed. H. M. Parshley (New York: Bantam, 1961).

La conciencia de la Mestiza: Towards a New Consciousness

Gloria Anzaldua*

Por la mujer de mi raza
hablará el espíritu.[1]

Jose Vascocelos, Mexican philosopher, envisaged *una raza mestiza, una mezcla de razas afines, una raza de color—la primera raza síntesis del globo.* He called it a cosmic race, *la raza cósmica*, a fifth race embracing the four major races of the world.[2] Opposite to the theory of the pure Aryan, and to the policy of racial purity that white America practices, his theory is one of inclusivity. At the confluence of two or more genetic streams, with chromosomes constantly 'crossing over', this mixture of races, rather than resulting in an inferior being, provides hybrid progeny, a mutable, more malleable species with a rich gene pool. From this racial, ideological, cultural and biological cross-pollenization, an 'alien' consciousness is presently in the making—a new *mestiza* consciousness, *una conciencia de mujer.* It is a consciousness of the Borderlands.

UNA LUCHA DE FRONTERAS/A STRUGGLE OF BORDERS

Because I, a *mestiza*,
continually walk out of one culture
and into another,
because I am in all cultures at the same time,
alma entre dos mundos, tres, cuatro,
me zumba la cabeza con lo contradictorio.
Estoy norteada por todas las voces que me hablan
simultáneamente.

* From Gloria Anzaldua, '*La Conciencia de la Mestiza*: Towards a New Consciousness' from *Borderlands: La Frontera: The New Mestiza* (The Crossing Press, 1987), 77–91,

The ambivalence from the clash of voices results in mental and emotional states of perplexity. Internal strife results in insecurity and indecisiveness. The mestiza's dual or multiple personality is plagued by psychic restlessness.

In a constant state of mental nepantilism, an Aztec word meaning torn between ways, *la mestiza* is a product of the transfer of the cultural and spiritual values of one group to another. Being tricultural, monolingual, bilingual or multilingual, speaking a patois, and in a state of perpetual transition, the *mestiza* faces the dilemma of the mixed breed: which collectivity does the daughter of a darkskinned mother listen to?

El choque de un alma atrapado entre el mundo del espíritu y el mundo de la técnica a veces la deja entullada. Cradled in one culture, sandwiched between two cultures, straddling all three cultures and their value systems, *la mestiza* undergoes a struggle of flesh, a struggle of borders, an inner war. Like all people, we perceive the version of reality that our culture communicates. Like others having or living in more than one culture, we get multiple, often opposing messages. The coming together of two self-consistent but habitually incompatible frames of reference[3] causes *un choque*, a cultural collision.

Within us and within *la cultura chicana*, commonly held beliefs of the white culture attack commonly held beliefs of the Mexican culture, and both attack commonly held beliefs of the indigenous culture. Subconsciously, we see an attack on ourselves and our beliefs as a threat and we attempt to block with a counterstance.

But it is not enough to stand on the opposite river bank, shouting questions, challenging patriarchal, white conventions. A counterstance locks one into a duel of oppressor and oppressed; locked in mortal combat, like the cop and the criminal, both are reduced to a common denominator of violence. The counterstance refutes the dominant culture's views and beliefs, and, for this, it is proudly defiant. All reaction is limited by, and dependent on, what it is reacting against. Because the counterstance stems from a problem with authority—outer as well as inner—it's a step towards liberation from cultural domination. But it is not a way of life. At some point, on our way to a new consciousness, we will have to leave the opposite bank, the split between the two mortal combatants somehow healed so that we are on both shores at once and, at once, see through serpent and eagle eyes. Or perhaps we will decide to disengage from the dominant culture, write it off altogether as a lost cause, and cross the border into a wholly new and separate territory. Or we might go another route. The possibilities are numerous once we decide to act and not react.

A TOLERANCE FOR AMBIGUITY

These numerous possibilities leave *la mestiza* floundering in uncharted seas. In perceiving conflicting information and points of view, she is subjected to a swamping of her psychological borders. She has discovered that she can't hold concepts or ideas in rigid boundaries. The borders and walls that are supposed to keep the undesirable ideas out are entrenched habits and patterns of behavior; these habits and patterns are the enemy within. Rigidity means death. Only by remaining flexible is she able to stretch the psyche horizontally and vertically. *La mestiza* constantly has to shift out of habitual formations; from convergent thinking, analytical reasoning that tends to use rationality to move toward a single goal (a Western mode), to divergent thinking,[4] characterized by movement away from set patterns and goals and toward a more whole perspective, one that includes rather than excludes.

The new *mestiza* copes by developing a tolerance for contradictions, a tolerance for ambiguity. She learns to be an Indian in Mexican culture, to be Mexican from an Anglo point of view. She learns to juggle cultures. She has a plural personality, she operates in a pluralistic mode—nothing is thrust out, the good the bad and the ugly, nothing rejected, nothing abandoned. Not only does she sustain contradictions, she turns the ambivalence into something else.

She can be jarred out of ambivalence by an intense, and often painful, emotional event which inverts or resolves the ambivalence. I'm not sure exactly how. The work takes place underground—subconsciously. It is work that the soul performs. That focal point or fulcrum, that juncture where the mestiza stands, is where phenomena tend to collide. It is where the possibility of uniting all that is separate occurs. This assembly is not one where severed or separated pieces merely come together. Nor is it a balancing of opposing powers. In attempting to work out a synthesis, the self has added a third element which is greater than the sum of its severed parts. That third element is a new consciousness—a mestiza consciousness—and though it is a source of intense pain, its energy comes from continual creative motion that keeps breaking down the unitary aspect of each new paradigm.

En unas pocas centurias, the future will belong to the mestiza. Because the future depends on the breaking down of paradigms, it depends on the straddling of two or more cultures. By creating a new mythos—that is, a change in the way we perceive reality, the way we see ourselves, and the ways we behave—*la mestiza* creates a new consciousness.

The work of *mestiza* consciousness is to break down the subject–object duality that keeps her a prisoner and to show in the flesh and through the images in her work how duality is transcended. The answer to the problem between the white race and the colored, between males and females, lies in healing the split that originates in the very foundation of our lives, our culture, our languages, our thoughts. A massive uprooting of dualistic thinking in the individual and collective consciousness is the beginning of a long struggle, but one that could, in our best hopes, bring us to the end of rape, of violence, of war.

LA ENCRUCIJADA/THE CROSSROADS

A chicken is being sacrificed
　　at a crossroads, a simple mound of earth
a mud shrine for *Eshu*,
　　Yoruba god of indeterminacy,
who blesses her choice of path.
　　She begins her journey.

Su cuerpo es una bocacalle. La mestiza has gone from being the sacrificial goat to becoming the officiating priestess at the crossroads.

As a *mestiza* I have no country, my homeland cast me out; yet all countries are mine because I am every woman's sister or potential lover. (As a lesbian I have no race, my own people disclaim me; but I am all races because there is the queer of me in all races.) I am cultureless because, as a feminist, I challenge the collective cultural/religious male-derived beliefs of Indo-Hispanics and Anglos; yet I am cultured because I am participating in the creation of yet another culture, a new story to explain the world and our participation in it, a new value system with images and symbols that connect us to each other and to the planet. *Soy un amasamiento*, I am an act of kneading, of uniting and joining that not only has produced both a creature of darkness and a creature of light, but also a creature that questions the definitions of light and dark and gives them new meanings.

We are the people who leap in the dark, we are the people on the knees of the gods. In our very flesh, (r)evolution works out the clash of cultures. It makes us crazy constantly, but if the center holds, we've made some kind of evolutionary step forward. *Nuestra alma el trabajo*, the opus, the great alchemical work; spiritual *mestizaje*, a 'morphogenesis',[5] an inevitable unfolding. We have become the quickening serpent movement.

Indigenous like corn, like corn, the *mestiza* is a product of crossbreeding, designed for preservation under a variety of conditions. Like an ear of corn—a female seed-bearing organ—the *mestiza* is tenacious, tightly wrapped in the husks of her culture. Like kernels she clings to the cob; with thick stalks and strong brace roots, she holds tight to the earth—she will survive the crossroads.

Lavando y remojando el maíz en agua de cal, despojando el pellejo. Moliendo, mixteando, amasando, haciendo tortillas de masa.[6] She steeps the corn in lime, it swells, softens. With stone roller on *metate*, she grinds the corn, then grinds again. She kneads and moulds the dough, pats the round balls into *tortillas*.

> We are the porous rock in the stone *metate*
> squatting on the ground.
> We are the rolling pin, *el maíz y agua*,
> *la masa harina. Somos el amasijo.*
> *Somos lo molido en el metate.*
> We are the *comal* sizzling hot,
> the hot *tortilla*, the hungry mouth.
> We are the coarse rock.
> We are the grinding motion,
> the mixed potion, *somos el molcajete.*
> We are the pestle, the *comino, ajo, pimienta,*
> We are the *chile colorado,*
> the green shoot that cracks the rock.
> We will abide.

EL CAMINO DE LA MESTIZA/THE MESTIZA WAY

Caught between the sudden contraction, the breath sucked in and the endless space, the brown woman stands still, looks at the sky. She decides to go down, digging her way along the roots of trees. Sifting through the bones, she shakes them to see if there is any marrow in them. Then, touching the dirt to her forehead, to her tongue, she takes a few bones, leaves the rest in their burial place.

She goes through her backpack, keeps her journal and address book, throws away the muni-bart metromaps. The coins are heavy and they go next, then the greenbacks flutter through the air. She keeps her knife, can opener and eyebrow pencil. She puts bones, pieces of bark, *hierbas*, eagle feather, snakeskin, tape recorder, the rattle and drum in her pack and she sets out to become the complete *tolteca.*[7]

Her first step is to take inventory. *Despojando, desgranando, quitando paja.* Just what did she inherit from her ancestors? This weight on her back—which is the baggage from the Indian mother, which the baggage from the Spanish father, which the baggage from the Anglo?

Pero es difícil differentiating between *lo heredado, lo adquirido, lo impuesto.* She puts history through a sieve, winnows out the lies, looks at the forces that we as a race, as women, have been a part of. *Luego bota lo que no vale, los desmientos, los desencuentos, el embrutecimiento. Aguarda el juicio, bondo y enraízado, de la gente antigua.* This step is a conscious rupture with all oppressive traditions of all cultures and religions. She communicates that rupture, documents the struggle. She reinterprets history and, using new symbols, she shapes new myths. She adopts new perspectives toward the darkskinned, women and queers. She strengthens her tolerance (and intolerance) for ambiguity. She is willing to share, to make herself vulnerable to foreign ways of seeing and thinking. She surrenders all notions of safety, of the familiar. Deconstruct, construct. She becomes a *nahual,* able to transform herself into a tree, a coyote, into another person. She learns to transform the small 'I' into the total Self. *Se hace moldeadora de su alma. Según la concepción que tiene de sí misma, así será.*

QUE NO SE NOS OLVIDE LOS BOMBRES

> '*Tú no sirves pa' nada—*
> you're good for nothing.
> *Eres pura vieja.*'

'You're nothing but a woman' means you are defective. Its opposite is to be *un macho*. The modern meaning of the word 'machismo', as well as the concept, is actually an Anglo invention. For men like my father, being 'macho' meant being strong enough to protect and support my mother and us, yet being able to show love. Today's macho has doubts about his ability to feed and protect his family. His 'machismo' is an adaptation to oppression and poverty and low self-esteem. It is the result of hierarchical male dominance. The Anglo, feeling inadequate and inferior and powerless, displaces or transfers these feelings to the Chicano by shaming him. In the Gringo world, the Chicano suffers from excessive humility and self-effacement, shame of self and self-deprecation. Around Latinos he suffers from a sense of language inadequacy and its accompanying discomfort; with Native Americans he suffers from a racial amnesia which ignores our common blood, and from guilt because the Spanish part of him took their land and oppressed them. He has an excessive compensatory hubris when around Mexicans from the other side. It overlays a deep sense of racial shame.

The loss of a sense of dignity and respect in the macho breeds a false machismo which leads him to put down women and even to brutalize them. Co-existing with his sexist behavior is a love for the mother which takes precedence over that of all others. Devoted son, macho pig. To wash down the shame of his acts, of his very being, and to handle the brute in the mirror, he takes to the bottle, the snort, the needle and the fist.

Though we 'understand' the root causes of male hatred and fear, and the subsequent wounding of women, we do not excuse, we do not condone, and we will no longer put up with it. From the men of our race, we demand the admission/acknowledgment/disclosure/testimony that they wound us, violate us, are afraid of us and of our power. We need them to say they will begin to eliminate their hurtful put-down ways. But more than the words, we demand acts. We say to them: We will develop equal power with you and those who have shamed us.

It is imperative that mestizas support each other in changing the sexist elements in the Mexican–Indian culture. As long as woman is put down, the Indian and the Black in all of us is put down. The struggle of the mestiza is above all a feminist one. As long as *los hombres* think they have to *chingar mujeres* and each other to be men, as long as men are taught that they are superior and therefore culturally favored over *la mujer*, as long as to be a *vieja* is a thing of derision, there can be no real healing of our psyches. We're halfway there—we have such love of the Mother, the good mother. The first step is to unlearn the *puta/virgen* dichotomy and to see *Coatlapopeuh–Coatlicue* in the Mother, *Guadalupe.*

Tenderness, a sign of vulnerability, is so feared that it is showered on women with verbal abuse and blows. Men, even more than women, are fettered to gender roles. Women at least have had the guts to break out of bondage. Only gay men have had the courage to expose themselves to the woman inside them and to challenge the current masculinity. I've encountered a few scattered and isolated gentle straight men, the beginnings of a new breed, but they are confused, and entangled with sexist behaviors that they have not been able to eradicate. We need a new masculinity and the new man needs a movement.

Lumping the males who deviate from the general norm with man, the oppressor, is a gross injustice. *Asombra pensar que nos hemos quedado en ese pozo oscuro donde el mundo encierra a las lesbianas. Asombra pensar que hemos, como femenistas y lesbianas, cerrado nuestros corazónes a los hombres, a nuestros hermanos los jotos, desheredados y marginales como nosotros.* Being the supreme crossers of cultures, homosexuals have strong bonds with the queer white, Black, Asian, Native American, Latino, and with the queer in Italy, Australia and the rest of the planet. We come from all colors, all classes, all races, all time periods. Our role is to link people with each other—the Blacks with Jews with Indians with Asians with whites with extraterrestrials. It is to transfer ideas and information from one culture to another. Colored homosexuals have more knowledge of other cultures; have always been at the forefront (although sometimes in the closet) of all liberation struggles in this country; have suffered more injustices and have survived them despite all odds. Chicanos need to acknowledge the political and artistic contributions of their queer. People, listen to what your *jotería* is saying.

The mestizo and the queer exist at this time and point on the evolutionary continuum for a purpose. We are a blending that proves that all blood is intricately woven together, and that we are spawned out of similar souls.

SOMOS UNA GENTE

Hay tantísimas fronteras
que dividen a la gente,
pero por cada frontera
existe también un puente.
Gina Valdés[8]

Divided Loyalties

Many women and men of color do not want to have any dealings with white people. It takes too much time and energy to explain to the downwardly mobile, white middle-class women that it's okay for us to want to own 'possessions', never having had any nice furniture on our dirt floors or 'luxuries' like washing machines. Many feel that whites should help their own people rid themselves of race hatred and fear first. I, for one, choose to use some of my energy to serve as mediator. I think we need to allow whites to be our allies. Through our literature, art, *corridos* and folktales we must share our history with them so when they set up committees to help Big Mountain Navajos or the Chicano farmworkers or *los Nicaragüenses* they won't turn people away because of their racial fears and ignorances. They will come to see that they are not helping us but following our lead.

Individually, but also as a racial entity, we need to voice our needs. We need to say to white society: We need you to accept the fact that Chicanos are different, to acknowledge your rejection and negation of us. We need you to own the fact that you looked upon us as less than human, that you stole our lands, our personhood, our self-respect. We need you to make public restitution: to say that, to compensate for your own sense of defectiveness, you strive for power over us, you erase our history and our experience because it makes you feel guilty—you'd rather forget your brutish acts. To say you've split yourself from minority groups, that you disown us, that your dual consciousness splits off parts of yourself, transferring the 'negative' parts onto us. (Where there is persecution of minorities, there is shadow projection. Where there is violence and war, there is repression of shadow.) To say that you are afraid of us, that to put distance between us, you wear the mask of contempt. Admit that Mexico is your double, that she exists in the shadow of this country, that we are irrevocably tied to her. Gringo, accept the doppelganger in your psyche. By taking back your collective shadow the intracultural split will heal. And finally, tell us what you need from us.

BY YOUR TRUE FACES WE WILL KNOW YOU

I am visible—see this Indian face—yet I am invisible. I both blind them with my beak nose and am their blind spot. But I exist, we exist. They'd like to think I have melted in the pot. But I haven't, we haven't.

The dominant white culture is killing us slowly with its ignorance. By taking away our self-determination, it has made us weak and empty. As a people we have resisted and we have taken expedient positions, but we have never been allowed to develop unencumbered—we have never been allowed to be fully ourselves. The whites in power want us people of color to barricade ourselves behind our separate tribal walls so they can pick us off one at a time with their hidden weapons; so they can whitewash and distort history. Ignorance splits people, creates prejudices. A misinformed people is a subjugated people.

Before the Chicano and the undocumented worker and the Mexican from the other side can come together, before the Chicano can have unity with Native Americans and other groups, we need to know the history of their struggle and they need to know ours. Our mothers, our sisters and brothers, the guys who hang out on street corners, the children in the playgrounds, each of us must know our Indian lineage, our afro-*mestisaje*, our history of resistance.

To the immigrant *mexicano* and the recent arrivals we must teach our history. The 80 million *mexicanos* and the Latinos from Central and South America must know of our struggles. Each one of us must know basic facts about Nicaragua, Chile and the rest of Latin America. The Latinoist movement (Chicanos, Puerto Ricans, Cubans and other Spanish-speaking people working together to combat racial discrimination in the market place) is good but it is not enough. Other than a common culture we will have nothing to hold us together. We need to meet on a broader communal ground.

The struggle is inner: Chicano, *indio*, American Indian, *mojado*, *mexicano*, immigrant Latino, Anglo in power, working-class Anglo, Black, Asian—our psyches resemble the border-towns and are populated by the same people. The struggle has always been inner, and is played out in the outer terrains. Awareness of our situation must come before inner changes, which in turn come before changes in society. Nothing happens in the 'real' world unless it first happens in the images in our heads.

EL DíA DE LA CHICANA

I will not be shamed again
Nor will I shame myself.

I am possessed by a vision: that we Chicanas and Chicanos have taken back or uncovered our true faces, our dignity and self-respect. It's a validation vision.

Seeing the Chicana anew in light of her history, I seek an exoneration, a seeing through the fictions of white supremacy, a seeing of ourselves in our true guises and not as the false racial personality that has been given to us and that we have given to ourselves. I seek our woman's face, our true features, the positive and the negative seen clearly, free of the tainted biases of male dominance. I seek new images of identity, new beliefs about ourselves, our humanity and worth no longer in question.

Estamos viviendo en la noche de la Raza, un tiempo cuando el trabajo se hace a lo quieto, en el oscuro. El día cuando aceptamos tal y como somos y para en donde vamos y porque—ese día será el día de la Raza. Yo tengo el conpromiso de expresar mi visión, mi sensibilidad, mi percepción de la revalidación de la gente mexicana, su mérito, estimación, honra, aprecio, y validez.

On December 2nd when my sun goes into my first house, I celebrate *el día de la Chicana y el Chicano*. On that day I clean my altars, light my *Coatlalopeuh* candle, burn sage and copal, take *el baño para espantar basura*, sweep my house. On that day I bare my soul, make myself vulnerable to friends and family by expressing my feelings. On that day I affirm who we are.

On that day I look inside our conflicts and our basic introverted racial temperament. I identify our needs, voice them. I acknowledge that the self and the race have been wounded. I recognize the need to take care of our personhood, of our racial self. On that day I gather the splintered and disowned parts of *la gente mexicana* and hold them in my arms. *Todas las partes de nosotros valen.*

On that day I say, 'Yes, all you people wound us when you reject us.

Rejection strips us of self-worth; our vulnerability exposes us to shame. It is our innate identity you find wanting. We are ashamed that we need your good opinion, that we need your acceptance. We can no longer camouflage our needs, can no longer let defenses and fences sprout around us. We can no longer withdraw. To rage and look upon you with contempt is to rage and be contemptuous of ourselves. We can no longer blame you, nor disown the white parts, the male parts, the pathological parts, the queer parts, the vulnerable parts. Here we are weaponless with open arms, with only our magic. Let's try it our way, the *mestiza* way, the Chicana way, the woman way.'

On that day, I search for our essential dignity as a people, a people with a sense of purpose—to belong and contribute to something greater than our *pueblo.* On that day I seek to recover and reshape my spiritual identity. *!Anímate! Raza, a celebrar el día de la Chicana.*

EL RETORNO

> All movements are accomplished in six stages,
> and the seventh brings return.
>
> I Ching[9]

> *Tanto tiempo sin verte casa mía,*
> *mi cuna, mi hondo nido de la huerta.*
>
> 'Soledad'[10]

I stand at the river, watch the curving, twisting serpent, a serpent nailed to the fence where the mouth of the Rio Grande empties into the Gulf.

I have come back. *Tanto dolor me costó el alejamiento.* I shade my eyes and look up. The bone beak of a hawk slowly circling over me, checking me out as potential carrion. In its wake a little bird flickering its wings, swimming sporadically like a fish. In the distance the expressway and the slough of traffic like an irritated sow. The sudden pull in my gut, *la tierra, los aguaceros.* My land, *el viento soplando la arena, ellagartijo debajo de un nopalito. Me acuerdo como era antes. Una región desértica de vasta llanuras, costeras de baja altura, de escasa lluvia, de chaparrales formados por mes quites y huizaches.* If I look real hard I can almost see the Spanish fathers who were called 'the cavalry of Christ' enter this valley riding their burros, see the clash of cultures commence.

Tierra natal. This is home, the small towns in the Valley, *los pueblitos* with chicken pens and goats picketed to mesquite shrubs. *En las colonias* on the other side of the tracks, junk cars line the front yards of hot pink and lavender-trimmed houses—Chicano architecture we call it, self-consciously. I have missed the TV shows where hosts speak in half and half, and where awards are given in the category of Tex–Mex music. I have missed the Mexican cemeteries blooming with artificial flowers, the fields of aloe vera and red pepper, rows of sugar cane, of corn hanging on the stalks, the cloud of *polvareda* in the dirt roads behind a speeding pickup truck, *el sabor de tamales de rez y venado.* I have missed *la yegua colorada* gnawing the wooden gate of her stall, the smell of horse flesh from Carito's corrals. *He hecho menos las noches calientes sin aire, noches de linternas y lechuzas* making holes in the night.

I still feel the old despair when I look at the unpainted, dilapidated, scrap lumber houses consisting mostly of corrugated aluminum. Some of the poorest people in the US live in the Lower Rio Grande Valley, an arid and semi-arid land of irrigated farming, intense sunlight and heat, citrus groves next to chaparral and cactus. I walk through the elementary school I attended so long ago, that remained segregated until recently. I remember how the white teachers used to punish us for being Mexican.

How I love this tragic valley of South Texas, as Ricardo Sánchez calls it; this borderland between the Nueces and the Rio Grande. This land has survived possession and ill-use by five countries: Spain, Mexico, the Republic of Texas, the US, the Confederacy and the US again. It has survived Anglo-Mexican blood feuds, lynchings, burnings, rapes, pillage.

Today I see the Valley still struggling to survive. Whether it does or not, it will never be as I remember it. The borderlands depression that was set off by the 1982 peso devaluation in Mexico resulted in the closure of hundreds of Valley businesses. Many people lost their homes, cars, land. Prior to 1982, US store owners thrived on retail sales to Mexicans who came across the border for groceries and clothes and appliances. While goods on the US side have become 10, 100, 1000 times more expensive for Mexican buyers, goods on the Mexican side have become 10, 100, 1000 times cheaper for Americans. Because the Valley is heavily dependent on agriculture and Mexican retail trade, it has the highest unemployment rates along the entire border region; it is the Valley that has been hardest hit.[11]

'It's been a bad year for corn', my brother, Nune, says. As he talks, I remember my father scanning the sky for a rain that would end the drought, looking up into the sky, day after day, while the corn withered on its stalk. My father has been dead for 29 years, having worked himself to death. The life span of a Mexican farm laborer is 50—he lived to be 38. It shocks me that I am older than he. I, too, search the sky for rain. Like the ancients, I worship the rain god and the maize goddess, but unlike my father I have recovered their names. Now for rain (irrigation) one offers not a sacrifice of blood, but of money.

'Farming is in a bad way', my brother says. 'Two to three thousand small and big farmers went bankrupt in this country last year. Six years ago the price of corn was $8.00 per hundred pounds,' he goes on. 'This year it is $3.90 per hundred pounds.' And, I think to myself, after taking inflation into account, not planting anything puts you ahead.

I walk out to the back yard, stare at *los rosales de mamá*. She wants me to help her prune the rose bushes, dig out the carpet grass that is choking them. *Mamagrande Ramona también tenís rosales*. Here every Mexican grows flowers. If they don't have a piece of dirt, they use car tires, jars, cans, shoe boxes. Roses are the Mexican's favorite flower. I think, how symbolic—thorns and all.

Yes, the Chicano and Chicana have always taken care of growing things and the land. Again I see the four of us kids getting off the school bus, changing into our work clothes, walking into the field with Papí and Mamí, all six of us bending to the ground. Below our feet, under the earth lie the watermelon seeds. We cover them with paper plates, putting *terremotes* on top of the plates to keep them from being blown away by the wind. The paper plates keep the freeze away. Next day or the next, we remove the plates, bare the tiny green shoots to the elements. They survive and grow, give fruit hundreds of times the size of the seed. We water them and hoe them. We harvest them. The vines dry, rot, are plowed under. Growth, death, decay, birth. The soil prepared again and again, impregnated, worked on. A constant changing of forms, *renacimientos de la tierra madre*.

This land was Mexican once
was Indian always
and is.
And will be again.

Notes

1. This is my own 'take off' on Jose Vasconcelos' idea. Jose Vasconcelos, *La Raza Cósmica: Misión de la Raza Ibero-Americana* (México: Aguilar S.A. de Ediciones, 1961).
2. Vasconcelos, *La Raza Cósmica.*
3. Arthur Koestler termed this 'bisociation', Albert Rothenberg, *The Creative Process in Art, Science, and Other Fields* (Chicago: University of Chicago Press, 1979), 12.
4. In part, I derive my definitions for 'convergent' and 'divergent' thinking from Rothenberg, *The Creative Process*, 12–13.
5. To borrow chemist Ilya Prigogine's theory of 'dissipative structures'. Prigogine discovered that substances interact not in predictable ways as it was taught in science, but in different and fluctuating ways to produce new and more complex structures, a kind of birth he called 'morphogenesis', which created unpredictable innovations. Harold Gilliam, 'Searching for a New World View', *This World* (January, 1981), 23.
6. *Tortillas de masa harina*: corn tortillas are of two types, the smooth uniform ones made in a tortilla press and usually bought at a tortilla factory or supermarket, and *gorditas*, made by mixing *masa* with lard or shortening or butter (my mother sometimes puts in bits of bacon or *chicharrones*).
7. Gina Valdés, *Puentes y Fronteras: Coplas Chicanas* (Los Angeles: Castle Lithograph, 1982), 2.
8. Richard Wilhelm, *The I Ching or Book of Changes*, trans. Cary F. Baynes (Princeton: Princeton University Press, 1950), 98.
9. '*Soledad*' is sung by the group, Haciendo Punto en Otro Son.
10. Out of the twenty-two border counties in the four border states, Hidalgo County (named for Father Hidalgo who was shot in 1810 after instigating Mexico's revolt against Spanish rule under the banner of *la Virgen de Guadalupe*) is the most poverty-stricken county in the nation as well as the largest home base (along with Imperial in California) for migrant farmworkers. It was here that I was born and raised. I am amazed that both it and I have survived.

10 Colonialism and Modernity: Feminist Re-presentations of Women in Non-Western Societies

Aihwa Ong*

WHO IS THE NON-FEMINIST OTHER?

[. . .] The irony of feminism is twofold: (i) As an oppositional subculture reproduced within the Western knowledge of the non-Western World, it is a field defined by historicism. This post-Enlightenment view holds that the world is a complex but unified unity culminating in the West. Liberal and socialist feminists alike apply the same incorporating world historical schemes to their understanding of women and men in the non-Western world. With common roots in the Enlightenment, masculinist and feminist perspectives share in the notion that enlightened reason has been a critical force in social emancipation. Western standards and goals—rationality and individualism—are thereby used to evaluate the cultures and histories of non-Western societies. Feminist voices in the social sciences unconsciously echo this masculinist will to power in its relation to non-Western societies. Thus, for feminists looking overseas, the non-feminist Other is not so much patriarchy as the non-Western woman. [. . .] (ii) When feminists look overseas, they frequently seek to establish *their* authority on the backs of non-Western women, determining for them the meanings and goals of their lives. If, from the feminist perspective there can be no shared experience with persons who stand for the Other, the claim to a common kinship with non-Western women is at best, tenuous, at worst, non-existent.

My concern here is to talk about the intersections between colonial discourse and feminist representations of non-Western women in what may be called 'women in development' studies. There are differ-

* From Aihwa Ong, 'Colonialism and Modernity: Feminist Re-presentations of Women in Non-Western Societies' from *Inscriptions* No's 3 and 4 (University College Santa Cruz, 1988), 79–93.

ent self-styled approaches within this feminism, linked by a basic concern with problems of sexual inequality and difference in non-Western societies, problems perceived as the failure to achieve modernity. The terms 'non-Western' and 'Third World' are used as a shorthand, and not to imply a monolithic world outside European and American societies which have collectively maintained hegemony over much of the globe in recent history.[1] By 'colonial discourse' I mean different strategies of description and understanding which were produced out of the historical emergence of this transnational network of power relations. Historically, distinct strands of colonial discourse circulating in particular colonial societies were linked to Western imperialist definitions of colonized populations.[2] Although there has been significant dismantling of this global political structure since the Second World War, neo-colonial preoccupations continue to haunt Western perceptions of ex-colonial societies. The following discussion suggests that well-known feminist studies on women in ex-colonial societies have not escaped this hegemonic world view.

FEMINIST DISCURSIVE POWER AND THE SILENCED OTHER

Albert Memmi characterizes the relationship between the colonizer and the colonized as one of 'implacable dependence'.[3] For the privilege of making cultural judgements which see their way into print, feminists often speak without reducing the silence of the cultural Other. George Marcus and Michael Fischer have recommended the repatriation of anthropology in order to defamiliarize the world view of middle-class Americans.[4] Much recent feminist study of Asian women already has had this function, producing epistemological and political gaps between us feminists and them 'oppressed' women. I will argue that although some kind of distance is necessary for arriving at a partial understanding of each other, this is not the kind of separation we should seek. We have to first divest ourselves of a cultural heritage whereby women in non-Western societies are fixed as various sexualities and natural capacities.

In the late nineteenth century, British traveller Isabella Bird passed through the Malay peninsula and made the following observation:

> The people lead strange and uneventful lives. The men are not inclined to much effort except in fishing or hunting, and, where they possess rice land, in ploughing for rice ... The women were lounging about the house, some

cleaning fish, others pounding rice; but they do not care for work, and the little money which they need for buying clothes they can make by selling mats or jungle fruits . . .[5]

Not a colonial official but an 'indomitable' explorer of the Eastern world recently brought under Western influence, Isabella Bird had already fixed her market lenses on the Malay (lack of) potential as a labor pool.[6] There are numerous other examples by less well known British observers in the 'tropical dependencies' where natives were constantly evaluated in terms of their 'natural' capacities and then dismissed as 'indolent'.[7]

What has this got to do with contemporary feminist perspectives on Asian women? Since the early 1970s, when feminists turned their attention overseas, our understanding of women and men in the Third World has been framed in essentialist terms: how their statuses may be explained in terms of their labor and reproductive powers. *The Role of Women in Economic Development* blazed a trail which has yet to spend itself.[8] Throughout the 1970s and 1980s, books on non-Western women emphasized their roles in capitalist development. Let me cite a few collections: *Women and National Development: The Complexities of Change*;[9] *African Women in The Development Process*;[10] *Of Marriage and the Market: Women's Subordination in International Perspective*;[11] *Women, Men and the International Division of Labor*;[12] and *Women's Work*[13]. Part of my own training as an anthropologist has been influenced by this kind of feminist literature largely shaped by a political economic perspective. By and large, non-Western women are taken as an unproblematic universal category; feminists mainly differ over whether modernization of the capitalist or socialist kind will emancipate or reinforce systems of gender inequality found in the Third World. The status of non-Western women is analyzed and gauged according to a set of legal, political and social benchmarks that Western feminists consider critical in achieving a power balance between men and women.

MODERNIZATION DISCOURSE ON THIRD WORLD WOMEN

Most of the literature in development studies falls within the framework of the so-called modernization school, as most clearly spelled out by William W. Rostow.[14] Each generation of scholars has reworked this model which opposes Western modernity to Third World traditionalism. In the 1960s, Raphael Patai in *Women in the Changing World* accounted for gender inequalities in terms of the degree to which 'age-old, custom-determining roles' were being broken down by 'Westernization', a process seen to favor women's access to wage work and higher social status.[15] This position was challenged by Laura Bossen who argued that Westernization has caused women to lose highly variable roles in the traditional economy. By placing structural limits on women's access to new production activities, the modernization process has reduced women's status relative to that of men in the Third World.

A recent revival of the modernization theory is expressed by Linda Lim in her paper on 'the dilemma of Third World women workers in multinational factories'.[16] She maintains that in societies 'where capitalist relations are least developed ... traditional patriarchy is sufficiently strong to maintain women in an inferior labor market position'.[17] Following from this logic, she maintains that by providing these women with wage employment, transnational companies contribute to their emancipation. This is an example of linear thinking which ignores the multiple and fluid nature of power relations. As my study shows, factory women freed from some forms of family control come under new systems of domination such as industrial discipline, social surveillance and religious vigilance. Patriarchal power is reconstituted in the factory setting and in the fundamentalist Islamic movement which induce both rebellion *and* self control on the part of women workers.[18] By using a traditional/modernity framework, these feminists view the destruction of 'traditional customs' as either a decline of women's status in a romanticized 'natural' economy, or as their liberation by Western economic rationality. This either/or argument reveals a kind of magical thinking about modernity which has proliferated in Third World governments, while confusing and obscuring the social meanings of change for people caught up in it.

DISCOURSE ON WOMEN IN CAPITALIST AND SOCIAL TRANSITIONS

For many socialist feminists, Asian societies are significant to the extent they possess or lack 'patriarchal' traditions which may be reproduced in the transition to a capitalist or socialist 'mode of production'. *Women's Work* is based on papers on the sexual division of labor initially published in *Signs* (Vol. 7, No. 2, 1981). Women's status worldwide is discussed within 'an evolutionary perspective on the gender division of labor'.[19] In their critique of Boserup, Lourdes Beneria and Gita Sen offer a 'capital accumulation' model to discuss 'the specific ways in which women are affected by the hierarchical and exploitative structure of production associated with capitalism's penetration in the Third World'.[20] Capitalism is personified and differentiated in terms of its varied effects on 'domestic work', production and reproduction, population control and birth control. In contrast, 'women' (in Africa, Latin America and Asia) are differentiated only in terms of their status as wives and workers in reproduction (i.e. the production of use values in the household), and production (of commodities). Beneria and Sen's claim to 'a richly textured understanding' may possibly describe their abstract formulation of 'tensions between gender and class',[21] but not their representation of 'women in the Third World'.

This substitution of understanding of women as cultural beings by an elaboration of feminist theory is also found in *Women, Men and the International Division of Labor.*[22] The papers taken as a whole tell us more about Marxist-feminist thinking about the capitalist world system than about the experience of women and men in the industrializing situation. Eleven papers fall under sections entitled 'global accumulation and the labor process', 'production, reproduction, and the household economy', and 'labor flow and capitalist expansion'. Seven essays (including my own) are 'case studies in electronics and textiles'. This organization is clearly an attempt to discuss changing women's positions in the encounter between global capitalist forces and the everyday life of paid and unpaid work. However, a consideration of the latter is subordinated to descriptions of the intersections of patriarchy and capitalism. Indeed, capitalism is delineated as a historically conditioned, polymorphous system; it has more contradictions and personalities than the women and men who are ostensibly the subjects of the volume. In most of the papers, the implied message is that even when women constitute the majority of workers in transnational industries, their practical and theoretical significance as 'a source of cheap labor' tends to take precedence over a more careful consideration of the social meanings these changes have for them. Except for essays by Bolles and Green, discourse on women's position is theoretically derived from their being acted upon in an unproblematic fashion by patriarchal and capitalist relations of domination. Even in the case studies, quotations cited are from Marxist scholars (e.g.

Braverman, Wolpe), and feminists like Heidi Hartmann are considered more significant in uncovering the social meanings of work relations than the words of women on the shop floor. The general effect of these papers is the fetishization of capital accumulation and the valorization of women and men as commodities.

By portraying women in non-Western societies as identical and interchangable, and more exploited than women in the dominant capitalist societies, liberal and socialist feminists alike encode a belief in their own cultural superiority. On the one hand, we have a set of Western standards whereby feminists and other scholars evaluate the degree of patriarchal oppression inflicted on women as wives, mothers and workers in the Third World. For instance, studies on women in post-1949 China inevitably discuss how they are doubly exploited by the peasant family and by socialist patriarchy,[23] reflecting the more immediate concerns of American socialist feminists than perhaps of Chinese women themselves. By using China as 'a case study' of the socialist experiment with women's liberation, these works are part of a whole network of Western academic and policy-making discourses on the backwardness of the non-Western, non-modern world. There is a scientific tendency to treat gender and sexuality as categories that are measurable, and to ignore indigenous meanings which may conceive of them as ideas inseparable from moral values.

On the other hand, feminist approaches which purport to understand indigenous traditions and meanings that have persisted over the course of modernization often betray a view of non-Western women as out of time with the West,[24] and therefore a vehicle for misplaced Western nostalgia. A recent ethnography, *Geisha*,[25] discussed the sexual aesthetics of Japanese women and yet is coy about their specific intention and techniques. Despite the rich ethnographic details, this view 'into a feminine community that has been the subject of rumor and fantasy for centuries in the West' (dustjacket) has managed to refreeze geishas as objects in Oriental erotica. Although their subculture is intended to create an illusion of an earlier time, one wishes the writer had situated her description of their images and working lives more firmly in late twentieth-century Japanese society.

Another modernist mode for treating exotic women out of their time context is presented in *Nisa: The Life and Words of a !Kung Woman*.[26] This book has become a popular text for introductory anthropology courses. Here is a feminist confrontation with a non-Western woman as an 'individual', i.e. someone seen as autonomous, in the moral sense of our modern (individualist) ideology. It seems inevitable that Nisa's life is re-presented as a sexual discourse that 'we' can appropriate for our post-modern consumption.

MODERN POSTURINGS WITH NONMODERN IMAGES

The feminist works cited above seek a modern form of individual freedom in their analyses of gender relations in the non-Western world. Furthermore, 'the non-Western woman' as a trope of feminist discourse is either non-modern or modern; she is seldom perceived as living in a situation where there is deeply felt tension between tradition and modernity. Two analytical strategies emerge in the feminist discourses discussed. First, even when, like Nisa, the non-Western woman speaks, she is wrenched out of the context of her society and inscribed within the concerns of Western feminist scholars. Secondly, however well-intended in their goal of exposing the oppression of Third World women, feminist scholars have a tendency to proceed by reversal: non-Western women are what we are not. These tendencies of projection and reversal situate non-Western women in a subordinate position within feminist theoretical and textual productions. These self-validating exercises affirm our feminist subjectivity while denying those of non-Western women.

What is peculiarly colonial in these feminist perspectives is the assumption that Western standards and feelings take precedence over those of their Third World subjects. In their naturalistic conceptualizations of non-Western women as labor power or sexuality, there is little interest (except in Dalby) about indigenous constructions of gender and sexuality. We miss the dense network of cultural politics that we demand of a study of women and men in Western societies. Thus, although a common past may be claimed by feminists, Third World women are often represented as mired in it, ever arriving at modernity when Western feminists are already adrift in postmodernism.

MODEST GOALS AND PARTIAL UNDERSTANDINGS

Despite my critical remarks, I remain convinced that feminists, because of their privileged positions as members of hegemonic powers, should speak out against female oppression at home and overseas. Surely an element of the current backlash against social science research by Third World governments[27] is their protests against our cultural assumptions and conceptual language.[28] Political elites in the Third World have their own representations and discourses which do not necessarily reflect a concern with women's or lower-class interests. However, this does not mean that the prescriptions of sympathetic Western feminists are inevitably more aligned with the ideas and values of Third World women. I mentioned earlier our need to maintain a respectful distance, to leave open the possibilities for an understanding not overly constructed by our own preoccupations. This 'privilege of distantiation'[29] also helps us accept that cultural struggles in the Third World may be for social and sexual destinies different from Western (male-dominated or feminist) visions.

I can suggest a few tentative leads for recognizing a mutuality of discourse in our encounter with women in non-Western societies. We can resist the tendency to write our subjectively defined world onto an Other that lies outside it. When we jettison our conceptual baggage, we open up the possibilities for mutual but partial, and ambiguous, exchange. With James Clifford, I am doubtful that we can achieve more than partial understandings. However, the multivocal ethnographic texts he would have anthropologists produce must also disclose a riot of social meanings embedded in the confrontation between tradition and modernity in Third World societies. Below, I attempt to show how cultural analysis in anthropology can produce an understanding of gender as constructed by, and contingent upon, the play of power relations in a cultural context.

In my study of Malay factory women, gender is revealed as a symbolic system not separable from domains such as the family, the economy and politics, but as embedded in discourses and images marking social boundaries and self-reflective identities. [. . .] The fluid and multiple nature of power relations becomes a part of the everyday life of young peasant women working in transnational factories. This making of a female labor force has been accompanied by an inflationary increase in the social meanings of gender and sexuality: these are negotiated and contested in relation to other discourses about social difference and domination in Malaysian society. I identify at least four overlapping sets of discourses about factory women: corporate, political, Islamic and personal. Corporate discourse elaborated on the 'natural' accommodation of 'oriental female' fingers, eyes and passivity to low-skilled assembly work. This instrumental–biological representation of women is part of the neo-colonial attitude towards development in Third World societies perceived as an international reservoir of cheap labor. Secondly, the emergence of a Malay female industrial labor force has produced a public debate over their sexuality, as expressed in individualistic ideas, behavior, and modern forms of consumption. The 'electronics woman' becomes a symbol of sexual threat to Malay culture and of working class defiance. Islamic pronouncements about factory women's morality betrays an anxiety over their crossing of social boundaries, and their flirtation with secularism and individualistic self-identity. They demand a greater religious vigilance to bring Malay working women back into the fold of Islamic womanhood. In this explosion of sexual discourses, many factory women internalize the cautionary tales and are induced to discipline themselves as Muslims and as workers. Others see themselves as modern women, and throwing caution to the winds, embrace Western images of sexual liberation. By looking at the politics of sexuality, I discovered conflicting sets of genders, and their embeddedness in political struggles over cultural identity and the transition to industrial modernization. In their own words and actions, which I cannot reproduce here, we see how meanings attached to gender can generate deep divisions, confusion and unresolved tensions between tradition and modernity.

Like Malay factory women, government bureaucrats and religious zealots, we may wish to deconstruct colonial categories and problematize modernization. By giving up our accustomed ways of looking at non-Western women, we may begin to understand better. We may come to accept their living according to their own cultural interpretations of a changing world, and not simply acted upon by inherited traditions and modernization projects. They may not seek our secular goal of individual autonomy, nor renounce the bonds of family and community. It seems to me that as feminists, we need to take into account the changing world community, and recognize the limits of our own traditions and explanations. We begin a dialogue when we recognize other forms of gender- and culture-based subjectivities, and accept that others often choose to conduct their lives separately from our particular vision of the future.

Notes

1. 'Western' is taken as a problematic construct, and is by no means used to suggest an undifferentiated and congealed form of global dominance. Since we are discussing texts in the English language, 'Western' is here taken to include European societies under prewar British and postwar American hegemonic leadership.

2. This definition of colonial discourse is thus broader than that used by Lata Mani in 'Contentious Traditions: The Debate on Sati in Colonial India', *Cultural Critique* 7 (Fall 1987), 119–156.
3. Albert Memmi, *The Colonized and the Colonizer* (Boston: Beacon Press, 1965).
4. George Marcus and Michael Fischer, *Anthropology as Cultural Critique* (Chicago: Chicago University Press, 1986).
5. Isabella Bird, *The Golden Chersonese* (Kuala Lumpur: Oxford University Press, 1967) [1886].
6. Isabella Bird's writings on her travels to the corners of the British empire and beyond have recently been printed in the United States because of the American market for 'travel literature'. See her *The Yangze Valley and Beyond* (New York: Beacon Press, 1987) and *Unbeaten Tracks in Japan* (New York: Beacon Press, 1987).
7. For a discussion of colonial discourse in the Malay world, see S. Hussein Alatas, *The Myth of the Lazy Native* (London: Frank Cass, 1977).
8. Ester Boserup, *Women's Role in Economic Development* (London: St Martin's Press, 1970).
9. Wellesley Editorial Board, 'Women and National Development: the Complexity of Change', Special issue of *Signs* (1977).
10. Nici Nelson (ed.), *African Women in the Development Process* (London: Routledge and Kegan Paul, 1981).
11. Kate Young, Carol Wolkowitz and Roslyn McCullagh (eds.). *Of Marriage and the Market: Women's Subordination in International Perspectives* (London: CSE Books, 1981).
12. June Nash and Maria Patricia Fernandez Kelly (eds.), *Women, Men and the International Division of Labor* (Albany, NY: State University of New York Press, 1983).
13. Eleanor Leacock and Helen Safa (eds.), *Women's Work: Development and the Division of Labor by Gender* (Massachusetts: Bergin and Garvey).
14. W. W. Rostow, *Stages of Economic Growth: A Non-Communist Manifesto* (New York: Free Press, 1960).
15. Raphael Patai, *Women in the Changing World* (New York: Free Press, 1967).
16. Linda Lim, 'Capitalism, Imperialism, and Patriarchy: The Dilemma of Third World Women Workers in Multinational Factories', in Nash and Kelly, (eds.), *Women, Men, and the International Division of Labor.*
17. Ibid., 79.
18. Aihwa Ong, *Spirits of Resistance and Capitalist Discipline: Factory Women in Malaysia* (New York: State University of New York, 1987).
19. Leacock and Safa, *Women's Work.*
20. Lourdes Beneria and Gita Sen, 'Accumulation, Reproduction, and Women's Role in Economic Development: Boserup Revisited', *Signs* (Winter 1981), vol. 7, no. 2, 279–98.
21. Ibid., 156.
22. Nash and Kelly, *Women, Men and the International Division of Labor.*
23. See Molyneux, 1981; Kay A. Johnson, *Women, Family and the Peasant Revolution in China* (Chicago: Chicago University Press, 1982); Judith Stacey, *Socialism and Patriarchy in China* (Berkeley. University of California Press, 1983);

Margery Wolf, *Revolution Postponed: Women and Socialism in China* (Stanford: Stanford University Press, 1986).

24. On circumventing 'coevalness' in ethnographies, see Johannes Fabian, *Time and the Other: How Anthropology Makes its Object* (New York: Columbia University Press, 1983).
25. Lisa Dalby, *Geisha* (Stanford: Stanford University Press, 1983).
26. Marjorie Shostak, *Nisa: The Life and Words of a !Kung Woman* (Cambridge, MA: Harvard University Press, 1983).
27. Cheryl Benard, 'Women's Anthropology Takes the Chador,' *Partisan Review* 2 (1986), 275–84.
28. Some feminists have criticized feminist categories projected onto non-Western women and men in the representation of indigenous meaning and experience (see Marilyn Strathern, 'Culture in a Netbag', *Man* (n.s.) 16 (December 1981), 165–88; and Deborah Gordon, 'Feminist Anthropology and the Invention of American Female Identities', paper presented at the 86th Annual Meeting of the American Anthropological Association, Chicago, November 1987).
29. Louis Dumont, *Essays on Individualism: Modern Ideology in Anthropological Perspective* (Chicago, IL: University of Chicago Press, 1986), 279–80.

Part II. **Engaging the Debates**

11 'Race', Gender and the Concept of 'Difference' in Feminist Thought

Mary Maynard*

This chapter is concerned with theorizing the interrelationships between 'race' and gender oppression and the extent to which this is furthered by using the concept of 'difference'. [. . .] Although the concept has no one connotation, as will be discussed, its implications of plurality and multiplicity have been regarded by many as providing the necessary antidote to the former unquestioning use of the unified terms 'woman' or 'women'. It is now commonplace to read books and articles, often written by white feminists, exhorting us to remember that there are differences between women and that these need to be taken account of in our work. Less likely to be found, however, are indications of what difference actually means and how it can be made a constructive part of empirical research, theoretical analysis or practical political action in order to bring about change.

My concern in this chapter is to question how useful the notion of 'difference' is for feminism, particularly when dealing with issues to do with 'race' and ethnicity. It should be pointed out from the beginning that I am certainly not denying the significance of diversity among women and the need for feminists to rethink their intellectual and political practice in the light of this. The problem is, rather, the extent to which using ideas about difference enables us to explore, not just the ways in which women may be distinguished from each other, but the mechanisms and processes through which distinct and specific forms of subordination are brought about. I argue that to focus on 'difference' alone runs the risk of masking the conditions that give

The author is grateful to Haleh Afshar, Anne Akeroyd, Sheila Allen, Bunie Matlanyane Sexwale, Bev Skeggs and Erica Wheeler for comments on an earlier draft of this chapter.

* From Mary Maynard, 'Race, Gender and the Concept of "Difference" in Feminist Thought' from *The Dynamics of 'Race' and Gender* by Heleh Afshar and Mary Maynard (Taylor & Francis, 1994), reprinted by permission of the publisher.

some forms of 'difference' value and power over others. In the context of 'race' and ethnicity this can lead to the marginalization of issues such as racism, racial domination and white supremacy.

The chapter has five sections. The first section briefly considers some linguistic and terminological difficulties. The second provides a context for those that follow by considering some problems with existing literature and the ways in which Western feminists have grappled with the 'race' and gender dynamic. The third section focuses on the idea of 'difference' and the main ways in which it has been used in the feminist literature of Britain and the United States. In the fourth, attention is turned to some of the problems in discussing 'difference', particularly when focusing on 'race'. The final section suggests some possible ways forward.

TERMINOLOGICAL DISPUTES

It is impossible to embark on any discussion of 'race' without first drawing attention to the problematic nature of the term, along with others associated with it. [. . .] It has long been recognized that races do not exist in any scientifically meaningful sense. None the less, in many societies people have often acted, and continue to act, as if 'race' is a fixed objective category. [. . .] Common-sense understandings of 'race' have concentrated on such variables as skin colour, country of origin, religion, nationality and language.

[. . .] Donald and Rattansi (1992) ask how does the category of 'race' operate?[1] Such an approach is useful because it can be used to chart the nature of the concept's shifting boundaries, while also permitting analysis of its ontological effects.

Another major confusion in the literature, as well as in everyday usage, is between the terms 'race' and ethnicity. Anthias distinguishes the two, defining 'race' as relying on 'notions of a biological or cultural immutability of a group that has already been attributed as sharing a common origin'.[2] She describes ethnicity as 'the identification of particular cultures as ways of life or identity which are based on a historical notion of origin or fate, whether mythical or "real"'. (*ibid*) The term ethnicity has been preferred to that of 'race' in some quarters, largely because it is viewed as supposedly having fewer essentialist connotations.[3] This overlooks the fact that it is quite possible for the concept to be used in an essentialist way, as Gilroy describes in his discussions of how black people's identification with ethnic absolutism has, indirectly, endorsed the explanations and politics of the new right.[4] The idea of ethnicity is also linked to liberal notions of multi-ethnic societies and multi-culturalism, which have a tendency to obscure the force of racism with their celebration of a benign pluralism. Yet, in as much as ethnicity can provide the grounds for inferiorization, oppression, subordination and exploitation, it too may constitute the basis for racism.[5] [. . .] In this chapter the term 'race' is used, with some reluctance, in the same way as by Omi and Winant who see it as 'an unstable and "decentred" complex of social meanings constantly being transformed by political struggle'.[6]

A further issue of language which requires clarification relates to the use of the term 'black'. Initially this was employed as a political category to signify a common experience of racism and marginalization and the gulf this creates between white people and those whom they oppress, on both an institutional and a personal basis. Hall has described, for example, how the idea of 'The Black Experience' provided the basis for a new politics of resistance and critique of the way black peoples were positioned as 'other', irrespective of their different histories, traditions and identities.[7] Recently, however, usage of the term 'black' has been criticized for the way in which it has tended to refer only to those of sub-Saharan African descent, for its American connotations, for its denial of the existence and needs of other cultural groups, and for assigning the label to those who do not necessarily define themselves in this way.[8] [. . .]

UNDERSTANDING 'RACE' AND GENDER: APPROACHES AND POSITIONS

One of the difficulties in trying to establish a perspective from which to consider how 'race' and gender interact is the polarized way in which research and thinking on the two subjects has previously developed. While white feminist work has been much criticized for its silence on matters of 'race', the fact that analyses of 'race' often disregard gender is frequently ignored.

[. . .] Although a vast body of literature on 'race' has been generated, little of it, with a few notable exceptions, has been gendered.[9] When women were included it was often in a highly stereotypical fashion as wives, mothers and daughters. Instead, the focus has been overwhelmingly on the lives of black men, which have also largely been discussed from a white male point of view. It has also tended to concentrate on the public zones of the economy, employment, policing and law and order. The contribution of this work to an understanding of black women's lives, as with that of much of the Western feminist literature, has been minimal.

One field of enquiry which is notable for its concern with non-white, non-Western women's lives has been Development Studies. Although very little of this was recognized before the publication in 1970 of Ester Boserup's *Women's Role in Economic Development*, a considerable body of work on the subject has now been produced. This has been not so much a polemic about the racism of white feminism as a major scholarly intervention which broadens our understanding of the nature of women's lives in various parts of the world. It demonstrates that notions such as the family, citizenship, nation and state mean different things to women in 'third world' situations to those in a white European or North American context. One change in the argument of this literature, which can be perceived over time, is from a perspective which aimed to integrate women into existing development theories and models to one designed to replace these with a more feminist framework.[10] It is interesting, however, that the academic studies of development and of 'race' rarely draw from each other and have tended to progress in parallel. (Work on colonialism and imperialism and, increasingly, on nationality and nationhood would be exceptions here.) In addition, mainstream feminist work, which has concentrated on women in the West, has paid little attention to the ideas and implications of the literature on women and development. Rather, it has tended to treat it as a separate concern, providing the comparative and contrasting examples to Western phenomena which are regarded as more central and mainstream. Thus the polarized nature of many approaches to issues of 'race' and of gender has obscured questions of the possible relationships which might exist between them.

It is the critiques of white feminism made by black feminists which have forced consideration of the implications of 'race' and racism for the study of women. Black feminists have pointed to the inherent racism of analyses and practices which assume white experiences to be the norm, use these as the basis from which to generate concepts and theories, and fail to acknowledge the internal differentiation of black women.[11] Yet early attempts to theorize the interconnection of 'race' and gender have themselves been criticized. These merely add 'race' into the already existing feminist theoretical frameworks. They imply that 'race' simply increases the degree of inequality and oppression which black women experience as women and that oppression can be quantified and compared.[12] This ignores the fact that 'race' does not simply make the experience of women's subordination greater. It qualitatively changes the nature of that subordination. It is within this context that writers have turned to the idea of 'difference' as a concept with the potential to encompass the diversities which ensue.

THE CONCEPT OF 'DIFFERENCE'

The concept, 'difference', has a long history in relation to Western feminism. Although the word was not used, as such, by first-wave feminists the degree to which women were the same as or different from men, as well as divided by factors such as class, formed the basis of discussions about their roles, their rights and their potentialities in nineteenth-century society.[13] [...] Recently, ... 'difference' has been used with another connotation by Western feminists, referring to the differences between women themselves, rather than just between two genders. There have been two formulations of this: one which focuses on the diversity of experience, the other concerned with difference as informed by postmodernist thinking.

One way of conceptualizing difference, then, is in experiential terms. The idea that women's experiences should be fundamental to its work has been one of feminism's central tenets. [...] Feminism must begin with experience, it has been argued, since it is only from such a vantage point that it is possible to see the extent to which women's worlds are organized in ways which differ from those of men.[14] Focusing on black women's experiences highlights the ways in which 'race' plays an important part in their social and economic positioning.

It has been shown, for example, how 'race' significantly affects black women's experiences of and treatment in areas such as education, the health service and the labour market.[15] The influence of 'race' on how black women are represented in popular culture and the mass media has also been demonstrated.[16] 'Race' also has profound consequences in terms of the kinds of environments and circumstances in which women live around the world, as witnessed by the appalling famines in Africa and ethnic cleansing in the former Yugoslavia. All these things are, of course, mediated by other factors, such as class, nationality and able-bodiedness.

Focusing on how different experiences can result from the influence of 'race', however ascribed and perceived, has also made difference visible in two other senses. The first is an acknowledgment that the impact of 'race' may mean that the chief sites of oppression are not the same for black and white women. [. . .] The second way in which a previously hidden form of difference has become visible is in the fact that 'race' is not a coherent category and that the lives of those usually classified together under the label 'black' can themselves be very different. Thus, culture, class, religion, nationality etc., in addition to gender, can all have an impact on women's lives. [. . .] The idea of difference, therefore, emphasizes differentation and diversity. It challenges the homogeneity of experience previously ascribed to women by virtue of being 'black'.

Some commentators, particularly those sympathetic to postmodernist thought, have argued against a notion of difference based on experiential diversity. Barrett, for instance, criticizes this formulation, in a general sense, for being rooted in an unproblematized and taken-for-granted notion of common sense and for its implicitly relativistic view of knowledge.[17] Black writers, however, have emphasized the importance of recognizing that experience does not necessarily equal 'truth'. [. . .]

The second way in which the concept of difference is employed is in the work of postmodernists. It goes without saying that there is little agreement over what the term means and much dispute as to whose work should or should not be included within its rubric.[18] While not dismissing the legitimacy of these debates, it is possible, for the purposes of this chapter, to describe some common themes.

The postmodernist position is, broadly speaking, characterized by the view that there is no objective social world which exists outside of our pre-existing knowledge of or discourse about it. There is, thus, much scepticism about the possibility of distinguishing between 'real' aspects of the social world, on the one hand, and the concepts, modes of understanding and meanings through which they are apprehended, on the other. Postmodernism is locked into confrontation with modernist modes of thought, which are premissed upon the search for grand theories and objectivity and the assumption of a rational and unified subject. In contrast, postmodernism emphasizes fragmentation, deconstruction and the idea of multiple selves. [. . .] Such an approach offers both a critique of conventional epistemology, of how we gain knowledge about the social world (this includes, at its extreme, a complete disavowal that this is possible), and a view of subjectivity as both ephemeral and transitory.

Postmodernism is, then, about difference in a number of senses. It can include 'difference' in the Derridean sense of the disjuncture between objects of perception and the meanings these have as symbols or representations.[19] Hence, phenomena such as objects or identities depend upon language, 'which simultaneously stands for and stands *in the place of* the things words represent'.[20] It can refer to the multiplicity of voices, meanings and configurations which need to be considered when trying to understand the social world and which, supposedly, negate the possibility of any particular authoritative account.[21] Postmodernism can also relate to the multitude of different subject positions which constitute the individual. It challenges the perceived essentialism of modernist thinking by positing difference as being at the centre of the postmodern world and by championing deconstruction as the method through which this is to be analysed. In all of the this *discourse*, rather than the supposedly modernist concern with structure, is the central conceptual preoccupation.[22] Although postmodernist writing tends to be very abstract, ungendered and indifferent to issues such as those of 'race', some black and white feminist writers have contemplated its significance for their work.[23]

The two connotations of difference which have been discussed, that based on experience and that on a postmodernist fragmentation, are clearly separate and rooted in what might be regarded as oppositional philosophies. Yet, their consequences for the study of 'race' and gender, and what makes them so appealing, are surprisingly similar. To begin with they both share an emphasis on heterogeneity, together with, quite rightly, a distrust of analyses which make sweeping generalizations and develop grandiose theoretical frameworks about the nature of 'race' and gender oppression. Both challenge the unquestioning, fixed polarizations of black versus white and the heterosexist male versus female. In the diversity-of-experience approach this enables consideration of oppressive relationships between women and between men, dispelling the idea that oppression only occurs between white and black people and between men and women.

Both formulations of difference, in varying ways, subvert the unity and meaning of terms such as 'race', 'black', 'patriarchy' and 'woman'. (It is interesting that 'white' and 'man' seem to have been relatively untouched by such deconstructionist treatment.) The implication is that these kinds of categories are too internally differentiated to be useful. This, in turn, has led to a concern with subjectivity and identity. [. . .] An emphasis on difference allows for multiple identities and can open up new possibilities for the construction of emancipatory selves. [. . .] One constructive consequence of this is that 'blackness' and 'womanhood' come to be associated with some positive connotations and are not just seen in terms of oppression.[24] Difference, then, not only challenges the passive labels of 'black woman' or 'white woman', it transcends such classifications, suggesting alternative subject formulations.

THE DANGERS OF DIFFERENCE

The previous discussion has indicated some of the reasons why Western feminists have seen the idea of difference as attractive, particularly when considering how to analyse the implications of 'race' and gender for each other. Yet there are dangers in accepting the concept uncritically in either of the two formulations described. [. . .] Numerous writers, for instance, have pointed to, and been critical of, the political conservatism that characterizes much postmodernist thinking, arguing that it is incapable of making any statements of an evaluative or ethical nature and has masculinist underpinnings.[25] Others have criticized the difference-as-experience approach because of its 'us' and 'them' connotation. It can imply the existence of a supposed norm that applies to some women but not to others, so that it is the women who are not white who are the different ones.[26] Whiteness here is not itself seen as a racialized identity and one that, additionally, may need to be deconstructed. White people are not racialized in the way that black people are and 'race' is seen to be a problem for the latter and not for the former. Such a stance leads to the proliferation of discrete studies of a wide variety of experiences, but makes no effective challenge to the categories or frameworks within which they are discussed. Acknowledging that 'race' gives rise to forms of difference, for example, is not the same as paying attention to *racism* as it exists in the social world or feminist work. [. . .]

Another difficulty inherent in using the idea of difference, in both the experience and postmodernist forms, is the endless possibilities for diversity which are created. There are several dangers associated with this. One relates to a potential slide towards the much critiqued position of liberal pluralism. [. . .] In such pluralism difference tends to be treated as existing all on one plane or on the same level. All forms of diversity are lumped together as examples of difference, implying that they are similar phenomena with similar explanations. [. . .] So many forms of difference are created that it becomes impossible to analyse them in terms of inequality or power, except in the Foucauldian sense of discourse. Under pluralism, differences in access to resources or life chances etc. become largely explicable in terms of personal culpability or luck. The possibility of offering more structured socio-political explanations disappears, except in a localized sense, because these, necessarily, must be rooted in generalizations which cannot be made. There is, therefore, the danger of being unable to offer any interpretations that reach beyond the circumstances of the particular.

There are other problems also related to the pluralistic assumptions of difference. For instance, it tends to emphasize what divides women, at the expense of those experiences that they might possibly share or have in common. Yet since cultural differences are not absolute, the similarities as well as the diversities need to be acknowledged. Pluralism also encourages a cultural relativism of the 'anything goes' variety in its approach to diversity. [. . .] There is a tendency in some of the current writing to discuss and deconstruct both 'race' and gender as if they have no links to racism and patriarchal oppression. It is the argument of this chapter that a focus on difference alone is not sufficient to take account of these latter dimensions of power. [. . .]

The deconstruction of the self into multiple modes and forms of identities, existing only at the intersection of discourses, raises questions about self-conscious activity. Paradoxically, although everything is about the subject, no one in postmodern analyses actually appears to *do* anything. Subjectivities are seemingly overdetermined by the discourses in which they are constituted, and thus lacking in both intentionality and will. [. . .] Are these discourses available to all women and black peoples in the same way? Or is it, perhaps, only some, the more privileged, who are in a better position to take advantage of and use the new forms of representation which ensue?

These are not intended to be idle questions, for behind them lies an important point. The deconstruction of categories such as race and gender may make visible the contradictions, mystifications, silences and hidden possibilities of which they are made up. But this is not the same as destroying or transcending the categories themselves, which clearly still play significant roles in how the social world is organized on a global scale. Thinking through and imagining beyond labels such as 'race' and gender, for those in a position to do so, is one important part of challenging both their legitimacy and their efficacy. A reworking of language alone, however, does not make them go away.

RETHINKING DIFFERENCE

The concept of difference is not sufficient or weighty enough to encompass all the dimensions that analyses of 'race' and gender need to include. [. . .] As an *analytical* tool its value is limited. Although usefully drawing attention to diversity, it cannot, on its own, account for power; how this comes to be constructed as inferiority and the basis for inequality and subordination. There is, therefore, a need to shift the focus of analysis from difference alone to the social relations which convert this difference into oppression.[27] [. . .]

Feminist analyses which are concerned with 'race' and gender, not just as subjects for study, but for the power relations to which they give rise and which need actively to be challenged, thus need to take account of several things. The first is the material, as well as the cultural, dimensions of social life and the social relations which emerge from and interact with these. This does not mean a return to the old mechanistic assumptions, embedded in non-Marxist as well as Marxist thought, in which culture, beliefs and subjectivity are determined by social structure or the economic. It *does* mean that access to and quality of resources (such as food, shelter, money, education), as well as the restrictions resulting from the lack of them and from violence, harassment and abuse, need to be taken into account. The interaction between these things, how they are represented and their relationship to more specifically cultural phenomena may be complex and contradictory. They are, nonetheless, mediating factors in any social circumstances and cannot be ignored in analysing the situations of black and white women.

A second important issue in considering race and gender is to problematize the label 'white'.[28] It was pointed out earlier that whiteness is not seen as a racial identity. When questions of 'race' are raised this usually means focusing on black peoples, its victims, who are thereby constructed as 'the problem'. Yet the processes of racism and racial oppression might be better understood by concentrating, as well, on the exercise and mechanisms of white privilege and power. This does not necessarily mean focusing only on situations where black and white peoples interact. It is as important to look at the taken-for-granted everydayness of white privilege, as well as circumstances in which it is more directly expressed. Also significant in this context is the process of unravelling what the term 'white' actually means, for it is by no means a homogeneous category. It should not be forgotten, for instance, that it is not necessary to be black to experience racism, as the experiences of the Jews and the Irish and current events in Europe testify. Further, the meanings of the categories black and white are not constant. Those labelled one way under certain socio-cultural conditions may find the label changes under others.

A third matter of significance in the analysis of 'race' and gender is the need to end the continual splitting of racial and gender identities and positions, as if they can be dichotomized. It is necessary, instead, to focus on the ways in which each is implied in and experienced through the other, and not separately. [. . .] It thus does not make sense to analyse 'race' and gender issues as if they constitute discrete systems of power. For this reason Gordon has suggested concentrating analytically, instead, on such questions as the racialized aspects of gender, gender as a concept with class characteristics, the racialized aspects of class, and so on.[29]

Such an approach is likely to involve concentrating on culturally and historically specific circumstances, reversing the flow of theory away from the grand abstract theorizing of the metanarrative type dismissed (yet still used) by postmodernists. [. . .] While it is clear that *universalizations*, with their implications for the whole world, are untenable, it is possible to talk in qualified terms about general properties, and through comparison to highlight differences and similarities, where these clearly arise from substantive material.

Finally, this chapter has argued that the current tendency to treat difference as *the* major organizing category in understanding 'race' and gender is misplaced. Although diversity is clearly one important element, to focus on this alone is to marginalize other issues, not least of which are those of racism, power and other forces of oppression. It is not the case that women are constructed differently in any absolute way and clearly evident that they share experiences across cultures. Nor is it necessary to abandon categories, such as woman or 'race', in order to recognize that they are internally differentiated. These categories may not be unitary, but this does not mean that they are now meaningless. [. . .] Discussions of difference have, rightly, drawn attention to serious problems which existed in the narrowly defined nature and overgeneralizations of previous work about women by Western feminists, one from which a concern for 'race' was almost entirely lacking. Their overemphasis on fragmentation, however, offers neither political nor intellectual support in confronting the oppressions with which feminism has historically been concerned. It runs the risk, in fact, of overlooking the very existence of such oppressions.

Notes

1. J. Donald and A. Rattansi (eds.), '*Race*', *Culture and Difference* (London: Sage, 1992).
2. F. Anthias, 'Race and Class Revisited—Conceptualising Race and Racisms', *Sociological Review* (1990), 20.
3. P. Rothenburg, 'The Construction, Deconstruction, and Reconstruction of Difference', *Hypatia*, 5/1 (1990).
4. P. Gilroy, *There ain't No Black in the Union Jack* (London: Hutchinson, 1987), and 'The End of Antiracism', in J. Donald and A. Rattansi (eds.), '*Race*', *Culture and Difference.*
5. Anthias, 'Race and Class Revisited'.
6. M. Omi and H. Winant, *Racial Formation in the United States* (London and New York: Routledge and Kegan Paul, 1986).
7. S. Hall, 'New Ethnicities', in J. Donald and A. Rattansi (eds.), '*Race*', *Culture and Difference* (London: Sage, 1992).
8. A. Brah, 'Difference, Diversity and Differentiation', in J. Donald and A. Rattansi (eds.), '*Race*', *Culture and Difference* (London: Sage, 1992).
9. Some of the notable exceptions would include A. Davis, *Women, Race and Class* (London: Women's Press, 1982); H. Gutman, *The Black Family in Slavery and Freedom, 1750–1925* (New York: Vintage, 1976); M. Morrissey, *Slave Women in the New World* (Lawrence, KS: University Press of Kansas, 1989); A. Phizacklea (ed.), *One Way Ticket: Migration and Female Labour* (London: Routledge, 1983), and *Unpacking the Fashion Industry* (London: Routledge, 1990); S. Westwood and P. Bachu (eds.), *Enterprising Women: Ethnicity, Economy and Gender Relations* (London: Routledge, 1988).
10. J. McFarland, 'The Construction of Women and Development Theory', *Canadian Review of Sociology and Anthropology*, 25/2 (1988).
11. See V. Amos and P. Parmar, 'Challenging Imperial Feminism', *Feminist Review* 17 (1984); F. Anthias and N. Yuval-Davis, 'Contextualising Feminism: Gender, Ethnic and Class Divisions', *Feminist Review* 15 (1983); P. H. Collins, *Black Feminist Thought* (London: Unwin Hyman, 1990); b. hooks, *Feminist Theory: From Margin to Centre* (Boston: South End Press, 1984).
12. Collins, *Black Feminist Thought.*
13. L. Gordon, 'On "Difference"', *Genders* 10 (1991).
14. D. Smith, *The Everyday World as Problematic* (Milton Keynes: Open University Press, 1988).
15. A. Brah, 'Questions of Difference and International Feminism', in J. Aaron and S. Walby (eds.), *Out of the Margins* (London: Falmer Press, 1991).
16. T. Modleski (ed.), *Studies in Entertainment: Critical Approaches to Mass Culture* (Bloomington: Indiana University Press, 1986).
17. M. Barrett, 'The Concept of Difference', *Feminist Review* 26 (1987).

18. J. Baudrillard, *Selected Writings* (M. Poster, ed.) (Cambridge: Polity Press, 1989); J. Baudrillard, *Revenge of the Crystal: A Baudrillard Reader* (London: Pluto Press, 1990); R. Felski, 'Feminist Theory and Social Change', *Theory, Culture and Society* 6 (1989); M. Foucault, *The Archeology of Knowledge* (London: Hutchinson, 1989); J.-F. Lyotard, *The Postmodern Condition* (Manchester: Manchester University Press, 1984). It is possible, for instance, to distinguish the post-structuralist work of someone like Foucault, which emphasizes how meanings and subjectivity are constituted through discourse, from the post-modernism of Baudrillard and Lyotard which sees the world in terms of wholesale disinformation and manipulation and the construction of language games. Felski points out that the latter are more likely to situate what they regard as a crisis of truth and representation as occurring within a particular period. Thus it may be linked to a supposedly new stage of capitalist development, variously described as late capitalism, post-capitalism or disorganized capitalism.
19. J. Derrida, *Writing and Difference* (London: Routledge and Kegan Paul, 1978).
20. M. Poovey, 'Feminism and Deconstruction', *Feminist Studies* 4 (1988), 51.
21. Lyotard, *The Postmodern Condition.*
22. S. Walby, 'Post-Post-Modernism? Theorizing Social Complexity', in M. Barrett and A. Phillips (eds.), *Destabilizing Theory* (Cambridge: Polity Press, 1992).
23. M. Barrett, 'Words and Things: Materialism and Method in Contemporary Feminist Analysis', in M. Barrett and A. Phillips (eds.), *Destabilizing Theory: Contemporary Feminist Debates* (Cambridge: Polity Press, 1992); J. Flax, 'Postmodernism and Gender Relations in Feminist Theory', *Signs* 12/4 (1987); Hall, 'New Ethnicities'; b. hooks, *Yearning* (London: Turnaround, 1991); L. Nicholson (ed.), *Feminism/Postmodernism* (London: Routledge, 1990); Poovey, 'Feminism and Deconstruction'; G. C Spivak, *In Other Worlds* (London: Routledge, 1988), and *The Post-Colonial Critic* (London: Routledge, 1990).
24. Brah, 'Questions of Difference and International Feminism'.
25. A. Callinicos, *Against Postmodernism: A Marxist Critique* (Cambridge: Polity Press, 1989); J. Habermas, *The Philosophical Discourse of Modernity* (Cambridge: Polity Press, 1987); N. Hartsock, 'Rethinking Modernism', *Cultural Critique* (Fall, 1987); C. Norris, *Uncritical Theory* (London: Lawrence and Wishart, 1992); B. Skeggs, 'Postmodernism: What is all the Fuss About?', *British Journal of the Sociology of Education* 12/2 (1991).
26. E. V. Spelman, *The Inessential Women* (London: The Women's Press, 1988).
27. C. L. Bacchi, *Same Difference: Feminism and Sexual Difference* (Sydney: Allen and Unwin, 1990).
28. V. Ware, *Beyond the Pale: White Women, Racism and History* (London: Verso, 1992).
29. Gordon, 'On "Difference"'.

12 Moving the Mountains, Making the Links

Mọlara Ogundipẹ-Leslie*

[. . .] I theorize that African women have six mountains on their back, over and above the four mountains proposed by Chairman Mao for Chinese women. From this concept of mountains, I have drawn the title of my introduction which proposes to show which mountains African women need to move and are moving. I also attempt to link their struggles in the various topographies where the mountains are being assailed.

My work represents a harvest of over two decades of theorizing, writing and organizing in Nigeria and abroad around the issues of women and transformations which I consider critical to their lives and their continent of Africa. The word 'critical' is being used in the sense of discriminating, evaluative and analytical; 'engaged' and perhaps not 'neutral' since most African women and myself are emotionally and spiritually committed to the wellbeing of their continent.

Added to the senses of 'careful judgement' or 'judicious evaluation' in 'critical', which I have evoked, are the sense of a crisis and that of 'being at a turning point or points', of 'reaching specially important junctures'. In many ways and particularly sociologically, historically and in terms of values, Africa is at a critical juncture, awaiting and demanding transformations.

What are some of these critical transformations that are required and necessary? Primarily, and at a very basic level, Africa needs economic transformation geared towards the interests of its populations. But African perspectives on this need are often ignored or suppressed. Africa needs to be recognized and re-introduced into discourses of world affairs, history and culture. Africa is always that place which gets

* From M. Ogundipẹ-Leslie, 'Moving the Mountains, Making the Links', from *Re-Creating Ourselves: African Women and Critical Transformations* (Africa World Press Inc, 1994), 9–25.

left out, forgotten and omitted in global discourses. Take a note of that and try to look for Africa in newspapers, anthologies, essay collections and books which claim to be globally inclusive. The African person is that person who does not have a 'self', who gets represented or spoken for by others. At the creative level, travellers and settlers in Africa become the spokespersons for the indigenous peoples. Where Africa comes up at all, it is either white South Africa, or 'English Kenya' (as a New Jersey high school teacher said to me in April, 1993) or Arab Africa. The black indigenous African is the international 'dirty secret'. He/She is that person who cannot participate in world discourse or action on his/her own behalf. In this problematic, we can imagine where the indigenous woman would be. Reading about Africa's place and role in world history from the beginnings of time should be part of the requisite education of every foreigner—for the sake of world peace.

An attitude, residual from nineteenth century racism and hegemonic, colonial times, still persists towards the indigenous black African (read 'negro'; if the secret be unmasked). It is that attitude which makes indigenous Africans (constructed as 'negroes' privately) left out of world discourses and disqualified from speaking for themselves or from being recognized in the gathering of the world's peoples as minds and agents of culture and history. This absence of indigenous Africans (indigenous as pre-Arab invasions of the 7th century AD) is at the heart of the discourses on voice and voicelessness which at the present moment suffuse scholarship and creativity in and about the African world.

Literary scholars in various perceptive ways have traced the absence of Africans from texts since the early days of European expansion and hegemony; from Elizabethan times where Othello's blackness is 'Moorish' not African; where scholars and theatre practitioners still debate Othello's Africanness; where not only Caliban's mother is absent[1] but also Caliban's mate,[2] that is, the archetypal helpmeet and woman owner of the land which is invaded and expropriated by Prospero and Miranda in Shakespeare's *The Tempest.* In a world constituted by surviving colonial visions and terminology into 'people' (read: white) and 'natives' (read: all other peoples)[3], the black woman's absence is ever central and taken for granted. At the heart of the discursive storms around voice and voicelessness, therefore, are African women.

But who are these African women? And how have they inserted themselves into the critical junctures to activate and participate in the transformations ongoing in Africa? . . . I attempt to answer some of these questions as they problematize the questions and reflect the dynamic contexts within which we tried, in the cataclysmic seventies and the more circumspect eighties, to re-vision our lives, re-create ourselves and re-examine received ideas and theories. All hegemonic perspectives and narratives of colonization went under questioning; methodologies too, as some of us, scholars in Nigeria, warred over 'concept and meaning, theory and method',[4] refining Marxist theory with African history, sociology and experience.

> Shall we say this war consumes the heart and enervates the soul? Shall we will the war, as we must, to clarify and guide us only? And shall we note the blue-eyed inertia, the glazed-eye indifference from passing weariness? . . . The passing weariness, born of tension and relax, the tension and relax which is the certain rhythm of life?[5]

African women were re-discovering themselves again, re-creating themselves and their lives in various social arena as the essays herein show. Through theory and practice, we tried to re-discover African women in the academy as speaker and spoken about, as critic and creator. We pursued women's episteme in society through research and activism. Through writing and organizing women, we tried to uncover and learn from how we know what we know and how we create what we do create socially and ideationally. [. . .]

Those were years of interjecting practice with theory when we questioned everything and created new visions. Criticisms went from the absurd (that Marx was a dead white male) to the psychological (that African Marxists were still in search of the great white father).[6] I have always wondered what being a 'dead white male' had to do with anything, considering that mortality is the inevitable fate of all of us and that some of the models of those who evoke that phrase are also dead. Are ideas valuable only in the instant? The critique of the Marxists was often either culturally nationalist (don't use ideas that come from Europe even as you ride European automobiles) or pathologically racist (if the inventor of the idea is white, then the idea must be pernicious). My hope, however, is that we can move beyond a viscerally racist reaction to the source of ideas, from a biological exclusionarism to a critical approach which looks for the relevance of ideas to our experiences, societies and history, and to our project at hand. Believing in culture and not race, I firmly hold that thought and ideas are products and the legacy of the possibilities of the human mind, to be claimed by all humankind.

Culture and cultural studies are, at the moment, receiving attention in the intellectual world. I hold that people's identities are determined by the cultures they carry, not by that nebulous category of race which is a political invention. [. . .] The area of culture is one where critical transformations must take place. Africans must now pay critical attention to what of their '*cultures*' must survive and through whom. Who will be the legitimate narrators of African cultures? Exiles, immigrants, part-children of cultural foreigners, some of whom were not raised with the experience of forms of African cultures, or middle-class indigenous children who are educated away from their languages? Some Westernized Africans are probably the only cultural types who think they can preserve their cultures by marrying culturally exogamously. Commonsensical people always knew this was bad for cultural survival. Africa is perhaps one of the only places where people marry spouses who do not care to learn their languages (language being a vehicle of culture), who despise the cultures of their marriage partners and identify away from them. We are perhaps the only people (compare Orientals and Jews) who marry spouses who cannot be cultural conduits and who produce children who are completely emotionally alienated from our cultures as we sing paeans to negritude, Africanity, or 'culture and heritage'. [. . .]

For the many reconstructions in which Africa has to engage, several of our ruling narratives of culture and epistemology have to be critically reviewed, if not abandoned. Our very view of ourselves, our knowledge of ourselves has to be constantly queried as not coming from what has been told to us, or from what has been constructed on our behalf. Sometimes we now see ourselves through the eyes of the Euro-American 'other', in narratives I call 'neo-colonial'.

There is the 'neo-colonial literary narrative' consisting of a paradigm and details which are now *de rigueur* for the African novel: some 'tribal' people involved with kolanuts and 'weird' rites of passage in some 'rural' place, away from their modern variety in 'the cities' who are poor (as constantly reiterated), speak some 'pidgin', ride around in mammy wagons with quaint and fetching sayings splashed across them, in a country where the political leaders are 'incomprehensibly' and 'uniquely' corrupt (as only Africans can be corrupt) and the intellectual/writer is in lonely and alienated angst. [. . .] When shall we get to see the real Africans as they actually live their lives in the complexity of continuity and change, tragedy and joy, not only in the gleefully, patronizingly reiterated poverty? Are there some Africans who are, in fact, happy to be alive and prefer to live in Africa, even with the hardship which they, of course, want to change on their own terms? Are there Africans who prefer to live in Africa but wish that their political leaders did not negotiate away their lives with such foreign institutions as the World Bank and IMF whose sharp practices and arm-twisting interactions with African governments are not protested by the owners of those same eyes that weep over the poverty of Africa?

Unfortunately, despite years of decolonizing research and scholarship, it still needs to be emphasized that paradigms for looking at Africa continue to require re-considerations and re-conceptualizing. Dichotomies of 'rural and urban', 'tradition and modernity', 'elite and people', and others continue to obfuscate knowledge about Africa. Many such analytical simplicities must change; particularly because they are predicated on Eurocentric assumptions. Africans themselves have inadequate self-constructed narratives to abandon and some of these are the narratives of victimhood in which we like to indulge, perhaps to harrow the conscience of Euro-America. [. . .]

One such narrative of victimhood, adopted by and popular among the African intelligentsia, is that of colonization as the fable of the bible and gun. It sounds touching to say while the 'white man' distracted us with the bible, he took away our lands with the gun. Yet, narratives of colonization consist more of interactions of commerce, resistance, negotiations, some conquest, administrative treachery, class collaborations, adaptations and more resistance, not only militarily but culturally.

Nowhere is the re-writing of narratives more mandatory than in discourses on African women. [. . .] Who are 'African women'? This is neither a trivial question as we shall see; nor is the phrase a truism. [. . .] There is no such thing as 'the African woman'. She cannot be essentialized in that way; rather she has to be considered, analysed and studied in the complexity of her existential reality [that include] her classes, cultures, races and ethnicities among other variables. African women are not a monolithic group of illiterate peasants sporting some twenty to thirty educated women who speak internationally and are discredited for being educated. Social stratification existed in pre-colonial (i.e. pre-nineteenth century) Africa just as there is social stratification, including traditional aristocrats and modern-day bourgeois elements in so-called rural Africa. A finely discriminating approach to African sociology still has to be developed . . .

It is important to note that in most Euro-American discourses about women, the term 'women' in Europe often refers to 'middle-class, educated white women' while 'women' in Africa refers to 'illiterate, peasant, working-class or poor women' or perhaps to a dark hole named 'women'—a primitive mass that manifests pristine, incomprehensible behaviour in ignorance and speechlessness. The middle-class educated African women are not somehow included in this referent of African women; neither are they equivalent to Euro-American women of the middle class. Therefore in discussing Africa, there is usually a 'rural Africa' where that pristine, undifferentiated, ahistorical mass of 'real' African women inhabit, in which context all theories about 'African women' are tested. No one can speak to this process, to this knowledge of this atavistic womanhood, not even African women from the continent themselves, but only Euro-American theorists and experts. In a way, it is ironically true that only these Euro-American experts know about that pristine and primitive 'mass' of atavistic African women who can also transform themselves into people, into history and modernization only if they heed the policies and ideas of their Euro-American 'knowers' and agencies, to whom they are exclusively 'knowable'.

From the foregoing problematic springs the so-called voicelessness of African women. We neither look for their voices where they utter them nor do we think it worthwhile to listen to their voices. We sometimes substitute our voices for their own and we do not even know when we do this nor are we able to recognize the differences in the mixed or substituted voices. Women of European descent are most prone to these ventriloquisms, frequently calling on African women to play the role of ventriloquists' puppets, speaking to other people's agenda. These are some of the issues burning still between Euro-American and AALA women.

Are African women voiceless or do we fail to look for their voices where we may find them, in the *sites* and forms in which these voices are uttered? One signal example is in the Ivorian movie *Faces of Women* by Desiré Ecaré (1985) in which so-called docile 'rural' women, allegedly subjugated by polygamy, amuse themselves about deceiving their husbands as they have extramarital sexual experiences. In what sites do the women express these emotional rebellions? In women's dance games during a very 'proper' village festival. We must look for African women's voices in women's spaces and modes such as in ceremonies and worksongs as some scholars like Kofi Agovi, Abu Barry, Helen Mugambi and others are beginning to do. We must look for them in places such as kitchens, watering sites, kinship gatherings, women's political and commercial spaces where women speak, often in the absence of men. It is not only in other modes such as in suicide that women speak, as acceptably argued by Gayatri Spivak;[7] women also speak in words where we do not hear them. They also speak in silences. [. . .]

Arguments such as African men occupied the public sphere while women occupied the private (read: domestic) still need to be challenged. Niara Sudarkasa puts it very clearly and correctly when she says 'a more appropriate conception (and by that I mean makes more sense of more of the realities of those societies) was to recognise two domains, one occupied by men and another by women—both of which were internally ordered in a hierarchical fashion and both of which provided personnel for domestic and extradomestic (or public) activities . . . there was considerable overlap between the public and domestic domains in pre-industrial societies.[8] [. . .]

African women feminists are being stigmatized as 'angry feminists' or 'frustrated women'. Needless to say, a woman who concerns herself with the negative conditions of African women and social justice for them reveals herself as being 'angry about nothing' and secretly sexually frustrated. None of her problems, however, cannot be solved by the indispensable phallus which has the undeniable power to keep her from lesbianism and her other potentially 'wayward' ways. 'The good African woman' is faithful to her 'culture and heritage' and as wife, acts submissive and accepts servitude and emotional abuse.

When trying to include gender issues in the intellectual movements in Nigeria in the seventies, feminists and progressive women received (and still receive) a great deal of flack. At times, I was personally called a 'black' white woman by Africans, and a 'brown' white woman by certain European friends and colleagues who thought they were naming me to a higher place. In such wise are African women constantly harassed today about 'culture', never mind that African men are not themselves fulfilling traditional demands; in marriage, such as burying their fathers-in-law, working on their farms, or working for them in any equivalent way. Without a blind adherence to the 'shibboleth' of 'culture and heritage', most African women and feminists are 'womanist' in Alice Walker's sense of being committed to survival and wholeness of entire peoples, male and female; being not in any way separatist or adversarial to men.[9] [. . .]

In fact, contemporary Africans have to resolve some contradictions between their inherited cultures and their modern conditions of life. We need to critically transform the contradictions between ethnicity and nation, between ethnic cultures which bind us emotionally at the level of family (the most defining area for Africans today) and the level of the state which has little meaning and less emotional significance, often commanding little loyalty. For instance, to whom does the body of a spouse belong in modern Africa today?[10] Does it belong to the birth family or the affinal (marital) family? It is not such a ridiculous question where in most countries in Africa, claims of consanguinity (which determine traditional law and behaviour at the personal level) still override claims of conjugality which are usually derived from Europe or Islam and characterize family laws at the state level.

Privileging conjugality over consanguinity, contrary to African realities, is responsible for misreadings of the statuses of African women and their conditions of life. We have reiterated, seemingly to no avail, that African women are more than wives. [. . .] The literature on African women, however, continues to focus solely on marriage as evidence for the inferior status of African women. It seems difficult for most outsiders to understand and accept that 'African women's relationships with men, within and outside conjugality, are not central to their self-inscription or to an understanding of our stories, lives and desires'.[11]

Observing the women in their various sites, paying attention to female bonding which is absent from much of African creative literature written by men would yield a more correct epistemology of women. In consanguineal relationships, women enjoy positions of deference, power and authority beyond gender; other variables being age, seniority as determined by order of birth, wealth and personal standing which is not always calculated by wealth. In some societies, men genuflect to women in many situations. Within marriage itself, statuses are marked by subtle and complex indices such as seniority based on the time of entry into the affinal family and personal achievements; such markers as are incomprehensible or invisible to some analysts. [. . .]

Other discourses of African women which need to change are those which insist on issues of polygamy and female circumcision (almost gleefully) over and above the other experiences of African women, while paying no equivalent attention or valuation to the violence done to women's bodies in Western cosmetic surgery for the same reason (pleasuring men); they totally ignore women's roles in other non-sexual domains. Is there some secret war against the myth of the superior sexual vitality of African women? In my view, coitus is given far too much attention in the discussion and appreciation of women's rights and conditions by some Western women; otherwise, how does one find surrogate motherhood less objectionable than polygyny? [. . .]

Some gender issues are not yet receiving the intellectual attention they should if we are to be comprehensive in our research and knowledge of women. [. . .] Africa has not yet given voice to her sexuality;[13] too many silences persist in the area of human sexuality in Africa. Sexual orientation is certainly one area that has not been opened up for research or discussion. In some countries of Africa, the death penalty awaits gay people; in others, the state does not persecute them. The experiences of sexual orientation in traditional arrangements require discovery still. It would seem, however, that some of the themes of female bonding, the search for female community and love between women so strong in lesbian literature already receive their expression in African societies, past and present, where non-sexual female bonding, community support and network exist as defining and basic characteristics.[14] Women in Africa have also always known the option of making *de facto* families, consisting only of themselves and their children, even within polygyny. More women in contemporary Africa are opting for motherhood without wifehood or independent wifehoods in matrilocal and polygynous arrangements as in the novel, *One is Enough* (1981) by Flora Nwapa.

Speaking of human sexuality in general, gender violence is another area of silence. African women tend to be protected by their larger families in the occurrence of violence within marriage through the possibility of the return of the bride wealth or the withdrawal of the woman by her male relatives who can also do a physical counterstrike of vengeance on the abusive husband. It can be argued that African kinship systems provided the abused woman the family and community support which feminist movements tried to give to Euro-American women through shelters for battered women. Police certainly give little protection in Africa as elsewhere. Unfortunately, African women in abusive situations are beginning to lose some of the protection they enjoyed from male relatives due to the nuclearization and Westernization of African families.

Finally, it must be indicated that patriarchy as understood and theorized in my work does not yield a simplistic paradigm of all women ranged against all men. African complex kinship structures and the day-to-day negotiations of our lives through gender, sex, and male and female relational experiences make us realize that patriarchy not only includes women but gains some of its force and effectiveness from the active participation of women too. We see a female patriarch in the Zimbabwean novel of Tsitsi Dangarembga.[15] We know of other African women more powerful in patriarchy than her Tete. Patriarchy takes different and complex forms in differing societies. We continue to examine critically our cultures and experiences as we transform them.

Notes

1. Abena Busia, 'Silencing Sycorax: on African Colonial Discourse and the Unvoiced Female', *Cultural Critique* 14 (Winter 1989–90), 81–104.
2. Maryse Conde, *La paroles des femmes: Essais sur les romancieres des Antilles des langues francaises* (Paris: Harmattan, 1979). Also cited in Sylvia Wynter, 'Afterword: Beyond Miranda's Meanings: Un/silencing the "Demonic Ground" of Caliban's "Woman" in Carol Boyce Davies and Elaine Fido (eds.), *Out of the Kumbla* (Trenton, NJ: Africa World Press, 1990) 355–72.
3. A Canadian woman professor once asked me in Toronto whether my dress was something worn by native Nigerians. Another European in Calgary said an archaeologist was at that time doing research on 'native' Nigerians. You wonder 'who are the *native* Nigerians' and who the 'non-native'? Why is it necessary to qualify Nigeria by 'native'? Take note of the use of 'native' from now on, when you read.
4. Molara Ogundipe-Leslie, 'Letter to a Loved Comrade, A Prose Poem', in *Sew the Old Days* (Ibadan: Evans Press, 1985) 26.
5. Ibid., 26.
6. Conversations with Ayi Kwei Armah.
7. Gayatri Spivak, 'Can the Subaltern Speak?', in Cary Nelson and Lawrence Grossberg (eds.), *Marxism and the Interpretation of Culture* (Urbana: University of Illinois Press, 1988), 271–313.
8. Niara Sudarkasa, 'The "Status of Women" in Indigenous African Societies,' in Terborg-Penn, Harley and Rushing (eds.), *Women in Africa and the African Diaspora* (Washington, DC: Howard, University Press, 1987), 28. This essay is highly recommended as a basic text on indigenous African women, conceptually and particularly on West African women.
9. Alice Walker, *In Search of Our Mothers' Gardens* (New York: Harcourt, 1983), xi.
10. Such questions will arise and drama such as surrounded burying Otieno in Kenya will continue to arise until Africans resolve conflicts in their emotional realities, resulting from contradictions between ethnicity and nation—ethnic culture and national culture. See Patricia Stamp, 'Burying Otieno,' *Signs* 16/4 (Summer 1991) 808–45, for a feminist perspective which still requires indigenous African feminist interventions. Otieno, a Kenyan Kikuyu, died and his wife, a Luo, had to resort to state legislation to contest the cultural claims of her in-laws concerning the burial remains.
11. Conversation with Kagendo Murungi, participant in The Colloquium on Women's Studies, the Laurie New Jersey Chair in Women Studies, 1992–93, Douglass College, Rutgers University.
13. Symposium on Gender Violence and Human Rights of Women in Africa, Paul

Robeson Center, Rutgers University, April 7, 1993. Panelists: Nahid Toubia (Sudan), Asma ben Halim (Sudan), Seble Dawit (Ethiopia), and Molara Ogundipe-Leslie (Nigeria); moderator, Abena Busia (Ghana).

14. For descriptions of the emotional characters of lesbians, see for instance the writings of the poet, Audre Lorde; and Rosemary Curb and Nancy Manahan, *Lesbian Nuns: Breaking the Silence* (Tallahassee, FL: The Naiad Press, 1985).
15. Tsitsi Dangarembga, *Nervous Conditions* (Seattle: The Seal Press, 1988).

13 The Persistence of Vision

Donna Haraway*

The names you uncaged primates give things affect your attitude to them forever after.

(Herschberger 1970 [1948])[1]

For thus all things must begin, with an act of love.

(Marais 1980)[2]

How are love, power and science intertwined in the constructions of nature in the late twentieth century? What may count as nature for late industrial people? What forms does love of nature take in particular historical contexts? For whom and at what cost? In what specific places, out of which social and intellectual histories, and with what tools is nature constructed as an object of erotic and intellectual desire? How do the terrible marks of gender and race enable and constrain love and knowledge in particular cultural traditions, including the modern natural sciences? Who may contest for what the body of nature will be? These questions guide my history of the modern sciences and popular cultures emerging from accounts of the bodies and lives of monkeys and apes.

The themes of race, sexuality, gender, nation, family and class have been written into the body of nature in Western life-sciences since the eighteenth century. In the wake of post-World War II decolonization, local and global feminist and anti-racist movements, nuclear and environmental threats, and broad consciousness of the fragility of earth's webs of life, nature remains a crucially important and deeply contested myth and reality. How do material and symbolic threads interweave in the fabric of late twentieth-century nature for industrial people?

Monkeys and apes have a privileged relation to nature and culture for Western people: simians occupy the border zones between those potent mythic poles. In the border zones, love and knowledge are richly ambiguous and productive of meanings in which many people have a stake. The commercial and scientific traffic in monkeys and apes is a traffic in meanings, as well as in animal lives. The sciences that tie monkeys, apes and people together in a Primate Order are built through disciplined practices deeply enmeshed in narrative, politics, myth, economics and technical possibilities. The women and men who have contributed to primate studies have carried with them the marks of their own histories and cultures. These marks are written into the texts of the lives of monkeys and apes, but often in subtle and unexpected ways. People who study other primates are advocates of contending scientific discourses, and they are accountable to many kinds of audiences and patrons. These people have engaged in dynamic, disciplined and intimate relations of love and knowledge with the animals they were privileged to watch. Both the primatologists and the animals on whose lives they reported command intense popular interest—in natural history museums, television specials, zoos, hunting, photography, science fiction, conservation politics, advertising, cinema, science news, greeting cards, jokes. The animals have been claimed as privileged subjects by disparate life and human sciences—anthropology, medicine, psychiatry, psychobiology, reproductive physiology, linguistics, neural biology, paleontology and behavioral ecology. Monkeys and apes have modeled a vast array of human problems and hopes. Most of all, in European, American and Japanese societies, monkeys and apes have been subjected to sustained, culturally specific interrogations of what it means to be 'almost human'.

Monkeys and apes—and the people who construct scientific and popular knowledge about them—are part of cultures in contention. Never innocent, the visualizing narrative 'technology' of this chapter draws from contemporary theories of cultural production, historical and social studies of science and technology, and feminist and anti-racist movements and theories to craft a view of nature as it is constructed and reconstructed in the bodies and lives of 'third world' animals serving as surrogates for 'man'. [. . .]

I am writing about primates because they are popular, important, marvelously varied and controversial. And all members of the Primate Order—monkeys, apes and people—are threatened. Late twentieth-century primatology may be seen as part of a complex survival literature in global, nuclear culture. Many people, including myself, have emotional, political and professional stakes in the production and stabilization of knowledge about the order of primates. This will not be a disinterested, objective study, nor a comprehensive one—partly because such studies are impossible for anyone, partly because I have stakes I want to make visible (and probably others as well). [. . .] Primates existing at the boundaries of so many hopes and interests are wonderful subjects with whom to explore the permeability of walls, the reconstitution of boundaries, the distaste for endless socially enforced dualisms.

FACT AND FICTION

Both science and popular culture are intricately woven of fact and fiction. It seems natural, even morally obligatory, to oppose fact and fiction; but their similarities run deep in western culture and language. Facts can be imagined as original, irreducible nodes from which a reliable understanding of the world can be constructed. Facts ought to be discovered, not made or constructed. But the etymology of facts refers us to human action, performance, indeed, to human feats (OED). Deeds, as opposed to words, are the parents of facts. That is, human action is at the root of what we can see as a fact, linguistically and historically. A fact is the thing done, a neuter past participle in our Roman parent language. In that original sense, facts are what has actually happened. Such things are known by direct experience, by testimony, and by interrogation—extraordinarily privileged routes to knowledge in North America.

Fiction can be imagined as a derivative, fabricated version of the world and experience, as a kind of perverse double for the facts or as an escape through fantasy into a better world than 'that which actually happened'. But tones of meaning in fiction make us hear its origin in vision, inspiration, insight, genius. We hear the root of fiction in poetry and we believe, in our Romantic moments, that original natures are revealed in good fiction. That is, fiction can be *true*, known to be true by an appeal to nature. And as nature is prolific, the mother of life in our major myth systems, fiction seems to be an inner truth which gives birth to our actual lives. This, too, is a very privileged route to knowledge in western cultures, including the United States. And finally, the etymology of fiction refers us once again to human action, to the act of fashioning, forming, or inventing, as well as to feigning. Fiction is inescapably implicated in a dialectic of the true (natural) and the counterfeit (artifactual). But in all its meanings, fiction is about human action. So, too, are all the narratives of science—fiction and fact—about human action.

Fiction's kinship to facts is close, but they are not identical twins. Facts are opposed to opinion, to prejudice, but not to fiction. Both fiction and fact are rooted in an epistemology that appeals to experience. However, there is an important difference; the word *fiction* is an active form, referring to a present act of fashioning, while *fact* is a descendant of a past participle, a word form which masks the generative deed or performance. A fact seems done, unchangeable, fit only to be recorded; fiction seems always inventive, open to other possibilities, other fashionings of life. But in this opening lies the threat of merely feigning, of not telling the true form of things.

From some points of view, the natural sciences seem to be crafts for distinguishing between fact and fiction, for substituting the past participle from the invention, and thus preserving true experience from its counterfeit. For example, the history of primatology has been repeatedly told as a progressive clarification of sightings of monkeys, apes, and human beings. First came the original intimations of primate form, suggested in the pre-scientific mists in the inventive stories of hunters, travelers and natives, beginning perhaps in ancient times, perhaps in the equally mythic Age of Discovery and of the Birth of Modern Science in the sixteenth century. Then gradually came clear-sighted vision, based on anatomical dissection and comparison. The story of correct vision of primate social form has the same plot: progress from misty sight, prone to invention, to sharp-eyed quantitative knowledge rooted in that kind of experience called, in English, experiment. It is a story of progress from immature sciences based on mere description and free qualitative interpretation to mature science based on quantitative methods and falsifiable hypotheses, leading to a synthetic scientific reconstruction of primate reality. But these histories are stories about stories, narratives with a good ending; i.e., the facts put together, reality reconstructed scientifically. These are stories with a particular aesthetic, realism, and a particular politics, commitment to progress.

From only a slightly different perspective, the history of science appears as a narrative about the history of technical and social means to produce the facts. The facts themselves are types of stories, of testimony to experience. But the provocation of experience requires an elaborate technology—including physical tools, an accessible tradition of interpretation, and specific social relations. Not just anything can emerge as a fact; not just anything can be seen or done, and so told. Scientific practice may be considered a kind of story-telling practice—a rule-governed, constrained, historically changing craft of narrating the history of nature. Scientific practice and scientific theories produce and are embedded in particular kinds of stories. Any scientific statement about the world depends intimately upon language, upon metaphor. The metaphors may be mathematical or they may be culinary; in any case, they structure scientific vision. Scientific practice is above all a story-telling practice in the sense of historically specific practices of interpretation and testimony.

Looking at primatology, a branch of the life sciences, as a story-telling craft may be particularly appropriate. First, the discourse of biology, beginning near the first decades of the nineteenth century, has been about organisms, beings with a life history; i.e., a plot with structure and function.[3] Biology is inherently historical, and its form of discourse is inherently narrative. Biology as a way of knowing the world is kin to Romantic literature, with its discourse about organic form and function. Biology is the fiction appropriate to objects called organisms; biology fashions the facts 'discovered' from organic beings. Organisms perform for the biologist, who transforms that performance into a truth attested by disciplined experience; i.e., into a fact, the jointly accomplished deed or feat of the scientist and the organism. Romanticism passes into realism, and realism into naturalism, genius into progress, insight into fact. Both the scientist and the organism are actors in a story-telling practice.

Second, monkeys, apes, and human beings emerge in primatology inside elaborate narratives about origins, natures and possibilities. Primatology is about the life history of a taxonomic order that includes people. Especially western people produce stories about primates while simultaneously telling stories about the relations of nature and culture, animal and human, body and mind, origin and future. Indeed, from the start, in the mid-eighteenth century, the primate order has been built on tales about these dualisms and their scientific resolution.

To treat a science as narrative is not to be dismissive, quite the contrary. [. . .] I am interested in the narratives of scientific fact—those potent fictions of science—within a complex field indicated by the signifier SF. In the late 1960s science fiction anthologist and critic Judith Merril idiosyncratically began using the signifier SF to designate a complex emerging narrative field in which boundaries between science fiction (conventionally, sf) and fantasy became highly permeable in confusing ways, commercially and linguistically. Her designation, SF, came to be widely adopted as critics, readers, writers, fans, and publishers struggled to comprehend an increasingly heterodox array of writing, reading, and marketing practices indicated by a proliferation of 'sf' phrases: speculative fiction, science fiction, science fantasy, speculative futures, speculative fabulation.

SF is a territory of contested cultural reproduction in high-technology worlds. Placing the narratives of scientific fact within the heterogeneous space of SF produces a transformed field. The transformed field sets up resonances among all of its regions and components. No region or component is 'reduced' to any other, but reading and writing practices respond to each other across a structured space. [. . .] The sciences have complex histories in the constitution of imaginative worlds and of actual bodies in modern and postmodern 'first world' cultures. [. . .]

FOUR TEMPTATIONS

Analyzing a scientific discourse, primatology, as story telling within several contested narrative fields is a way to enter current debates about the social construction of scientific knowledge without succumbing completely to any of four very tempting positions . . . I use the image of temptation because I find all four positions persuasive, enabling, and also dangerous, especially if any one position finally silences all the others, creating a false harmony in the primate story.

The first resourceful temptation comes from the most active tendencies in the social studies of science and technology. For example, the French prominent analyst of science, Bruno Latour, radically rejects all forms of epistemological realism and analyzes scientific practice as thoroughly social and constructionist. He rejects the distinction between social and technical and represents scientific practice as the refinement of 'inscription devices', i.e., devices for transcribing the immense complexity and chaos of competing interpretations into unambiguous traces, writings, which mark the emergence of a fact, the case about reality. [. . .] The accounts of the scientists about their own processes become ethnographic data, subject to cultural analysis.

[. . .] This approach can explain scientific contests for the power to close off debate, and it can account for both successful and unsuccessful entries in the contest. Scientific practice is negotiation, strategic moves, inscription, translation. A great deal can be said about science as effective belief and the world-changing power to enforce and embody it.[4] What more can one ask of a theory of scientific practice?

The second valuable temptation comes from one branch of the marxist tradition, which argues for the historical superiority of particular structured standpoints for knowing the social world, and possibly the 'natural' world as well. Fundamentally, people in this tradition find the social world to be structured by the social relations of the production and reproduction of daily life, such that it is only possible to see these relations clearly from some vantage points. This is not an individual matter, and good will is not at issue. From the standpoint of those social groups in positions of systematic domination and power, the true nature of social life will be opaque; they have too much to lose from clarity.

Thus, the owners of the means of production will see equality in a system of exchange, where the standpoint of the working class will reveal the nature of domination in the system of production based on the wage contract and the exploitation and deformation of human labor. Those whose social definition of identity is rooted in the system of racism will not be able to see that the definition of human has not been neutral, and cannot be until major material–social changes occur on a world scale. Similarly, for those whose possibility of adult status rests on the power to appropriate the 'other' in a socio-sexual system of gender, sexism will not look like a fundamental barrier to correct knowledge *in general*. The tradition indebted to Marxist epistemology can account for the greater adequacy of some ways of knowing and can show that race, sex and class fundamentally determine the most intimate details of knowledge and practice, especially where the appearance is of neutrality and universality.[5]

These issues are hardly irrelevant to primatology, a science practiced in the United States nearly exclusively by white people, and until quite recently by white men, and still practiced overwhelmingly by the economically privileged. [. . .] For example, perhaps most primatologists in the field in the first decades after World War II failed to appreciate that the interrelationships of people, land and animals in Africa and Asia are at least partly due to the positions of the researchers within systems of racism and imperialism. Many sought a 'pure' nature, unspoiled by contact with people; and so they sought untouched species, analogous to the 'natives' once sought by colonial anthropologists.

But for the observer of animals, the indigenous peoples of Africa and Asia were a nuisance, a threat to conservation—indeed, encroaching 'aliens'—until decolonization forced white Western scientists to restructure their bio-politics of self and other, native and alien. The boundaries among animals and human beings shift in the transition from a colonial to a post- or neo-colonial standpoint. Insisting that there can be less deformed contents and methods in the natural as well as social sciences, the Marxist, feminist and anti-racist accounts reject the relativism of the social studies of science. Explicitly political accounts take sides on what is a more adequate, humanly acceptable knowledge. But these analyses have limits for guiding an exploration of primate studies. Wage labor, sexual and reproductive appropriation, and racial hegemony are structured aspects of the human social world. There is no doubt that they affect knowledge systematically, but it is not clear precisely how they relate to knowledge about the feeding patterns of patas monkeys or about the replication of DNA molecules.

Another aspect of the Marxist tradition has made significant progress in answering that kind of question. In the 1970s, people associated with the British *Radical Science Journal* developed the concept of science as a labor process in order to study and change scientific mediations of class domination in the relations of production and reproduction of human life.[6] [. . .] Every aspect of scientific practice can be described in terms of the concept of mediation: language, laboratory hierarchies, industrial ties, medical doctrines, basic theoretical preferences, and stories about nature. The concept of labor process seems cannibalistic, making the social relations of other basic processes seem derivative. For example, the complex systems of domination, complicity, resistance, equality and nurturance in gendered practices of bearing and raising children cannot be accommodated by the concept of labor. But these reproductive practices visibly affect more than a few contents and methods in modern primate studies. But even an extended concept of mediation and systematic social process, one that does not insist on the reduction to labor in a classic Marxist sense, leaves out too much.

The third temptation comes from the siren call of the scientists themselves; they keep pointing out that they are, among other things, watching monkeys and apes. In some sense, more or less nuanced, they insist that scientific practice 'gets at' the world. They claim that scientific knowledge is not simply about power and control. They claim that their knowledge somehow translates the active voice of their subjects, the objects of knowledge. Without necessarily being compelled by their aesthetic of realism or their theories of representation, I believe them in the strong sense that my imaginative and intellectual life and my professional and political commitments in the world respond to these scientific accounts. Scientists are adept at providing good grounds for belief in their accounts and for action on their basis. Just how science 'gets at' the world remains far from resolved. What does seem resolved, however, is that science grows from and enables concrete ways of life, including particular constructions of love, knowledge and power. That is the core of its instrumentalism and the limit to its universalism.

Evidence is always a question of interpretation; theories are accounts *of* and *for* specific kinds of lives. I am looking for a way of telling a story of the production of a branch of the life sciences, a branch which includes human beings centrally, that listens very carefully to the stories themselves. My story must listen to the practices of interpretation of the primate order in which the primates themselves—monkeys, apes, and people—all have some kind of 'authorship'. I would suggest that the concept of constrained and contested story-telling allows an appreciation of the social construction of science, while still guiding the hearer to a search for the other animals who are active participants in primatology. I want to find a concept for telling a history of science that does not itself depend on the dualism between active and passive, culture and nature, human and animal, social and natural.

The fourth temptation intersects with each of the other three; this master temptation is to look always through the lenses ground on the stones of the complex histories of gender and race in the constructions of modern sciences around the globe. That means examining cultural productions, including the primate sciences, from the points of view enabled by the politics and theories of feminism and anti-racism. The challenge is to remember the particularity as well as the power of this way of reading and writing. But that is the same challenge that should be built into reading or writing a scientific text. Race and gender are not prior universal social categories—much less natural or biological givens. Race and gender are the world-changing products of specific, but very large and durable, histories. The same thing is true of science. The visual system of this book depends upon a triple filter of race, gender, and science. This is the filter which traps the marked bodies of history for closer examination.[7] [. . .]

PRIMATOLOGY IS (JUDEO-) CHRISTIAN SCIENCE

Western Jews and Christians or post-Judeo-Christians are not the only practitioners of primate sciences. [. . .] In these stories, there is a constant refrain drawn from salvation history; primatology is about primal stories, the origin and nature of 'man', and about reformation stories, the reform and reconstruction of human nature. Implicitly and explicitly, the story of the Garden of Eden emerges in the sciences of monkeys and apes, along with versions of the origin of society, marriage, and language.

From the beginning, primatology has had this character in the west. If the eighteenth-century Swedish 'father' of modern biological classification, Linnaeus, is cited at all by twentieth-century scientists, he is noted for placing human beings in a taxonomic order of nature with other animals, i.e., for taking a large step away from Christian assumptions. [. . .] But there is quite another way to see Linnaeus's activity as the 'father' of a discourse about nature. He referred to himself as a second Adam, the 'eye' of God, who could give true representations, true names, thus reforming or restoring a purity of names lost by the first Adam's sin.[8] Nature was a theatre, a stage for the playing out of natural and salvation history. The role of the one who renamed the animals was to ensure a true and faithful order of nature, to purify the eye and the word. The 'balance of nature' was maintained partly by the role of a new 'man' who would see clearly and name accurately, hardly a trivial identity in the face of eighteenth-century European expansion. Indeed, this is the identity of the modern authorial subject, for whom inscribing the body of nature gives assurance of his mastery.

Linnaeus's science of natural history was intimately a Christian science. Its first task, achieved in Linnaeus's and his correspondents' life work, was to announce the kinship of 'man' and beast in the modern order of an expanding Europe. Natural man was found not only among the 'savages', but also among the animals, who were named primates in consequence, the first Order of nature. Those who could bestow such names had a powerful modern vocation; they became scientists. Taxonomy had a secular sacred function. [. . .] The stories produced by such practitioners have a special status in a repressed protestant biblical culture like that of the United States.

Nature for Linnaeus was not understood 'biologically', but 'representationally'. In the course of the nineteenth century, biology became a discourse about productive, expanding nature. Biology was constructed as a discourse about nature known as a system of production and reproduction, understood in terms of the functional division of labor and the mental, labor, and sexual efficiency of organisms. [. . .] The primate body, as part of the body of nature, may be read as a map of power. Biology, and primatology, are inherently political discourses, whose chief objects of knowledge, such as organisms and ecosystems, are icons (condensations) of the whole of the history and politics of the culture that constructed them for contemplation and manipulation. The primate body itself is an intriguing kind of political discourse.

PRIMATOLOGY IS SIMIAN ORIENTALISM

[. . .] The two major axes structuring the potent scientific stories of primatology are defined by the interacting dualisms, *sex/gender* and *nature/culture.* Sex and the west are axiomatic in biology and anthropology. Under the guiding logic of these complex dualisms, western primatology is simian orientalism.

Edward Said (1978) argued that western (European and American) scholars have had a long history of coming to terms with countries, peoples, and cultures in the Near and Far East that is based on the Orient's special place in western history—the scene of origins of language and civilization, of rich markets and colonial possession and penetration, and of imaginative projection. The Orient has been a troubling resource for the production of the Occident, the 'East's' other and periphery that became materially its dominant. The west is positioned outside the Orient, and this exteriority is part of the Occident's practice of representation. Said quotes Marx, 'They cannot represent themselves; they must be represented' (xiii). These representations are complex mirrors for western selves in specific historical moments. The west has also been positioned mobilely; westerners could be *there* with relatively little resistance from the other. The difference has been one of power. The structure has been limiting, of course, but more importantly, it has been *productive.* That productivity occurred within the structured practices and discourses of orientalism; the structures were a condition of having anything to say. There never is any question of having anything truly original to say about origins. Part of the authority of the practices of telling origin stories resides precisely in their intertextual relations.

Without stretching the comparison too far, the signs of orientalist discourse mark primatology. But here, the scene of origins is not the cradle of civilization, but the cradle of culture, of human being distinct from animal existence. If orientalism concerns the western imagination of the origin of the city, primatology displays the western imagination of the origin of sociality itself, especially in the densely meaning-laden icon of 'the family'. Origins are in principle inaccessible to direct testimony; any voice from the time of origins is structurally the voice of the other who generates the self. That is why both realist and postmodernist aesthetics in primate representations and simulations have been modes of production of complex illusions that function as fruitful generators of scientific facts and theories. 'Illusion' is not to be despised when it grounds such powerful truths.

Simian orientalism means that western primatology has been about the construction of the self from the raw material of the other, the appropriation of nature in the production of culture, the ripening of the human from the soil of the animal, the clarity of white from the obscurity of color, the issue of man from the body of woman, the elaboration of gender from the resource of sex, the emergence of mind by the activation of body. To effect these transformative operations, simian 'orientalist' discourse must first construct the terms: animal, nature, body, primitive, female. [. . .] Primatology is western discourse, and it is sexualized discourse. It is about potential and its actualization. Nature/culture and sex/gender are not loosely related pairs of terms; their specific form of relation is hierarchical appropriation, connected as Aristotle taught by the logic of active/passive, form/matter, achieved form/resource, man/animal, final/material cause. Symbolically, nature and culture, as well as sex and gender, mutually (but not equally) construct each other; one pole of a dualism cannot exist without the other.

Said's critique of orientalism should alert us to another important point: neither sex nor nature is the truth underlying gender and culture, any more than the 'East' is really the origin and distorting mirror of the 'West'. Nature and sex are as crafted as their dominant 'others'. But their functions and powers are different. [. . .] It matters to know precisely how sex and nature become natural–technical objects of knowledge, as much as it matters to explain their doubles, gender and culture. It is not the case that no story could be told without these dualisms or that they are part of the structure of the mind or language. For one thing, alternative stories within primatology exist. But these binarisms have been especially *productive* and especially *problematic* for constructions of female and race-marked bodies; it is crucial to see how the binarisms may be deconstructed and maybe redeployed.

It seems nearly impossible for those who produce natural sciences and comment on them for a living really to believe that there is no *given* reality beneath the inscriptions of science, no untouchable sacred center to ground and authorize an innocent and progressive order of knowledge. Maybe in the humanities there is no recourse from representation, mediation, story-telling, and social saturation. But the sciences succeed that other faulty order of knowledge; the proof is in their power to convince and reorder the whole world, not just one local culture. The natural sciences are the 'other' to the human sciences, with their tragic orientalisms. But these pleas do not survive scrutiny.

The pleas of natural scientists do not convince because they are set up as the 'other'. The claims are predictable and seem plausible to those who make them because they are built into the taxonomies of western knowledge and because social and psychological needs are met by the persistent voices of the divided knowledge of natural and human sciences, by this division of labor and authority in the production of discourses. But these observations about predictable claims and social needs do not reduce natural sciences to a cynical 'relativism' with no standards beyond arbitrary power. Nor does my argument claim there is no world for which people struggle to give an account, no referent in the system of signs and productions of meanings, no progress in building better accounts within traditions of practice. That would be to reduce a complex field to one pole of precisely the dualisms under analysis, the one designated as ideal to some impossible material, appearance to some forbidden real.

The point of my argument is rather that natural sciences, like human sciences, are inextricably *within* the processes that give them birth. And so, like the human sciences, the natural sciences are culturally and historically specific, modified, involved. They matter to real people. It makes sense to ask what stakes, methods, and kinds of authority are involved in natural scientific accounts, how they differ, for example, from religion or ethnography. It does not make sense to ask for a form of authority that escapes the web of the highly productive cultural fields that make the accounts possible in the first place. The detached eye of objective science is an ideological fiction, and a powerful one. But it is a fiction that hides—and is designed to hide—how the powerful discourses of the natural sciences really work. Again, the limits are *productive*, not reductive and invalidating. [. . .]

Part of the difficulty of approaching the embedded, interested, passionate constructions of science non-reductively derives from an inherited analytical tradition, deeply indebted to Aristotle and to the transformative history of 'White Capitalist Patriarchy' (how may we name this scandalous Thing?) that turns everything into a resource for appropriation. As 'resource' an object of knowledge is finally only matter for the seminal power, the act, of the knower. Here, the object both guarantees and refreshes the power of the knower, but any status as *agent* in the productions of knowledge must be denied the object. It—the world—must, in short, be objectified as thing, not agent; it must be matter for the self-formation of the only social being in the productions of knowledge, the human knower. Nature is only the raw material of culture, appropriated, preserved, enslaved, exalted, or otherwise made flexible for disposal by culture in the logic of capitalist colonialism. Similarly, sex is only the matter to the act of gender; the productionist logic seems inescapable in traditions of western binarisms. This analytical and historical narrative logic accounts for my nervousness about the sex/gender distinction in the recent history of feminist theory as a way to approach reconstructions of what may count as female and as nature in primatology—and why those reconstructions matter beyond the boundaries of primate studies. It has seemed all but impossible to avoid the trap of an appropriationist logic of domination built into the nature/culture binarism and its generative lineage, including the sex/gender distinction.

READING IN THE BORDERLANDS

[. . .] That monkeys and apes, and human beings as their taxonomic kin, exist on the boundaries of so many struggles to determine what will count as knowledge. Primates are not nicely boxed into a specialized and secured discipline or field. Even in the late twentieth century, many kinds of people can claim to know primates, to the chagrin and dismay of many other contestants for official expertise. The cost of destabilizing knowledge about primates remains within reach not only for practitioners of several fields in the life and human sciences, but for people on the fringes of any science—like science writers, philosophers, historians, and zoo goers. In addition, story telling about animals is such a deeply popular practice that the discourse produced within scientific specialties is appropriated by other people for their own ends. The boundary between technical and popular discourse is very fragile and permeable. Even in the late twentieth century, the language of primatology is accessible in contentious political debate about human nature, history, and futures. This remains true despite a transformation of specialized discourses in primatology into the language of mathematics, systems theories, ergonomic analysis, game theory, life history strategies, and molecular biology.

Some of the interesting border disputes about primates, who and what they are (and who and what they are for), are between psychiatry and zoology, biology and anthropology, genetics and comparative psychology, ecology and medical research, agriculturalists and tourist industries in the 'third world', field researchers and laboratory scientists, conservationists and multinational logging companies, poachers and game wardens, scientists and administrators in zoos, feminists and anti-feminists, specialists and lay people, physical anthropologists and ecological–evolutionary biologists, established scientists and new Ph.Ds, women's studies students and professors in animal behavior courses, linguists and biologists, foundation officials and grant applicants, science writers and researchers, historians of science and real scientists, marxists and liberals, liberals and neo-conservatives. [. . .] I want to set new terms for the traffic between what we have come to know historically as nature and culture.

Notes

1. Ruth Herschberger, *Adam's Rib* (New York: Harper and Row, 1970 [1948]).
2. Eugene Marais, 'Soul of the White Ant', South Africa Radio Broadcasting, 1980.
3. Michel Foucault, *The Birth of the Clinic: An Archeology of Medical Perception* (transl. A. M. Sheridan Smith) (New York: Pantheon, 1973); William R. Albury, 'Experiment and Explanation of Bichat and Magendie', *Studies in the History of Biology* 1 (1977), 47–131; Georges Canguilhem, *On the Normal and the Pathological* (transl. C. R. Fawcett) (Dordrecht: Reidel, 1978); Karl Figlio, 'The Metaphor of Organization: An Historiographical Perspective on the Bio-Medical Sciences of the Early 19th Century', *History of Science* 14 (1976), 17–53.
4. Bruno Latour, 'Give Me a Laboratory and I Will Raise the World', in Karin D. Knorr-Cetina and Michael Mulkay (eds.), *Science Observed: Perspectives on the Social Study of Science* (London: Sage, 1983), 141–70; *Science in Action: How to Follow Scientists and Engineers Through Society* (Cambridge: Harvard University Press, 1987) and *The Pasteurization of France* (transl. A. Sheridan and J. Law) (Cambridge: Harvard University Press, 1988); Wiebe E. Bijker, Thomas P. Hughes and Trevor Pinch (eds.), *The Social Construction of Technological Systems. New Directions in the Sociology and History of Technology*

(Cambridge: MIT Press, 1987); Michel Callon and Bruno Latour 'Unscrewing the Big Leviathan, or How Do Actors Microstructure Reality?', in Karin D. Knorr-Cetina and A. Cicourel (eds.), *Advances in Social Theory and Methodology: Toward an Integration of Micro and Macro Sociologies* (London: Routledge and Kegan Paul, 1981); Karin D. Knorr-Cetina, 'The Ethnographic Study of Scientific Work: Towards a Constructivist Interpretation of Science', in Knorr-Cetina and Mulkay, *Advances in Social Theory and Methodology*; Sharon Traweek, *Beamtimes and Lifetimes: The World of High Energy Physics* (Cambridge: Harvard University Press, 1988).

5. Nancy Hartsock, 'The Feminist Standpoint: Developing the Ground for a Specifically Feminist Historical Materialism', in S. Harding and M. Hintikka (eds.), *Discovering Reality: Feminist Perspectives on Epistemology, Metaphysics, Methodology, and Philosophy of Science* (Dordrecht: Reidel, 1983), 283–310; Sandra Harding, *The Science Question in Feminism* (Ithaca: Cornell University Press, 1986); Hilary Rose, 'Hand, Brain, and Heart: A Feminist Epistemology for the Natural Sciences', *Signs* 9 (1983), 73–90.
6. Robert M. Young, 'Science *Is* Social Relations', *Radical Science Journal* 5 (1977), 65–129 and 'Is Nature a Labour Process?', in Les Lividow and R. M. Young (eds.), *Technology and the Labour Process: Marxist Studies*, vol. 2 (London: Free Association Books, 1985), 206–32; Edward J. Yoxen, 'Life as a Productive Force: Capitalising the Science and Technology of Molecular Biology', in Les Lividow and R. M. Young (eds.), *Technology and the Labour Process: Marxist Studies*, vol. 1 (London: CSE Books, 1981), 66–122; Karl Figlio, 'The Historiography of Scientific Medicine: An Invitation to the Human Sciences', *Comparative Studies in Society and History* 19 (1977), 262–86.
7. Elizabeth Fee, 'Critiques of Modern Science: The Relationship of Feminism to Other Radical Epistemologies', in Ruth Bleier (ed.), *Feminist Approaches to Science* (New York: Pergamon, 1986), 42–56; Stephen J. Gould, *The Mismeasure of Man* (New York: Norton, 1981); Evelyn Hammonds, 'Race, Sex, and AIDS: The Construction of "Other"', *Radical America* 20/6 (1986), 28–38; Ruth Hubbard, M. S. Henifin and B. Fried (eds.), *Biological Woman—the Convenient Myth.* (Cambridge: Schenkman, 1982); Sander L. Gilman, 'Black Bodies, White Bodies: Towards an Iconography of Female Sexuality in Late Nineteenth-Century Art, Medicine, and Literature', *Critical Inquiry* 12 (1985), 204–42; Marian Lowe and Ruth Hubbard (eds.), *Woman's Nature: Rationalizations of Inequality* (New York: Pergamon, 1983); Evelyn Fox Keller, *Reflections on Gender and Science* (New Haven: Yale University Press, 1985).
8. I owe this analysis of Linnaeus as the Eye/I of God to Camille Limoges, Université de Québec à Montréal.

14 Bold Omissions and Minute Depictions

Trinh T. Minh-ha*

Thanks to Ayi Kwei Armah, I know the screens of life you have left us: veils that rise in front of us, framing the world in neat pieces. Until we have grown tall enough to look over the next veil, we believe the little we see is all there is to see. From veil to veil, the bitter taste of surprise in disfranchisement keeps on renewing. But again and again, we hold fast to what our eyes perceive; again and again we fool ourselves, convinced at each step, that we have grown wise.

Recently, in a casual conversation, two visiting writers from Martinique and Guadeloupe remarked with a certain bewilderment that the question of migration was again enjoying a great vogue in the States and that 'they all talk about identity and marginality'. Finding myself deeply implied in this 'they' despite the fact that my friends tacitly included me on their side while talking, I was suddenly hit by a brief but sharp feeling of confusion as to where my identity lay. Since *they*, in this context, pointed both to the trendy Euro-American intellectuals eager to recycle strands of subversion and to those for whom the migrant's condition continued to be an everyday reality and an ongoing border struggle, it was difficult to react quickly without speaking simply for or against. Caught between two fixed closures—American and Asian—I was at the same time grateful to be treated as an outsider to the passing trends of discursive thought in North America, and repelled by my friends' apparent refusal to identify (even strategically) with the fight against marginalization. However, their remarks did have a strong destabilizing effect. I was assaulted by intense skepticism as I realized the intricacy of my own participation in what had been indirectly pointed to here as a spurious, fashionable

* From Trinh T. Minh-ha, 'Bold Omissions Minute Depictions' from *When the Moon Waxes Red* by Trinh T. Minha-ha (Taylor & Francis, Inc/Routledge, Inc, 1991), 155–166, copyright © 1991, reprinted by permission of the publisher.

preoccupation of the West raised up for the sake of Western vanguardism and its desire to conserve itself as sovereign Subject of radical knowledge. For the above writers, the word 'marginality' clearly did not make sense, nor did its juxtaposition with the notion of 'identity' seem any more revealing. They thus reacted to its use with astonishment, if not with sarcasm: 'What marginality? Marginal in relation to whom? to where? to what?'

Perhaps vindicating and interrogating identity takes on a peculiarly active significance with displacement and migration. It becomes inevitable with the questioning of established power relations, or with the daily meddling with the ruling culture. For those who feel settled at home in their land (or in other lands) where racial issues are not an everyday challenge, perhaps self-retrieval and self-apprehension are achieved without yielding to the urge to assimilate, to reject, or to fight for a space where identity is fearlessly constructed across difference. A familiar story of 'learning in America' is, for example, the one lived by artist Wen Yi Hou when she left Mainland China to further her education in the States:

> I became aware of my minority status only in America . . . I asked people there [at the University of California San Diego], 'Why did the school select me?' They said when they saw my slides, they were surprised by my paintings. They were modern and very western. How could that happen in Red China? I was surprised that shortly after I started the program, I was asked why my paintings were not traditional Chinese paintings. I was depressed. I did not have any value as a Chinese artist in their minds. My feelings of worthlessness as an artist intensified in San Diego. There was a group of American graduate students who talked about the Eastern influence on Western art. I was in the seminar, but no one talked to me or looked at me. I worried about how they could talk about Eastern cultures and yet they would not even look at a person from the East. I was the subject of the lecture but was excluded.[1]

Hear how the story happened again; watch the scenario of disfranchisement repeat itself across generations; smell the poison taking effect in the lives of those who dare mix while differing. The predicament of crossing boundaries cannot be merely rejected or accepted. It has to be confronted in its controversies. There is indeed little hope of speaking this simultaneously outside-inside actuality into existence in simple, polarizing black-and-white terms. The challenge of the hyphenated reality lies in the hyphen itself: the *becoming* Asian-American; the realm in between, where predetermined rules cannot fully apply. Presumedly, the Real Chinese artist should abide by Chinese aesthetics, the authenticity of which is naturally defined on *their*

(Euro-American) terms. After all, who would dispute the fact that Western influence should be challenged in its global domination? But again, who never hesitates to take the licence to decide what is Western and what is Eastern in this context? Indeed, no statements about the negative nature of such an influence could be more dogmatic than those often made by Euro-Americans for the benefit of their non-Western *protégés*. 'Yes, the white world is still a pretty dark one for the man of color', noted Ezekiel Mphahlele.[2] It is always mind-boggling to recognize how readily opposed liberal Westerners are to any discrimination in the public treatment of people of color while remaining blind to it in more individualized relationships or when dealing with difference on a one-to-one basis.

A lesson learned from the failure of Negritude is that any attempt at pegging things and reclaiming a denied heritage to construct a positive identity should remain at its best, diacritical and strategical, rather than dogmatic and originary. (The term *négritude*, created by poet Aimé Césaire to denote a quality common to the thought and behavior of black people, was championed in the fifties by the Society of African Culture in Paris as a concept capable of defining and exalting the negroness of artistic activity.) Racial and sexual discriminations are based on assumptions of biological essences, and with such an affirmation as 'Emotion is completely Negro as reason is Greek' (Léopold Sédar Senghor), Negritude, like 'Feminitude' (or reactive feminism), ends up trapping itself in what remains primarily a defensive stance.

In my struggle to overcome the artistic difficulty that arises when one is angry most of the time and when one's sense of values is continually being challenged by the ruling class, I have never thought of calling my *negritude* to my aid, except when writing protest material. But is not this elementary—shall I call it 'underdoggery'?—that Senghor is talking about? Even he must know, however, that his philosophy will contain his art only up to a point: it won't chain his art for long.[3]

If Negritude tended to oversimply and to re-entrench black values in its assertion, it was mainly because it heavily indulged in binary oppositional thinking. [. . .] Separatism as a strategy, *not* as an end point, is at times necessary for the emergence of a framework that promotes and entitles second-class citizens to articulate problems related to their condition. Highly privileged are those who can happily afford to remain comfortable in the protected world of their own, which neither seems to carry any ambiguity nor does it need to question itself in its mores and measures—its utter narrowness despite its global material expansion. When the footprints made by the shoes are not readily confused with the shoes themselves, what Negritude has also achieved can never be belittled. Due to it, the creation of a new multicultural alliance with the world's dispossessed became possible. It is in having to confront and defy hegemonic values on an everyday basis, in other words, in assuming the between-world dilemma, that one understands both the predicament and the potency of the hyphen. Here, the becoming Asian-American affirms itself at once as a transient and constant state: one is born over and over again as hyphen rather than as fixed entity, thereby refusing to settle down in one (tubicolous) world or another. The hyphenated condition certainly does not limit itself to a duality between two cultural heritages. It leads, on the one hand, to an active 'search of our mother's garden' (Alice Walker)—the consciousness of 'root values' or of a certain Asianness—and on the other hand, to a heightened awareness of other 'minority' sensitivities, hence of a Third World solidarity, and by extension, of the necessity for new alliances. Unavoidably, the step backward is constantly also a step forward. The multidimensional desire to be both here(s) and there(s) implies a more radical ability to shuttle between frontiers and to cut across ethnic allegiances while assuming a specific and contingent legacy.

Cultural difference is not a totemic object. It does not always announce itself to the onlooker; sometimes it stands out conspicuously, most of the times it tends to escape the commodifying eye. Its visibility depends on how much one is willing to inquire into the anomalous character of the familiar, and how engaged one remains to the politics of continuous doubling, reversing, and displacing in marginality as well as to the necessity of changing both oneself-as-other and other-as-oneself.

> Fervently we have wanted to belong somewhere at the same time that we have often wanted to run away. We reached out for something, and when by chance grasped it, we often found that it wasn't what we wanted at all. There is one part of us that is always lost and searching. It is an echo of a cry that was a longing for warmth and safety. And through our adolescent fantasies, and however our adult reasoning may disguise it, the search continues.[4]

The quest for this other in us can hardly be a simple return to the past or to the time-honored values of our ancestors. Changes are inevitably implied in the process of restoring the cultural lineage, which combines the lore of the past with the lore of the complex present in its histories of migrations. As soon as we learn to be 'Asians in America'—that is, to come to a rest in a place supposedly always there, waiting to be discovered—we also recognize that we can't simply be Asians any longer. The fight has to focus on our physical and political hereabouts, so that 'here in San Francisco/there is Saigon/ their locks of mouths/damming the Pacific!'[5] Listening to new sounds in the attempt to articulate a specific and transcultural between-world reality requires again, that the step backward be simultaneously a step forward. As Al Robles puts forth in these lines: 'A Filipino fisherman once said/that looking for your roots/will get you all tangled up/with the dead past . . . /If the mind bothers with the roots/It'll forget all about the weeds . . . '[6]

I am not a painter who has come to America to paint China.
I am a painter from China who came to America to continue painting.

Why paint?

People need to paint and painting needs people.[7]

What is Chinese in America? An artistic event is often presented as a thought, a feeling that has found its form in its formless nature. To paint is to continue painting. The becoming is not a becoming something; it remains active and intransitive. While, for example, for Thomas Mann 'a spiritual—that is, significant—phenomenom is "significant" precisely because it exceeds its own limits', for Andrei Tarkovsky the film image as acute observation of life is linked to the Japanese Haiku, which he wrote, 'cultivates its images in such a way that they mean nothing beyond themselves, and at the same time express so much that it is not possible to catch their final meaning . . . the great function of the artistic image is to be a detector of infinity . . . [and to give] the beholder a simultaneous experience of the most complex, contradictory, sometimes even mutually exclusive feelings'.[8] People need to paint and painting needs people for, in this mutual need, they both exceed their limits as people and as painting. This is the challenge of the hyphen. Chinese artist Shih-t'ao (1630–c. 1717/1720) evolved his philosophy of painting around the fundamental notions of 'the form of the formless' and 'the sound of the soundless'.[9] The basic urge to manifest (*not* to arrest) the Formless in form seems, indeed, to be what Tarkovsky yearns for through the many words he uses to explicate an aesthetic that remains implicitly admiring of the Haiku as well as of other Asian sources, such as Kurosawa's poetic approach in his *Macbeth*. What Tarkovsky tries to retain and 'make it incarnate, new each time', is the Formless, or as he said it, the life principle itself, *unique* in each moment of life. Thus, form is not intended to express form, but rather, formlessness. The non-consumable relationship between form and formlessness or between art and life defies every binarist attempt at reducing it to the old dichotomy of form and content. In Tarkovsky's definition, 'the image is not a certain *meaning*, expressed by the director, but an entire world reflected as in a drop of water'.[10]

Transformation requires a certain freedom to modify, appropriate, and reappropriate without being trapped in imitation. Chinese traditional arts, for example, do not speak so much of beauty or of aesthetic, as of the spirit—the *ch'i*. What can be taught and assimilated, indeed, is technical knowledge; not the *ch'i*—the principle of life that is unique to each artistic moment, event, and manifestation; or the breath that sustains all processes of movement and change. To excel only in the mechanics of a language, be it verbal, visual, or musical, is to excel in imitation—the part that can be formulated, hence enclosed in formulas. Form as formulas can only express form; it cannot free itself from the form–content divide. However, a film can be made the way a tale is spun by many storytellers of Asian and African cultures. Nothing is explained, everything is evoked. When explanations were requested, the storyteller would pause, listen carefully, and after due consideration, repeat exactly the passage relevant to the question. No more, no less. Here, there is no necessity to reduce the plural meaning of the story to some flat explanatory answer, and the questioner is invited to listen again more mindfully to what he or she has missed. Since form cannot be separated from content—the form of the story being (integral to) the story itself—there is no other way to say it without reforming it (that is, un/intentionally modifying, augmenting, or narrowing it). One of the characteristics of Shih-T'ao's principles in painting is precisely the *yugen*, translated as 'subtle profundity' or 'deep reserve'. The quality emphasized here is the ability to imply, rather than to expose something in its entirety; to suggest and evoke, rather than to delineate laboriously. 'Such works', wrote Shih-T'ao, 'enable us to imagine the depth of content within them and to feel infinite reverberations, something that is not possible with detail painted minutely and distinctly'.[11]

The realm of a film is that of a mediating elsewhere, albeit one deeply rooted in reality. It seeks the truth of reality, or the *ch'i* of life's fictions, but is neither dream nor reality. Its meaning is never simply true or false. For it is thanks to its falsity (recreation through the mediation of the cinematic apparatus) that a truth is made perceptible to the spectator. In confusing meaning with truth or imposing it as truth, a form of literalism, of narrow-mindedness and of ensuing terrorism is accorded the name of 'realism'. Such glaring 'misnaming' in film history ultimately serves to mask the process in filmmaking by which meaning is fixed and formulas are prescribed. Thereby, the oppressive cinematic conventions that serve the ideology of power are naturalized, and representation, lacking *yugen*, no longer vibrates; it ceases to be political, while meaning becomes merely a pawn in the game of power. 'The stereotype is not a simplification because it is a false representation of a given reality. It is a simplification because it is an arrested, fixated form of representation . . . '[12] To disturb the comfort, the security, the fanaticism of meaning is a critical task that allows film to partake in the politics of everyday life as well as in the challenge of the dominant ideology of world cinema.

One of the ways by which feminism defines itself as a politics of everyday life, thereby breaking down the barriers separating the public and the private spheres of activity, is precisely to continue redefining the nature and boundaries of the political in relation to the personal. Much has been said concerning the 'misuse' of the personal in attempts to radicalize consciousness. And much has also been voiced on how sexual politics can lead straight to identity politics, which tends to collapse the personal and the political instead of maintaining the tension between the two so that, in the absence of the one or the other, the state of depoliticization that occurs can no longer go unnoticed. Still, feminism continues to be a political critique of society and what it has contributed is the possibility of a new way of understanding subjectivity, a radically different aesthetic, a rewriting of culture in which women are addressed as social and political subjects. As bell hooks remarks, 'to begin revisioning we must acknowledge the need to examine the self from a new, critical standpoint. Such a perspective, while it would insist on the self as site for politicization, would equally insist that simply describing one's experience of exploitation or oppression is not to become politicized. It is not sufficient to know the personal but to know—to speak it in a different way.'[13]

Listening to new sounds, speaking in a different way, manifesting the Formless. There would be no 'new', no 'different' possible if it were not for the Formless, which is the source of all forms. The belief that there can exist such a thing as an outside foreign to the inside, an objective, unmediated reality about which one can have knowledge once and for all, has been repeatedly challenged by feminist critics. For centuries, this belief has most perniciously served to reduce the world to the dominant's own image, and the fight against 'realism' is, in fact, not a denial of reality and of meaning, but rather, a determination to keep meaning creative, hence to challenge the fixity of realism as a style and an arrested form of representation. Claire Johnston argued in her famous essay on 'Women's Cinema As Counter-Cinema':

> Within a sexist ideology and a male-dominated cinema, woman is presented as what she represents for man . . . What the camera in fact grasps is the 'natural' world of the dominant ideology . . . Any revolutionary strategy must challenge the depiction of reality: it is not enough to discuss the oppression of women within the text of the film: the language of the cinema/the depiction of reality must also be interrogated, so that a break between ideology and text is affected.[14]

Realism as one form of representation defined by a specific attitude toward reality is widely validated to perpetuate the illusion of a stable world (even when it depicts sickness, poverty, and war), in which the same 'how-to-do's' are confidently standardized and prescribed for different realities. Gaps and cracks of the systems of filmmaking and filmviewing are carefully made invisible so that the flow of events can continue to provide the spectator with a sense of gradual, linear acquisition of knowledge. This is, in fact, the way the West has envisioned much of its art for centuries. If eighteenth-century Chinese artists used to judge Westerners' skill in engraved illustrations as 'nothing but artisanry' and their methods 'good only for catching likeness', the 'Chinese image' long remained an example of what the Western painter should avoid, since it was viewed as being deficient in three-dimensionality. It was not until the late nineteenth century, when the rejection of illusionism spread among artists of the West, that the non-illusionistic art of the Chinese started to 'make sense' to them. History abounds with instances where, for example, established representational devices used by early Europeans for picture-maps to display or isolate the object of study in its most readable and informative aspect, were adopted by the Chinese for purposes other than legibility and information. The illusionism of exactitude in representation and of three-dimensionality on a two-dimensional medium could hardly be what the Chinese would search for at the time, no matter how intrigued they could be with the European pictures. Not only did they consider the Europeans to be quite incapable of depicting landscape (rocks, trees, rivers, mountains, which demanded more than illusionistic technique), but they also did not accept these pictures as true representations of real scenes.[15] Imitation of the forms of nature (or rather the viewing of nature as arrested forms) had apparently little to do with manifestation of the *ch'i* and the Formless that is life or the source of all forms. In working with the sense of the unknown instead of repressing it, in bringing infinity within sight, traditional Chinese arts choose to suggest always *more than what they represent*. Thus, 'if one wishes to paint a high mountain, one should not paint every part, or it will not seem high; when mist and haze encircle its haunches, then it seems tall'.[16]

> The work of the mountain does not lie just with the mountain, but with its quiescence . . . the work of the water does not lie just with the water, but with its movement. Moreover, the work of antiquity does not lie with just antiquity, but with its freedom from error. The work of the present does not lie with just the present, but with its freedom.[17]

The Chinese are known to their neighbors (the Vietnamese, for example) as a strongly practical and realistic people. Realism in this context requires that life be intimately understood both in its flow and its temporary pauses or specific instances. To face reality squarely and sensitively, without positive or negative escapism, is to see 'the small in the large and the large in the small; the real in the illusory and the illusory in the real' (Shen-Fu). The idea of realism in art, and more particularly in realistically powerful media like photography and film, should be linked with the principle of life (and death) by which things, endowed with existential and spiritual force and never static, continue to grow, to change, to renew, and to move. The freedom implied in the internal and external projection of these 'landscapes of life' on canvas, on celluloid, or on screen, lies in the availability of mind—and heart—that declines to limit one's perception of things and events to their actual forms. Such freedom also allows for the fearless assumption of the hyphen—the fluid interplay of realistic and non-realistic modes of representation, or to quote a Chinese opera expert, of 'bold omissions and minute depictions'.[18]

Notes

1. Wen Yi Hou, 'Being in America', Master thesis. University of California San Diego, 1990, 1, 14–15.
2. Ezekiel Mphahlele, *The African Image* (New York: Praeger, 1962), 15.
3. Mphahlele, *The African Image*, 54.
4. Mai-mai Sze, *Echo of a Cry, A Story Which Began in China* (New York:

Harcourt Brace, 1945), 202; quoted in Amy Ling, *Between Worlds: Women Writers of Chinese Ancestry* (Elmsford, NY: Pergamon Press, 1990), 108.

5. Stella Wong, 'The Return', poem quoted in Russell Leong, 'Poetry Within Earshot', *Amerasia Journal* 15 (1989), 172.
6. Al Robles, 'Tagatac on Ifugao Mountain', quoted in *Amerasia Journal* 15(1989), 175.
7. 'Being in America', 27.
8. Andrei Tarkovsky, *Sculpting in Time: Reflections on the Cinema,* (trans. K. Hunter-Blair) (New York: Alfred A. Knopf, 1987). The quote from Mann is on p. 104; the rest is on p. 109.
9. In Earle J. Coleman, *Philosophy of Painting by Shih T'ao: A Translation and Exposition of his Hua-P'u* (New York: Mouton Publishers, 1978).
10. Tarkovsky's italics, *Sculpting In Time,* 104, 110.
11. Coleman, *Philosophy of Painting,* 15.
12. Homi Bhabha, 'The Other Question: Difference, Discrimination and The Discourse of Colonialism', in F. Baker *et al.* (eds.), *Literature, Politics and Theory* (London: Methuen, 1986), 163.
13. bell hooks, *Talking Back: Thinking Feminist, Thinking Black* (Boston, MA: South End Press, 1989), 107.
14. Claire Johnston, 'Women's Cinema As Counter-Cinema', in B. Nichols (ed.), *Movies and Methods: An Anthology,* Vol. 1 (Berkeley: University of California Press, 1976), 211, 214.
15. See James Cahill, *The Compelling Image* (Cambridge: Harvard University Press, 1982), 72, 74, 82, 96. The complexities of Cahill's discussion on the influences from Europe among Chinese artists cannot be conveyed in the few general lines I have written here.
16. Quoted in George Rowley, *Principles of Chinese Painting* (Princeton: Princeton University Press, 1947), 66.
17. Coleman, *Philosophy of Painting,* 142–3.
18. Huang Shang, *Tales from Peking Opera* (Beijing: New World Press, 1985), 7.

15 'Race', identity and cultural criticism

Lola Young*

[. . .] Here, I will elucidate the potential of black feminist cultural analyses and examine the absence of black women and the ways in which they may be considered as Other for both black men and white people. I go on to summarize why I have felt it necessary to embark on this project through an examination of how 'whiteness' is under-elaborated in cultural analysis. I then argue that white film-makers have continually constructed black women and men as Other and attempt to account for this using psychoanalytic theory. [. . .] The question of how the work of black film-makers might be addressed is discussed in some detail in order to clarify points about black subjectivities and cultural criticism. The final section suggests some further areas where critical debate and scholarly research would be of benefit in the development of this field of study.

THE WORK OF BLACK FEMINIST CRITICISM

One of the central concerns of this study has been to attempt to establish a conceptual framework for the study of racial difference in the cinema which is able to engage with issues of gender and sexuality. Crucially the impetus for discussing all the films has been the conspicuous lack of critical feminist voices prepared to consider colonialism's implication in the construction of notions of femininity and sexuality in British cinema. The separation of issues relating to 'race', gender and class and the privileging of one over another has contributed to the lack of attention to the points at which these politically

* From Lola Young, '"Race", Identity and Cultural Criticism' from *Fear of the Dark: 'Race', Gender and Sexuality in the Cinema* (Routledge, 1996), 175–192, reprinted by permission of the publisher.

constructed categories intersect. Although I have argued for a consideration of the interconnections of gender and 'race', I have not posited that there is any advantage to be gained from thinking of them as the same. The constant juxtaposition of gender, 'race' and class should not lead to a presumption that they are reducible to one another.

[. . .] Black feminists have consistently drawn attention to European history's construction of black women as hypersexual, or as desexualized characters, there to serve the interests of white women and men. In the field of visual culture, bell hooks and Michelle Wallace in particular have made constructive observations regarding white feminist cultural theorists' avoidance of discussing the specificities of racial privilege and subordination embedded in gender issues.[1]

Representations of white women have often served to support and legitimate the narcissistic illusion of the centrality of white masculine, middle-class identity through their acceptance of patriarchal/heterosexual conventions and lifestyles. A critical perspective which analyses the role of white women in terms of their ethnicity as well as their gender would give fresh insight into their instrumentality in such texts. It is the case that where white feminists have analysed the socio-sexual colonial matrix, they have emphasized the similarity of their positioning by white men, with that of black or 'primitive' people. They have stopped short of more detailed analysis of their relative power and shifting status within that matrix. [. . .] It has not been my intention to construct a hierarchy of oppression but to suggest that a more reflective critical practice needs to be developed in order to analyse the complex ways in which these systems of oppression may be destabilized.

One aspect of the dominant form of white feminism which is important in regard to black women's absence from cinematic representation is the continued use of the 'dark continent' trope, the metaphorical status of which serves to naturalize a whole set of ideas about Africa, its inhabitants and its diaspora. For example, Mary Ann Doane (1991),[2] although she problematizes the term, continues to use it in a way which perpetuates its mythic status. Similarly, Ella Shohat (1991)[3] points to the ways in which the term elides the land and the people and ascribes the 'dark continent' and its peoples hypersymbolic status. This is an important point to reiterate since I argue that there has been white feminist overinvestment in the gender component of the 'dark continent', which has resulted in the virtual elimination of the racial and colonial implications. Thus this most racialized of sexual metaphors has become synonymous with the concerns of white women.

Particular importance in this study has been accorded to the way in which European history has constructed black female sexuality and femininity, characterizing women of African descent as 'lacking' those 'feminine' qualities which have been attributed to white European women. The function of both black and white women in cinema is most often sexualized, and for each of them, their representational status is frequently that of repositories for the continuation of their respective 'races'. For black women, conventional patriarchal and Eurocentric notions of femininity have been particularly problematic. This stems from being doubly inscribed with Otherness, as black and female.

[. . .] When it comes to black male productions, audiences are presented with scenarios which regard the male expression of oppression and political resistance as being the representative black experience. This black masculinist view of the problematic position of black women is also evident in Fanon's *Black Skin, White Masks* (1986). In this psychoanalytic account of the processes which contribute to Negrophilia and Negrophobia, it is evident that Fanon concentrates on male experiences. Indeed, echoing Freud's 'dark continent' comment in relation to white women, Fanon confesses that he knows little about black women's psychosexuality.[4] The chapters in *Black Skin, White Masks* which discuss 'The Woman of Color and the White Man' and 'The Man of Color and the White Woman' attribute quite different significance to the relations foregrounded in the titles. The 'woman of colour' is said to be motivated by self-hatred, and by a contempt of black people in general, and of black men in particular; she is greedy, wishing to deny her social and racial origins in exchange for social and economic status. On the other hand, black men's sexual relationships with white women are represented as political acts, stealing and tainting the white woman—conceptualized purely in terms of her status as the white man's possession—as an act of revenge on white men. [. . .] Thus black women, due to the disturbance they provoke, remain cinematically peripheral.

In the white-authored texts considered here, I have pointed out that white men derive their status from their assumed superior relation to black men: white women may be used to confirm this status and to emphasize their heterosexuality. Where black women have been portrayed by white film-makers in Britain, the black woman is frequently sexualized, objectified and associated with both the primal and the inappropriately oversophisticated (meaning overcivilized). The latter is signified [. . .] in *Mona Lisa* (1986) through Simone's use of stockings, corsets, whips and so on. She is designated the origin of perverse forms of sexual behaviour . . . There is a sense in which Sister Louise in *Pressure* (1974) may be included here because of her involvement in male-dominated politics and her seduction of the much younger, and sexually naive Tony.

Within a supremacist representational schema, black women are marginal. Unlike black men, black women represent no *present* threat to established hierarchies of privilege, since black women have so little political and social power; however, black women represent a *potential* threat, a danger yet to come since they—because of their responsibility in continuing the black 'race'—carry the future dissidents against subordinate status. Unlike white middle-class women whose 'capture' confers prestige on the 'captor', black women's sexual and racial Otherness has only exotic or economic value for white men. The question of desire across racial lines is then difficult to broach since it entails relinquishing so much.

[. . .] In their texts, black male directors and writers seem to have found it difficult to accord black women economic independence, autonomy or agency without problematizing their status as mothers or as politicized black individuals. Where black women are present in British films they are portrayed by white film-makers as victims, purveyors of transgressive sexuality or emblematic silent bystanders, and as politically naive and assimilationist by black male directors and writers: most frequently, though they are marginal or absent. Black male film-makers, in resisting the hegemony of middle-class white men, should not seek to relocate that hegemony elsewhere, but to work towards gender equity within their cultural practices.

Black feminists' interrogations of black male prerogative in defining black subjectivity and the identification of masculinist analyses of the struggle for political and social autonomy and freedom have been crucial in critiquing essentialist notions of blackness. I would not wish to claim that only black women have the authority to advance understanding of the complexities of 'race', sexuality and gender in cultural forms, but I do think it is necessary for black women to assert themselves in the academy as elsewhere. Due to the cultural constructions of gender and racial differences, attitudinal differences do occur in terms of what are seen as the priorities for critical attention and analysis. Although nothing is guaranteed by the presence of black women film-makers or critics, it is important for them to be empowered to make more interventions in the construction and criticism of images in Britain.

RACIAL IDENTITIES, REPRESENTATION AND CULTURAL ANALYSIS: THE SUBJECT OF SILENCE

White identity has managed to assume a normativeness which has left it underinterrogated and part of what I have been concerned with here has been to indicate the extent to which constructions of notions of whiteness are available for analysis in a variety of films. In regard to contemporary cultural practices, Cornel West has identified the need to defamiliarize whiteness as an important political project and he urges that black cultural critics:

> must investigate and interrogate the other of Blackness–Whiteness. One cannot deconstruct the binary oppositional logic of images of Blackness without extending it to the contrary condition of Blackness/Whiteness itself . . . what is needed [is] to examine and *explain* the historically specific ways in which 'Whiteness' is a politically constructed category parasitic on 'Blackness'.[5]

Indicated here is the way in which analyses of racial and cultural identity have come to revolve around 'blackness' as the object of fascination leaving unspoken issues of differentiated white ethnicities. Having argued against essentialist positions in regard to questions of 'race' and subjectivity, I would say that it is necessary for white cultural critics to address the ways in which questions of ethnicity and racial difference are structured into texts and their analyses. However, it is especially important for black people to become involved in the analysis of media and culture and to produce knowledge and cultural theory in order to challenge the hegemony of white and male critics.

In her discussion of 'Whiteness as Absent Centre', Claire Pajaczkowska has indicated that the 'emotional state produced by denial is one of blankness' and it is this blankness which helps to sustain White identity as normal and as undefined.[6] The blankness at the centre of the denial of racism, colonialism and imperialism serves to obscure a set of contradictory actions and fantasies which are often unconscious, and are manifested in the representations created of the African Other: representations which are the projections of the 'good' and 'bad' split off parts of the self. This blankness of whiteness is the consequence of an identity without a centre since its existence acquires meaning only because of its relationship with the Other. Acknowledging how the idea of blackness constructs the idea of whiteness, just as the notion of femininity assists in the construction of the idea of masculinity is a small but significant step in demystifying those processes. [. . .]

Being dependent or 'parasitic' on the notion of Otherness for a conceptualization of the self is problematic for both self and Other. The recognition of the self in the Other remains at root an alienated identity, an 'identity-in-Otherness'. Self-determination is a precondition for self-recognition or self-conscious identity. This assertion of self-determination may be thought to require that the Other—literally the Other's otherness—be negated or cancelled. Where this 'identity-in-the-Other' is racially predicated or defined by racialized discourses, the drive to self-consciousness may result in the negation or reduction of the racial Other, the Other's exclusion.[7]

There is a long historical tradition of black people being constituted by whites as:

> the fantasy of a fantasy—not cold, pure, clean, efficient, industrious, frugal, rational (that is, not the pantheon of anal-negative ego traits which are the *summum bonum* of the bourgeois order) but rather warm, dirty, sloppy, feckless, lazy, improvident and irrational, all those traits that are associated with Blackness, odor and sensuality.[8]

These fantasies which emerge from the psychical mechanisms of repression and projection are recognized at a popular, common sense level by many black people who see themselves as 'scapegoats' for white society's problems which arise regarding, for example, housing, crime and unemployment.

Those who embody Otherness and difference are often the focus for the projection of white societies' rages, fears and anxieties. [. . .] For those whose relationship to Africa is a textual one, the knowledge and information gained not only from films and television but also from school history and geography books, anthropological discourses and other colonialist perspectives will have a cumulative effect on their perceptions of racial Otherness.

I have shown how, in many white-authored films . . . there are elements of centuries old racialized discourses comprised of a set of assumptions about black people: black male sexuality as a threat to white womanhood and cultural superiority; black intellectual inferiority and fecklessness; and, derived from that, unmotivated irrational behaviour as the natural state of blackness. I have argued that in many white film-makers' depictions of black people there are sets of values and attitudes towards 'race' and sexuality which have their roots in long-established ideologies. The traces of these ideologies are evident in film texts where black people are annihilated, criminalized and labelled as sexually deviant, and where sexual behaviour is monitored and regulated. The perceived threat is consistently contained or diminished by rendering black people invisible, infantile, desexualized or by eliminating black subjects from texts altogether. [. . .]

BLACK FILM, THEORY AND CULTURAL CRITICISM

The shift in ways of conceptualizing black identity has been a crucial component of discussions about black cultural production. During the 1980s, debates about black people, representation and history centered around absences and invisibility, and cultural activists sought to redress imbalances by rewriting the histories through both practical and theoretical work.[9] This critique has consisted not only of pointing out and coming to terms with absences, it has also consisted of evaluations of the ways in which black people have been made visible and in particular how media discursive practices have been a major component in determining and defining the 'problem' of blackness. For black film-makers, struggling against such representations, the perceived necessity for creating 'accurate' images is understandable.

Through the construction of a black identity which has as its reference points the cultures of both the colonized and the colonizer, one textual strategy has been to create characters which appear to conform to white European stereotypes but which may also be read as a set of masculine identities designed to be the antithesis of white male propriety. [. . .]

To a significant extent, black identities in Britain have been adopted as modes of resistant self-identification and political affiliation in order to counter the hegemony of Eurocentrism and racist ideologies and practices relating to difference. For black film-makers, identity—as structured through the experience of the subordination and inferiorization of colonialism—is an important issue. The mode of discussing identity and blackness has developed in ways which can be differentiated from those associated with whiteness.

Defining identity as being a coherent sense of self, both on an individual and group level, it is the threat of that dissolution of self-constructed identity which fuels racial supremacy, homophobia and misogyny. Identity is about having a sense of belonging, about recognizing what 'we' have in common with some people and what differentiates 'us' from others. This may be an identity constructed in order to fit in with the demands of a particular community but none the less, it retains a potency which is continually exploited by those who have a stake in the maintenance of absolutist notions of ethnicity and racial authenticity. The feelings of 'belongingness' which develop as a result of these group identifications may well be illusory since individual identities are not necessarily fixed or consistent, and there are occasions when the different aspects of individual subjectivities are in conflict with each other. The relationship between 'our' constructed group or cultural identity and those of 'Others' is often one in which the realities of that other group's experiences and cultural values seem to be 'alien' to 'our' own.

In his analysis of xenophobia, Memmi points to the interdependence of the subjective positions constructed through the prism of colonialism.[10] However, as a direct relationship between diaspora peoples and the experience of colonialism recedes, to what extent do issues of identity need to be reconceptualized? The idea of diaspora is one which is made from fragments of identity derived from a colonial construction, so where does that leave the notion of a diaspora aesthetic? Again, the necessity of opposition in the first instance is shaped and formed by the experience of marginality and the discourse is developed in direct relation to its opposite. It should be remembered that it was globalized racism which created the necessity for the supranational flag of diaspora and cultural nationalism.

As I have argued throughout, white people have seen the black Other as an object of and for investigation, and the subject of 'race' relations discourse. In contrast to the effacement and naturalizing of their ethnic location by white film-makers, black cultural practitioners have continually examined their position as specifically black subjects within white cultures. Black film-makers' constant self-analysis and the investment in carrying out such analyses begins to explain the intensity of debates about black film within black communities and the desire to construct and develop critical and interpretive frameworks such as Third Cinema and post-colonial critiques.[11] An important point to consider here is the extent to which the field itself has become a significant aspect of the cultural and critical life of Britain; black culture has become less marginal, more self-confident, more clear about the need to articulate self-determined critical analysis. There has been no equivalent theoretical debate regarding racial identities amongst white film-makers and theorists in this country. Thus, there is a sense in which black film may be placed as a discrete practice in British cinema as is suggested by the title of ICA Document 7, *Black Film, British Cinema*, since there is a marked difference in approach to the issue of racialized identities. This difference is centred around how black and white people have located themselves ethnically.

Some of the fiercest debates about black cultural politics and artistic expression have centred on the appropriateness or otherwise of what are characterized as Eurocentric textual strategies and modes of analysis. The approach used in this study has been to attempt to modify what are often casually referred to as 'Eurocentric' theories of culture by recasting them through the prism of 'race'. I have not advocated a refusal of theories the provenance of which is Europe in favour of an Afrocentric mode of analysis. The position which regards black cultural 'authenticity' as a desirable objective raises the question of racial essentialism. [. . .] Anti-essentialist critical interventions should provide more insight than those which exclusively privilege class, 'race', gender or sexual orientation because they avoid the fixity of monolithic essentializing critical discourses, and are able to analyse the interconnections and 'dialogic strategies'. [. . .]

CONCLUSION

Cultural production, the dissemination of historical information and the pursuit of knowledge in Western Europe should be understood and analysed within a framework which recognizes the centrality of racial difference in the construction of colonial and post-colonial black and white identities. The small number of critical accounts of British cinema which have addressed racial concerns have tended to privilege 'race' without adequately exploring or indicating the place of gender, sexuality and class. With regard to the latter, although I have attempted to draw attention to the ways in which class is implicated in the interactions depicted on screen, I am aware that this analysis has been uneven. [. . .]

During the course of this study, I have referred to both African-American and white North American cultural theorists and critics although I have voiced some reservations about the applicability of some of the work. Such 'cultural borrowings' are inevitable given that much of the work on images of blackness and whiteness has been focused on North American cinema. The vastness of the North American film industry, North America's cultural centrality, the burgeoning African-American feminist literature, and the development of African-American and black British diasporic sensibilities have also contributed to it being necessary to rely on a black North American input. Increasingly though, the differences in approach and in historical circumstances in regard to racism and colonialism have become apparent and whilst I do think it both necessary and productive to draw on cultural criticism from the USA, it is desirable that a feminist praxis that recognizes the specificity of British experiences be nurtured. This would involve going beyond the basic thinking of black women as the victims of white and male oppressors to considering when and how images of black women are used and the ways that they are implicitly and explicitly contrasted with white women. It would also entail thinking in more detail about how white women's and men's racial identity may be coded or unconsciously structured into a text, when there are few or no significant black characters present.

Given black women's central role as economic linchpins in the development of western Eurocapitalism—as producers, as 'breeders', as labourers, as wet-nurses and so on—black women's actual presence and significance cannot easily be cast aside. Yet it is still the case that few films give prominent roles to women of African descent in either North American or British cinema. The potentially transgressive seductions between men, between white man and black woman, and black woman and white woman are not realized in most mainstream narratives. As previously indicated, there has long been an association between 'race' and sex and it is notable that sexual relationships between black and white people are still rarely openly discussed on film: the subject still arouses fierce debate and controversy in both black and white communities and this is reflected in the content and treatment of the issue in films by both blacks and whites. The avoidance of serious, reflective discussions about such relationships generally is underlined by the prohibitions associated with overt interracial sexuality on film. It seems that interracial sexual activity is still contentious in a racist society: if the sexual activity is homoerotic and interracial, then it is virtually unspeakable. The prohibition of this aspect of sexual behaviour is reflected in the absence or superficial nature of portrayals of such relationships on the screen. Two recent examples of exceptions to the interdiction on interracial homosexual relationships are *My Beautiful Launderette* (1985), and *Young Soul Rebels* (1991).

Ideas about racial and sexual difference have long been a part of British intellectual thought. There are other factors which come into play, not least those of class, and sexual orientation and expression which make for a complex matrix of possibilities of interaction. Whatever the basis on which discussions about identity or cultural diversity are made it is the question of the distribution of power with which we have to grapple, together with an understanding of how cultural politics are articulated through and with the everyday politics of the distribution of power, of everyday injustice and racism. In the face of the escalation of reactionary political forces, and the continuation of racism and fascism which represent dangerous threats to the development of progressive social forces, people need cultural practices which question and stimulate. Proposing that the conventions or signifying practices of film be changed is not in itself an adequate strategy since spectators' existing belief systems may still restrict their perceptions. There needs to be a multiplicity of discursive practices which serve to disrupt the stability of deeply held beliefs, and a continual public and social questioning of imagery and representations to which people have become habitualized. [. . .]

As regards audiences, how the desires of black viewers may or may not differ in absolute terms from those of white audiences, or how this concept of 'black spectatorship' might be fractured or differentiated along class, gender and generational lines, is just beginning to be investigated within British cultural studies. Questions of audience are marginalized from much theoretical work on black film, so the matter of pleasure and identification become peripheral: there is also the question of mainstream, popular cinema and black audiences' relation to that, not to mention televisual forms.

The material conditions in which films are produced also need to be considered, not as apologies for poor work but in order to be able to understand adequately how a text acquires meaning in the context in which it is produced and consumed. Also the possibilities of realist strategies as radical interventions should be broached. Of course a politics of deconstruction seeks to challenge the validity and dominance of particular ways of making sense which exclude and marginalize other forms: none the less there has to be a recognition of the pleasures afforded by realism and Hollywood-style cinema [. . .]

Despite the eagerness to subscribe to post-structuralist accounts of reality, it is necessary to retain a grasp on social/material reality, which is, after all, what most people live by. Viewers bring to texts their personal and cultural knowledge which mediates their perception of the 'reality' depicted on screen. Even if it is accepted that there is no direct access to that which is called 'the real', that there is nothing outside discourse or representation, it is still the case that many texts encourage conclusions about historical events and particular issues. The struggles over representation and the demand for positive images to counteract the debilitating effects of negative ones is grounded in everyday experience of the reality of racism, sexism, homophobia, notions of 'perfect' bodies and so on.

In regard to black film, I would argue that the deployment of discursive practices which speak of the 'reality' of lived experience is legitimate as a strategy for documenting events, perspectives and perceptions. Such forms articulate the concerns of many black people for whom the reconstruction of the past and the structuring of the present seems to necessitate a certain amount of mythmaking.

I have argued that examining texts for negative and positive images is not in itself the most productive model for attempting to understand images since such analyses are unable to address adequately the complex processes which occur at the sites of the production and consumption of images of blackness and whiteness. It is, however, still necessary to examine images in racialized terms whilst noting the necessity for a continued interrogation of the binary oppositions of black and white. To deny that blackness and whiteness still have significance as ontological symbols is to deny the existence of the many ways that racism operates in contemporary British society.

The production of arts and culture in Britain is structurally inscribed with questions of racism and sexism, discrimination, domination and subordination, forged in the period of colonialism. Thus, all such work is inscribed with questions of power. The power relations embedded in the right to look or not to be looked at constitute the politics of cultural production and ensure that film-making and the resulting critical work is a crucial political activity.

Notes

1. bell hooks, *Yearnings: Race, Gender, and Cultural Politics* (London: Turnaround, 1991); and *Black Looks: Race and Representation* (London: Turnaround, 1992); Wallace, 1993.
2. Mary Ann Doane, *Femmes Fatales: Feminism, Film Theory, Psychoanalysis* (New York: Routledge, 1991).
3. Ella Shohat, 'Gender and the Culture of Empire: Toward a Feminist Ethnography of the Cinema', *Quarterly Review of Film and Video* 13 (1991), 45–84.
4. F. Fanon, *Black Skin, White Masks* (transl. C. L. Markmann) (London: Pluto Press, 1986), 177. Originally published in 1952.
5. Cornel West, 'The New Cultural Politics of Difference', in R. Ferguson *et al.* (eds.), *Out There: Marginalization and Contemporary Culture* (New York: New Museum of Contemporary Art, 1990), 29.
6. C. Pajaczkowska and L. Young, 'Racism, Representation, Psychoanalysis', in J.

Donald and A. Rattansi, *'Race', Culture and Difference* (London: Sage, 1992), 202.

7. D. T. Goldberg, *Racist Culture: Philosophy and the Politics of Meaning* (Cambridge, MA: Blackwell, 1993), 59.
8. J. Kovel, *White Racism: A Psychohistory* (London: Free Association Books, 1988), 61.
9. L. Young, 'Identity, Realism and Black Photography', in M. Sealy (ed.), *Vanley Burke: A Retrospective* (London: Lawrence and Wishart, 1993), 80.
10. A. Memmi, *The Colonizer and the Colonized* (transl. H. Greenfield) (London: Earthscan Publications, 1990), 196–7. Originally published in 1957.
11. It should be noted that each of these books refers to films made in the USA.

16 The Social Construction of Black Feminist Thought

Patricia Hill Collins*

Sojourner Truth, Anna Julia Cooper, Ida Wells Barnett, and Fannie Lou Hamer are but a few names from a growing list of distinguished African-American women activists. Although their sustained resistance to Black women's victimization within interlocking systems of race, gender, and class oppression is well known, these women did not act alone.[1] Their actions were nurtured by the support of countless, ordinary African-American women who, through strategies of everyday resistance, created a powerful foundation for this more visible Black feminist activist tradition.[2] Such support has been essential to the shape and goals of Black feminist thought.

The long-term and widely shared resistance among African-American women can only have been sustained by an enduring and shared standpoint among Black women about the meaning of oppression and the actions that Black women can and should take to resist it. Efforts to identify the central concepts of this Black women's standpoint figure prominently in the works of contemporary Black feminist intellectuals.[3] Moreover, political and epistemological issues influence the social construction of Black feminist thought. Like other subordinate groups, African-American women not only have developed distinctive interpretations of Black women's oppression but have done so by using alternative ways of producing and validating knowledge itself.

Special thanks go out to the following people for reading various drafts of this manuscript: Evelyn Nakano Glenn, Lynn Weber Cannon, and participants in the 1986 Research Institute, Center for Research on Women, Memphis State University; Elsa Barkley Brown, Deborah K. King, Elizabeth V. Spelman, and Angelene Jamison-Hall; and four anonymous reviewers at *Signs*.

* From Patricia Hill Collins, 'The Social Construction of Black Feminist Thought' from *Signs* 14:4 (The University of Chicago Press, 1989), 745–73, reprinted by permission of the publisher.

A BLACK WOMEN'S STANDPOINT

The Foundation of Black Feminist Thought

Black women's everyday acts of resistance challenge two prevailing approaches to studying the consciousness of oppressed groups.[4] One approach claims that subordinate groups identify with the powerful and have no valid independent interpretation of their own oppression.[5] The second approach assumes that the oppressed are less human than their rulers and, therefore, are less capable of articulating their own standpoint.[6] Both approaches see any independent consciousness expressed by an oppressed group as being not of the group's own making and/or inferior to the perspective of the dominant group.[7] More important, both interpretations suggest that oppressed groups lack the motivation for political activism because of their flawed consciousness of their own subordination.

Yet African-American women have been neither passive victims of nor willing accomplices to their own domination. As a result, emerging work in Black women's studies contends that Black women have a self-defined standpoint on their own oppression.[8] Two interlocking components characterize this standpoint. First, Black women's political and economic status provides them with a distinctive set of experiences that offers a different view of material reality than that available to other groups. The unpaid and paid work that Black women perform, the types of communities in which they live, and the kinds of relationships they have with others suggest that African-American women, as a group, experience a different world than those who are not Black and female.[9] Second, these experiences stimulate a distinctive Black feminist consciousness concerning that material reality.[10] In brief, a subordinate group not only experiences a different reality than a group that rules, but a subordinate group may interpret that reality differently than a dominant group.

Many ordinary African-American women have grasped this connection between what one does and how one thinks. Hannah Nelson, an elderly Black domestic worker, discusses how work shapes the standpoints of African-American and white women: 'Since I have to work, I don't really have to worry about most of the things that most of the white women I have worked for are worrying about. And if these women did their own work, they would think just like I do—

about this, anyway.'[11] [. . .] While an oppressed group's experiences may put them in a position to see things differently, their lack of control over the apparatuses of society that sustain ideological hegemony makes the articulation of their self-defined standpoint difficult. Groups unequal in power are correspondingly unequal in their access to the resources necessary to implement their perspectives outside their particular group.

One key reason that standpoints of oppressed groups are discredited and suppressed by the more powerful is that self-defined standpoints can stimulate oppressed groups to resist their domination. [. . .]

The Significance of Black Feminist Thought

The existence of a distinctive Black women's standpoint does not mean that it has been adequately articulated in Black feminist thought. [. . .] Black feminist thought's potential significance goes far beyond demonstrating that Black women can produce independent, specialized knowledge. Such thought can encourage collective identity by offering Black women a different view of themselves and their world than that offered by the established social order. This different view encourages African-American women to value their own subjective knowledge base.[12] By taking elements and themes of Black women's culture and traditions and infusing them with new meaning, Black feminist thought rearticulates a consciousness that already exists.[13] More important, this rearticulated consciousness gives African-American women another tool of resistance to all forms of their subordination.[14]

Black feminist thought, then, specializes in formulating and rearticulating the distinctive, self-defined standpoint of African-American women. One approach to learning more about a Black women's standpoint is to consult standard scholarly sources for the ideas of specialists on Black women's experiences.[15] But investigating a Black women's standpoint and Black feminist thought requires more ingenuity than that required in examining the standpoints and thought of white males. Rearticulating the standpoint of African-American women through Black feminist thought is much more difficult since one cannot use the same techniques to study the knowledge of the dominated as one uses to study the knowledge of the powerful. This is precisely because subordinate groups have long had to use alternative ways to create an independent consciousness and to rearticulate it through specialists validated by the oppressed themselves.

THE EUROCENTRIC MASCULINIST KNOWLEDGE-VALIDATION PROCESS[16]

All social thought, including white masculinist and Black feminist, reflects the interests and standpoint of its creators. [. . .] Two political criteria influence the knowledge-validation process. First, knowledge claims must be evaluated by a community of experts whose members represent the standpoints of the groups from which they originate. Second, each community of experts must maintain its credibility as defined by the larger group in which it is situated and from which it draws its basic, taken-for-granted knowledge.

When white males control the knowledge-validation process, both political criteria can work to suppress Black feminist thought. [. . .] The experiences of African-American women scholars illustrate how individuals who wish to rearticulate a Black women's standpoint through Black feminist thought can be suppressed by a white-male-controlled knowledge-validation process. Exclusion from basic literacy, quality educational experiences, and faculty and administrative positions has limited Black women's access to influential academic positions.[17] Thus, while Black women can produce knowledge claims that contest those advanced by the white male community, this community does not grant that Black women scholars have competing knowledge claims based in another knowledge-validation process. As a consequence, any credentials controlled by white male academicians can be denied to Black women producing Black feminist thought on the grounds that it is not credible research.

Those Black women with academic credentials who seek to exert the authority that their status grants them to propose new knowledge claims about African-American women face pressures to use their authority to help legitimate a system that devalues and excludes the majority of Black women.[18] One way of excluding the majority of Black women from the knowledge-validation process is to permit a few Black women to acquire positions of authority in institutions that legitimate knowledge and to encourage them to work within the taken-for-granted assumptions of Black female inferiority shared by the scholarly community and the culture at large. Those Black women who accept these assumptions are likely to be rewarded by their institutions, often at significant personal cost. Those challenging the assumptions run the risk of being ostracized.

African-American women academicians who persist in trying to rearticulate a Black women's standpoint also face potential rejection of their knowledge claims on epistemological grounds. Just as the material realities of the powerful and the dominated produce separate standpoints, each group may also have distinctive epistemologies or theories of knowledge. It is my contention that Black female scholars may know that something is true but be unwilling or unable to legitimate their claims using Eurocentric masculinist criteria for consistency with substantiated knowledge and Eurocentric masculinist criteria for methodological adequacy. [. . .]

THE CONTOURS OF AN AFROCENTRIC FEMINIST EPISTEMOLOGY

Africanist analyses of the Black experience generally agree on the fundamental elements of an Afrocentric standpoint. In spite of varying histories, Black societies reflect elements of a core African value system that existed prior to and independently of racial oppression.[19] Moreover, as a result of colonialism, imperialism, slavery, apartheid, and other systems of racial domination, Blacks share a common experience of oppression. These similarities in material conditions have fostered shared Afrocentric values that permeate the family structure, religious institutions, culture, and community life of Blacks in varying parts of Africa, the Caribbean, South America, and North America.[20] This Afrocentric consciousness permeates the shared history of people of African descent through the framework of a distinctive Afrocentric epistemology.[21]

Feminist scholars advance a similar argument. They assert that women share a history of patriarchal oppression through the political economy of the material conditions of sexuality and reproduction.[22] These shared material conditions are thought to transcend divisions among women created by race, social class, religion, sexual orientation, and ethnicity and to form the basis of a women's standpoint with its corresponding feminist consciousness and epistemology.[23]

Since Black women have access to both the Afrocentric and the feminist standpoints, an alternative epistemology used to rearticulate a

Black women's standpoint reflects elements of both traditions.[24] [. . .] The parallels between the two conceptual schemes raise a question: Is the worldview of women of African descent more intensely infused with the overlapping feminine/Afrocentric standpoints than is the case for either African-American men or white women?[25] While an Afrocentric feminist epistemology reflects elements of epistemologies used by Blacks as a group and women as a group, it also paradoxically demonstrates features that may be unique to Black women. On certain dimensions, Black women may more closely resemble Black men, on others, white women, and on still others, Black women may stand apart from both groups. Black feminist sociologist Deborah K. King describes this phenomenon as a 'both/or' orientation, the act of being simultaneously a member of a group and yet standing apart from it. [. . .] Bonnie Thornton Dill's analysis of how Black women live with contradictions, a situation she labels the 'dialectics of Black womanhood', parallels King's assertions that this 'both/or' orientation is central to an Afrocentric feminist consciousness.[26] Rather than emphasizing how a Black women's standpoint and its accompanying epistemology are different than those in Afrocentric and feminist analyses, I use Black women's experiences as a point of contact between the two.

Viewing an Afrocentric feminist epistemology in this way challenges analyses claiming that Black women have a more accurate view of oppression than do other groups. [. . .]

African-American women do not uniformly share an Afrocentric feminist epistemology since social class introduces variations among Black women in seeing, valuing, and using Afrocentric feminist perspectives. While a Black women's standpoint and its accompanying epistemology stem from Black women's consciousness of race and gender oppression, they are not simply the result of combining Afrocentric and female values—standpoints are rooted in real material conditions structured by social class.[27]

Concrete Experience as a Criterion of Meaning

Carolyn Chase, a thirty-one-year-old inner city Black woman, notes, 'My aunt used to say, "A heap see, but a few know."'[28] This saying depicts two types of knowing, knowledge and wisdom, and taps the first dimension of an Afrocentric feminist epistemology. Living life as Black women requires wisdom since knowledge about the dynamics of race, gender, and class subordination has been essential to Black women's survival. African-American women give such wisdom high credence in assessing knowledge. [. . .]

Black women need wisdom to know how to deal with the 'educated fools' who would 'take a shotgun to a roach'. As members of a subordinate group, Black women cannot afford to be fools of any type, for their devalued status denies them the protections that white skin, maleness, and wealth confer. This distinction between knowledge and wisdom, and the use of experience as the cutting edge dividing them, has been key to Black women's survival. In the context of race, gender, and class oppression, the distinction is essential since knowledge without wisdom is adequate for the powerful, but wisdom is essential to the survival of the subordinate.

For ordinary African-American women, those individuals who have lived through the experiences about which they claim to be experts are more believable and credible than those who have merely read or thought about such experiences. Thus, concrete experience as a criterion for credibility frequently is invoked by Black women when making knowledge claims.

[. . .] Even after substantial mastery of white masculinist epistemologies, many Black women scholars invoke their own concrete experiences and those of other Black women in selecting topics for investigation and methodologies used. For example, Elsa Barkley Brown subtitles her essay on Black women's history, 'how my mother taught me to be an historian in spite of my academic training'.[29] Similarly, Joyce Ladner maintains that growing up as a Black woman in the South gave her special insights in conducting her study of Black adolescent women.[30]

[. . .] June Jordan's essay about her mother's suicide exemplifies the multiple levels of meaning that can occur when concrete experiences are used as a criterion of meaning. Jordan describes her mother, a woman who literally died trying to stand up, and the effect that her mother's death had on her own work:

> I think all of this is really about women and work. Certainly this is all about me as a woman and my life work. I mean I am not sure my mother's suicide was something extraordinary. Perhaps most women must deal with a similar inheritance, the legacy of a woman whose death you cannot possibly pinpoint because she died so many, many times and because, even before she became your mother, the life of that woman was taken . . . I came too late to help my mother to her feet. By way of everlasting thanks to all of the women who have helped me to stay alive I am working never to be late again.[31]

While Jordan has knowledge about the concrete act of her mother's death, she also strives for wisdom concerning the meaning of that death.

[. . .] In valuing the concrete, African-American women may be invoking not only an Afrocentric tradition, but a women's tradition as well. Some feminist theorists suggest that women are socialized in complex relational nexuses where contextual rules take priority over abstract principles in governing behaviour. This socialization process is thought to stimulate characteristic ways of knowing.[32] For example, Canadian sociologist Dorothy Smith maintains that two modes of knowing exist, one located in the body and the space it occupies and the other passing beyond it. She asserts that women, through their child-rearing and nurturing activities, mediate these two modes and use the concrete experiences of their daily lives to assess more abstract knowledge claims.[33]

[. . .] Many Black women intellectuals invoke the relationships and connectedness provided by use of dialogue. When asked why she chose the themes she did, novelist Gayle Jones replied: 'I was . . . interested . . . in oral traditions of storytelling—Afro-American and others, in which there is always the consciousness and importance of the hearer.'[34] In describing the difference in the way male and female writers select significant events and relationships, Jones points out that 'with many women writers, relationships within family, community, between men and women, and among women—from slave narratives by black women writers on—are treated as complex and significant relationships, whereas with many men the significant relationships are those that involve confrontations—relationships outside the family and community.'[35]

[. . .] Their centrality in Black churches and Black extended families provides Black women with a high degree of support from Black institutions for invoking dialogue as a dimension of an Afrocentric feminist epistemology. However, when African-American women use dialogues in assessing knowledge claims, they might be invoking a particularly female way of knowing as well. Feminist scholars contend that males and females are socialized within their families to seek different types of autonomy, the former based on separation, the latter seeking connectedness, and that this variation in types of autonomy parallels the characteristic differences between male and female ways of knowing.[36] For instance, in contrast to the visual metaphors (such as equating knowledge with illumination, knowing with seeing, and truth with light) that scientists and philosophers typically use, women tend to ground their epistemological premises in metaphors suggesting speaking and listening.[37]

While there are significant differences between the roles Black women play in their families and those played by middle-class white women, Black women clearly are affected by general cultural norms prescribing certain familial roles for women. Thus, in terms of the role of dialogue in an Afrocentric feminist epistemology, Black women may again experience a convergence of the values of the African-American community and woman-centered values.

The Ethic of Caring

'Ole white preachers used to talk wid dey tongues widdout sayin' nothin', but Jesus told us slaves to talk wid our hearts.'[38] These words of an ex-slave suggest that ideas cannot be divorced from the individuals who create and share them. This theme of 'talking with the heart' taps another dimension of an alternative epistemology used by African-American women, the ethic of caring. Just as the ex-slave used the wisdom in his heart to reject the ideas of the preachers who talked 'wid dey tongues widdout sayin' nothin',' the ethic of caring suggests that personal expressiveness, emotions, and empathy are central to the knowledge-validation process.

One of three interrelated components making up the ethic of caring is the emphasis placed on individual uniqueness. Rooted in a tradition of African humanism, each individual is thought to be a unique expression of a common spirit, power, or energy expressed by all life.[39] This belief in individual uniqueness is illustrated by the value placed on personal expressiveness in African-American communities.[40] [. . .]

A second component of the ethic of caring concerns the appropriateness of emotions in dialogues. Emotion indicates that a speaker believes in the validity of an argument.[41] Consider Ntozake Shange's description of one of the goals of her work: 'Our [Western] society allows people to be absolutely neurotic and totally out of touch with their feelings and everyone else's feelings, and yet be very respectable. This, to me, is a travesty . . . I'm trying to change the idea of seeing emotions and intellect as distinct faculties.'[42] Shange's words echo those of the ex-slave. Both see the denigration of emotion as problematic, and both suggest that expressiveness should be reclaimed and valued.

A third component of the ethic of caring involves developing the capacity for empathy. Harriet Jones, a sixteen-year-old Black woman, explains why she chose to open up to her interviewer: 'Some things in my life are so hard for me to bear, and it makes me feel better to know that you feel sorry about those things and would change them if you could.'[43]

These three components of the ethic of caring—the value placed on individual expressiveness, the appropriateness of emotions, and the capacity for empathy—pervade African-American culture. One of the best examples of the interactive nature of the importance of dialogue and the ethic of caring in assessing knowledge claims occurs in the use of the call and response discourse mode in traditional Black church services. In such services, both the minister and the congregation routinely use voice rhythm and vocal inflection to convey meaning. The sound of what is being said is just as important as the words themselves in what is, in a sense, a dialogue between reason and emotions. As a result, it is nearly impossible to filter out the strictly linguistic–cognitive abstract meaning from the sociocultural psycho-emotive meaning.[44] [. . .]

There is growing evidence that the ethic of caring may be part of women's experience as well. Certain dimensions of women's ways of knowing bear striking resemblance to Afrocentric expressions of the ethic of caring. Belenky, Clinchy, Goldberger, and Tarule point out that two contrasting epistemological orientations characterize knowing—one, an epistemology of separation based on impersonal procedures for establishing truth, and the other, an epistemology of connection in which truth emerges through care. While these ways of knowing are not gender specific, disproportionate numbers of women rely on connected knowing.[45]

The parallels between Afrocentric expressions of the ethic of caring and those advanced by feminist scholars are noteworthy. The emphasis placed on expressiveness and emotion in African-American communities bears marked resemblance to feminist perspectives on the importance of personality in connected knowing. Separate knowers try to subtract the personality of an individual from his or her ideas because they see personality as biasing those ideas. In contrast, connected knowers see personality as adding to an individual's ideas, and they feel that the personality of each group member enriches a group's understanding.[46] Similarly, the significance of individual uniqueness, personal expressiveness, and empathy in African-American communities resembles the importance that some feminist analyses place on women's 'inner voice'.[47]

The convergence of Afrocentric and feminist values in the ethic-of-care dimension of an alternative epistemology seems particularly acute. While white women may have access to a women's tradition valuing emotion and expressiveness, few white social institutions except the family validate this way of knowing. In contrast, Black women have long had the support of the Black church, an institution with deep roots in the African past and a philosophy that accepts and encourages expressiveness and an ethic of caring. While Black men share in this Afrocentric tradition, they must resolve the contradictions that distinguish abstract, unemotional Western masculinity from an Afrocentric ethic of caring. The differences among race/gender groups thus hinge on differences in their access to institutional supports valuing one type of knowing over another. Although Black women may be denigrated within white-male-controlled academic institutions, other institutions, such as Black families and churches, which encourage the expression of Black female power, seem to do so by way of their support for an Afrocentric feminist epistemology.

The Ethic of Personal Accountability

An ethic of personal accountability is the final dimension of an alternative epistemology. [. . .] Zilpha Elaw's description of slavery reflects this notion that every idea has an owner and that owner's identity matters: 'Oh, the abominations of slavery! . . . Every case of slavery, however lenient its inflictions and mitigated its atrocities, indicates an oppressor, the oppressed, and oppression.[48] For Elaw, abstract definitions of slavery mesh with the concrete identities of its perpetrators and its victims. Blacks 'consider it essential for individuals to have personal positions on issues and assume full responsibility for arguing their valididty'.[49]

Assessments of an individual's knowledge claims simultaneously evaluate an individual's character, values, and ethics. African-Americans reject Eurocentric masculinist beliefs that probing into an individual's personal viewpoint is outside the boundaries of discussion. Rather, all views expressed and actions taken are thought to derive from a central set of core beliefs that cannot be other than personal.[50] From this perspective, knowledge claims made by individuals respected for their moral and ethical values will carry more weight than those offered by less respected figures.[51]

[. . .] The ethic of personal accountability is clearly an Afrocentric value, but is it feminist as well? While limited by its attention to middle-class, white women, Carol Gilligan's work suggests that there is a female model for moral development where women are more inclined to link morality to responsibility, relationships, and the ability to maintain social ties.[52] If this is the case, then African-American women again experience a convergence of values from Afrocentric and female institutions.

The use of an Afrocentric feminist epistemology in traditional Black church services illustrates the interactive nature of all four dimensions and also serves as a metaphor for the distinguishing features of an Afrocentric feminist way of knowing. The services represent more than dialogues between the rationality used in examining biblical texts/stories and the emotion inherent in the use of reason for this purpose. The rationale for such dialogues addresses the task of examining concrete experiences for the presence of an ethic of caring. Neither emotion nor ethics is subordinated to reason. Instead, emotion, ethics, and reason are used as interconnected, essential components in assessing knowledge claims. In an Afrocentric feminist epistemology, values lie at the heart of the knowledge-validation process such that inquiry always has an ethical aim.

EPISTEMOLOGY AND BLACK FEMINIST THOUGHT

Living life as an African-American woman is a necessary prerequisite for producing Black feminist thought because within Black women's communities thought is validated and produced with reference to a particular set of historical, material, and epistemological conditions.[53] African-American women who adhere to the idea that claims about Black women must be substantiated by Black women's sense of their own experiences and who anchor their knowledge claims in an Afrocentric feminist epistemology have produced a rich tradition of Black feminist thought.

Traditionally, such women were blues singers, poets, autobiographers, storytellers, and orators validated by the larger community of Black women as experts on a Black women's standpoint. Only a few unusual African-American feminist scholars have been able to defy Eurocentric masculinist epistemologies and explicitly embrace an Afrocentric feminist epistemology. Consider Alice Walker's description of Zora Neale Hurston: 'In my mind, Zora Neale Hurston, Billie Holiday, and Bessie Smith form a sort of unholy trinity. Zora *belongs* in the tradition of Black women singers, rather than among "the literati". . . . Like Billie and Bessie she followed her own road, believed in her own gods, pursued her own dreams, and refused to separate herself from "common" people.'[54]

[. . .] In establishing the legitimacy of their knowledge claims, Black women scholars who want to develop Black feminist thought may encounter the often conflicting standards of three key groups. First, Black feminist thought must be validated by ordinary African-American women who grow to womanhood 'in a world where the saner you are, the madder you are made to appear'.[55] To be credible in the eyes of this group, scholars must be personal advocates for their material, be accountable for the consequences of their work, have lived or experienced their material in some fashion, and be willing to engage in dialogues about their findings with ordinary, everyday people. Second, if it is to establish its legitimacy, Black feminist thought also must be accepted by the community of Black women scholars. These scholars place varying amounts of importance on rearticulating a Black women's standpoint using an Afrocentric feminist epistemology. Third, Black feminist thought within academia must be prepared to confront Eurocentric masculinist political and epistemological requirements.

The dilemma facing Black women scholars engaged in creating Black feminist thought is that a knowledge claim that meets the criteria of adequacy for one group and thus is judged to be an acceptable knowledge claim may not be translatable into the terms of a different group. [. . .] Once Black feminist scholars face the notion that, on certain dimensions of a Black women's standpoint, it may be fruitless to try to translate ideas from an Afrocentric feminist epistemology into a Eurocentric masculinist epistemology, then the choices become clearer. Rather than trying to uncover universal knowledge claims that can withstand the translation from one epistemology to another, time might be better spent rearticulating a Black women's standpoint in order to give African-American women the tools to resist their own subordination. The goal here is not one of integrating Black female 'folk culture' into the substantiated body of academic knowledge, for that substantiated knowledge is, in many ways, antithetical to the best interests of Black women. Rather, the process is one of rearticulating a pre-existing Black women's standpoint and recentering the language of existing academic discourse to accommodate these knowledge claims. [. . .]

Black feminist scholars offering knowledge claims that cannot be accommodated by both frameworks face the choice between accepting the taken-for-granted assumptions that permeate white-male-controlled academic institutions or leaving academia. [. . .]

Black feminist scholars offering knowledge claims that can be partially accommodated by both epistemologies can create a body of thought that stands outside of either. Rather than trying to synthesize competing worldviews that, at this point in time, may defy reconciliation, their task is to point out common themes and concerns. By making creative use of their status as mediators, their thought becomes an entity unto itself that is rooted in two distinct political and epistemological contexts.[56]

Those Black feminists who develop knowledge claims that both epistemologies can accommodate may have found a route to the elusive goal of generating so-called objective generalizations that can stand as universal truths. [. . .]

Alternative knowledge claims, in and of themselves, are rarely threatening to conventional knowledge. Such claims are routinely ignored, discredited, or simply absorbed and marginalized in existing paradigms. Much more threatening is the challenge that alternative epistemologies offer to the basic process used by the powerful to legitimate their knowledge claims. If the epistemology used to validate knowledge comes into question, then all prior knowledge claims validated under the dominant model become suspect. An alternative epistemology challenges all certified knowledge and opens up the question of whether what has been taken to be true can stand the test of alternative ways of validating truth. The existence of an independent Black women's standpoint using an Afrocentric feminist epistemology calls into question the content of what currently passes as truth and simultaneously challenges the process of arriving at that truth.

Notes

1. For analyses of how interlocking systems of oppression affect Black women, see Frances Beale, 'Double Jeopardy: To Be Black and Female', in Toni Cade Bambara (ed.), *The Black Woman*, (New York: Signet, 1970); Angela Y. Davis, *Women, Race and Class* (New York: Random House, 1981); Bonnie Thornton Dill, 'Race, Class, and Gender: Prospects for an All-Inclusive Sisterhood', *Feminist Studies* 9 (1983), 131–50; bell hooks, *Ain't I a Woman? Black Women and Feminism* (Boston: South End Press, 1981); Diane Lewis, 'A Response to Inequality: Black Women, Racism, and Sexism', *Signs: Journal of Women in Culture and Society* 3 (Winter 1977), 339–61; Pauli Murray, 'The Liberation of Black Women', in Mary Lou Thompson (ed.), *Voices of the New Feminism* (Boston: Beacon, 1970), 87–102; and the introduction in Filomina Chioma Steady, *The Black Woman Cross-Culturally* (Cambridge, MA: Schenkman, 1981), 7–41.
2. See the introduction in Steady, *The Black Woman*, for an overview of Black

women's strengths. This strength–resiliency perspective has greatly influenced empirical work on African-American women. See, e.g., Joyce Ladner's study of low-income Black adolescent girls, *Tomorrow's Tomorrow* (New York: Doubleday, 1971); and Lena Wright Myers's work on Black women's self-concept, *Black Women: Do They Cope Better?* (Englewood Cliffs, NJ: Prentice-Hall, 1980). For discussions of Black women's resistance, see Elizabeth Fox-Genovese, 'Strategies and Forms of Resistance: Focus on Slave Women in the United States', in Gary Y. Okihiro (ed.), *In Resistance: Studies in African, Caribbean and Afro-American History* (Amherst, MA: University of Massachusetts Press, 1986), 143–65; and Rosalyn Terborg-Penn, Black Women in Resistance: A Cross-Cultural Perspective', in Okihiro *In Resistance* 188–209. For a comprehensive discussion of everyday resistance, see James C. Scott, *Weapons of the Weak: Everyday Forms of Peasant Resistance* (New Haven: Yale University Press, 1985).

3. See Patricia Hill Collin's analysis of the substantive content of Black feminist thought in 'Learning from the Outsider Within: The Sociological Significance of Black Feminist Thought', *Social Problems* 33/6 (1986), 14–32.
4. Scott describes consciousness as the meaning that people give to their acts through the symbols, norms and ideological forms they create.
5. This thesis is found in scholarship of varying theoretical perspectives. For example, Marxist analyses of working-class consciousness claim that 'false consciousness' makes the working class unable to penetrate the hegemony of ruling-class ideologies. See Scott's critique of this literature.
6. For example, in Western societies, African-Americans have been judged as being less capable of intellectual excellence, more suited to manual labor and therefore as less human than whites. Similarly, white women have been assigned roles as emotional, irrational creatures ruled by passions and biological urges. They too have been stigmatized as being less than fully human, as being objects. For a discussion of the importance that objectification and dehumanization play in maintaining systems of domination, see Arthur Brittan and Mary Maynard, *Sexism, Racism and Oppression* (New York: Basil Blackwell, 1984).
7. The tendency for Western scholarship to assess Black culture as pathological and deviant illustrates this process. See Rhett S. Jones, 'Proving Blacks Inferior: The Sociology of Knowledge', in Joyce Ladner (ed.), *The Death of White Sociology*, (New York: Vintage, 1973), 114–35.
8 The presence of an independent standpoint does not mean that it is uniformly shared by all Black women or even that Black women fully recognize its contours. By using the concept of standpoint, I do not mean to minimize the rich diversity existing among African-American women. I use the phrase 'Black women's standpoint' to emphasize the plurality of experiences within the overarching term 'standpoint'. For discussions of the concept of standpoint, see Nancy M. Hartsock, 'The Feminist Standpoint: Developing the Ground for a Specifically Feminist Historical Materialism', in S. Harding and M. Hintikka (eds.), *Discovering Reality*, (Boston: Reidel, 1983), 283–310, and *Money, Sex, and Power* (Boston: Northeastern University Press, 1983); and Alison M. Jaggar, *Feminist Politics and Human Nature* (Totowa, NJ: Rowman and Allanheld, 1983), 377–89. My use of the standpoint epistemologies as an organizing concept in this essay does not mean that the concept is problem

free. For a helpful critique of standpoint epistemologies, see Sandra Harding, *The Science Question in Feminism* (Ithaca: Cornell University Press, 1986).

9. One contribution of contemporary Black women's studies is its documentation of how race, class and gender have structured these differences. For representative works surveying African-American women's experiences, see Paula Giddings, *When and Where I Enter: The Impact of Black Women on Race and Sex in America* (New York: William Morrow, 1984); and Jacqueline Jones, *Labor of Love, Labor of Sorrow: Black Women, Work, and the Family from Slavery to the Present* (New York: Basic, 1985).
10. For example, Judith Rollins, *Between Women: Domestics and Their Employers* (Philadelphia: Temple University Press, 1985); and Bonnie Thornton Dill, '"The Means to Put My Children Through": Child-Rearing Goals and Strategies among Black Female Domestic Servants', in LaFrances Rodgers-Rose (ed.), *The Black Woman*, (Beverly Hills: Sage Publications, 1980), 107–23, report that Black domestic workers do not see themselves as being the devalued workers that their employers perceive and construct their own interpretations of the meaning of their work. For additional discussions of how Black women's consciousness is shaped by the material conditions they encounter, see Ladner (n. 2 above); Myers (n. 2 above); and Cheryl Townsend Gilkes, '"Together and in Harness": Women's Traditions in the Sanctified Church', *Signs: Journal of Women in Culture and Society* 10 (Summer 1985), 678–99. See also Marcia Westkott's discussion of consciousness as a sphere of freedom for women in 'Feminist Criticism of the Social Sciences', *Harvard Educational Review* 49 (1979), 422–30.
11. John Langston Gwaltney, *Drylongso: A Self-Portrait of Black America* (New York: Vintage, 1980), 4.
12. See Michael Omi and Howard Winant, *Racial Formation in the United States* (New York: Routledge and Kegan Paul, 1986), esp. 93.
13. In discussing standpoint epistemologies, Hartsock, in *Money, Sex, and Power*, 132, notes that a standpoint is 'achieved rather than obvious, a mediated rather than immediate understanding'.
14. See Scott (n. 2 above); and Hartsock, *Money, Sex, and Power*.
15. Some readers may question how one determines whether the ideas of any given African-American woman are 'feminist' and 'Afrocentric'. I offer the following working definitions. I agree with the general definition of feminist consciousness provided by Black feminist sociologist Deborah K. King: 'Any purposes, goals, and activities which seek to enhance the potential of women, to ensure their liberty, afford them equal opportunity, and to permit and encourage their self-determination represent a feminist consciousness, even if they occur within a racial community' (in 'Race, Class and Gender Salience in Black Women's Womanist Consciousness' [Dartmouth College, Department of Sociology, Hanover, NH, 1987, typescript], 22). To be Black or Afrocentric, such thought must not only reflect a similar concern for the self-determination of African-American people, but must in some way draw upon key elements of an Afrocentric tradition as well.
16. The Eurocentric masculinist process is defined here as the institutions, paradigms, and any elements of the knowledge-validation procedure controlled by white males and whose purpose is to represent a white male standpoint. While this process represents the interests of powerful white males, various

dimensions of the process are not necessarily managed by white males themselves.

17. Maxine Baca Zinn, Lynn Weber Cannon, Elizabeth Higginbotham and Bonnie Thornton Dill, 'The Cost of Exclusionary Practices in Women's Studies', *Signs: Journal of Women in Culture and Society* 11 (Winter 1986), 290–303.
18. Peter L. Berger and Thomas Luckmann. *The Social Construction of Reality* (New York: Doubleday, 1966) notes that if an outsider group, in this case African-American women, recognizes that the insider group, namely, white men, requires special privileges from the larger society, a special problem arises of keeping the outsiders out and at the same time having them acknowledge the legitimacy of this procedure. Accepting a few 'safe' outsiders is one way of addressing this legitimation problem. Collins's discussion (n. 3 above) of Black women as 'outsiders within' addresses this issue. Other relevant works include Franz Fanon's analysis of the role of the national middle class in maintaining colonial systems, *The Wretched of the Earth* (New York: Grove, 1963); and William Tabb's discussion of the use of 'bright natives' in controlling African-American communities, *The Political Economy of the Black Ghetto* (New York: Norton, 1970).
19. For detailed discussions of the Afrocentric worldview, see John S. Mbiti, *African Religions and Philosophy* (London: Heinemann, 1969); Dominique Zahan, *The Religion, Spirituality, and Thought of Traditional Africa* (Chicago: University of Chicago Press, 1979); and Mechal Sobel, *Trabelin' On: The Slave Journey to an Afro-Baptist Faith* (Westport, CT: Greenwood Press, 1979), 1–76.
20. For representative works applying these concepts to African-American culture, see Niara Sudarkasa, 'Interpreting the African Heritage in Afro-American Family Organization', in Harriette Pipes McAdoo (ed.) *Black Families* (Beverly Hills: Sage, 1981); Henry H. Mitchell and Nicholas Cooper Lewter, *Soul Theology: The Heart of American Black Culture* (San Francisco: Harper and Row, 1986); Robert Farris Thompson, *Flash of the Spirit: African and Afro-American Art and Philosophy* (New York: Vintage, 1983); and Ortiz M. Walton, 'Comparative Analysis of the African and the Western Aesthetics', in Addison Gayle (ed.) *The Black Aesthetic* (Garden City, NY: Doubleday, 1971), 154–64.
21. One of the best discussions of an Afrocentric epistemology is offered by James E. Turner, 'Foreword: Africana Studies and Epistemology; a Discourse in the Sociology of Knowledge', in James E. Turner (ed.) *The Next Decade: Theoretical and Research Issues in Africana Studies* (Ithaca: Cornell University Africana Studies and Research Center, 1984), v–xxv. See also Vernon Dixon, 'World Views and Research Methodology', summarized in Harding, *The Science Question*, 170.
22. See Hester Eisenstein, *Contemporary Feminist Thought* (Boston: G. K. Hall, 1983). Nancy Hartsock's *Money, Sex, and Power*, 145–209, offers a particularly insightful analysis of women's oppression.
23. For discussions of feminist consciousness, see Dorothy Smith, 'A Sociology for Women', in Julia A. Sherman and Evelyn T. Beck (eds.), *The Prism of Sex: Essays in the Sociology of Knowledge* (Madison: University of Wisconsin Press, 1979); and Michelle Z. Rosaldo, 'Women, Culture, and Society: A Theoretical Overview', in Michelle Z. Rosaldo and Louise Lamphere (ed.), *Woman,*

Culture, and Society (Stanford: Stanford University Press, 1974), 17–42. Feminist epistemologies are surveyed by Jaggar, *Feminist Politics.*

24. One significant difference between Afrocentric and feminist standpoints is that much of what is termed women's culture is, unlike African-American culture, created in the context of and produced by oppression. Those who argue for a women's culture are electing to value, rather than denigrate, those traits associated with females in white patriarchal societies. While this choice is important, it is not the same as identifying an independent, historic culture associated with a society. I am indebted to Deborah K. King for this point.
25. Harding, *The Science Question,* 166.
26. Bonnie Thornton Dill, 'The Dialectics of Black Womanhood', *Signs: Journal of Women in Culture and Society* 4 (Spring 1979), 543–55.
27. Class differences among Black women may be marked. For example, see Paula Giddings's analysis (n. 9 above) of the role of social class in shaping Black women's political activism; or Elizabeth Higginbotham's study of the effects of social class in Black women's college attendance in 'Race and Class Barriers to Black Women's College Attendance', *Journal of Ethnic Studies* 13 (1985), 89–107. Those African-American women who have experienced the greatest degree of convergence of race, class and gender oppression may be in a better position to recognize and use an alternative epistemology.
28. Gwaltney, *Drylongso,* 83.
29. Elsa Barkley Brown, 'Hearing Our Mothers' Lives' (paper presented at the Fifteenth Anniversary Faculty Lecture Series, African-American and African Studies, Emory University, Atlanta 1986).
30. Ladner, *Tomorrow's Tomorrow.*
31. June Jordan, *On Call: Political Essays* (Boston: South End Press, 1985), 26.
32. Hartsock, *Money, Sex and Power,* 237; and Nancy Chodorow, *The Reproduction of Mothering* (Berkeley and Los Angeles: University of California Press, 1978).
33. Dorothy Smith, *The Everyday World as Problematic* (Boston: Northeastern University Press, 1987).
34. Claudia Tate, *Black Women Writers at Work* (New York: Continuum, 1983), 91.
35. Ibid., 92.
36. Evelyn Fox Keller, *Reflections on Gender and Science* (New Haven: Yale University Press, 1985); Chodorow, *The Reproduction of Mothering.*
37. Mary Belenky, Blythe Clinchy, Nancy Goldberger and Jill Tarule, *Women's Ways of Knowing* (New York: Basic, 1985), 16.
38. Thomas Webber, *Deep Like the Rivers* (New York: Norton, 1978), 127.
39. In her discussion of the West African Sacred Cosmos, Mechal Sobel (*Trabelin' On*), notes that Nyam, a root word in many West African languages, connotes an enduring spirit, power, or energy possessed by all life. In spite of the pervasiveness of this key concept in African humanism, its definition remains elusive. She points out: 'Every individual analyzing the various Sacred Cosmos of West Africa has recognized the reality of this force, but no one has yet adequately translated this concept into Western terms' (13).
40. For discussions of personal expressiveness in African-American culture, see Geneva Smitherman, *Talkin and Testifyin: The Language of Black America* (Detroit: Wayne State University Press, 1986); Thomas Kochman, *Black and*

White: Styles in Conflict (Chicago: University of Chicago Press, 1981), esp. ch. 9; and Mitchell and Lewter, *Soul Theology.*

41. For feminist analyses of the subordination of emotion in Western culture, see Arlie Russell Hochschild, 'The Sociology of Feeling and Emotion: Selected Possibilities', in M. Millman and R. Kanter, *Another Voice: Feminist Perspectives on Social Life and Social Science* (Garden City, NY: Anchor, 1975).
42. Tate (n. 70 above), 156.
43. Gwaltney, *Drylongse,* 11.
44. Smitherman, *Talkin and Testifyin,* 135 and 137.
45. Belenky *et al.*, *Women's Ways of Knowing,* 100–130.
46. Ibid., 119.
47. See ibid., 52–75, for a discussion of inner voice and its role in women's cognitive styles. Regarding empathy, Belenky *et al.* note: 'Connected knowers begin with an interest in the facts of other people's lives, but they gradually shift the focus to other people's ways of thinking. . . . It is the form rather than the content of knowing that is central. . . . Connected learners learn through empathy' (115).
48. William L. Andrews, *Sisters of the Spirit: Three Black Women's Autobiographies of the Nineteenth Century* (Bloomington: Indiana University Press, 1986), 98.
49. Kochman, *Black and White,* 20 and 25.
50. Ibid., 23.
51. The sizable proportion of ministers among Black political leaders illustrates the importance of ethics in African-American communities.
52. Carol Gilligan, *In a Different Voice* (Cambridge: Harvard University Press, 1982). Carol Stack critiques Gilligan's model by arguing that African-Americans invoke a similar model of moral development to that used by women (see 'The Culture of Gender: Women and Men of Color', *Signs: Journal of Women in Culture and Society* 11 (Winter 1986), 321–4). Another difficulty with Gilligan's work concerns the homogeneity of the subjects she studied.
53. Black men, white women and members of other race, class and gender groups should be encouraged to interpret, teach and critique the Black feminist thought produced by African-American women.
54. Alice Walker, *In Search of Our Mothers' Gardens* (New York: Harcourt Brace Joranovich, 1974)
55. Gwaltney, *Drylongso,* 7.
56. Collins, 'Learning from the Outsider Within'.

Practising Feminist Research: The Intersection of Gender and 'Race' in the Research Process

Ann Phoenix*

INTRODUCTION

An increasing number of feminists have written about their experiences of conducting research and what it means to be a feminist researcher.[1] The complex relationships to be negotiated at each stage of the research process (obtaining funding; negotiating access to respondents; data collecting; analysis and dissemination) are now more clearly recognized than formerly. However, there are still a number of themes that have been neglected. For example, most published material has discussed projects over which the researcher had some control rather than the more common experience where the feminist researcher has no control over the research process. Another gap in the literature on feminist methodology relates to the ways in which the gender, 'race' and social class positions of respondents intersect with those of the researcher.

This chapter will touch on the first issue, but will focus on the second. It will use two studies—one of Mothers Under Twenty and one of Social Identities in young people—to explore aspects of racialized and gendered relationships in the practice of feminist research.[2] It will focus particularly on interviewers' contact with respondents and participants' feelings about taking part in the studies. It will be argued that 'race' and gender positions, and hence the power positions they entail, enter into the interview situation but that they do not do so in any unitary or essential way. As a result the impact of 'race' and gender within particular pieces of research cannot easily be predicted. Prescriptions for matching the 'race' and/or gender of interviewers and respondents are thus too simplistic.

* From Ann Phoenix 'Practising Feminist Research' from *Researching Women's Lives* by Mary Maynard and June Purvis (Taylor & Francis, 1994), 49–71, reprinted by permission of the publisher.

CONTACT WITH RESPONDENTS

Feminist writing on the place of the 'subject' within feminist research has tended to concentrate on what it means for women to interview other women.[3] In the 1980s the focus of much of this writing was on the contradiction between the differential power status of researchers and interviewees and the fact that women respondents often enjoyed talking to women interviewers without apparently recognizing or minding the differential power positions inherent in the interview situation. [. . .]

It is easy to see why the emotional dynamics of the interview situation are potentially important to feminist researchers. First, the establishing of friendly relations and the willingness of the researcher to give of herself by answering any questions the respondent poses can create a situation of easy intimacy which feels (and perhaps is) less exploitative and more equally balanced in power terms.[4] Secondly, and more instrumentally, rapport established in the interview situation may well have a direct impact on how forthcoming respondents are and hence the quantity (if not the quality) of the data collected.

Friendly relations between interviewers and researchers are, of course, not only established in the interview itself. Researchers generally have contact with respondents both before and after interviews. At the very least there is some discussion of appointments (either for the researcher to discuss the study or to do the interview). In addition, prior to the interview and after its conclusion, there is often preamble and informal talk, sometimes over refreshment and at the end of the research there may also be contact when the results of the study are disseminated. [. . .]

The complexity and range of respondents' reasons for taking part in a study means that the woman interviewer—woman interviewee situation does not always produce rapport through gender identification. Nor are the power positions between researcher and researched fixed dichotomies; the balance of power between interviewers and interviewees shifts over the course of a study. For example, at recruitment, respondents have the ultimate power to refuse to be involved in a study. In the interview situation power does not only lie with researchers but shifts and varies, while during the analysis of the data and writing-up of the study, researchers are almost always more powerful than their respondents.

Doing Interviews

[. . .] Interviews *are* frequently enjoyable. However, the dynamics of 'race', social class, the issue being researched, and the intersection of the agendas of interviewers and interviewees all have as much impact as gender on the interview situation.[5] Instances where the interview situation becomes uncomfortable and where rapport is disrupted (however slightly or temporarily) all help to identify, by contrast, the elements that make woman–woman interviews comfortable.

Negative reaction to oneself

It has sometimes been obvious that following appointments made on the telephone, a minority of white interviewees are visibly shocked to see me when I turn up on the doorstep. Since I am expected, known by name and not wearing anything unusual, it seems reasonable to assume that it is my colour that is unexpected. It is not unusual for black researchers and academics to encounter reactions of surprise[6] and it is not a novel experience for me. The temporary consternation that I engender seems to have little impact on the conduct of interviews because people recover themselves fairly quickly and it is generally easy to establish rapport. However, I cannot rule out the possibility that for some white interviewees having a black woman in their home, perhaps for the first time, has an impact on how forthcoming they are. That impact is not necessarily inhibitory. For it is possible that some white respondents may feel more disinhibited than they otherwise would when talking to someone of a different colour from themselves. For black respondents who are surprised (although less visibly so) that the university researcher who has turned up to see them is black, the reasons for surprise and their subsequent reactions are likely to differ from those of white respondents but to be equally complex and multi-faceted.

Kum-Kum Bhavnani argues that the inversion of the more usual balance of power in research studies when a black woman interviews white respondents is interesting in itself and that its subversion of traditional power relations can help make explicit the power relations within the research situation.[7] While this is undoubtedly true, the simultaneity of 'race', social class, gender, (assumed) sexuality and age make it extremely difficult to tease apart the aspects of the interviewer which are having an impact on the interviewee or on the power dynamics between interviewer and interviewee.[8]

Negative feelings evoked by respondents' accounts

One of the standard textbook notions of interviewing is that the interviewer absorbs all that the interviewee says; reflecting some statements back for clarification or expansion but always accepting it, rather in the style of client-centred therapy. However, depending on the characteristics of the two people in the interviewer–interviewee relationship and the topic being explored, the interviewer can obviously sometimes have negative reactions to the interviewee or to some aspect of their accounts (just as interviewees can to interviewers—see below). This can happen when interviewees rail against a category that the interviewer fits into (e.g., employed mothers; feminists; black people) or make sexist or racist comments. Since the whole point of interviews is to evoke respondents' accounts rather than to hear one's own discourses reflected back, I would argue that this is usually interesting data rather than upsetting and that it is manageable within the interview context. However, I would like to cite examples of two situations in which it can be more difficult to be dispassionate about what respondents say.

If, as a feminist researcher, one has established a warm, intimate interview relationship with a woman, it can be more difficult to have no personal reaction to accounts one does not like. For example, the occasion I most minded what an interviewee said to me was outside the interview situation. I had interviewed this particular woman three times over a period of two years. At the third interview she was very upset about her husband's behaviour (she had just allowed him back into the home having excluded him for a while). When the tape recorder was turned off at the end of the interview, she explained that she was worried about being pregnant by someone other than her husband and that her husband would 'kill her' if she was. She did not want to go to her general practitioner and could not afford to pay for a pregnancy test and yet was worried and wanted to know one way or another. I paid for her to have a pregnancy test. Over a cup of tea she began talking graphically about her distaste for black people (mainly men) in the area in which I live without ever seeming to become aware that she, a white woman, was talking to me, a black woman. She may, of course, have considered that I was not implicated in her account since most of her venom was directed at black young men. Alternatively, since she clearly liked me, she may have made the more usual 'exception' for me.[9] [. . .]

The fact that I found this particular incident upsetting was probably because I had established a warm feminist interviewing relationship with this woman and gone beyond the interviewee/interviewer relationship in attempting to help her begin to sort out a potential predicament. It is more difficult to deal with instances of racism in situations where one has begun to empathize (rather than simply sympathize) with respondents. [. . .]

The other case in which it may be difficult for researchers to deal with respondents' comments is when respondents are critical of a research study on which interviewers are employed to collect data, but to which they have had minimal input at the design stage (a situation not generally explored in writing on feminist methodology, but one that can and does divide women researchers depending on their position in the research hierarchy). At the end of both studies described here, interviewees were asked to discuss their feelings about the interview. In the Social Identities study there were generally no complaints about the ways in which social class or gender were discussed, but some respondents (white and black) did not like the emphasis on 'race' and racism. A few black mothers were hostile to the study design and this was uncomfortable for the black woman interviewer who was not the grant holder.[10]

Q: How did you feel about the interview?
A: Pretty boring. I don't personally think that is quite necessary.
Q: What's not necessary?
A: The whole interview.
Q: And why don't you think it's necessary?
A: Well because you know all these questions about asking people about colour and you know your race and racism and you know. I mean to say what does it really matter? . . . I look at everybody as the same human being as myself . . . (Black mother whose account made it clear that she considered there to be a great deal of racism in Britain, that it does matter to her and that she is entirely opposed to it).

The following comment is extracted from pages of largely negative comment about the study from another black mother:

Some of the questions you could actually feel was a white person asking them, and some of them were so stupid that you could get the feeling that somebody was trying to get inside black people to find out what it is like . . . (Black mother)

Equally some white mothers who were interviewed by a black researcher expressed hostility to some of the questions on racism (sometimes because they considered the answers to questions to be self-evident):

Q: Do you think there is much racism in Britain at the moment?
A: Well that's a bloody stupid question. Of course there is. (White mother of mixed-parentage daughter)

The white interviewer on the project also had to deal with reluctance from some white young people to discuss issues of 'race' at all since they considered them irrelevant to their lives. She did not like hearing expressions of racism from young white people and found them difficult to deal with.

Janet Finch[11] suggests that feminist researchers side with the 'subject' when doing interviews with women and that she (the researcher) shares the powerless position of the women that she interviews. Arguably, however, this is an instance where lack of recognition of differences between women is not helpful for, in many ways, women who are interviewers are relatively powerful in comparison with many other women.[12] The intersection of 'race' and social class with gender leads to a dynamic situation of shifting similarities and differences and hence shifting sympathies. Furthermore, the women participants in a study are not equally powerless[13] and some can oppress others. Thus, the feminist aim of empowering *all* women cannot mean the taking of sides with women in general.

Offending the respondent

It is often unpredictable which issues will irritate or offend a particular respondent since most interviewees will readily answer questions about the most personal issues while a few will bridle at being asked what seem to be fairly innocuous questions on one occasion but not another. [. . .]

RESPONDENTS' VIEWS OF AND RESPONSES TO THE RESEARCH

It has been well documented that many women enjoy being interviewed by women interviewers.[14] In the studies reported here, many women also said that they had enjoyed taking part in the research. For example, when asked what they felt about the first interview in the study of Mothers Under Twenty, half of the sample said that they had enjoyed it and that it was good. More than a third (36 per cent) said that it had been 'all right'; 11 per cent had both good and bad things to say about the interview and only two women said that they had not liked it. The majority of the women reported that they had welcomed the opportunity to be listened to with interest and without interruption, even apparently deriving some therapeutic benefit from this.

[. . .] Those who mentioned bad things about the interview generally mentioned the intrusiveness of some questions and the length of time that interviews had taken.

[. . .] Young people of both sexes in the Social Identities study were also asked about how they had found the interview. They gave similar responses to the women in the Mothers Under Twenty study. Four per cent were negative about the interview; 42 per cent were positive about it; two-fifths said that it was 'all right' or they 'didn't mind it' and 11 per cent gave mixed responses. White respondents were slightly more likely to give negative responses than black or mixed-parentage respondents (8 per cent, 0 and 4 per cent respectively). The same was true of middle-class respondents in comparison with working-class respondents (6 per cent as against 3 per cent) and young men in comparison with young women (6 per cent as against 3 per cent).

In the Social Identities study, a few of those interviewees who did not like the interview said that they found it boring and 'too long' but some disliked it because it asked too many questions about colour. A couple of the black mothers interviewed were sceptical that the study was worth doing because they considered that it would not change anything for black people and so was pointless. [. . .]

Many parents and young people who liked, or did not mind, being interviewed were concerned about what we would do with the data that we had collected. [. . .] Lack of certainty about what the study was about and what we were going to do with the data may have been because respondents in the Social Identities study were recruited from schools where initial permission was given by headteachers, and students were selected and then asked whether they wanted to take part. It may be that in some schools the students were not as informed about the study as they should ideally have been. However, in the Mothers Under Twenty study women were recruited directly by researchers who explained the study to them and gave them handouts about the research at each interview. Nonetheless, at the end of the study it was apparent that some interviewees had not understood what the study was about, and so could not be said to have given informed consent:

Q: Do you feel that you were given enough information about the study?
A: I don't know why I'm being interviewed or—you know—maybe I was told, but I can't remember (laughs). Why did you pick on me?

Julia Brannen suggests that 'participants respond favourably to some methods especially where there is overlap between the concerns of researchers and those of participants, and where both parties are in search of similar explanations'.[15] While this is true, it is also the case that the overlap is itself complex in that some respondents are really not sure what explanations they should give in answer to specific questions and are discomfited by the fear (at least when 'race' is being discussed) that there is a 'politically correct' answer that they are ignorant of. The quote above from a black mother indicates the felt vulnerability of respondents who have said potentially compromising things to interviewers they have trusted.

Interviewee Questions to Interviewer

One of the important contributions made by feminist researchers to thinking about the interview situation is the recognition that it is not 'bad science' to allow the balance of power within interviews to be shifted by giving respondents opportunities to ask questions which the researcher answers rather than parries.[16] Yet, even this important innovation has different meaning and impact depending on the positioning of the two people in the interview and the topic being investigated. For example, three-quarters of pregnant women's questions to Ann Oakley in her study of the transition to motherhood were requests for clarification of the process of birth. Such questions are probably more likely to be made to sympathetic women researchers than to men (and indeed most of the personal questions asked to Ann Oakley were about her own experiences of childbirth and motherhood).[17] In this instance gender as a shared characteristic was of prime importance.

In neither the study of Mothers Under Twenty nor the Social Identities study was the style of interviewing a conversational one. [. . .]

In the Social Identities study 44 per cent of the young people in the study asked questions when invited to do so by interviewers at the end of their interviews. Questions were asked by almost equal percentages of black and white, but slightly more by mixed-parentage young people; by more middle-class than working-class young people (53 per cent as against 38 per cent), and by more young women than young men (50 per cent as against 35 per cent). The most frequent questions asked were about what the study was really about, what was going to be done with the data and where the study would be published. However, both black and white respondents were more likely to ask general and personal questions about racism to the black researchers than to the white researchers who had asked the same things.[18] It is interesting to speculate to what extent this would have occurred if black men had been conducting the interviews. However, the fact that all the interviewers were women and not men may have accounted for the readiness of young women respondents to ask questions.

It would appear that respondents asked questions for *four* main types of reasons which differed both within as well as between colour groupings. These reasons were as follows.

Curiosity about how their peers had responded . . .

Curiosity about the black interviewers
Both white and black young people expressed curiosity about the life and experiences of an adult black stranger whom they expected to have views on the issue of racism and on what they had said:

Q: How did you feel about the interview?
A: (Pause) It was a nice interview. I think it probably got me to talk about things more than I would have otherwise, and yes, I think it covered a lot. I think it was quite good.
Q: Is there anything you would like to ask me?
A1: What do you feel as a black person? About living in Britain? / . . . /
A2: Do you have problems? Do you get racism thrown at you? / . . . /
A3: What do you think about social backgrounds? . . . / . . . / (Black young woman/black woman interviewer)

Q: Okay, well we are at the end of the interview. How did you feel about it?
A: Quite enjoyed it. At first I thought 'Oh no. I don't want to do this!' But I quite enjoyed it.
Q: Well I am really grateful that you spent, well almost the entire lunch break with me. That's been really nice. Are there any questions you would like to ask me?
A: What is your background?
Q: What do you mean?
A: Well where do your parents come from? (Black young man/black interviewer)

Seeking approval for their views
Some young people (both black and white) also sought reassurance that what they said was 'right' by either gaining evidence that they were not racist (white young people); that racism is a diminishing problem in Britain (mainly white young people); or that they were

correct to view racism as an important social problem (black and mixed-parentage young people).

It was sometimes also evident from white young people's post-interview talk that they had found it anxiety-provoking to be asked questions by a black woman interviewer. This anxiety was exacerbated if respondents felt a general lack of confidence:

Q: Right. Well, is there anything that you would like to ask me?
A: Yes, what do you think about—I mean we're going on about racism. What do you think my attitude is, personally I mean.
Q: How do you mean?
A: Do you think I have a good attitude about racism?
Q: Yes I do.
A: You do? It's just I was very conscious because obviously you're black. You know I think—because I've never talked about it much, I'm very mixed up in my own ideas. So, and it's something that I think I'd probably have to have a little more time to think about.
Q: Would it have been easier to talk to someone white . . . ?
A: No. I don't think so, because I think you were very neutral . . . It was quite difficult, but I'm not sure really . . . / . . . / So I mean what do you think? It's quite—I mean I'd quite like to listen to the other interviewers, interviewees just to compare myself with other people.
Q: . . . How did you find being interviewed?
A: Well I don't think I'm extremely good talking about myself because I don't know myself very well at all, so it's very hard and I think I'm not a very easy person, a bit of a closed book really rather than an open one. So I'm sort of sorting ideas out in my head rather than ready just to put them over. So it's—I probably came over very vague . . . (White young woman/black woman interviewer)

In the above extract the interviewee–interviewer colour difference seems to be more salient for this respondent than their shared gender.

Retribution for having been asked questions about racism

There were a few white respondents whose tone of questioning appeared partly to be exacting revenge from a black person who had subjected them to questions they found awkward while perhaps secretly sitting in judgment on them. A few others were impatient with being asked a lot of questions about 'race' and racism by a white interviewer when they did not consider that these issues were relevant to them. Such retributive questioning or demonstrated impatience may, to some extent, shift the balance of power from the interviewer to the interviewee, but it does not necessarily make either for a comfortable situation or for an equal relationship between them.

It must also be remembered that interviewing in a school is very different from interviewing in people's homes in that information shared in a respondent's home is not likely to be passed around other members of the sample nor to officials in the institution which granted permission to contact respondents. In schools, it was not uncommon for students who had been interviewed to tell others what they had been asked and, unlike the interviewers, respondents are not bound by ethical guidelines on confidentiality.

That 'race' is a particularly controversial and thought-provoking issue is demonstrated by the fact that neither gender and sexism nor social class (which were asked about in the same interview) produced much interviewee questioning of black or white interviewers. It also demonstrates that, despite attending schools with black people, many white young people do not have an easy familiarity either with issues of racism or with black people. Although Ann Oakley was also asked a fair number of personal questions in her study of 'becoming a mother', the differences between her subject matter (motherhood) and ours ('race' and racism, gender and social class) made many of our respondents' responses more emotionally marked.

'Race'/Gender Matching of Interviewees and Interviewers

The argument that black interviewers are best used for black interviewees is sometimes rooted in a realist epistemology, the central tenet of which is that there is a unitary truth about respondents and their lives which interviewers need to obtain. Black interviewers are considered to 'blend in' better with black interviewees and thus to be more likely than white interviewers to get data which is 'good' because it captures 'the truth'. Some studies have found that the colour of the interviewer does have an impact on the data collected. For example, black people have been found to express more radical opinions about their lives when interviewed by a black interviewer than when interviewed by a white one.[19]

Constructivist theories of knowledge differ from realist ones in that they treat accounts as constructions rather than repositories of a unitary truth. They thus argue that it is not possible to 'read off' attitudes from talk.[20] As a result accounts have to be analyzed within the context of the interview itself. This necessitates analysis of the interview situation as the site where specific accounts are produced, rather than the taking for granted of interviews as productive of 'truths'. Even the narrative form of the story produced in an interview is considered to require analysis.[21]

The discussion above has explored some ways in which the intersection of the 'race'/gender positions of interviewers and interviewees can have an impact on the interview itself and on respondents' reactions to it. The complexity of this impact, however, makes it difficult to be clear whether the matching of interviewees with interviewers on particular characteristics will produce 'better' or 'richer' data than not matching. If different types of accounts about 'race' and racism are produced with black and with white interviewers this is in itself important data and may be good reason for using interviewers of both colours whenever possible since it illustrates the ways in which knowledges are 'situated'.[22] It is, therefore, not methodologically 'better' *always* to have black interviewers interviewing black interviewees. Politically, this strategy may also lead to the marginalization of research on black people and of black researchers since it is then easy for white researchers to consider that black interviewers can only contribute to research on black informants.[23] In addition it renders invisible any contributions they make to research which is not only on black samples or on 'race'. It is potentially exploitative in that some black respondents may believe that the research for which they have been recruited is genuinely in the control of black researchers or forget that this may not be the case when, in fact, the black interviewer has little control over the trajectory of the research or the analysis of the data.

The employment of women only to interview women informants is a comparable situation. The very notion of conducting feminist research presupposes that the feminists doing the research have some power in and hence control over the research process. Yet the majority of women working within research are at the bottom of research hierarchies where, as interviewers, their input to the research process is limited. The use of women only as interviewers of women respondents can be a cynical and exploitative ploy simply to get the 'best' possible data by encouraging respondents to speak rather than being an attempt to empower women.

It is, of course, helpful in the issue of control of the research process for women (black and white) to move up research hierarchies. However, the employment of a minority of women and black people in senior research positions does not necessarily change the status quo with regard to control of the research process. Nor does it ensure that research is *for* women or black people and hence the empowering of them. However, women at the top of research hierarchies are differentially positioned with regard to research from the women employed to conduct the interviews.

Preference for interviewers of particular gender and colour

Whatever the theoretical debates about the impact of the colour of interviewers, respondents' expressed preferences for colour of interviewers are important in themselves. In the study of 16-to-19-year-old first-time mothers there was no attempt to match the colour of the respondent with the colour of the participant although (since I am black and there were white interviewers) this happened sometimes. We therefore asked the young women what they felt about the colour, age and gender of interviewers. Age of interviewer produced no clear-cut preference in that the biggest response (44 per cent) was for 'no preference', while a quarter of the women said that they preferred interviewers not to be their own age and 30 per cent said that they did prefer to be interviewed by someone nearer their age, that is, younger than their interviewers had been.

Sixty-four per cent of the women said that they preferred to be interviewed by women. . . . A further 19 per cent said that they had no preference while the remaining 17 per cent said that they would have preferred to be interviewed by a man.

With regard to colour and ethnicity, most of the women (71 per cent) said that they had no preference for the colour of their interviewers; a fifth said that they preferred to be interviewed by someone of their own colour (they were mainly black) and three women (all black) said that they would prefer to be interviewed by someone who was not their colour.

The less common answers with regard to gender and colour of interviewer are worth exploring. In both cases, the reason for this seems to be that respondents did not wish to be judged by people like themselves and felt that they would get less disapproval and a more dispassionate hearing if the people who interviewed them were clearly different from themselves and not in the same social groups. In addition, some of those women who said that they would have preferred to talk to men as interviewers reported that this was because they considered women to be 'catty' or 'bitchy'.

Expressed preferences for interviewers of particular colour or gender do not necessarily mean that respondents will not readily talk to interviewers who do not fit those characteristics. In the study of

Mothers Under Twenty, for example, one black woman said at the final interview:

If——[white interviewer] had been doing the interview I would have had to tell her that the questions were too nosey because white people don't understand what a typical black family is like . . .

However, the transcript of her previous interview with a white interviewer did not appear different in quality from the two interviews with a black interviewer. The colour of interviewer may have made a difference to how she felt, but that difference was not analytically discernible. A study by Michael Rutter and his colleagues done twenty years ago also found no differences in black interviewee/interviewer rapport according to whether the interviewer was white or black.[24] In a similar way, the only two respondents in the study to be interviewed by men (at the first interview) expressed no preference for gender of interviewer and seemed to answer the most personal questions readily. In the study of Mothers Under Twenty, all the women interviewers were themselves mothers and some interviewees said that they wished to be interviewed by women who were mothers. However, they only asked (and hence learned) that we were mothers after at least one interview. It is thus questionable whether it would have made any difference to their responses if we had not been.

This does not rule out the possibility that respondents are more comfortable with interviewers of particular colour or gender and that they may even consciously alter their accounts depending on interviewer gender and colour. Some of the spontaneous remarks of black young people in the Social Identities study would seem to indicate that this might be the case. [. . .]

Q: How did you feel about being interviewed?
A: I thought it was good, sort of like you can talk, say what you want to say about what you think about other people, other races. I mean it is good, sort of like a black person interviewing a white person, because then they can share their feelings between each other, what they feel about other colours and things like that.
Q: So you didn't mind answering those questions with a black interviewer?
A: No.
Q: Anything you would like to ask me?
A: Have you ever been picked on because of your colour? (White young man)

Q: Well thank you very much. How did you find being interviewed?
A: I found it comfortable cos you're a black person I can talk to you like more easily than I could talk to a white person. (Black young man) [. . .].

CONCLUSION

This chapter has explored interviewer–interviewee relationships within the research process. It has argued that while contact between women participants and women researchers is frequently pleasurable for both, it is important not to mistake shared enjoyment of conversational exchanges with gender identification through shared positioning. Instances where positive, warm relationships in interviews are disrupted or fail to be established illustrate the ways in which factors beyond the interview relationship enter into interviewer–interviewee relationships as well as into the negotiation of researcher access to respondents. Thus, there are a number of factors which may have an impact on whether potential respondents participate in a study and, if they do, how they feel about their participation. These include other people, women's living circumstances, the topic of the research, their concerns about what the research will mean for the groups to which they belong as well as the colour, gender, social class and age of interviewers in comparison with those of interviewees. However, the strategy of matching interviewers and respondents on particular characteristics (such as gender and 'race') does not produce 'better' data. Indeed, since respondents are not positioned in any unitary way, it does not avoid the necessity for analysis of the ways in which wider social relations enter into the interview relationship.

The chapter has further argued that issues of 'race' and racism are particularly uncomfortable or thought-provoking for many respondents and that, as a result, colour differences may be more salient than shared gender for some young women respondents. However, respondents who are of the same colour and gender can have very different reactions to being asked the same questions. It is, therefore, important to recognize differences and commonalities between people who are socially constructed as belonging to the same group as well as across groups, a project which is consonant with feminist concerns over the last decade.[25]

Notes

1. For a recent account, see S. Reinharz (with L. Davidman), *Feminist Methods in Social Research* (Oxford: Oxford University Press, 1992).
2. The first study included a sample of seventy-nine 16-to-19-year-old women who gave birth in the mid-1980s. The women were given in-depth interviews in late pregnancy and as many as possible were followed up six months and

twenty-one months after birth. It is written up most fully in Ann Phoenix, *Young Mothers?* (Cambridge: Polity Press, 1991). The second study was completed in the early 1990s. It explored the social identities of 'race', gender and social class in a sample of 248 mixed-parentage, black and white 14-to-18-year olds and seventy of their parents. See B. Tizard and A. Phoenix, *Black, White or Mixed-Race? Race and Racism in the Lives of Young People of Mixed Parentage* (London: Routledge, 1993).

3. See for example, A. Oakley, 'Interviewing Women: A Contradiction in Terms', in H. Roberts (ed.), *Doing Feminist Research* (London: Routledge, 1981); J. Finch, '"It's Great to Have Someone to Talk To": The Ethics and Politics of Interviewing Women', in C. Bell and H. Roberts (eds.), *Social Researching: Politics, Problems, Practice* (London: Routledge and Kegan Paul, 1984). The conduct of feminist research with men as respondents has not been subjected to the same scrutiny.
4. See Oakley, 'Interviewing Women'.
5. See for example, J. Brannen, 'Research Note: The Study of Sensitive Subjects: Notes on Interviewing', *Sociological Review* 36 (1988), 552–63 and 'Research Note: The Effects of Research on Participants: Findings from a Study of Mothers and Employment', *Sociological Review* 41 (1993), 328–46; R. Edwards, 'Connecting Method and Epistemology: A White Woman Interviewing Black Women', *Women's Studies International Forum* 13 (1990), 477–90; and A. Phoenix, 'Social Research in the Context of Feminist Psychology', in E. Burman (ed.), *Feminists and Psychological Practice* (London: Sage, 1990).
6. See Jaquelyn Mitchell, 'Reflections of a Black Social Scientist: Some Struggles, Some Doubts, Some Hopes', *Harvard Educational Review* 52 (1982), 27–44; M. de la luz Reyes and J. Halcon, 'Racism in Academia: The Old Wolf Revisited', *Harvard Educational Review* 58 (1988), 299–314; Centre for Staff Development in Higher Education, *Through a Hundred Pairs of Eyes*, anti-racist video and accompanying guide (London: CSDHE, 1985).
7. Kum-Kum Bhavnani, 'What's Power Got to Do With It? Empowerment and Social Research', in I. Parker and J. Shotter (eds.), *Deconstructing Social Psychology* (London: Routledge, 1990).
8. For example, three black respondents in the Mothers Under Twenty study reported, to the white interviewers who asked them, that they preferred to be interviewed by white people. The reason they gave for this preference was that they wanted to avoid having people who are black like themselves making judgements about whether or not their behaviour is appropriate for black people.
9. See Michael Billig, *Ideology and Social Psychology* (Oxford: Basil Blackwell, 1982), for discussion of how white people can be close friends with black people while expressing racist views about black people in general.
10. There were two black women and one white woman who did interviews on this project.
11. Finch, '"It's Great To Have Someone to Talk To"'.
12. See J. Cook and M. Fonow, 'Knowledge and Women's Interests: Issues of Epistemology and Methodology in Feminist Sociological Research', *Sociological Inquiry* 56 (1986), 2–29 (reprinted in J. Nielsen and J. McCarl (eds.), *Feminist Research Methods: Exemplary Readings in the Social Sciences* (London: Westview Press, 1990)).

13. For example, in the study of 16-to-19-year-old first-time mothers, there were a minority who were economically more powerful than the majority. Two, who came from middle-class backgrounds, also had some advantages that other members of the study did not have.
14. Brannen, 'The Effects of Research on Participants', 329.
15. Ibid., 329.
16. Oakley, 'Interviewing Women'; Ann Oakley, *Social Support and Motherhood* (Oxford: Blackwell, 1993).
17. See Ann Oakley, *Becoming a Mother* (Oxford: Martin Robertson, 1979).
18. The aim in this study had been to colour-match interviewers and interviewees but this was sometimes not possible.
19. See Tim May, *Social Research: Issues, Methods and Process* (Buckingham: Open University Press, 1993); and S. Reese, W. Danielson, P. Shoemaker, T. Chang and H. Hsu, 'Ethnicity-of-Interviewer Effects Among Mexican-American and Anglos', *Public Opinion Quarterly* 35 (1986), 48–68.
20. Jonathan Potter and Margaret Wetherall, *Discourse and Social Psychology: Beyond Attitudes and Behaviour* (London: Sage, 1987); and Margaret Wetherall and Jonathan Potter, *Mapping the Language of Racism* (Basingstoke: Harvester Wheatsheaf, 1992).
21. Martine Burgos, 'Life Stories, Narrativity, and the Search for Self', *Life Stories/Recits de Vie* 5 (1989), 29–37.
22. Donna Haraway, 'Situated Knowledges: The Science Question in Feminism and the Privilege of the Partial Perspective', *Feminist Studies* 14 (Fall, 1988), 573–99.
23. Penny Rhode, 'Race-of-Interviewer Effects: A brief comment', *Sociology*, 28 (2), 547–58.
24. M. Rutter, W. Yule, M. Berger, B. Yule, J. Morton and C. Bagley, 'Children of West Indian Immigrants—I. Rates of Behavioural Deviance and of Psychiatric Disorder', *Journal of Child Psychology and Psychiatry* 15 (1974), 241–54; Reyes and Halcon, 'Racism in Academia'.
25. See for example, Avtar Brah, 'Difference, Diversity, Differentiation', in J. Donald and A. Rattansi, *'Race', Culture and Difference* (London: Sage, 1992).

18 'Somebody Forgot to Tell Somebody Something': African-American Women's Historical Novels

Barbara Christian*

The title of my essay is taken from a radio interview Ntozake Shange did with Toni Morrison in 1978, just after she had published *Song of Solomon.*[1] Morrison's comment referred to a generation of Afro-Americans of the post-World War II era who had seen the new possibilities that period seemed to promise for their children and who thought that knowledge of their history—one of enslavement, disenfranchisement, and racism—might deter the younger generation's hopes for the future. As Morrison put it, the older generation of that era sometimes X'd out the southern grandfather who had been a sharecropper and tried to forget the brutality of the African-American past. Margaret Walker tells a similar story of how her mother resented the stories about slavery her grandmother told the young Margaret . . .[2] Alice Walker tells us in a BBC documentary that her family spoke 'in whispers' about certain parts of their history, whispers which she said fascinated her.[3] These African-American writers, as well as many others, comment on the ambivalence their families felt toward the African-American past.

In the eighties, Morrison, Alice Walker, as well as Sherley Anne Williams, previously a poet and playwright, have written African-American historical novels, a sign of these writers' desire to re-vision African-American history from their imaginative and informed point of view. This trend, I think, indicates the fascination not only of novelists and scholars but also of many other women who share the experiences of African-American women in the nineteenth and early twentieth centuries . . .

This is not to say that as a group, contemporary African-American

* From Barbara Christian: 'Somebody Forgot to Tell Somebody Something' by Barbara Christian from *Wild Women in the Whirlwind* edited by Joanne M. Braxton and Andree Nicola McLaughlin (Rutgers University Press, 1990),

women writers had not previously recalled the past. However, generally speaking, they had reached back to the period of their mothers' lives, from the 1920s to the 1960s, to a past that often involved shifts of values in African-American communities, sometimes migration from the rural South or West Indies to the small-town or urban North. So, for example, Morrison's first three novels, *The Bluest Eye* (1970), *Sula* (1974), *Song of Solomon* (1977), much of Walker's short fiction as well as her novels, Paule Marshall's *Brown Girl, Brownstones* (1959), Gloria Naylor's 'Mattie Michaels' section of *The Women of Brewster Place* (1982) explore the twenties, thirties and forties from the African-American women's perspective. [. . .] All were propelled by the stories their mothers told them about their lives.

During the last decade, these writers have also probed their own contemporary context. Toni Cade Bambara's *Gorilla, My Love* (1971) and Alice Walker's *Meridian* (1976) ask pivotal questions about girls and women who were living in the decade of the intense 'black consciousness', the 1960s. Morrison, in *Tar Baby* (1981), Bambara in *The Sea Birds Are Still Alive* (1974) and Shange in *Sassafrass, Cypress, and Indigo* (1982) explore the relationships of women and men as affected by the second wave of feminism, although from very different points of view. Marshall in *Praisesong for the Widow* (1982), Morrison in *Tar Baby*, Naylor in *Linden Hills* (1985) examine the effects of middle-class mobility among some blacks during the 1960s and 1970s, while in *The Women of Brewster Place* (1982), Naylor tells the story of underclass contemporary African-American women. African-American women have even extended the present into the future, as Susan Willis pointed out in her study, *Specifying* (1982), the most overt work being Bambara's *The Salt Eaters* (1980). As a group then, contemporary African-American women have written about every decade of the twentieth century, and about every region of this country—the North, the Midwest, the South and the West, the country, small town and inner city—as well as the underclass and the middle class. And they have even traveled in their fiction beyond the geographical borders of this country to the Caribbean, to Europe and to Africa.

Yet, even as many of these writers have, in their earlier novels, focussed on the twentieth century, they have, in these same novels, taken us back in time [. . .] Even when major characters resist the past, as Macon and Milkman Dead do in *Song of Solomon*, or Avey Johnson does in *Praisesong for the Widow*, it intrudes itself upon their consciousness through dream and/or song and especially the sense of dis-ease they feel in the present. The use of history in the novels of contemporary African-American women writers, then, is constant and consistent.

Although previous novels have used history within the context of the present and the future, however, most of them would not have been properly called historical novels. In the last few years, novels by African-American women have explored those very periods that some post-World-War II African-Americans had attempted to erase. So, *The Color Purple* (1982) is set in Reconstruction Georgia, *Beloved* (1987) in the post-slavery years and *Dessa Rose* (1986) in the 1840s at the height of American slavery. These three novels are historical in that they recall a life that no longer exists and recreate societies that are apparently past. In examining this trend in African-American women's writing, I am not only interested in the novels themselves but also in why they are appearing at this particular time.

In order to understand the ways these contemporary novels revision history, first it is necessary, I think, to emphasize that historical novels by African-American women have appeared before and that there are pieces written by African-American women during the periods about which these three contemporary novels are written.

There is a small but important body of female slave narratives in which successful runaway slaves record aspects of their experience. Perhaps the most notable of these is *Incidents in the Life of a Slave Girl* (1861) written by Harriet Jacobs under the pseudonym, Linda Brent. [. . .] Jacobs codes her narrative and often tells the reader that because of modesty, a specifically female term, and her desire not to offend her audience, a specifically African-American consideration, she had to omit certain details of her life story.

In the introductory remarks to her reading of *Beloved* at the University of California at Berkeley in October 1987, Toni Morrison emphasized the consistency with which the slave narrators made such statements.[4] Morrison pointed out that their omissions were partly due to the fact that these ex-slaves addressed a white audience. Even more important, she suggested, they omitted events too horrible and too dangerous for them to recall. Morrison went on to state that these consistent comments made by nineteenth-century ex-slaves about the deliberate omissions in their narratives intrigued her and that this was the initial impulse for her writing the novel that would become *Beloved*. Clearly one of the major themes of this masterpiece is the paradox of 're-memory'. Morrison emphasizes this theme throughout the novel and reiterates it in the last words of *Beloved*: 'This was not a story to pass on.'[5] [. . .]

Not only were the slave narrators restrained by 'modesty' and by 'audience' from not passing on some stories, so were African-American nineteenth-century novelists. In *Clotel* (1851), the first novel published by an African-American writer in this country, William Wells Brown made palatable the experience of his quadroon slave heroine by fashioning her character according to the acceptable ideal image of woman at that time. Thus, Clotel is beautiful/fair, thoroughly Christian and European upper class in her demeanor and language. African-American women writers also used this construct, most notably Frances Harper in *Iola LeRoy* (1892) . . .

What is *not* focused on in these novels is as important as the images these writers emphasized. For in these novels, little light is shed on the experiences and cultures of 'ordinary' slaves like Sethe or on their relationships or communities. Clotel grows up with her mother who, because she is the 'natural wife' of her master, lives in a fairy-tale-like cottage completely apart from other slaves. Nor is she subjected to the hard labor usually exacted from other slaves. Iola LeRoy is a slave, but only for a short time and had, as a 'white' woman, been educated in fine schools. While Brown and Harper give us hints through some minor characters of the physically and psychologically harsh conditions under which most slaves lived, they reserved privileged positions for their heroines, thus exhibiting even more modesty than the slave narrators. For the sentimental romance form demanded not only a beautiful refined heroine but also that the story be entertaining and edifying.

An idea such as the one that generates *Beloved*, the existence of a 'haint', a visitor from the past in which the major characters naturally believe, though an important belief in African-American culture, could not possibly have been seriously considered by these nineteenth century novelists. They would have been fully cognizant of the detrimental effects that such a 'superstitious', or non-Christian concept would have had on their own people. Nor could nineteenth century audiences react favorably to a contrary slave like Dessa Rose who attacks her master and leads a slave rebellion that results in the death of many whites.[6] Such audiences would have been even more alarmed by the presentation of a 'crazy' slave like Sethe who would kill her own child rather than have her returned to slavery. Clearly Brown and Harper, leading activists of their day would have heard about such events—certainly, the story of Margaret Garner, on which *Beloved* is based, was sensational enough to be known by Harper.[7] But she, as well as other African-American writers, could not muddy the already murky waters of sentiment toward the Negro by presenting characters who might terrify their readers.

That these nineteenth-century writers were constrained by the socio-political biases of their time is graphically demonstrated by the disappearance of Harriet Wilson's *Our Nig* (1858). Although Mrs Wilson wrote a fluent, strong-voiced novel which is obviously autobiographical, although she employed a form which fused elements of the slave narrative and sentimental romance that readers expected in works written by Blacks and by women, *Our Nig* did not cater to the accepted mores of the time. By emphasizing the racism of Mrs Bellmont, her northern white mistress, by exposing racism in the North, as well as by ending her story with her desertion by her fugitive-slave husband, Frado, the protagonist of *Our Nig*, questioned the progressive platform of her time—that white northern women were the natural allies of blacks, that the North was not racist, that all Black men were devoted to the women of their race.

Equally important, Frado herself is the result of an interracial marriage between a white woman and a Black man, a type of union that was simply not supposed to have existed. Readers could cope with Clotel and Iola's ancestry—that their father was white, their mother Black. But acknowledging that white women would willingly be sexually involved with Black men was opposed to white women's sacred position—that they were a treasure to be possessed only by white men. The reception of *Dessa Rose* in this decade illustrates the longevity of this taboo. For many readers, Black and white, are stunned, sometimes offended by the sexual relationship between Mis Rufel, a white mistress, and Nathan, a runaway slave, despite the historical evidence that such relationships existed.

The disappearance of *Our Nig* for some one hundred years was also due to doubts raised about its authorship. Like *Incidents in the Life of a Slave Girl*, *Our Nig* was thought to have been written by a white woman because of its point of view and its excellent style. So, in his 1983 introduction to this newly discovered classic, Henry Louis Gates had to spend many pages establishing Mrs Wilson's existence, that she was a free Black woman, and that the incidents in *Our Nig* are based on her life. When nineteenth-century African-Americans wrote in a manner that did not correspond to deeply held opinions of their time, their very authorship was put in question. Such a restriction, the ultimate one for writers in that it obliterates their very existence, would certainly have affected the way they wrote about African-Americans.

One critical area in which these writers were restricted is their very medium, that of language. Since slaves were hardly conceived of as human beings who had a culture, their language was emphatically discredited. Such a devaluation is central to what experiences could be passed on, for language is the repository of anyone's point of view on experience, whether it is that of oppression, resistance to it, or a value system. Yet African-American language could not be seriously fashioned by nineteenth-century writers to dramatize their characters' essence; for that language was considered at best to be comic, at worst, a symbol of ignorance. Nineteenth-century writers like Brown and Harper imbued their heroines and heroes with a language that indicated their superiority, a language that was in no way distinguished from the language of well-bred white Americans. When these writers do use 'dialect', minor characters employ it for comic effect. If one compares Celie, Dessa Rose or Sethe's language to the language of Clotel or Iola, one immediately feels what is missing. For it is difficult to communicate the authenticity of a character without investing her language with value. If there is any one false sounding note in nineteenth-century novels about slavery and reconstruction it is the language of the characters, the way the imagination of the authors is constrained by the language their characters use.

Language is not only an expression of one's everyday experience but also of those deeper labyrinths of dream and memory, dimensions to which nineteenth-century slave characters had little access. If memory were central to Clotel or Iola, it would take them back to the past, beyond their personal history to stories their mothers told them, possibly back to the Middle Passage, so horrendous a memory that Morrison dedicated *Beloved* to those anonymous '60 million or more'. Memory might take them even further back to an African man, like the one who taught Kaine, in *Dessa Rose*, to play the banjo. To acknowledge that slaves had memory would threaten the very ground of slavery, for such memory would take them back to a culture in Africa where they existed, [. . .] 'in terms other than the ones' imposed upon them in America.[8] [. . .]

So, memory when it does exist in nineteenth-century African-American novels about slavery goes back but one generation, to one's mother, but certainly not much further back than that. Slave-owners were aware of the power of memory, for they disrupted generational lines of slaves in such a way that many slaves did not *know* even their own parents or children. Nineteenth-century writers like Brown and

Harper, too, were certainly aware of the power of memory, for their protagonists, above all else, cling to the memory of parent, child, loved one. In Brown's first version of *Clotel*, he has his heroine give up her freedom to search for her child, only to have her drown herself rather than be re-enslaved. Her story is the other side of Sethe's action in the shed, in that one mother kills herself for her child, while the other mother 'saves the best part of herself' by freeing her child through death. Brown does not linger long on the personal and emotional aspects of Clotel's suicide for his purpose is to illustrate the evils of the *institution* of slavery. Morrison, on the other hand, is riveted on the use of memory in all her characters' search for self-understanding. Nineteenth-century novelists could not be as much concerned with the individual slave as a subject as they were with the institution itself. They therefore had to sacrifice the subjectivity and, therefore, the memory of their characters to an emphasis on the slaveholders and their system.

Re-memory is a critical determinant in how we value the past, what we remember, what we select to emphasize, what we forget, as Morrison has so beautifully demonstrated in *Beloved*. But that concept could not be at the center of a narrative's revisioning of history until the obvious fact that African-Americans did have a history and culture was firmly established in American society, for writers would be constrained not only by their readers' points of view but also by the dearth of available information about the past that might give their work authenticity.

In her essay on how she wrote her historical novel, *Jubilee* (1966), Margaret Walker pointed to these difficulties. On the one hand, she made it clear that memory was the impetus for her novel, since it grew out of her promise to her grandmother to write *her* mother's story. On the other hand, as an African-American in the 1940s who wanted to write a historical novel about her past, she knew that few people, black or white, were informed about slavery and early Reconstruction, the contexts in which Vyry, her great-grandmother, lived. She tells us that she found in her research at least three historical versions of slavery: the southern white version in which the institution was benevolent, necessary and paternalistic; the northern white version, which often emphasized the horrors of slavery but was not particularly interested in the lives of the slaves; and the African-American version, of which there were few accounts, and which tended to focus on the lives of extraordinary slaves, almost always men.[9] In each version, the institution of slavery, meaning the slaveholders themselves, was pivotal, while the slaves were reduced to a voiceless mass. How, then, was Walker to write a novel which gave sufficient information about slaves to the reader who was either ignorant about the period or believed in false myths such as the ones featured in *Gone With the Wind?* How was she to do that *and* focus on Vyry, an ordinary slave woman who knew little about the larger political struggles that determined her life—a woman who could not read or write, and who had not been more than twenty miles from the place where she was born?

Margaret Walker decided that her historical novel would take the form of a folk novel. It would emphasize the fact that African-American slaves had a culture and a community, even as it sketched the outline of more specifically historical data, like the Fugitive Slave Law, or the legal conditions that determined a free Black's status in early nineteenth-century Georgia. She would have to give readers history lessons; she would have to invest with meaning the apparently mundane everyday experiences of her protagonist; and she would have to convince her reader that a viable culture and community existed among slaves.

Confronted with needing to cover so much territory to render Vyry's story, Walker, not surprisingly, created characters, Black and white, who are not subjects so much as they are the means by which we learn about the culture of slaves and slave holders and the historical period. Vyry, for example, hardly speaks in the first half of the novel, although she becomes more vocal in the Reconstruction section. Despite the many historical details about which she informs her readers, her characters have little internal life, perhaps because Walker, who is writing her historical novel in the forties and fifties before the rise of the black culture movements of the sixties, could not give slaves the right to claim those events they do not want to remember—not only what was done to them but what they might have had to do, given their precarious context. So Vyry is not complex in the way that Sethe and Dessa Rose are, for we are seldom privy to her internal conflicts and to the doubts she might have about her relations to others. Interestingly, one of the few times when we do feel her ambivalence about what she should do is when she must choose between escape for herself and leaving her children behind in slavery. As in *Beloved* and *Dessa Rose*, motherhood is the context for the slave woman's most deeply felt conflicts.

What Walker accomplished so effectively in *Jubilee* is the establishment of an African-American culture which enabled the ordinary slave to survive. In building her novel around Vyry, a hard-working mulatto slave, she revised the image of the beautiful, refined mulatto heroine of the nineteenth century, an image that her grandmother's stories refuted.

That image is further revised in Barbara Chase-Riboud's *Sally Hemings* (1979), a fictional biography of the African-American woman reputed to be Jefferson's mistress for some forty years.[10] Brown's first version of *Clotel*, which was sensationally subtitled 'The President's Daughter' was based in part on the fact that Hemings was Jefferson's mistress. But Brown used this slave mulatta's existence to cast shadows on the great Jefferson who, at once, had a black mistress and children he would not free and who nonetheless championed freedom and democracy. In contrast to Brown, Chase-Riboud uses a romantic frame to dig into the myth of Sally Hemings and to reveal this complex woman's bond to her master both as a slave and as a lover. Because Chase-Riboud is interested not only in the contradiction between Jefferson's personal and political life, and in the institution of slavery, but also in the way the nineteenth-century definition of love is related to the definition of enslavement—she revisions Brown's sentimental romance. Still, Chase-Riboud has her protagonist tell her story to a white man who is trying to rationalize slavery so that at times Sally's narrative seems as censored as the slave narratives of the nineteenth century. [. . .]

Not so with Morrison's *Beloved* and Williams's *Dessa Rose*, both of which are based on historical notes yet are not controlled by them. Although *Beloved* is based on the sensational story of Margaret Garner, a runaway slave woman who attempted to kill herself and her children rather than be returned to slavery, Morrison leaves the historical facts behind to probe a not easily resolvable paradox—how the natural and personal emotion, mother love, is traumatically affected by the political institution of slavery. Morrison has said that she did not inquire further into Garner's life other than to note the event for which this slave woman became famous.[11] And indeed Margaret Garner did not achieve freedom as Morrison's Sethe does. Instead she was tried, not for attempting to kill her child, but for the 'real crime', of attempting to escape, of stealing property, herself, from her master. For that crime, she was tried, convicted, and sent back to slavery, thus restoring his property. But Morrison takes us beyond the world of the slaveholders into the world of slaves as complex human beings. In creating Sethe, who must remember her killing of her own child and must reflect upon whether she had a right to commit so destructive an act against her child which also, paradoxically, is for her an expression of her love for her child, Morrison raises disturbing questions about mother love. And in giving Sethe her legal freedom Morrison is able to explore the nature of freedom . . .

Sherley Anne Williams also based her novel on historical notes. As often happens in historical research, the discovery of one source leads us to another. *Dessa Rose* originates with two brief notes about a southern woman, one a Black slave, the other a free white woman who lived in the first half of the nineteenth century. Williams discovered in Angela Davis's 'Reflections on a Black Woman's Role in the Community of Slaves', a pregnant slave woman who helped to lead an uprising and whose death sentence was delayed until after the birth of her child. That note led Williams to another source, Herbert Aptheker's *American Slave Revolts*, in which Williams learned about a white woman living on an isolated farm who was reported to have given sanctuary to runaway slaves. In response to these two women, whose actions appeared to refute what we have been told about both African-American and white southern women of the nineteenth century, Williams refined her point of view. Like *Beloved*, *Dessa Rose* is based on recorded historical facts but is not determined by them. 'How sad', Williams comments in her introduction to the novel 'that these two women never met' (*Dessa Rose*, p. 5).

[. . .] In *Beloved*, Morrison underlines the way that literary tradition is buttressed by an intellectual one. Schoolteacher not only exploits slaves, he is fascinated by the intellectual arguments he constructs to rationalize that exploitation. Throughout the nineteenth century, American intellectuals performed this function—that of providing intellectual arguments for a profitable legal *and* dehumanizing institution. Nehemiah and Schoolteacher's curiosity about the slave was indeed 'scientific'; their historical counterparts did measure the various parts of the slaves' bodies, did observe their 'characteristics', did interpret their behavior and did write serious treatises on them. Morrison stresses these activities—the apparently neutral ways in which intellectuals and 'scientists' were fascinated with slaves—by having the most terrible act done to Sethe, the milking of her body for Schoolteacher's scientific observation, be a bleeding wound in her memory.

Williams and Morrison then indict the American literary and intellectual tradition. And clearly, neither of their novels would be what they are if it were not for previous historical fiction by African-American women. Nor, paradoxically, would their novels be as vivid as they are if during the last decade there had not been an intense interest, among scholars, in the history of African-American women from their point of view. [. . .]

In both these novels, such remembering, such re-imagining centers on motherhood, on mothering and being mothered. On the one hand for slave women, motherhood was denied, devalued, obliterated by slavery since it was considered to be breeding, while on the other hand, it was critical to the concept of self and to the very survival of one's self. It is through the memory of *their* mothers, their reflections on that precarious role, and whether they themselves were able to be mothered, that Sethe and Dessa Rosa delve into themselves as subjects. In *Beloved*, this is true of all the major women characters: Baby Suggs, Sethe, Denver, Beloved, even Amy Denver the white girl, who helps Sethe give birth to Denver. Sethe knows 'what it is to be without the milk that belongs to you; to have to holler and fight for it'. (*Beloved*, p. 200) Denver knows what it is to see her mother in a terrible place, for she drinks her mother's milk with her sister's blood. Beloved yearns for complete union with her mother, the mother who kills her and saves her in one stroke. For her, her mother's face is her face and without her mother's face 'she has no face'. (*Beloved*, p. 216)

While Morrison moves us into the chaotic space of mother-love/mother-pain, daughter-love/daughter-pain, a space that can barely be sketched in terms of historical data, Williams takes us in another direction: she explores the concept of that double-edged term 'mammy,' which slaveowners used for African-American mothering. By reversing the usual image, that of the black mammy nursing the white baby, Williams creates a different context for that term. Rufel, the white mistress and the only nursing woman on her neglected farm feels obliged, because of her own womanhood, to nurse the baby of the ailing darky, Dessa Rose. But the white woman would not have felt she had permission to do such a thing if she were under her husband's control and not isolated from other whites. As she nurses that Black baby, she dreams aloud about what she considers to be the source of her own mother-love, her mammy, who is not her mother but her darky slave. In an exchange that emphasizes the way these two women interpret that love, Williams shows us how power relations affect mothering. When Rufel claims that *her* mammy loved her, Dessa Rose retorts, 'You ain't got no mammy . . . What her name then? . . . Child don't know its own mammy's name?' (*Dessa Rose*, p. 119)

In listing the names of *her* mammy's children, names she can remember, Dessa Rose also establishes the existence of a slave community with relationships that provided occasions for the heroism and love that Williams reminds us about in her preface. Her novel opens up the spaces in which that heroism and love can be explored. So Dessa Rose attacks her master because he has killed her lover Kaine. She and the men on the coffle are able to plan an uprising together and that action binds them forever in friendship. Later they are able, in an adventure as exciting as any in American lore, to free themselves and go West. Nevertheless, when she tells her story, many years later to one of her grandchildren, the freed Dessa Rose recalls her mother braiding her hair and her love for Kaine, events that precede the escape adventure. Williams ends the novel with this focus on re-memory, for Dessa Rose insists on having her story written down: '"Oh," she says, "we have paid for our children's place in the world again, and again . . . "'. (*Dessa Rose*, p. 236)

But while Dessa Rose may remember her mother's name, Sethe, Paul D., and Baby Suggs cannot. For Sethe, her mother is a mark, since she knows her only by the circle with a cross branded into her skin, a sign Sethe cannot even find when her mother's rotting body is cut down from the hanging rope. Morrison's novel, then, moves us into those spaces that we do not want to remember, into the spaces where there are no names *but* Beloved—those forgotten ones of the past even to the sixty million anonymous ones of the Middle Passage, those terrible spaces, those existing spaces which for slave women, men, and children can divide them as much as they can bring them together. So in her novel, the adventure is not an exterior one, but the more dangerous internal one of the self-remembering and even understanding its past—of Paul D. who lives through the terror of a chain gang which almost distorts his manhood, of Sethe who kills her own child which almost distorts her womanhood. Of Baby Suggs who cannot remember her own children, of Denver who does not want to remember her mother's act, of Beloved who *is* that part of their past that they all attempt to forget.

In the last pages of the novel Morrison leaves us with that Beloved, 'a loneliness that roams' . . . 'that is alive on its own', but 'by and by is gone', for 'remembering seems unwise'. 'The story of Beloved, of all the beloveds, was not a story to pass on', or one that could be passed on in the records of historians or the slave narrators. And yet it remains in dream, in the 'folk tale', 'in the wind', in the imagination, in fiction. Paradoxically, only when history is explored and evaluated is memory free to flow. Then, although 'somebody forgot to tell somebody something', the past finds its way back into our memory lest, like Beloved, we risk erupting into separate parts. Perhaps that is one reason why African-American women writers are now writing African-American historical novels. As we move into another century when Memory threatens to become abstract history. they remind us that if we want to be whole, we must recall the past, those parts that we want to remember, those parts that we want to forget.

Notes

1. Toni Morrison interviewed by Ntozake Shange on Steve Cannon's show 'It's Magic', WBAI, New York, 1978.
2. Margaret Walker, *How I Wrote Jubilee* (Chicago: Third World Press, 1972).
3. 'Alice Walker and *The Color Purple*', BBC TV Documentary, 1986.
4. Toni Morrison, 'Distinguished University of California Regent's Lecture', University of California, Berkeley, 13 October 1987.
5. Toni Morrison, *Beloved* (New York: Alfred A. Knopf, Inc., 1987), 275. (All subsequent quotations from novel will be cited in the text.)
6. Sherley Anne Williams, *Dessa Rose* (New York: William Morrow and Co., 1986).
7. See Gerda Lerner (ed.), *Black Women in White America: A Documentary History* (New York: Vintage, 1973), 60–3, for the Margaret Garner story.
8. See June Jordan, 'The Difficult Miracle of Black. Poetry in America or Something Like a Sonnet for Phillis Wheatley', in *On Call: Essays* (Boston: South End Press, 1985). Also reprinted in this volume.
9. Walker, *How I Wrote Jubilee.*
10. Barbara Chase-Riboud, *Sally Hemings* (New York: Avon Books, 1979).
11. Morrison, 'Regent's Lecture'.

19 The Occult of True Black Womanhood: Critical Demeanor and Black Feminist Studies

Ann duCille*

> *The Black Woman; The Black Woman: An Anthology; The Black Woman in America; The Black Woman in American Society; The Black Woman Cross-Culturally; Black Women in America; Black Women in White America; Black Women in the Nineteenth Century; Black Women in Nineteenth-Century American Life; Black Women Writers; Black Women Writers at Work; Black Women Writing Autobiography; Black Women Writing the American Experience; Black Women Novelists; Black Women Novelists in the Wake of the Civil Rights Movement; Black Women, Fiction, and Literary Tradition; The Sexual Mountain and Black Women Writers; Ain't I a Woman?; Arn't I a Woman?*

For reasons that may already be obvious, the books named above and numerous others like them have led me to think of myself as a kind of sacred text. Not me personally, of course, but me black woman object, Other. Within and around the modern academy, racial and gender alterity has become a hot commodity that has claimed black women as its principal signifier. I am alternately pleased, puzzled, and perturbed—bewitched, bothered, and bewildered—by this, by the alterity that is perpetually thrust upon African-American women, by the production of black women as infinitely deconstructable 'othered' matter. Why are black women always already Other? I wonder. To myself, of course, I am not Other; to me it is the white women and men so intent on theorizing my difference who are the Other. Why are

I wish to thank the many friends, colleagues, and readers whose insights and critiques helped shape this essay, including Elizabeth Weed, Laura Kipnis, and *Signs's* anonymous reviewers. I am particularly indebted to Indira Karamcheti, Laura Santigian, and Sharon Holland for their wisdom and their willingness to talk me through the many lives (and deaths) of what was for me a very difficult article to write and what will be for some, I am sure, a very difficult article to read.

* From Ann duCille, 'The Occult of True Black Womanhood: Critical Demeanor and Black Feminist Studies' from *Signs* 19:3 (The University of Chicago Press, 1994), 591–629, reprinted by permission of the publisher.

they so interested in me and people who look like me (metaphorically speaking)? Why have we—black women—become the subjected subjects of so much contemporary scholarly investigation, the peasants under glass of intellectual inquiry in the 1990s? [. . .]

Black feminist theorist bell hooks calls the contemporary version of this preoccupation with alterity 'the commodification of Otherness' or 'eating the Other'.[1] [. . .]

Where gender and racial difference meet in the bodies of black women, the result is the invention of an other Otherness, a hyperstatic alterity. Mass culture, as hooks argues, produces, promotes, and perpetuates the commodification of Otherness through the exploitation of the black female body. In the 1990s, however, the principal sites of exploitation are not simply the cabaret, the speakeasy, the music video, the glamour magazine; they are also the academy, the publishing industry, the intellectual community. [. . .] Of course, one of the dangers of standing at an intersection—particularly at such a suddenly busy, three-way intersection—is the likelihood of being run over by oncoming traffic.

Michele Wallace likens the traffic jam that has built up around Zora Neale Hurston, in particular, to a 'rainbow coalition' of critics, who, 'like groupies descending on Elvis Presley's estate,' are engaged in 'a mostly ill-mannered stampede to have some memento of the black woman',[2] who is, at least to some degree, a figment of their individual and collective critical imaginations.

Precisely the question I want to explore in this essay is what it means for black women academics to stand in the midst of the 'dramatically charged field'—the traffic jam—that black feminist studies has become. Are we in the way of the critical stampede that accompanies what I am calling here 'the occult of true black womanhood'? Are we in danger of being trampled by the 'rainbow coalition' of critics—'black, white, male, female, artists and academics, historicists and deconstructionists'—that our own once isolated and isolating intellectual labors have attracted to the magnetic field of black feminist studies?

'HURSTONISM' AND THE BLACK FEMINIST PHENOMENON

In her foreword to the 1978 University of Illinois Press reprint of *Their Eyes Were Watching God*, black poet, novelist, and critic Sherley Anne

Williams tells of first encountering Zora Neale Hurston and *Their Eyes* while a graduate student enrolled in a two-semester survey of black poetry and prose. 'Afro-American literature was still an exotic subject then,' Williams writes, 'rarely taught on any regular basis'.[3] She goes on to describe how she and her classmates fought over the pitifully few copies of African-American texts, long out of print, that they were able to beg, borrow, and otherwise procure from musty basements, rare book collections, and reserved reading rooms. When it finally became her turn to read *Their Eyes Were Watching God*, Williams says she found in the speech of Hurston's characters her own country self and, like Alice Walker and numerous others, became Zora Neale's for life.

For many of us who came of intellectual age in the late sixties and early seventies, Sherley Anne Williams's 'discovery' of Zora is an almost painfully familiar textual encounter of the first kind. While Hurston was not the first black woman writer I encountered or claimed as my own (that was Ann Petry), it was during this same period—1971, in fact—that I, too, discovered Zora. I was introduced to her and to her work by my friend and fellow graduate student, another gifted black woman writer, Gayl Jones. When I began my teaching career a few years later at a college in upstate New York, Gayl was again generous enough to lend me her well-worn, oft-read copy of *Their Eyes.* Only a lingering fear of being prosecuted for copyright infringement prevents me from detailing how I went about sharing among the dozen or so students in my seminar, none of whom had heard of Hurston, the fruits that bloomed within the single, precious, tattered copy of *Their Eyes Were Watching God.*

Twenty years later, African-American studies courses and black women writers such as Hurston are once again exotic subjects. They are exotic this time out, however, not because they are rarely taught or seldom read, but because in the midst of the present, multicultural moment, they have become politically correct, intellectually popular, and commercially precious sites of literary and historical inquiry. Long either altogether ignored as historical and literary subjects or badly misfigured as magnanimous mammies, man-eating matriarchs, or immoral Jezebels, black women—that is, certain black women—and their texts have been taken up by and reconfigured within the academy, elevated and invoked by the intellectual elite as well as the scholarly marginal. Currently in print in several editions, *Their Eyes Were Watching God* has become quasi-canonical, holding a place of honor on syllabi of mainstream history, social science, literature, and

American studies courses, as well as of perhaps more marginalized disciplines such as African American studies and women's studies. Much the same holds true for Alice Walker's *The Color Purple* and Toni Morrison's *Beloved*, each of which has been awarded the Pulitzer Prize for fiction.

It is important to note that black women critics and scholars have played a crucial role in bringing to the academic fore the works of 'lost' writers such as Hurston and Nella Larsen and in opening up spaces within the academy both for the fiction of contemporary African-American women writers and for the study of black and other women of color more generally. While I am usually suspicious of efforts to define benchmarks and signposts, there are nevertheless a number of important essays, anthologies, and monographs that I think can be rightly claimed as the founding texts of contemporary black feminist studies. Toni Cade Bambara's anthology *The Black Woman* (1970), for example—which showcased the prose and poetry of writers such as Nikki Giovanni, Audre Lorde, Paule Marshall, Alice Walker, and Sherley Anne Williams—stands as a pivotal text along with critical essays and literary, historical, and sociological studies by Barbara Smith, Barbara Christian, Frances Beal, Joyce Ladner, Jeanne Noble, Darlene Clark Hine, Angela Davis, Frances Foster, Filomina Chioma Steady, Sharon Harley and Rosalyn Terborg-Penn, and Mary Helen Washington.[4]

While keepers of (dominant) culture have given the lion's share of credit for the development of black literary and cultural studies to male scholars such as Houston Baker, Henry Louis Gates, and Cornel West, Mary Helen Washington nevertheless has been a key player in efforts to define and institutionalize the fields of African American literature and black feminist studies for more than twenty years.[5] [. . .]

Much the same can and must be said of Barbara Christian and Barbara Smith, whose essays on African-American women writers began appearing in print in the mid and latter 1970s. Christian's first book, *Black Women Novelists: The Development of a Tradition, 1892–1976* (1980, see Note 4), which brilliantly analyzed the work of black women writers from Frances Harper to Marshall, Morrison, and Walker, remains a foundational text. . . . Nor have the more than fifteen years since its publication dulled the impact and significance of Barbara Smith's pivotal essay 'Toward a Black Feminist Criticism' ([1977] 1985), a widely reprinted, often anthologized black lesbian feminist critical declaration that, gave name, definition, and political persuasion to the perspective from which Bambara, Washington, and others had been writing.[6] Smith's work in literary criticism and that of her sister Beverly Smith in the area of black women's health have played crucial roles in developing the fields of black feminist and black lesbian feminist studies.

Within the realm of literary studies alone, the names making up even a partial list of pioneering black feminist scholars include Deborah McDowell, Nellie McKay, Hortense Spillers, Gloria Hull, Patricia Bell Scott, Cheryl Wall, Valerie Smith, Mae Henderson, Gloria Wade-Gayles, Thadious Davis, Trudier Harris, Frances Smith Foster, Hazel Carby, Joyce Joyce, and Claudia Tate, as well as Christian, Washington, Smith . . .[7] Toni Morrison, too, has played a particularly dramatic role in opening up spaces for and directing critical attention toward African-American women.

While I, as a beneficiary of their research and writing, am anxious to give credit where credit is long overdue, this essay is not intended as a praisesong for black women scholars, critics, and artists, or even as a review of the literature they have generated.[8] Rather, I would like to examine critically some of the implications and consequences of the current explosion of interest in black women as literary and historical subjects. Among the issues I hope to explore are the ways in which this interest—which seems to me to have reached occult status—increasingly marginalizes both the black women critics and scholars who excavated the fields in question and their black feminist 'daughters' who would further develop those fields.

What does it mean, for example, that many prestigious university presses and influential literary publications such as the *New York Times Book Review* regularly rely not on these seasoned black women scholars but on male intellectuals—black and white—to read, evaluate, and review the book manuscripts of young black women just entering the profession? What does it mean for the black female professoriate that departments often ask powerful senior black male scholars to referee the tenure and promotion cases of the same black women scholars who have challenged or affronted these men in some way? What does it mean for the field in general and for junior African Americanists in particular that senior scholars, who are not trained in African-American studies and whose career-building work often has excluded (or at least not included) black women, are now teaching courses in and publishing texts about African-American literature and generating supposedly 'new scholarship' on black women writers? What does it mean for the future of black feminist studies that a large portion of the growing body of scholarship on black women is now being written by white feminists and by men whose work frequently achieves greater critical and commercial success than that of the black female scholars who carved out a field in which few 'others' were then interested?

My questions are by no means new; nor do I claim to have any particularly insightful answers. I only know that as an African Americanist who has been studying the literature and history of black women for almost thirty years and teaching it for more than twenty, I have a burning need to try to work through on paper my own ambivalence, antipathy, and, at times, animosity over the new-found enthusiasm for these fields that I readily think of as my own hard-won territory. . . .

Elsewhere I have argued against territoriality, against racial, cultural, and gender essentialism, against treating African-American studies as the private property of what Gayatri Spivak calls 'black blacks'.[9] Yet questions of turf and territoriality, appropriation and cooptation persist within my own black feminist consciousness, despite my best efforts to intellectualize them away. Again, this is not a new dilemma. The modern, academic version of the ageless argument over who owns the sacred text of me and mine is at least as old as the work of white anthropologists Melville and Frances Herskovits dating back to the 1920s and reaching a controversial peak in 1941 with the publication of *The Myth of the Negro Past*, a study of African cultural retensions scorned by many black intellectuals.[10] [. . .]

One hundred thirty years ago, former slave Harriet Jacobs was able to publish her life's story only with the authenticating stamp of the well-known white abolitionist Lydia Maria Child as editor and copyright holder. 'I have signed and sealed the contract with Thayer & Eldridge, in my name, and told them to take out the copyright in my name,' Child wrote in a letter to Jacobs in 1860. 'Under the circumstances *your* name could not be used, you know'.[11] The circumstances to which Child alluded (but did not name) were of course the conditions of slavery under which Jacobs had lived for most of her life and from which she had not completely escaped. Now, as then, it often seems to take the interest and intervention of white scholars to legitimize and institutionalize African-American history and literature or such 'minority discourses' as post-coloniality and multiculturalism. Let me offer two examples: Gerda Lerner's *Black Women in White America* and Shelley Fisher Fishkin's *Was Huck Black?*.[12]

Black feminist critic Gloria Wade-Gayles has identified Toni Cade Bambara's *The Black Woman* as 'the first book that pulled together black women's views on black womanhood' and Jeanne Noble's *Beautiful, Also, Are the Souls of My Black Sisters* as the 'first history of black women in America written by a black woman'.[13] Yet, despite the recovery and reconnaissance missions of Bambara, Noble, Joyce Ladner, and other black women intellectuals who did groundbreaking work in the seventies, it is white feminist historian Gerda Lerner whom the academy recognizes as the pioneer in reconstructing the history of African-American women.

With the 1972 publication of her documentary anthology *Black Women in White America*, Lerner became by many reckonings the first historian to produce a book-length study devoted to African-American women. Her goal, as she outlined in her preface, was to call attention to such 'unused sources' as black women's own records of their experiences and 'to bring another forgotten aspect of the black past to life'. In drawing on such first-person accounts as diaries, narratives, testimonies, and organizational records and reports, Lerner endeavored in her volume, she says, 'to let black women speak for themselves'.[14]

While the notion of letting someone speak for herself is surely problematic, I want to note as well that Lerner was by no means the first to draw on what she implies were unexamined resources. Black artists, activists, and intellectuals had made use of these kinds of resources since the nineteenth century. Former slave William Wells Brown, for one, drew on such sources in the many novels, narratives, and histories he published between 1847 and his death in 1884.[15] Although written in a vein admittedly different from Lerner's work, Mrs. N. F. Mossell's *The Work of the Afro-American Woman*, first published in 1894, represents an early effort on the part of an African-American woman to acknowledge the accomplishments and contributions of her black sisters.[16] Black activist, educator, and 'race woman' Anna Julia Cooper wrote of the 'long dull pain' of the 'open-eyed but hitherto voiceless Black Women of America' in *A Voice from the South*, published in 1892.[17] [. . .]

Nor should we ignore the intellectual labors of black literary scholar Charles Nichols, whose masterwork *Many Thousand Gone: The Ex-Slaves' Account of Their Bondage and Freedom* (1963) has directed two generations of researchers interested in slavery to a significant source: the 'forgotten testimony of its victims'.[18] In fact, the methodology Lerner employed in *Black Women in White America* is one perfected by Nichols.

To take up a more contemporary example, I might point out that for decades black writers, critics, and scholars have attempted to delineate the tremendous impact African-American culture has had on the mainstream American literary tradition. Their efforts, however, have received little attention from the academy. But when a white scholar recently asked, 'Was Huckleberry Finn Black?' the academy, the publishing industry, and the media sat up and took notice. I am referring, of course, to the hoopla over Shelley Fisher Fishkin's book *Was Huck Black*? As much as a year before it appeared in bookstores, Fishkin's study was lauded in such influential publications as the *New York Times, Newsweek*, and the *Chronicle of Higher Education*. In fact, according to the London *Times*, more than fifty news items on the book appeared across the country, sporting such headlines as: 'Scholar Concludes That Young Black Was Model for Huck Finn's Voice; Huck Finn Speaks "Black," Scholar Says; and Theory Might Warm Foes to Twain's Novel'.[19] [. . .]

I do not mean to make little or light of Shelley Fishkin's research and conclusions: hers is important and provocative work. What I am intrigued by, however, is the response from the white intellectual establishment. Why is the conclusion that 'we need to pay more attention to African-American culture, even when we study the canon' suddenly being greeted as news? Black scholars have long argued the reflexive nature of cultural appropriation and the interrelatedness of so-called minor and major traditions. Speaking at a socialist conference in 1917, James Weldon Johnson, whom David Levering Lewis calls the 'dean of Afro-American letters,' reportedly shocked his audience by declaring that '"the only things artistic in America that have sprung from American soil, permeated American life, and been universally acknowledged as distinctively American" were the creations of the Afro-American'.[20] No African Americanist I know has been surprised at being told at this late date what many of us have argued for a long time: that Twain, like many major white American writers, drew canon fodder from 'the black experiences' that are a fundamental, if often unacknowledged, part of American culture.

These and numerous other examples suggest to me a kind of color line and intellectual passing within and around the academy: black culture is more easily intellectualized (and canonized) when transferred from the danger of lived black experience to the safety of white metaphor, when you can have that 'signifying black difference' without the difference of significant blackness. Fishkin's work, like

Lerner's, is undeniably important, but it does not stand alone as revolutionary. 'Sociable Jimmy,' the young black boy on whose vernacular speech Twain may have based Huck's colorful language, may never have gotten to speak for himself in print, but black women had been speaking for themselves and on behalf of each other long before Gerda Lerner endeavored 'to let' them do so.

The question of who speaks for me, who can write my sacred text, is as emotionally and politically charged as it is enduring and controversial. Asked about the explosion of interest in the lives and literature of black women among male scholars and white feminists, Barbara Christian responded in part: 'It is galling to me that after black women critics of the 1970s plowed the neglected field of Afro-American women's literature when such an act was academically dangerous, that some male and white feminist scholars now seem to be reaping the harvest and are major commentators on this literature in influential, though not necessarily feminist journals such as *The New York Review of Books.* Historical amnesia seems to be as much a feature of intellectual life as other aspects of American society'.[21]

[. . .] Christian's remarks imply black women's expressivity is not merely discourse; it has become lucre in the intellectual marketplace, cultural commerce. What for many began as a search for our mothers' gardens, to appropriate Alice Walker's metaphor,[22] has become for some a Random House harvest worth millions in book sales and prestigious university professorships. Sensitive as the issue is, it must be said at some point and even at the risk of hurt feelings that the explosion of interest in the black female subject is at least in some measure about economics—about jobs. White feminist scholar Elizabeth Abel has acknowledged as much. 'This new attentiveness [to texts by women of color] has been overdetermined', she argues, 'by the sheer brilliance and power of this writing and its escalating status in the literary marketplace and, consequently, the academy; [and] by white feminist restlessness with an already well-mined white female literary tradition'.[23] For many scholars trained in these well-mined fields, the shift to African-American studies has yielded more prominent positions at more prestigious institutions.

But is this, as it seems to be for Barbara Christian, necessarily a bitter harvest? We—'we' being here African-American women scholars—have complained long and loud about exclusion, about the degree to which white feminists and male critics have ignored the work of black women. Can we now legitimately complain that they are taking up (and taking over?) this important work? And what do such complaints tell us about ourselves and our relationship to what many of us continue to speak of as *our* literature?[24]

While, as I have acknowledged, I, too, am troubled, even galled by what at times feels like the appropriation and co-optation of black women by white feminists and by men, what I ultimately want to get at in this article is not simply about property rights, about racial or gender territoriality. It is by no means my intention to claim Hurston, Morrison, Walker, et al. as the private property of black women readers who, like Sherley Anne Williams, see themselves in their characters. In fact, I have argued elsewhere that rather than liberating and valorizing black female voices, the celebration of African-American women's literature and history as the discursively familiar, as a 'truth' to which black women scholars have privileged access rooted in common experience, both delimits and demeans those discourses. For, however inadvertently, it restricts this work to a narrow orbit in which it can be readily validated only by those black and female for whom it reproduces what they already know.[25]

Undeniably critical contributions to the study of black women and their literature and history have been made by scholars who are neither black nor female. The name of William L. Andrews comes to mind immediately, as does that of Robert Hemenway.[26] That we have increased access to the autobiographical writings of nineteenth-century African-American women is due in part to Andrews's effort. That Hurston's work is now so readily accessible is due in no small measure not only to the efforts of black feminist writer Alice Walker, but also to those of white male scholar Robert Hemenway. Through the research and publishing efforts of white feminist scholar Jean Fagan Yellin and black male theorist Henry Louis Gates, to cite two other examples, we now have authentification of and access to two fundamental texts from the nineteenth century: Harriet Jacob's *Incidents in the Life of a Slave Girl, Written by Herself* and Harriet Wilson's *Our Nig*.[27] [. . .]. The recent work of white feminist scholar Elizabeth Ammons also represents a positive turn in literary studies. In its intercultural readings of works by African, Asian, Native, Jewish, and white American women, her book *Conflicting Stories: American Women Writers at the Turn into the Twentieth Century*[28] represents a model we all would do well to follow.

Surely this is great work and good news. Why, then, am I and so many other black feminist scholars left wrestling with such enduring questions about co-optation and exploitation? Why are we haunted by a growing sense that we are witnessing (and perhaps even have inspired in some way) the commodification of the same black womanhood we have championed? It is a mistake, I think, to define this persistent (but perhaps inherently unresolvable) debate over who can read black female texts as strictly or even perhaps primarily racial or cultural or gendered: black/white, male/female, insider/outsider, our literature/your theory, my familiar/their foreign. The most important questions, I have begun to suspect, may not be about the essentialism and territoriality, the biology, sociology, or even the ideology about which we hear so much but, rather, about professionalism and disciplinarity; about cultural literacy and intellectual competence; about taking ourselves seriously and insisting that we be taken seriously not as objectified subjects in someone else's histories—as native informants—but as critics and as scholars reading and writing our own literature and history.

DISCIPLINARY MATTERS: WHEN DEMEANOR DEMEANS

So I have arrived at what for me is at the heart of what's the matter. Much of the newfound interest in African-American women that seems to honor the field of black feminist studies actually demeans it by treating it not like a discipline with a history and a body of rigorous scholarship and distinguished scholars underpinning it, but like an anybody-can-play pick-up game performed on a wide-open, untrammeled field. [. . .] Moreover, many of the rules that the academy generally invokes in doing its institutional business—in making appointments, assigning courses, and advancing faculty—are suddenly suspended when what is at stake is not the valorized, traditional disciplines of Western civilization but the more marginal, if extremely popular, fields within African-American studies.

Among those elements considered when English departments hire Medievalists, Victorianists, Americanists, and so on, at least in my experience in the academy, are school(s) attended, the nature of one's graduate training, the subject of one's dissertation, and not only what one has published but where one has published as well. Were the articles refereed? Were they published in reputable academic journals? Are the journals discipline specific, edited and juried by experts in the candidate's field, scholars who know whereof they read? I have seen these valorized criteria relaxed time and time again, however, when these same traditionally trained, nonblack scholars are being hired not in the fields in which they were educated but in African-American studies. Interestingly enough, the same loosening of standards does not readily occur when black scholars—particularly young black scholars—apply for positions as generalists in American or world literature. The fact that the educational system is such that it is still largely impossible to specialize in African-American literature without first being trained in the European and Anglo-American canons does not keep the powers that be from questioning the preparedness of blacks who apply for jobs as generalists. A dissertation on Toni Morrison or C. L. R. James or W. E. B. Du Bois does not necessarily qualify one as an Americanist, but a thesis on Chaucer or the Brontës or Byron is not an impediment to an appointment as an African-Americanist. [At the same time] black scholars duly and properly trained and credentialed in traditional fields—medieval studies, for example—are often assumed or expected to be ready, willing, and able to teach black studies courses. [. . .] Moreover, black scholars on predominantly or overwhelmingly white campuses are rarely authorized simply as scholars. Rather, our racial difference is an authenticating stamp that, as Indira Karamcheti has argued, often casts us in the role of Caliban in the classroom 'as traveling icons of culture,'[29]

[. . .] This is particularly true for black women scholars on white college campuses where they experience both a hypervisibility and a superisolation by virtue of their racial and gender difference. Unfortunately, icons are not granted tenure automatically; when their canonical year rolls around, all too often these same black women faculty members who have been drawn on as exemplars and used up as icons will find themselves chewed up and spit out because they did not publish. [. . .] Sympathetic white colleagues lament their black colleagues' departures from the university: 'Why didn't she just say "no"?' they ask each other, rarely remembering the many times they implored her to just say 'yes,' . . .

Given the occult of true black womanhood, to be (not so) young, female, and black on today's college campuses is difficult, to be sure. But more troubling still is the fact that commodified, Calibanized black women intellectuals, whose authority as academicians has often been questioned at every turn in their careers, are not supposed to resent, or even to notice, the double standard that propels others forward even as it keeps them back. For the most part, however, black women in the academy not only have noticed, we have refused to suffer in silence; our complaints are by now old news. Many ears, once sympathetic to 'the black woman's plight', her 'double jeopardy', her 'exceptional burdens', have been frozen by the many winters of our discontent. Our grievances have begun to be heard only as 'anti-intellectual identity politics' and 'proprietary claims'. What Houston Baker describes as our 'black feminist manifestos'—our 'admonitions, injunctions, and cautions to those who wish to share the open road'[30]—reveal us to be, even to our most supportive colleagues, small-minded, mean-spirited, and downright petty.

Of course, my point is that for many of us . . . , questioning the race, ethnicity, culture, and credentials of those the academy authorizes to write *our* histories and to teach and interpret *our* literature is anything but petty. Rather, it is a concern that rises from the deepest recesses of who we are in relation to where we live and work. Black women have pioneered a field that even after more than twenty years remains marginalized within the university, regardless of how popular both the field and its black women practitioners are with students. Our at once precarious and overdetermined positions in the academy and our intimate knowledge of social, intellectual, and academic history prompt us not simply to guard our turf, as often accused, but also to discipline *our* field, to preserve its integrity and our own.

I have emphasized the pronoun *our* in order to problematize the admitted possessiveness of our disciplinary concerns. For no matter how compelling—no matter how historically resonant—the sense of personal stake that permeates the scholarship by black women about black women just may be an aspect of the insider/outsider problematic for which African-American women academics have to take responsibility. It may be time for us to interrogate in new and increasingly clinical ways our proprietary relationship to the field many of us continue to think of as *our own*.

Such internal review presents its own problematic, however. To claim privileged access to the lives and literature of African-American women through what we hold to be the shared experiences of our black female bodies is to co-operate with our own commodification, to buy from and sell back to the dominant culture its constitution of our always already essentialized identity. On the other hand, to relinquish claim to the experiences of the black body and to confirm and affirm its study purely as discourse, simply as a field of inquiry equally open to all, is to collaborate with our own objectification. We become objects of study where we are authorized to be the story but have no special claim to decoding that story. We can be, but someone else gets to tell us what we mean.

This conundrum operates, of course, in realms beyond the either/or options I have established here. But how to find the middle ground, that happier medium? How do we negotiate an intellectually charged space for experience in a way that is not totalizing and essentializing—a space that acknowledges the constructedness of and the differences within our lived experiences while at the same time attending to the inclining, rather than the declining, significance of race, class, culture, and gender? [. . .]

CRITICAL APOLOGIA: THE DRIVING MISS DAISY CRAZY SYNDROME

[. . .] If a Ph.D. in British literature is not a title deed to the African-American text, neither is black skin. Romantic fantasies of an authentic, cohesive, magical, ancient, all-knowing black female folk are certainly not unique to white academics who would read black women. Some might argue that what is at issue is not simply the color or culture of the scholar but the kind, quality, and cultural competence of the scholarship. Black historian Carter Woodson reportedly welcomed the contributions of white scholars, 'so long as they were the products of rigorous scholarship and were not contaminated by the venom of racial [and, I would add, gender] bias'.[31] Unfortunately, however, such biases are ideologically inscribed and institutionally reproduced and as such are not easily elided—not even by the most liberal, the most sensitive, the most well-intentioned among us. I think, for example, of Adrienne Rich.

I had long been a fan of Rich's poetry, but I was rather late in coming to her prose. *Of Woman Born: Motherhood as Experience and Institution*, originally published in 1976, was more than a dozen years old before I gave myself the pleasure of reading it. For once, however, my timing could not have been better, for I 'discovered' this essential book at a critical moment in my life and in the development of my feminism: on the eve of my fortieth birthday, as I wrestled with the likelihood of never having a child. Rich's brilliant analysis of motherhood as an instrument of patriarchy helped me come to terms with the constructedness of what I had been reared to believe were natural maternal instincts without which I was no woman. But for all that Rich's book gave me, it also took something away . . .[32]

For a moment in the penultimate chapter of this passionate and painful critique of motherhood, Rich turns her remarks toward the black woman who helped raise her. To this woman, who remains nameless, Rich assigns the designation 'my Black mother'. 'My Black mother was "mine"', she writes, 'only for four years, during which she fed me, dressed me, played with me, watched over me, sang to me, cared for me tenderly and intimately'. Rich goes on to describe poetically the physical presence of her Black mother, from whom she 'learned—*nonverbally*—a great deal about the possibilities of dignity in a degrading situation' (my emphasis). Unaware of the degrading situation she creates with her words, she continues: 'When I began writing this chapter I began to remember my Black mother again: her calm, realistic vision of things, her physical grace and pride, her beautiful soft voice. For years, she had drifted out of reach, in my searches backward through time, exactly as the double silence of sexism and racism intended her to do. She was meant to be utterly annihilated'.[33]

To the double silences of sexism and racism Rich adds a third: the silence (and the blindness) of feminism. . . . Although she no doubt means to honor the woman who cared for her as a child, the poetry of her prose should not mask the annihilating effect of her claim on the being she resurrects and recreates as 'my Black mother'. Silent and nameless in Rich's book, 'my Black mother' has no identity of her own and, in fact, does not exist beyond the care and nurture she gave exclusively to the young Adrienne.

'"Childless" herself, she *was* a mother', Rich writes. Her . . . attempt to thrust motherhood upon a childless black woman domestic worker are all the more ironic because of what she claims for all women in the introduction to the anniversary edition of *Of Woman Born*: 'The claim to personhood; the claim to share justly in the products of our labor, not to be used merely as an instrument, a role, a womb, a pair of hands or a back or a set of fingers; to participate fully in the decisions of our workplace, our community; to speak for ourselves, in our own right'.[34] Even in the midst of her own extended critique of the mystification of motherhood and the objectification of women as mothers, Rich has both mystified and objectified someone she can see only in the possessive case as 'my Black mother'. 'My Black mother' is a role, a pair of hands; her function is to instruct the white child 'nonverbally' in the ways of the world, even as she cannot speak 'in [her] own right'.[35]

The kind of transformative move Rich makes in invoking the silent racial, maternalized Other is in no way unique to her prose. The child may be father of the man in poetry, but frequently when white scholars reminisce about blacks from their past it is black mammy (metaphorically speaking, even where the mammy figure is a man) who mothers the ignorant white infant into enlightenment. Often as the youthful, sometimes guilty witness to or cause of the silent martyrdom of the older Other, the privileged white person inherits a wisdom, an agelessness, perhaps even a racelessness that entitles him or her to the raw materials of another's life and culture but, of course, not to the Other's condition.

Such transformative moves often occur in the forewords, afterwords, rationales, even apologias white scholars affix to their would-be scholarly readings of the black Other—discussions that methinks just may protest too much, perhaps suggesting a somewhat uneasy relationship between author and objectified subject. These prefaces acknowledge the 'outsider' status of the authors—their privileged positions as white women or as men—even as they insist on the rightness of their entry into and the significance of their impact on the fields of black literature and history. [. . .]

In the opening chapter of his study Callahan takes us on a sentimental journey through his Irish-American youth, which was *colored* not only by his being likened to niggers—('"Do you know the definition of an Irishman?"' the eight-year-old Callahan was asked by a much bigger Italian boy. '"A Nigger turned inside-out"'[36])—but also by the black male guardians and protectors who 'taught [him] a great deal about the hard work of becoming a man'.[37] The teaching tools used by one of these guardians—Bill Jackson, the chauffeur for the insurance company for which Callahan worked while in college—include a 'prolonged *silent* challenge' after Callahan called him a black bastard[38] and his 'trickster's way' of teaching Callahan certain lessons.

Like Adrienne Rich, Callahan describes his black guide as 'silent,' even as he credits the chauffeur with teaching him many things 'essential to [his] own evolving voice and story'.[39] Indeed Bill Jackson, the stereotypical black trickster, remains silent as he is employed by Callahan to claim not only Callahan's own Irish-American voice but also entitlement to African-American fictions of voice, fictions that in the author's words 'connect and reconnect generations of Americans—African-American, yes and preeminently, but all others too, Irish-Americans like me, for instance—with those past and present oral traditions behind our evolving spoken and written voices'.[40]

Here again a critical posturing that means to celebrate a literature to my mind actually demeans it by leveling and universalizing it. Callahan's introduction suggests that we are all brothers not only under the skin but under the book jacket as well. The white scholar understands 'the African American experience' not in its own right, not on its own terms, but because he can make it like his own. With his voice, he can translate another's silence into his speech. He speaks through and for the Other. Bill Jackson's silence is telling in this translative move, but so too is his profession. It is altogether fitting and proper that Jackson is a chauffeur, for indeed Callahan's introduction and Jackson's role in it invoke for me what I call the *Driving Miss Daisy* syndrome: an intellectual sleight of hand that transforms power and race relations to make best friends out of driver and driven, master and slave, boss and servant, white boy and black man.

When Callahan overhears the company vice-president lumping together Irish and African-Americans as 'contemptible, expendable lower caste,' he wishes for the craft, strength, skill, and smarts of a black football player he admires from a distance to help him speak up for himself (though apparently not for the niggers with whom he is compared). 'My fate linked to African-Americans by that Yankee bank officer', Callahan writes, 'I became more alert and sympathetic to black Americans my own age and younger who, though cursed, spat upon, and beaten, put their lives and voices on the line to uphold the law of the land and integrate public schools in the South'.[41]

I feel as if I am supposed to applaud this declaration of allegiance, empathy, and understanding, but instead the claim of fellow feeling and universality—of linked fates and shared voice—makes me profoundly angry and mars my reading of what is actually a very fine book. Ultimately, Callahan's personal narrative, like Rich's, takes symbolic wealth from the martyred, romanticized black body but retains the luxury of refusing, erasing, or ignoring its material poverty. Twenty-five years later, John Callahan is a well-respected university professor while, as he tells us in his introduction, Roy Fitch—the protective black mailroom manager under whom he once worked—'looks after' a building near the 'plebeian end' of the city green.[42] Intent as he is on using Fitch to tell his story, Callahan does not comment on or I suspect even see the historical irony of their relative positions. Nor does he grasp the ironic implications of his own storytelling. 'Don't climb no mountain on my back', he recalls Fitch saying to him years before in response to his awkward attempt to apologize for yet another racial slur. Had Callahan understood the signifying significance of Fitch's word—were he as good at interpreting speech as silence—he could not possibly have written the introduction he did. [. . .]

I know I am misbehaving. I know I should be more patient, more sisterly, more respectful of other people's discoveries. I know my bad attitude comes from what in this instance might be called the arrogance of 'black privilege' . . . But I mean my criticism as a kindness. Perhaps if I can approximate in words—however haltingly—what is so profoundly offensive about these *Driving-Miss-Daisy*/some-of-my-best-friends-are-black/I-once-was-a-racist confessionals, I will do the field and all those who want to work in it a genuine favor. Perhaps if I can begin to delineate the difference between critical analysis that honors the field and guilty conscience rhetoric that demeans it, I can contribute something positive to the future production of scholarship on African-American women. Unfortunately, the words do not come easily and the heart of what's the matter is a difficult place to get to. How do you tell people who do not get it in the first instance that it is only out of the arrogance of white privilege and/or male prerogative that they assume that it is an honor for a black woman to be proclaimed their black mother or their black friend or their black guardian or their black conscience?

It would be a mistake, however, for me to imply that these demeaning gestures are solely the product of white privilege and racial difference. For my money, the occult of true black womanhood has generated few more offensive renderings of African-American women writers and critics than that offered by black literary theorist Houston Baker in *Workings of the Spirit: The Poetics of Afro-American Women's Writing*. Having largely ignored black women as cultural producers throughout his long and distinguished career, Baker suddenly takes them up in *Workings*.

[. . .] Baker also has included an introduction that calls attention to himself as outsider. He begins his study by acknowledging the prior claim and what he calls the justifiably 'cautious anxieties' of black feminist critics such as Barbara Smith, Barbara Christian, and Mary Helen Washington, who long ago mined the 'provinces of Afro-American women's expressivity' that he is just now entering. A 'blackmale' scholar 'will find cause to mind his steps in a demanding territory', he asserts, seemingly unaware of the step he misses with his province/metropole metaphor. Baker's language here works linguistically to confirm him in the very role he wants most to avoid—that of colonizing, come-lately 'blackmale' critic. His diction is a small example of what I found to be a big problem with *Workings of the Spirit:* the hierarchical relation between what he inevitably treats as master (male) and minor (female) narrative traditions, even in this book dedicated to exploring black female expressivity. Rather than building on the work of black women scholars who excavated the field he is just now entering, Baker, for the most part, either ignores or dismisses what he implies is their primarily historical (as opposed to theoretical) feminist criticism in favor of his own masculinist theorizing and the black male writers and white male theorists he champions.

In *Workings of the Spirit*, our mothers' gardens are populated by what Baker terms *phenomenological* white men such as Gaston Bachelard along with the phenomenal black women—Hurston, Morrison, and Shange—who are the book's announced subjects. Indeed, Baker's study of black women writers marginalizes its female objectified subjects as male writers, critics, theorists, and male experience prevail as the text's principal referents. In *Workings*'s third chapter, for example, to even get to Baker's reading of Toni Morrison's *Sula*, one must first wade through thirty pages on Richard Wright. The attention to Wright (and other male artists and intellectuals) is justified, Baker argues, because 'classic Afro-American male texts' provide a touchstone from which 'to proceed by distinctions' in exploring the provinces of black female expressivity.

Baker's posterior positioning of Morrison within a chapter supposedly devoted to her work intersects the problematic I have been working with in this article. Like much of the new 'new scholarship' that has come out of the occult of true black womanhood, Baker's book fails to live up to its own postmodern, deconstructive principles. It achieves neither inversion nor subversion; black women writers and the black feminist critics who read them remain fetishized bodies juxtaposed against analytical white or superior male minds. As objects of investigation in studies like Baker's, black women are constructed in terms of their difference from or (in the name of sisterhood) similarity to the spectator, whether the spectator is a black male theorist or a white feminist critic. In other words, the black female Other is made only more Other by the male theorist or by the 'white female academic' (to use Jane Gallop's phrase) who views the objectified subject from a position of unrelinquished authority.

This failure of inversion is particularly alarming in Baker's case because of the enormous power he wields in the academy and the publishing industry. That *Workings of the Spirit* was published as part of a series Baker edits under the University of Chicago imprint suggests just how absolutely absolute power authorizes and reproduces itself. For black feminist studies, the ramifications of this power dynamic are potentially devasting: black feminist critics can be deauthorized with a roll of the presses, even as black women are deployed in a decidedly masculinist project that claims to 'enter into dialogue' with them.

Baker is, of course, free to disagree with black women scholars (as we frequently do with each other), but his failure to take seriously their critical insights ultimately undermines his effort to enter into what he acknowledges is an already established dialogue. His privileging of male subjects in this book supposedly about black women writers becomes an act of silencing and makes his text the victim of its own intentional phallacy. By 'intentional phallacy,' I mean the gap between Baker's stated wish to avoid appropriating and objectifying the work and images of African-American women through a 'blackmale' gaze and the degree to which his text fosters rather than avoids such appropriations.

His essential and, I think, essentializing metaphors—black women as 'departed daughters' and 'spirit workers'—taken together with the uncontextualized photographs of black women interspersed throughout his book, raise questions about the gaze, about specularization and objectification, that Baker, despite his desire not to 'colonize' the female subject, does not address or, I suspect, even see. This is both ironic and unfortunate, since Mae Henderson—one of the black feminist critics Baker faintly praises for her 'fine theorizing'—called his attention to the problematic of the gaze generated by his work in a critique of an earlier essay of his that was the prototype for *Workings of the Spirit.* The danger, she warned, 'is not only that of essentializing but of reinforcing the most conventional constructs of (black) femininity.' Henderson was troubled in particular by the '*specularity* of [Baker's] rather spectacular theory' of black female spirituality. She cautioned him to rethink his treatment of black women in terms that would not objectify and idealize them.[43]

While the words of praise from Henderson excerpted on *Workings*'s back cover imply her endorsement of Baker's finished project, she in fact has offered the author both an elegantly incisive critique and an eloquently pointed admonition. Her cautionary tale has been little heeded, however; *Workings of the Spirit,* I would argue, continues the idealization and specularization of black women that its prototypical essay began. The book's complementary phototext seems to me, in fact, to evoke precisely what Henderson identified as 'the male activity of scopophilia'. Largely unremarked except for occasional captioned quotations from Baker's written word, the images of black women interspersed throughout the text objectify graphically those whom the book objectifies linguistically. But in another example of Baker's strategic deployment of women, this objectification is made *okay* by the author's claim that the phototext is the handiwork not of senior 'blackmale' theorist Houston Baker but of junior female scholars Elizabeth Alexander and Patricia Redmond. This, in fact, is Baker's final point, his 'last word':

> The phototext is the artistry of two young scholars. Their complementary text is a rich enhancement of the present work, and I cannot thank Elizabeth Alexander and Patricia Redmond enough for their collaboration. It seems to me that the intertextuality represented by their effort makes the present work more engaging than it would otherwise have been. My initial idea was that such a text would comprise a type of countercurrent of signification, soliciting always my own words, qualifying their 'maleness.' What emerged from the labors of Redmond and Alexander, however, is a visualization of an Afro-American women's poetics. Eyes and events engage the reader/viewer in a solicitous order of discourse that asks: 'Who reads here?'[44]

If these photos indeed could ask such a question, I suspect that their answer would be, 'A man.' Baker means for the photographs to speak for themselves of 'the space, place, and time of Afro-American women'[45], but it is unclear how they are to do so placed unproblematically in the midst of what is—despite his claims about the collaborative efforts of Alexander and Redmond—*his* project. Whose project the phototext is becomes even clearer when we know that at the time the book was compiled Alexander and Redmond were graduate students to whom Baker assigned the task of assembling a complementary photo essay. The image that Alexander and Redmond presented to Baker as the 'parting shot' of his book is of a young black woman, her mouth open wide as if in a scream. I wonder what it means that the black woman depicted in midscream is literally, physically, clinically mute.

TOWARD A CONCLUSION

I am not quite certain what to make of the ground I have covered in this article or where to go from here. More bewitched, bothered, and bewildered than ever by my own problematic, I find myself oddly drawn to (gulp) William Faulkner. The griefs of great literature, Faulkner suggested in his Nobel Prize acceptance speech, must grieve on universal bones. I realize that I have heard this before—and not just from Faulkner. The Self recognition spontaneously generated by the literature of the ennobled Other is the essence of Callahan's professed link to African-American 'fictions of voice' and the medium of Baker's claimed connection to the texts of black women. And they are not alone in this kind of association with the ennobled Other. In the words of three white feminist academics who claim to identify closely with the explicit depiction of physical and psychic abuse in the fiction of black women writers such as Toni Morrison, Alice Walker, and Gayl Jones: 'We, as white feminists, are drawn to black women's visions because they concretize and make vivid a system of oppression'. Indeed, they continue, 'it has not been unusual for white women writers to seek to understand their oppression through reference to the atrocities experienced by other groups'.[46] For these feminists, the lure of black women's fiction is, at least in part, its capacity to teach others how to endure and prevail, how to understand and rise above not necessarily the pain of black women but their own.

Is this usage of black women's texts a bad thing? If Faulkner is right—if it is the writer's duty to help humankind endure by reminding us of our capacity for courage and honor and hope and pride and compassion and pity and sacrifice and survival—black women writers have done the job particularly well. The griefs of African-American women indeed seem to grieve on universal bones—'to concretize and make vivid a system of oppression'. But it also seems (and herein lies the rub) that in order to grieve 'universally', to be 'concrete', to have 'larger meaning', the flesh on these bones ultimately always must be white or male.

This, then, is the final paradox and the ultimate failure of the evidence of experience: to be valid—to be true—black womanhood must be legible as white or male; the texts of black women must be readable as maps, indexes to someone else's experience, subject to a seemingly endless process of translation and transference. Under the cult of true black womanhood, the colored body, as Cherríe Moraga has argued, is 'thrown over a river of tormented history to bridge the gap',[47] to make connections—connections that in this instance enable scholars working in exhausted fields to cross over into the promised land of the academy.

Both black women writers and the black feminist critics who have brought them from the depths of obscurity into the ranks of the academy have been such bridges. The trouble is that, as Moraga points out, bridges get walked on over and over and over again. This sense of being a bridge—of being walked on and passed over, of being used up and burnt out, of having to 'publish while perishing', as some have described their situations—seems to be a part of the human condition of many black women scholars. While neither the academy nor mainstream feminism has paid much attention to the crisis of black female intellectuals, the issue is much on the minds of black feminist scholars, particularly in the wake of the Thomas/Hill hearings, the critique of professional women and family values, and the loss of Audre Lorde and Sylvia Boone in a single year. So serious are these issues that the state and fate of black women in and around the university were the subjects of a national conference held at the Massachusetts Institute of Technology in January 1994. Entitled 'Black Women in the Academy: Defending Our Name, 1894–1994', this conference, the first of its kind, drew together nearly two thousand black women from institutions across the country. The conference organizers have said that they were overwhelmed by the response to their call for papers: they were instantly bombarded by hundreds of abstracts, letters, faxes, and phone calls from black women describing the hypervisibility, superisolation, emotional quarantine, and psychic violence of their precarious positions in academia.

I do not mean to imply that all black women scholars see themselves as what Hurston called 'tragically colored', but I think that it is safe to say that these testimonies from across the country represent a plaintive cry from black women academics who see themselves and their sisters consumed by exhaustion, depression, loneliness, and a higher incidence of such killing diseases as hypertension, lupus, cancer, diabetes, and obesity. But it also seems to me that the white feminist's concern that there is no position from which a middle-class white woman can speak about race without being offensive, and Houston Baker's desire for dialogue with black women scholars also represent plaintive cries. Clearly both white women and women and men of color experience the pain and disappointment of failed community.

As much as I would like to end on a positive note, I have little faith that our generation of scholars—black and nonblack, male and female—will succeed in solving the problems I have taken up in this article. We are too set in our ways, too alternately defensive and offensive, too much the products of the white patriarchal society that has reared us and the white Eurocentric educational system that has trained us. If ever there comes a day when white scholars are forced by the systems that educate them to know as much about 'the Other' as scholars of color are required to know about so-called dominant cultures, perhaps black women will no longer be treated as consumable commodities.

Until that day, I see a glimmer of hope shining in the bright eyes of my students who seem to me better equipped than we to explore the intersection of racial and gender difference. I was impressed by the way young women—black and white—and one lone white man in a seminar I offered on black feminist critical theory were able to grapple less with each other and more with issues, to disagree without being disagreeable, and to learn from and with each other. I wonder if there is a lesson for us older (but not necessarily wiser) academics in their interaction. I wonder what it would mean for feminist scholarship in general if 'woman' were truly an all-inclusive category, if 'as a woman' ceased to mean 'as a white woman'. I wonder what it would mean for women's studies, for black studies, for American studies, if women of color, white women, and men were truly able to work together to produce the best of all possible scholarship. [. . .]

Notes

This chapter was edited by Ann duCille and Kum-Kum Bhavnani.

1. bell hooks, *Black Looks: Race and Representation* (Boston: South. End Press, 1992).
2. Michele Wallace, 'Who Owns Zora Neale Hurston? Critics Carve Up the Legend', in her *Invisibility Blues* (New York: Verso, 1990), 172–86.
3. Sherley Anne Williams, 'Foreword', in Zora Neale Hurston, *Their Eyes Were Watching God.* (Urbana University of Illinois Press, 1978), vi.
4. See, among many others: Toni Cade Bambara, *The Black Woman.* (New York: New American Library, 1970); Beal, Frances 'Double Jeopardy: To Be Black and Female', in Robert Morgan (ed.), *Sisterhood Is Powerful* (New York: Random House, 1970), 340–52; Angela Davis, 'Reflections on the Black Woman's Role in the Community of Slaves', *Black Scholar* 3 (December 1971), 3–15; Angela Davis, *Women, Race and Class* (New York: Random House, 1981); Joyce Ladner, *Tomorrow's Tomorrow: The Black Woman* (New York: Doubleday, 1972); Mary Helen Washington, 'Zora Neale Hurston: The Black Woman's Search for Identity', *Black World* (August 1972), 68–75; Mary Helen Washington, 'Their Fiction Becomes Our Reality: Black Women Image Makers', *Black World* (August 1974), 10–18; Mary Helen Washington, 'Introduction', in *Black-Eyed Susans: Classic Stories by and about Black Women*, Mary Helen Washington (ed.), (Garden City, NY: Anchor, 1975), ix–xxxii; Mary Helen Washington, 'In Pursuit of Our Own History', in M. H. Washington (ed.), *Midnight Birds: Stories of Contemporary Black Women Writers* (Garden City, NY: Anchor), xiii–xxv; Frances Foster, 'Changing Concept of the Black Woman'. *Journal of Black Studies* (June 1973), 433–52; Sharon J., Skeeter, 'Black Women Writers: Levels of Identity'. *Essence* 4 (May 1973), 3–10; Barbara Christian, 'Images of Black Women in Afro-American Literature: From Stereotype to Character', in her *Black Feminist Criticism: Perspectives on Black Women Writers* (New York: Pergamon, 1975/1985), 1–30; Barbara Christian.

Black Women Novelists: The Development of a Tradition, 1892–1976 (Westport, CT: Greenwood, 1980); Barbara Christian, Ann duCille, Sharon Marcus, Elaine Marks, Nancy K. Miller, Sylvia Schafer and Joan W. Scott. 'Conference Call', *Differences* 2 (Fall 1990), 52–108; Barbara Smith, 'Toward a Black Feminist Criticism', in Elaine Showalter (ed.), *The New Feminist Criticism: Essays on Women, Literature, and Theory* (New York: Pantheon, 1985 (1977)); Barbara Smith, 'Notes for Yet Another Paper on Black Feminism, or Will the Real Enemy Please Stand Up?' *Conditions: Five* (1979), 123–7; Sharon Harley and Rosalyn Terborg-Penn, (eds.) *The Afro-American Woman: Struggles and Images* (New York: Kennikat, 1978); Jeanne Noble, *Beautiful, Also, Are the Souls of My Black Sisters* (Englewood Cliffs, NJ: Prentice-Hall, 1978); Roseanne P., Bell, Bettye J. Parker and Beverly Guy-Sheftall (eds.), *Sturdy Black Bridges: Visions of Black Women in Literature* (Garden City, NY: Anchor, 1979); Bonnie Thornton Dill, 'Across the Barriers of Race and Class: An Exploration of the Relationship between Female Domestic Servants'. Ph.D. dissertation, New York University, 1979; B.T. Dill, 'The Dialectics of Black Womanhood'. *Signs* 4 (Spring, 1979), 543–55; B.T. Dill, 'Race, Class, and Gender: Prospects for an All-inclusive Sisterhood', *Feminist Studies* 9 (Spring 1983), 131–50; Darlene Clark Hine, 'The Four Black History Movements: A Case for the Teaching of Black History', *Teaching History: A Journal of Methods* 5 (Fall 1980), 115. Quoted in Meier and Rudwick 1986; Darlene Clark Hine, *When the Truth Is Told: A History of Black Women's Culture and Community in Indiana, 1875–1950* (Indianapolis: National Council of Negro Women, 1981); Darlene Clark Hine, and Kate Wittenstein, 'Female Slave Resistance: The Economics of Sex', *Western Journal of Black Studies* 3 (1983), 123–7; bell hooks, *Ain't I a Woman?* (Boston South End Press, 1981); Filomina Chioma Steady, (ed.), *The Black Woman Cross-Culturally* (Cambridge, MA: Schenkman, 1981); Gloria Hull, Patricia Bell Scott and Barbara Smith (eds.), *All the Women Are White, All the Blacks Are Men, but Some of Us Are Brave.* (Old Westbury, NY: Feminist Press, 1982).

5. For whatever it may suggest about the crisis and the production of the black intellectual, it is interesting to note that the intellectual labors of Baker, Gates and West have been chronicled and lauded in cover stories and feature articles in such publications as the *New York Times*, the *Boston Globe*, *Newsweek*, the *Washington Post*, and *Time* magazine. I recall seeing only one article on Mary Helen Washington, in the 'Learning' section of the Sunday *Globe* (although, of course, there may have been others). The article was dominated by a stunning picture of Washington, accompanied by a caption describing her as a scholar-teacher who 'helps restore sight to the "darkened eye" of American literary tradition'. Despite this very fitting and promising caption, the article went on to say remarkably little about Washington's actual scholarship and its impact on American literary studies. See Elizabeth New Weld, 'The Voice of Black Women', *Boston Globe* (February 14, 1988), 98, 100.
6. Cheryl Wall (ed.), 'Taking Positions and Changing Words', in her *Changing Our Own Words: Essays on Criticism, Theory, and Writing by Black Women* (New Brunswick, NJ): Rutgers University Press, 1989), 1–15.
7. These black feminist critics have produced essays, articles, and books too

numerous to name. In addition to a wealth of critical essays, Thadious Davis, Trudier Harris, and Deborah McDowell, e.g., have made tremendous contributions to the fields of African-American and black feminist literary studies through their editorial work on a number of important projects, including vol. 51 of the Dictionary of Literary Biography series, Trudier, Harris, (ed.), *Afro-American Writers from the Harlem Renaissance to 1940,* Dictionary of Literary Biography, vol. 51 (Detroit: Gale Research, 1986) and Beacon Press's Black Women Writers Series (McDowell). See among many other pivotal essays, introductions and books: Hazel Carby, 'It Jus' Be's Dat Way Sometime: The Sexual Politics of Women's Blues', *Radical America* 20 (1986), 9–22; Hull, Scott and Smith, *All the Women are White*; Joyce A. Joyce, 'The Black Canon: Reconstructing Black American Literary Criticism', *New Literary History* 18 (Winter 1987), 335–44; Deborah McDowell, 'New Directions for Black Feminist Criticism', in Elaine Showalter (ed.), *The New Feminist Criticism: Essays on Women, Literature, and Theory* (New York: Pantheon, 1980/1985); Nellie McKay, *Jean Toomer, Artist: A Study of His Literary Life and Work, 1894–1936* (Chapel Hill: University of North Carolina Press, 1984); Valerie Smith, *Self-Discovery and Authority in Afro-American Narrative* (Cambridge: Harvard University Press, 1987); Hortense Spillers, 'Mama's Baby, Papa's Maybe: An American Grammar Book', *Diacritics* 17 (Summer 1987), 65–81; Claudia Tate, *Interviews with Black Women Writers* (New York: Continuum, 1981); Gloria Wade-Gayles, *No Crystal Stair: Visions of Race and Sex in Black Women's Fiction* (New York: Pilgrim Press, 1984); Cheryl A. Wall, 'Poets and Versifiers, Singers and Signifiers: Women Writers of the Harlem Renaissance', in Kenneth W. Wheeler and Virginia Lee Lussier (eds.), *Women, the Arts, and the 1920s in Paris and New York* (New Brunswick, NJ: Transaction, 1982), 74–98.

8. For such a review of the critical literature, see Carby, *Reconstructing Womanhood: The Emergence of the Afro-American Woman Novelist* (New York: Oxford University Press, 1987) and Wall, 'Taking Positions and Changing Words'.
9. Gayatri Chakravorty Spivack, *In Other Worlds: Essays in Cultural Politics* (New York: Routledge, 1988). See, for example, the introduction to Ann duCille, *The Coupling Convention: Sex, Text, and Tradition in Black Women's Fiction* (New York: Oxford University Press, 1993).
10. Melville J. Herskovits, *The American Negro: A Study in Racial Crossing* (Westport, CT: Greenwood, 1985 (1928)); *Dahomey* (New York: Augustin, 1938); *The Myth of the Negro Past* (Boston: Beacon Press, 1941); and Melville J. Herskovits, and Frances Herskovits, *Suriname Folklore* (New York: Columbia University Press, 1936).
11. Harriet Jacobs, (Jean Fagan Yellin, ed.), *Incidents in the Life of a Slave Girl, Written by Herself* (Cambridge: Harvard University Press, 1861/1987), 246.
12. Gerda Lerner, *Black Women in White America: A Documentary History* (New York: Random House, 1972); Shelley Fisher Fishkin, *Was Huck Black? Mark Twain and African American Voices* (New York: Oxford University Press, 1993).
13. Wade-Gayles, *No Crystal Stair*, 41–2.
14. Lerner, *Black Women in White America*, xviii, xx.
15. William Wells Brown, *Clotel; or, The President's Daughter: A Narrative of Slave Life in the United States*, with an introduction by William Farrison (London: Pattidge & Oakey; New York: Carol Publishing, 1989 (1853)).

16. Mrs. N. F. Mossell, *The Work of the Afro-American Woman*, with an introduction by Joanne Braxton (New York: Oxford University Press, 1988 (1894)).
17. Anna Julia Cooper, *A Voice from the South*, with an introduction by Mary Helen Washington (Zenia, OH. Aldine Printing House; reprint, New York: Oxford University Press, 1988 (1892)).
18. Charles Nichols, *Many Thousand Gone: The Ex-Slaves' Account of Their Bondage and Freedom* (Bloomington: Indiana University Press, 1963). Lerner does mention Nichols briefly in the bibliographical essay on p. 620 of *Black Women in White America*. Nichols's book, she writes, 'offers an excellent synthesis of the literature of slave narratives and evaluates their authenticity'.
19. Stephen Fender, 'African Accents, Tall Tales,' review of *Was Huck Black? Mark Twain and African-American Voices*, by Shelley Fisher Fishkin, and *Mark Twain and the Art of the Tall Tale*, by Henry B. Wonham, *Times Literary Supplement* (July 16 1993), 27.
20. David Levering Lewis, 'Parallels and Divergences: Assimilationist Strategies of Afro-American and Jewish Elites from 1910 to the Early 1930s', *Journal of American History* 71 (December 1984), 543–64.
21. Christian *et al.*, 'Conference Call', 61.
22. Alice Walker, 'In Search of Our Mothers' Gardens', *Ms.* 2 (May 1974): 64–70, 105.
23. Elizabeth Abel, 'Black Writing, White Reading: Race and the Politics of Feminist Interpretation', *Critical Inquiry* 19 (Spring 1993), 470–98.
24. White deconstructivist Barbara Johnson has called Henry Louis Gates on his repeated use of the term 'our own'. Johnson notes that in a single discussion 'Gates uses the expression "our own" no fewer than nineteen times'. She goes on to query the meaning behind his ambiguous phrase: 'Does Gates mean all black people (whatever that might mean)? All Afro-Americans? All scholars of Afro-American literature? All black men? All scholars trained in literary theory who are now interested in the black vernacular?' See Henry Louis Gates, Jr, 'Canon-Formation and the Afro-American Tradition', in Houston Baker, Jr and Patricia Redmond (eds.), *Afro-American Literary Studies in the 1990s* (Chicago: University of Chicago Press, 1989); and Barbara Johnson, 'Response to Gates', in Baker and Redmond, *Afro-American Literary Studies.*
25. For those of us tempted to make common (black female) experience the essence of critical interpretation or to view black women's fiction as expressive realism, Belsey's words may be prohibitively instructive: 'The claim that a literary form reflects the world is simply tautological,' she writes. 'What is intelligible as realism is the conventional and therefore familiar. . . . It is intelligible as "realistic" precisely because it reproduces what we already seem to know'. Catherine Belsey, *Critical Practices* (New York: Routledge, 1980), 47.
26. Robert Hemenway, *Zora Neale Hurston: A Literary Biography.* (Urban: University of Illinois Press, 1977): William L. Andrews, (ed.), *Sisters of the Spirit: Three Black Women's Autobiographies of the Nineteenth Century* (Bloomington: Indiana University Press, 1986.
27. Harriet Wilson, *Our Nig; or, Sketches from the Life of a Free Black* (New York: Vintage, 1983 (1859)).
28. Elizabeth Ammons, *Conflicting Stories: American Women Writers at the Turn into the Twentieth Century* (New York: Oxford University Press, 1992).

29. Indira Karamcheti, 'Caliban in the Classroom', *Radical Teacher* 44 (Winter 1993), 13–17.
30. Baker, *Workings of the Spirit*, 11.
31. Quoted by August Meier, and Elliot Rudwick, *Black History and the Historical Profession, 1915–1980* (Urbana: University of Illinois Press, 1986), 289.
32. Adrienne Rich, *Of Woman Born*. Tenth anniversary edn. (New York: Norton, 1986 (1976)).
33. Ibid., 254–55, for all the quotes in this paragraph.
34. Ibid., xxviii
35. In the tenth anniversary revised edition of *Of Woman Born*, a wiser, reflective Adrienne Rich attempts to expand and adjust her vision in light of 1980s concerns and considerations. To her discussion of 'my Black mother' she appends a footnote that reads in part: 'The above passage overpersonalizes and does not, it seems to me now, give enough concrete sense of the actual position of the Black domestic worker caring for white children' (255). Even ten years later, Rich has failed to recognize that she is talking about another woman—another woman who is not her black mother but a laborer whose role as mammy is also socially, politically, and economically constructed.
36. John F. Callahan, *In the African-American Grain: Call-and-Response in Twentieth-Century Black Fiction*. 2nd edn. (Middletown, CT: Wesleyan University Press, 1989), 5.
37. Ibid., 9.
38. Ibid., 9, my emphasis.
39. Ibid., 10.
40. Ibid., 21.
41. Ibid., 8.
42. Ibid., xi.
43. Mae Henderson, 'Commentary on "There is No More Beautiful Way: Theory and the Poetics of Afro-American Women's Writing" by Houston Baker', in Baker and Patricia Redmond (eds.), *Afro-American Literary Studies*, 159.
44. Baker and Redmond, *Afro-American Literary Studies*, 212.
45. Ibid., 213.
46. Patricia F. E. Sharpe, Mascia-Lee and C. B. Cohen, 'White Women and Black Men: Different Responses to Reading Black Women's Texts', *College English* 52 (February 1990), 142–53, 146
47. Cherríe Moraga, 'Preface', in Cherríe Moraga and Gloria Anzaldúa (eds.), *This Bridge Called My Back: Writings by Radical Women of Color* (New York: Kitchen Table Women of Color Press, 1981), xiii–xix, xv.

20 US Third World Feminism: The Theory and Method of Oppositional Consciousness in the Postmodern World[1]

Chela Sandoval *

The enigma that is US third world feminism has yet to be fully confronted by theorists of social change. To these late twentieth century analysts it has remained inconceivable that US third world feminism might represent a form of historical consciousness whose very structure lies outside the conditions of possibility that regulate the oppositional expressions of dominant feminism. In enacting this new form of historical consciousness, US third world feminism provides access to a different way of conceptualizing not only US feminist consciousness but oppositional activity in general: it comprises a formulation capable of aligning such movements for social justice with what have been identified as world-wide movements of decolonization.

Both in spite of and yet because they represent varying internally colonized communities, US third world feminists have generated a common speech, a theoretical structure which, however, remained just outside the purview of the dominant feminist theory emerging in the 1970s, functioning within it—but only as the unimaginable. Even though this unimaginable presence arose to reinvigorate and refocus the politics and priorities of dominant feminist theory during the 1980s, what remains is an uneasy alliance between what appears on the surface to be two different understandings of domination, subordination, and the nature of effective resistance—a shot-gun arrangement at best between what literary critic Gayatri Spivak characterizes as a 'hegemonic feminist theory'[2] on the one side and what I have been naming 'US third world feminism' on the other.[3] I do not mean to suggest here, however, that the perplexing situation that exists between US third world and hegemonic feminisms should be understood

* From Chela Sandoval, 'U.S. Third World Feminism: The Theory and Method of Oppositional Consciousness in the Postmodern World' from *Genders* No. 10 (University of Texas Press, 1991), 1–23.

merely in binary terms. On the contrary, what this investigation reveals is the way in which the new theory of oppositional consciousness considered here and enacted by US third world feminism is at least partially contained, though made deeply invisible by the manner of its appropriation, in the terms of what has become a hegemonic feminist theory.

US third world feminism arose out of the matrix of the very discourses denying, permitting, and producing difference. Out of the imperatives born of necessity arose a mobility of identity that generated the activities of a new citizen-subject, and which reveals yet another model for the self-conscious production of political opposition. In this essay I will lay out US third world feminism as the design for oppositional political activity and consciousness in the United States. In mapping this new design, a model is revealed by which social actors can chart the points through which differing oppositional ideologies can meet, in spite of their varying trajectories. This knowledge becomes important when one begins to wonder, along with late twentieth century cultural critics such as Fredric Jameson, how organized oppositional activity and consciousness can be made possible under the co-opting nature of the so-called 'post-modern' cultural condition.[4] [. . .]

I want to apply Althusser's general theory of ideology to the particular cultural concerns raised within North American liberation movements and develop an extended theory of ideology which considers consciousness not only in its subordinated and resistant yet appropriated versions—the subject of Althusser's theory of ideology[5]—but in its more effective and persistent oppositional manifestations. In practical terms, this theory focuses on identifying forms of consciousness in opposition that can be generated and coordinated by those classes self-consciously seeking affective oppositional stances in relation to the dominant social order. The idea here, that the subject-citizen can learn to identify, develop, and control the means of ideology, that is, marshal the knowledge necessary to 'break with ideology', while also speaking in and from within ideology, is an idea which lays the philosophical foundations enabling us to make the vital connections between the seemingly disparate social and political aims which drive yet ultimately divide liberation movements from within. From Althusser's point of view, then, the theory I am proposing would be considered a 'science of oppositional ideology.'

This study identifies five principal categories by which 'oppositional consciousness' is organized, and which are politically effective means for changing the dominant order of power. I characterize them as 'equal rights', 'revolutionary', 'supremacist', 'separatist', and 'differential' ideological forms. All these forms of consciousness are kaleidoscoped into view when the fifth form is utilized as a theoretical model which retroactively clarifies and gives new meaning to the others. Differential consciousness represents the strategy of another form of oppositional ideology that functions on an altogether different register. Its power can be thought of as mobile—not nomadic but rather cinematographic: a kinetic motion that maneuvers, poetically transfigures, and orchestrates while demanding alienation, perversion, and reformation in both spectators and practitioners. Differential consciousness is the expression of the new subject position called for by Althusser—it permits functioning within yet beyond the demands of dominant ideology. This differential form of oppositional consciousness has been enacted in the practice of US third world feminism since the 1960s.

This essay also investigates the forms of oppositional consciousness that were generated within one of the great oppositional movements of the late twentieth century, the second wave of the women's movement. What emerges in this discussion is an outline of the oppositional ideological forms which worked against one another to divide the movement from within. I trace these ideological forms as they are manifested in the critical writings of some of the prominent hegemonic feminist theorists of the 1980s. In their attempts to identify a feminist history of consciousness, many of these thinkers believe they detect four fundamentally distinct phases through which feminists have passed in their quest to end the subordination of women. But viewed in terms of another paradigm, 'differential consciousness', here made available for study through the activity of US third world feminism, these four historical phases are revealed as sublimated versions of the very forms of consciousness in opposition which were also conceived within post-1950s US liberation movements.

These earlier movements were involved in seeking effective forms of resistance outside of those determined by the social order itself. My contention is that hegemonic feminist forms of resistance represent only other versions of the forms of oppositional consciousness expressed within all liberation movements active in the United States during the later half of the twentieth century. What I want to do here is systematize in theoretical form a theory of oppositional consciousness as it comes embedded but hidden within US hegemonic feminist theoretical tracts. At the end of this essay. I present the outline of a corresponding theory which engages with these hegemonic feminist theoretical forms while at the same time going beyond them to produce a more general theory and method of oppositional consciousness.

The often discussed race and class conflict between white and third world feminists in the United States allows us a clear view of these forms of consciousness in action. The history of the relationship between first and third world feminists has been tense and rife with antagonisms. My thesis is that at the root of these conflicts is the refusal of US third world feminism to buckle under, to submit to sublimation or assimilation within hegemonic feminist praxis. This refusal is based, in large part, upon loyalty to the differential mode of consciousness and activity outlined in this essay but which has remained largely unaccounted for within the structure of the hegemonic feminist theories of the 1980s.

Differential consciousness is not yet fully theorized by most contemporary analysts of culture, but its understanding is crucial for the shaping of effective and ongoing oppositional struggle in the United States. Moreover, the recognition of differential consciousness is vital to the generation of a next 'third wave' women's movement and provides grounds for alliance with other decolonizing movements for emancipation. My answer to the perennial question asked by hegemonic feminist theorists throughout the 1980s is that yes, there *is* a specific US third world feminism: it is that which provides the theoretical and methodological approach, the 'standpoint' if you will, from which this evocation of a theory of oppositional consciousness is summoned. [. . .]

The logic of hegemonic feminism is dependent upon a common code that shapes the work of such a diverse group of thinkers as Julia Kristeva, Toril Moi, Gerda Lerner, Cora Kaplan, Lydia Sargent, Alice Jardine, or Judith Kegan Gardiner. Here I follow its traces through the 1985 writings of the well-known literary critic Elaine Showalter,[6] the now classic set of essays published in 1985 and edited by Hester Eisenstein and Alice Jardine on *The Future of Difference* in the 'women's movement': Gale Greene and Coppelia Kahn's 1985 introductory essay in the collection *Making a Difference: Feminist Literary Criticism*,[7] and the great self-conscious prototype of hegemonic feminist thought encoded in Allison Jaggar's massive dictionary of feminist consciousness, *Feminist Politics and Human Nature*, published in 1983.[8] [. . .]

We have just charted our way through what I hope to have demonstrated is a commonly cited four-phase feminist history of consciousness consisting of 'liberal', 'Marxist', 'radical/cultural', and 'socialist' feminisms, and which I schematize as 'women are the same as men', 'women are different from men', 'women are superior', and the fourth catchall category, 'women are a racially divided class'. I contend that this comprehension of feminist consciousness is hegemonically unified, framed, and buttressed with the result that the expression of a unique form of US, third world feminism, active over the last thirty years, has become invisible outside of its all-knowing logic. Jaggar states this position quite clearly in her dictionary of hegemonic feminist consciousness when she writes that the contributions of feminists of color (such as Paula Gunn Allen, Audre Lorde, Nellie Wong, Gloria Anzaldua, Cherrie Moraga, Toni Morrison, Mitsuye Yamada, bell hooks, the third world contributors to *Sisterhood Is Powerful*, or the contributors to *This Bridge*, for example) operate 'mainly at the level of description', while those that *are* theoretical have yet to contribute to any 'unique or distinctive and comprehensive theory of women's liberation'.[9] For these reasons, she writes, US third world feminism has not been 'omitted from this book' but rather assimilated into one of the 'four genera' of hegemonic feminism I have outlined earlier.

US third world feminism, however, functions just outside the rationality of the four-phase hegemonic structure we have just identified. Its recognition will require of hegemonic feminism a paradigm shift which is capable of rescuing its theoretical and practical expressions from their exclusionary and racist forms. I am going to introduce this shift in paradigm by proposing a new kind of taxonomy which I believe prepares the ground for a new theory and method of oppositional consciousness. The recognition of this new taxonomy should also bring into view a new set of alterities and another way of understanding 'otherness' in general, for it demands that oppositional actors claim new grounds for generating identity, ethics, and political activity.

Meanwhile, US third world feminism has been sublimated, both denied yet spoken about incessantly, or, as black literary critic Sheila Radford Hill put it in 1986, US third world feminism is 'used' within hegemonic feminism only as a 'rhetorical platform' which allows white feminist scholars to 'launch arguments for or against' the same four basic configurations of hegemonic feminism.[10] It is not surprising, therefore, that the writings of feminist third world theorists are laced through with bitterness. [. . .] Clearly, the theoretical structure of hegemonic feminism has produced enlightening and new feminist intellectual spaces, but these coalesce in what Spivak characterizes as a 'high feminist norm' which culminates in reinforcing the 'basically isolationist' and narcissistic 'admiration' of hegemonic feminist thinkers 'for the literature of the female subject in Europe and Anglo America'.[11] [. . .]

Despite the fundamental shift in political objectives and critical methods that is represented by hegemonic feminism, there remains in its articulations a limited and traditional reliance on what are previous, *modernist* modes of understanding oppositional forms of activity and consciousness. The recognition of a specific US third world feminism demands that feminist scholars extend their critical and political objectives even further. During the 1970s, US feminists of color identified common grounds upon which they made coalitions across profound cultural, racial, class, and gender differences. The insights perceived during this period reinforced the common culture across difference comprised of the skills, values, and ethics generated by subordinated citizenry compelled to live within similar realms of marginality. During the 1970s, this common culture was reidentified and claimed by US feminists of color, who then came to recognize one another as countrywomen—and men—of the same psychic terrain. It is the methodology and theory of US third world feminism that permit the following rearticulation of hegemonic feminism, on its own terms, and beyond them.

TOWARD A THEORY OF OPPOSITIONAL CONSCIOUSNESS

Let me suggest, then, another kind of typology, this one generated from the insights born of oppositional activity beyond the inclusive scope of the hegemonic women's movement. It is important to remember that the form of US third world feminism it represents and enacts has been influenced not only by struggles against gender domination, but by the struggles against race, class, and cultural hierarchies that mark the twentieth century in the United States. It is a mapping of consciousness in opposition to the dominant social order which charts the white and hegemonic feminist histories of consciousness we have just surveyed, while also making visible the different ground from which a specific US third world feminism rises. It is important to understand that this typology is not necessarily 'feminist' in nature, but is rather a history of oppositional consciousness. Let me explain what I mean by this.

I propose that the hegemonic feminist structure of oppositional consciousness be recognized for what it is, reconceptualized, and replaced by the structure that follows. This new structure is best thought of not as a typology, but as a '*topography*' of consciousness in opposition, from the Greek word 'topos' or place, insofar as it represents the charting of realities that occupy a specific kind of cultural region. The following topography delineates the set of critical points around which individuals and groups seeking to transform oppressive powers constitute themselves as resistant and oppositional subjects. These points are orientations deployed by those subordinated classes which have sought subjective forms of resistance other than those forms determined by the social order itself. They provide repositories within which subjugated citizens can either occupy or throw off subjectivities in a process that at once both enacts and yet decolonizes their various relations to their real conditions of existence. This kind of kinetic and self-conscious mobility of consciousness is utilized by US third world feminists as they identify oppositional subject positions and enact them differentially.

What hegemonic feminist theory has identified are only other versions of what I contend are the various modes of consciousness that have been most effective in opposition under modes of capitalist production before the postmodern period, but in their 'feminist' incarnations. Hegemonic feminism appears incapable of making the connections between its own expressions of resistance and opposition and the expressions of consciousness in opposition enacted amongst other racial, ethnic, cultural, or gender liberation movements. Thus, I argue that the following topography of consciousness is not necessarily 'feminist' in nature, but represents a history of oppositional consciousness.

Any social order that is hierarchically organized into relations of domination and subordination creates particular subject positions within which the subordinated can legitimately function.[12] These subject positions, once self-consciously recognized by their inhabitants, can become transformed into more effective sites of resistance to the current ordering of power relations. From the perspective of a differential US third world feminism, the histories of consciousness produced by US white feminists are, above all, only other examples of subordinated consciousness in opposition. In order to make US third world feminism visible within US feminist theory, I suggest a topography of consciousness which identifies nothing more and nothing less than the modes the subordinated of the United States (of any gender, race, or class) claim as politicized and oppositional stances in resistance to domination. The topography that follows, unlike its hegemonic feminist version, is not historically organized, no enactment is privileged over any other, and the recognition that each site is as potentially effective in opposition as any other makes possible another mode of consciousness which is particularly effective under late capitalist and postmodern cultural conditions in the United States. I call this mode of consciousness 'differential'—it is the ideological mode enacted by US third world feminists over the last thirty years.

The first four enactments of consciousness that I describe next reveal hegemonic feminist political strategies as the forms of oppositional consciousness most often utilized in resistance under earlier (modern, if you will) modes of capitalist production. The following topography, however, does not simply replace previous lists of feminist consciousness with a new set of categories, because the fifth and differential method of oppositional consciousness has a mobile, retroactive, and transformative effect on the previous four forms (the 'equal rights', 'revolutionary', 'supremacist', and 'separatist' forms) setting them into new processual relationships. Moreover, this topography encompasses the perimeters for a new theory of consciousness in opposition as it gathers up the modes of ideology–praxis represented within previous liberation movements into the fifth, differential, and postmoderm paradigm.[13] This paradigm can, among other things, make clear the vital connections that exist between feminist theory in general and other theoretical modes concerned with issues of social hierarchy, race marginality, and resistance. US third world feminism, considered as an enabling theory and method of differential consciousness, brings the following oppositional ideological forms into view:

(i) Under an 'equal rights' mode of consciousness in opposition the subordinated group argue that their differences—for which they have been assigned inferior status—are only in appearance, not reality. Behind their exterior physical difference, they argue, is an essence the same as the essence of the human already in power. On the basis that all individuals are created equal, subscribers to this particular ideological tactic will demand that their own humanity be legitimated, recognized as the same under the law, and assimilated into the most favored form of the human in power. The expression of this mode of political behavior and identity politics can be traced throughout the writings generated from within US liberation movements of the post-World War II era. Hegemonic feminist theorists have claimed this oppositional expression of resistance to social inequality as 'liberal feminism'.

(ii) Under the second ideological tactic generated in response to social hierarchy, which I call 'revolutionary', the subordinated group claim their differences from those in power and call for a social transformation that will accommodate and legitimate those differences, by force if necessary. Unlike the previous tactic, which insists on the similarity between social, racial, and gender classes across their differences, there is no desire for assimilation within the present traditions and values of the social order. Rather, this tactic of revolutionary ideology seeks to affirm subordinated differences through a radical societal reformation. The hope is to produce a new culture beyond the domination/subordination power axis. This second revolutionary mode of consciousness was enacted within the white women's movement under the rubric of either 'socialist' or 'Marxist' feminisms.

(iii) In 'supremacism', the third ideological tactic, not only do the oppressed claim their differences, but they also assert that those very differences have provided them access to a superior evolutionary level than those currently in power. Whether their differences are of biological or social origin is of little practical concern, of more importance is the result. The belief is that this group has evolved to a higher stage of social and psychological existence than those currently holding power; moreover, their differences now comprise the essence of what is good in human existence. Their mission is to provide the social order with a higher ethical and moral vision and consequently a more effective leadership. Within the hegemonic feminist schema 'radical' and 'cultural' feminisms are organized under these precepts.

(iv) 'Separatism' is the final of the most commonly utilized tactics of opposition organized under previous modes of capitalist development. As in the previous three forms, practitioners of this form of resistance also recognize that their differences have been branded as inferior with respect to the category of

> the most human. Under this mode of thought and activity, however, the subordinated do not desire an 'equal rights' type of integration with the dominant order, nor do they seek its leadership or revolutionary transformation. Instead, this form of political resistance is organized to protect and nurture the differences that define it through complete separation from the dominant social order. A utopian landscape beckons these practitioners . . . their hope has inspired the multiple visions of the other forms of consciousness as well.

In the post-WWII period in the United States, we have witnessed how the maturation of a resistance movement means not only that four such ideological positions emerge in response to dominating powers, but that these positions become more and more clearly articulated. Unfortunately, however, as we were able to witness in the late 1970s' white women's movement, such ideological positions eventually divide the movement of resistance from within, for each of these sites tend to generate sets of tactics, strategies, and identities which historically have appeared to be mutually exclusive under modernist oppositional practices. What remains all the more profound, however, is that the differential practice of US third world feminism undermines the appearance of the mutual exclusivity of oppositional strategies of consciousness; moreover, it is US third world feminism that allows their reconceptualization on the new terms just proposed. US feminists of color, insofar as they involved themselves with the 1970s' white women's liberation movement, were also enacting one or more of the ideological positionings just outlined, but rarely for long, and rarely adopting the kind of fervid belief systems and identity politics that tend to accompany their construction under hegemonic understanding. This unusual affiliation with the movement was variously interpreted as disloyalty, betrayal, absence, or lack: 'When they were there, they were rarely there for long' went the usual complaint, or 'they seemed to shift from one type of women's group to another'. They were the mobile (yet ever present in their 'absence') members of this particular liberation movement. It is precisely the significance of this mobility that most inventories of oppositional ideology cannot register.

It is in the activity of weaving 'between and among' oppositional ideologies as conceived in this new topological space where another and fifth mode of oppositional consciousness and activity can be found.[14] I have named this activity of consciousness 'differential' insofar as it enables movement 'between and among' the other equal rights, revolutionary, supremacist, and separatist modes of oppositional consciousness considered as variables, in order to disclose the distinctions among them. In this sense the differential mode of consciousness operates like the clutch of an automobile: the mechanism that permits the driver to select, engage, and disengage gears in a system for the transmission of power.[15] Differential consciousness represents the variant, emerging out of correlations, intensities, junctures, crises. What is differential functions through hierarchy, location, and value enacting the recovery, revenge, or reparation; its processes produce justice. For analytic purposes I place this mode of differential consciousness in the fifth position, even though it functions as the medium through which the 'equal rights', 'revolutionary', 'supremacist', and 'separatist' modes of oppositional consciousness became effectively transformed out of their hegemonic versions. Each is now ideological and *tactical* weaponry for confronting the shifting currents of power.

The differences between this five-location and processual topography of consciousness in opposition, and the previous typology of hegemonic feminism, have been made available for analysis through the praxis of US third world feminism understood as a differential method for understanding oppositional political consciousness and activity. US third world feminism represents a central locus of possibility, an insurgent movement which shatters the construction of any one of the collective ideologies as the single most correct site where truth can be represented. Without making this move beyond each of the four modes of oppositional ideology outlined above, any liberation movement is destined to repeat the oppressive authoritarianism from which it is attempting to free itself and become trapped inside a drive for truth which can only end in producing its own brand of dominations. What US third world feminism demands is a new subjectivity, a political revision that denies any one ideology as the final answer, while instead positing a *tactical subjectivity* with the capacity to recenter depending upon the kinds of oppression to be confronted. This is what the shift from hegemonic oppositional theory and practice to a US third world theory and method of oppositional consciousness requires.

Chicana theorist Aida Hurtado explains the importance of differential consciousness to effective oppositional praxis this way: 'by the time women of color reach adulthood, we have developed informal political skills to deal with State intervention. The political skills required by women of color are neither the political skills of the White power structure that White liberal feminists have adopted nor the free spirited experimentation followed by the radical feminists'. Rather, 'women of color are more like urban guerrillas trained through everyday battle with the state apparatus'. As such, 'women of color's fighting capabilities are often neither understood by white middle-class feminists' nor leftist activists in general, and up until now, these fighting capabilities have 'not been codified anywhere for them to learn'.[16] Cherrie Moraga defines US third world feminist 'guerrilla warfare' as a way of life: 'Our strategy is how we cope' on an everyday basis, she says, 'how we measure and weigh what is to be said and when, what is to be done and how, and to whom . . . daily deciding/risking who it is we can call an ally, call a friend (whatever that person's skin, sex, or sexuality'. Feminists of color are 'women without a line. We are women who contradict each other'.[17]

In 1981, Anzaldua identified the growing coalition between US feminists of color as one of women who do not have the same culture, language, race, or 'ideology, nor do we derive similar solutions' to the problems of oppression. For US third world feminism enacted as a differential mode of oppositional consciousness, however, these differences do not become 'opposed to each other'.[18] Instead, writes Lorde in 1979, ideological differences must be seen as 'a fund of necessary polarities between which our creativities spark like a dialectic. Only within that interdependency', each ideological position 'acknowledged and equal, can the power to seek new ways of being in the world generate, as well as the courage and sustenance to act where there are no charters'.[19] This movement between ideologies along with the concurrent desire for ideological commitment are necessary for enacting differential consciousness. Differential consciousness makes the second topography of consciousness in opposition visible as a new theory and method for comprehending oppositional subjectivities and social movements in the United States.

The differential mode of oppositional consciousness depends upon the ability to read the current situation of power and of self-consciously choosing and adopting the ideological form best suited to push against its configurations, a survival skill well known to oppressed peoples.[20] Differential consciousness requires grace, flexibility, and strength: enough strength to confidently commit to a well-defined structure of identity for one hour, day, week, month, year; enough flexibility to self-consciously transform that identity according to the requisites of another oppositional ideological tactic if readings of power's formation require it; enough grace to recognize alliance with others committed to egalitarian social relations and race, gender, and class justice, when their readings of power call for alternative oppositional stands. Within the realm of differential consciousness, oppositional ideological positions, unlike their incarnations under hegemonic feminist comprehension, are tactics—not strategies. Self-conscious agents of differential consciousness recognize one another as allies, country women and men of the same psychic terrain. As the clutch of a car provides the driver the ability to shift gears, differential consciousness permits the practitioner to choose tactical positions, that is, to self-consciously break and reform ties to ideology, activities which are imperative for the psychological and political practices that permit the achievement of coalition across differences. Differential consciousness occurs within the only possible space where, in the words of third world feminist philosopher Maria Lugones, 'cross-cultural and cross-racial loving' can take place, through the ability of the self to shift its identities in an activity she calls 'world traveling'.[21]

Perhaps we can now better understand the overarching utopian content contained in definitions of US third world feminism, as in this statement made by black literary critic Barbara Christian in 1985 who, writing to other US feminists of color, said: 'The struggle is not won. Our vision is still seen, even by many progressives, as secondary, our words trivialized as minority issues', our oppositional stances 'characterized by others as divisive. But there is a deep philosophical reordering that is occurring' among us 'that is already having its effects on so many of us whose lives and expressions are an increasing revelation of the INTIMATE face of universal struggle.'[22] This 'philosophical reordering', referred to by Christian, the 'different strategy, a different foundation' called for by hooks are, in the words of Audre Lorde, part of 'a whole other structure of opposition that touches every aspect of our existence at the same time that we are resisting'. I contend that this structure is the recognition of a five-mode theory and method of oppositional consciousness, made visible through one mode in particular, differential consciousness, or US third world feminism, what Gloria Anzaldua has recently named 'la conciencia de la mestiza' and what Alice Walker calls 'womanism'.[23] For Barbara Smith, the recognition of this fundamentally different paradigm can 'alter life as we know it' for oppositional actors.[24] In 1981, Merle Woo insisted that US third world feminism represents a 'new framework which will not support repression, hatred, exploitation and isolation, but will be a human and beautiful framework, created in a community, bonded not by color, sex or class, but by love and the common goal for the liberation of mind, heart, and spirit'.[25] It has been the praxis of a differential form of oppositional consciousness which has stubbornly called up utopian visions such as these.

In this essay I have identified the hegemonic structure within which US feminist theory and practice are trapped. This structure of consciousness stands out in relief against the praxis of US third world feminism, which has evolved to center the differences of US third world feminists across their varying languages, cultures, ethnicities, races, classes, and genders. I have suggested that the 'philosophical reordering' referred to by Christian is imaginable only through a new theory and method of oppositional consciousness, a theory only visible when US third world feminist praxis is recognized. US third world feminism represents a new condition of possibility, another kind of gender, race and class consciousness which has allowed us to recognize and define differential consciousness. Differential consciousness was utilized by feminists of color within the white women's movement; yet it is also a form of consciousness in resistance well utilized among subordinated subjects under various conditions of domination and subordination. The acknowledgment of this consciousness and praxis, this thought and action, carves out the space wherein hegemonic feminism may become aligned with different spheres of theoretical and practical activity which are also concerned with issues of marginality. Moreover, differential consciousness makes more clearly visible the equal rights, revolutionary, supremacist and separatist, forms of oppositional consciousness, which when kaleidescoped together comprise a new paradigm for understanding oppositional activity in general.

The praxis of US third world feminism represented by the differential form of oppositional consciousness is threaded throughout the experience of social marginality. As such it is also being woven into the fabric of experiences belonging to more and more citizens who are caught in the crisis of late capitalist conditions and expressed in the cultural angst most often referred to as the postmodern dilemma. The juncture I am proposing, therefore, is extreme. It is a location wherein the praxis of US third world feminism links with the aims of white feminism, studies of race, ethnicity, and marginality, and with postmodern theories of culture as they crosscut and join together in new relationships through a shared comprehension of an emerging theory and method of oppositional consciousness.

Notes

1. This is an early version of a chapter from my hook in progress on 'Oppositional Consciousness in the Postmodern World'. A debt of gratitude is owed the friends, teachers, and politically committed scholars who made the publication of this essay possible, especially Hayden White, Donna Haraway, James Clifford, Ronaldo Balderrama, Ruth Frankenberg, Lata Mani (who coerced me into publishing this now), Rosa Maria Villafane-Sisolak, A. Pearl Sandoval, Mary John, Vivian Sobchak, Helene Moglan, T. de Lauretis, Audre Lorde, Iraci Chapman and the Student of Color Coalition. Haraway's own commitments to social, gender, race, and class justice are embodied in the fact that she discusses and cites an earlier version of this essay in her own work. See especially her 1985 essay where she defines an oppositional postmodern consciousness grounded in multiple identities in her 'A Manifesto for Cyborgs: Science, Technology, and Socialist Feminism in the 1980s', *Socialist Review*, No. 80 (March 1985). At a time when theoretical work by women of color is so frequently dismissed, Haraway's recognition and discussion of my work on oppositional consciousness has allowed it to receive wide critical visibility, as reflected in references to the manuscript that appear in the works of authors such as Sandra Harding, Nancy Hartsock, Biddy Martin, and Katherine Hayles. I am happy that my work has also received attention from Caren Kaplan, Katie King, Gloria Anzaldua, Teresa de Lauretis, Chandra Mohanty, and Yvonne Yarboro-Bejarano. Thanks also are due Fredric Jameson, who in 1979 recognized a theory of 'oppositional consciousness' in my work. It was he who encouraged its further development.

   This manuscript was first presented publicly at the 1981 National Women's Studies Association conference. In the ten years following, five other versions have been circulated. I could not resist the temptation to collapse sections from these earlier manuscripts here in the footnotes: any resulting awkwardness is not due to the vigilance of my editors. This essay is published now to honor the political, intellectual, and personal aspirations, of Rosa Maria Villafane-Sisolak, 'West Indian Princess,' who died April 20, 1990. Ro's compassion, her sharp intellectual prowess and honesty, and her unwavering commitment to social justice continue to inspire, guide, and support many of us. To her, to those named here, and to all new generations of US third world feminists, this work is dedicated.
2. Gayatri Spivak, 'The Rani of Sirmur,' in F. Barker (ed.), *Europe and its Others* vol. 1 (Essex: University of Essex, 1985), 147.
3. Here US third world feminism represents the political alliance made during the 1960s and 1970s between a generation of US feminists of color who were separated by culture, race, class, or gender identifications but united through similar responses to the experience of race oppression.

   The theory and method of oppositional consciousness outlined in this essay is visible in the activities of the recent political unity variously named 'US third world feminist', 'feminist women of color', and 'womanist'. This unity has coalesced across differences in race, class, language, ideology, culture, and color. These differences are painfully manifest: materially marked physiologically or in language, socially value laden, and shot through with power. They confront each feminist of color in any gathering where they serve as constant reminders of their undeniability. These constantly speaking differences stand at the crux of another, mutant unity, for this unity does not occur in the name of all 'women', nor in the name of race, class, culture, or 'humanity' in general. Instead, as many US third world feminists have pointed out, it is unity mobilized in a location heretofore unrecognized. As Cherrie Moraga argues, this unity mobilizes 'between the seemingly irreconcilable lines—class lines, politically correct lines, the daily lines we run to each other to keep difference and desire at a distance,' it is between these lines 'that the truth of our connection lies'. This connection is a mobile unity, constantly weaving and reweaving an interaction of differences into coalition. In what follows I demonstrate how it is that inside this coalition, differences are viewed as varying survival tactics constructed in response to recognizable power dynamics. See Cherrie Moraga. 'Between the Lines: On Culture, Class and Homophobia in Cherrie Moraga and Gloria Anzaldua (eds.), *This Bridge Called My Back. A Collection of Writings by Radical Women of Color.* (Watertown, MA: Persephone Press, 1981), 106.

During the national conference of the Women's Studies Association in 1981, three hundred feminists of color met to agree that 'it is white men who have access to the greatest amount of freedom from necessity in this culture, with women as their "helpmates" and chattels, and people of color as their women's servants. People of color form a striated social formation which allow men of color to call upon the circuits of power which charge the category of "male" with its privileges, leaving women of color as the final chattel, the ultimate servant in a racist and sexist class hierarchy. US third world feminists seek to undo this hierarchy by reconceptualizing the notion of "freedom" and who may inhabit its realm'. See Sandoval, 'The Struggle Within: A Report on the 1981 NWSA Conference,' published by the Center for Third World Organizing, 1982, reprinted by Gloria Anzaldua in *Making Faces Making Soul, Haciendo Caras* (San Francisco: Spinsters/Aunt Lute, 1990), 55–71. See also 'Comment on Krieger's *The Mirror Dance*: a US Third World Feminist Perspective', in *Signs* 9 (Summer 1984); 725.

4. See Fredric Jameson's 'Postmodernism, or the Cultural Logic of Late Capitalism,' *New Left Review* 146 (July–August 1984). Also, footnote no 50, this essay.
5. Louis Althusser, 'Ideology and Ideological State Apparatuses (Notes Towards an Investigation)', in *Lenin and Philosophy and Other Essays* (London: New Left Books, 1970).
6. Elame Showaller, (ed.), *The New Feminist Criticism: Essays on Women, Literature and Theory* (New York: Pantheon Books, 1985). See especially the following essays: 'Introduction: The Feminist Critical Revolution,' 'Toward a Feminist Poetics', and 'Feminist Criticism in the Wilderness', 3–18. 125–43 and 243–70.
7. Gayle Greene and Copelia Kahn, eds., *Making a Difference: Feminist Literary Criticism* (New York: Methuen, 1985). See their chapter 'Feminist Scholarship and the Social Construction of Woman,' 1–36.
8. Alison Jaggar, 'Feminist Politics and Human Nature.' Uncorrected Proof (New York: Rowman and Allanfield, 1983).
9. Jaggar, *Feminist Politics.*
10. Sheila Radford-Hall, 'Considering Feminism as a Model for Social Change'.

in Teresa de Lauretis (ed.), *Feminist Studies Critical Studies* (Bloomington: Indiana University Press, 1986). 160.

11. Gayatri Chakravorty Spivak, 'Three Women's Texts and a Critique of Imperialism', *Critical inquiry* 12 (Autumn 1985), 243–61.
12. In another essay I characterize such legitimated idioms of subordination as 'human', 'put', 'game', and 'wild'.
13. The connection between feminist theory and decolonial discourse studies occurs within a contested space claimed but only superficially colonized by first world theorists of the term 'postmodernism.' Within this zone, it is generally agreed that Western culture has undergone a cultural mutation unique to what Frederic Jameson calls 'the cultural logic of late capital'. There is, however, prolound *disagreement* over whether the new cultural dominant should be opposed or welcomed. Jameson's essay on postmodernism, for example, is a warning which points out how the new cultural dominant creates a citizen who is incapable of any real oppositional activity, for all novelty including opposition, is welcomed by its order. Forms of oppositional consciousness, he argues, the 'critical distance' available to the unitary subjectivities of a Van Gogh or a Picasso under previous modernist conditions, are no longer available to a postmodern subject. The critical distance by which a unitary subjectivity could separate itself from the culture it lived within, and which made parodic aesthetic expression possible, has become erased, replaced by an 'exhilaratory' superficial effect, 'schizophrenic' in function, which turns all aesthetic representations into only other examples of the plethora of difference available under advanced capital social formations Given these conditions, Jameson can only see the first world citizen as a tragic subject whose only hope is to develop a new form of opposition capable of confronting the new cultural conditions of postmodernism. For Jameson, however, the catch is this: 'There may be historical situations in which it is not possible at all to break through the net of ideological constructs' that make us subjects in culture and this is 'our situation in the current crises'. Jameson's own attempt to propose a new form of 'cognitive mapping' capable of negotiating postmodern cultural dynamics dissipates under the weight of his hopelessness, and in my view, his essay coalesces into a eulogy to passing modes of Western consciousness.

    What Jameson's essay does not take into account, however, is the legacy of decolonial discourse which is also permeating the cultural moment first world subjects now inherent in the intersections between the critical study of decolonial discourse and feminist theory and is a form of consciousness in opposition once only necessary to the socially marginalized citizen, but which postmodern cultural dynamics now make available to all first world citizens. The content of this form of oppositional consciousness is rather naively celebrated and welcomed by other (primarily white, male) first world theorists of postmodernism. But whether welcoming or rejecting the variously construed meanings of the new cultural dominant, both camps share the longing for a regenerated hope and new identity capable of negotiating the crumbling traditions, values, and cultural institutions of the West, in the first example by celebrating a passing modernist form of unitary subjectivity, in the second by celebrating an identity form whose contours are comparable to the fragmenting status of present Western cultural forms.

Interesting to certain third world scholars is the coalescing relationship between these theories of postmodernism (especially between those which celebrate the fragmentations of consciousness postmodernism demands) and the form of differential oppositional consciousness which has been most clearly articulated by the marginalized and which I am outlining here. The juncture I am analyzing in this essay is that which connects the disoriented first world subject, who longs for the postmodern cultural aesthetic as a key to a new sense of identity and redemption, and the form of differential oppositional consciousness developed by subordinated and marginalized Western or colonized subjects, who have been forced to experience the aesthetics of a 'postmodernism' as a requisite for survival. It is this constituency who are most familiar with what citizenship in this realm requires and makes possible.

The juncture between all of these interests is comprised of the differential form of oppositional consciousness which postmodern cultural conditions are making available to all of its citizenry in an historically unique democratization of oppression which crosses class, race, and gender identifications. Its practice contains the possibility for the emergence of a new historical moment—a new citizen—and a new arena for unity between peoples. See Jameson, 'Postmodernism', 53–92.

14. Gloria Anzaldua writes that she lives 'between and among' cultures in 'La Prieta', *This Bridge Called My Back*, 209.
15. Differential consciousness functioning like a 'car clutch' is a metaphor suggested by Yves Labissiere in a personal conversation.
16. Aida Hurtado. 'Reflections on White Feminism. A Perspective from a Woman of Color' (1985), 25, from an unpublished manuscript. Another version of this quotation appears in Hurtado's essay. 'Relating to Privilege Seduction and Rejection in the Subordination of White Women and Women of Color', in *Signs* (Summer 1989), 833–55.
17. Moraga and Anzaldua, xix. Also see the beautiful passage from Margaret Walker's *Jubilee* which enacts this mobile mode of consciousness from the viewpoint of the female protagonist. See the Bantam Books edition (New York, 1985). 404–7.
18. Gloria Anzaldua, 'La Prieta', *This Bridge Called My Back*, 209.
19. Audre Lorde, 'Comments at "The Personal and the Political Panel"' Second Sex Conference. New York, September 1979. Published in *This Bridge Called My Back*, 98. Also see 'The Uses of the Erotic', in *Sister Outsider* (New York: The Crossing Press, 1984), 58–63, which calls for challenging and undoing authority in order to enter a utopian realm only accessible through a processual form of consciousness which she names the 'erotic'.
20. Anzaldua refers to this survival skill as 'la facultad, the capacity to see in surface phenomena the meaning of deeper realities' in *Borderlands, La Frontera: The New Mestiza* (San Francisco: Spinsters/Lute), 38.

The consciousness which typifies la facultad is not naive to the moves of power: it is constantly surveying and negotiating its moves. Often dismissed as 'intuition' this kind of 'perceptiveness', 'sensitivity,' consciousness if you will, is not determined by race, sex, or any other genetic status, neither does its activity belong solely to the 'proletariat', the 'feminist', nor to the oppressed, if the oppressed is considered a unitary category, but it is a learned emotional and intellectual skill which is developed amidst hegemonic powers. It is the recognization of 'la facultad' which moves Lorde to say that it is marginally, 'whatever its nature . . . which is also the source of our greatest strength,' for the cultivation of la facultad creates the opportunity for a particularly effective form of opposition to the dominant culture within which it is formed. The skills required by la facultad are capable of disrupting the dominations and subordinations that scar US culture. But it is not enough to utilize them on an individual and situational basis. Through an ethical and political commitment, US third world feminism requires the development of la facultad to a methodological level capable of generating a political strategy and identity politics from which a new citizenry arises.

Movements of resistance have always relied upon the ability to read below the surfaces—a way of mobilizing—to resee reality and call it by different names. This form of la facultad inspires new visions and strategies for action. But there is always the danger that even the most revolutionary of readings can become bankrupt as a form of resistance when it becomes reified, unchanging. The tendency of la facultad to end in frozen, privileged 'readings' is the most divisive dynamic inside of any liberation movement. In order for this survival skill to provide the basis for a differential and unlying methodology, it must be remembered that la facultad is a process. Answers located may be only temporarily elective, so that wedded to the process of la facultad is a flexibility that continually woos change.

21. Maria Lugones. 'Playfulness. World-Travelling, and Loving Perception', from *Hypatia. A Journal of feminist Philosophy* 2 (2, (1987)).

Differential consciousness is comprised of seeming contradictions and difference, which then serve as tactical interventions in the other mobility that is power. Entrance into the realm 'between and amongst' the others demands a mode of consciousness once relegated to the province of intuition and psychic phenomena, but which now must be recognized as a specific practice. I define differential consciousness as a kind of anarchic activity (but with method) a form of ideological guerrilla warfare, and a new kind of ethical activity which is being privileged here as the way in which opposition to oppressive authorities is achieved in a highly technologized and disciplinized society. Inside this realm resides the only possible grounds of unity across differences. Entrance into this new order requires an emotional commitment within which one experiences the violent shattering of the unitary sense of self, as the skill which allows a mobile identity to form takes hold. As Bernice Reagon has written, 'most of the time you feel threatened to the core and if you don't, you're not really doing no coalescing'. Citizenship in this political realm is comprised of strategy and risk. Within the realm of differential consciousness there are no ultimate answers, no terminal utopia (through the imagination of utopias can motivate its tactics), no predictable final outcomes. Its practice is not biologically determined, restricted to any class or group, nor must it become static. The fact that it is a process capable of freezing into a repressive order—or of disintegrating into relativism—should not shadow its radical activity.

To name the theory and method made possible by the recognition of differential consciousness 'oppositional' refers only to the ideological effects its activity can have under present cultural conditions. It is a naming which signifies a realm with constantly shifting boundaries which serve to delimit, for differential consciousness participates in its own dissolution even as it is in action. Differential consciousness under postmodern conditions is not possible without the creation of another ethics, a new morality, which will bring about a new subject of history. Movement into this realin is heralded by the claims of US third world feminists, a movement which makes manifest the possibility of ideological warfare in the form of a theory and method, a praxis of oppositional consciousness. But to think of the activities of US third world feminism thus is only a metaphorical avenue which allows one conceptual access to the threshold of this other realm, a realm accessible to all people.

22. Barbara Christian, 'Creating a Universal Literature: Afro-American Women Writers,' *KPFA Folio.* Special African History Month Edition, February 1983, front page. Reissued in *Black Feminist Criticism: Perspectives on Black Women Writers* (New York: Pergamon Press, 1985), 163.
23. Alice Walker coined the neologism 'womanist' as one of many attempts by feminists of color to find a name which could signal their commitment to egalitarian social relations, a commitment which the name 'feminism' had seemingly betrayed. See Walker, *In Search of Our Mother's Gardens. Womanist Prose* (New York: Harcourt Brace Jovanovich, 1983), xi–xiii, Anzaldua, *Borderlands, La Nueva Frontera.*
24. bell hooks, *Feminist Theory From Margin to Center* (Boston: South End Press, 1984), 9, Audre Lorde, 'An Interview: Audre Lorde and Adrienne Rich' held in August 1979. *Signs* 6 (Summer 1981); and Barbara Smith, *Home Girls. A Black Feminist Anthology*, xxv.
25. Merle Woo, *This Bridge Called My Back*, 147.

Decolonizing Feminism

Marnia Lazreg*

> It has already formed its concepts; it is already certain of their truth; it will assign to them the role of constitutive schemata. Its sole purpose is to force the events, the persons, or the acts considered into prefabricated molds.
>
> Jean-Paul Sartre on institutional Marxism.[1]

Writing about women in Algeria has been the most challenging task I have undertaken so far. Not only did it concretize for me the difficulty of doing interdisciplinary research, and raise theoretical/methodological issues, it has also led me to question the feasibility of writing and communicating across cultures about the subject of women. My project is not to entertain readers with one more exotic tale or shock them with another astounding revelation about womanhood in a faraway place. All I wish to do is communicate in intelligible terms another mode of being female. But this is more easily said than done.

Dealing with a subject with which people in this country are unfamiliar threatens to turn me into a social translator of sorts, a bona fide native anthropologist, writing for others about others. I have always resisted the quasiheroic stance assumed by experts on other cultures, and I have far too many questions about the validity of their knowledge claims to find comfort in mimicking them. My predicament takes on a more complex turn when it is realized that I am not writing 'just' about another culture but about women from a culture with a history of distortion. Indeed, Algerian women and their culture have been mystified by more or less well-intentioned social scientists and feminists moved by something akin to missionary zeal.

Difference, whether cultural, ethnic or racial, has been a stumbling block for Western social science from its very inception. Nineteenth-

* From Marnia Lazreg, 'The Eloquence of Silence: Algerian Women in Question' from *The Eloquence of Silence* (Taylor & Francis, Inc/Routledge, Inc, 1994), 6–19, copyright © 1994, reprinted by permission of the publisher.

century European ethnology and anthropology were established precisely to study different peoples and their institutions. However, regardless of the conceptual, theoretical and methodological inadequacies and uncertainties in the works of many classical anthropologists and ethnologists, their interest in 'difference' was a function of their desire to understand their own institutions better. This was the case with Durkheim's work on religion, Mauss on exchange and Malinowski on the Oedipus complex, to cite only a few. Although I do not wish to absolve Western anthropology of its Eurocentrism, it showed, at least in its heyday, some awareness of a common denominator between people of different cultures, a *human* bond. The notion of 'cultural universals' or that of the 'human mind', no matter how problematical, are expressions of such a common link between various peoples.

Contemporary American academic feminism has rejected, if not forgotten, this part of its intellectual heritage. Yet it has failed to do away with the evolutionary bias that characterizes social science in one form or another. In feminist scholarship (with a few exceptions) this bias is embedded in the objectification of 'different' women as the unmediated 'other', the embodiments of cultures presumed inferior and classified as 'traditional' or 'patriarchal'. This would ordinarily be seen as a theoretical mishap were it not for the fact that academic feminists have generally denounced conventional social science as being biased against women both in its theory and its practice. They have specifically shown that it has reduced women to one dimension of their lives (for example, reproduction and housework) and failed to conceptualize their status in society as a historically evolving phenomenon. Hence, academic feminism has brought a breath of fresh air into the social science discourse on women, and has held the promise of a more evenhanded, more holistic practice. Surprise is in order when one sees that women in Algeria (or in any other part of the Middle East) are still dealt with largely in ways that academic feminists do not wish to be dealt with.[2]

Women in Algeria are subsumed under the less-than-neutral labels of 'Muslim women', 'Arab women' or 'Middle Eastern women', giving them an identity that may not be theirs. Whether the so-called Muslim women are devout, or their societies are theocracies, are questions that the label glosses over.

The one-sidedness of the prevailing discourse on difference between women would appear intolerably grotesque if it were suggested, for example, that women in Europe and North America be studied as Christian women! Similarly the label 'Middle Eastern women', when counterposed with the label 'European women', reveals its unwarranted generality. The Middle East is a geographical area covering some twenty-one countries (if one counted members of the Arab League) that display a few similarities and as many differences. Yet a book on Moroccan women and another on Egyptian women were both subtitled 'Women in the Arab World'.[3]

This reductive tendency to present women as an instance of a religion, nation, ethnicity or race is carried over from American feminists' uneasy relations with minority women. African-, Chinese- and Mexican-American women as well as Puerto Rican women have denounced their exclusion from feminist scholarship and/or the distortions of their lived reality by 'white', middle-class feminists. They have also noted that academic feminism reproduces the social categorizations and prejudices that are prevalent in the larger society.

Objecting to definitions that reduce women to their skin color, Rosario Morales emphasizes that she wants 'to be whole', and reminds her readers that 'we are all in the same boat'.[4] Going one step further, Mitzuye Yamada inveighs against the burden placed upon individual Asian-American women to 'represent' their racial group and speak 'in ways that are not threatening to our audiences'. In this sense they are made to reinforce the stereotype of the Asian woman.[5]

These relatively new voices express the underside of difference between women, and are a welcome reminder that feminism as an intellectual practice cannot merely rest on the consciousness of wrongs done to *some* women by men. It points to the necessity of developing a form of consciousness among feminists in North America (and in Europe) that transcends their sense of specialness and embraces what is human at the heart of womanhood across cultures and races. Decentering as well as deracializing one's self is a precondition for such a venture. However, it is a complex and difficult one, as it requires giving up a sense of entitlement for some and overcoming disability for others that is undoubtedly grounded in the racialization of one's self. It is remarkable that academic feminists do not tire of referring to themselves as 'white' or 'of color'. Damning the Algerian revolution with a stroke of a pen (over exactly fourteen pages), Sheila Rowbotham, who refers to herself as a 'white middle-class woman', sums a complex history as the battle between whites and nonwhites. Although she writes about them, she surprisingly asserts that 'I do not know what it is like to be Vietnamese, or Cuban, or Algerian'—all women she classifies as 'Black, yellow, and brown'.[6] If her color is a barrier to understanding the special circumstances of these women, whence comes the authority that made her define their lives and characterize their roles in history? What gives legitimacy to her work on women whom she admits she does not understand? Is it the very color she uses as a shield to both empower herself to write and protect herself from criticism?

Third World women in the United States who have expressed their anger and disappointment at being objectified as the irrevocably unmediated other have also assumed that very otherness. They refer to themselves as 'women of color', another linguistic sleight of hand ostensibly meant to supplant but which in fact merely recycles the old expression 'colored women', the racist connotations of which need no elaboration. This expression has acquired common currency and is used by academic feminists apparently as a way of recognizing the existence of difference between women. The inability to examine the language in which difference is expressed renders ineffective objections to academic feminists' failures to address difference in adequate terms. The language of race belongs to the history of social segregation. To argue that minority and Third World women have adopted the term 'women of color' as a liberating means to assert their difference and escape a homogenizing Anglo-American feminist discourse begs the question. By using this label they accept its referent and bow to the social group that gives it currency. [. . .] It is not 'women of color' who have the authority to impose the language of race but the women who implicitly claim to have no color and need to be the standard for measuring difference. 'Color' does not determine sex, but, like sex, it does become an opportunity for discrimination. Like sex, color ought to be questioned as a significant category in understanding human beings. Why select color and not hair texture, shape of eyes or length of nails to define women? Who is subsumed under the awkwardly expressed and marginally grammatical expression 'women of color?' Does it include women who are pink, pasty or sallow-skinned?

This cumbersome term grounds difference among women in biology, thereby presenting academic feminism with one of its most telling contradictions. Feminists have been waging a battle against sociobiology, yet they find themselves reasoning along similar lines when faced with 'different' women! The term has become widespread even among feminists who claim to pursue a Marxist or socialist tradition that should have sensitized them to the pitfalls of using race or color as a defining criterion of human beings. The captivating power of the label 'women of color' *reinscribes*, with the complicity of its victims, the racialization of social relations that it purports to combat.

Michel Foucault's assertion that 'knowledge is not made for understanding; it is made for cutting' illustrates the knowledge effect of this biological language.[7] If there is little knowledge to be gained by identifying difference with color, the process of 'cutting', or establishing divisions among individual women, of measuring the distance that separates them from one another, is made easier. Knowledge as cutting is politically grounded and pervades feminist scholarship. The expression, 'the personal is political', ought to be amended by substituting race, ethnicity or nationality for the personal.

There is, to a great extent, continuity in American feminists' treatment of difference between women, whether it originates within American society or outside of it. There is, however, an added feature to feminists' modes of representation of women from the Third World: they reflect the dynamics of global politics. The political attitudes of the powerful states are mirrored in feminists' attitudes towards women from economically marginal states in a world rent asunder by the collapse of communism.

The political bias in representations of difference is best illustrated by feminists' search for the sensational and the uncouth. Mary Daly selected infibulation as the most important feature of African women as reported to her by Audre Lorde.[8] Local customs such as polygamy and/or veiling, wherever they take place, appear decontextualized and are posited as normative absolutes.

The search for the disreputable which reinforces the notion of difference as objectified otherness is often carried out with the help of Third World women themselves. Academic feminism has provided a forum for Third World women to express themselves and vent their anger at their societies. But the Western mode of feminist practice is no free gift, any more than anger is conducive to lucid inquiry. Individual Third World women are made to appear on the feminist stage as representatives of the millions of women in their own societies.

The dissenting voice that objects to the gynocentric language of difference unwittingly reinforces the prevailing representation of herself, if only because she acquiesces in the notion of difference as opposition, as polarity. The totalitarian character of the existing representation of difference appropriates differential items haphazardly, and incorporates them into a structure that becomes autonomous and stands for the lived reality of Third World women. An abstract anthropological subject deemed 'oppressed' is thus created. Studying this constructed subject is not for the purpose of understanding her as such as it is to gather documentary evidence of her 'oppression'. Ironically, the language of liberation *reinscribes* relations of domination.

In assessing the issue of writing about Third World women, Gayatri C. Spivak points out that 'First World women' and 'Western-trained women' are complicitous in contributing to the continued 'degradation' of Third World women whose 'micrology' they interpret without having access to it.[9] Although essentially correct, this view obscures the fact that complicity is often a conscious act involving the interplay of social class position, psychological identification and material interests. To include all the 'Western-trained' women in the plural 'we', which also incorporates 'First World' women, is to simplify the reality of the feminist encounter between Western and non-Western women. Some Third World women find comfort in acquiring a Western-style feminist identity that presumably dissolves their cultural selves and enables them to take their distance from those who resist looking at themselves through Western feminists' eyes. The problem for Third World women is that their writing is constrained by the existence of an imperious feminist script. Thus, instead of being emancipatory, writing for them is often alienating. Their satisfaction, if any, derives from the approval they receive from their Western counterparts, or the ire they draw from them if they attempt to rewrite the script.

IDENTITY POLITICS AND FEMINIST PRACTICE

Asian-American feminists have pointed out that Third World feminists feel under pressure to choose between their feminism and their ethnicity or culture. This identification of feminist practice with Western culture has resulted in a contest between those who affirm their ethnicity or culture against 'feminism' seen as a monolithic system of thought and behavior, and those who flaunt their feminism against their culture, implying that feminism stands above culture. Thus Third World female intellectuals find themselves either defending their culture against feminist misrepresentations or reveling in the description of practices deemed disreputable, but always sensational, in an attempt to reaffirm the primacy, validity and superiority of Western feminism.

A focus on the phenomenal manifestations of difference between women has also resulted in a crude politicization of race, ethnicity, color and/or nationality. Women speak as embodiments of these categories. It is only when a feminist's practice is racialized, ethnicized or nationalized that it somehow becomes worthy of interest. This form of identity feminism is sustained by the extension of standpoint theories to larger constituencies of women. Standpoint knowledge is in effect a *representation* of activity instead of the situated truth it purports to be.[10] By claiming standpoint as a foundation of knowledge, academic feminists have *produced* an activity that stands above and beyond a simple intervention of women's experience in constituted knowledge. When used by racialized women, standpoint knowledge yields an inverted double representation. They represent themselves in terms that already subsume and contain their representation.

The politicization of race, color, ethnicity and nationality is also the expression of a form of adaptation to the salience of racial thinking in the post-Civil Rights, post-Cold War era. The prevailing racialization of power relations in American society (which the corrective of affirmative action had already made palpable) is countered by the use of race/color, ethnicity and nationality as grounds and strategies of contention and resistance.

Among Third World academics this trend transcends the bounds of a simple awareness of ethnocentrism and cultural imperialism. It seeks to recenter existing knowledge, whether feminist or not. For example, Indian scholars have in the last few years focused on colonialism and post-colonialism to account for their own realities. Based on their understanding of the British colonial venture in India, they make generalizations that embrace other colonial situations which thus become ancillary props to buttress the Indian model.[11] The Indian experience, presented as normative, mediates our understanding of colonialism, a phenomenon as multiple and diverse in its expression as it was in its consequences. Such sanskritization of knowledge (feminist or otherwise) is perhaps a welcome change in centuries of Eurocentric knowledge, but it does not transform it. By focusing on India's colonial past, seen as constitutive of Indians' identity, it strikes a nostalgic note for a system of relations that needs to be overcome. In the same vein, the accommodation of African-American feminists to 'white', middle-class feminism takes the form of an assertion of Black feminist epistemology grounded in the experience of slavery.[12]

Given this framework, is it possible to do scholarly work on women in the Third World that goes beyond documenting existing stereotypes? How does one put an end to the fundamental dismissal of what Third World women say when they speak a non-stereotypical language? How does one overcome the incipient ghettoization of knowledge about Third World women, who now figure in last chapters of anthologies in a space reserved for 'women of color'?

Academic feminist scholarship on American women is generally critical without being denigrating, and therefore leaves hope for a better future for its subjects. American culture is not rejected wholesale, but presented as perfectible. In this respect, feminist critical practice takes on an air of normalcy that is missing in the scholarship on Third World women, especially those from North Africa and the Middle East. It appears as part of a reasonable project for greater equality. Conversely, the Third World feminist critique of gender difference acquires a maverick dimension. It is not carried out from within, with a full knowledge and understanding of the history and the dynamics of the institutions it rejects. It unfolds within an external conceptual frame of reference and according to equally external standards. It may provide explanations but little understanding of gender difference. In this sense, it reinforces the existing '*méconnaissance*' of these societies and constitutes another instance of knowledge as 'cutting'. Only this time, the cutters are also those who are generally 'cut out' of the fellowship of sisterhood.

BEYOND THE RELIGION PARADIGM

I have explained in the past that there is continuity between the body of literature produced by colonial scholars and contemporary feminist studies of Algerian women.[13] Colonial critiques of native women and men centered on Islam (as a religion and culture), which also happens to play a predominant role in contemporary feminists' scholarship. Visions of Islam constitute links in a long chain that ties colonial and feminist practices over the past hundred years. They are articulated in a paradigm I have referred to as the 'religion paradigm', which continues to monopolize and constrain writers' and their critics' thoughts (including my own) by compelling them to address its parameters or submit to them. This paradigm has recently been reinforced by the emergence of religiose movements throughout North Africa and the Middle East, thereby giving credence to a self-fulfilling prophecy.

The religion paradigm is steeped in a dual intellectual tradition, orientalist and evolutionary, resulting in an ahistorical conception of social relations and institutions. The orientalist tradition supports the notion that Islam is an archaic and backward system of beliefs that determines the behavior of the peoples who adhere to it. In the popular culture Islam also conjures up a medley of images ranging from the exotic splendor of the Arabian Nights, sequestered odalisques, to circumcized virgins. Fancy and fact mix to create a notion of massive difference. The language used to define women in North Africa and the Middle East creates and sustains their irremediable difference from other women. For example, a translation of French feminist Juliette Minces's book *Women in the Arab World* (the original title) bore the title *The House of Obedience* in an attempt to frame the reader's judgment.[14]

The veil has had an obsessive impact on many a writer. Frantz Fanon, the revolutionary, wrote about 'Algeria unveiled'. Reaction to the abusive imagery of the veil fails to escape its attraction. Fatima Mernissi entitled her first book, *Beyond the Veil.* In the spring of 1990 Condé Nast published an advertisement in the *Sunday New York Times* portraying a blonde woman modeling a bathing suit. She stood up waving a diaphanous white scarf above the heads of a group of veiled Moroccan women crouched at her feet. During the Gulf War the media were replete with contrasting images of veiled Saudi women and American women in combat gear. The persistence of the veil as a symbol that essentially stands for women illustrates researchers' as well as laypeople's inability to transcend the phenomenal expression of difference. Besides, veiling is close to masquerading, so that writing about women where veiling exists is a form of theater. Ironically, while the veil plays an inordinate role in representations of women in North Africa and the Middle East, it is seldom studied in terms of the reality that lies behind it. Women's strategic uses of the veil and what goes on under the veil remain a mystery.

Religion is perceived as the bedrock of the societies in which Islam is practised. In an uncanny way, the feminist discourse on women mirrors that of the theologians. Writers invoke religion as the main cause (if not *the* cause) of gender inequality, just as it is made the source of underdevelopment in much of modernization theory. Two extreme interpretations of women have ensued. Women are seen either as embodiments of Islam, or as helpless victims forced to live by its tenets. Illustrating this second interpretation, a French-Algerian woman named an association she founded the 'association of women living *under* Islamic law'.

To break out of the totalitarianism of the religion paradigm requires a conception of religion as a process. It is misleading and simplistic to look upon Islam as a text that is learned and faithfully applied by all members of the society in which it is practiced. Emile Durkheim pointed out long ago that even a society of saints would produce its deviants. From a sociological perspective, religion may provide motivation for social action. It may then become secularized. Max Weber explained how this process took place in his controversial study, *The Protestant Ethic and the Spirit of Capitalism.* Religion may also be used as a mechanism of legitimation of inequality, or as a protest against it. Islam should not be analyzed differently from the ways in which other religions have been, without making it meaningless. If it were possible to isolate an independent variable that holds the key to all social ills (as is usually done in the case of Islam) we would undoubtedly have reached the utopia of a positive society that Auguste Comte, the founder of sociology, had in mind.

The point is neither to dismiss the role that Islam plays in women's and men's lives, nor to inflate it. More importantly, it is to study the historical conditions under which religion *becomes significant* in the production and reproduction of gender difference and inequality. The historicization of the relationship between gender and religion permits an appreciation of the *complexity* of the lives of women hitherto subsumed under the homogenizing and unitary concept of 'Muslim'. This approach further introduces a phenomenological dimension by relying on the lived experiences of women rather than textual injunctions and prescriptions made for them. It also helps to identify and explain lags that often develop between lived experience (in its social, political and economic forms) and religious dogma.

In the Algerian case, to place religion within a historical framework means introducing other equally powerful factors, such as colonialism, development policy, socialism, democratization and so on, that interact with religion in complex ways. Historicizing religion and gender is different from determining how each phenomenon appeared at various points in time. It sheds light on conclusions based on such a limited view of history. For example, one trend of thought maintains that where local customs survived the advent of Islam, women are freer.[15] Another trend points to the deleterious effects that the survival of pre-Islamic customs has had on women whose rights as spelled out in the *Quran* have been violated.[16] What matters is not so much that customs inimical to the Islamic spirit have survived, but through what process religion accommodates practices that appear to contradict its principles.

THINKING DIFFERENTLY ABOUT WOMEN

I began my book ten years ago, when I became interested in feminist theory and the role it assigns 'other' women. Unhappy with the culturalist conception that attributed to Islam a powerful causative significance, I initially inquired into the conditions under which religious norms did not affect women's behavior by looking at women's involvement in the war of decolonization that took place from 1954 to 1962. As I proceeded to study the social changes that had taken place among women since 1962, it became clear to me that to understand the present I had to understand the past, especially the colonial past which still haunts the present. Colonialism and its interface with the economy and religion overdetermine any study of Algerian women in complex ways that have yet to be understood. I am thus compelled to revisit two formidable realities, colonialism and Islam, that have defeated more than one scholar.

To write intelligibly about colonialism, for a formerly colonized person such as myself, is as difficult as it is to search one's childhood for possible clues to things that happen in adulthood. Besides, the cacophony of voices clamoring about colonial and 'postcolonial' discourses has recently filled academic halls so pervasively that it has trivialized references to this most important event of the nineteenth century, and placed an additional burden on those seeking to come to terms with it. Finally, the intractability of the effects of colonial domination on natives' minds and behavior well after its institutional structures were dismantled makes its analysis always frustratingly tentative.

Apart from confronting all the issues pertaining to Third World women discussed above, writing about Algerian women must deal with the crucial problem of the audience it necessarily assumes. I am writing in English about a reality that is generally unfamiliar to an English-speaking audience. The problem is not only linguistic; it is also one of sharing with an audience a history and culture, a frame of mind, significant silences, and a multitude of things that are said but dispense with explanations—all that makes writing a fulfilling and emancipatory act. A solution to the assumption of an audience, without which I could not write this article, came to mind as I remembered a discussion I had in Algiers in 1988 with a young female sociology instructor who had given me her doctoral dissertation to read. In answering a question I had asked her about her lack of reference to the role played by family law during the colonial period, she asserted that 'they had no such law then'. I suddenly realized how misunderstood and remote was a past that was in fact quite recent for the generation of women who came of age after the colonial era. It is that generation that I have chosen to keep in mind as a fictitious audience that might become real should my book be translated some day. It is a different generation that does not share with its parents a memory of the colonial past, and is increasingly detached from the old agrarian and community-based value system. Through a combination of ill-devised school curricula and exposure to culturally hybrid media messages, it is very naive about its history and cultural roots.

The critical approach here and its virtual audience make it an act of transgression. I assume no race, color, ethnicity or nationality as a legitimating ground for writing it. It has no identity politics and does not aim at being politically correct. Algerian women including myself have no privileged 'standpoint' or perspective that makes them closer to a feminist truth than any other women. Like many women and men, they are caught up in an intricate historical web from which they are trying to disentangle themselves with the means available to them. [. . .]

Notes

1. Jean-Paul Sartre, *Search for a Method* (New York: Vintage, 1963), 37.
2. The use of the concept 'Western' in this book does not connote any ontological meaning. It refers to individuals who inhabit the space identified as the 'West' which happens to coincide with industrialization and/or past colonial empires. The concept of 'Third World' is as inadequate as 'West' especially now that the so-called 'Soviet Bloc,' which occupied the space of a Second World, no longer fits the Cold War terminology.
3. Fatima Mernissi, *Beyond the Veil* (New York: Shenkman, 1975); Nawal El-Saadawi, *The Hidden Face of Eve* (Boston: Beacon Press, 1980).
4. Rosario Morales, 'We Are All In The Same Boat', in Cherrie Moraga and Gloria Anzaldua (eds.), *This Bridge Across My Back* (New York: Kitchen Table, Women of Color Press, 1983), 91.
5. Mitsuye Yamada, 'Asian Pacific American Women and Feminism', ibid., 71.
6. Sheila Rowbotham, *Women, Resistance, and Revolution* (New York: Vintage, 1974), 244–7.
7. Michel Foucault (D. F. Bouchard, ed.) *Language, Counter-Memory, Practice,* (Ithaca, NY: Cornell University Press, 1977), 154.
8. Audre Lorde, 'An Open Letter to Mary Daly', in Elly Bulkin, M. B. Pratt and B. Smith, *Yours in Struggle* (New York: Long Haul Press, 1984), 94–7.
9. Gayatri Chakravorty Spivak, 'Draupad' by Mahasveta Devi', in Elizabeth Abel

(ed.), *Writing and Sexual Difference* (Chicago: University of Chicago Press, 1982), 261–82, especially translator's foreword.

10. Pierre Bourdieu, *Outline of a Theory of Practice* (Cambridge: Cambridge University Press, 1977), 2.
11. See Ranajit Guha (ed.) *Subaltern Studies VI: Writings on South Asian History and Society* (Delhi, Oxford and New York: Oxford University Press, 1989).
12. Patricia Hill Collins, *Black Feminist Thought: Knowledge, Consciousness and the Politics of Empowerment* (New York: Routledge, Chapman and Hall, 1991).
13. See Marnia Lazreg, 'Feminism and Difference: The Perils of Writing as a Woman on Women in Algeria', in *Feminist Studies* 14 (Spring 1988).
14. Juliette Minces, *The House of Obedience: Women in the Arab World.* (London: Zed Press, 1980).
15. Margaret Smith, *Rabi'a the Mystic and Her Fellow Saints in Islam* (Armsterdam: Philo Press, 1974), 148–54.
16. Reuben Levy, *The Social Structure of Islam* (Cambridge: Cambridge University Press, 1959).

Part III. Shifting the Debates

Black Women's Employment and the British Economy

Gail Lewis *

INTRODUCTION

In recent years it has become a commonplace . . . to accept that it is black people[1] in general, and black women in particular, who have borne the brunt of the effects of the economic crisis. More particularly, the factors that give rise to this condition are said to be the interlocking of massive unemployment, government legislation and growing racialism in local areas. For black women the added burden of domestic work combined with long hours of paid employment is also alluded to as is the fact that racist government legislation is often predicated on, and reinforces sexist divisions and stereotypes. A strong case in point is the Nationality Act of 1981. In this Act not only is the citizenship status of much of the population redefined, but the ability of black female citizens to confer entry and residency rights on their husbands is denied.[2] [. . .]

In my view the context in which to view black women's employment patterns and prospects is the sexual division of labour (in relation to both the private market economy and domestic production); the long-term relative decline of the British economy: the present recession and government policy as it relates to: monetarism and public sector cuts; and control of the black communities at central and local government level.

A mediating category is 'racism', which we can define as the organization of society on the basis of an ideology of inferiority grounded in

Although originally published in the 1990s, this article was written in the mid-1980s.

* From Gail Lewis, 'Black Women's Employment and the British Economy' from *Inside Babylon: The Caribbean Diaspora in Britain* edited by Winston James and Clive Harris (Verso, 1993), 73–96, reprinted by permission of the author.

'race' or colour (i.e. biological differences) and/or ethnic (i.e. cultural) differences, which then gives rise to a distribution of the labour force in certain ways. However, we cannot analyse the role and experiences of black women in the British economy in ideological terms alone. . . . In other words we begin from an analysis of the workings of the British capitalist economy in general and move, more specifically, to the ways in which the sexual division of labour, racialism and government policy intersect with the economic factors against a background of relative decline and cyclical crisis. [. . .]

PATTERNS OF BLACK WOMEN'S EMPLOYMENT

One of the characteristics of the British economy in the immediate post-war period was the mobilization of two sources of relative surplus population: the mass of workers in the Caribbean and Indian subcontinent,[3] and indigenous women workers. By drawing on these pools of labour British capital was in fact attempting to overcome the effects of its long-term comparative decline by intensifying the rate of exploitation.[4] Therefore cheap labour was substituted for capital investment in Britain. This approach was to have the effect of determining the sectors into which the two pools of workers were to be concentrated. For women workers (undifferentiated in terms of 'race') there was the added dimension of the sexual division of labour whose operation was to determine the occupations into which they were absorbed. For black women the ideology of racism and the practice of racialism were to intertwine with the ideology and practice of sexism, both of which were to impact on the structural characteristics of the British economy to determine the industrial and occupational location of black women workers.

As one would expect from the foregoing, the geographical distribution of Britain's black population mirrors that of the traditional industries into which they were recruited. Thus 40 per cent of black people live in the Greater London area, though for Afro-Caribbeans this is 59 per cent, and a substantial number of the remainder live in the major conurbations of the Midlands and North East. [. . .] Black women also display a similar concentration into what is considered 'women's work', . . . and within these industries black women tend to be concentrated in the lowest-paid, least skilled jobs with bad conditions of work. Furthermore, they have very high economic activity rates and a large majority work full-time, as will be discussed below. It is, however, important to note that the contrast between black and white women workers in terms of type and conditions of work is less than that which exists between black and white men. In part this is due to the low employment status of women generally and because of the high incidence of white women who are in unskilled jobs because they work part-time.

More generally this less wide discrepancy is due to the fact that women as a category were themselves brought into the labour market on conditions similar to those of black people, i.e., as cheap labour. Having said this Brown[5] shows that when we compare Afro-Caribbean women with white women the former are still concentrated in the lowest status positions in both manual and non-manual occupations. This is so despite a slight increase in the numbers of black women in non-manual occupations between 1974 and 1982.

The sexual division of labour was also to determine the ways in which women in general were to match their domestic responsibilities with their participation in paid employment. However, the ways in which women combined these dual responsibilities were subject to 'racial' differentiation. For many white women the way to do this was to do part-time work. For example, 36 per cent of white women in the London area were engaged in part-time work in the late 1970s.[6] This compares to a national average of 43 per cent for all women. By contrast the same NDHS survey showed that only 19 per cent of West Indian women worked part-time, and only 12 per cent of Asian women. (In 1988, when the national average was 40 per cent, the figure for West Indian women was 25 and 23 for Indian women.) This means that for black women the worrying task of combining domestic responsibilities with paid employment had to be done within the constraints imposed by full-time paid employment. One way out has been to do full-time hours on a regular shift basis. Brown shows that 18 per cent of West Indian women work shifts regularly, compared with 11 per cent for white women.[7]

As a result of these differences wage levels are different, although once again the discrepancy between black and white men is much greater than that between black and white women. In the PSI study the average for Caribbean women was slightly higher than that for white women, though that of Asian women was slightly lower, albeit only slightly. This is in part caused by the age composition of the workforce: 47 per cent of white women workers are in the under twenty-five and over fifty-four age groups compared with 28 per cent of black women workers. This difference has the effect of deflating average earnings of white women workers because it is these age groups that have the worst pay rates. Thus if these two age groups are excluded from the calculations we get a reversal of the differential 'from £1.50 in favour of black women to £10.40 in favour of white women'.[8] However, even with this adjustment white women do not tend to have higher wages within employment categories.

Overall therefore white women have better wages because there are more of them in better-paid jobs. Thus black women's earnings are the result partly of their concentration in particular occupations and partly because their concentration in large, better-unionized workplaces and the public sector cushions them from the worst levels of pay.

Having outlined the broad characteristics of black women's employment patterns let us now turn to the context in which to consider them.

THE SEXUAL DIVISION OF LABOUR

The concentration of women workers in particular occupations and sectors of the economy is one manifestation of the sexual division of labour which pervades all aspects of society. Primarily the sexual division of labour in British society is based on the ideological separation of the spheres of production and reproduction into 'work' and 'home/family'. The former is considered the sphere of men and the latter that of women, with the wage acting as the mediating factor between the two spheres. Moreover the assumed 'naturalness' and desirability of this ideological division is presented as though it were a historical constant which matched contemporary social reality.

In fact the development of the concept of the ideal family type, desirable and attainable for people of all classes in Britain, itself grew out of the changes that accompanied the development of capitalism.[9] A full discussion of the processes which gave rise to the articulation between the extension of capitalist social relations and the ideology of 'separate spheres' is beyond the scope of this chapter. However, for our purposes it is important to note two points. The first is that the idea of separate spheres accompanied that of the single family wage which was earned by the 'male breadwinner'. This means that while the preservation and reproduction of the household was more firmly wedded to market relations as articulated by the wage, women were less able to directly influence developments in the wage labour or production sphere.[10] Meanwhile men were tied more deeply to the necessity to earn a wage and an ideology of masculinity, and as a result they were expected to be able to provide singlehandedly the ever-expanding supply of household commodities which the expansion of productive capacity and the changing domestic economy gave rise to.

The inadequacy of many individual 'family' wage rates for these purposes was to act as a contributory factor in the demand for state-provided welfare services, since these were essential if women were to be freed for the labour market and new standards for the reproduction of labour were to be met. The possibility of the state providing some level of welfare services was increased by the expansion of the domestic productive base from which some surplus could be redirected for these purposes, together with that portion of surplus which came from the extraction of super-profits in the colonial world.

However, a second consequence of the increase in the production of consumer goods and the provision of welfare services was an increase in the demand for labour in the immediate post-Second World War period. This increase was partly the result of the tensions between production and reproduction which were generated by the ideology of separate spheres for men and women. Importantly this was one contributory factor in the expansion of the demand for labour in those manufacturing and service sectors into which black workers were recruited in the 1950s and early 1960s. Examples are the transport, construction, food and drink manufacture (particularly of convenience and snack foods) and the NHS.

[. . .] Thus the second point to note is that by the 1950s the ideology of separate spheres included the notion and fact of 'dual roles' for women. At one level this was a representational shift based on the need to incorporate women into the labour force which the expansion of productive capacity and the requirement of an increased number of commodities for the domestic economy gave rise to. Women became wage workers in both intensive production processes and the expansion of office work. At another level, however, the concept of the dual role was itself related to the continuation of the idea that women's primary responsibility was that of the home and the family. [. . .]

Taken as a total ideological construct then the notion of 'separate spheres' serves to reinforce a sexual division of labour both within and outside the household and acts to determine which occupations women are most commonly found in as well as preserving their position within the industrial reserve army of labour. Moreover changes within the ideology of the sexual division of labour not only mirrored developments within the accumulation of capital but also had material repercussions which were to partially determine the industrial location of black workers in the British economy. This is an important point which is more often than not overlooked by writers concerned with the position of black people in Britain because they fail to see the relevance of gender divisions within society as a whole and between individual men and women.

From the foregoing it is clear that an analysis of the role of black women workers in the British economy must be contextualized within an understanding of the dynamic and impact of the sexual division of labour. This is so not just because such an understanding helps to explain the occupational and sectoral concentration of all women workers but also because it helps us to understand the forces which give rise to the expansion of these occupations and sectors themselves.

This is not to presume that the effects of the sexual division of labour on women's employment experience is uniform. Gender categories need to be disaggregated by 'race'; and when this is done disparities emerge.

Two further points need to be mentioned. On the one hand whatever the wider 'economic' effects of the ideology of separate spheres, this notion gave rise to an additional assumption that all migrants who came to Britain with the primary purpose of finding paid work were men, since it is men who are universally deemed to be the main breadwinners. On the other hand to the extent that it was recognized that black women came seeking work in their own right, it was assumed that these women had no family/domestic responsibilities whose fulfilment required an 'adequate' wage. Their very migrant status was assumed to mean that the problems associated with the 'dual role' were absent as far as these women were concerned. Of course in the 1950s and early 1960s this was to some extent partly true and was reflected in the overconcentration of black women workers in occupations where part-time work is less common, for example in manufacturing as opposed to office work.

Moreover, whether or not the assumption about the lack of domestic responsibilities within Britain was true at that time, it was more often than not the case that early black women migrants had financial responsibilities for dependants in the Caribbean or elsewhere. The number of Caribbean-born young women and men who remember the departure of their mothers for England while they were left with a grandmother or aunt, is eloquent testimony to this. Consequently the low wage rates paid here often acted as a fetter on her ability to fulfil these commitments, particularly given the relatively high cost of living in Britain. It is not therefore surprising that the burden of dual responsibilities together with low wages acted as a compulsion to work overtime and shifts to maximize the weekly pay packet. Indeed such is often the case in the 1980s. Black women workers are thus caught by the low wages associated with the assumption that women work for 'pin money', the effects of racialism as practised by employers (and in some cases unions), and the downward pressure on wages that the physical separation of black workers' productive capacity from the previous site of their reproduction (i.e. home) gave rise to.

By the mid-1960s the situation was changing as it became clear that black people were here as settlers and it was increasingly impossible to assume that black women workers did not have 'dual role' functions to perform at home and 'work'. Indeed in some measure this fact was itself the outcome of government attempts to restrict the size of the black population by the introduction of immigrant controls. The change in the status of black workers was itself accompanied by the development of a different kind of racism which was directed at the level of reproduction (e.g. concerns over housing, community facilities, education, etc.) and the so-called 'problems' that it was anticipated would arise within this sphere because of the presence of black families in Britain. This new racism covered all aspects of social life and included hysterical 'rivers of blood' type speeches by leading politicians and alarming developments in the policing of inner city areas where the majority of the black population lives. An important additional element from the point of view of black women was the rise of the notion of the 'pathological' black family, a notion which is nothing other than a racially specific ideological assault on the black population in general and black women in particular. Its roots lay, at least in part, in the tensions associated with the particular way in which black women are forced to bridge the 'separate spheres' (e.g. full-time hours in shifts) and, importantly, the community-based struggles in which these women are engaged in the attempt to alter the terms on which they performed their dual roles. Consequently the ideological assault has been accompanied by a host of institutional practices by 'welfare' agencies. Indeed it is the struggle within this arena which has been the sharp edge of black people's political action for some time and it is often even at the core of many of the industrial struggles that black women have engaged in over the years. Hence the common scenario of a mobilization of the community behind strikes, Grunwick being a classic example.

Taken as a whole then, developments within the sexual division of labour have acted in concert with developments within the wider economy, which together with the ideology of racism and the practice of racialism have determined the place of black women workers in the British economy. Moreover, the effects of the cyclical crisis have led to a period of major restructuring in all spheres of social life which will have material affects on black women's employment prospects.

THE CRISIS IN THE BRITISH ECONOMY

The continuation of the capitalist mode of production depends on the constant accumulation of capital and on the reproduction of the conditions, within and outside of production, which facilitate that accumulation. This includes the continual accumulation of labour itself, employed or unemployed and categorized according to different skill levels. It has meant that periodically the spheres of production and reproduction have had to be restructured, as has the relationship between these two spheres. It goes without saying that this restructuring is itself the subject of struggle in which the working class, defined in its different categories, i.e. as women, black, youth, etc., attempts to ensure that the process occurs in their interests and not those of capital. This in part is what 'community' struggles are about.[11] Indeed such a process of restructuring is occurring during the present crisis. However, within this general picture of periodic crisis it is arguable that in terms of international comparison the British economy has been in one form of crisis since the end of the last century.[12] For example Britain remained the world's leading country in terms of international trade until well into this century (not least because of the 'captive' markets which the colonies represented), accounting for 25 per cent of the world manufactured exports in 1950. However, in production terms Britain was overtaken as early as the 1880s by the USA and the 1890s by Germany. As one would expect this situation has continued into the present so that by 1978 Britain's Gross Domestic Product was less than half that of

Germany's while in terms of output per person of goods and services, only Italy, Greece and Ireland were lower. This is a function of low investment levels: a 93 per cent fall (in constant 1975 prices) in net investment in Britain between 1970 and 1981 illustrates the point.

Within this more long-term relative decline, however, the British economy (like all capitalist economies) has been subject to long cycles of boom and slump in tandem with, but more pronounced than, the international economy as a whole. More particularly for our purposes we need to note that these distinct but inter-related forms of crisis have given rise to two factors. First, Britain's long-term relative decline has led to structural features which have determined the conditions under which black workers in general, and black women workers in particular, were brought into the labour force. Since these conditions were also to affect the relationship between production and reproduction they were to give rise to additional tensions which were gender specific. I will return to this point below. Secondly the more medium-term, but nevertheless endemic, structural crises such as those of 1974 and 1978–79 onwards, have meant a more pronounced period of restructuring which has impinged heavily on the pattern and prospects of black women's employment.

This restructuring, itself a response to a crisis of profitability (for example as a percentage of income gross profit rates fell from 20 per cent in 1966 to below 4 per cent in 1974—Anderson *et al.*[13]), has involved widespread bankruptcies and voluntary closure of plants, massive unemployment and a switch to new branches of production. The figure of 5500 bankruptcies in the first half of 1982, a 75 per cent increase on 1981, is illustrative of the extent of the problem. Moreover employment loss is particularly severe in those sectors of the economy in which black women are concentrated. It has also meant a cut in wage levels and a reduction in the social wage. A few simple facts illustrate these trends.

Britain's long-term decline as a producer of manufactured goods has continued so that by the end of the 1970s Britain's share of world manufactured exports was below 10 per cent and by 1982 Britain was a net importer of manufactures. Moreover, manufactured output had declined even in absolute terms so that by 1981 it was below its 1967 level. As one would expect, this has been matched by a decline in the numbers employed in manufacturing in both absolute and proportionate terms. Thus, while 8.8 million people were employed in manufacturing in 1951 this figure had dropped to 5.8 million by 1981. In percentage terms this represented 45 per cent and 27.5 per cent respectively.[14]

While this decline in manufacturing has been accompanied by an expansion in the service sector of the economy—especially during the 1960s—it was not enough to compensate for the loss of employment in the manufacturing sector. Notwithstanding this there is some evidence to suggest that until recently the growth in certain parts of the service sector has helped to cushion women as a whole from the worst effects of employment loss.[15] Thus for example growth in the professional and scientific, and miscellaneous services categories has helped to offset the loss of women's jobs in manufacturing, which, between 1974 and 1977, fell by 9 per cent. Factors such as these are attributable to the sexual division of labour in employment whereby certain sectors and occupations are almost exclusively defined as 'women's jobs' (e.g. 70 per cent of all women wage workers are employed in service industries, while in manufacturing they account for 76 per cent, 46 per cent and 40 per cent of the work force in clothing and footwear, textiles and food and drink).

However, there is also some evidence to suggest that this cushioning effect was not proportionately shared by black women workers. This is because of the higher concentration of black women in semi- and unskilled manual work, together with their under-representation in routine white-collar work such as clerical work. Annie Phizacklea[16] for example, has concluded that the comparative figures for 'all women' (including all migrant women workers) and 'Caribbean women' in four occupational categories are as shown in Table 22.1. Such discrepancies might be analysed within a 'racialized' sexual division of labour, the effects of which are more fundamental than is

Table 22.1 Occupational Distribution of Women by Ethnic Origin (%)

	All women	*Caribbean women*
Clerical workers	27.2	11.0
Sales workers	11.6	1.3
Service, sports and recreation	22.3	21.0
Professional and technical (incl. nurses)	11.7	25.0
Total	72.8	58.3

Source: Phizacklea 'Migrant Women and Wage Labour'.

conveyed by a simple notion of discrimination, as I have attempted to show.

More recently the service sector as a whole has also begun to decline. Between 1979 and 1982 well over half a million jobs were lost in the service sector. In addition during the last decade the main inner city areas where black people are concentrated have experienced an increase in the rate of loss of service sector jobs (Cambridge Economic Policy Review 1982[17]).

Added to this the loss in total employment has declined faster than registered unemployment has increased. Nearly 2.5 million jobs have been lost between mid 1979 and mid 1982, compared with a 1.9 million increase in the numbers of people registered as unemployed during the same period.[18] This is in part due to the fact that even in those industries where there has been increased investment in plant during the recession, employment levels have often declined. For example in the chemical industry investment increased by 70 per cent between 1964 and 1973 yet employment declined by 8 per cent. Overall then the restructuring associated with the recession has meant 'changes in where people work, how they work and if they work'[19] and the process of shedding the number of workers it requires to produce an expanded amount of goods will only increase unless action by workers stops it.

To approach the question of employment in this way suggests that the concept of 'crisis' implies more than a restructuring of relations at the workplace and of how things are produced. It also suggests that 'crisis' implies a necessity to try and restructure relations within reproduction as well, as was suggested in the section dealing with the sexual division of labour. In other words the struggles of working-class people in general and black workers in particular that take place in the community (over home, policing, education, immigration, health, social security benefit) are as much a problem for capital as it tries to overcome the crisis in its own favour, as are strikes over pay or the length of the working day. Indeed it is only by adopting an integrated approach such as this that we will be able to understand the impact on black women's employment of the recession and the interventionist strategies of the state on behalf of capital. Similarly and more importantly only by adopting this approach will we be able to develop the appropriate strategies by which to defeat the attacks being made on us as black people.

Let us now look at government policy.

MONETARISM

Against the picture of the crisis painted above it becomes clear that the Thatcher government's economic strategy has been a radical intervention aimed at hastening the process of restructuring which is required if profitability is to be restored to acceptable levels for British capital as a whole.

At one level crises within capitalism are an inevitable consequence of the pursuit for continued and expanded accumulation on the one hand, and the attempt by workers to subvert this process in their own interests on the other. Thus while investment in more plant as against labour may improve productivity and profit levels for individual capitals by increasing the extraction of relative surplus-value,[20] at the level of collective capital it only serves to eliminate the source of profit, i.e. the workers themselves. Therefore for capital as a whole the effect of an increase in the proportion of machines to workers[21] is that too many firms chase too little profit. Moreover with a strong, well-organized labour force, itself partly the result of full employment during the boom period, the easy reorganization of production by the introduction of new technology or different working hours, etc., is prohibited as is a decline in real wage rates. However, as the effects of long-term relative decline and cyclical structural crisis take hold, weaker (and usually, though not always, smaller) firms begin to go broke. At this point the emergence of a full-blown crisis acts as a means to re-establish the basis of a renewed cycle of accumulation. This process if successful is inevitably at the cost to workers who are themselves engaged in a struggle to force the terms of restructuring in their favour. There are, however, also casualties among capital, i.e. those weaker firms that are driven out of production.

In this context monetarism is a way of hastening the process by which weaker, i.e. less competitive and profitable, firms go bust, thereby reducing the total number chasing profits. It is important to note that the strategy does not cause the recession but it does quite deliberately exacerbate it by manipulating fiscal and monetary policies in order to bring to bear the sharp point of competition and to blunt the edge of working-class struggle for its own interests. Moreover, this process not only affects different sections of the workforce in different ways (e.g. higher levels of unemployment among some groups, changes in which sections of the workforce work where, etc.), but also divisions within the workforce are often manipulated in order to hasten and ease (for capital) the process of restructuring. For example, the introduction of new methods of production may be done by employing more vulnerable sections of labour for these tasks, as happened at Ford's or as is happening with the increased employment of black women workers in offices at the time that new technology is being introduced.

Monetarism is also a cheap labour strategy. Therefore an additional effect of tightening the supply of money is that those firms that do survive must both shed labour, thereby increasing unemployment, and lower average wage levels for those still employed. Given that black women workers are overconcentrated in those backward, declining sectors most affected by the crisis it is not surprising that the employment effects of the recession are being disproportionately felt by black women workers.

The monetarist cheap labour strategy also has additional prongs which impact still further on black women workers. These include the attempt, in the main via the MSC (now Employment Department), to restructure the level and type of skill training available, as well as the sections of the workforce who have access to such training. For example, the abolition of sixteen of the twenty-three Industrial Training Boards, the herding of young black people on to mode B schemes of YTS with the result that their 'training' is worse than no training at all, and the longer-term demise of any high-quality apprenticeship are all indicators of the attempt to restructure what training exists and for whom.

At one level this is related to the long-term relative decline of the British economy which was to predetermine that the daughters and sons of those who migrated as workers from the 1950s onwards were never to have access to plentiful and highly skilled occupations. At another level the restrictions and transformations in skill training are related to developments in the technology of production. Such developments have made it possible to deskill larger and larger numbers of workers. This has the effect of both lowering average wage levels and subordinating the worker to the machine (lathe or word-processor) and to further fragment the production process. Both of these impinge on the ability of the workforce to control the production process by collective action.

Important from the point of view of women's employment is the fact that technological developments in the processing and storing of information are rapidly changing the nature of work in the office, making conditions more like those in the factory which had already undergone 'rationalization' with the application of Fordist and Taylorist production methods.[22] For black women who have recently gained any noticeable degree of entry into office work (the 1984 PSI study shows a 10 per cent shift from manual to non-manual occupations for black women) this means that entry into these jobs does not necessarily represent an escape from the bad, hazardous and low-paid conditions of manufacturing, but simply their resurfacing at new sites of employment.

Another effect of the monetarist strategy with potentially dire effects for black women is its impact on the growth of homeworking and sweatshops. Homeworkers are perhaps the least documented sector of workers since by the very nature of their work they tend to be excluded from government and trade union statistics. Despite this the CIS report on *Women in the '80s*[23] estimated that in 1980 there were between 200,000 and 400,000 homeworkers. Such workers are predominantly women and many are employed in those manufacturing industries in which black women workers are concentrated, such as clothing. Consequently it is not surprising to find that clothing manufacturers in the East End of London themselves estimate that 30–50 per cent of all homeworkers engaged by them are black women (this figure includes Cypriot women).[24]

These workers are employed on low wages, usually piece rate, with 85 per cent earning less than £1.06 per hour in 1979.[25] Engaged in homeworking largely because of their geographical immobility, which is itself the result of dual roles, racism in the streets and sometimes additional cultural or linguistic factors, homeworkers often find it difficult to organize either within or outside of the trade union movement. As such this section of cheap female labour may well prove increasingly attractive to employers. This is particularly true at a time of recession and when technological developments make it at least theoretically possible to put out more and more office or manufacturing tasks to homeworkers. Thus for example developments in information technology are opening up new avenues for homeworking as when visual display units or micro-computers are installed in a home and linked to a main-frame at the regional or head office of the employing firm wherever in the world that may be. Yet clearly this type of homeworking is at present both spatially and qualitatively removed from the domestic manufacture of the clothing industry. The middle-class, university-trained housewife, expert in computer programming and based in her Berkshire detached, is far removed from her homeworking counterpart in the inner city areas of London or Bradford.

Yet the political link lies in the fact that both these sources of labour have been sought by capital in the attempt to recruit what it assumes to be a docile or passive labour force in the hope that its (capital's) interests can be pursued unhindered by the collective action of sections of the working class. In this sense therefore the widening use of homeworkers and the development of the technology which facilitates it, is an outcome of the continuing dynamic of the class struggle to control production.

The other side of the homeworking coin often tends to be the sweatshop, expansion of which can be expected as the inevitable outcome of successful monetarist intervention in the process of recession and the process of restructuring. Once again black women workers can be expected to be disproportionately affected by this development since it is in some of the manufacturing sectors where black women are concentrated that sweatshops predominate, for example in clothing and footwear. Moreover such sweatshops are not the exclusive preserve of the white petty bourgeois superexploiting black women's labour. It is often the case that such sweatshops are themselves black-owned businesses utilizing family and community labour. George Ward's Grunwick is a classic case in point, while Barbara Hoel[26] has documented the experience of Asian women workers in sweatshops in Coventry. In both these cases the conditions and level of exploitation were appalling and there is no prior reason, theoretical or otherwise, to assume that such conditions are not or would not be duplicated in existing or developing Caribbean-owned and run businesses. Indeed it is factors such as these which demand an organized political response by black progressives against the current ideological promotion of the development of an Afro-Caribbean small business sector.[27]

THE RE-CREATION OF A SURPLUS POPULATION WITHIN THE BLACK COMMUNITIES

If industrial restructuring is indicative of a crisis in the economic sense, the need for restructuring is also indicative of a crisis in the political sense in that there is a crisis in the power of relations between classes. Thus the need for economic restructuring to restore the basis for a renewed cycle of accumulation and valorization also includes a need to restructure the working class and in particular divisions between workers.

Restructuring also means then the way in which capital as a whole attempts to create new forms of accumulation in which the needs of the working classes, as expressed through their economic/political demands, are either incorporated into the new dynamic of accumulation or completely marginalized. An essential element in this process is the attempt by capital to restructure the various elements within the working class, thereby reproducing the divisions within the class. Necessarily therefore the struggle of capital to restore its domination is not confined to the site of production alone but is carried out in the sites of reproduction, i.e. those of the home and 'community' together with parts of the 'welfare' state. Thus the struggles of black women workers against the conditions of their exploitation in the workplace and their conditions of oppression in the community, are manifestations of a political crisis (for capital) acted out within the locus of 'racialized gender/class relations'. Moreover it is struggles such as these which have contributed to the very onset of crisis and demanded a response from capital. This was particularly true because such struggles represented a rebellion of a section of the 'working class', considered the most docile and marginal (by employers and trade unions alike). The consequence of this was that internal divisions within the class themselves threatened to become undermined, suggesting at least the potential for harmonization and greater unity of working-class struggles. Indeed it was this fact, together with struggles elsewhere and the increasing severity of the economic crisis, that was to provide the impetus for the state to introduce a plethora of measures designed to control the black communities.

These measures included the integration of various government departments in the policing of inner city communities. Under the guise of tackling 'crime', state agencies were to co-ordinate and share information on local populations. The Home Office, responsible for the police and immigration, was to work in conjunction with the DHSS, the DES, and the DoE in order to develop so-called crime prevention strategies at the local level. In other words information passed on by the public at the dole office, in the hospital, at the school or in the housing office was to become readily available to the police on request. Integrated surveillance brought 'big brother' into the heart of the community via these state agencies and it did so precisely at a time when the relationship of the working class as a whole to these welfare agencies was itself being changed as a result of public expenditure cuts. Increasing queues at the dole and social security office; destruction of services provided by welfare agencies; and the increasing corporatization of delivery and administration of state services were further tools in the armoury of restructuring.[28] The agencies of welfare and coercion were coming together to attack the working class at the level of the community, but they were doing so by targeting specific fragments of the working class in specific localities.

In short the process is one in which capital is attempting to recreate a relative surplus population, with large chunks of the black population being assigned to this category of people.

Friend and Metcalfe[29] identify this surplus population as a group more extensive than the unemployed. As a category it also includes temporary and casual workers; those working on the margins outside the tax system; the low paid, especially in the state service sector and the sweated industries; and those dependent on state benefits. The importance of this definition lies precisely in the fact that it embraces those employed in sectors of the economy where the wages and overall conditions are well below the average endured by the bulk of the working class. Examples of such sectors are homeworking, the sweated industries, cleaning, or some of the worst part of the catering industry or the fast food trade. As we already know it is precisely these areas where many black women work.[30]

The creation of surplus population is a necessary outcome of changes in the process of production caused by technological developments and the resultant changes in the way work is carried out and products are made. But if the creation of surplus population is located in the sphere of production, its shape and the terrain of its political control occur within the 'community'. In other words when women do battle over the level or form of payment of welfare benefit or the quality of service from a council department, and when black youths opt for unemployment rather than be herded into the worst jobs on offer, they are both engaged in more than a form of protest over conditions of working-class life outside of work. They are also engaged in struggles which affect the potential of capital to transform segments of the relative surplus population into a reserve army of labour which, by competing for jobs, will act as a downward pressure on wages. Additionally such struggles are also indicative of their refusal to accept incorporation into the more highly exploited occupations.

This can be seen more clearly when considering the effects of cuts on welfare and other public expenditure. Such cuts are aimed at lowering the amount the government needs to raise in order to carry out its redistributive functions. They also serve to entrench the sexual division of labour in the home by making women assume greater responsibility for domestic duties and dependants.[31] (This is what the current debate about 'Community Care' is all about.) However, precisely by lowering or removing some of the 'social' wage, these cuts force more and more people to seek some form of paid employment and therefore compete for jobs that are scarce. In all probability the sectors where these people will compete for jobs will be those where the process of deskilling and the erosion of pay and conditions, including unionization, have been carried to the furthest extent.

Such competition only serves to entrench divisions between sections of employed and unemployed workers even though the levels of income between them may be extremely slight. Indeed it is precisely where the margins are narrow that the desire to maintain the distinction between employment and unemployment is most keenly felt by those employed in low-paid work.

This highlights the relationship between the re-creation of a surplus population and the trend towards the peripheralization of major areas of work. Peripheralization of the economy simply means that the conditions which prevail in the most highly exploited and worst-organized sectors of the economy (see note 31) become more and more widespread. This development can be seen in the growing trend towards casualization and part-time employment, abolition of wages councils, anti-trade union legislation, and decentralization, by which industries are removed from the orbit of legal control so that forms of employment protection are relaxed. Consequently larger and larger numbers of people will become part of a surplus population as a result of the conscious intervention on the part of capital and the state into the internal dynamics of capitalist production.

From this perspective we can see that just as the success of working-class struggles within the factory, office or shop influence the levels, distribution and conditions of employment, so too the success of struggles within the 'community' will have an impact on who gets work, where and under what circumstances. Consequently the struggles of black women outside of the workplace are an important influence on their future role in the British economy.[32]

PROSPECTS

Taken as a whole the employment effects of the recession and the associated restructuring of both the economy and class relations paint a rather gloomy picture for the employment prospects of black women in the immediate future. On the one hand plant closure, rationalization and relocation, together with cuts and restructuring in the public sector, mean that unofficial unemployment levels will at best remain at the three million mark. On the other hand for those who continue to be engaged in waged employment, the conditions of service will continue to deteriorate as the introduction of new technology serves to deskill, fragment and control the worker. This is true in both manufacturing and office work in both the public and private sectors. Moreover as we have already seen, for those employed in the public sector, the development of multi-agency policing will mean that black people, mostly women, employed by the 'welfare' services will be expected to carry out surveillance tasks on other black people. Conditions will therefore worsen in both the traditional sense of pay and terms and in the political sense of being stooges in the process of policing the black communities, and creating divisions between working-class people as capital attempts to reassert its control.

In short, the economic and political processes by which the black population is being restructured, if successful, will mean that an ever-growing proportion will become part of the relative surplus population; a prospect which was in many senses predetermined by the specific form of capital accumulation within an economy which was both growing but in long-term relative decline, the contradictions of which were exacerbated by the political struggles of black workers in the 1960s and 1970s.

This place within the surplus population is true for those both outside of and within waged labour as we have seen in the case of homeworkers, a form of waged work which may well expand as technological developments and relocation of production facilitate it. Similarly the expansion of this and similar forms of employment is very likely to be predicated on the sexual division of labour since it gives rise to a cheap and relatively immobile female labour force. In addition then to new types of homeworking other occupations may well become 'feminized' as employers relocate to cheaper, more flexible (for capital) sources of labour. Thus restructuring involves not only changes in the amount and value of the wage, in the occupational and sectoral composition of employment, it also involves changes in the 'racial' and sexual composition of employment. Indeed changes in the sexual composition of employment (undifferentiated in terms of 'race') associated with economic restructuring have already been documented.[33]

However, an increase in women's employment in some regions does not necessarily mean that all women workers gain access to these new employment opportunities. The spatial unevenness of the process inevitably means that the employment impact is regionally specific and reflects the contours of classes in struggle. When analysing black women's employment prospects this is of particular importance since the ruralization of production which is occurring at present means that these new avenues of employment are precisely not in the inner cities where the bulk of the black population lives.

Thus even where restructuring throughout the economy is leading to the proliferation of working conditions familiar to many black women, the spatial and political aspects of restructuring may well serve to limit the employment opportunities of black working-class women, confined as they are to the inner cities which were the industrial centres of another era of accumulation.

Thus the present situation is one in which a number of trends are occurring. Whilst many existing areas of employment for black women are closing altogether or experiencing major decline, others are opening up (e.g. fast food, some office work, especially in 'equal opportunity establishments'). However, the extent to which these potential opportunities can be turned into real jobs, which show some movement towards qualitatively better jobs for black women, is less sure.

One thing is clear, however, and that is that the outcome will depend, at least in part, on the success of black women's autonomous organization both on the shop floor and outside, in the 'community'. The sooner this lesson is learnt by all sections of the black population and indeed all sectors of the working class as a whole, the better.

Notes

1. Note that throughout this paper the term 'black' will be used to refer to women and men who have immigrant or refugee status (and their descendants) and who are from the New Commonwealth or other parts of the 'Third World', unless otherwise stated.
2. Recently this aspect of the Act was ruled as sexually discriminatory by the European Court of Human Rights. The British government's response has been to bring women's status in line with that of men, thereby eliminating sexual discrimination but reinforcing racism.
3. Together with workers from the underdeveloped southern Mediterranean.
4. That is, it was at least in part an attempt to increase the extraction of absolute surplus value. This is not to say that no increase in the extraction of relative

surplus value occurred, but that in comparison with its international competitors the rate of increase of absolute surplus value was higher. Hence the continued use of outmoded equipment and the high degree of mobility of British capital overseas.

5. Colin Brown, *Black and White Britain: The Third PSI Survey* (The Policy Studies Institute, 1984).
6. NDHS (National Dwelling and Household Survey) 1977–8.
7. Brown, *Black and White Britain.*
8. Ibid., 168.
9. Mackenzie, S. and D. Rose (1983), 'Industrial Change, the Domestic Economy and Home Life,' in J. Anderson, S. Duncan and R. Hudson (eds.), *Redundant Spaces in Cities and Regions* (London: Academic Press, 1983), 155–200; E. Wilson, *Women and the Welfare State*, (London: Tavistock Press, 1977); Michele Barrett, *Women's Oppression Today* (London: Verso, 1981).
10. Mackenzie and Rose, 'Industrial Change', 172.
11. This is not to suggest the *a priori* existence of a 'community'. Indeed, it is often the case that such struggles reflect the common aspirations of a collectivity and are the process by which that is formed into a 'community'.
12. Cecil Gutzmore, 'Imperialism and Racism: The Crisis of the British Capitalist Economy and the Black Masses in Britain', *The Black Liberator*, 2(4), (1975–6), 76.
13. Anderson *et al.*, *Redundant Spaces in Cities and Regions*, 5.
14. Ibid.
15. Irene Breugel, 'Women as a Reserve Army of Labour: A Note on Recent British Experience', *Feminist Review*, No. 3 (1979) 12–23.
16. A. Phizacklea, 'Migrant Women and Wage Labour: The Case of West Indian Women in Britain', in J. West (ed.), *Work, Women and the Labour Market* (London: Routledge and Kegan Paul, 1982), 104;
17. Cambridge Economic Policy Review (1982), *Employment Problems in the Cities and Regions of the United Kingdom: Prospects for the 1980s*, vol. 8(2), December 1982, Cambridge University Press, Cambridge.
18. Anderson *et al.*, *Redundant Spaces in Cities and Regions.* The changes in the way in which government departments classified people as active or inactive are shown here.
19. D. Byrne and D. Parson (1983), 'The State and the Reserve Army: the Management of Class Relations in Space', in Anderson *et al.*, *Redundant Spaces in Cities and Regions*, 128.
20. Relative surplus-value is the production of a greater amount of value created by the worker without extending the length of the working day or the number of workers employed to produce the same amount of goods. In the main, technological developments and/or the reorganization of the work process are the means by which this increase in the extraction of surplus-value is achieved.
21. This is sometimes called an increase in the organic composition of capital. This term refers to a technical relation in that it means the amount of machinery to the number of workers. It is also a value relation in that it refers to the ratio between the value of the machinery and the value of the worker as measured by the cost of the average bundle of goods which workers buy to keep themselves going (i.e. reproduce themselves), i.e. the wage.

22. See for example Jane Barker and Hazel Downing. 'Word Processing and the Transformation of the Patriarchal Relations of Control and the Office', *Capital and Class*, No. 10 (1980). Fordist production methods refer to the application of conveyor belt or 'line' production as existed in car production, biscuit manufacture or the production of in-flight meals at British Airways. Taylorist methods refer to the application of 'scientific' methods to production, as for example the breaking down of the different aspects of producing a commodity into discrete operations.
23. Counter Information Services, *Women in the '80s* (London: CIS Publications, 1981).
24. Quoted in GLC Committee Report, IEC 1011, 1983.
25. Counter Information Services, *Women in the '80s*.
26. West, *Work, Women and the Labour Market*.
27. There is a whole plethora of schemes aimed at encouraging black people to solve their unemployment problem by going into business. Central and local government schemes for advice and/or financial assistance exist as do private sector ones. There is also a vociferous lobby from some sections of the black community: Business in the Community or The First Partnership Bank being two examples. An important and revealing aspect of all the rhetoric surrounding these schemes is the emphasis placed by all concerned on the supposed relationship between the development of a thriving black business sector and the cessation of inner city uprisings. The argument is that if young black people (and note here that the emphasis is on Caribbean youth) see some evidence of black investment in the country they won't protest at police harassment and brutality!
28. Cynthia Cockburn, *The Local State* (London: Pluto Press, 1977).
29. A. Friend and A. Metcalfe, *Slump City: The Politics of Mass Unemployment* (London: Pluto, 1981).
30. Marx included these workers in his discussion of the Reserve Army of Labour and described it in this way: 'The third category of the relative surplus population, the stagnant, forms a part of the active army, but with extremely irregular employment . . . Its conditions of life sink below the average normal level of the working class; this makes it at once the broad basis of special branches of capitalist exploitation. It is characterised by a maximum of working time and a minimum of wages' (Karl Marx, *Capital* vol. 1 (London: Lawrence and Wishart, 1974), 602).
31. Cuts in public expenditure are also accompanied by the construction of more and more people as 'scroungers'. Simultaneously it undermines or removes the notion of people's 'rights' to state-provided welfare and redefines who is entitled to these rights.
32. For example the extent to which black women were successful in gaining improvements in the education received by their children (as measured by formal academic qualifications) affected the type of jobs these black children would then expect or demand.
33. D. Massey, *Spatial Divisions of Labour* (London: Macmillan, 1985), especially ch. 5.

23 Women, Migration and the State

Annie Phizacklea *

INTRODUCTION

Over the last fifteen years or so there has been an increased recognition, amongst women researchers at least, of the need to provide a gendered account of migratory processes. Nevertheless, despite a recognition of the importance of women's role in migration, many accounts of contemporary migratory processes continue to fail to take on board what this means at an analytical level. [. . .]

In what follows I want to explore the relationship between women's migration, employment and state practice in three globalized industries—clothing, sex and the maids industry. These case studies throw light on how a world market for women's labour and services continues to be mediated by the policies of individual nation-states which have not only been constructed in highly masculinist ways but which contribute to the reproduction of women's subordination and dependency in traditional forms. Concerns of this kind have become increasingly unfashionable in Western feminist analyses where a post-structuralist concern with identity, difference and diversity amongst women has become more widespread. Given Western feminism's tendency to universalize the experience of Western, affluent women, a focus on the diversity of women's experiences is welcome. Nevertheless it needs to be emphasized that there are also real dangers in an emphasis on diversity if it obscures the continuing material inequalities between women in racialized hierarchies of power; these have not gone away . . .

In fact one of the purposes of this paper is to highlight specific

* From Annie Phizacklea, 'Women, Migration and the State' from *Women and the State: International Perspectives* by Shirin Rai and Geraldine Lievesley (Taylor & Francis, 1996), reprinted by permission of the publisher.

situations which raise uncomfortable and pressing questions for feminists in affluent societies. A recognition of difference and diversity does not however mean that coalitions cannot be built between women of different class, ethnic and national backgrounds. The structure of this chapter is as follows: it begins with a brief overview of the ways in which women's migration has been conceptualized and the global forces that have shaped women's migratory experiences; it then goes on to the case studies; and it concludes with a very brief consideration of organization and coalition building.

THEORIZING MIGRATION—VOLUNTARIST VERSUS STRUCTURALIST ACCOUNTS

In this chapter I am not concerned with the migration of well-qualified, usually professional migrant workers whose relatively scarce skills can be sold for generous rewards on the world labour market. My concern is with those migrants (and this includes refugees) who through poverty, unemployment or war are forced to seek a livelihood outside their country of origin.

Women constitute half of the world's migrants and 80 per cent of the world's refugee population. This includes women living permanently or for long periods of time outside their country of origin as well as those migrating for relatively short periods of time on fixed-term work contracts. Others may have migrated in order to join husbands or relatives already working abroad and still others are forced to leave their home countries due to unrest, persecution and violence. But none of these women just wake up one morning and decide to migrate from their homes; rather, the causes of migration are complex, and they are very often different for men and for women.

While there is not the space here to present a literature review on women and migration, I want to suggest that there have been two main models. One I will call voluntarist, because it stresses the role of human agency and the potentially emancipatory effects of migration for women, particularly when this is related to the pursuit of increased wage-earning opportunities. The alternative structuralist model regards women's migration, whether it be individual or family related, as determined by economic necessity and the migratory experience shaped by external forces leaving little space for 'choice' to be exercised. I want to suggest that, given the type of migratory flows that I am addressing in this chapter, the latter model is the most appropriate, and I will emphasize the role of the state in shaping migratory projects. Migration has always been and continues to be an expression of uneven economic development on a global scale. In describing South–North migrations in the 1960s, Castles and Kosack[1] suggested that we might regard such migrations as a form of development aid to the North. With the demise of the 'communist bloc' and rapid capitalist development in many south-east Asian countries our binary shorthands of 'North–South' or the always pejorative notion of First, Second and Third Worlds have limited value even at a descriptive level. Some of us have now started to refer simply to affluent and poor countries of the world, though it is important to remember the historic linkages that explain why some are affluent and some are poor. The unevenness was established in its clearest forms under colonization by European nation-states from the fifteenth century onwards. Colonization meant the enrichment of the European nation-states at the expense of the colonized economy and population, often the latter's destruction and its substitution with imported slave labour. The European colonial powers went on to impose their domination on to large tracts of the world. In many cases the colonized, dispossessed of their land either through compulsory acquisition or changes in communal land holding, were forced to work on estates or in mines producing food and raw materials for export. Political independence from the colonizer rarely brought with it economic independence because the legacy of colonialism was economic underdevelopment, a distorted economy, degraded land and structural unemployment. These same countries continued to be economically dependent on their ex-colonizers and other affluent developed countries through the presence of multinational companies, external debt and a dependence on export led growth.

The economic and social dislocation which arises from this distorted development process is not gender-neutral—deprived of traditional subsistence activities on and around the land it is often women who become a 'relative surplus' population in the poorer, 'developing' countries of the world. Up until the end of the 1970s women's migration from poor countries was very often bound into these colonial linkages as they migrated in search of work to the affluent metropolitan society.

From the mid-1970s this pattern began to change as multinational companies in the affluent countries began to site more and more of their production in the poor countries themselves. This change is often referred to as the move, to 'capital to labour' rather than 'labour to capital'. Most affluent countries introduced strict immigration controls on the entry of new workers by the mid-1970s as their need for migrant labour was reduced. Nevertheless the demand for low-waged female labour in manual service jobs has remained and many countries have permitted the entry of family members if those workers already in the migration setting can prove that they are able to support their families without 'recourse to public funds'.

At the same time the demand for manufacturing workers increased in newly industrializing countries such as Hong Kong, South Korea, Singapore, Malaysia and Taiwan. Dispatched to earn cash in the world market in factories located in urban areas, young women have been targeted by multinational companies for their cheapness, vulnerability and supposed 'nimble fingers' since the 1960s.[2] In their search for foreign investment, developing country governments have encouraged this. [. . .]

This rural–urban migration is often the first step in what becomes an international migration because many poor, developing country governments encourage their surplus population to work abroad and send home remittances to ease internal poverty and help service foreign debt.

In addition the Gulf States began to recruit large numbers of personal service workers. In countries such as Kuwait the rapid increase in the numbers of professional and managerial women has been paralleled by an equally significant rise in demand for maids, the vast majority of whom migrate from southern Asia, particularly Sri Lanka. The demand for personal service workers has risen throughout affluent societies.[3]

Often it is very difficult to distinguish between what may be considered to be 'individual' choices governing migratory decisions and economic factors. For instance, migration may be regarded by some women as offering the possibility of escape from oppressive patriarchal cultures where notions regarding appropriate behaviour for women are strictly defined. But Morokvasic has shown the greater number of divorced, separated and widowed women in labour migrations in comparison with men with those statuses.[4] Women have greater difficulty surviving economically with that status or changing it; thus while the migratory decision may appear to be an individual's 'choice' it is underwritten by economic necessity. In many cases it is women who are left behind as heads of households in war zones.

Family men may have left to fight or been killed, resulting in the situation where 80 per cent of the world's refugee populations are now female.[5]

STATE MASCULINISM

The vast majority of women migrating from poor, usually formerly colonized, countries are not entering an ideological vacuum when migrating to affluent parts of the world. A major feature of the colonization process was the development of an ideology alleging the innate inferiority of the dominated. Within this context, women from poor countries are stereotyped as illiterate beasts of burden, the bearers of many children and the guardians of 'tradition'.[6] [. . .] All women migrating legally as workers are controlled by the work permit system which not only stipulates the type of work but usually the actual employer. In cases where the woman has entered as the spouse of an employed male or 'mail-order' bride she may be bound to an unhappy, even violent marriage by immigration laws which render her right of residence dependent upon her husband.[7] If a woman in this situation divorces she is liable to deportation. The legal entry of spouses and dependants is only allowed if a sponsor can provide evidence that he or she can support and accommodate them without recourse to 'public funds'. Not only is the family then forced to settle without state support, in many cases there is a waiting period before legal access to the labour market is granted. This forces many migrant women into unregistered work such as homeworking. They cannot work in registered jobs because they do not have a work permit. Even when they do have a legal right to work, racial discrimination and disadvantage may still confine migrant and immigrant women to low-paid homeworking jobs, as we shall see in the clothing industry case study. These stereotypes also have serious implications for women in other areas of their lives. For instance, unsafe methods of contraception, such as Depo Provera, abortion and sterilization have often been forced on migrant women in the name of 'emancipation'.[8]

As we have seen, racial discrimination often further constrains the labour market and therefore the earning opportunities of migrant women. This in turn is reflected in the kind of housing migrants can afford and the increased likelihood of overcrowding. But again this is not just a reflection of low incomes; in Europe at least there is plenty of evidence to show how the differential access to employment, housing, education, social and health services which is experienced by immigrants as compared with European nationals can be traced to institutionalized racism.[9]

It is within this context that we consider three specific cases of women's migration and the role of the state in shaping their migratory experience.

THE SEX AND MARRIAGE INDUSTRIES

Over the last twenty years we have witnessed the rapid growth of the sex-related entertainment industry in affluent and newly industrializing countries. Prostitution and other forms of sex-related 'entertainment' have become very big business for many countries where the industry has become an integral part of tourism. While women from many parts of south-east Asia and Africa have been deceived and 'trafficked' by the sex industry, now women from Eastern Europe and the former Soviet Union are finding their way into the clubs and brothels of north-west Europe in particular. The traffic in women is largely illegal and undocumented. Many women are recruited as entertainers, but when they arrive in the migration setting they realize that the only entertainment they are expected to provide is sex. Others indebted in their home country may be trafficked as bonded labour, but because they are very often illegal migrants any attempt to break free of the trafficker or pimp will result in deportation.[10]

A related growth industry is that of 'mail-order' brides. Whereas in the past women from south-east Asia were 'favoured' for their 'submissiveness', now Eastern European women are being promoted on cost grounds[11] as the following extract from a German newspaper indicates: 'whereas a Thai is unprepared for cold German winters—one has to buy her clothes—a Pole brings her own boots and fur coat. And she is as good in bed and industrious in the kitchen'.[12]

Truong and del Rosario[13] put forward a compelling theoretical framework with which to analyse the nature of power relations governing the lives of trafficked women, but I would want to argue that it has a broader applicability to the situation of migrant women generally and particularly all those who are undocumented or who have gained entry to the migration setting as a spouse.

They argue that the state is pivotal to such power relations in so far as it encompasses so many institutionalized dimensions of masculinism including the juridical–legislative, the capitalist, the prerogative and the bureaucratic dimension. Brown's argument is that the juridical–legislative dimension of the state is based on a public/private distinction, placing the family, and women's place within it, firmly within a male-regulated private domain.[14] Truong and del Rosario argue that this has serious implications for the way that trafficked women in the sex industry and mail-order brides are treated by the state. To reiterate, trafficked women are often deceived or coerced into an illegal migration and remain under the physical control of procurers in the migration setting. If they come to the notice of the state, deportation is likely to be the result for the worker as an illegal alien while the procurer may hide behind the many different forms of legal sex-related services.[15] The burden of proof is shifted to the woman; in the eyes of the state she is an undesirable alien. In the same way if a mail-order bride wishes to leave the relationship that secured her entry into the migration setting, she too will be liable to deportation. In this way Truong and del Rosario argue that 'state practices buttress the interests and power of individual men as husbands, fiancés or pimps'.[16] As they point out, once women are shifted out of the private sphere it is immigration law that determines their status, not family law or the laws against trafficking. The capitalist dimension of the state restricts the level of state intervention and regulation of the sex and marriage industries which are regarded as being part of the private domain in any case. Exactly the same 'logic' applies to the state's attitude to the maids industry.

THE MAIDS INDUSTRY

By the early 1980s it was estimated that less than 15 per cent of families in the US conformed to the idealized notion of breadwinning husband, housewife and 2.4 children. The vast majority of households either contained dual-earner couples or were single-headed.[17] Other affluent societies have followed suit and the reality of the working mother and a diminishing role for the state in the care of the very young and the elderly has resulted in a massively increased demand for domestic workers in affluent societies. In the US the work of Hertz and Hochschild and Machung[18] indicates very clearly that more affluent women can buy their way out of performing many reproductive tasks traditionally associated with women's 'role' in the private sphere by employing poorer (often undocumented) migrant women to perform them instead.

Anderson's work shows how in the Gulf States and in Britain also migrant domestic workers are treated by the state as members of households: they have no immigration status in their own right. This non-recognition as an employee leaves such workers, virtually all of whom are women, vulnerable to all sorts of abuse, physical, mental and material. [. . .] They are trapped by an immigration law that ties them into what can be a wholly unsatisfactory, even physically dangerous relationship with their employer. If they leave their employment they will be liable to deportation.[19]

Thus women from poor countries such as Mexico, Sri Lanka and the Philippines allow women in affluent countries to escape the drudgery of housework in conditions that sometimes approximate a contemporary form of state-facilitated slavery. In the final case study we examine some of the experiences of migrant women in the clothing industry.

MAKING CLOTHES

To reiterate, by the late 1970s we had witnessed a changing pattern of female migration in affluent societies. Rather than manufacturing industries in the higher-wage countries importing labour, they began to export certain labour-intensive stages of production to lower-wage poor and newly industrializing countries instead. While the electronics industry pioneered this trend, the clothing industry was quick on its heels, seizing the opportunity of reducing labour costs by shifting production to 'off-shore' sites. There were a number of incentives to do so, such as tax holidays, unrestricted repatriation of profits, and laws restricting the organization and bargaining power of trade unions, though lower labour costs were the biggest incentive.

In 1980 the English-language version of the influential study by Frobel, Heinrichs and Kreye, *The New International Division of Labour*, was published. They argued that the majority of clothing firms in what was then West Germany had relocated their production to low-wage countries to reduce labour costs in an industry where further mechanization was deemed too risky.[20] While their thesis is compelling and the trend towards a global relocation of labour-intensive manufacturing a continuing reality, there remain national differences which I would want to argue are closely related to differing immigration policies. A comparison between Britain and what was then the Federal Republic of Germany makes this clear.[21]

By the early 1970s both the British and German clothing industries were faced with declining profitability and both looked to subcontracting as a way of reducing labour costs. While Germany subcontracted abroad, British firms found new domestic subcontracting sources in the growing number of small, often 'family' dominated, inner-city factories run by ethnic minority entrepreneurs and labour.

While Germany had tied its migrant workers to specific jobs, had restricted the right of foreigners to set up businesses and had discouraged family re-union, Britain had imposed no such restrictions on migrant workers from ex-colonies entering prior to the restrictions of 1962. But the situation has been very different since then with even family re-union becoming increasingly difficult. The entry of spouses and family is only allowed if a sponsor can provide evidence that she or he will not have recourse to public funds. To reiterate, this forces many families to settle in poverty; it forces migrant women to find whatever work is available. In a 1990 study of homeworking in the English city of Coventry, my colleague Carol Wolkowitz and myself found that not only was the Asian-dominated clothing industry the only manufacturing growth industry in the city, it was also a major employer of Asian immigrant women, many of whom work for very low wages in their homes assembling garments. When we asked these women if they preferred to work at home, virtually all of them responded that working at home made them neither 'happier' nor 'unhappier'; they felt that they had no other choice.[22]

What the case studies indicate is, first, the extent to which the structural model of women's migration continues to have very real explanatory power and, secondly, the continuing importance of state immigration policies in shaping the migratory experience of women from poor countries.

ORGANIZING

Within the context of an unashamedly structural analysis I hope to have indicated not only the diversity of migratory experiences but also what that means in terms of the persistence of inequalities between women on a global scale. One of the most pressing questions this leaves us with is what the possibilities are of organization and coalition building between women of different classes, ethnic groups and nationalities when these categories represent hierarchies of power and privilege.

Self-organization and activity has often been forced upon migrant workers. In many cases organizations representing particular nationality groupings have been set up initially with a social function. Yet it is these very organizations that have shown themselves capable of transforming their role through networking to take on a political campaigning function, for example Filipina women's organizations in Europe. In 1979 the Commission for Filipino Migrant Workers was set up to support Filipino migrants in Britain, many of whom are maids and totally isolated. In the words of one woman, 'I went back to normal. Before when I was alone, I didn't trust anyone. My experience with my employers meant that I couldn't speak up. It makes you silent and not open. When I began to talk to people in similar situations and I saw that I was not alone, I realised that the problem was not just to do with me, that it was the Philippines and Britain and the government in those countries'.[23]

Women who escaped from abusive employers, whatever their nationality, have been helped by the Commission, but it became increasingly clear that a campaign to change the immigration law relating to the position of domestics was vital. Kalayaan was formed, representing a coalition of migrant and immigrant groups, trade unions and concerned individuals who have campaigned to change the law as well as providing practical help for migrant domestic workers in Britain.[24]

The National Group on Homeworking in Britain (which now has links with homeworking groups worldwide) represents another coalition campaigning in the interests of homeworkers. While the National Group has campaigned for years to achieve employee status for all homeworkers, it recognizes that if the majority of homeworkers are to achieve something approximating equal opportunities then many structural obstacles must be tackled, such as racist and sexist immigration legislation and the opening up of real alternative employment possibilities for homeworkers, in some cases looking towards successful initiatives established by casualized women workers in poor countries. Swasti Mitter has examined a number of organizations including the Self-Employed Women's Association in India (SEWA) as models.

SEWA was set up in 1972 as a workers' association for homeworkers and petty traders and vendors. As a trade union it organizes campaigns around conditions of work and childcare; it provides leadership training and has encouraged the formation of women's savings banks and producer co-operatives. As Mitter emphasizes, perhaps the most important role that SEWA has carried out is in bringing the plight of casualized workers to the notice of national and international policy-makers.[25]

In the Netherlands local women's groups have taken up the cause of illegal migrant sex workers who would face deportation if they were to personally publicize and campaign against the bonded conditions under which they work.[26] There are many other instances of coalition building amongst diverse groups which only go to underline the point that a recognition of diversity and difference does not preclude collective organization across class and ethnic boundaries that challenges state practices and ideology.

Notes

1. S. Castles and G. Kosack, *Immigrant Workers and Class Structures in Western Europe* (Oxford: Oxford University Press, 1973).
2. R. Hancock, 'Transnational Production and Women Workers', in A. Phizacklea (ed.), *One Way Ticket: Migration and Female Labour* (London: Routledge, 1983).
3. Bridget Anderson, *Britain's Secret Slaves* (Anti-Slavery International, 1993).
4. Mirjana Morokvasic, 'Women and Migration: Beyond the Reductionist Outlook', in Phizacklea, *One Way Ticket.*
5. Susan Forbes-Martin, *Refugee Women* (London: Zed Press, 1991).
6. Morokvasic, 'Women and Migration'.
7. L. Potts, *The World Labour Market* (London: Zed Press, 1990).
8. Beverley Bryan, Stella Dadzie and Suzanne Scafe, *The Heart of the Race* (London: Virago, 1985).
9. Eleonore Kofman and Rosemary Sales, 'Towards Fortress Europe', *Women's Studies International Forum* 15, Nos 5/6 (1992), 29–40.
10. Thanh-Dam Truong, *Sex, Money and Morality: Prostitution and Tourism in Southeast Asia* (London: Zed Press, 1990); Thanh-Dam Truong and Virginia del Rosario, 'Captive Outsiders: Trafficked Sex Workers and Mail-Order Brides in the European Union', in J. Wiersma (ed.), *Insiders and Outsiders: On the Making of Europe II* (Kampen: Pharos, 1994).
11. Truong and del Rosario, 'Captive Outsiders'.
12. *Bild,* 9 January 1991, cited in Mirjana Morokvasic, 'Fortress Europe and Migrant Women', *Feminist Review* 39 (Winter 1991), 69–84.
13. Truong and del Rosario, 'Captive Outsiders'.
14. W. Brown, 'Finding the Man in the State', *Feminist Studies* 18 (1992), 20.
15. Truong and del Rosario, 'Captive Outsiders', 5.

16. Truong and del Rosario, 'Captive Outsiders', 11.
17. M. Andersen, *Thinking About Women: Sociological Perspectives on Sex and Gender* (New York: Macmillan, 1988).
18. R. Hertz, *More Equal Than Others* (Berkeley: University of California Press, 1986); A. Hochschild and A. Machung, *The Second Shift* (New York: Viking, 1989).
19. Anderson, *Britain's Secret Slaves.*
20. L. Frobel, J. Heinrichs and O. Kreye, *The New International Division of Labour* (Cambridge: Cambridge University Press, 1980).
21. Annie Phizacklea, *Unpacking the Fashion Industry: Gender, Racism and Class in Production* (London: Routledge, 1990).
22. Annie Phizacklea and Carol Wolkowitz, *Homeworking Women: Gender, Racism and Class at Work* (London: Sage, 1995).
23. Quoted in Anderson, *Britain's Secret Slaves*, 59.
24. Anderson, *Britain's Secret Slaves.*
25. S. Rowbotham and S. Mitter, *Dignity and Daily Bread: New Forms of Organization Amongst Poor Women in the Third World* (London: Routledge, 1994).
26. Truong and del Rosario, 'Captive Outsiders'.

24 People or Population: Towards a New Ecology of Reproduction

Maria Mies and Vandana Shiva *

POPULATION, ENVIRONMENT AND PEOPLE

Some years ago the continuing and increasing poverty in the countries of the South was attributed to the population explosion and population growth is seen increasingly as the main cause of environmental deterioration on a global scale. This assumed causal connection between the rising numbers of people and the destruction of the earth's ecological foundations was strongly emphasized in the political discourse around the June 1992 Earth Summit (UNCED) in Rio de Janeiro. Arguments supporting this view were propagated worldwide by the media, and more and more outright cynical and inhuman population control policies were proposed, including coercive contraceptive technologies for women and denial of basic health care for children, for example in a proposal by Maurice King in 1990.[1]

That industrialization, technological progress and the affluent lifestyle of the developed nations have precipitated the acceleration of environmental degradation worldwide can no longer be ignored. The main threats are: (1) degradation of land (for example, desertification, salination, loss of arable land); (2) deforestation, mainly of tropical forests; (3) climate change, due to the destruction of the ozone layer; and (4) global warming, due mainly to increasing rates of carbon dioxide and other gaseous emissions. But instead of looking into the root causes of these threats which it is feared are approaching catastrophic thresholds, they are today almost universally attributed to a single cause: population growth. Not only the affluent North and dominant political and economic interests but UN organizations also

* From Maria Mies and Vandana Shiva, 'People or Population: Towards a New Ecology of Reproduction' from *Ecofeminism* (Zed Books, 1993), 277–96, reprinted by permission of the publisher.

subscribe to this view. Thus the United Nations Fund for Population Action (UNFPA), in its report of 1990 *The State of World Population 1990* states:

For any given type of technology, for any given level of consumption or waste, for any given level of poverty or inequality, the more people there are the greater the impact on the environment.[2]

In the affluent North there is a decline in the birth-rate, but this is balanced by immigrations; the culprits are seen as people living in the poor countries of the South. No less than 95 per cent of global population growth over the next thirty-five years will be in the developing countries of Africa, Asia and Latin America.

The UNFPA argues that world population is growing at a rate of three people per second—or a quarter of a million people per day. This is faster than at any time in history. The most rapid growth is in developing countries. But will the earth's damaged environment be able to sustain such numbers in the 1990s and beyond? No account is taken of the exploitative and colonial world system, of the prevailing development paradigm or of the wasteful production and consumption patterns of the industrialized societies which are responsible for most of the environmental destruction, as, in fact, is admitted in the UNFPA report:

By far the largest share of the resources used, and waste created, is currently the responsibility of the 'top billion' people, those in the industrialized countries. These are the countries overwhelmingly responsible for the damage to the ozone layer and acidification, as well as for roughly two-thirds of global warming.[3]

Despite these insights, however, the main policy to stem these threatening trends is to halt population growth. This means that it is not the rich, who have caused the problems, who must take action, but the poor, in the exploited countries of the South.

Arguments to support this Malthusian logic are usually based on statistical projections, which in turn are based on the assumption that the social and economic model of the industrialized North, the growth model, will eventually be followed by all people living in the South. Such arguments are always introduced by such phrases as: 'If present trends continue' . . . 'If the pattern of the past is repeated' . . . . One example is the projection with regard to the growth of car production:

As incomes grow, lifestyles and technologies will come to resemble those of Europe, North America or Japan . . . There will be an increase in car ownership. Since 1950 the human population has doubled, but the car population [sic] has increased seven times. The world car fleet is projected to grow from present 400 million to 700 million over the next twenty years—twice as fast as the human population.

After such a statement it might be expected that a reduction in the North's rate of car production would follow, but instead we read: 'If past trends continue, developing countries will be emitting 16.6 billion tonnes of carbon annually by 2025, over four times as much as the developed countries today.'[4]

The real threat, therefore, is considered to be that a growing world population would emulate the life-style of the average person in the North, with as many cars, TVs, refrigerators, and so on. [. . .] The 'car population' must grow, but in order to curb the environmental damage this causes, the South's human population (those who will not buy cars) must decrease. This is the industrial system's real dilemma. It does not want to abandon its growth therefore it lays the blame for the damage it causes on its victims: the South's poor, particularly the women who produce too many children. [. . .]

In patriarchal society women are responsible for the production and maintenance of everyday life, of subsistence, for water, fuel, food and fodder as well as for land preservation. But with more 'development' and more modernization propagated by the North they are pushed ever closer to the margins of their life-sustaining systems. They are accused of destroying the forests in search of fuel, polluting and exhausting water sources in search of drinking water, and exhausting the land resources by producing too many additional mouths to feed.

All the methods proposed in the UNFPA Report to curb overpopulation are directed towards women. The responsibility of men, and their cult of machismo, for the large number of births is mentioned only *en passant.* It is stated that most women in the South want fewer children, but the men are not addressed when it comes to contraceptive methods. It seems to be feared that to directly attack and attempt to change patriarchal culture would probably be interpreted as interference and the imposition of cultural imperialism by the North.

[. . .] As the world's political leaders dare not openly oppose the system based on permanent growth and demand drastically reduced consumption patterns in the North, the solution is increasingly seen in a kind of lifeboat or triage philosophy. This philosophy is even promulgated by local family-planning workers in Bangladesh:

> You see, there are only nine cabins in the steamer launch which comes from Dhaka to Pathuakhali [a Bangladeshi village]. In the nine cabins only 18 people can travel. The ticket is expensive, so only the rich people travel in the cabins. The rest of the common passengers travel in the deck. The latrine facility is only provided for the cabin passengers. But sometimes cabin passengers allow them to use the latrine because they are afraid that if the poor deck passengers get angry then they might go down and make a hole in the launch. Then the launch will sink: they will die no doubt but the rich cabin passengers will not survive either. So, my dear sisters, do not give birth to more children as they cause a problem for the cabin passengers.[5]

The North's cabin passengers' fear of the South's population explosion is shared by the South's affluent middle classes. Population control policy mobilizes these imperialist and class fears.

Discourses on population and poverty and on population and environment are permeated by several fundamental anomalies inherent in capitalist partiarchal society. These are the assumed contradictions between people and the environment, the individual and society, production and reproduction, and sexuality and procreation. For capitalist philosophy the basic economic unit is the isolated individual with his/her egotistic and aggressive self-interest, which is perceived as fundamentally antagonistic to that of other such self-interested individuals. Therefore, there is a conflict of interests between the individual and the community which, according to the Hobbesian concept of man and society, can only be solved by an all-powerful state. Adam Smith tried to solve this dilemma by his famous 'invisible hand', which means allowing aggressive competition between these self-interested egotistic individuals for their economic gains, which eventually would result in optimal wealth for all.

Already underlying this concept of the human being and society is a statistical view or a 'political arithmetic', first developed by William Petty in 1690. Quantifying society, people and their relationship to nature (today one would say resources), became necessary for rising capitalism. Following Bacon, Petty saw a parallel between the 'body natural' and the 'body politic' and he tried to demonstrate that the wealth and power of the state depends on the number and character of its subjects.[6]

According to Barbara Duden, however, it was not before 1800 that statistics became the new language of all modern science, particularly economics, and that the term 'population' lost its tie to actual people.[7]

Meanwhile, actual living persons, real people, real communities, their history, culture and diversity have vanished behind the abstraction of aggregate numbers, expressed in population figures, growth rates, pressures and policies. The term population can refer, as Barbara Duden writes, as much to 'mosquitoes as to humans'.[8] This concept of population, which transforms living people into mere numbers makes it possible, as we have noted, even for a UN document to compare the growth of the 'car population' with that of the 'human population'.

But not only did people disappear when populations were identified as mainly responsible for underdevelopment, poverty and environmental destruction, but other, different anomalies emerged with the new capitalist population policies, namely: in the relationship between the sexual and reproductive behaviour of individuals and the well-being of the community; and between production and reproduction. In capitalist patriarchy's liberal philosophy the sexual behaviour of individuals is assumed to be determined by natural laws expressed as biological drives, whereby, as in the case of economic self-interest, people simply follow their egotistic pleasure-seeking, careless of the well-being of others or the community, and of the consequences of sexual activity for women. It is assumed that eventually this individual sexual self-interest, unless checked by external forces, technologies, the state and new contraceptive devices, will result in 'overpopulation'.

The same liberal philosophy is applied to justify not only the separation between sexuality and procreation but also to conceptualize an individual's sexual and reproductive activity as a purely individual affair, rather than as the expression of a social relation, interconnected with other social, economic and cultural spheres and relations. This is why many women put emphasis only on women's individual reproductive rights, without demanding changes in the overall political and economic structures of the present world (dis)order. They see only the individual woman and the need to protect her reproductive freedom or 'choice'.[9] The population controllers, however, see women only as aggregated uteruses. Both views stem from the same philosophy and both are based on abstractions which ignore the real social relations through which people—real men and women—interact with themselves, with each other and with nature as producers and reproducers. The separation between production and reproduction facilitated by capitalist patriarchy is such that producers conceive of themselves as separate from and superior to the nature around and within them, and women as reproducers experience themselves as passive and alienated from their own bodies, their procreative capacities and from any subjectivity.

Feminists in the North subscribe to the people and population anomaly by their demand for 'control over our own body' and safe contraceptives, without asking who controls the production of contraceptives, for what purposes and within which political and economic framework. Women of the South, however, experience this anomaly in the fact that they are increasingly reduced to numbers, targets, wombs, tubes and other reproductive parts by the population controllers.

The aim in this chapter is to show that these apparent anomalies are based not only on false assumptions but also on a viewpoint that blames the planet's ills on victims, mainly poor women.

WHO CARRIES WHOM?

Most people assume that local population pressure is the only pressure on ecosystems, that there is a straightforward carrying capacity calculus for human societies as there is for non-human communities.

Most ecosystems in the Third World, however, do not only carry local populations; they also carry the North's demands for industrial raw material and consumption. This demand on Third World resources means that the threshold for the support of local populations is lowered. In other words, what would be a sustainable population size on the basis of local production, consumption and life-style patterns becomes non-sustainable due to external resource-exploitation. The theoretical and conceptual challenge is to find the roots of non-sustainable use not only in visible local demand but also in the invisible, non-local resource demand; otherwise, the search for sustainable population rates will become an ideological war declared against the victims of environmental degradation in the Third World, without removing the real pressures on the environment inflicted by the global economic system.

The 'carrying capacity' in the case of human societies is not simply a matter of local population size and local biological support systems. It is a more complex relationship of populations in the North to populations and ecosystems in the South. The South's ecosystems (E) carry a double burden: supplying commodities and raw materials to the global market (G); and supporting the survival of local communities (L).

Reducing L, and ignoring G, cannot protect E. Moreover, most analyses of the relationship between population and the environment ignore non-local demand for resources, as does Garett Hardin in his seminal essay, 'Tragedy of the Commons'. What he failed to notice about the degradation of the commons is that it is accelerated when the commons are enclosed, that is, when they stop being commons and become privatized.

Enclosure of the commons separates people from resources; people are displaced and resources exploited for private profit. In England, enclosure of the commons forced peasants off the land in order to pasture sheep. 'Enclosures make fat beasts and lean people', 'Sheep eat men' were two of the sayings that characterized the consequences of the enclosure. 'Carrying capacity' had been problematized because the land was no longer available to support people but sheep, largely to provide wool for Britain's emerging textile industry. The disenfranchised people were turned into a resource, worth only the market price of their labour power. Displacement from land makes a necessity of growth in numbers.

But not all these poor peasants and craftsmen, driven from their land and robbed of the commons, were absorbed by the rising industry as free wage labourers. Many had to migrate to the new colonies in America and Canada or, for petty thefts and the like, were deported to Australia. After the violent clearing of people from the Scottish Highlands to make room for sheep, many Highlanders were forced to migrate to Canada to work as lumberjacks or were recruited into the British army to fight in the new colonies.

Similar processes—privatization of the commons, eviction of the rural poor—took place in the other industrializing countries of Europe, and its pauperized masses were exported to the colonies. After the mid-19th century there was a wave of mass migration of poor Europeans to North America, and to other colonies, such as Brazil and South Africa. A wave of out-migration after World War II was not, however, confined to the poor. It was this out-migration of Europe's poor (and the ambitious) rather than advances in medicine, the rise of general living standards and the invention of new contraceptives, that led to a demographic decline in Europe. [. . .]

Population growth is not a cause of the environmental crisis but one aspect of it, and both are related to resource alienation and destruction of livelihoods, first by colonialism and then continued by Northern-imposed models of maldevelopment. Until 1600 India's population was between 100 and 125 million: till 1800 it remained stable. Then it began to rise: 130 million in 1845; 175 million in 1855; 194 million in 1867; 255 million in 1871. The beginning of the 'population explosion' dove-tailed neatly with the expansion of British rule in India, when the people's resources, rights and livelihoods were confiscated.

What is also ignored in this 'carrying capacity' discourse is the history of colonial intervention into people's reproductive behaviour. This intervention was initially motivated, as in Europe, by the need for more disposable labour, labour freed from subsistence activities and forced to work 'productively' on plantations, farms, roads, in mines and factories for the benefit of capital. This policy vacillated between a largely anti-natalist regime for slaves in most of the Caribbean, who were cheaper to purchase than to breed,[10] and a pro-natalist approach later implemented in South Africa—when the white farmers needed more labour. After the Herero rebellion, South African women were punished if they aborted or used contraceptives. This pro-natalist policy was supported throughout the colonial period by christian missionaries who everywhere campaigned against indigenous institutions, family forms and methods and sexual practices which, women in particular, had used for centuries to regulate their procreative potential to maintain a balance with the ecological limits of the region that provided their livelihood.

The focus on population as the cause of environmental destruction is erroneous at two levels: (1) it blames the victims—mainly women; and (2) by failing to address economic insecurity and by denying rights to survival, the current policy prescriptions avoid the real problem. False perceptions lead to false solutions. As a result, environmental degradation, poverty creation and population growth continue unabated, despite the billions of dollars spent on population control programmes.

It might then well be more fruitful to address directly the roots of the problem: the exploitative world market system which *produces* poverty. Giving people rights and access to resources so that they can generate sustainable livelihoods is the only solution to environmental destruction and the population growth that accompanies it.

FALSE ASSUMPTIONS, FALSE CONCLUSIONS

The discourse on the prime responsibility of the 'population explosion' for environmental destruction is also erroneous in so far as it is based on a number of patriarchal and Eurocentric assumptions and theories which, in the light of careful socio-historical analysis, are untenable.

The first of these is the well-known Malthusian 'population law', according to which population grows geometrically, while food production proceeds arithmetically. This 'law' is based on what demographers have later called the concept of 'natural fertility'; that is, unchecked, uncontrolled human fertility, with no recourse to contraception or birth control, implying a purely unconscious, biological process.

Such a concept can only mean that, after a certain stage, there will be neither enough space nor food to 'carry' the people. The discourse on the ecological carrying capacity of the earth is based on this Malthusian logic. But it is also based on what we have called the myth of catching-up development. This means population growth is seen not only as a biological and statistical process, but implies that all people worldwide, now and in the future, will aspire to and eventually attain the level of consumption now prevailing in the North and in the rich classes of the South.

The Malthusian logic underpinning most demographic analyses and population policies of such UN organizations as the UNFPA, and of the World Bank, the Population Council and other national and international agencies, is augmented by the concept of 'natural fertility' employed by some demographers in regard to pre-modern, pre-industrial, traditional societies. When these demographers characterize the reproductive behaviour of modern, industrial society in Europe, the USA and Japan they apply the concept of 'controlled fertility behaviour'. They assume that 'natural fertility behaviour' prevailed in all pre-industrial societies before the end of the eighteenth century, meaning that contraception was unknown in these societies, in and outside Europe. 'Natural fertility' was assumed always to have been high and generally stable, checked only by 'biological factors': diseases; epidemics; wars; low standards of living; and institutional constraints such as sex taboos.

In Europe, however, after what the demographers have called the period of transition in the eighteenth and nineteenth centuries, natural fertility is said to have been replaced by controlled fertility; mid-nineteenth century high fertility rates gave way to lower ones in the twentieth century. Increased population in nineteenth-century Europe is usually attributed to industrial progress: better medicines; improved hygiene and standards of living; lower mortality rates. Similar modernization technology, particularly in the field of medicine, has supposedly led to the South's population explosion, because it is said to have checked epidemics and diseases, the so-called 'natural' controls on population growth. But whereas this sudden population growth in Europe was supposedly checked by the invention of modern contraceptives, and by education, particularly of women, with gainful employment and more consumer goods bought by the masses, the same did not happen in the South. (The fact that Europe exported its poor to the colonies is usually disregarded.) Since the mid-1970s, feminists and other scholars have challenged the assumptions of overall natural fertility in pre-modern societies and convincingly demonstrated that women knew and practised methods of contraception and birth control before the invention of the pill.

In her history of birth control in America, Linda Gordon showed that as early as 1877, it existed long before modern contraceptives were invented:

> There is a prevalent myth in our technological society that birth control technology came to us with modern medicine. This is far from the truth, as modern medicine did almost nothing until the last twenty years to improve on birth control devices that were literally more than a millenium old.[11]

From ancient times, women almost everywhere have known of methods and techniques of birth control; men, too, were aware of practices that precluded conception. As Wacjman argues, modern contraceptives were developed with a view to population control rather than motivated by a desire to further women's self-determination.[12] Feminist historians have provided ample evidence that the so-called witches, who for several centuries were persecuted and brutally murdered in Europe, were in fact the wise-women, well-versed in medicine and midwifery, who knew many methods whereby women were enabled to balance the number of their children [. . .] With the annihilation of these women went the disappearance of their birth-control and other knowledge.[13] According to Heinsohn and Steiger, it was the systematic destruction of these women and their knowledge together with the modern capitalist states' deliberate pro-natalist population policy, which led to rapid population growth in nineteenth-century Europe, and not advances in medicine, hygiene and nutrition.[14]

This critical historical research has been barely noticed by modern demographers and the population control establishment. [. . .]

To give one example: B. F. Mussalam has shown that the theory that pre-modern societies were ignorant of methods of contraception is false even for medieval Islam, a society which supposedly is more strongly traditional and patriarchal than European society. In a detailed socio-historical analysis, Mussalam shows that birth control, particularly the method of *coitus interruptus* was not only permitted by the Koran and Islamic law but also widely practised in Islamic society. In addition, techniques, mainly barrier methods, were employed by women. The concept of natural fertility cannot, therefore, be upheld, even for medieval Islamic society,[15] any more than it can be upheld for pre-industrial Europe or for other traditional societies in the South.

[. . .] After World War II, modern contraceptives were developed by transnational pharmaceutical corporations in order to fight overpopulation in the South. Unlike traditional methods, modern contraceptive technology is totally controlled by scientists, the profit interests of pharmaceutical corporations, and the state. [. . .]

WOMEN AS WOMBS AND TARGETS

The process whereby people become populations is to be understood not only as a mere epistemological change. In practice it meant and means a direct and usually coercive intervention into people's lives—particularly women's, because they have been identified as responsible for population growth.

Following the quantitative and divisive logic of modern reductionist science and capitalist patriarchy, population controllers and developmentalists both conceptualize people as separated from their resource base and women as separated from their reproductive organs. The population control establishment, including the producers of contraceptive devices, the multinational pharmaceutical corporations, are not concerned with real women, but only with the control of some of their reproductive parts: their wombs, tubes, their hormones and their eggs.

In the process of developing ever-more effective technical fixes to depopulate the South,[16] women's dignity and integrity, their health and that of their children are of little concern. This accounts for the fact that most of the contraceptives produced for and introduced into the South have, and continue to have negative side-effects on women. Moreover, hormonal contraceptives (Depo-provera, Net-OEN, and the latest, Norplant or RU 486) increasingly take away from women control over reproduction processes and put it into the hands of doctors and the pharmaceutical industry. The latest in this process of alienating women from their reproductive capacities is the research into anti-fertility vaccines.[17] Apart from these, sterilization, mainly of women, is seen as the most efficient method of population control. [. . .]

Today, while an increase in population is held responsible for environmental degradation, the Sarawak forests are being cleared and their peoples made homeless in their own land, in order that Japan can have its supply of disposable chopsticks; Indonesian forests are being felled to make toilet paper and tissues; and Amazon forests are burnt down to create cattle ranches to provide beefburgers. The plunder of such countries continues under unjustifiable world trade practices, loan servicing terms, and unrealistic interest rates on debts. As poverty increases and concomitantly, social insecurity, the poor and the illiterate will tend to look for security in numbers, and national governments will have to apply increasingly coercive measures in order to comply with the population control conditions linked to foreign aid.

In 1951, with its first Five Year Plan, India was the first country to formulate a National Population Policy. Typically 'top down', it was centrally planned, financed and monitored, to be applied at state and local levels. Guided, formulated and designed by external agencies it was to be implemented by India's government and its employees. [. . .] After the failure of the coercive sterilization campaign during the Emergency (1975–77), which was mainly targetted at men, the programme's title changed from 'family planning' to 'family welfare', but the strategies and approaches in respect of women remained unchanged. Women were seen as ignorant, illiterate and stupid beings who wanted only to produce children—curbing their fertility was obviously needed. For those involved in health-care, Indian population control policies were a double tragedy: first, because they failed to understand and cater to women's contraceptive needs; and second, because they marginalized and eclipsed all other health-care work.

The current population control policy in the South has been criticized not only by people concerned about the exploitative patriarchal and imperialist world order, but also by health workers and feminists, particularly in the South. Thus, regarding India's population policy which treats women not as human beings but as 'tubes, wombs and targets', Mira Shiva draws attention to the total lack of accountability that characterized the drive for women to undergo tubectomies, for which financial incentives are on offer not only for those who accept sterilization 'but also for the family planning workers'. [. . .] The costs borne by women were all too apparent in a violation of their dignity and a denial of their right to unbiased information, to safe and effective contraceptive care and to follow-up services to make the whole process accountable to those involved. 'The deterioration of the health status of women in several regions and a [skewed] sex ratio call for intervention in several areas, contraceptive needs being only one among several components of human welfare.' Mira Shiva, a health activist, writes about the side-effects of the various contraceptive devices tried out on Indian women, all advertised as safe and 100 per cent effective:

> Lippes Loop was first introduced into India following a strong advertising blitz announcing it as the wonder contraceptive for women. Again, when Dalkon Shield was introduced in the '60s, it was pronounced 'safe' until litigation in the U.S., following the death of seven women users, brought to light the intrauterine infections that had developed in thousands of women users across the world. In India, the problem is inevitably compounded by the fact that due to a lack of access to their own medical records, no compensation is possible even when women develop serious complications. Even if access was possible, the almost non-existent follow up would have nullified any gains made through a control over their own medical records.

The method of female sterilization by means of the costly imported laparoscope was seen as a revolutionary step in the Indian family planning programme. Yet, Indian doctors' callous use of this technology, citing with pride the number of sterilizations performed within the hour, caused it to fall into grave disrepute.

Curiously, long-acting injectable contraceptives are considered safe and effective for anaemic, malnourished and underweight Third World women, while in the North, recognition of the hazards of hormonal doses have led to minimizing their use in the contraceptive pill. [. . .]

POPULATION CONTROL AND COERCION

The population–environment discourse gave rise to panic in some quarters and nullified any ethical, humanistic opposition to an open policy of coercive interventions into people's reproductive behaviour. Such interventions, of course, are not new—India, during the (1975–77) Emergency, and Bangladesh have been subjected to them. Farida

Akhter from Bangladesh is one of the most outspoken critics of this 'coercive depopulation policy'. In numerous speeches and articles she has shown convincingly that population control programmes were devised to serve the commercial interests of the multinational pharmaceutical companies; forced on the Bangladeshi people as a pre-condition for aid and credit; and that, increasingly, coercion is applied in the implementation of these programmes. Additionally, in Bangladesh, sterilization is performed without prior examination of the women; even pregnant women are sterilized. But the government, which is responsible for enforcing these programmes, has no programme to treat the resultant health problems that women experience. In India and in Bangladesh, women are used as guinea-pigs to test new hormonal contraceptives: Norplant was administered to 1,000 women in Bangladesh, none of whom were told that they were participating in a test sponsored by the Bangladesh Fertility Research Programme.[18]

Farida Akhter has also pointed out the contradiction between this coercive policy *vis-à-vis* the South and the marketing rhetoric of 'free-choice' and 'reproductive freedom' in respect of new contraceptives and reproductive technologies in the North. She shows how the population control establishment increasingly co-opts the slogans of the North's Reproductive Rights Movement to legitimize depopulating strategies in the South. She also criticizes those feminists of the North who emphasize individualistic 'rights' and seemingly forget that reproduction as well as production is integral to social relations. To isolate the individual sexual and reproductive behaviour from the social fabric can only be harmful to women, in the South and the North.[19]

A NEW ECOLOGY OF REPRODUCTION

Our critique of an anti-human, anti-woman, anti-poor, racist, imperialist and coercive population control policy, however, does not imply that no one, particularly women, should have access to birth control and contraceptive methods. From an ecofeminist perspective, it is essential that women be asked what they themselves want. [. . .]

An ecofeminist perspective is not to look at reproduction in isolation, but to see it in the light of men–women relations, the sexual division of labour, sexual relations and the overall economic, political and social situation, all of which, at present, are influenced by patriarchal and capitalist ideology and practice. Therefore a primary demand is that women regain greater autonomy with regard to their sexuality and procreative capacities.

This implies first, that women must begin to overcome the alienation from, and learn again to be one with their bodies. This alienation, brought about by capitalist, patriarchal reproduction relations and technologies has affected women in the North more than poor women in the South. Poor, rural women in the South may still be knowledgeable in respect of their bodily cycles and evidence of fertility and infertility, but women in the North have virtually lost this intimate knowledge and instead increasingly depend on medical experts to tell them what is happening in their bodies. A new ecology of reproduction would mean that women reappropriate this 'fertility awareness', as Mira Sadgopal calls it,[20] and realize that traditional as well as modern sources can show them the way. Secondly, men too, must begin to be educated in women's fertility awareness and to respect it, which implies a new, creative interaction of the procreative potential of women and men.

It is essential to bear in mind that the sexual relationship must also be understood as an ecological one, embedded in overall production relations. Unless these relationships are freed from exploitation and dominance, the oppressors, as well as the oppressed, will face ruinous consequences. Liberating sexual relationships from patriarchal dominance and exploitation is not solely a matter of contraceptive technology, but demands a change in attitudes/life-style, institutions, and the everyday conduct of men and women. Clearly the introduction of new contraceptive devices has not resulted in the expected fundamental change in sexual relationships, even in the North. Social change cannot be brought about by technological fixes; neither can production relations, or the earth, be freed from exploitation and dominance by technology alone.

If men and women begin to understand sexual intercourse as a caring and loving interaction with nature, of their own and of their partners, then they will also be able to find birth control methods that do not harm women. Such a loving and caring relationship would lead to a new understanding of sexuality—not as a selfish, aggressive 'drive' but as the human capacity for love, relatedness to ourselves, to each other and, by implication, the earth and all its inhabitants.

Development of this new sexual and reproductive ecology is essential if women are to be enabled to maintain their human dignity; it is even more important for men who, in militaristic, patriarchal society are taught to identify their sexuality with aggression. This aggression, however, is directed not only against their sexual partners, but also against themselves. To conquer the 'enemy', 'nature', women, other people, they must first learn to conquer themselves, which means they must reject and destroy in themselves the caring, loving, nurturing characteristics that are generally attributed to women, and for which women are devalued.

This new understanding of non-patriarchal sexuality can develop only together with changes in the sexual division of labour, the economy and politics. Only when men begin seriously to share in caring for children, the old, the weak, and for nature, when they recognize that this life-preserving subsistence work is more important than work for cash, will they be able to develop a caring, responsible, erotic relationship with their partners, be they men or women.

Such relationships will enable the opposition between 'people' and 'population' to be resolved, thus: individuals' sexual and procreative activity need not be opposed to a community's need for a 'sustainable' number of children. We have shown that the concept of 'natural fertility' is a Eurocentric, patriarchal myth propagated since the eighteenth century. Women, in particular, have always known methods and techniques of birth control and contraception. A new ecology of reproduction within the context of economic and political eco-regions will lead to new and/or rediscovered ways to ensure a balanced ratio of people to the environment, without coercive national or international intervention. From an ecofeminist perspective we demand the exclusion of state interference in the sphere of reproduction.

Notes

1. King, Maurice: 'Health is a Sustainable State,' in *Lancet*, 15 September 1990, abridged version in *Third World Resurgence* No. 16, 31–2.
2. Nafis Sadik (ed.), *The State of World Population* 1990. (New York: United Nations Population Fund (UNFPA)) 1990, 10.
3. Ibid., 1–2.
4. Ibid., 12.
5. F. Akhter, 'New Reasons to Depopulate the Third World,' in *Third World Resurgence*, No 16, 21–3.
6. Barbara Duden, 'Population,' in W. Sachs (ed.), *Development Dictionary*. (London: Zed Books, 1992), 147.
7. Ibid.
8. Ibid. 148.
9. For a critique of this narrow and individualistic concept of 'reproductive rights' see F. Akhter: 'On the Question of Reproductive Right,' in F. Akhter,

Depopulating Bangladesh. Essays on the Politics of Fertility. (Dhaka: Narigrantha Prabartana, 1992), 33.

10. Rhoda Reddock, *Women, Labour and Politics in Trinidad and Tobago: A History* (London: Zed Books, 1994).
11. Linda Gordon, *Woman's Body, Woman's Right: A Social History of Birth Control in America* (Harmondsworth: Penguin, 1977), 25.
12. J. Wajcman, *Feminism Confronts Technology.* (Philadelphia: Pennsylvania State University Press, 1991), 76.
13. For a discussion of the witch-hunt and its impact on women see M. Mies, *Patriarchy and Accumulation on a World Scale: Women in the International Division of Labour.* (London Zed Books, 1991).
14. G. Heinsohn and O. Steiger *Die Vernichtung der Weisen Frauen, Hexenverfolgung, Bevolkerungspolitik.* (Herbstein: Marz-Verlag, 1984).
15. B. F. Mussalam, *Sex and Society in Islam* Cambridge: Cambridge University Press, 1986).
16. Akhter, 'New Reasons to Depopulate the World'.
17. Dr Talwar in Bombay is one of the researchers who is working on the development of an anti-fertility vaccine. (See Video Documentary 'Something like a War' by Deepa Dhanraj and Abha Bhaiya.)
18. Akhter 'New Reasons to Depopulate the World'. 26–32.
19. Ibid., 41–56.
20. Mira Sadgopal, 'Fertility Awareness Education in the Context of Development Issues'. Paper presented at a Seminar on Women and Development, Pune University, 6 February 1992.

25 Women and the Politics of Fundamentalism in Iran

Haleh Afshar *

This chapter is concerned with understanding what Islamic fundamentalism means to women who choose to adopt it and how, if at all, it could be used as a means for political struggles. The intention is to move away from the usual condemnatory approach to Islamic fundamentalism and consider it in the light of the views and activities of its adherents. Specific examples will be given with reference to Iran and the women's organizations and their activities in that country.

WHAT IS FUNDAMENTALISM?

Fundamentalism has for long been associated with greater or lesser degrees of oppression of women. Given the rise of fundamentalism and the decision of many women to consciously reject feminisms of various kinds and adopt the creed, it is important for some of us to consider what it is and why so many have chosen it. [. . .]

Part of the problem of understanding fundamentalism has been in terms of definitions and terminology. Muslims themselves do not use the term 'fundamentalist' at all; the twentieth-century Islamists argue that they are revivalists, and are returning to the sources of Islam to regain a purified vision, long since lost in the mire of worldly governments. Shiias, who are a minority school of Islam, but form 98 per cent of the Iranian population, have for long seen themselves as the guardians of the poor, the dispossessed and those trampled on by unjust governments.[1] For them revivalism is merely a matter of succeeding in their centuries-long struggle against injustice.

* From Haleh Afshar, 'Women and the Politics of Fundamentalism in Iran' from *Women & Politics in the Third World* by Haleh Afshar (Taylor & Francis, 1996), 121–141, reprinted by permission of the publisher and the author.

Thus fundamentalism for the Muslims is a return to the roots and a recapturing of both the purity and the vitality of Islam as it was at its inception. In this pursuit of the past, the Muslims, like all those glorifying their histories, are returning to an imaginary golden episode to lighten the difficulties of their present-day existence.[2] The golden age for the Shiias is the short-term rule of the Prophet, about a decade long, and the even shorter one of his nephew and son-in-law Ali, who ruled for less than five years. The Sunnis, who accept the first four caliphs of Islam as being pure and worthy of emulating, can lay claim to about forty years of just rule; from the *hijrat*, the Prophet's move to Madina in 622 to Ali's death in AD 661. In addition all Muslims claim to adhere absolutely to the Koranic laws and accept the Koran as representing the very words of God as revealed to his Prophet Muhammad.

> The Koran which is divided into 114 Suras, contains expressly or impliedly, all the divine commands. These commands are contained in about 500 verses and of these about 80 may be regarded by WESTERN lawyers as articles of a code.[3]

Thus in their pursuit of the golden age the Muslims are equipped with fifty years of history and 500 verses of a holy book, and a clutch of legal clauses, perhaps as good a resource as those offered by any other ideologies or utopists' vision.

But like all utopias the past and the holy book have difficulties adjusting to the present. It is in the domain of interpretation and adjustments to history that Islam is deemed to have become degraded. Yet without such adjustments, it would find it hard to survive as a creed. Thus the notions of return and revivalism are very much anchored in the processes of interpretations and adjustments. They seek to present new interpretations, puritanical interpretations, interpretations that wipe out the centuries of misdeed and hardship and open the way for the future.

WOMEN AND REVIVALISM

In the twentieth-century domain of interpretations, women have been active in their own right. Although the bulk of Islamic theology has been adapted and interpreted by male theologians, who have claimed exclusive rights to instituting the Islamic laws, *Shari'a*, women have always maintained a presence, albeit a small one, in the domains of politics and theology.[4] They have consistently and convincingly argued that Islam as a religion has always had to accommodate women's specific needs. [. . .]

Thus some fourteen centuries ago Islam recognized women's legal and economic independence as existing and remaining separate from that of their fathers or husbands and sons. Islamic marriage was conceived as a matter of contract between consenting partners (Koran 4.4, 4:24), and one that stipulated a specific price, *mahre*, payable to the bride before the consummation of marriage. Women must be maintained in the style to which they have been accustomed (2:238, 4:34) and paid for suckling their babies (2:233).

Beside having personal and economic independence, women were also close confidantes and advisers to the Prophet. Khadija supported him in the early years and undoubtedly her influence protected the Prophet against the various Meccan nobles who wished to quench Islam at its inception. After her death Muhammad's favourite wife Aishah, who married him as a child and grew up in his household, became not only his spouse, but also his closest ally and confidante. She is known as one of the most reliable interpreters of Islamic laws.

Besides being a renowned source for the interpretation and extension of Islamic laws, Aishah was also an effective politician and a remarkable warrior; like many of the Prophet's wives, she accompanied him on his campaigns. After his death she ensured that her father Abu Bakre, and not Muhammad's nephew Ali, succeeded to the caliphate, and led the Muslim community. Subsequently, when Ali became the Caliph, Aishah raised an army and went to battle against him, taking to the field herself. Although she was defeated, Ali treated her with respect, but begged her not to interfere in politics.

Thus, if fundamentalism is about returning to the golden age of Islam, Muslim women argue that they have much reason for optimism and much room for manoeuvre. Furthermore, many highly educated and articulate Muslim women regard Western feminism as a poor example and have no wish to follow it. Not only do they dismiss Western feminism for being one of the many instruments of colonialism, but also they despise the kind of freedom that is offered to women under the Western patriarchy.[5] [. . .] They have failed to alter the labour market to accommodate women's needs and at the same time have lost the benefits that women had once obtained in matrimony. Thus Western feminists have made women into permanent second-class citizens. Not a model that most women, in the West as elsewhere, would choose to follow.

By contrast the Islamist women argue that they can benefit by returning to the sources of Islam. They are of the view that Islamic dictum bestows complementarity on women, as human beings, as partners to men and as mothers and daughters. They argue that Islam demands respect for women and offers them opportunities, to be learned, educated and trained, while at the same time providing an honoured space for them to become mothers, wives and homemakers. They argue that unlike capitalism, and much of feminist discourse, Islam recognizes the importance of women's life cycles: they have been given different roles and responsibilities at different times of their lives and at each and every stage they are honoured and respected for that which they do. They argue that Islam at its inception has provided them with exemplary female role models and has delineated a path that can be honourably followed at each stage. For all Muslims Khadija is a powerful representative of independence as well as being a supportive wife. Muhammad's daughter Fatima, for the Shiias in particular, provides an idealized and idolized role model as daughter to the Prophet and wife to the imam, Ali. The Sunnis admire Aishah for her powerful intellect as well as her political leadership. [. . .]

Islamist women are particularly defensive of the veil. The actual imposition of the veil and the form that it has taken is a contested domain.[6] Nevertheless many Muslim women have chosen the veil as the symbol of Islamification and have accepted it as the public face of their revivalist position. For them the veil is a liberating, and not an oppressive, force. They maintain that the veil enables them to become the observers and not the observed; that it liberates them from the dictates of the fashion industry and the demands of the beauty myth. In the context of the patriarchal structures that shape women's lives the veil is a means of bypassing sexual harassment and 'gaining respect'[7] [. . .]

IRAN AND THE PRACTICAL POLITICS OF ISLAMIST WOMEN

Like all political theories, the Islamist women's has had difficulties in standing the test of time. Although Islam does provide a space for women, it has been as difficult for Muslim women, as for their Western counterparts, to obtain and maintain their rights. The throng of women who supported the Islamic revolution in Iran were no exception to this rule. On its inception the Islamic Republic embarked on a series of misogynist laws, decrees and directives which rapidly curtailed the access of women to much of the public domain. Female judges were sacked, the faculty of law closed its door to female applicants and Article 163 of the Islamic constitution stated that women cannot become judges.

Subsequently the Islamic laws of retribution, *Qassas*, severely eroded women's legal rights. Not only are two women's evidence equated with that of one man, as required by the Koran (2.82), but women's evidence, if uncorroborated by men, is no longer accepted by the courts. Women who insist on giving uncorroborated evidence are judged to be lying and subject to punishment for slander (Article 92 of the *Qassas* laws). Murder is now punished by retribution; but the murderer can opt for the payment of *dayeh*, blood money, to the descendants of the murdered, in lieu of punishment (Article 1 of the *Qassas* laws). Furthermore the murderer can be punished only if the family of the victim pays the murderer's blood money to his descendants:

> Should a Muslim man wilfully murder a Muslim woman, he must be killed, the murderer can be punished only after the woman's guardian has paid half of his *dayeh* (blood money, or the sum that the man would be worth if he were to live a normal life; this is negotiated with and paid to the man's family;)
>
> (Article 5 of the *Qassas* laws)

Whereas killing a man is a capital offence, murdering a woman is a lesser crime. The same logic dictates that women murderers should have little or no blood money and must be executed (Article 6). Similarly if a man attacks a woman, and maims or severely injures her, he can be punished only if the injured or her family pay retribution money so that the assailant can be similarly mutilated; this is to ensure that his dependants have secured the income lost through the implementation of the retribution laws: No such money is paid to the dependants of women assailants (Article 60).

What is worse, fathers, who are recognized as the automatic guardians of the household, have the right of life and death over their children. Fathers who murder their children are 'excused' from punishment, provided they pay blood money to the inheritors (Article 16); however, there is no specific blood money stipulated for children.

Fathers who murder one or more of their children, are to pay themselves the blood money! Khomeini decided to return to all fathers their Islamic automatic right of custody of children on divorce, which they had lost under the 1976 Family Laws in Iran. By doing so and legislating the *Qassas* laws, the post-revolutionary state endowed fathers with the undisputed right of life and death over their children. Men gained the right to kill anyone who 'violated their harem'. Men who murder their wives, or their sisters or mothers, on the charge of adultery, are not subject to any punishment. But women are not given any such rights. Nor do they have the right of life and death over their children.

In addition the access of women to almost 50 per cent of university departments was barred and they were encouraged to abandoned paid employment.[8] They could not be employed without the formal consent of their husband, a rule that after much struggle was extended to apply to both marriage partners before the revolution, but was revised in favour of men afterwards. Politically too women were marginalized; Article 115 of the Islamic constitution follows Ayatollah Khomeini's instructions in insisting that the leader of the nation, *Valayateh Faqih*, would be a man, and so would the president. Since its inception the Islamic Republic has never had a female member of the cabinet and the numbers of female *Majlis* (parliamentary) representatives had been fewer than five in all but the last *Majlis*, when they reached twelve.

Thus with the arrival of the Islamic Republic, with the notable exception of the vote, Iranian women lost all they had struggled for over a century. The situation seemed grim indeed.

THE POLITICS OF FEMINIST FUNDAMENTALISM

But to despair of the plight of women is to fail to recognize the formidable resilience of Iranian women. [. . .] Although some bowed to the pressures of the Islamic Republic, many remained firm, both as women and as believers in the faith. There has been a long and determined struggle by secularist women. But it was as devout Muslims that elite women in Iran[9] have most successfully countered the demands made of them by the Islamic Republic. Given the Islamic nature of the national political discourse,[10] the defenders of the faiths of women took the republic to task for failing to deliver its Islamic duties. For post-revolutionary Iranian elite women, revivalism has almost literally been a God-send. They have used it to fight against their political, legal and economic marginalization. [. . .]

Using the Koranic instruction that all Muslims must become learned, women have finally succeeded in removing many of the bars placed on their education. Women who gained their training and expertise in the pre-revolutionary days of equality now command high salaries and many run their own successful businesses in the private sector.[11] Private sector schools have simply defied the laws of gender segregation and employed male science and mathematics teachers to teach girls. As a result Iranian girls regularly come top in the university entrance examinations in most subjects.

THE STRUGGLE FOR EQUAL EMPLOYMENT OPPORTUNITY

Before the revolution Iranian women had, at least on paper, obtained the right to equal employment. But although the post-revolutionary state accepted this right, in practice Islamification has led to a severe cut-back in female employment rates.[12] Nevertheless neither the public nor the private sector could operate without female employees, nor for that matter could most households survive without the women's income. Thus despite the government's policies, women continue to have a presence in the workforce, though in terms of percentage, it is much lower than before the revolution; whereas according to the 1966 and 1976 censuses some 13 to 14 per cent of women of working age were in paid employment, the post-revolutionary census of 1986 indicated that only 9 per cent were in paid employment. This was a clear reflection of the government's policies, which disapproved of the entry of women into all but a few 'suitable' professions such as teaching and nursing and the refusal of the civil service to employ women in other fields. In addition the segregation of work places and public transport, the cutting back on child care provisions and unfavourable tax systems all made it harder for women to participate fully in paid employment.

These discriminatory practices were legitimized by some women appointees who had no difficulty in using Khomeini's teachings to support such activities. A clear example is Shahla Habibi who, in 1991, was appointed to the newly created post of presidential adviser on women's affairs.

Typically her previous post had been with the national Islamic Propaganda Organization. She reminded the public that Khomeini had placed women in the home and had declared that:

Women, whatever qualifications they may have or however learned they may be, must remain the pivotal core of the family and play their parts as exemplary housewives.[13]

In this she was fully supported by the government-sponsored Women's Organization. In December 1990 it had already declared:

As the imam [Khomeini] has repeatedly said good men are raised in the laps of good women. If we follow this example then we'd find our true station in life and recognise that motherhood is a sacred and holy duty of women.[14]

This view was shared by the High Council of Women's Cultural and Social Affairs which was appointed by the High Council of Cultural Revolution to coordinate government policies on women. It was staffed with women like Soraya Maknoun, university professor who headed the Council's Employment Research Group. Maknoun chose to disregard her own highly paid position and blithely denounced all demands for equal opportunities as corruptive and pro-Western:

I am totally against the view that women's success depends on gaining access to equal opportunities in all sectors of the economy . . . The truth is that our society does not have a women's problem and it's just pro-Western critics who have invented such a problem and imposed it on our lives.[15] [. . .]

But the women supporters of the government have been firmly and continuously opposed by women such as Azam Taleqani, the campaigning daughter of the late Ayatollah Taleqani and member of the first post-revolutionary *Majlis.* Azam Taleqani founded the Women's Society of Islamic Revolution, which has been ceaselessly defending women's rights.

Two-thirds of women in this country live and work in the rural areas and carry a major burden of agricultural activity. Nevertheless we do not allow our women to study agricultural sciences at the University.[16]

Similarly Zahra Rahnavard, a leading Islamic feminist and the wife of a previous Iranian Prime Minister, Mir Hussein Mussavi, denounced discrimination against women on religious and political grounds:

Our planners say 'we don't have the means to invest equally in men and women and must spend our limited resources on those who provide the highest return for our society. Therefore as women's natural obligations, in giving birth and raising their children, means that they work less, we cannot allocate too great a portion of our resources to them.'

We respond that this is wrong since all Muslims are required to pursue knowledge regardless of their gender. It is of the essence, in terms of religious requirement and social well-being, that no barriers be put between women and their quest for knowledge.[17]

By placing the argument squarely in the Islamic domain, Rahnama, Taleqani and others succeeded in gaining the support of some of the leading politicians, like the long-serving, enlightened Minister of Interior, Hojatoleslam Nateq Nouri. He declared: 'Islam places no limitation whatever on the participation of women in the public, political and cultural domains.'[18] In fact women have retained their entitlement to equal rights of access to the labour market in Iran after the revolution. They had even been promised a less discriminatory future at the inception of the Islamic Republic. Article 43 of the constitution undertakes to provide employment opportunities for all and states that full employment is a fundamental aim of the revolution. Thus, even after the revolution, the constitution, labour laws and the State Employment Laws make no distinction between men and women. [. . .]

Of course in practice women do not benefit from equal pay for equal work provisions. Married women pay higher taxes on their incomes than do married men; and women pay higher child insurance premiums than do men. It is the men who benefit from the married man's entitlement whereas it is usually women who end up paying for nursery care of their children. Men get larger bonuses, because it is assumed that they are the head of household, and they are entitled to cheap goods from the civil service co-operatives; their share increases with the numbers of their children. Not so for women who do not even get a share for themselves.[19]

Zahra Rahnavard . . . had to admit that at least the government, if not the revolution, had failed women:

We have no strategy for including women in this country's destiny and in this respect we have fallen far short of our political aspiration . . . In the five year plan women are only mentioned once . . . despite all our protests we have remained invisible. It is essential that women's role in the development process is clearly delineated.[20]

THE POLITICS OF ACTIVISM, RESISTANCE AND COMPROMISE

Activists such as Rahnavard and Taleqani persevered and eventually found a foothold in the High Council of Cultural Revolution, which determines policies at a national level. There they managed to formulate an Islamic female employment policy. [. . .] Its statement applauded the revolution for returning women to the pedestal of honour and respectability:

> Women in society who under the past regime had, in the name of freedom, suffered great oppression and lost many of their human and Islamic rights have had the opportunity to free themselves of the cheap Westoxificated voyeuristic societal gaze and find their real and pure Islamic status . . . Thus the Muslim Iranian woman is on the one hand faithfully fulfilling her pivotal social task in the familial context . . . On the other hand where there has been a need and a correct context Iranian women have remained active in the educational, social and economic domains.

The High Council accepted that women's first priority was to remain within the home and care for the family. But it argued that Islam offered women the opportunity of fulfilling all their potentials and was capable of enabling them to live their life cycles to the full. Therefore the Committee requested that 'suitable jobs' be provided for women in fields such as:

> midwifery and similar medical posts as well as teaching (Article 5A).
>
> Jobs which best suit the nature and temperament of women such as laboratory work, electronic engineering, pharmacology, welfare work and translation work (Article 5B).
>
> Employment where men and women are equally suitable such as simple workers in service and technical industries. In such cases experience and qualifications, rather than gender must be the determining factor for selection of the work force (Article 5C).

Where the Council's resolution is of interest is that it argues that the government should enable women to fulfil both their domestic and their paid duties. In addition to equal pay for equal work, in the segment of the labour market allocated to women, the government should also allow women paid time off to enable them to fulfil their 'mothering obligations'. They should be entitled to shorter working hours and an earlier retirement age; measures which would recognize women's double burden of unpaid domestic work and paid employment. [. . .]

If, as the Council has suggested, the recognition of 'mothering duties' results in some flexibility in working hours, without cut-backs in pay, then women workers would indeed fare much better. At the moment, despite all the lipservice paid to complementarity in marriage and women's special qualities, Iranian women workers have to work as a 'manpower' in an inflexibly male labour market. For example, work and schools start at the same time, as do nurseries; there are few workplace nurseries... Most factories have two fortnight-long holidays, one for the Persian new year in late March and one during the summer. The factories close for that period. Women are not allowed to use their paid holiday leave in small portions to deal with a sick child or do their 'mothering' duties; all such obligations have to be shouldered as unpaid leave. Furthermore anyone who accumulates more than four months' unpaid leave in any working year can be sacked, even from tenured posts.

If the High Council's recommendations go through, at least some of these problems may be alleviated. In addition the proposal demanded that working women be entitled to job security, unemployment benefits and welfare provisions (Article 10). Women who are heads of household are to be entitled to special retraining programmes to enable them to return to the labour market (Article 11) and the government is urged to provide co-operative type organizations to facilitate home working for women who wish to combine their paid and unpaid jobs (Article 12). Thus, in return for accepting women's domestic obligations, the Council's proposal sought to extract concessions which would enable women to fulfil both their paid and unpaid duties. Its declaration forms part of the slow, but continuous progress of women in Iran in clawing back the rights that were summarily curtailed by the post-revolutionary state.

WOMEN IN PUBLIC AND POLITICS

Although they fought shoulder to shoulder with men, women were not given high office by the revolutionary government. It has never appointed a woman to a ministerial post. [. . .]

But getting elected is only the first step; women members of *Majlis* are severely constrained by the ideological views that designate them as inferior, demands on them to be modest, silent and invisible,[21] and defines them as interlopers in the public domain. [. . .] Azam Taleqani, who gained a seat in the first post-revolutionary *Majlis*, explained that women were expected to be 'naturally modest' and this prevented them from 'saying too much in the *Majlis*'.[22] [. . .]

In the 1991 *Majlis* twelve women were elected. They have been fighting hard on women's issues. [. . .] In a remarkable move, *Majlis* representatives Behrouzi, Monireh Nobakht and Marzieh Vahid Datgerdi managed to alter the divorce laws to make it more expensive for men to leave their wives at will. [. . .] By using the marriage contract, and insisting on the Koranic right to fair treatment, many Iranian women had continued using the Family Courts as bargaining counters in their divorce proceedings.[23] On the whole the courts favoured the men and on divorce women were not entitled to any of their husband's property. Activists such as Azam Taleqani had gone on arguing fiercely against the gender-blind attitudes of the courts:

> Unfortunately after the revolution . . . the government and the religious institution have not paid enough attention to women as full human beings. All their efforts has been concentrated on making women stay at home, at all costs; to make them accept self sacrifice, oppression and submission. Even when they go to court to get their due, I am not saying that the courts are totally patriarchal; but unfortunately there are these tendencies. So the problem is presented in a way that does not illuminate the truth.[24]

[. . .] The 1993 Bill sought to curtail men's automatic right of divorce, by demanding that men who 'unjustly' divorce their 'obedient' wives should do their Koranic duty and pay 'wages' for the wife's domestic services during their married years.

Behrouzi also succeeded in pushing through a Bill that allowed women to retire after twenty years of active service, while the men still had to serve twenty-five years. Her success was in part achieved because it permitted women to return to their proper sphere, that of domesticity, all the sooner. [. . .]

WOMEN'S ORGANIZATIONS

It was in quangos and organizations outside the direct control of the government that women activists were most successful in struggling for better economic and political opportunities. Although in the public domain success depended on espousing an Islamic stance, Islam itself is sufficiently flexible to allow a diversity of interpretation and much leeway for women. Azam Taleqani, for example, set up the

Women's Society of Islamic Revolution, a non-governmental activist group, whose members have included Zahra Rahnavard, the path-breaking Islamist writer and the wife of the long-serving post-revolutionary Prime Minister Musavi, as well as more conservative women such as *Majlis* representative Gohar Dastqeib, and Monireh Gorgi, a woman representative in the Assembly of Experts, which is responsible for nominating the national leader.

Within the civil service it was younger women in the lower echelons of the governmental organizations who fought effectively for the cause. [. . .] A good example is Jaleh Shahrian Afshar, a member of Western Azarbaijan's women's committee, who told the press that first and foremost the women wished to be independent, furthermore they sought better employment opportunities and needed more facilities to embark on a wide-ranging family planning programme.[25] [. . .]

THE POPULATION DEBATE

By 1987 the Statistical Centre of Tehran was indicating that 96 per cent of the urban women of child-bearing age were married and only 1 per cent had never married. The non-literate women married at around 16 and literate women at 17.5. But only 7 per cent of married women used any form of family planning. The average age for the first birth was 19, but it increased to 21 for women with secondary education. On average mothers had four live births, rather more than their stated desired average of two in urban areas and three in rural areas. Interestingly over half of the women questioned did not mind whether they had a son or a daughter; 14 per cent actually preferred to have a daughter and only 31 per cent had a marked son preference.[26]

Thus by 1990 the Iranian population reached 59.5 million and was growing at an average annual rate of 3.9 per cent. Although there was some disquiet, the devout were not panicking. Nevertheless both the high birth rates and temporary marriages came under new scrutiny. The daily newspapers warned that the country had only 12 million hectares of cultivable land which would feed 30 million people at most.[27] [. . .]

The population crisis posed a severe dilemma for the Islamic government. It had long since outlawed the pre-revolutionary abortion law and dismantled the family planning clinics. Suddenly it found itself with families averaging five or more children and no clear policy for halting the momentum. In July 1991 the government decreed that for a fourth birth, working women were not entitled to their three months' paid maternity leave, nor could a fourth child be allowed any rations or a ration card. Any family that chose to have a fourth child would have to share out its resources and spread it more thinly, with no help from the state. At the same time the Minister of Health Dr Reza Malekzadeh suggested to husbands that they should choose to have a vasectomy. A year later the courts decided to reconsider the abortion laws:

> It remains absolutely illegal to have an abortion or to carry out an abortion. Article 91 of the Criminal code imposes the death penalty, according to the Islamic laws, for anyone murdering an unborn child 'if that child possesses a soul'. But 'before the soul enters the body of a being' if a doctor is of the opinion that it is dangerous to continue with the pregnancy and issues a certificate to that effect; then the pregnancy can be terminated.[28]

At the same time the newspapers published a list of fifty hospitals in the country offering free vasectomy and female sterilization.

By 1993 the Ministry of Health had its own population control bureau, with a 20 billion rials budget that was 300 per cent higher than that of the previous year. Assisted by an additional $300 million loan from the World Bank the bureau launched a massive population control campaign offering free services at national, provincial and rural levels. The aim was to reduce population growth to 2.7 per cent per annum.[29]

A year later academia was mobilized to provide evidence in support of population control. Dr Mohab Ali Professor and head of research on productivity and efficiency *bahrevari* of Alameh Tabatabyi University announced that

> Women who have too many children would not find the time to think and work properly and have to devote themselves to cleaning and feeding the household. For a woman to have time to think properly about the education of her children and to create a suitable home environment she must have few children—ideally a maximum of two adults and two children per family—since the fewer the children the more time a mother has for each and the higher the rate of efficiency and productivity of that mother.[30]

Azam Taleqani seized the opportunity to point out the close links between polygamy and increasing birth rates. Before the revolution Iranian women had managed to curb men's right to polygamy, by making remarriage subject to the consent of the first wife and ratification by Family Courts. Khomeini had restated men's right to permanent and temporary marriages and his successor Rafsanjani had endorsed this position during the war.

But women's opposition to polygamy continued. In this they were assisted by the Koranic dictum that no man, other than the Prophet of Islam, could treat all his wives equally and therefore it was advisable for them to take only one (4:3, 4:4, 4:129). [. . .]

As yet polygamy has not been outlawed. But the prospects of curbing it have improved. What has been a marked success is the decision in the summer of 1993 to revise the *Qassas* laws and make honour killings punishable. The newly elected women members of *Majlis*, Azam Taleqani's Women's Movement and Zahra Rahnavard, all made a concerted effort to outlaw honour killings. They documented the growing numbers of murders and atrocities committed by husbands, fathers and brothers on their unsuspecting womenfolk and demanded that the judiciary defend women. Finally the head of the judiciary Ayatollah Mohamad Yazdi issued a decree revising the laws and making male murders, be they kin or not, subject to state prosecution. He agreed to remove the requirement that made the male 'guardians' responsible for seeking justice in such cases. The decision was a landmark; it demonstrated that the *Qassas* laws, supposedly Islamic and eternal, were, like other aspects of the Islamic rule, responsive to pressure and subject to change.

SELF-IMMOLATION

Although it is the Islamist women who have succeeded in changing some of the more repressive anti-feminist laws they have been assisted in their battle by secular women's resistance groups as well as the rising numbers of tragic self-immolations. Increasingly Iranian women are choosing to burn themselves rather than tolerate the misogynist rules concerning their private and public lives. Daughters forced into unacceptable marriages, young brides caught in difficult marriages, wives faced with their husbands' polygamous marriages, and more recently women barred from employment for failing to observe the Islamic dress code.

A tragic example was Professor Homa Darabi Tehrani, who set herself on fire to protest against the draconian misogynist rule of the Islamic government; she died as she had lived, campaigning for liberty. On 21 February 1994, Darabi tore off her headscarf and her Islamic long coat in a public thoroughfare near Tajrish Square in the Shemiran suburb of Tehran. She gave an impassioned speech against the government's oppressive measures which disempower and undermine women; calling for liberty and equality she poured petrol on herself and set herself alight. Homa Darabi, a popular teacher and respected researcher, had been dismissed from her post as Professor of Psychology in Tehran University for 'non-adherence to Islamic conduct and dress code' in December 1991. Although in May 1993 the decision was overturned by the 'Employment and Grievance Tribunal' the university refused to reinstate her.

Her death led to widespread protests in Iran and abroad. An estimated thirty thousand people attended her memorial service on 24 February 1994, at the Aljavad Mosque in Tehran. The meeting was held despite the government's intention to ban it. A letter of condemnation signed by about seventy leading Iranian academics working in the West was sent to the government in Tehran and activists abroad organized well-attended protest meetings in her memory in London, Paris, Los Angeles and other cities in the USA and Canada. They have also been writing letters condemning the denial of human rights to Iranian women.

CONCLUSION

The rule of Islam in Iran has not been easy on women. They lost much of the ground that they had won over the previous century and the way to recapturing some of those rights has been slow and barred by prejudice and patriarchal power. Undaunted, Iranian women have struggled on. Some have actively opposed the Islamic dress codes and put their own lives on the line in support of their principles. Others have for the moment conceded the veil and its imposition in the name of Islam, though they have done so reluctantly and have continued the discussions about its validity, relevance and the extent to which it should be imposed. But the bargain that they have struck[31] has enabled them to negotiate better terms. They have managed to revert the discriminatory policies on education, they are vociferously attacking the inequalities in the labour market and demanding better care and welfare provisions for working mothers. Of course in this, as in all other issues concerning women, the demise of Khomeini was in itself of the essence. Although the road to liberty is one that is strewn with difficulties, Iranian women, as ever, have come out fighting and have proved indomitable.

Notes

1. M. Momen, *An Introduction to Shii Islam* (New Haven: Yale University Press, 1985).
2. A. Chhachhi, (1991) 'Forced Identities: The State, Communalism, Fundamentalism and Women in India', in D. Kandiyoti (ed.), *Women, Islam and the State* (Philadelphia: Temple University Press).
3. H. Afshar, 'The Muslim Concept of Law', *International Encyclopedia of Comparative Law* (Tubingen, The Hague and Paris: J. C. B. Mohr, 1987), 86.
4. N. Abbott, *Aishah The Beloved of Mohamad* (Chicago: University of Chicago Press, 1942); L. Ahmed, *Women and Gender in Islam* (New Haven and London: Yale University Press, 1992); R. Keddie and B. Baron (eds.), *Women in Middle Eastern History: Shifting Boundaries in Sex and Gender* (New Haven and London: Yale University Press, 1991); F. Mernissi, *Women and Islam: An Historical and Theological Enquiry* (Oxford: Blackwell, 1991) H. Afshar, *Islam and Feminisms* (Macmillan, 1998).
5. Z. al-Ghazali, *Ayam min hayati* (Cairo: Dar al-shurua, n.d.), quoted by V. J. Hoffman, 'An Islamic Activist: Zeinab al-Ghazali', in E. Warnok Fernea (ed.), *Women and the Family in the Middle East* (Austin, TX: University of Texas Press, 1985) and L. Ahmed, *Women and Gender in Islam* (New Haven and London: Yale University Press, 1992); Z. Rahnavard, *Toloueh Zaneh Mosalman* (Tehran: Mahboubeh Publication, n.d.).
6. Mernissi, *Women and Islam.*
7. As one of many examples this statement was made by a woman interviewee in Algeria, for the *Today* programme (21 September 1993).
8. H. Afshar, 'Khomeini's Teachings and their Implications for Women', in A. Tabari and N. Yeganeh (eds.) *In the Shadow of Islam* (London: Zed Books, 1982), 79–90; H. Afshar, 'Women and Work: Ideology not Adjustment at Work in Iran', in H. Afshar and C. Dennis (eds.) *Women and Adjustment Policies in the Third World* (London: Macmillan Women's Studies at York Series, 1992); A. Tabari and N. Yeganeh (compilers), *In the Shadow of Islam* (London: Zed Books, 1982).
9. H. Moghissi, '*hoquqeh zan v bonbasthayeh farhangi, ejtemayi jomhurieyeh eslami*' [Women's Rights and the Sociocultural Problems in the Islamic Republic], *Cesmandaz* 13 (spring 1773 [1994], 42–53.
10. It is worth noting that some commentators such as Ghassan Salame are of the view that the 'the Islam of the Islamists may be nothing but a discourse'. G. Salame, *Democracy Without Democrats: The Renewal of Politics in the Muslim World* (London: Tauris, 1994), 7–8.
11. Afshar, 'Women and Work'.
12. Ibid.
13. *Zaneh Rouz,* 7 January 1992.
14. Ibid., 25 December 1990.
15. Ibid., 27 January 1990.

16. Ibid., 25 December 1990.
17. Ibid., 10 February 1990.
18. Ibid., 14 March 1985.
19. Jaleh Shahriar Afshar, feminist researcher interviewed by *Zaneh Rouz*, 29 August 1992.
20. *Zaneh Rouz*, 10 February 1990.
21. F. Milani, *Veils and Words: The Emerging Voices of Iranian Women Writers* (London: Tauris, 1992).
22. *Zaneh Rouz*, 20 January 1991.
23. Z. Mir-Hosseini, 'Women, Marriage and the Law in Post-revolutionary Iran', in H. Afshar (ed.), *Women in the Middle East* (London: Macmillan, 1993); and *Marriage on Trial, A Study of Islamic Family Law* (London: Tauris, 1993).
24. *Zaneh Rouz*, 25 December 1990.
25. Ibid., 29 August 1992.
26. The 1978 sample survey of childbearing women, carried out by the Statistical Centre and reported in February 1987.
27. *Zaneh Rouz*, 18 September 1991.
28. Ibid., 1 August 1992.
29. Ibid., 18 April 1993.
30. Ibid., 4 May 1994.
31. D. Kandiyoti, 'Bargaining with Patriarchy', *Gender and Society* 2 (1988), 271–90.

26 Jewish Fundamentalism and Women's Empowerment

Nira Yuval-Davis *

Owing to the specific history of the Jewish people, Jewish fundamentalist movements (and the position of women inside them) embrace forms of religious fundamentalism common among both majorities and minorities both in the West and in post-colonial countries. Two different perspectives and political interests have determined the definition of Jewish fundamentalism as reflected in the literature: the Messianic Zionist *Gush Emunim* and its satellites[1] and the individualistic spiritual *khazara bitshuva* ('Born-Again') movement.[2] I share with Lustick his political definition of fundamentalism:

> A belief system is defined as fundamentalist in so far as its adherents regard its tenets as uncompromisable and direct transcendental imperatives to political action oriented toward the rapid and comprehensive reconstruction of society. (p. 6)

Jewish fundamentalism is not, therefore, just about being, or even becoming, ultra-Orthodox, and is not necessarily present everywhere where a Jewish community exists. At the same time, examination of some of the *khazara bitshuva* movements, especially the one led by the Lubavitch Rebbe, reveals that they are fundamentalist movements in the political sense as well. Individual redemption in the Jewish

I would like to thank all the many people who helped me to obtain material relevant to this chapter—they are too numerous for me to mention them all here. In particular I would like to thank all those within the Jewish Orthodox community who agreed to supply me with material and to be interviewed, even knowing that I do not share their world-view. I am not mentioning any of their names, to avoid associating them in any way with this chapter. But I would like to mention by name some of the friends who helped me, knowing that I do share some of their views: Dena Attar, Julia Bard, Gail Chester, Neil Collins, Ora Davis, Sue Katz, Janet Kufperman, Rami Levy, Pragna Patel, Israel Shahak. The responsibility for the chapter and its views, however, is all mine.

* From Nira Yuval-Davis, 'Jewish Fundamentalism and Women's Empowerment' from *Refusing Holy Orders* edited by Gita Sahgal and Nira Yuval-Davis (Virago Press, 1992), 198–222, reprinted by permission of the author.

religion is but a means towards collective redemption. Although these different forms of Jewish fundamentalism developed separately and often with antagonistic interrelationships, they have deeply affected each other and cannot be fully understood without each other.

The Lubavitch Women's Organization (the most active 'missionary' movement in contemporary Judaism) published a book aimed at women, trying to convince single American Jewish women that they should 'return' to Judaism. The Hebrew expression is *khazara bitshuva*—return to repentance; for everyone born to a Jewish mother is Jewish according to the *halakha* (the religious law)—even if they never practise or believed in the Jewish religion. As the *mitzvot* (commandments) that women have to practise in Judaism all relate to their roles as wives and mothers (single girls do not even have to cover their hair), and as early arranged marriage is the normal practice among the ultra-Orthodox, the task of targeting single women is not as simple as it could have been had Judaism been aimed at individual (gender-neutral) redemption. The argument used in the book emphasizes the collective nature and collective responsibility of the Jewish people, which transcends even their gender differences:

Every Jew—no matter what one's physical, spiritual, sexual or marital status—critically affects every other Jew, the world and G-d Himself, so to speak.[3]

While this is an elegant formulation which has obviously been effective among single 'returning' women, the different construction of men and women in Judaism is crucial. It is no coincidence that the second article in the above collection is called 'Changing Careers' and claims that:

Shifting gears from the contemporary professional world to the traditional roles of wife and mother can be unexpectedly fulfilling.[4]

The following twenty-eight articles deal with women as Jewish wives and as mothers.

In this chapter it is virtually impossible to do justice to such a complex background, as well as to explore the ways in which women are empowered and disempowered by the Jewish fundamentalist movements. I shall therefore resort to wide generalizations, drawing only in very general terms the history of British Jewry, as well as that of the major fundamentalist movements that have affected it. I shall then concentrate on issues relating to women's position and empowerment within these movements and, in particular, on factors that push women towards and away from Jewish Orthodoxy.

Britain has not spawned a unique or even particularly intense Jewish fundamentalist movement. However, the effects of Jewish fundamentalist movements which have emerged both within Israel and within the USA, and have been operating in Britain, are transforming the character of British Jewry. At the same time, it is impossible to understand fundamentalist activities in Britain without analysing them within the particular context of British multiculturalism and state structures.

[. . .] Unlike many other ethnic minorities in Britain, Jews as a whole (except Orthodox Jews in Hackney during the last few years) have remained outside the British 'Race Relations Industry'. One reason is the particular construction of the 'Industry', which emerged mainly as a response to immigration from Britain's imperial domains.[5] Another reason, however, is the continued reluctance of most Jews to be 'unnecessarily' visible, so as not to become an easy target for discrimination and *numerus clausus* (quotas which used to limit the number of Jews who could have access to higher education in Tsarist Russia).

A further reason is the fact that, despite several debates in the British Parliament regarding the legal status of Jews in Britain, no agreement was ever reached on the subject, so that Jewish legal and political rights were achieved largely as a side-effect of rights given to Catholics and other non-Established Churches during the eighteenth and nineteenth centuries. This, of course, applies to the Jews who settled in Britain from the sixteenth century onwards. Before that period there were no Jews in Britain for about three hundred years; and earlier, their legal position had been very clearly delineated. Jews first reached Britain during Roman times and settled in large numbers in England after the Norman occupation. In medieval times they constituted what Abraham Leon has called 'a people-caste'[6] and fulfilled specific socio-economic roles within the feudal estate society. They were excluded from agriculture as well as from the city guilds, so their occupations were necessarily concentrated in the money economy, from pawning to the poor to lending huge sums to the aristocracy. [. . .]

Things came to a head during the Crusades, both as a result of general social destabilization and religious mobilization and because of the heavy economic burdens the campaign imposed. After a period of persecutions and pogroms, and with the weakening of the economic resources of the British Jewish community, Jews were expelled from Britain in 1290 by a royal decree from Edward I—the first of a series of Jewish expulsions which took place in Western European countries, with the general rise of mercantile capitalism and national bourgeoisies.

[. . .] The biggest influx of Jews to come to Britain in modern time took place towards the end of the nineteenth century and at the beginning of the twentieth, when they escaped persecutions and pogroms in Eastern Europe, the last part of Europe to emerge into modernity. Jewish refugees continued to arrive in Britain before and after World War II, but their numbers were greatly reduced by a developing machinery of immigration controls. The first law of this kind—the Aliens Act 1905—was prompted as a direct response to the Jewish immigration from Eastern Europe.[7]

It is difficult to estimate the exact number of Jews in Britain. Waterman and Kosmin, who conducted a statistical and demographic study of contemporary British Jewry, estimate their number to be around 330,000.[8]

Although Jews can be found in virtually every part of Britain and in every class group—from poverty-stricken East Enders to members of the lower aristocracy—there are still certain demographic trends which characterize British Jewry. They are mostly concentrated in Britain's large cities, especially in certain parts of Greater London; the percentage of those who have achieved high levels of education is somewhat greater than among other sections of the population; and a higher proportion are either self-employed or professionals.

The organized Jewish community is formally led by the Board of Deputies, which, [. . .] while it represents a wider constituency than it used to do in the days when the Cousinhood (the Jewish aristocracy which used to intermarry[9]) used to dominate it, is still far from being representative of the Jewish community as a whole. It has no relation to Jews who are not members of any established organization (including some 'alternative' synagogues), nor does it include formal representation from the ultra-Orthodox. In the controversy regarding appropriate reactions to anti-Semitic attacks, the Board of Deputies has always taken the line that minimizing and turning attention away from such attacks would be best—although this might be changing gradually, given the recent upsurge of anti-Semitic attacks in Britain, and much more so in other parts of Europe.

Jewish education in Britain is usually associated with the different kinds of synagogue—Orthodox and Progressive. About half of Jewish schooling is carried out by part-time, after-school and Sunday schools, and half in full-time Jewish day schools, . . . having increased from one third in 1964. [. . .]

Upwardly mobile Jews have been moving to the suburbs, where they have often chosen to join liberal/reform synagogues in order to avoid the cumbersome daily observance rules which constitute the basis of Orthodox observance (the Jewish adult male is supposed to follow 613(!) different *mitzvot*). Assimilation becomes a dominant pattern in a neighbourhood that lacks a support network of kosher food shops and a synagogue within walking distance (observant Jews are forbidden to travel in a vehicle on the Sabbath), and has a class-homogeneous but religiously and ethnically mixed population. This assimilation can take place either on an individual basis, accompanied by secularization, or on a more collective basis. Liberal and reform synagogues have constructed kinds of Judaism which are much more compatible with Protestant denominations and do not intrude significantly (except on Jewish holidays) into the daily lives of their adherents.

On the other hand, more and more Jews who grew up in the United Synagogues, the mainstream Orthodox strand of Judaism, are moving towards a more Orthodox lifestyle. Again, this movement can be on an individual or family basis, when they become *khozrim bitshuva* ('born-again Jews'), or on a more collective basis—when the synagogue's rabbi, or the Jewish school, develops a much more Orthodox style. [. . .]

JEWISH FUNDAMENTALIST MOVEMENTS

It is difficult, especially in Israel, to determine which Orthodox movements are fundamentalist and which are not. In a sense they all are—both those who define themselves as Zionist and those who do not (except, probably, the small groups of the extreme anti-Zionist Neturei Karta and the Satmar Rebbe Hassids, who consistently continue to oppose the Israeli state and to boycott any participation in its politics). Although Zionism generally presented itself as a modern alternative to Orthodox Jewishness, the two were never completely separated.[10] The Zionist movement needed the legitimation of Orthodox Judaism for both its claims on the country and its claim to represent the Jewish people as a whole. The Orthodox movements used the Israeli state both to gain more resources for their institutions and to impose as many religious practices as possible on Israeli society. Central to their strategy was the control of women's position in Israeli personal law.[11] [. . .]

Some of the Orthodox—although by now a minority among the religious voters in Israel—have been actively Zionist. The religious ideologue during the early days of Zionism was HaRav Kook,[12] who saw the Zionist settlers, secular as they were, as instruments in the hands of God. He considered building the Israeli state as a necessary step, a precondition for the return of the Messiah.

The Messianic element is central to contemporary fundamentalist Jewish movements, both in Israel and in the Diaspora. Although the individual motivation of people who become *khozrim bitshuva* is often totally subjective and personal, Judaism is a communal religion. The general political message of these movements as a whole is Messianic; therefore, 'the Promised Land'—Israel and the Occupied Territories—is central to them. In all versions, the ultimate aim is constructed in terms of the coming of the Messiah, in which all these splits within Jewish existence would heal—the people of Israel would be in the land of Israel, in a state of Israel, with the Messiah as its ruler. [. . .]

British Jewish youth have been affected by these Messianic movements in Israel, especially members of right-wing or religious youth movements such as Betar and B'nai Akiva. Paradoxically, however, their influence in Britain was curtailed in the 1980s because of the nature of their ideology—the zealous immigrated to Israel, and those who remained had to adopt a more pragmatic approach and became incorporated into mainstream Jewish political and religious life. As in Israel and the USA, however, the political message of these movements has moved the political discourse within the general Jewish community to the Right. [. . .]

WOMEN AND JUDAISM

The position of women in Judaism depends, of course, not only on the particular religious ideology within which they are operating but also on their class position and other sociological determinants. Although all Jewish Orthodox would claim that there is an inherent Jewish position on women, their degree of freedom and empowerment varies from one community to another, a function of the different interpretations that are given to common laws. The difference between a middle-class professional American woman, say, and a poor housewife in a development town in Israel is immense, even if both are Orthodox, married and have four or five children. Similar—although probably somewhat less striking—differences also exist among Orthodox Jewish women who live in Britain, from different neighbourhoods and in different class positions.

However, these differences are not only contextual but also depend on different constructions of the religious duties themselves. A somewhat superficial yet illustrative example of this are the variations concerning women's dress.

Women and men are forbidden to 'cross-dress'—for a man, to wear women's clothes; for a woman, to wear men's clothes. Women who wear trousers and walk in ultra-Orthodox neighbourhoods in Jerusalem are cursed and sometimes even stoned. When I went to interview college girls from B'nai Akiva, the Zionist Orthodox youth movement, I saw many of them wearing not only trousers but even jeans. When asked, however, they claimed that these jeans were made especially for women; therefore they did not 'sin'. [. . .]

There are some basic inequalities in the position of men and women in Orthodox Judaism that crosscut all trends. Women are not counted as part of a Jewish 'public'; they are not allowed to lead prayers, to become rabbis, dayans (judges) or hold any other public religious position; their evidence is not acceptable in court and they cannot—unlike men—obtain a divorce against their spouses' will, even if their case is conceded to be just.

In their daily prayers every morning, Jewish men pray: 'Bless Thee that did not make me a woman'. Women pray: 'Bless Thee that has made me according to Thy will' . . . Orthodox Jews, however, claim that women's position is not inferior to men's but different, and equally important. Since the rise of the feminist movement, a lot of energy has been expended to show that in actuality the Jewish woman's position is 'really' even more important and powerful than the man's. [. . .]

Women cannot go near and be touched by their husbands during (and seven days after) their monthly period. Only then, and after taking a ritual bath (the *mikve*), are they considered purified enough to be touchable again. Protofeminist explanations for this argue that this is a proof that Jewish women are not just sex objects for their husbands. This might be so, but it is also a very improbable coincidence that the two weeks in a month in which men can have sexual relationships with their wives are those in which the woman is most likely to become pregnant. Moreover, such an argument can hardly explain the fact that when a woman gives birth to a baby boy she can be purified after forty days, whereas when she has a baby girl she is untouchable for eighty days.

The religious commandments that are specific to women relate to her duties as a wife, a housewife and a mother. [. . .]

FUNDAMENTALISM AND WOMEN'S EMPOWERMENT

The construction of women as wives and mothers, and the drudgery of domestic labour, were at the heart of the feminist rebellion of the 1970s and 1980s. It is interesting to look in this context, at the elements within Orthodox Jewish practice that have attracted women, some of them with a feminist 'past'. From interviews with such women several points emerge, some of which are common to both men and women *khozrim bitshuva* and some specific to women.

The first reason—both women and men—have given me is:

> 'At last, I know who I am. I know what it is to be a Jew. Before that I knew I was different from the others, but I did not know how . . . And when I went to a reform synagogue, it all looked so artificial to me. Here there are finally people who can teach me who I am, who really understand about Judaism.'

Since the Jewish emancipation and the break-up of 'classical Judaism' in eighteenth-century Europe, the question of 'who' or 'what' is a Jew has become a major debate—is Jewishness a religion? Is it a nationality? Is it a culture? Is it a race? Jewish experience has been heterogeneous in different countries, and a confusing variety of movements and ideologies, developed both by Jews and by non-Jews, attempted to answer this question.[13]

The delegitimization of open anti-Semitism since World War II has enabled assimilation on a much wider scale, but the sense of being different and 'the Other' has continued to be reproduced. Jews who are not Israelis or religious often feel that their identity has boundaries but no content. Zionism has offered an easy 'modern' way of being Jewish via identification with Israel. However, in the developing political reality of post-1967 Israel, this has gradually become more difficult, as a non-critical support of Israel became morally more and more problematic. Ultra-Orthodox Judaism offers the illusion of authenticity, homogeneity and an ahistoric, unchanging Judaism, at least until the arrival of the Messiah. [. . .]

Part of the attraction of that knowledge is that it is composed from a duality of security and challenge. The sense of security derives from its offer of a total way of life, in which there is always a right way to approach and do everything, from the most profound to the most trivial things in life. And if one is confused and does not know what the right way is—the rabbi is always available for prescription. [. . .] It is a welcome antidote to what they believe to be the malaise of our time: the meaninglessness of a life where everything is permitted. [. . .]

The emphasis in Jewish ultra-Orthodoxy is on the 'natural' difference between men and women. They were created differently, and they have different religious duties and life careers:

> 'When I sometimes become tired and fed up with cleaning the house, I remember that this is not just a dreary cleaning—it is cleaning of a Jewish home and it's part of how God wants me to worship Him.'
>
> 'In every other society I think it is not fair. But in my society it is fair that when both the man and the woman work out all day, the woman comes home and does all the cooking and cleaning. Because my husband doesn't come home and watch the telly—he studies the Torah. And we were taught that that's what gives eternity for women—that you encourage the men to learn and you remove the petty worries in their life.'

In addition to containment and clarity of gender roles, Jewish Orthodox lifestyle often offers its *khozrot bitshuva* an escape from loneliness. Many of the women (and men) I talked to described the feeling of warmth that encompassed them when they first started to spend their Sabbath with an Orthodox Jewish family. [. . .]

The naturalization of the sexual division of labour, in terms of religious duties, in the family and in the community, creates a very strong separate women's community. Moreover, because of the system of arranged marriage and the fact that except on Sabbath and holidays, husbands and wives spend very little time together as a rule, a lot of the emotional bonding is between women. Debra Kaufman (and, in a much less reserved way, Tariq Modood in relation to Muslim fundamentalists [at a conference in Warwick, April 1990]), has pointed out a similarity between the sense of empowerment of Jewish women fundamentalists and that of radical feminists:

Like women-centred feminists, many *ba'alot tshuva* and indeed other women of the new religious right celebrate gender differences. For many radical feminists and for newly orthodox women, women represent a source of special strength, knowledge and power.[14]

For me, such a view mixes form with purpose, separateness with segregation, autonomy with male-defined women's space. It is easy to talk about women's empowerment as emanating from their difference without relating to the actual reality of their lives. It is not only about warmth and smiling faces and a sense of solidarity.

The other facet of the warmth and support is the harshness directed against 'deviants' who do not adhere to the very strict rules of internal authority and closed ranks. [. . .]

There is no Orthodox Jewish 'battered women's' refuge, and family conflicts are usually handled by the rabbi, who attempts to re-establish *shlom bayit*—domestic peace. Recently, however, the Jewish Marriage Bureau has started to train volunteers to become marriage guidance counsellors, for the need has become so acute. [. . .] However, the conception of what constitutes acceptable social relations between husband and wife is very narrowly determined. [. . .]

Social workers who work among ultra-Orthodox Jews, as well as the ultra-Orthodox women with whom I talked, reported many cases of physical and mental exhaustion and extreme post-natal depression among ultra-Orthodox Jewish women who bore many children in conditions of serious overcrowding and inadequate housing.

As in other cases of oppression, however, it is not those who are most oppressed who rebel. The women whom I interviewed, who broke away from Jewish Orthodoxy during the process of becoming feminists, did not grow up under these extreme conditions. [. . .]

They had regular contacts as girls with non-Jews or non-Orthodox Jews as a result of having at least part of their education in regular state schools or non-parochial Jewish schools. In other words, they were exposed—at least to some degree—to *Weltanschauungen* other than the ones they grew up with.

Rebelling against such close control was one of the major factors mentioned by those who have broken away from Orthodoxy: 'I wanted to live my own life, to find my own way. It was very warm in the family bosom, but too often suffocatingly so . . . ' This stifling feeling was not just the familial control, nor were the strict rules and regulations of observance always the most difficult things to bear. [. . .]

When she was seventeen, in the year before she broke away, Dena Attas wrote a poem:

> Tree you have grown old
> I have no more use for you tree
> for your insolent arms sky groping
> reach wrapping folding intruding
> into my own close held my-life
> I remember days without you tree . . .
> no stifle-green swaying possessing . . .
> tree I have grown old
> have grown old grown apart
> have no more no more use for you tree.[15]

It was not easy to break away. One of the women I interviewed described her feeling of dread in the beginning:

> 'When I danced for the first time with this tall handsome Catholic boy, I was sure I was going to be struck down by God. Nothing happened. It was all crap.' [. . .]

What can the acquired freedom give those who have broken away from Orthodoxy? As with the main character in the novel on Christian fundamentalism, Jeanette Winterson's *Oranges Are Not the Only Fruit*, the sense of being stifled and of being cast in a different mould from that demanded by the religious orthodoxy can be particularly enhanced by developing a different sexuality from the norm—not just lesbianism, but also a wish to remain single and/or not to become a mother to a big family. Freedom to become 'different', then, has been essential. Getting in touch with the feminist movement has played a significant role in the lives of many of the women who have broken away from religious orthodoxy.

Not surprisingly, however, some of them can be critical of attempts by other Jewish feminists, who have come from liberal or assimilated homes, to develop a Jewish feminism which draws on the traditional framework, while eliminating anything which is explicitly offensive to women but does not challenge the whole patriarchal framework. Unlike them, the Jewish feminist liberation theologian Judith Plaskow has claimed that to transform Judaism into a non-patriarchal religion would require a revolution as extensive as the one which transformed Judaism from a religion that sacrificed animals in the Jewish Temple in Jerusalem into the abstract monotheistic system of classical Judaism which has developed during the last 2,000 years.[16]

Some of the women I interviewed, however, go even further and see feminism as inherently incompatible with any religious order. One of them, Gail Chester, wrote an article on the subject entitled 'A

Women Needs a God like a Fish Needs a Bicycle'.[17] [. . .] One woman told me:

'What started my questioning, even more than God, was the question of Israel. Discovering that non-Jews were also living there and what happened to them.'

Minority women often face the dilemma that the same particularistic collective identity which they seek to defend against racism and subordination—and from which they gain their empowerment to resist dominant oppressive systems and cultures—also oppresses them as women and can include many reactionary and exclusionary elements. In the Jewish case the picture is even more complicated, because the same collective identity that constructed them as a persecuted minority is also the one which, via the hegemony of Zionism and Israel, links them to a collective identity that is racist and exploitative of others. [. . .] The search of the Lubavitch *khozrot bitshuva* for a secure identity not only raises pertinent questions about the kinds and limits of any empowerment they could get in man-made spaces, but also puts them in a position that supports the kind of Messianism that is racist and expansionist. This is so even if they never move to Israel, and even if they never make the connections themselves. [. . .]

It might be appropriate, therefore, to finish this chapter with a few excerpts from the songs the girls in the Lubavitch Youth Movement sing (found in song sheets at the Lubavitch Women's Centre):

'Oh mother, oh graceful queen
Your life your sacrifice supreme
So royal such holiness therein
Tell me please where do I come in.
  Daughter dear it doesn't take much
  To share a smile a soul to touch
  The role the goal of a Jewish mother
  Set aside yours for another.'

'Father, father, how can we return once more
The guards are all surrounding the door.
  Children, children, Torah you should learn
  Then Biyas Hamoshiach [the coming of the Messiah] you will
    surely earn.'

'G-d will save Zion and will build cities in Judea
and the descendants of His slaves will inherit them
and the lovers of His name will dwell there.

> How happy we are, how good is our fortune
> How lovely is our fate and how beautiful our heritage
> How happy we are, Jews we are, Lubavitch Hassids we are
> of our Lord, our teacher, our Rebbe.
> If you would build everywhere the House of Lubavitch,
> I shall show you the House of Lubavitch in Zion.'

[The third quote was translated by me from Hebrew. The first two songs are originally in English.]

The different themes in the different excerpts are not linked in the songs. But *we have* to make the link.

Notes

1. I. S. Lustick, *For the Land and the Lord: Jewish Fundamentalism in Israel* (New York: Council on Foreign Relations, 1988).
2. D. Kaufmann, 'Patriarchal Women: A Case Study of Newly Orthodox Jewish Women', *Symbolic Interaction* 12 (2) (1989).
3. Shaina Sara Handelmann, 'On Being Single and Jewish' (NY: Lubavitch Women's Publication, 1981). Orthodox people avoid using the full name of God and therefore use G-d instead.
4. Ibid., abstract in the Table of Contents.
5. N. Yuval-Davis, 'Ethnic/Racial and Gender Divisions in Britain and Australia', in R. Nile (ed.), *Multi-culturalism in Britain and Australia* (London: Institute of Commonwealth Studies, 1991).
6. A. Leon, *The Jewish Question* (Pathfinder Press, 1970).
7. S. Cohen, *From the Jews to the Tamils: Britain's Mistreatment of Refugees* (Manchester: South Manchester Law Centre, 1988).
8. S. Waterman and B. Kosmin, *British Jewry in the Eighties: A Statistical and Demographic Study* (London: Board of Deputies of British Jews, 1986).
9. C. Bermant, *The Cousinhood* (London: Eyre and Spottiswoode, 1971).
10. N. Yuval-Davis, 'The Jewish Collectivity and National Reproduction in Israel', in *Khamsin: Women in the Middle East* (London: Zed Books, 1987).
11. N. Yuval-Davis, 'The Bearers of the Collective: Women and Religious Legislation in Israel', *Feminist Review* No. 4 (1980).
12. Lustick, *For the Land and the Lord.*
13. N. Yuval-Davis, 'The Jewish Collectivity'; W. Evron (ed.), *A National Reckoning* (Tel-Aviv: Devir Publishing House (Hebrew), 1988).
14. Kaufmann, 'Patriarchal Women', 18
15. Dena Attar, 'The Selfish Tree'. Unpublished paper, 1985, 3.
16. J. Plaskow, *Standing Again at Sinai* (New York: Harper Collins, 1991).
17. G. Chester, 'A Woman Needs a God Like a Fish Needs a Bicycle', in S. Maitland and J. Garcia (eds.), *Walking on the Water* (London: Virago, 1983).

27 Black (W)holes and the Geometry of Black Female Sexuality

Evelynn Hammonds *

> The female body in the West is not a unitary sign. Rather, like a coin, it has an obverse and a reverse: on the one side, it is white; on the other, not-white or, prototypically, black. The two bodies cannot be separated, nor can one body be understood in isolation from the other in the West's metaphoric construction of 'woman.' White is what woman is; not-white (and the stereotypes not-white gathers in) is what she had better not be. Even in an allegedly postmodern era, the not-white woman as well as the not-white man are symbolically and even theoretically excluded from sexual difference. Their function continues to be to cast the difference of white men and white women into sharper relief.
>
> (O'Grady 14)[1]

When asked to write for the second special issue of *differences* on queer theory I must admit I was at first hesitant even to entertain the idea. Though much of what is now called queer theory I find engaging and intellectually stimulating, I still found the idea of writing about it disturbing. When I am asked if I am queer I usually answer yes even though the ways in which *I* am queer have never been articulated in the *body* of work that is now called queer theory. Where should I begin, I asked myself? Do I have to start by adding another adjective to my already long list of self-chosen identities? I used to be a black lesbian, feminist, writer, scientist, historian of science, and activist. Now would I be a black, queer, feminist, writer, scientist, historian of science, and activist? Given the rapidity with which new appellations are created I wondered if my new list would still be up to date by the time the article came out. More importantly, does this change or any

My thanks to Joan Scott, Mary Poovey, Donna Penn, and Geeta Patel for their support and for their thoughtful and incisive critiques of the ideas in this essay.

* From Evelynn Hammonds, 'Black (W)holes and the Geometry of Black Female Sexuality' from *differences* 6: 2+3 (Indiana University Press, 1995), 126–45, reprinted by permission of the publisher.

change I might make to my list convey to anyone the ways in which I am queer?

Even a cursory reading of the first issue of *differences* on queer theory or a close reading of *The Lesbian and Gay Studies Reader*[2] —by now biblical in status—would lead me to answer no. So what would be the point of my writing for a second issue on queer theory? Well, I could perform that by now familiar act taken by black feminists and offer a critique of every white feminist for her failure to articulate a conception of a racialized sexuality. I could argue that while it has been acknowledged that race is not simply additive to, or derivative of sexual difference, few white feminists have attempted to move beyond simply stating this point to describe the powerful effect that race has on the construction and representation of gender and sexuality. I could go further and note that even when race is mentioned it is a limited notion devoid of complexities. Sometimes it is reduced to biology and other times referred to as a social construction. Rarely is it *used* as a 'global sign', a 'metalanguage', as the 'ultimate trope of difference, arbitrarily contrived to produce and maintain relations of power and subordination'.[3] [. . .]

For example, the issue of silence about so-called deviant sexuality in public discourse and its submersion in private spaces for people of color is never addressed in theorizing about the canonical categories of lesbian and gay studies in the reader. More important, public discourse on the sexuality of particular racial and ethnic groups is shaped by processes that pathologize those groups, which in turn produce the submersion of sexuality and the attendant silence(s). Lesbian and gay theory fails to acknowledge that these very processes are connected to the construction of the sexualities of whites, historically and contemporaneously.

QUEER WORDS AND QUEER PRACTICES

I am not by nature an optimist, although I do believe that change is possible and necessary. Does a shift from lesbian to queer relieve my sense of anxiety over whether the exclusionary practices of lesbian and gay studies can be resolved? [. . .]

Maybe I had found a place to explore the ways in which queer, black, and female subjectivities are produced.[4] Of course, I first had to gather more evidence about this shift before I jumped into the fray.

In her genealogy of queer theory, de Lauretis argues that the term was arrived at in the effort to avoid all the distinctions in the discursive protocols that emerged from the standard usage of the terms *lesbian* and *gay*. The kind of distinctions she notes include the need to add qualifiers of race or national affiliation to the labels, 'lesbian' and 'gay'. De Lauretis goes on to address my central concern. She writes:

> The fact of the matter is, most of us, lesbians and gay men, do not know much about one another's sexual history, experiences, fantasies, desire, or modes of theorizing. And we do not know enough about ourselves, as well, when it comes to differences between and within lesbians, and between and within gay men, in relation to race and its attendant differences of class or ethnic culture, generational, geographical, and socio-political location. *We do not know enough to theorize those differences.*

She continues:

> Thus an equally troubling question in the burgeoning field of 'gay and lesbian studies' concerns the discursive constructions and constructed silences around the relations of race to identity and subjectivity in the practices of homosexualities and the representations of same sex desire.[5]

In my reading of her essay, de Lauretis then goes on to attribute the problem of the lack of knowledge of the experiences of gays and lesbians of color to gays and lesbians of color. While noting the problems of their restricted access to publishing venues or academic positions, she concludes that 'perhaps, to a gay writer and critic of color, defining himself gay is not of the utmost importance; he may have other more pressing priorities in his work and life'.[6] This is a woefully inadequate characterization of the problem of the visibility of gays and lesbians of color. Certainly institutional racism, homophobia, and the general structural inequalities in American society have a great deal more to do with this invisibility than personal choices. I have reported de Lauretis's words at length because her work is symptomatic of the disjuncture I see between the stated goals of the volume she edited and what it actually enacts.

[. . .] Thus, queer theory has so far failed to theorize the very questions de Lauretis announces that the term 'queer' will address. I disagree with her assertion that we do not know enough about one another's differences to theorize differences between and within gays and lesbians in relation to race. This kind of theorizing of difference, after all, isn't simply a matter of empirical examples. And we do know enough to delineate what queer theorists *should* want to know. For me it is a question of knowing specifically about the production of black female queer sexualities: if the sexualities of black women have been shaped by silence, erasure, and invisibility in dominant discourses, then are black lesbian sexualities doubly silenced? What methodologies are available to read and understand this perceived void and gauge its direct and indirect effects on that which is visible? Conversely, how does the structure of what is visible, namely white female sexualities, shape those not-absent-though-not-present black female sexualities? . . . And, finally, how do these racialized sexualities shaped by silence, erasure, and invisibility coexist with other sexualities, the closeted sexualities of white queers, for example? It seems to me that there are two projects here that need to be worked out. White feminists must refigure (white) female sexualities so that they are not theoretically dependent upon an absent yet-ever-present pathologized black female sexuality. I am not arguing that this figuration of (white) female sexuality must try to encompass completely the experiences of black women, but that it must include a conception of the power relations between white and black women as expressed in the representations of sexuality.[7] This model of power, as Judith Butler has argued, must avoid setting up 'racism and homophobia and misogyny as parallel or analogical relations', while recognizing that 'what has to be thought through, is the ways in which these vectors of power require and deploy each other for the purpose of their own articulation'.[8] Black feminist theorists must reclaim sexuality through the creation of a counternarrative that can reconstitute a present black female subjectivity and that includes an analysis of power relations between white and black women and among different groups of black women. In both cases I am arguing for the development of a complex, relational but not necessarily analogous, conception of racialized sexualities.[9] In order to describe more fully what I see as the project for black feminist theorists, I want to turn now to a review of some of the current discussions of black women's sexuality.

THE PROBLEMATIC OF SILENCE

> To name ourselves rather than be named we must first see ourselves. For some of us this will not be easy. So long unmirrored, we may have forgotten how we look. Nevertheless, we can't theorize in a void; we must have evidence.
>
> (O'Grady 14)

Black feminist theorists have almost universally described black women's sexuality, when viewed from the vantage of the dominant discourses, as an absence. In one of the earliest and most compelling discussions of black women's sexuality, the literary critic Hortense Spillers wrote: 'black women are the beached whales of the sexual universe, unvoiced, misseen, not doing, awaiting *their* verb'.[10] For writer Toni Morrison, black women's sexuality is one of the 'unspeakable things unspoken', of the African-American experience. Black women's sexuality is often described in metaphors of speechlessness, space, or vision, as a 'void' or empty space that is simultaneously ever visible (exposed) and invisible and where black women's bodies are always already colonized. In addition, this always already colonized black female body has so much sexual potential that it has none at all.[11] Historically, black women have reacted to this repressive force of the hegemonic discourses on race and sex with silence, secrecy, and a partially self-chosen invisibility.

Black feminist theorists, historians, literary critics, sociologists, lawyers, and cultural critics have drawn upon a specific historical narrative which purportedly describes the factors that have produced and maintained perceptions of black women's sexuality (including their own). Three themes emerge in this history: first, the construction of the black female as the embodiment of sex and the attendant invisibility of black women as the unvoiced, unseen everything that is not white; second, the resistance of black women both to negative stereotypes of their sexuality and to the material effects of those stereotypes on their lives; and, finally, the evolution of a 'culture of dissemblance' and a 'politics of silence' by black women on the issue of their sexuality.

The historical narrative begins with the production of the image of a pathologized black female 'other' in the eighteenth century by European colonial elites and the new biological scientists. By the nineteenth century, with the increasing exploitation and abuse of black women during and after slavery, US black women reformers began to develop strategies to counter negative stereotypes of their sexuality and their use as a justification for the rape, lynching, and other abuses of black women by whites. Although some of the strategies used by black women reformers might have initially been characterized as resistance to dominant and increasingly hegemonic constructions of their sexuality, by the early twentieth century black women reformers promoted a public silence about sexuality which, it could be argued, continues to the present.[12] This 'politics of silence', as described by historian Evelyn Brooks Higginbotham, emerged as a political strategy by black women reformers who hoped by their silence and by the promotion of proper Victorian morality to demonstrate the lie of the image of the sexually immoral black woman.[13] Historian Darlene Clark Hine argues that the 'culture of dissemblance' that this politics engendered was seen as a way for black women to 'protect the sanctity of inner aspects of their lives'.[14] She defines this culture as 'the behavior and attitudes of Black women that created the appearance of openness and disclosure but actually shielded the truth of their inner lives and selves from their oppressors'.[15] 'Only with secrecy', Hine argues, 'thus achieving a self-imposed invisibility, could ordinary Black women accrue the psychic space and harness the resources needed to hold their own'. And by the projection of the image of a 'super-moral' black woman, they hoped to garner greater respect, justice, and opportunity for all black Americans.[16] Of course, as Higginbotham notes, there were problems with this strategy. First, it did not achieve its goal of ending the negative stereotyping of black women. And second, some middle-class black women engaged in policing the behavior of poor and working-class women and any who deviated from a Victorian norm in the name of protecting the 'race'.[17] My interpretation of the conservatizing and policing aspect of the 'politics of silence' is that black women reformers were responding to the ways in which any black woman could find herself 'exposed' and characterized in racist sexual terms no matter what the truth of her individual life, and that they saw this so-called deviant individual behavior as a threat to the race as a whole. Finally, one of the most enduring and problematic aspects of the 'politics of silence' is that in choosing silence black women also lost the ability to articulate any conception of their sexuality.

Without more detailed historical studies we do not know the extent of this 'culture of dissemblance', and many questions will remain to be answered.[18] Was it expressed differently in rural and in urban areas; in the north, west, or south? How was it maintained? Where and how was it resisted? How was it shaped by class? And, furthermore, how did it change over time? How did something that was initially adopted as a political strategy in a specific historical period become so ingrained in black life as to be recognizable as a culture? Or did it? What emerges from the very incomplete history we have is a situation in which black women's sexuality is ideologically located in a nexus between race and gender, where the black female subject is not seen and has no voice. [. . .]

It should not surprise us that black women are silent about sexuality. The imposed production of silence and the removal of any alternatives to the production of silence reflect the deployment of power against racialized subjects. . . . It is this deployment of power at the level of the social and the individual which has to be historicized. It seems clear that we need a methodology that allows us to contest rather than reproduce the ideological system that has up to now defined the terrain of black women's sexuality. [. . .] To date, through the work of black feminist literary critics, we know more about the elision of sexuality by black women than we do about the possible varieties of expression of sexual desire.[19] Thus what we have is a very narrow view of black women's sexuality. [. . .] The restrictive, repressive, and dangerous aspects of black female sexuality have been emphasized by black feminist writers while pleasure, exploration, and agency have gone under-analyzed.

I want to suggest that black feminist theorists have not taken up this project in part because of their own status in the academy. Reclaiming the body as well as subjectivity is a process that black feminist theorists in the academy must go through themselves while they are doing the work of producing theory. Black feminist theorists are themselves engaged in a process of fighting to reclaim the body—the maimed immoral black female body—which can be and still is used by others to discredit them as producers of knowledge and as speaking subjects. [. . .] Ann duCille notes:

> Mass culture, as hooks argues, produces, promotes, and perpetuates the commodifcation of Otherness through the exploitation of the black female body. In the 1990s, however, the principal sites of exploitation are not simply the cabaret, the speakeasy, the music video, the glamour magazine; they are also the academy, the publishing industry, the intellectual community.[20]

In tandem with the notion of silence, black women writers have repeatedly drawn on the notion of the 'invisible' to describe aspects of black women's lives in general and sexuality in particular. Lorde writes that 'within this country where racial difference creates a constant, if unspoken distortion of vision, Black women have on the one hand always been highly visible, and on the other hand, have been rendered invisible through the depersonalization of racism'.[21] The hypervisibility of black women academics means that visibility too can be used to control the intellectual issues that black women can and cannot speak about. [. . .] I want to stress here that the silence about sexuality on the part of black women academics is no more a 'choice' than was the silence practiced by early twentieth-century black women. [. . .] While hypervisibility can be used to silence black women academics it can also serve them. [. . .]

Yet, while invisibility may be somewhat useful for academicians, the practice of a politics of silence belies the power of such a stance for social change. Most important, the outsider-within stance does not allow space for addressing the question of other outsiders, namely black lesbians. Black feminist theorizing about black female sexuality, with a few exceptions—Cheryl Clarke, Jewelle Gomez, Barbara Smith, and Audre Lorde—has been relentlessly focused on heterosexuality. The historical narrative that dominates discussion of black female sexuality does not address even the possibility of a black lesbian sexuality, or of a lesbian or queer subject.

[. . .] For example, since discussions of black female sexuality often turn to the issue of the devastating effects of rape, incest, and sexual abuse, I want to argue that black queer female sexualities should be seen as one of the sites where black female desire is expressed.

Discussions of black lesbian sexuality have most often focused on differences from or equivalencies with white lesbian sexualities, with 'black' added to delimit the fact that black lesbians share a history with other black women. However, this addition tends to obfuscate rather than illuminate the subject position of black lesbians. One obvious example of distortion is that black lesbians do not experience homophobia in the same way as do white lesbians. Here, as with other oppressions, the homophobia experienced by black women is always shaped by racism. What has to be explored and historicized is the specificity of black lesbian experience. I want to understand in what way black lesbians are 'outsiders' within black communities. This, I think, would force us to examine the construction of the 'closet' by black lesbians. Although this is the topic for another essay, I want to argue here that if we accept the existence of the 'politics of silence' as an historical legacy shared by all black women, then certain expressions of black female sexuality will be rendered as dangerous, for individuals and for the collectivity. [. . .] Yet there are exceptions. Lorde's claiming of her black and lesbian difference 'forced both her white and Black lesbian friends to contend with her historical agency in the face of [this] larger racial/sexual history that would reinvent her as dead'.[22] I would also argue that Lorde's writing, with its focus on the erotic, on passion and desire, suggests that black lesbian sexualities can be read as one expression of the reclamation of the despised black female body. Therefore, the works of Lorde and other black lesbian writers, because they foreground the very aspects of black female sexuality which are submerged—that is, female desire and agency—are critical to our theorizing of black female sexualities. Since silence about sexuality is being produced by black women and black feminist theorists, that silence itself suggests that black women do have some degree of agency. A focus on black lesbian sexualities, I suggest, implies that another discourse—other than silence—can be produced.

I also suggest that the project of theorizing black female sexualities must confront psychoanalysis. Given that the Freudian paradigm is the dominant discourse which defines how sexuality is understood in this postmodern time, black feminist theorists have to answer the question posed by Michele Wallace: 'is the Freudian drama transformed by race in a way that would render it altered but usable?'[23] While some black feminists have called the psychoanalytic approach racist, others such as Spillers, Mae Henderson, and Valerie Smith have shown its usefulness in analyzing the texts of black women writers. [. . .]

It can readily be acknowledged that the collective history of black women has in some ways put them in a different relationship to the canonical categories of the Freudian paradigm, that is, to the father, the maternal body, to the female-sexed body.[24] On the level of the symbolic, however, black women have created whole worlds of sexual signs and signifiers, some of which align with those of whites and some of which do not. None the less, they are worlds which always have to contend with the power that the white world has to invade, pathologize, and disrupt those worlds. In many ways the Freudian paradigm implicitly depends on the presence of the black female other. One of its more problematic aspects is that in doing so it relegates black women's sexuality to the irreducibly abnormal category in which there are no distinctions between homosexual and heterosexual women. By virtue of this lack of distinction, there is a need for black women, both lesbian and heterosexual, to, as de Lauretis describes it, 'reconstitute a female-sexed body as a body for the subject and for her desire'[25] [. . .]. Disavowing the designation of black female sexualities as inherently abnormal, while acknowledging the material and symbolic effects of the appellation, we could begin the project of understanding how differently located black women engage in reclaiming the body and expressing desire.

What I want to propose requires me to don one of my other hats, that of a student of physics. As I struggled with the ideas I cover in this essay, over and over again I found myself wrestling with the juxtaposed images of 'white' (read normal) and 'black' (read not white and abnormal) sexuality. In her essay, 'Variations on Negation', Michele Wallace invokes the idea of the black hole as a trope that can be used to describe the invisibility of black creativity in general and black female creativity specifically.[26] As a former physics student, I was immediately drawn to this image. Yet it also troubled me.[27] As Wallace rightfully notes, the observer outside of the hole sees it as a void, an empty place in space. However, it is not empty; it is a dense and full place in space. There seemed to me to be two problems: one, the astrophysics of black holes, i.e. how do you deduce the presence of a black hole? And second, what is it like inside of a black hole? I don't want to stretch this analogy too far so here are my responses. To the first question, I suggest that we can detect the presence of a black hole by its effects on the region of space where it is located. One way that physicists do this is by observing binary star systems. A binary star system is one that contains two bodies which orbit around each other under mutual gravitational attraction. Typically, in these systems one finds a visible apparently 'normal' star in close orbit with another body such as a black hole, which is not seen optically. The existence of the black hole is inferred from the fact that the visible star is in orbit and its shape is distorted in some way or it is detected by the energy emanating from the region in space around the visible star that could not be produced by the visible star alone.[28] Therefore, the identification of a black hole requires the use of sensitive detectors of energy and distortion. In the case of black female sexualities, this implies that we need to develop reading strategies that allow us to make visible the distorting and productive effects these sexualities produce in relation to more visible sexualities. To the second question—what is it like inside of a black hole?—the answer is that we must think in terms of a different geometry. Rather than assuming that black female sexualities are structured along an axis of normal and perverse paralleling that of white women, we might find that for black women a different geometry operates. For example, acknowledging this difference I could read the relationship between Shug and Celie in Alice Walker's *The Color Purple*[29] as one which depicts desire between women and desire between women and men simultaneously, in dynamic relationship rather than in opposition. This mapping of the geometry of black female sexualities will perhaps require black feminist theorists to engage the Freudian paradigm more rigorously, or it may cause us to disrupt it.

CAN I GET HOME FROM HERE?

> I see my lesbian poetics as a way of entering into a dialogue—from the margins—with Black feminist critics, theorists and writers. My work has been to imagine an historical Black woman-to-woman eroticism and living—overt, discrete, coded, or latent as it might be. To imagine Black women's sexuality as a polymorphous erotic that does not exclude desire for men but also does not privilege it. To imagine, without apology, voluptuous Black women's sexualities.
>
> (Clarke, 224)[30]

So where has my search taken me? And why does the journey matter? I want to give a partial answer to the question I posed at the beginning of this essay. At this juncture queer theory has allowed me to break open the category of gay and lesbian and begin to question how sexualities and sexual subjects are produced by dominant discourses and then to interrogate the reactions and resistances to those discourses. However, interrogating sites of resistance and reaction did not take me beyond what is generally done in gay and lesbian studies. The turn to queer should allow me to explore, in Clarke's words, the 'overt, discrete, coded, or latent' and 'polymorphous' eroticism of differently located black women. It is still not clear to me, however, that other queer theorists will resist the urge to engage in a re-ranking, erasure, or appropriation of sexual subjects who are at the margins of dominant discourses.

Why does my search for black women's sexuality matter? Wallace once wrote that she feared being called elitist when she acted as though cultural criticism was as crucial to the condition of black women as health, the law, politics, economics, and the family. 'But', she continued, 'I am convinced that the major battle for the 'other' of the 'other' [Black women] will be to find voice, transforming the construction of dominant discourse in the process'.[31] It is my belief that what is desperately needed is more rigorous cultural criticism detailing how power is deployed through issues like sexuality and the alternative forms that even an oppressed subject's power can take. Since 1987, a major part of my intellectual work as an historian of US science and medicine has addressed the AIDS crisis in African-American communities. The AIDS epidemic is being used, as Simon Watney has said, to 'inflect, condense and rearticulate the ideological meanings of race, sexuality, gender, childhood, privacy, morality and nationalism'.[32] The position of black women in this epidemic was dire from the beginning and worsens with each passing day. Silence, erasure, and the use of images of immoral sexuality abound in narratives about the experiences of black women with AIDS. Their voices are not heard in discussions of AIDS, while intimate details of their lives are exposed to justify their victimization. In the 'war of representation' that is being waged through this epidemic, black women are victims that are once again the 'other' of the 'other', the deviants of the deviants, regardless of their sexual identities or practices. While white gay male activists are using the ideological space framed by this epidemic to contest the notion that homosexuality is 'abnormal' and to preserve the right to live out their homosexual desires, black women are rendered silent. The gains made by queer activists will do nothing for black women if the stigma continues to be attached to their sexuality. The work of black feminist critics is to find ways to contest the historical construction of black female sexualities by illuminating how the dominant view was established and maintained and how it can be disrupted. This work might very well save some black women's lives. I want this epidemic to be used to foment the sexual revolution that black Americans never had.[33] I want it to be used to make visible black women's self-defined sexualities.

[. . .] The appeal to the visual and the visible is deployed as an answer to the legacy of silence and repression. As theorists, we have to ask what we assume such reflections would show. Would the mirror black women hold up to themselves and to each other provide access to the alternative sexual universe within the metaphorical black hole? Mirroring as a way of negating a legacy of silence needs to be explored in much greater depth than it has been to date by black feminist theorists. An appeal to the visual is not uncomplicated or innocent. As theorists we have to ask how vision is structured, and, following that, we have to explore how difference is established, how it operates, how and in what ways it constitutes subjects who *see* and *speak* in the world.[34] This we must apply to the ways in which black women are seen and not seen by the dominant society and to how they see themselves in a different landscape. But in overturning the 'politics of silence' the goal cannot be merely to be seen: visibility in and of itself does not erase a history of silence nor does it challenge the structure of power and domination, symbolic and material, that determines what can and cannot be seen. The goal should be to develop a 'politics of articulation'. This politics would build on the interrogation of what makes it possible for black women to speak and act.

Finally, my search for black women's sexuality through queer theory has taught me that I need not simply add the label queer to my list as another naturalized identity. As I have argued, there is no need to reproduce black women's sexualities as a silent void. Nor are black queer female sexualities simply identities. Rather, they represent discursive and material terrains where there exists the possibility for the active production of speech, desire, and agency.

Notes

1. Lorraine O'Grady, 'Olympia's Maid: Reclaiming Female Black Subjectivity', *Afterimage* (1992), 14–23.
2. Henry Abelove, Michèle Barale and David Halperin (eds.), *The Lesbian and Gay Studies Reader* (New York: Routledge, 1993).
3. Evelyn Brooks Higginbotham, 'African-American Women's History and the Metalanguage of Race', *Signs* 17 (1992), 255.
4. Teresa de Lauretis, 'Queer Theory: Lesbian and Gay Sexualities: An Introduction', *differences: A Journal of Feminist Cultural Studies* 3.2 (1991), iv–v.
5. Ibid., viii, emphasis added.
6. Ibid., ix.
7. Higginbotham, 'African-American Women's History', 252. Here, I am referring to the work of Stuart Hall and especially Hazel Carby: 'We need to recognize that we live in a society in which dominance and subordination are structured through processes of racialization that continuously interact with other forces of socialization. . . . But processes of racialization, when they are mentioned at all in multicultural debates are discussed as if they were the sole concern of those particular groups perceived to be racialized subjects. Because the politics of difference works with concepts of individual identity, rather than structures of inequality and exploitation, processes of racialization are marginalized and given symbolic meaning only when subjects are black', Hazel Carby, 'The Multicultural Wars', in Michele Wallace and Gina Dent (eds.), *Black Popular Culture* (Seattle: Bay, 1992), 193.
8. Judith Butler, *Bodies That Matter: On the Discursive Limits of 'Sex'* (New York : Routledge, 1993), 18.
9. Abdul JanMohamed, 'Sexuality On/Of the Racial Border: Foucault, Wright, and the Articulation of "Racialized Sexuality"', in Domna Stanton (ed.), *Discourses of Sexuality: From Aristotle to AIDS* (Ann Arbor: University of Michigan Press, 1992), 94.
10. Hortense Spillers, 'Interstices: A Small Drama of Words', in Carole Vance (ed.), *Pleasure and Danger: Exploring Female Sexuality* (London: Pandora, 1989), 74.
11. Ibid., 85.
12. See Higginbotham, 'African-American Women's History'; Darlene Clark Hine, 'Rape and the Inner Lives of Black Women in the Middle West: Preliminary Thoughts on the Culture of Dissemblance', *Signs* 14 (1989), 915–20; Paula Giddings, 'The Last Taboo', in Toni Morrison (ed.), *Race-ing Justice,*

En-gendering Power: Essays on Anita Hill, Clarence Thomas and the Construction of Social Reality (New York: Pantheon, 1992), 462; Hazel Carby, *Reconstructing Womanhood: the Emergence of the Afro-American Woman Novelist* (New York: Oxford University Press, 1987); and Elsa Barkley Brown, '"What Has Happened Here": The Politics of Difference in Women's History and Feminist Politics', *Feminist Studies* 18 (1992), 295–312.

13. Higginbotham, 'African-American Women's History', 262.
14. Hine, 'Rape and the Inner Lives of Black Women', 915.
15. Ibid., 915.
16. Ibid., 915.
17. See Hazel Carby, 'Policing the Black Woman's Body in the Urban Context', *Critical Inquiry* 18 (1992), 738–55. Elsa Barkley Brown, in 'Negotiating and Transforming the Public Sphere: African American Political Life in the Transition From Slavery to Freedom', *Public Culture* 7 (1994), 144, argues that the desexualization of black women was not just a middle-class phenomenon imposed on working-class women. Though many working-class women resisted Victorian notions of womanhood and developed their own notions of sexuality and respectability, some also, from their own experiences, embraced a desexualized image.
18. The historical narrative discussed here is very incomplete. To date there are no detailed historical studies of black women's sexuality.
19. See analyses of novels by Nella Larsen and Jessie Fauset in Carby, *Reconstructing Womanhood*; Deborah E. McDowell, '"It's Not Safe, Not Safe At All": Sexuality in Nella Larsen's Passing', in Abelove, Barale and Halperin, *The Lesbian and Gay Studies Reader*, and others.
20. Ann duCille, 'The Occult of True Black Womanhood: Critical Demeanor and Black Feminist Studies', *Signs* 19 (1994), 592.
21. Audre Lorde, "Transformation of Silence into Language and Action", *Sister Outsider: Essays and Speeches* (Trumansburg, NY: Crossing Press, 1984), 91.
22. Karla Scott quoted in Teresa de Lauretis, *The Practice of Love: Lesbian Sexuality and Perverse Desire* (Bloomington: Indiana University Press, 1994), 36.
23. Michele Wallace, *Invisibility Blues: From Pop to Theory* (New York: Verso, 1990), 231.
24. Hortense Spillers, 'Mama's Baby, Papa's Maybe: An American Grammar Book', *Diacritics* 17 (Summer 1987), 65–81.
25. de Lauretis, *The Practice of Love*, 200.
26. Wallace, *Invisibility Blues*, 218.
27. I was disturbed by the fact that the use of the image of a black hole could also evoke a negative image of black female sexuality reduced to the lowest possible denominator, i.e. just a 'hole'.
28. The existence of the second body in a binary system is inferred from the periodic Doppler shift of the spectral lines of the visible star, which shows that it is in orbit, and by the production of X-radiation. My points are taken from the discussion of the astrophysics of black holes in Robert Wald, *Space, Time and Gravity: The Theory of the Big Bang and Black Holes*. 2nd edn. (Chicago: University of Chicago Press, 1992), ch. 8 and 9.
29. Alice Walker, *The Color Purple* (New York: Harcourt, 1982).
30. Cheryl Clarke, 'Living the Texts Out: Lesbians and the Uses of Black Women's Traditions', in Abena Busia and Stanlie James, *Theorizing Black Feminisms:*

The Visionary Pragmatism of Black Women (New York: Routledge, 1993), 214–27.

31. Wallace, *Invisibility Blues*, 236.
32. Simon Watney, *Policing Desire: Pornography, AIDS and the Media* (Minneapolis: University of Minnesota Press, 1989), ix.
33. Giddings, 'The Last Taboo', 462.
34. Donna Haraway, 'The Promises of Monsters: A Regenerative Politics for Inappropriate/d Others', in Lawrence Grossberg, Cary Nelson and Paula Treichler (eds.), *Cultural Studies* (New York: Routledge, 1992), 313.

28 I'm a feminist but . . . 'Other' women and postnational feminism

Ien Ang *

For some time now, the problematic of race and ethnicity has thrown feminism into crisis. I am implicated in this crisis. As a woman of Chinese descent, I suddenly find myself in a position in which I can turn my 'difference' into intellectual and political capital, where 'white' feminists invite me to raise my 'voice', *qua* a non-white woman, and make myself heard. Anna Yeatman[1] suggests that voices such as mine are needed to contest and correct the old exclusions of the established feminist order, and that they will win non-white women authorship and authority within a renewed, less exclusionary feminism. In this sense, feminism acts like a nation: just like Australia, it no longer subscribes to a policy of assimilation but wants to be multicultural.

I want to complicate this scenario by looking at the *problems* of such a desire. Rather than positively representing a 'Chinese' or 'Asian' contribution to Australian feminism—which would only risk reinforcing the objectification and fetishization of 'Asianness'—I want to argue that the very attempt to construct a voice for self-presentation in a context already firmly established and inhabited by a powerful formation (what is now commonly called, rather unreflexively, 'white/Western feminism') is necessarily fraught with difficulty. To me, non-white, non-Western women in 'white/Western' societies can only begin to speak with a hesitating 'I'm a feminist, but . . . ', in which the meaning and substance of feminism itself become problematized. Where does this leave feminism? Feminism must stop conceiving itself as a nation, a 'natural' political destination for all women, no matter how multicultural. Rather than adopting a politics of inclusion (which

* From Ien Ang, 'I'm a Feminist But . . . "Other" Women and Postnational Feminism' from *Transitions: New Australian Feminisms* by Barbara Caine and Rosemary Pringle (St Martin's Press, 1995), 57, copyright © Barbara Caine and Rosemary Pringle, reprinted by permission of the publisher.

is always ultimately based on a notion of commonality and community), it will have to develop a self-conscious politics of partiality, and imagine itself as a *limited* political home, which does not absorb difference within a pre-given and predefined space but leaves room for ambivalence and ambiguity. In the uneven, conjunctural terrain so created, white/Western feminists too will have to detotalize their feminist identities and be compelled to say: 'I'm a feminist, but . . . '

THE POLITICS OF DIFFERENCE AND ITS LIMITS

In the early days of the second wave, feminist theory and practice were predicated on the assumptions of women's common identity *as* women, and of a united global sisterhood. It was the universalization of white, middle-class women's lives as representative of *the* female experience that made it possible for modern Western feminism to gather momentum and become such an important social movement. [. . .]

Today, it is precisely this homogenizing idea of sisterhood that has come under increasing attack within feminism itself. After all, not all women share the same experience of 'being a woman', nor is shared gender enough to guarantee a commonality in social positioning. [. . .] It is now widely acknowledged that differences between women undermine the homogeneity and continuity of 'women' as a social category: differences produced by the intersections of class, race, ethnicity, nationality, and so on. So 'difference' has become an obligatory tenet in feminist discourse in the 1990s, and feminism's ability to 'deal with it' is often mentioned as a condition for its survival as a movement for social change. The so-called politics of difference recognizes the need to go beyond the notion of an encompassing sisterhood, and acknowledges that feminism needs to take account of the fact that not all women are white, Western and middle class and take into consideration the experiences of 'other' women as well. [. . .]

What does it mean, however, to 'deal with difference'? Pettman suggests among other things that it means 'recognising unequal power and conflicting interests while not giving up on community or solidarity or sisterhood'.[2] But this sounds all too deceptively easy, a formula of containment that wants to have it both ways, as if differences among women could unproblematically be turned into a 'unity in diversity' once they are 'recognised' properly. [. . .]

The way difference should be 'dealt with', then, is typically imagined by the feminist establishment through such benevolent terms as 'recognition', 'understanding' and 'dialogue'. The problem with such terms is first of all that they reveal an overconfident faith in the power and possibility of open and honest communication to 'overcome' or 'settle' differences, of a power-free speech situation without interference by entrenched presumptions, sensitivities and preconceived ideas. It is a faith in our (limitless?) capacity not only to speak, but, more importantly, to listen and hear. [. . .]

Therefore, I want to stress here the *difficulties* of 'dealing with difference'. These difficulties cannot be resolved through communication, no matter how complex the dialogue. Indeed, the very desire to resolve them in the first place could result in a premature glossing-over of the social irreducibility and inescapability of certain markers of difference and the way they affect women's lives. To focus on *resolving* differences between women as the ultimate aim of 'dealing with difference' would mean their containment in an inclusive, encompassing structure which itself remains uninterrogated; it would mean that 'these differences must comply with feminism's (. . .) essentialising frame'.[3] In such a case, difference is 'dealt with' by absorbing it into an already existing feminist community without challenging the naturalized legitimacy and status of that community *as* a community. By dealing with difference in this way, feminism resembles the multicultural nation—the nation that, faced with cultural differences within its borders, simultaneously recognizes and controls those differences amongst its population by containing them in a grid of pluralist diversity.[4] However, reducing difference to diversity in this manner is tantamount to a more sophisticated and complex form of assimilation. [. . .]

To take difference seriously, then, we need to focus on how the gulf between mainstream feminism and 'other' women is constructed and reproduced, and paying attention to, rather turning our gaze away from, those painful moments at which communication seems unavoidably to *fail*[5]. Rather than assuming that ultimately a common ground can be found for women to form a community—on the *a priori* assumption that successful communication is guaranteed—we might do better to start from point zero and realize that there are moments at which no common ground exists whatsoever, and when any communicative event would be nothing more than a speaking past one another. I want to suggest, then, that these moments of ultimate failure of communication should not be encountered with regret, but rather should be accepted as the starting point for a more modest feminism, one which is predicated on the fundamental *limits* to the very idea of sisterhood (and thus the category 'women') and on the necessary *partiality* of the project of feminism as such.

In other words, I suggest that we would gain more from acknowledging and confronting the stubborn solidity of 'communication barriers' than from rushing to break them down in the name of an idealized unity. Such an idealized unity is a central motif behind a politics of difference which confines itself to repairing the friction between white women and 'other' women. The trouble is that such reparation strategies often end up appropriating the other rather than fully confronting the incommensurability of the difference involved. This is the case, for example, in well-intentioned but eventually only therapeutic attempts on the part of white women to overcome 'our own racism' through consciousness-raising, a tendency particularly strong in some strands of American liberal feminism. White feminists worried about their own race privilege typically set out to overcome their feelings of guilt by identifying with the oppressed other. [. . .] This form of appropriation only reinforces the security of the white point of view as the point of reference from which the other is made same, a symbolic annihilation of otherness which is all the more pernicious precisely because it occurs in the context of a claimed solidarity with the other. The very presumption that race-based oppression can be understood by paralleling it with gender-based oppression results in a move to reinstate white hegemony. Such a move represses consideration of the cultural repercussions of the structural ineluctability of white hegemony in Western societies. (I have used the terms 'white' and 'Western' in an overgeneralizing way here, but will specify them later.)

Of course, the most powerful agents of white/Western hegemony are white middle-class males,[6] but white middle-class females too are the bearers of whiteness which, because of its taken for grantedness, is 'a privilege enjoyed but not acknowledged, a reality lived in but unknown'.[7] [. . .]

The extent to which this white self-exnomination permeates mainstream feminism should not be underestimated. It is a core, if unconscious, aspect of (white/Western) feminism, which appears unaware that even some of its apparently most straightforward ideas and beliefs reveal its embeddedness in particular orientations and tendencies derived from 'white/Western' culture. For example, the well-known maxim 'When a woman says no, she means no!' to articulate the feminist stance on rape and sexual harassment invokes an image of the ideal feminist woman as assertive, determined, plain-speaking and confrontational. The slogan does not just speak to men (who are commanded to take no for an answer), but also implicitly summons women to take up these feministically approved qualities and mean no when they say it. However, these qualities are far from culturally neutral: they belong to a repertoire of rules for social interaction which prizes individualism, conversational explicitness, directness and efficiency—all Western cultural values which may not be available or appeal to 'other' women. Asian women, for example, may well deal with male dominance in culturally very different, more circuitous (and not necessarily less effective) ways. In other words, far from being culturally universal, 'When a woman says no, she means no!' implies a feminist subject position and style of personal politics that are meaningful chiefly for those women who have the 'right' cultural resources. I am not saying that the maxim itself is ethnocentric; what is ethnocentric is the assumption that it represents all women's experiences and interests in sexual relations (arguably it doesn't even represent those of all 'white/Western' women). Even more perniciously, this universalist feminist assumption implicitly finds wanting all women who do *not* have these cultural resources. [. . .]

In acknowledgement of the need to deconstruct such universalizing assumptions of white/Western feminism, feminist theorists have begun to concern themselves with the issue of representation, of 'who is permitted to speak on behalf of whom'. If speaking in the name of the other is no longer politically acceptable, how then should the other be represented? Or should white feminists refrain from representing 'other' women at all? Would the problem be gradually solved if more 'other' women would start raising their voices and presenting 'their' points of view? Here again, the implicit assumption is that a diversification of discourse would eventually lead to a broader, more inclusive representation of 'all' women. However, what implications the resulting contestatory discourses can and should have for feminist politics remain glaringly unresolved. In other words, where does the emanating 'complexity of dialogue' lead us?

Let me address this question through an example, again derived (mainly) from American feminist criticism. As is well known, there has been much controversy in the academy about the cultural and sexual politics of the pop singer Madonna. Her many white feminist defenders see her as a postmodern protofeminist heroine, a woman who manages to create a cultural space where she can invent and play with daring representations of feminine sexuality while remaining in control and in charge.[8] While white critics have generally appreciated Madonna in terms of her clever subversion of male dominance,[9] however, the black feminist critic bell hooks argues that Madonna's gender politics can only be interpreted as liberating from a 'white' perspective:

> In part, many black women who are disgusted by Madonna's flaunting of sexual experience are enraged because the very image of sexual agency that she is able to project and affirm with material gain has been the stick this society has used to justify its continued beating and assault on the black female body.[10]

According to hooks, what Madonna's white feminist fans applaud her for—namely her power to act in sexually rebellious ways without being punished—cannot be experienced as liberating by the vast majority of black women in the USA, as dominant myths of black females as sexually 'fallen' force them to be 'more concerned with projecting images of respectability than with the idea of female sexual agency and transgression'.[11] In other words, hooks contends, Madonna's status as a feminist heroine makes sense only from a white woman's perspective, and any deletion of this specification only slights the black woman's perspective.

The point I want to make is not that the white feminist interpretation is wrong or even racist, or that hooks's view represents a better feminism, but that we see juxtaposed here two different points of view, constructed from two distinct speaking positions, each articulating concerns and preoccupations which make sense and are pertinent within its own reality. The meaning of Madonna, in other words, depends on the cultural, racially marked context in which her image circulates, at least in the USA. Nor can either view be considered the definitive white or black take on Madonna; after all, any interpretation can only be provisional and is indefinitely contestable, forcing us to acknowledge its inexorable situatedness.[12] [. . .] What we see exemplified here is a fundamental *incommensurability* between two competing feminist knowledges, dramatically exposing an irreparable chasm between a white and a black feminist truth. No harmonious compromise or negotiated consensus is possible here.

This example illuminates the limits of a politics of difference focused on representation. The voice of the 'other', once raised and taken seriously in its distinctiveness and specificity, cannot be assimilated into a new, more totalized feminist truth. The otherness of 'other' women, once they come into self-representation, works to disrupt the unity of 'women' as the foundation for feminism. [. . .] That is, there are situations in which 'women' as signifier for commonality would serve more to impede the self-presentation of particular groups of female persons—in this case African-American women struggling against racist myths of black female sexuality—than to enhance them. White women and black women have little in common in this respect. [. . .] So we can talk with each other, we can enter into dialogue—there is nothing wrong with learning about the other's point of view—provided only that we do not impose a premature sense of unity as the desired outcome of such an exchange.

CONSIDERING WHITE/WESTERN HEGEMONY

But there is more. It is clear that, while white critical discourse could afford to be silent about the racial dimension of the cultural meaning(s) of Madonna and could assume a stance of seeming racial neutrality,[13] hooks is only too aware of the marginal situatedness of her own point of view.[14] She does not share the sense of entitlement which empowers white women to imagine a world in which they are 'on top', as it were, successfully turning the tables on men (white and black). Yet this is the quintessence of the all-powerful fantasy Madonna offers white women. Black women like hooks operate in the certainty that they will *never* acquire the power to rule the world; they know that this world—white-dominated, Western, capitalist modernity—is quite simply *not theirs*, and can never be. [. . .]

It is important to emphasize, at this point, that white/Western hegemony is not a random psychological aberration but the systemic consequence of a global historical development over the last 500 years—the expansion of European capitalist modernity throughout the world, resulting in the subsumption of all 'other' peoples to its economic, political and ideological logic and mode of operation. Whiteness and Westernness are closely interconnected; they are two sides of the same coin. Westernness is the sign of white hegemony at the international level, where non-white, non-Western nations are by definition subordinated to white, Western ones. It is the globalization of capitalist modernity which ensures the structural insurmountability of the white/non-white and Western/non-Western divide, as it is cast in the very infrastructure—institutional, political, economic—of the modern world.[15] In other words, whether we like it or not, the contemporary world system is a *product* of white/Western hegemony, and we are all, in our differential subjectivities and positionings, implicated in it.

We are not speaking here, then, of an *ontological* binary opposition between white/Western women and 'other' women. Nor is it the case that white feminists are always-already 'guilty' (another psychologizing gesture which can only paralyse). But the fracturing of the category of 'women' is historically and structurally entrenched, and cannot be magically obliterated by (white) feminism through sheer political will or strategy. [. . .] In other words, it is important to realize that the white/'other' divide is a historically and systemically imposed structure which cannot yet, if ever, be superseded.

Until now I have deliberately used the term 'other' to encompass all the disparate categories conjured up to classify these 'others': for example, 'black women', 'women of colour', 'Third World women', 'migrant women' or, a specifically Australian term circulating in official multicultural discourse, 'NESB (non-English-speaking-background) women'. Of course these different categories, themselves labels with unstable and shifting content and pasting over a multitude of differences, cannot be lumped together in any concrete, historically and culturally specific sense. In structural terms, however, they occupy the same space insofar as they are all, from a white perspective, relegated to the realm of racialized or ethnicized 'otherness', a normalizing mechanism which is precisely constitutive of white/Western hegemony. As we have seen, feminism in Australia and elsewhere is not exempt from such hegemonizing processes: in most feminist theory, too, whiteness is the unmarked norm against which all 'others' have to be specified in order to be represented. [. . .]

What difference can a politics of difference make in the face of this fundamental, binary asymmetry? Sneja Gunew claims that '[t]he dismantling of hegemonic categories is facilitated by the proliferation of difference rather than the setting up of binary oppositions that can merely be reversed, leaving structures of power intact'.[16] This postmodern celebration of a 'proliferation of difference' as a utopian weapon in the destruction of hegemonic structures of power is also proposed by Jane Flax, as in this oft-quoted statement:

> Feminist theories, like other forms of postmodernism, should encourage us to tolerate and interpret ambivalence, ambiguity, and multiplicity as well as expose the roots of our needs for imposing order and structure no matter how arbitrary and oppressive these needs may be. If we do our work well, reality will appear even more unstable, complex and disorderly than it does now.[17]

For reasons that will become clear, I am generally sympathetic to Flax's emphasis on ambivalence, ambiguity and multiplicity as theoretical principles in our approach to 'reality'. But she surreptitiously displays another form of psychological reductionism when she ascribes the imposition of order and structure to the obscurity of 'our needs', and suggests that we should learn to 'tolerate' ambivalence, ambiguity and multiplicity. To be sure, the consequence of Flax's postmodern equation of 'doing our work well' with making reality 'appear even more unstable, complex and disorderly' is an underestimating of the historical tenacity and material longevity of oppressive orders and structures, such as those entailing sedimented consequences of white/Western hegemony. This postmodern optimism, I suspect, can only be expressed from a position which does not have to cope with being on the receiving end of those orders and structures. Flax's 'we', therefore, can be read as a white 'we': it is white needs for order and structure which she implicitly refers to and whose roots she wants to expose (and, by implication, do away with), and it is only from a white perspective that 'tolerating' ambivalence and disorder would be a 'progressive', deuniversalizing step. The problem is, of course, that the order and structure of white/Western hegemony cannot be eliminated by giving up the 'need' for it, simply because its persistence is not a matter of 'needs'.

From the perspective of 'other' women (and men), then, there is no illusion that white, Western hegemony will wither away in any substantial sense, at least not in the foreseeable future. The nature of global capitalist modernity is such that these 'other' peoples are left with two options: either enter the game or be excluded. At the national level, either integrate/assimilate or remain an outsider; at the international level, either 'Westernize' or be ostracized from the 'world community', the 'family of nations'. This ensures that the position of the non-white in a white-dominated world and the non-Western in a Western-dominated world is always necessarily and inescapably an 'impure' position, always dependent on and defined *in relation to* the white/Western dominant.[18] Any resistance to this overwhelming hegemony can therefore only ever take place from a position always-already 'contaminated' by white/Western practices, and can therefore only hope to carve out spaces of *relative* autonomy and freedom *within* the interstices of white/Western hegemony.

It is in this historical sense that the hierarchical binary divide between white/non-white and Western/non-Western should be taken account of as a master-grid framing the potentialities of, and setting limits to, all subjectivities and all struggles. Feminists and others need to be aware of this systemic inescapability when 'dealing with difference'. This is where I find Flax's insistence on ambivalence, ambiguity and multiplicity useful, not to celebrate 'difference' as a sign of positive postmodern chaos, but to describe the *necessary condition of existence* of those who are positioned, in varying ways, as peripheral others to the white, Western core. There is no pure, uncontaminated identity outside of the system generated by this hegemonic force.[. . .] Contemporary Aboriginal 'identity' in Australia cannot erase the effects of 200 years of contact and conflict with European colonizers,[19] and the 'identity' of Third World nations, mostly post-colonial, cannot be defined outside the parameters of the international order put in place by the unravelling of European colonial and imperial history. The irony is that while all these 'identities' are effected by the objectification of 'others' by white/Western subjects, they have become the necessary and inescapable points of identification from which these 'others' can take charge of their own destinies in a world not of their own making. Ambivalence, ambiguity and multiplicity thus signal the unfinished and ongoing, contradictory, and eternally unresolved nature of this double-edged process of simultaneous objectification/subjectification. Seen this way, the politics of difference, while bitterly necessary now that 'other' voices are becoming increasingly insistent, has not resulted in a new feminist consensus and never will. There will always be a tension between difference as benign diversity and difference as conflict, disruption, dissension.

AUSTRALIAN WHITENESS, THE POST-COLONIAL AND THE MULTICULTURAL

I have used the terms 'white' and 'Western' rather indiscriminately so far. This is problematic, especially given the rapidity with which these terms have become 'boo-words', signifying irredeemable political incorrectness. To counter such sloganeering and to clarify my argument, I should stress that I have used these concepts first of all as generalizing categories which describe *a position in a structural, hierarchical interrelationship* rather than a precise set of cultural identities. Thus, being white in Australia is not the same as being white in Britain, France or the United States, as whiteness does not acquire meanings outside of a distinctive and overdetermined network of concrete social relations. Even who counts as white is not stable and unchanging—we should not forget, for example, that in the postwar period Southern European immigrants to Australia (Italians, Greeks) were perceived as non-white, thus 'black'! Whiteness, then, is not a biological category but a political one. Therefore, we need to go beyond the generalizations of generic whiteness and undifferentiated Westernness if we are to understand the specific cultural dynamics in which these interrelationships are played out in any particular context. In other words, analysing and interrogating the culturally specific ways in which whiteness, including white femininity, has been historically constructed and inflected in Australia is a necessary condition if Australian feminism is to effectively deuniversalize the experience of white women in feminist theory and practice.[20]

Australia is implicated in the global configuration of white/Western hegemony in ways which are particular to its history—of European settlement and Aboriginal genocide, of the White Australia policy, official multiculturalism, and the current 'push toward Asia'. Despite this, Australia remains predominantly populated by Anglo-Celtic people, who inhabit exnominated whiteness in this country. Its main social institutions and basic cultural orientations are identifiably Western, and as a nation it is categorized in the international order as a part of 'the West'. Yet it is important to note that Australian whiteness is itself relatively marginal in relation to world-hegemonic whiteness. The fact that Australia itself is on the periphery of the Euro-American core of 'the West' (and as such is often forgotten or ignored by that core), produces a sense of non-metropolitan, post-colonial whiteness whose structures of feeling remain to be explored. Meaghan Morris has begun to capture the distinctive ambiguities of Australian whiteness with the term 'white settler subjectivity', a subject position which, Morris notes, oscillates uneasily between identities as colonizer and colonized.[21] In this respect, Australian whiteness is itself steeped in a deep sense of the ambivalence, ambiguity and multiplicity so valued by Flax. Here again, however, it doesn't get us very far to celebrate these conditions as inherently positive principles. Rather, they signal a historically specific cultural predicament which has led Morris to describe the Australian social formation as both 'dubiously postcolonial' and 'prematurely postmodern'.[22] I want to suggest that the precariousness and fragility of this antipodean whiteness, so different from (post)imperial British whiteness or messianic, superpower American whiteness, inscribes and affects the way in which white

Australia relates to its non-white 'others'. I will finish this essay then, by sketching briefly how Australian feminism is implicated in this.

Being Asian in Australia necessarily implies a problematic subject positioning. It is well known that the White Australia policy effectively excluded Asian peoples from settling in the country, because Australia wanted to be white, an outpost of Europe. Since the abandonment of this policy, however, 'we' are allowed in. And the politics of multiculturalism even encourages us to contribute to the cultural diversity of Australia. Still, the presence of Asians is not naturalized. A while ago I bumped into a middle-aged white woman in the supermarket. Such small accidents happen all the time; they are part of the everyday experience of sharing a space, including national space. But she was annoyed and started calling me names. 'Why don't you go back to your own country!' she shouted. I am familiar with this exhortation: it is a declaration of exclusion racialized and ethnicized people have to put up with all the time. But what does such a comment mean in Australia? I want to suggest that, placed in the larger context of Australian cultural history, the racism expressed here is not just ordinary prejudice. There is a measure of spite in the insistence with which this white woman proclaims Australia as her 'home' while emphatically denying me the right to do the same thing. It shocked me, because I thought this kind of thing was possible in Europe, not in a settler society such as Australia. In declaring herself to be a native threatened by alien immigrants, she displays an historical amnesia of (British) colonialism which actively erases the history of Aboriginal dispossession of the land. In other words, in her claim that Asians don't belong in this country, she simultaneously reproduces, in a single appropriative gesture, the exclusion of Aboriginal people. A disturbing bunker mentality is expressed in this peculiar double-edgedness of white Australian ethnocentrism, a mentality of tenaciously holding on to what one has which, I suggest, is sourced precisely in the precariousness and fragility, the moot legitimacy and lack of historical density of white settler subjectivity.[23]

Australian feminism has to take into account this two-sided antagonism, in which white Australia constitutes and asserts itself by demarcating itself from the immigrant on the one hand and the indigene on the other by racializing and/or ethnicizing both, naturalizing its own claim to nativeness in the process. It is clear that an Australian feminist politics of difference needs to dismantle and deconstruct the hierarchical relations involved in this complex and contradictory, three-pronged structure of mutual exclusivism, in which 'white' is the constitutive centre. This quotation from anthropologist Margaret Jolly typifies the problematic as it is currently seen through 'white' feminist eyes:

> There is the general problem of white feminists dealing with Australian women of colour, the rainbow spectrum of ethnic identities resulting from a long process of migration. *But the problem is more acute* with indigenous women because they identify us not so much as Anglo-inhabitants of Australia, but as the white invaders of their land. There is a strong and persistent sense of racial difference and conflict born out of the history of colonialism in our region.[24]

My quarrel with this comment is that it reinstates the white feminist subject as the main actor, for whom the Aboriginal other and the migrant other are two competing interlocutors, kept utterly separate from each other. One result of this is that the differing relations between indigenous peoples and various groups of settlers remains unaddressed,[25] and that the Anglo centre—*its* problems and concerns pertaining to identity and difference—remains the main focus of attention. In intellectual terms, this amounts to a non-dialogue between the post-colonial and the multicultural problematic, the serial juxtapositioning of the two conditional entirely upon the distributive power of the hegemonic Anglo centre. From a white (Anglo) perspective, it may be understandable that priority be given to Anglo-Aboriginal relations (as Jolly suggests), as it is this relationship which marks the original sin foundational to Australian white settler subjectivity, which can now no longer be repressed. However, this intense investment in the post-colonial problematic—which is the locus of the distinctively Australian quandary of 'white guilt'—may be one important reason why there is so little feminist engagement with the challenge of constructing a 'multicultural Australia'. 'Migrant women', lumped together in homogenizing and objectifying categories such as NESB, are still mostly talked about, not spoken with and heard;[26] they remain within the particularist ghetto of ethnicity and are not allowed an active, constitutive role in the ongoing construction of 'Australia'.[27] Multiculturalism remains, as Gunew complains, 'the daggy cousin of radical chic postcolonialism'.[28]

It is this context which makes it problematic to construct an 'Asian' voice in Australian feminism. Despite the regular presence of Asians in contemporary Australia and despite the recurrent official rhetoric that Australia is 'part of Asia', Asianness remains solidly defined as external to the symbolic space of Australianness, in contrast to Aboriginality which—certainly since Mabo—has now been accepted by white Australia, albeit reluctantly, as occupying an undeniable place, however fraught by the injustices of history, in the heart of Australian national identity. To define myself as Asian, however, necessarily means writing myself out of the boundaries of that identity and into the margins of a pregiven, firmly established Australian imagined community. The only escape from this ghetto, from this perspective, would be the creation of a symbolic space no longer bounded by the idea(l) of national identity; a space, that is, where 'Australia' no longer has to precede and contain, in the last instance, the unequal differences occurring within it. Of course, such a space is utopian, given the fact that 'Australia' is not a floating signifier but the name for an historically sedimented nation-state. Yet the imagination of such a space is necessary to appreciate the permanent sense of displacement experienced by racialized and ethnicized people, including, I want to stress, Aboriginal people.[29]

What does this tell us, finally, about the feminist politics of difference? As I have already said, too often the need to deal with difference is seen in the light of the greater need to save, expand, improve or enrich feminism as a political home which would ideally represent all women. In this way, the ultimate rationale of the politics of difference is cast in terms of an overall politics of *inclusion*: the desire for an overarching feminism to construct a pluralist sisterhood which can accommodate all differences and inequalities between women. It should come as no surprise that such a desire is being expressed largely by white, Western, middle-class women, whom Yeatman calls the 'custodians of the established order' of contemporary feminism.[30] Theirs is a defensive position, characterized by a reluctance to question the status of feminism *itself* as a political home for all women, just as Australia will not—and cannot, in its existence as a legislative state—question its status as a nation despite its embrace of multiculturalism. [. . .] Feminism functions as a nation which 'other' women are invited to join without disrupting the ultimate integrity of the nation. But this politics of inclusion is born of a liberal pluralism which can only be entertained by those who have the *power* to include [. . .]

Taking difference seriously necessitates the adoption of a politics of *partiality* rather than a politics of inclusion. A politics of partiality implies that feminism must emphasize and consciously construct the *limits* of its own field of political intervention. While a politics of inclusion is driven by an ambition for universal representation (of all women's interests), a politics of partiality does away with that ambition and accepts the principle that feminism can never ever be an encompassing political home for all women, not just because different groups of women have different and sometimes conflicting interests, but, more radically, because for many groups of 'other' women other interests, other identifications are sometimes more important and politically pressing than, or even incompatible with, those related to their being women.

It is this structural incommensurability that feminists need to come to terms with and accept as drawing the unavoidable limits of feminism as a political project. In short, because all female persons 'do not inhabit the same sociohistorical spaces',[31] (white/Western) feminism's assumption of a '"master discourse" position'[32] can only be interpreted as an act of symbolic violence which disguises the fundamental structural divisions created by historical processes such as colonialism, imperialism and nationalism. [. . .] It compels us to say, 'I'm a feminist, but . . .'

Notes

1. A. Yeatman, 'Interlocking Oppressions', in B. Caine and R. Pringle (eds.), *Transitions: New Australian Feminisms* (New York: St Martin's Press, 1995), ch. 4.
2. J. Pettman, *Living in the Margins* (Sydney: Allen and Unwin, 1992), 158.
3. V. Kirby, '"Feminisms, Reading, Postmodernisms": Rethinking Complicity', in S. Gunew and A. Yeatman (eds.), *Feminism and the Politics of Difference* (Sydney: Allen and Unwin, 1993), 29.
4. H. Bhabha, 'The Third Space', in J. Rutherford (ed.), *Identity: Community, Culture, Difference* (London: Lawrence and Wishart, 1991).
5. On the theoretical importance of emphasizing failure rather than success in communication, see I. Ang, 'In the Realm of Uncertainty: The Global Village in the Age of Capitalist Postmodernity', in D. Crowley and D. Mitchell (eds.), *Communication Theory Today* (Oxford: Polity Press, 1994).
6. For an historical analysis of the construction of this hegemonic masculine identity in imperial Britain, see C. Hall, *White, Male and Middle Class* (Oxford: Polity Press, 1992).
7. Cathy Thomas, quoted in R. Frankenberg, *White Women, Race Matters* (Minneapolis: University of Minnesota Press, 1993).
8. See C. Schwichtenberg (ed.), *The Madonna Connection: Representational Politics, Subcultural Identities and Cultural Theory* (Sydney: Allen and Unwin, 1993).
9. While most white feminist critics have come out as Madonna enthusiasts, there are exceptions; see, for example, S. Bordo, '"Material Girl": The Effacements of Postmodern Culture', in Schwichtenberg, *The Madonna Connection.*
10. b. hooks, *Black Looks: Race and Representation* (Boston: South End Press, 1992), 159–60.

11. Ibid., 160.
12. D. Haraway, 'Situated Knowledges: The Science Question in Feminism and the Privilege of Partial Perspective', *Feminist Studies* 14 (1988), 575–99.
13. See, however, C. Patton, 'Embodying Subaltern Memory: Kinesthesia and the Problematics of Gender and Race', in Schwichtenberg, *The Madonna Connection.*
14. hooks, *Black Looks.*
15. I. Wallerstein, *The Modern World System* (London: Academic Press, 1974).
16. S. Gunew, 'Feminism and the Politics of Irreducible Differences: Multiculturalism/Ethnicity/Race', in S. Gunew and A. Yeatman, *Feminism and the Politics of Difference,* 1.
17. J. Flax, *Thinking Fragments: Psychoanalysis, Feminism, and Postmodernism in the Contemporary West* (Berkeley: University of California Press, 1990), 56–7.
18. It should be added that 'whiteness', too, is a structurally impure position, deriving its very meaning from suppressing and othering that which is not white. But while the centre, by virtue of its being the centre, can subsequently repress the marginalized other in its sense of identity, the margin(alized) always has to live under the shadow of the centre and be constantly reminded of its own marginality.
19. See B. Attwood, *The Making of the Aborigines* (Sydney: Allen and Unwin, 1989).
20. For this kind of interrogation by white feminists in Britain and the USA, see V. Ware, *Beyond the Pale: White Women, Racism and History* (London: Verso, 1992) and Frankenberg, *White Women, Race Matters.*
21. M. Morris, 'Afterthoughts on "Australialism"', *Cultural Studies* 6 (1992), 468–75.
22. Ibid., 471.
23. I would suggest that it is for this reason that the scare campaign against Mabo relied so much on a populist hysteria focused around 'people's backyards'.
24. M. Jolly, 'The Politics of Difference: Feminism, Colonialism and the Decolonisation of Vanuatu', in G. Bottomley *et al.* (eds.), *Intersexions: Gender/Class/Culture/Ethnicity* (Sydney: Allen and Unwin, 1991), 56, emphasis added.
25. For example, I have not come across any discussion about the relationship between Asian and Aboriginal women.
26. J. Martin, 'Multiculturalism and Feminism', in Bottomley *et al., Intersexions.*
27. See, for example, A. Curthoys, 'Feminism, Citizenship and National Identity', *Feminist Review* No. 44 (1993), 19–38.
28. Gunew, 'Feminism and the Politics of Irreducible Differences', 54.
29. In this sense, the theme of reconciliation is more important to the peace of mind of white Australians than to Aboriginal people, for whom reconciliation will never compensate for their permanent displacement from their land.
30. A. Yeatman, 'Voice and Representation in the Politics of Difference', in Gunew and Yeatman, *Feminism and the Politics of Difference.*
31. R. Chow, 'Violence in the Other Country: China as Crisis, Spectacle, and Woman', in C. T. Mohanty *et al.* (eds.), *Third World Women and the Politics of Feminism* (Bloomington: Indiana University Press, 1991), 93.
32. Ibid., 98.

Environmental Management, Equity and Ecofeminism: Debating India's Experience

Bina Agarwal *

There is today a widespread recognition that for effectively managing local forests and commons, we need the active involvement of village communities. But what shape should community institutions for environmental management take? Many favour the revival or replication of traditional ones. But what would this imply for social equity? Indeed are even the newly emergent institutions challenging traditionally unequal social relations? While the issue of appropriate institutions for environmental management is still being debated, there is a striking absence of a gender perspective within the debate. This neglect of gender continues in the face of a substantial parallel literature (and movement) that has grown under the banner of 'ecofeminism'. Why has ecofeminism failed to provide a corrective? To what extent can it so serve?

It is argued here that rather than challenging traditional inequities and revivalist tendencies, the historical representations, premises and prescriptions of ecofeminism (especially its Indian variant) could, in specific contexts, strengthen institutions that entrench gender inequalities. The experience of environmental management institutions in India bear this out. To transform gender relations, and relations between people and nature, will need enhancing the bargaining power of women *vis-à-vis* men and of those seeking to conserve the environment *vis-à-vis* those causing its degradation. Although illustrated from India's experience, conceptually these arguments would have wider relevance.

INTRODUCTION

A significant consensus has emerged in recent years, in many parts of the world, that the effective management of local natural resources, especially forests and village commons, requires the active involve-

* From Bina Agarwal, 'Environmental Action, Equity and Ecofeminism: Debating India's Experience' from *Journal of Peasant Studies* vol. 25 no. 4 (Frank Cass & Company, 1998), 55–95, reprinted by permission of the publisher.

ment of user communities.[1] This is a notable (and welcome) shift away from the top-down State-dependent approach to natural resource management that prevailed widely less than two decades ago.

The question, however, is: what shape should community institutions for environmental management take? Should the traditional ones be revived and even be replicated elsewhere, as many are arguing, in a romantic construction of the past? If so, what would this imply for equality of participation and benefit sharing, given embedded social (especially gender) inequities? Equally, are newly emergent community institutions challenging inegalitarian aspects of traditional social relations and values, or are they unwittingly strengthening them?

While questions regarding appropriate and feasible institutional forms are still very much a matter of intellectual debate and local experimentation, what is striking about much of this debate and emergent literature is the virtual absence of gender as a significant analytical perspective. In fact most of the analysis and policy discussion on the environment ignores the question of gender inequalities. At best what receives an occasional mention is women's actual or potential role in environmental projects. As a result, many of the new institutional arrangements for local resource management that are being encouraged by governments and non-governmental bodies are entrenching, even exacerbating, gender inequalities.

This neglect of gender as an analytical concern in mainstream environmental writing and policy formulation continues in the face of a substantial parallel literature which claims universal relevance and a significant feminist following—literature that has grown under the broad banner of 'ecofeminism', with both Western and Indian variants.[2] Why has this literature (and movement) failed to serve as a corrective? To what extent can it so serve?

It will be argued here that although ecofeminism is becoming increasingly important in shaping views on women and the environment in international and national forums and among donor agencies,[3] its premises seriously limit its effectiveness as an analytical tool and its potential for promoting gender equality, both within and outside the context of environmental concerns. By its overdependence on ideological constructions to historically infer the situation of women and of the environment, by being selective even as regards ideology, and by romanticizing specific periods of the past, ecofeminism has tended to obscure, rather than grapple with, the political economy factors underlying women's subordination, nature's degradation, and their interlinks. It has also mostly ignored gender inequalities that are independent of the environment question. And it has paid little attention to institutional change and the processes for transforming gender relations. As a result, rather than challenging traditional inequities and revivalist tendencies, its premises and prescriptions could, in specific contexts, bolster institutions and practices that increase gender inequalities. Although these arguments will be illustrated from rural India's experience, in conceptual terms they would have relevance for many other regions and contexts.

After briefly outlining (by way of background) the nature, causes and effects of environmental decline in India, and contesting romanticized representations of pre-colonial ecology and society, the study will detail some of the conceptual and empirical weaknesses of the ecofeminist formulation (and especially of its Indian variant) which impinge centrally on the issue of gender and institutions for environmental change today. It will then spell out the nature of gender inequalities that are emerging in new community institutions for natural resource management in India, and how this experience further contradicts several ecofeminist assumptions. In conclusion, the chapter will highlight a more promising approach to understanding the process by which gender inequities are constructed and could be contested, so that institutional interventions can further the goals of both greening and social equity.

BACKGROUND: THE INDIAN CONTEXT

In largely agrarian economies, forests and village commons have always been important for subsistence, either as primary or as supplementary sources. They provide a diverse range of products for everyday use (fuelwood, wild vegetables, herbs, thatching for roofs, timber for house building, and so on); and they provide items necessary for subsistence farming (such as green manure and fodder for cattle). In addition, they contribute to rural livelihoods through the role they play in replenishing groundwater supplies, preventing soil erosion, and maintaining air purity.

Although all rural households in India use communal resources in various ways, poor households with little or no private land are especially dependent. In the mid-1980s, landless households collected from the local commons some 90 per cent of their firewood (a fuel which provided 65 per cent or more of domestic energy in large parts of the rural north), and depended on the commons for 69–89 per cent (varying by region) of their grazing needs, compared with the relative self-sufficiency of landed households.[4]

But within poor households women's dependence on non-privatized resources is particularly high, given (i) their limited ownership of private property resources, especially land, and their lesser access to employment;[5] (ii) the gender division of labour (women and female children do much of the collection of firewood and non-timber forest products);[6] and (iii) the gender unequal distribution of basic resources, such as for health care and often even food, within households.[7] It is poor rural women (and female children) living in environmentally vulnerable regions, such as arid and semi-arid zones, who are therefore typically the most adversely affected by environmental decline.[8]

This decline has a long history, but it has been especially apparent over the past century. In India today, forests cover only 19.5 per cent of the geographic area, and village commons about 18 per cent (even this latter figure is likely to be an overestimate).[9] The land under commons has been falling dramatically: it fell by 45–60 per cent between 1950 and 1984, in many states.[10] In addition, there has been a substantial thinning out of what was earlier dense forest or rich pasture, with an associated fall in productivity and biodiversity.

Underlying this decline are a complex range of factors:[11] the expansion of area under agriculture and plantations, especially but not only during British colonial rule; the commercial exploitation of forests first by the colonial State to build ships, railways, etc., and subsequently for various uses in the post-colonial period; the submersion of land under large hydro-electric and irrigation projects; population growth; urban spread; the substantial privatization of village common land; crop production technologies which are soil and water depleting; and the erosion of community institutions which monitored village resource use. While there is no clear consensus on the relative importance of these factors, there is today a growing recognition of an environmental crisis which, especially in the rural context, is linked critically to the sustainability of livelihood systems.

Less widely recognized or documented are the particular implications of this for poor rural women. These implications, which I have traced in some detail elsewhere,[12] cover a wide range. With a decline in village commons and local forests, for instance, there tends to be an increase in the time and energy women spend in collecting firewood, fodder, and non-timber forest products. In addition, incomes (the household's and women's) tend to decline with fewer items to gather, and less time at the woman's command for cultivation, especially where women's labour is critical for the crops grown, or where the household is *de facto* female headed. With the fall in incomes and food-supplementing gathered items, nutrition is adversely affected. Nutrition is also affected if firewood shortages become acute and women have to economize by shifting to less nutritious food items which need less fuel to cook, or by missing meals altogether. Similarly, fodder shortages which cause a decline in household milch cattle can have negative nutritional consequences. Although, as a result of the nutritional effects, the entire household suffers to some degree, women and female children are affected to a greater extent, given the gender bias in the sharing of subsistence goods within households. In addition there is a gradual erosion of knowledge of local plants and species, as the forests and commons which are the basis of this knowledge disappear. While rural women are by no means the sole repositories of this knowledge, they are often the significant bearers of information on the particular items they collect or use, such as information about local trees, grasses and food-related forest produce which cushion families under severe food shortage conditions.[13] And where large irrigation works or substantial deforestation uproot entire communities, they also destroy the local support networks—the social capital—which women in particular build up and draw upon during crises. These effects have been experienced, albeit in varying degree, across the country.

State response to the environmental and livelihood crisis associated with the decline of forests and commons has been slow and has varied over time. In the mid to late 1970s, responses took the form of top-down tree planting programmes. These involved both direct planting by the State and encouraging private farmers ('farm forestry') and village communities to plant. Although promoted under the banner of 'social forestry', much of what the State directly planted were fast-growing commercial species such as eucalyptus (used largely for paper and rayon production), rather than species which provided for the villagers' varied needs. Undertaken on land which the villagers often used for multiple purposes, and without any attempt to ensure their consent or participation, the schemes led to widespread local resistance (including people uprooting saplings) and a high failure rate. The State's attempts to promote tree planting by communities were similarly top-down and had little success; while farm forestry, which *was* successful in terms of tree survival, favoured commercial trees for profits rather than species for domestic use.[14] In particular these schemes raised serious doubts about the ability of the State or of individual farmers to regenerate communal resources, without the involvement of the community and user groups.

In contrast to State efforts were the more successful attempts by villagers themselves and by non-governmental organizations (NGOs) in many parts of the country to protect the local resource base. Some of these were spontaneous initiatives by populations living in or near the forests, others took the form of popular movements such as Chipko, and some few were initiated by innovative forest officials as 'joint' ventures involving both villagers and the forest department. There was also a considerable push from environmental academics, activists and journalists emphasizing the importance of local participation for successful environmental regeneration.

As a result, today we are seeing an emerging consensus, both among scholars and among government and non-governmental agencies, that local resources should be managed by village communities.[15] There is less clarity,[15] however, on whether the most appropriate institutional form would be management by an elected village council, or by traditional village councils (based on tribal or caste affiliations), or by representatives of households, or by all village adults; and the extent to which the State should be involved. What is notable in this discussion, however, is the little attention given to the possible effects of different institutional arrangements on social relations,[16] especially gender relations.[17] The absence of such a critical perspective has led many influential environmental thinkers to favour the strengthening, reviving, or replicating of old community institutions, partly from practical considerations—it is often easier to bring about co-operative action where it has existed before[18]—but particularly from an assumption that the past from which these institutions emerged constituted a period of ecological stability and social harmony.

A number of environmental scholars (termed by Sinha as the 'new traditionalists'[19]), for instance, have reconstructed the pre-colonial period as one of relative ecological and social balance, suffused with a conservation ethic grounded in religion (e.g., the tradition of maintaining sacred groves) and/or culture. Indeed, Madhav Gadgil represents the entire period from '500 BC to AD 1860' as one of relative stability in the natural environment, where caste and associated occupational divisions provided a nonconflictual basis for sharing communal resources.[20] The pre-colonial period is also represented by

Gadgil, and others such as Agarwal and Narain,[21] as one in which communal institutions for resource management were the norm rather than the exception, which were then substantially destroyed under colonialism: 'The British established their control over an India of largely self-sufficient, self-governing village communities which managed the natural resources on communally held lands, often with great restraint and prudence'.[22]

Existing evidence provides quite a different picture. Undoubtedly colonialism contributed in notable ways to environmental degradation, especially through deforestation (for various purposes, mentioned earlier), and through increasing State takeover of forests and communal land which eroded community property rights and would also have undermined village resource management institutions in many areas. But, as a growing body of work on environmental history shows, the pre-colonial period was far from one of ecological stability and subsistence balance, given the growth in human and animal populations, agricultural extensification, and pre-British State interventions.[23] Nor was it a period of social harmony: caste and class divisions were deeply oppressive, especially as experienced by the poorest and lowest castes, and caste (and class)-linked sexual exploitation of and violence against women was common,[24] aspects to which neither Gadgil, nor Gadgil and Guha[25] pay much attention. In addition, although various types of community resource management institutions clearly did exist in pre-colonial India, there is little to suggest that these were universal, nor can their erosion be attributed only to colonial policies.[26]

Historical representation apart, what is especially problematic in this romantic reading of the past is its uncritical *prescriptive use.* Gadgil and Iyer, for instance, suggest the revitalizing of caste groupings: 'We have to work with the caste groups and rebuild the resource base'.[27] They further suggest that the new institutions should 'attempt to ensure that *a small number of individuals* interacting with each other on a long-term basis . . . should have control over access to the resources of a given locality', and that 'local communities would increasingly come to *reassert* their key role in the management of common-property resources'.[28] This formula has all the dangers of reproducing old hierarchies as well as creating new ones along gender, caste, and class lines (depending on who that 'small number of individuals' is). Moreover, the revivalist agenda is not confined to a few. Guha and Gadgil observe that in almost all parts of India, social activists—'Gandhians, Marxists and wholly apolitical social workers'—are looking to tradition for answers in various ways, including many who wish to 'revive the rich traditions of prudent use'.[29]

Some writers, such as Fisher, distinguish between 'traditional' and 'indigenous' institutions, arguing that the former would go back in time while the latter could be of more recent origin.[30] What is at issue here, however, is not whether the institutions are of ancient or recent origin, but whether they embody and reinforce inegalitarian social relations and values. Notwithstanding and not denying the lessons tradition could offer on other counts, these discussions fail to problematize unequal gender relations which characterize most village communities and institutions, and which tend to get reproduced in the new ventures.

At the same time a large body of ecofeminist literature (to which I will now turn), which focuses directly on women and the environment, also fails to provide an adequate challenge to these institutional inequalities. Indeed it unwittingly provides scope for strengthening them.

ECOFEMINISM: MISLEADING REPRESENTATIONS, PROBLEMATIC PRESCRIPTIONS

Over the past two decades, a significant body of work has emerged in the West with some Third World variants, under the broad banner of 'ecofeminism'.[31] Although ecofeminist discourse embodies several strands, these share many common features. Most emphasize that women have a special relationship with nature which gives them a particular stake in environmental conservation. The domination of women and the exploitation of nature are seen as interrelated and as having historically emerged together from a common world view. The connection between the two forms of domination (of women and of nature) is typically traced to ideology; to the identification within patriarchal thought of women with nature (= inferior) and men with culture (= superior).[32] This link is seen to give women a special motivation in ending the domination of nature, and by implication their own subordination.

To bring about this change, ecofeminism calls upon women and men to reconceptualize themselves and their relationships to one another and to the nonhuman world, in non-hierarchical ways.[33] In this, the feminist movement and the environmental movement are seen to work together, on the assumption that they both stand for egalitarian, non-hierarchical systems. Indeed the liberation of women and of nature are seen as intimately linked.

Elsewhere[34] I have critiqued aspects of the ecofeminist position on several counts which cannot be detailed here, as have a number of other scholars from various other viewpoints.[35] Here I will outline some problems with the ecofeminist analysis (focusing especially on the Indian variant) which are of particular relevance in the present discussion, and have received inadequate attention earlier. These relate broadly to three aspects: (i) their inaccurate historical characterization of the situation of women and of nature, and their tracing the subordination of both to common and largely ideological origins; (ii) their insistence on the necessary simultaneity of the emancipation of women and of nature; and (iii) their assumptions about women's agency. All three elements are problematic. This is especially well illustrated by the works of Carolyn Merchant and Vandana Shiva.

The Question of Origins and Historical Representation

Both Merchant and Shiva locate the domination of women and of nature primarily in a shift in ideas and representations of women and nature, at a particular period in history (variously specified). Merchant traces the subordination of women and of nature to the beginning of the Scientific Revolution, and especially to the accompanying ideas (such as those of Francis Bacon) which gained prominence in Europe in the sixteenth and seventeenth centuries.[36] Vandana Shiva—whose work constitutes an influential Indian variant of ecofeminism—also traces this subordination to ideas associated with modern science and their manifestation in India with the advent of British colonialism in the mid-eighteenth century.[37] Both authors give primacy to what they see as resultant shifts in ideologies, representations and values.

(a) Examples from merchant

Merchant[38] argues that in pre-modern Europe the conceptual connection between women and nature rested on the coexistence of two divergent images (both identified with the female sex), one which constrained the destruction of nature and the other which sanctioned it. The dominant image identified nature, especially the earth, with the nurturing mother, and culturally restricted 'the types of socially and morally sanctioned human actions allowable with respect to the earth'. The opposing image of nature as a wild and uncontrollable force which could render violence, droughts and general chaos, culturally sanctioned human dominance over nature.

Between the sixteenth and seventeenth centuries, Merchant suggests, the scientific revolution and a market-oriented culture in Europe undermined the image of an organic cosmos with a living female earth at its centre, replacing it with a mechanistic world view in which nature was seen as something to be mastered and controlled by humans. The twin ideas of mechanism and of dominance over nature supported both the denudation of nature and male dominance over women. Merchant observes:

> The ancient identity of nature as a nurturing mother links women's history with the history of the environment and ecological change . . . In investigating the roots of our current environmental dilemma and its connections to science, technology, and the economy, we must reexamine the formation of a world view and a science that, *by reconceptualising reality as a machine rather than a living organism sanctioned the domination of both nature and women.*[39]

Merchant's historical tracing of these ideological shifts is illuminating, but several aspects of her analysis are also problematic. For instance, she does not grapple with gender inequalities (such as in economic rights and the division of labour) in pre-industrial Europe, or with the institutions that perpetuated them. Although she mentions such inequalities in passing—such as the custom of primogeniture which disinherited women and younger sons, and women's limited presence in public office—she does not note that these contradict her claim that women's subordination originated with the scientific revolution. Moreover, she says little about other disabilities women faced in premodern Europe, such as England's common law doctrine of coverture by which women lost control over all their property to their husbands on marriage, and were unable to sign contracts, sue, or obtain credit in their own names.[40]

In fact, Merchant, like Shiva (discussed below) pays little attention to earlier gender inequalities, and projects women's role in subsistence production in the best possible light: she sees women as economic partners to their husbands, assumes that farm profits are shared by the whole family, and views women's substantial work input as a positive indicator of their status, notwithstanding its backbreaking and undervalued character.[41] Merchant also downplays some of the positive features of women's position in the sixteenth century that she herself notes, namely greater opportunities for education and for public speaking on religious matters.

Equally, it is not clear how Merchant reconciles tracing the origins of the environmental crisis to the sixteenth–seventeenth centuries, with her observation that already in the twelfth–thirteenth centuries considerable ecological strains were emerging in Europe, with population growth, substantial deforestation, the conversion of pastures into fields, feudal extraction of surplus, and technological shifts (including the use of watermills and windmills). Would these technologies not represent 'dominance over nature'; and if they do, what would we make of her proposed causal link with the shift in ideas that came later?

In other words, even from the historical details Merchant herself provides, in pre-industrial Europe (i) women's position was by no means one of equality with men, nor did it become unambiguously worse in the subsequent period; and (ii) there were already notable pressures on the environment, especially on forests and commons. Apart from this disjunction between the ideological shifts that Merchant traces and the situation in practice, it is also not obvious that there was a historical conjunction between the subordination of women and the degradation of nature.

(b) Examples from Shiva: ideological selectivity

Vandana Shiva's propositions,[42] although set in the Indian context, problematically parallel those of Merchant on several counts, while being very much thinner in historical detail. She too links the subordination of women and of nature historically: 'With the violation of nature is linked the violation and marginalisation of women especially in the Third World'.[43] She generalizes for the Third World but her discussion is basically on India. Like the 'new traditionalists', Shiva dichotomizes history into pre-colonial and after, presenting the pre-colonial period as one of ecological sustainability and social harmony, and, like other ecofeminists, she infers women's position in that period mostly from a selective reading of ideology.[44]

> [T]he world views of ancient civilizations and diverse cultures which survived sustainably over centuries . . . were based on an ontology of the feminine as the living principle, and on an ontological continuity between society and nature . . . the humanization of nature and the naturalization of society. Not merely did this result in an ethical context which *excluded possibilities of*

exploitation and domination, it allowed the creation of an earth family [1988; 41, emphasis mine].

In this world she sees women's position in relation to men as being complementary and equal: '[U]nder conditions of subsistence, the interdependence and complementarity of the separate male and female domains of work is the characteristic mode, *based on diversity, not inequality*' [1988; 5, emphasis mine]. In other words, Shiva characterizes the pre-colonial world as one where (i) there was a strong ideological and material basis for harmony with nature and equality in social relations; (ii) women's position in relation to men was different and equal; and (iii) not only did inequality not exist, it was a world in which *exploitation was not even possible.*

This harmonious society, Shiva argues, was disrupted by colonialism which imposed on it a Western development model and caused a radical conceptual shift away from the Indian cosmological view of nature as Prakriti—a manifestation of Shakti [energy], 'the feminine and creative principle of the cosmos'. In this shift, the living nurturing relationship of man with nature as earth mother was replaced by the idea of man as dominating over nature. The shift, she argues, was violent, causing the death of the feminine principle, and so causing the devaluation of nature and of women 'embedded in nature': 'The ecological crisis is, at its roots, the death of the feminine principle'.[45] Indeed she generalises further:

All ecological societies of forest-dwellers and peasants, whose life is organised on the principle of sustainability and the reproduction of life in all its richness, also embody the feminine principle. Historically, however, when such societies have been colonised and broken up the men have usually started to participate in life-destroying activities or have had to migrate.

The western concept of masculinity that has dominated development and gender relations has excluded all that has been defined by culture as feminine and has legitimized control over all that counts as such.[46]

This view of history is untenable in its representation of pre-colonial India, and so in its attributing solely to colonialism what were in fact complex processes of gender subordination, environmental degradation, and a search for livelihoods. Certainly, neither in terms of ideas nor of practice were ecological sustainability and social equality the universal guiding principles of pre-colonial Indian society.

Consider, in particular, gender inequality. Shiva characterizes male–female relations in Indian tradition as complementary, interdependent and equal. She states this clearly in her representation of the gender division of labour under subsistence (on which more later), and it can be inferred from her discussion on 'Indian' cosmology. In relation to the latter, she argues (among other things) that Shakti, the feminine principle of the cosmos (as manifest in Prakriti), in conjunction with the masculine principle (Purusha), created the world. She amplifies this by invoking another manifestation of Shakti (in the Śiva–Shakti tradition), namely as the consort of the male deity, Śiva, arguing that Śiva is the passive and Shakti the active element.[47] Indeed, she notes: 'Without Shakti, [Śiva], the symbol for the force of creation and destruction, is as powerless as a corpse. The quiescent aspect of [Śiva] is, by definition, inert'.[48]

Although Vandana Shiva does not explicitly conflate Shakti with woman, such a gendering is implicit in her discussion, especially in her close identification of women with nature/Prakriti, and in her invoking the Śiva–Shakti representation. But the gender relations implicit in the symbolic Śiva–Shakti representation can be interpreted in ways contrary to Shiva's. For instance, in a different context, anthropologist Kapadia argues that in the Tamil Nadu village she studied, in the Brahminical discourse on Śiva–Shakti, Śiva's passivity implies his superiority:

> The message of this Brahminical discourse is that wisdom is 'still' and 'passive' and that this 'stillness' is a superior mode of being to the 'restlessness' of Shakti. Further, in this discourse it is clear that Wisdom or Knowledge is gendered as male and is hierarchically related to Power or Energy, which is gendered as female. Wisdom controls and directs the exuberant creativity of Power. When divinely possessed, men are both wise and powerful, male and temporarily female too. Consequently, it is only men who can autonomously represent Divinity completely.[49]

In this interpretation, the relationship of Śiva and Shakti, while one of complementarity, is not that of equality, nor of Shakti's superiority; rather the opposite.

Again, within Tantric Buddhism, in the period AD 1000–1300, it is noted that the male principle, Upaya (akin to Śiva and Purusha), was regarded as the active agent, and the female principle, Prajna (akin to Shakti and Prakriti), as a passive spectator.[50] This is the exact opposite of the Śiva-Shakti attributes in the Shakta religious tradition which Vandana Shiva largely draws upon.

In other words, representations of the Purusha–Prakriti, Śiva–Shakti relationships (and any hierarchies symbolized therein) differed in important ways within and between different religious traditions:

Hindu, Hindu-influenced, as also tribal. And these representations changed appreciably over the centuries, through a process of both contestation and assimilation. For instance, there was a gradual elevation of Purusha in the Purusha-Prakriti depiction,[51] an undermining of Prakriti from a symbol of creativity to that of 'devalued materiality',[52] the emergence of Shakti as a spouse goddess, and so on. Such shifts, however, are noted to have begun already under Brahmanical influence in the ancient period,[53] rather than been precipitated specifically by the advent of colonialism. Indeed, in the colonial period, countershifts, with various forms of revivalism of the Shakti cult, were observed.[54] And in present-day India, the process of contestation and assimilation continues around the attributes of particular deities, the concepts of male and female (or masculine and feminine) principles and their depictions, and so on. But notwithstanding all such shifts, neither under colonialism nor since has there been any clear unification of depictions across regions or communities. Ethnographic studies, both of the colonial and contemporary periods, show that even within one village the religious discourses of different castes and communities have tended to diverge significantly.[55]

Basically, Vandana Shiva's claims to the universality of particular representations of Shakti, of Śiva–Shakti, or of Purusha–Prakriti, and to their unchanging character before the British arrived, are difficult to sustain. Moreover, their presentation by Shiva as *pan-Indian* symbols ignores not only the co-existing alternative traditions within Hinduism and the temporal shifts therein, but also India's multi-religious character (encompassing Islam, Christianity, etc.). It is difficult to derive from all this any straightforward or widely applicable ideological depictions of women, of nature, or of gender relations.

For understanding the ideological construction of gender in pre-colonial and colonial India, what are likely to be of greater importance and relevance are the depictions of women in popular versions of epics such as *the Ramayana*; and in non-religious legends, folk songs, proverbs, etc. These too suggest a plural tradition, but one nevertheless steeped, in most part, in a hierarchical construction of male–female relationships.[56]

All in all, it is difficult to support the argument that in pre-colonial society there was some universalistic ontology and ethical context which would have precluded the possibility of social exploitation and domination. Nor can the particular philosophic interpretations that

Shiva emphasizes be linked readily with observed social relations (as outlined below).

At a more general level, ecofeminist formulations (and not just those of Merchant and Shiva), by depending in most part on a selective and largely ideological interpretation of women's position and their relationship with nature, neglect the institutions and forms through which social relations get played out in practice.

(c) Shiva: ignoring historical practice

In practice, there is enormous evidence historically of women's subordinate position existing long before the advent of the scientific revolution in Europe or of the British in India. These inequalities relate in particular to three aspects: (i) the gender division of labour; (ii) property rights, especially in land; and (iii) jural authority and access to public decision-making forums. These by no means exhaust all dimensions of women's unequal situation, but they are especially relevant for the present discussion.[57]

In the Indian context, all three types of inequality continue in the present period (even though their extent and form has altered in various ways), and critically influence where women get placed in relation to institutions for environmental change today.

The gender division of labour. That women bear the double burden of productive and reproductive work requires little elaboration, given the very substantial documentation and discussion on this in the feminist literature. Contemporary studies of course provide detailed information on the time division of labour by gender in peasant households in the Indian subcontinent.[58] But even for the nineteenth and early twentieth centuries there are many ethnographic descriptions which reveal the burden and importance of subsistence tasks performed by poor peasant women.[59] Buchanan, for instance, when describing what he saw in his travels through southern India, repeatedly emphasizes the 'industriousness' of women in agriculture, food processing, kitchen gardening, spinning, cattle tending, trading, and working as wage labourers. In one tribal community he notes that 'as the women are so industrious . . . the more wives [the man] can get, the more he lives at his ease'.[60] Allen *et al.* [1996] observe women in Assam (north east India) transplanting rice: 'up to their knees in mud, stooping for hours together in the burning sun.'[61] Chowdhry describes peasant women's heavy work in north-west India in the late nineteenth and early twentieth centuries.[62] Shiva's claim that women and men occupy complementary but equal domains in subsistence conditions, ignores the substantial and typically greater input of time and energy by women for household sustenance relative to men, *particularly* in subsistence contexts.

The problem is not simply that women's work in subsistence is 'treated as having no economic value' or of an 'ideological' divide between productive and unproductive work, as Shiva[63] argues, it is also the *extra effort* women *actually* expend, taking account of both their non-domestic and domestic work (the latter largely unshared by men). Moreover, perceptions about relative contributions influence the division of resources, such as for health care and food, within households. Hence, the economic undervaluation of women's work under subsistence can also affect their share in basic necessities.[64]

Inequality in property rights. Historically, Indian women had very limited rights in property under traditional law and practice. As detailed in Agarwal,[65] the *Dharmashastras*, the ancient Hindu treatises, and the many commentaries on them (especially the eleventh–twelfth-century *Mitakshara* and *Dayabhaga* legal doctrines), constituted the basis of traditional patrilineal Hindu law, and also strongly influenced the formulation of contemporary law. These gave Hindu women few rights of inheriting or controlling property. Women could inherit immovable property, such as land, only in the absence of four generations of males in the male line of descent, and even then they received only a limited interest in the property—they could enjoy it in their lifetime but had few rights of disposal. Actual practice deviated from this prescription in women's favour in south and west India, but the deviation was not substantial enough to make much difference to most women. Effectively few women owned or controlled property in the pre-colonial period. This was true even of tribal patrilineal communities: they customarily permitted women only use rights in land, and typically as wives or widows, which meant that these were usually rights mediated through marriage.[66] For many Hindu women, village citizenship itself was mediated through marriage, since women were often not married into their natal village (indeed were socially barred from doing so in large parts of northern India).

Muslim women, although allowed greater property rights by their religious laws than Hindu women by theirs, fared very similarly in practice, since in most regions local customs differed little in this regard between the two religious communities.[67] The only notable exceptions to women's general exclusion from landed property were a few matrilineal communities (found among tribals, caste-Hindus, as well as Muslims) in north-east and south-west India, which gave women significant rights in land.[68] But even they vested managerial control over land largely in male relatives.

Decision-making. Equally debilitating under customary practice has been women's exclusion from jural authority and public decision-making. Traditional forums of decision-making in the village, such as clan or caste councils, admitted only men.[69] Even in matrilineal communities, despite women's considerable rights of inheritance, the basic management of property lay with maternal uncles, brothers or sons; and membership, voice and representation in public forums was also typically limited to men.[70] This not only implied women's exclusion from the political domain, it also meant that during the colonial period when property and marriage laws began to be changed, women's ability to influence the direction of these changes, which profoundly affected their lives, was severely constrained. Among matrilineal communities such as the Nayars of Kerala this had particularly dramatic implications for women, as legal changes instituted in male forums shifted inheritance rights from matrilineal to increasingly bilateral.[71]

There is, therefore, little to suggest that women occupied a position of complementary equality in pre-colonial India. Inequalities existed in varying degrees in most cultures, and even tribal communities, although typically less gender unequal, were not immune. The assumption in some ecofeminist writing[72] that tribal cultures in non-Western societies are gender equal is questionable, as is the assumption that at some historical point in time when an organic world view of nature is presumed to have prevailed, gender equality also prevailed. The pre-colonial period was clearly characterized by strong gender hierarchies. Rendering these hierarchical structures historically invisible also makes invisible their continuation in various forms in the post-colonial period.

What survives today is a complex legacy of colonial, pre-colonial and post-colonial interactions. But the three central aspects of gender inequalities discussed above persist, even though their sharpness has typically declined and their manifestations sometimes altered, due to a range of factors, including State and non-State interventions in the colonial and post-colonial periods.[73] The gender division of labour, for instance, continues to be unequal, with most rural women bearing a double work burden. Although inheritance laws (as a result of legal reform, especially in the 1930s and 1950s) now allow Indian women even of patrilineal communities to legally own and fully control immovable property as individuals, significant inequalities remain, especially in relation to landed property. Moreover, in practice, few women own land and even fewer control any. A recent sample survey by development sociologist, Marty Chen, of rural widows in seven states, found that only 13 per cent of the 470 women whose fathers owned land inherited any as daughters, and only 51 per cent of the 280 women whose husbands owned land inherited any as widows. Hence 87 per cent of the women eligible to inherit as daughters and 49 per cent of those eligible to inherit as widows, did not get their due.[74] And in terms of public decision-making power, despite an improvement in women's representation in public forums, there is still a wide gap in relation to men at all levels, but especially at higher levels of decision-making.[75]

These three elements of gender inequality not only underlie in substantial degree the noted negative gender effects of environmental degradation, they also underlie the little attention being given to women's concerns in the emergent village institutions for environmental protection. As noted, the gender division of labour underlies the increase in women's time and energy in fuel and fodder collection. Women's lack of ownership in private land critically increases their dependence on common property resources. And their marginal representation in public decision-making forums, makes them mostly takers not makers of laws and rules for natural resource management currently being framed.

A misleading representation of the past prevents the identification and hence the challenging of the institutional and social constraints that women continue to face, and allows traditional inequities to persist in emergent institutions for environmental change. Prescribing the revival of traditional community structures, or extolling subsistence production systems, further compounds these tendencies. In this, the implications of Shiva's position closely parallel those of the new traditionalists, notwithstanding her declared concern for women's emancipation and the latter's virtual silence on it.

A Common Emancipatory Agenda?

The second important problematic in ecofeminist discourse is the claim by Merchant, Shiva, and many others, that the women's movement and the environmental movement both stand for egalitarian, non-hierarchical systems, and share a common emancipatory agenda.

Merchant[76] proposes, for instance, that 'common to both [movements] is an egalitarian perspective' and that juxtaposing the goals of the women's movement and the environmental movement can suggest 'new values and social structures, based not on the domination of women and nature as resources but on the full expression of both male and female talent and on the maintenance of environmental integrity'. While the desirability of this objective is indisputable, the assumption of a shared egalitarian perspective in the two movements is contestable. Likewise, Shiva notes: 'Women and nature are intimately related, and their domination and liberation similarly linked. The women's and ecology movements are therefore one'.[77]

Flying in the face of this belief is the continued absence in both theory and practice of a gender perspective in most streams of environmentalism, and of an environmental perspective in most streams of feminism. Basically Merchant, Shiva, and many other ecofeminists *assume* what in fact is an issue for *challenge*: they assume a necessary congruity in the goals of the two sets of movements when in fact that congruity needs to be brought about. It is also by no means obvious what an egalitarian perspective might translate into in relation to the environment.

Moreover, structures of gender inequalities are complex, and interlinked with other structures of social hierarchy such as class, caste and race. The dimensions of women's subordination are many, and are by no means all (or even in large part) connected with the question of man's dominance over nature. Hence they cannot be resolved simply by movements focused on the environmental crisis.

The Question of Women's Agency

The third major problematic in ecofeminist analysis that impinges on this discussion is the issue of women's agency. Ecofeminism romanticizes the notion of agency and in effect constructs women as fully fledged agents. Arguing that women have a special stake in environmental protection, ecofeminism assumes that women are therefore effective agents of change. But is having an interest in changing something enough to initiate the process of change? Ecofeminist discourse takes little account of a possible gap between women having an interest in environmental protection, and their ability to translate that interest into effective action.

Much of the literature on women's resistance is also wanting in this respect. Although it insightfully demonstrates that women, even under severely oppressive conditions, often resist their subordinate position in various (typically covert) ways,[78] examples of this resistance alone cannot serve to demonstrate that women have ceased to be victims or have become 'agents', as many assume. The unqualified extolling of such resistance obscures the fact that women, even if not passive, may still be victims of larger processes and structures of dominance.[79] More commonly, the inherent limitations of particular forms of resistance in undermining material and ideological dominance, as well as the possible constraints on women's ability to exercise agency (or what Sen terms 'agency-freedom') are seldom examined.[80]

Elsewhere[81] I have suggested that women's resistance to gender inequity can range from individual-covert to group-overt (with individual-overt and group-covert resistance coming in between); and that individual-covert resistance is the least likely and group-overt the most likely to be effective in seriously challenging structures of male dominance. But women's ability to move from one form of resistance to another—from covert to overt, individual to group, informal to formal—is not unconstrained.

In the present context, I would like to argue that women (especially of poor peasant and tribal households) are indeed victims of environmental degradation, although they are usually not 'passive' victims in that they often recognize the need for environmental protection and many seek to take action in various, typically informal, ways. To be effective agents for changing their own situation, however, requires also the ability to challenge and transform in their own interest the formal structures that control natural resource use and abuse.

The fact that women are often visibly present, sometimes even in the forefront of protests organized by environmental groups, is no guarantee that this will further women's interests or change gender relations. The history of peasant movements is witness to this. Women have typically been present in a major way in these movements, in various capacities, but have seldom occupied significant decision-making positions in the organizations spearheading these movements. This is poignantly brought out in the Tebhaga and Telangana movements of the 1940s in India.

In the Tebhaga struggle for land by sharecroppers, against feudal landlords in Bengal, women's efforts are noted to have assumed heroic proportions in disarming police parties, resisting arrests, and rescuing people. But unequal gender relations persisted both within and outside the movement. For instance, women's claims to land independent of their husbands were not even discussed by the peasant organization; male activists accused by their spouses of domestic violence got off lightly; women were largely excluded from membership and decision-making in the organization; and once the struggle ended women were forced back into domesticity. The same happened in the Telangana peasant struggle for land and against feudal rule in Hyderabad state, as recorded in the oral testimonies of women who participated in it.[82] Women's claims to even joint titles with husbands were not recognized, and women were seldom admitted as members of the Communist Party that catalysed the movement. As Dayana Priyamvada, one of the women activists put it: '[Women] would feed the comrades, giving up their own meals . . . carry letters . . . get beaten up . . . and yet there was no question of membership for [them]'.[83] Also, after the struggle, they had to return home to the same unremitting domestic labour. Brij Rani[84] asks with bitterness: 'What do you think it means, to wield weapons in the struggle and sit before sewing machines now?'

Even in the much-publicised Chipko movement (catalysed by villagers in the UP hills in 1973 to protest against the commercial exploitation of their local forests), women's domestic work burden, rights in property and many other aspects of gender relations have not been taken up as issues, although women have been central to the protests, and their mobilization against alcoholism and associated domestic violence preceded the movement. On occasion, during the movement, women have taken stands in opposition to the men, as in 1980 when women in Dungri-Paintoli successfully prevented the local oak forest (their major source of firewood) from being axed for building a potato seed farm that the village men wanted for its potential cash benefits.[85] But such stands remain sporadic, and have led to intra-family tensions, while important decision-making positions within the movement (barring a few exceptions) remain with men.

There are thus many aspects of gender inequity which will need contestation both within and outside the domain of environmental movements. This also raises the question (to which I will return): what factors might constrain women's exercise of agency in terms of environmental action, and how might these constraints be overcome? To illustrate these issues further, consider women's experience within emergent community institutions for forest management, detailed in Agarwal[86] and summarized below.

GENDER, GREENING, AND COMMUNITY INSTITUTIONS

A range of initiatives for forest management have emerged in India in recent years, especially in the form of micro-level forest protection groups. Some are State initiated under the Joint Forest Management (JFM) programme, in which village communities and the government share the responsibility and benefits of protecting and regenerating degraded local forest land, protection being done typically by forest protection committees constituted of the villagers. Other groups have been initiated autonomously in the village by a youth club, elder, or village council. Yet others are focused around the *van panchayats* or forest councils in the UP hills, created by the British in the 1930s to manage those forests which were deemed to be of little commercial value, but of importance as watersheds and as sources of fuel and fodder to local communities. Many of these *van panchayats* are being revived by NGOs or by villagers. By one estimate, some 10,000 such groups (including both the JFM and other initiatives) exist in India today, covering about two million hectares of degraded forest land. These are in addition to the protection efforts spearheaded by environmental movements such as Chipko.

In terms of regeneration, many of these initiatives have had notable successes. Where the rootstock is undamaged, natural regeneration begins apace. Several tracts being protected under the JFM programme that I visited in Gujarat (west India) in March 1995 showed impressive results. Areas which five years earlier consisted of little more than barren hillsides, from which it was difficult to obtain much except dry twigs and monsoon grass, were covered with young trees. Biodiversity was also reported to have increased, incomes risen, and seasonal outmigration fallen. Several other areas report similar benefits from protection.[87]

But the results are far from impressive in terms of gender equity in resource management and benefit sharing. Few women are members of the forest protection groups. They constituted only 3 per cent of some 8,000 members in the JFM committees studied in West Bengal,[88] and 7 per cent of some 22,000 committees studied in Tamil Nadu.[89] In general, women constitute under 10 per cent of the members in most areas. The JFM programme has specified rules of membership, and several states allow membership to only one person per household. This is invariably the male head. The autonomous groups have no formal rules of membership, but traditional norms which excluded women from village decision-making bodies, continue to prevail. Typically, women are not called to conflict-resolution meetings even where the dispute directly involves them.[90]

Membership apart, even where women are members, usually few attend; those that do rarely speak out; and when they do speak their views are seldom taken seriously or their interests and expertise recognized.

Before probing the factors which constrain women's participation, consider why it is important for women to participate in their own right, as below.

Gender-unequal Participation: Implications

Women's lack of direct membership and participation in decision-making adversely affects theirs and the family's welfare, efficient functioning of the institutions, and scope for women's empowerment.

In women's absence from the protection groups, the rules framed for forest management by the all-male groups tend to take little account of women's concerns. In many villages in eastern and western India, women have been barred from collecting even dry twigs. Where earlier they could fulfil at least a part of their needs from the protected area, they are now forced to travel to neighbouring sites, spending many extra hours and also risking humiliation as intruders. In some protected sites in Gujarat and West Bengal, many women who prior to protection spent one to two hours to collect a headload of firewood, now spend four to five hours, and journeys of half a kilometre have lengthened to eight to nine kilometres.[91] Some women seek additional help from young daughters, with negative effects on the latter's schooling. In one Gujarat village women commented on a recent award for environmental conservation conferred on their village, as follows: 'What forest? . . . Since the men have started protecting it they don't even allow us to look at it!'.[92]

Many of the self-initiated autonomous groups are even more male-biased than the JFM ones. A number of all-male youth clubs which are protecting the forests in eastern India, for instance, have not only banned entry, they have been selling the forest products obtained from thinning and cleaning operations. Many poor households cannot afford to buy this firewood and other forest products (which they had earlier collected free), and women again have to bear most of the burden of finding alternative collection sites. Moreover, cash generated through the sale of timber or grass from the protected sites is often put in a collective fund and used by the groups as they deem fit. In a number of cases the money has been spent on building a clubhouse or for club functions.[93]

Even where the groups, be it the JFM or the autonomous ones, distribute the cash benefits to participating households through the male members, there is no guarantee these will be shared equitably within the family, or even shared at all. In many cases, the men have been known to use the money for gambling, liquor or personal items.[94] Outside the context of forestry initiatives, in fact, there is a good deal of evidence that in poor households men tend to spend a significant percentage of their earnings on personal goods. In contrast, women in poor households tend to spend almost all their incomes on basic household needs.[95] Hence where women are not part of the formal protection committees and get excluded from receiving the benefits *directly*, it is not just their welfare which gets affected adversely, but also that of the children.

Not surprisingly, when the question of benefit sharing was discussed in a meeting of three JFM villages of West Bengal in which both women and men were present, all the women unequivocally wanted equal and separate shares for husbands and wives. 'There was no vote for "joint accounts" or the husband being more eligible as the "head of the household"'.[96] These women were responsible for a major part of household sustenance and wanted direct control over their share of the income.

Welfare apart, women's exclusion from the decision-making forums can adversely affect the long-term efficiency and sustainability of these initiatives (whatever the immediate gains). It can also obstruct the full realization of potential benefits from protection. Since it is typically women who have to collect firewood and grasses regularly, their lack of involvement in framing workable rules for protection and use, can cause them to circumvent the rules in order to fulfil essential household needs. In some cases, male committee members have threatened their wives with beatings if they break the rules, thus asserting their existing positions of power.[97] Its reprehensibility apart, this form of control is hardly enforceable in the long run, given that women's collection activities are necessary for household subsistence. In addition, excluding women means that replantation plans lack the benefit of their particular knowledge of plants and species which would enrich the selections made, enhance biodiversity, and increase the overall productivity of the commons.

In some cases, village men recognize the importance of involving women in the forestry programmes, but they seldom take steps for facilitating this. Overall, women's absence from formal participation in these new initiatives not only reinforces pre-existing gender inequalities, it further reduces women's bargaining power within and outside the household.

Thus what initially appears to be a success story of participative community involvement in resource regeneration is found to be largely non-participatory and highly inequitable in relation to women. This highlights too the problem of treating 'communities' as ungendered units and 'community participation' as an unambiguous step toward equity.

What constrains women's formal participation?

Constraints to Women's Formal Participation

In addition to the JFM rules of membership in several states, and the traditional norms of exclusion followed by many self-initiated groups, several other factors restrict women's participation in the formal forest protection groups, even where the rules are inclusive. These factors, detailed in Agarwal[98] and briefly outlined below, include the following:

(i) Logistical constraints associated with women's double work burdens: women have longer workdays than men, and meetings are often called when they are busy with domestic chores or fieldwork. Women (especially younger ones with children) are thus rarely able to attend long meetings, unless family or friends can cover such responsibilities.[99]

(ii) Official male bias: In government schemes, male forest officers rarely consult women, be it regarding the choice of trees or the village-level micro-plans for forest development.[100] Many women also complain that the officers 'always crosscheck with the men to verify the truth of [women's] words. And if ever there is any conflict or contradiction between the women and the men, the foresters always settle the disputes in favour of the men'.[101]

(iii) Social constraints: These take various forms: female seclusion practices or a more subtle disapproval of women's presence in public spaces; specification of appropriate female behaviour and forms of public interaction; social perceptions, articulated in various ways, that women are less capable than men, or that their participation in public forums is not appropriate or necessary; and so on.[102] Village women claim that the committee meetings are considered to be only for men, whose 'opinions and consent are taken as representative of the whole family'.[103]

(iv) The absence of 'a critical mass' of women: Women are often reluctant to attend meetings if there are only a few of them. Most women also feel they cannot change procedures by acting individually, and that individual women would be better able to speak up in their own interest if they were present in large numbers.[104]

(v) Women's lack of recognized authority: many women find that when they do attend meetings their opinions are disregarded—they thus become 'discouraged dropouts'. The experience of a woman member in a *van panchayat* is indicative: 'I went to three or four meetings . . . No one ever listened to my suggestions. They were uninterested'.[105] There are similar complaints by women about JFM functioning.[106]

Exceptions to the general picture of women's virtual absence from forest protection committees do exist. Both under JFM and in the *van panchayats*, for instance, there are cases where a third or half of the participants in the formal committees are women. There are even some all-women *van panchayats*. This suggests that the above constraints are not entirely insurmountable. But such cases are few and far between, and occur under specific enabling circumstances (highlighted later).

More common are the *informal* patrol groups that women form where men's groups are ineffective.[107] This enhances the efficiency of protection groups, but it also adds to women's work burden and responsibility, without increasing their authority: such informal groups typically still have to report offenders to the formal (typically all-male) bodies, in whom vests the authority for punishments.

Correctives and Alternatives to Ecofeminism

How does the ecofeminist formulation hold up in the light of women's experiences in the emergent community institutions?

To begin with, these experiences call to question the claim that the women's movement and the environment movement both stand for egalitarian, non-hierarchical systems. As this experience shows, an agenda for 'greening' need not include one for transforming gender relations; indeed efforts at greening by male-biased institutions might sharpen gender inequalities and (as noted) even bring threats of violence upon women.

Second, in relation to the ecofeminist claim that women have a special stake in environmental protection and regeneration, it is clear that women alone do not have such a stake. Both women and men whose livelihoods are threatened by the degradation of forests and commons are found to be interested in conservation and regeneration, but from *different (and at times conflicting)* viewpoints, stemming from differences in their respective responsibilities and the nature of their dependence on these resources. Men's interests can be traced mainly to the threat to their livelihood systems, their dependence on the local forests for supplementary income, and/or their need for small timber for house repairs and agricultural tools, which are their responsibility. Women's interests are linked more to the availability of fuel, fodder, and non-timber products, for which they are more directly responsible, and the depletion of which has meant ever-lengthening journeys. In other words, there is clearly a link between the gender division of labour and the gendered nature of the stakes.

The women I interviewed from some Gujarat villages were unambiguous about this:

Q: On what issues do men and women differ in forest protection committee meetings?

A: Men can afford to wait for a while because their main concern is timber. But women need fuelwood daily.

Third, women's concerns, even if pressing, do not necessarily translate into effective environmental action by the community or by women themselves. Case studies of several autonomous forest-management initiatives in Orissa (east India) highlight both the gendered motivation for forest protection and the unequal distribution of power which has enabled men's interests to supersede women's:

In most of the cases protection efforts started only when the forest had degraded and communities faced shortages of small timber for construction of houses and agricultural implements. Although there was a scarcity of fuelwood, it hardly served as an initiating factor.[108]

Although firewood is a household necessity and not just a women-specific one, since it is women's unpaid labour that goes into providing it any additional cost in terms of women's time and energy remains invisible or of insufficient importance to generate a community response.

Women's own responses too are far from automatic. The experience of an NGO in Rajasthan, working on the regeneration of village commons, as described by Sarin and Sharma, illustrates this well:

> [T]here is nothing 'automatic' in the extent of women's active participation in the development of village common lands, no matter how acute their hardship of searching for fuel and fodder. Even in the villages where women took the initiative and played a leadership role, this was preceded by enabling them to interact with other women's groups . . . Continuous interaction with [the NGO's] women staff has been another crucial input for facilitating women's genuine participation.[109]

It is notable that even in the Chipko movement, the specific incident which served as catalyst was the conflict between a sports goods manufacturer who was granted government permission to cut a tract of oak forest and the village co-operative which was refused permission to cut even a few trees for agricultural implements. The growing firewood and fodder shortage that was causing women enormous hardship did not elicit the same kind of response from the community or from the women.[110]

These experiences are in keeping with the alternative theoretical perspective to ecofeminism which I had spelt out elsewhere under the formulation, *feminist environmentalism.*[111] As I had argued then, and as the above discussion also indicates, people's relationship with nature, their interest in protecting it, and their ability to do so effectively, are significantly shaped by their material reality, their everyday dependence on nature for survival, and the social, economic and political tools at their command for furthering their concerns. Ideological constructions of gender, of nature, and of the relationship between the two, would impinge on how people respond to the environmental crisis, but cannot be seen as the central determinants of their response, as emphasised in ecofeminist discourse.[112]

To the extent that both women and men of poor peasant and tribal households are substantially dependent on natural resources for their needs, they would both have a stake in environmental regeneration. However, whether this leads them to initiate environmental action, and what benefits they derive from such action, would be contingent, among other things, on their ability to act in their own interest. Gender-specific interest in alleviating the environmental crisis, as also the ability to do something about it, would typically be linked to the division of labour, property and power between women and men. This formulation appears to be a better predictor of the environmental action we are observing, than the perspective provided by ecofeminism.

Feminist environmentalism also points to a different approach to effective change. On the feminist front it points to the need to challenge and transform not just ideas about gender but also the actual division of work, resources, and political space between the genders. On the environmental front it points to the need not only to transform notions about nature, but also to grapple with the material factors (economic, institutional, etc.) which determine how people interact with nature.

To move from being the main victims of environmental degradation to being effective agents of environmental regeneration, poor women will thus need to overcome not just disabling gender ideology, but social and political barriers. They will also have to contend with the pre-existing advantages that men as a gender (albeit not all men as individuals) enjoy, in terms of greater access to economic resources and public decision-making forums.

ON THE PROCESS OF CHANGE

Representations of the past seldom remain just that. They inform prescriptions for the future, either directly or indirectly. In the Indian context, representation and prescription have been explicitly linked by a number of scholars and activists in calls to revive or replicate traditional practices and institutions. As shown in this study, this approach can prove deeply problematic, since traditional understandings of family, community, and institutional interactions were not universally based on the idea of social equality, even less of gender equality. Although a study of past community institutions can provide lessons on a number of counts (for example, forms of co-operation, and norms of trust and reciprocity) typically they are not the best models for furthering equality along class, caste, and especially gender lines. In fact the uncritical preservation or revival of such institutions can further entrench such inequalities.

Moreover, even if the past does not serve as an explicit model, embedded inequalities can persist by virtue of being unchallenged. The examples analysed here provide early warnings that this is indeed happening in many cases. Most environmental institutions that have emerged in recent decades have made few significant breaks from earlier traditions in terms of gender relations. As a result, we are in danger not only of replicating old gender biases, but of creating new inequities in institutions, property rights, and social relations. To this, a number of environmental thinkers are contributing. Ironically, this includes not just those for whom gender is of peripheral concern but also many who claim it as their central concern.

Typically the work of environmentalists advocating community participation today is not informed by a gender perspective. Two influential thinkers, Madhav Gadgil and Ramachandra Guha, for instance, devote their 1995 book *Ecology and Equity* specifically to the connections between these two concerns, yet pay little attention to gender equity. Hence while they recognise that women's formal participation in forest protection groups is the exception rather than the rule, they still assume that 'as primary gatherers and collectors of forest produce, women stand to gain most from forest protection and regeneration'.[113] The possibility that women might be barred from collection by formal male committees, or that the forest produce generated might be appropriated solely or mostly by the male members, is not considered. In fact the authors endorse the forest protection committees of West Bengal (most of which we noted were gender exclusionary and inequitable) as 'a perfect vindication of the core message of [the] book, the need to blend ecology and equity'.[114] Their otherwise compelling vision for the future, which seeks to synthesize Gandhism (on restraining consumption and empowering village communities), liberal capitalism (on democratic institutions and publicly accountable private enterprises), and Marxism (on equity),[115] remains uncontaminated by feminism!

Others more cognizant of women's concerns still stop short of incorporating a gender perspective. For instance, Agarwal and Narain in their pioneering monograph *Towards Green Villages*, unequivocally state that 'it is absolutely vital that women play an important role in the affairs of village communities'.[116] But even their concern appears to stem more from considerations of efficiency, than of gender equality. They note: 'women's participation will make a crucial difference for ecological regeneration programmes'. Why? Because women are the 'fuel, fodder and water carriers' and therefore 'despite the extraordinary work burden that hill women have to bear, the members of the Mahila Mangal Dals [women's groups] organized by the Chipko Movement *willingly* find the time to take on the extra burden of planting and caring for trees and grasslands'.[117] The need to reduce women's excessive work burden, while giving them greater claims in resources, receives no mention here. Rather women get viewed instrumentally. This highlights the importance of monitoring not just whether women are taken into account, but *in what ways* they are taken into account.

This appears especially necessary, given that women's role in ecological regeneration is beginning to receive some recognition in global fora, but, due largely to ecofeminist advocacy, the ground for this recognition is commonly the view that women have a special way of knowing and nurturing nature. Braidotti *et al.* note that Shiva has been particularly influential in shaping thinking on women and the environment among Northern NGOs, and Jackson observes that 'ecofeminist approaches have colonized the views of development agencies'.[118] Under this influence, 'the idea of women's privileged position in environmental management and their closer connection with nature' is 'embraced wholeheartedly' by many,[119] at times even being expressed in ecofeminist metaphors of women 'healing' or 'reweaving' the world. This influence has also extended to global agendas, such as that drawn up at the 'World Women's Congress for a Healthy Planet' in 1991 and spelt out in *Women's Action Agenda 21*.[120] Although this document also talks of factors such as women having rights in resources, this gets obscured in the overarching message that 'our wounded planet needs [the] healing touch of women'. Hence what gets picked up by policy advocates is the idea of women's naturalized roles, not rights.

Maurice Strong (Secretary General of the United Nations Conference on Environment and Development 1992), for instance, in his remarks to the World Women's Congress, reiterated what he understood were the central messages of the Congress, namely 'it is time for women to mother Earth'; and that 'women have a special relationship with nature'. He went on to emphasize the need to 'generate global awareness about the important role of women in promoting sustainable development'.[121] All this highlights the trap of the ecofeminist position, since a recognition of women's special ability to 'heal nature' can easily translate into schemes which increase women's work burden, without any assurance of a greater share in resources, or of men sharing women's workloads.

German ecofeminist Maria Mies and Vandana Shiva in their recent offering, *Ecofeminism*, concede (albeit in passing) the need to change the gender division of labour toward a greater sharing of domestic and subsistence work by men, but say little about the means by which this might be achieved. It is doubtful that this can happen merely by calling upon men to 'redefine their identity' and to 'share unpaid subsistence work: in the household, with children, with the old and sick'.[122] Nor is it apparent how the rural women whom Shiva praises for being 'not owners of their own bodies or of the earth, but [who] cooperate with their bodies and with the earth in order "to let grow and to make grow"',[123] can change a long-entrenched division of labour in their own favour. In fact, in romanticizing subsistence economies and prescribing their revival in various ways, as Mies and Shiva (and some 'new traditionalists') are doing, there is a real risk of further entrenching women in unremitting, undervalued labour.

Basically, therefore, while most mainstream environmental discourses and interventions neglect gender concerns, most ecofeminist writings tend to essentialize them, and neglect *the process* by which these concerns can be addressed effectively.

The analysis in this article suggests that if environmental movements and institutions are to become more gender sensitive and inclusive, women will need to negotiate this both from within these initiatives and from an independent position of strength outside them. If environmental thinking is to incorporate a gender perspective, that too will need to be negotiated. As noted, women's subordinate position existed long before there was an observable environmental crisis, and greening does not appear impossible without women's emancipation. To assume that the one is organically linked to the other appears unrealistic and unduly self-limiting.

Women's negotiating strength in relation to environmental concerns would be enhanced by simultaneous struggles to change gender relations not just in the context of the environment but more fundamentally—in particular, to change the gender division of labour, of property, and of political power. While the specific factors that could bring about these changes need more probing and cannot be detailed here, the *process* of change can be conceptualized. I would suggest that changes in these elements would depend on women's ability to 'bargain' for a better deal within the household, as well as with the community, the market, and the State.[124]

The idea that market relations are characterized by forms of bargaining is a familiar one, but a conceptual shift is needed to recognize intra-household interactions too as forms of bargaining. The bargaining approach (elaborated variously by some economists and anthropologists in recent years), can provide an important insight into the process by which gender disadvantages are constituted and contested within the family. In this approach, household dynamics are seen to involve both co-operation and conflict, and the allocation of resources, tasks, and so on, are seen to result from the differential bargaining power of family members. Gender and age are two major sources of such differentials. Women in relation to men (and children in relation to adults) typically have lower bargaining power. It is notable that bargaining power is revealed not only in explicit negotiation but also implicitly. For example, the fact that men can often get a favourable outcome (such as sisters forfeiting their property shares in favour of brothers in India) without overt negotiation, suggests men's considerable implicit bargaining strength.

The bargaining approach, or 'bargaining as process', represents an important theoretical shift from the unitary concept of the household that has long dominated economic and social analyses and policy. Stated very broadly, this characterizes the household as an undifferentiated unit in which members share common preferences and interests, pool incomes, and an altruistic household head ensures that resources are allocated equitably among the members. Despite substantial evidence of intra-household gender inequalities and of differences in interests and preferences among members, the unitary household model continues to be highly influential. This is complemented by social perceptions that men are the sole or primary breadwinners and women the dependants or supplementary workers. Hence, except in households without adult men, male members are still seen as the appropriate claimants in transfers of important resources such as land to families, or for vesting decision-making powers over communal resources such as local commons and forests. A shift from a unitary to a bargaining approach could prove critical for planning effective interventions to promote gender equity within households and so help transform families into more women-supportive institutions.

A similar shift is needed in conceptualizing communities, which, like households, are neither unitary nor ungendered.[125] Hence while decentralization and the strengthening of community control over resources would empower local groups, this can also strengthen local pockets of power, including patriarchal power. Here support from State institutions, NGOs, and political formations outside the local power nexus would prove important for strengthening women's bargaining power, in relation to the community and the family.

It needs emphasis here that the idea of strengthening women's bargaining power places a premium on increasing women's independence and autonomy *vis-à-vis* the family and community. This does not imply, however, as Mies[126] suggests, 'severing all communal relations'.[126] In fact it is necessary precisely to enable women to get a better deal *within* the family and community, so that both institutions might emerge as more egalitarian. Mies' claim on behalf of 'Third World Women' that the idea of an independent, autonomous 'female individual' is 'not attractive' to village women, is in fact contrary to what many Third World rural women themselves indicate when, for instance, they ask for independent and not joint shares in forest protection benefits, or for independent and not joint land titles with husbands.[127] Mies poses false alternatives in assuming that independence and autonomy necessarily imply isolation from family and community.

Basically, for transforming the relationship between women and men and between people and nature, we need to enhance the bargaining power of women in relation to men, and of those seeking to protect the environment in relation to those causing its destruction. At the most general level, three interlinked aspects are likely to be especially important in determining women's bargaining power: (i) women's independent economic and legal status; (ii) the external support (economic, social and political) they receive from kin and friends, as well as from the State and gender-progressive groups;[128] and (iii) gender ideology (gendered norms and perceptions about men's and women's appropriate roles, rights, abilities, etc.).[129] On the one hand, these aspects are themselves in effect the result of past bargaining outcomes. On the other hand, they impinge in different ways on women's future ability to change the gender division of labour, property, and political power. Although the importance of particular factors within each category would vary by context,[130] one factor which appears important in most contexts is support from gender-progressive organizations, especially women's organizations.

In terms of public voice, for instance, we had noted that within the larger picture of women's exclusion from decision-making in the community forest management institutions, there are pockets of substantial participation, even of all-women protection committees. This is usually where there is a gender-progressive organization, often a women's organization. Women belonging to such organizations (even those unrelated to forest protection) are found to be more assertive in joining protection committees (thus creating a critical mass), to have greater self-confidence and awareness of their rights, and to be more vocal in mixed forums.[131] In the Rajasthan example mentioned earlier, and in several other cases, women's organizations have also helped village women respond collectively to their fuel and fodder crises.[132]

Again, at a more macro-level, women's political participation received a push when, in 1992, pressure from women's groups led to the Seventy-third Constitutional Amendment in India, under which one-third of the seats in village and block level elected bodies are now reserved for women.[133] Although women's presence alone cannot guarantee that their interests, especially poor women's interests, will be upheld in these bodies, it does provide the potential for furthering that goal.

Indian women's organizations have also helped negotiate with the State and with the community (albeit with varying degrees of success) for more gender-just property laws and for women's greater access to economic resources.[134] Changing the gender division of labour is of course the most difficult. But women who are economically independent and have a political voice would also be in a better position to negotiate some change on this count.

What most women's groups in India have so far paid inadequate attention to, however, is environmental issues as issues of central feminist concern. An important focus of future effort on this count needs to be on institutions for environmental change and management. As argued in this study, the philosophical and ethical principles on which new institutions for environmental change are structured will require some breaks with the past. They will require new building blocks, a central one being gender equity. If this could be ensured, perhaps then it could be argued with greater justification that there is substantial and concrete congruity, and not just a presumed one, in the goals of the women's movement and the environmental movement.

Notes

1. See among others M. Poffenberger, P. Walpole, E. D'Silva, K. Lawrence and A. Khare (1997) 'Linking Government Policies and Programs with Community Resource Management Systems: What is Working and What is Not', Research Network Report No. 9, A Synthesis Report of the Fifth Asia Forest Network Meeting held at Surajkund, India, Dec. 1996; J. M. Baland and J. P. Platteau, *Halting Degradation of Natural Resources: Is There a Role for Rural Communities?* (Oxford: Clarendon Press, 1996); and F. Berkes (ed.), *Common Property Resources: Ecology and Community Based Sustainable Development* (London: Belhaven Press, 1989).
2. Under 'ecofeminism' I do not include the largely descriptive literature on women and the environment. As formulated theoretically, the central strands of ecofeminism (for all their diversity) share some basic premises, which that literature does not share. There has been a tendency among some

scholars in recent years to include under the banner of 'ecofeminism' virtually any study or movement that deals with women and the environment (e.g. Gaard and Gruen). I believe this is a misrepresentation. G. Gaard and L. Gruen, 'Ecofeminism: Toward Global Justice and Planetary Health', *Society and Nature: The International Journal of Political Economy* 2, No. 1 (1993).

3. See, for example, R. Braidotti, E. Charkiewicz, S. Hausie, and S. Wieringa, *Women, the Environment and Sustainable Development: Towards a Theoretical Synthesis* (London: Zed Books, 1994); C. Jackson 'Women/Nature or Gender/History? A Critique of Ecofeminist "Development"', *The Journal of Peasant Studies* 20 (1993), 389–419; and WEDO, *World Women's Congress for a Healthy Planet, Official Report, including Women's Action Agenda 21, and Findings of the Tribunal* (Women's Environment and Development Organization, New York, 1992).
4. N.S. Jodha, 'Common Property Resources and the Rural Poor', *Economic and Political Weekly* 21 (1986), 1169–81.
5. On property rights, see for example, B. Agarwal, *A Field of One's Own: Gender and Land Rights in South Asia* (Cambridge: Cambridge University Press, 1994). On employment, see B. Agarwal, 'Disinherited Peasants, Disadvantaged Workers: A Gender Perspective on Land and Livelihood', *Economic and Political Weekly,* 28 March, Review of Agriculture, 33 (1998, No. 13), A2–14; K. Bardhan, 'Rural Employment. Wages and Labour Markets in India: A Survey of Research', *Economic and Political Weekly* 2, (1977, No. 26) A34–A18; 12 (No. 27), 1062–74; and 12 (No. 28) 1101–18; and G.K. Chadha, 'Gender differences in Some Aspects of Non-farm Employment in Rural India', paper presented at the IEG-ISLE Seminar on 'Gender and Employment in India: Trends, Patterns and Policy Implications', Institute of Economic Growth, Delhi, 11 December, 1996.
6. See especially R. Kaur, 'Women in Forestry in India', World Bank, Women in Development, Working Paper WPS 714, Washington, DC, 1991; B. Agarwal 'Gender, Environment and Poverty Interlinks: Regional Variations and Temporal Shifts in Rural India 1971–1991', *World Development* 25 (1997), 23–52; and B. Agarwal, 'Environmental Action, Gender Equity, and Women's Participation', *Development and Change* (1997), 1–44.
7. See for example B. Agarwal, 'Women, Poverty and Agricultural Growth in India', *The Journal of Peasant Studies* 13 (1986), 165–220; B. Harriss, 'The Intrafamily Distribution of Hunger in South Asia', in J. Drèze and A. K. Sen (eds.), *The Political Economy of Hunger* (Oxford: Clarendon Press, 1990), 351–424; and J. Drèze and A. K. Sen, *Hunger and Public Action* (Oxford: Clarendon Press, 1989).
8. See also Agarwal, 'Gender, Environment and Poverty Interlinks'.
9. See Agarwal, *A Field of One's Own*, 49.
10. Jodha, 'Common Property Resources'.
11. Detailed in B. Agarwal, *Cold Hearths and Barren Slopes: The Woodfuel Crisis in the Third World* (London: Zed Books; Delhi: Allied Publishers, 1986) and Agarwal, 'Gender, Environment and Poverty Interlinks'.
12. B. Agarwal, 'The Gender and Environment Debate: Lessons from India', *Feminist Studies* 18 (1992), 119–58, and 'Gender, Environment and Poverty Interlinks'.

13. Although there is little to support romanticized views such as Vandana Shiva's that rural women everywhere are the main possessors of knowledge about biodiversity, there is substantial evidence of location and use-related gender-specific knowledge. V. Shiva *Staying Alive: Women, Ecology and Survival* (London: Zed Books, 1988); V. Shiva 'Women's Indigenous Knowledge and Biodiversity Conservation', special issue on 'Indigenous Vision: People of India's Attitudes to the Environment', *India International Quarterly* 19 (1992), 205–14. On gender-specific knowledge, see K. K. Gaul, Negotiated Positions and Shifting Terrains: Apprehension of Forest Resources in the Western Himalaya, doctoral dissertation, Department of Anthropology, University of Massachusetts, Amherst, 1994; M. Chen, 'Women and Wasteland Development in India: An Issue Paper', in A. Singh and N. Burra (eds.), *Women and Wasteland Development in India* (Delhi: Sage Publishers, 1993), 21–90; S. Pandey, 'Women in Hattidunde Forest Management in Dhading District, Nepal', MPE Series No. 9, International Center for Integrated Mountain Development (ICIMOD), Kathmandu, Nepal, 1990; and B. Agarwal, 'Social Security and the Family: Coping with Seasonality and Calamity in Rural India', *Journal of Peasant Studies* 17 (1990), 341–412.
14. Agarwal, *Cold Hearths and Barren Slopes.*
15. For a useful discussion of the theoretical issues, see especially Baland and Platteau, *Halting Degradation.* On more country-specific discussion, for India, see in addition, A. Agarwal and S. Narain, *Towards Green Villages,* Monograph, (Delhi: Center for Science and Environment, 1989); M. Gadgil, 'The Indian Heritage of a Conservation Ethic', in B. Allchin, E. R. Allchin and B. K. Thapar (eds.), *Conservation of the Indian Heritage* (New Delhi: Cosmo Publications, 1989), 13–22; M. Gadgil and P. Iyer, 'On the Diversification of Common Property Resource Use by the Indian Society', in F. Berkes (ed.) *Common Property Resources: Ecology and Community Based Sustainable Development* (London: Belhaven Press, 1989), 240–55; M. Gadgil and R. Guha, *This Fissured Land: An Ecological History of India* (Delhi: Oxford University Press, 1993); M. Gadgil and R. Guha, *Ecology and Equity* (New Delhi: Penguin Books, 1995); M. Poffenberger and B. McGean (eds.), *Village, Voices, Forest Choices: Joint Forest Management in India* (Delhi: Oxford University Press, 1996) and the substantial literature on 'joint forest management' (some reviewed in Agarwal, 'Environmental Action, Gender Equity'). For Nepal, see R.J. Fisher, 'Indigenous Systems of Common Property Forest Management', EAPI Working Paper No. 18, Environment and Policy Institute, East-West Center, Honolulu, III, 1989; J. G. Campbell and J. Denholm, and *Inspirations in Community Forestry.* Report of the Seminar on Himalayan Community Forestry, ICIMOD, Kathmandu, Nepal, 1–4 June, 1992.
16. In contrast, there has been considerable discussion on the possible impact of existing equal or unequal social relations on the success of institutional interventions (e.g. Bardhan, 1993; Seabright, 1997), but this discussion too does not cover gender inequality. P. Bardhan, 'Analytics of the Institutions of Informal Cooperation in Rural Development', *World Development* 21 (1993), 633–9; and P. Seabright, 'The Effect of Inequality on Collective Action', draft paper, Department of Applied Economics, University of Cambridge, 1997.
17. The few exceptions include M. Sarin, 'Regenerating India's Forest: Reconciling

Gender Equity and Joint Forest Management', *IDS Bulletin* 26 (1995), 83–91; Agarwal, 'Environmental Action, Gender Equity'; C. Britt, 'Out of the Wood? Local Institutions and Community Forest Management in two Central Himalayan Villages', draft monograph, Cornell University, Ithaca, NY, 1993; and some very recent writings on the Joint Forest Management Programme in India.

18. For an interesting theoretical exposition on this see, P. Seabright, 'Is Co-operation Habit-Forming?', in P. Dasgupta and K.-G. Maler (eds.), *The Environment and Emerging Development Issues* (Oxford: Clarendon Press, 1997), 283–307.
19. S. Sinha, S. Gururani and B. Greenberg, 'The "New Traditionalist" Discourse of Indian Environmentalism', *The Journal of Peasant Studies* 24 (1997), 65–99.
20. See also Gadgil, 'The Indian Heritage of a Conservation Ethic'; and Gadgil and Guha, *This Fissured Land.*
21. Gadgil, 'The Indian Heritage'; Agarwal and Narain, *Towards Green Villages.*
22. Gadgil, 'The Indian Heritage', 18.
23. See M. Rangarajan, 'Imperial Agendas and India's Forests: The Early History of Indian Forestry, 1800–1878', *The Indian Economic and Social History Review* 31 (1994, No 2); S. Guha, 'Kings, Commoners and the Commons: People and Environments in Western India: 1600–1900', mimeo, Nehru Memorial Museum and Library, New Delhi, 1995; B. Greenberg, 'Sustainable Futures and Romantic Pasts: Political Ecology and Environmental History in North India', paper presented at the Institute of Economic Growth, University of Delhi, 6 February, 1996; and R. Grove, 'Conserving Eden: The (European) East India Companies and their Environmental Policies on St. Helena, Mauritius and in Western India: 1660 to 1854', *Comparative Study of Society and History* 35 (1993), 318–35. Greenberg also cites detailed studies which indicate very significant changes, largely due to human intervention, in the local vegetation of Kashmir and Himachal Pradesh, some going as far back as 1200 years or more.
24. There is substantial evidence of such exploitation. In feudal Bengal, for example, the sharecropper's daughters and daughters-in-law were seen by the landlord as his own property, to be summoned to his house at will. See, A. Cooper, *Sharecropping and Sharecroppers: Struggles in Bengal: 1930–1950* (Calcutta: K. Bagchi & Co, 1988), 102. Similarly, during the Nizam of Hyderabad's feudal rule, Lalita *et al.* note: 'Everything the men suffered under the system, the women suffered twice over. If the [upper-caste] landlord fancied a woman, she was taken. When she got married, it was the prerogative of the landlord to sleep with her on the first night.' (*We Were Making History: Life Stories of Women in the Telangana People's Struggle* (Delhi: Kali for Women, 1989).)
25. Gadgil and Guha, *This Fissured Land.*
26. Fisher ('Indigenous Systems of Common Property') makes an important conceptual point that typically community institutions for forest management are likely to emerge from an experience of scarcity, and suggests that in Nepal most would date from the 1950s. Also see S. Guha ('Kings, Commoners') on India's environmental situation during 1600–1900, and for a nuanced environmental history of India under British colonialism see

R. Grove, *Green Imperialism: Colonial Expansion. Tropical Island Edens and the Origins of Environmentalism: 1600–1860* (Delhi: Oxford University Press, 1995).

27. Gadgil and Iyer, 'On the Diversification of Common Property'.
28. Ibid., 253, emphasis mine.
29. Gadgil and Guha, *Ecology and Equity*, 188–9.
30. Fisher, 'Indigenous Systems of Common Property'.
31. Detailed in Agarwal, 'The Gender and Environment Debate'.
32. Some ecofeminists suggest that women are not just conceptualized as closer to nature than men, they are in fact closer to nature. Shiva (*Staying Alive*), for instance, sees women as 'embedded in nature'. She and some others also suggest that women's closeness with nature can affirm more nurturing and caring values both between humans and between human and non-human nature. Shiva traces this closeness both to biology and to historical and cultural factors; some others (A.K. Saleh, 'Deeper than Deep Ecology: The Eco-Feminist Connection', *Environmental Ethics*, 16 (Winter 1984), 339–45) place primary emphasis on women's biology.
33. The arguments highlighted above are fairly characteristic of ecofeminist formulations, even given their differences on other counts. See, for example, Y. King, 'Feminism and the Revolt', *Heresies*, No. 13 (1981), 12–16; Y. King, 'The Ecology of Feminism and the Feminism of Ecology', in J. Plant (ed.), *Healing the Wounds: The Promise of Ecofeminism* (Philadelphia, PA: New Society Publishers, 1989); Saleh, 'Deeper than Deep Ecology'; C. Merchant, 1980, *The Death of Nature: Women, Ecology and the Scientific Revolution* (San Francisco, CA: Harper & Row); C. Merchant, 1990, 'Ecofeminism and Feminist Theory', in I. Diamond and G. Orenstein (eds.), *Reweaving the World: The Emergence of Ecofeminism* (San Francisco: Sierra Club Books, 1990); S. Griffin, *Women and Nature: The Roaring Within Her* (New York: Harper and Row, 1978); Shiva, *Staying Alive*; Introduction in M. Mies, V. Shiva, *Ecofeminism* (Delhi: Kali for Women, 1993); and various articles in J. Plant (ed.), *Healing the Wounds: Feminism, Ecology and the Nature/Culture Dualism.* (Philadelphia, PA: New Society Publishers, 1989), and Diamond and Orenstein, *Reweaving the World.* For further discussions on some of the central arguments on which ecofeminists agree, see also, J. K. Warren and J. Cheney, 'Ecological Feminism and Ecosystem Ecology', *Hypatia* (Spring 1991), 179–97; V. Davion, 'Is Feminism Feminist?', in K. J. Warren (ed.), *Ecological Feminism* (London and New York: Routledge, 1994), 8–28; and J. Birkeland, 'Ecofeminism: Linking Theory and Practice', in G. Gaard (ed.), *Ecofeminism: Women, Animals, Nature* (Philadelphia: Temple University Press, 1993). While most generalise about all women, Shiva distinguishes between Third world women and the rest, but does not differentiate between women by class, caste, race, or ecological location.
34. Agarwal, 'The Gender and Environment Debate'.
35. See, for example J. Biehl, *Rethinking Ecofeminist Politics* (Boston South End Press, 1991); J. Chency, 'Ecofeminism and Deep Ecology', *Environmental Ethics*, 9 (1987), 115–45; Jackson, 'Women/Nature or Gender/History?'; M. Leach and C. Green, 'Gender and Environmental History: From Representations of Women and Nature to Gender Analysis of Ecology and Politics', *Environment and History*, 3(3) (1997), 343–70; Li Huey-li, 'A Cross-cultural Critique

of Ecofeminism', in G. Gaard (ed.), *Ecofeminism: Women, Animals, Nature* (Philadelphia, PA: Temple University Press, 1993), 272–94; H. Longino, Book Review, *Environmental Ethics*, 3 (Winter 1981), 365–9; and M.E. Zimmerman, 'Feminism, Deep Ecology and Environmental Ethics', *Environmental Ethics*, 9 (Spring 1987), 21–44. For reasons not entirely clear, Li ends with a polemical statement supporting ecofeminism, in contradiction of her strong criticisms of ecofeminism in the body of her paper. Also Li, Birkeland ('Ecofeminism'), and several others who identify particular problems with Western ecofeminism ignore similar problems in non-Western ecofeminist arguments, most notably in the work of Shiva (*Staying Alive*). For an important critique of Shiva's views on science, see M. Nanda, 'Is Modern Science a Western Patriarchal Myth? A Critique of the Populist Orthodoxy', *Social Science Bulletin* 11 (1991), 32–60. See also Davion ('Is Feminism Feminist') and S. Sinha, S. Gururani and B. Greenberg, 'The "New Traditionalist" Discourse of Indian Environmentalism', *Journal of Peasant Studies* 24 (April 1997), 65–99.

36. Merchant, *The Death of Nature.*
37. Shiva, *Staying Alive.*
38. Merchant, *The Death of Nature*, 2–3.
39. Ibid., xx, emphasis mine.
40. A. L. Erickson, *Women and Property in Early Modern England* (London: Routledge, 1995), 3.
41. Merchant, *The Death of Nature*, 150–1; also Merchant, 'Ecofeminism and Feminist Theory'.
42. Shiva, *Staying Alive.*
43. Ibid., 42.
44. Sinha *et al.*, 'The "New Traditionalist" Discourse', include Shiva among the 'new traditionalists'. I feel it is necessary to distinguish between the two, both because the central point of feminist discourse, namely the relationship between women and nature, is not shared by the new traditionalists, and the meeting points of many ecofeminists and the new traditionalists (for example, the romanticization of certain historical periods and of subsistence production) themselves need to be noted, as indicated at various points in the paper.
45. Shiva, *Staying Alive*, 42.
46. Ibid., 42.
47. The name of the god Śiva can also be spelt as Shiva, but Śiva is used here to preclude confusion with Vandana Shiva's name.
48. Shiva, *Staying Alive*, 39.
49. K. Kapadia, *Siva and Her Sisters: Gender, Caste and Class in Rural South Asia* (Boulder, CO: Westview Press, 1995), 159.
50. N. N. Battacharyya, *History of Sakta Religion* (New Delhi: Munshiram Manoharlal, 1996), 141.
51. Ibid.
52. Lynne E. Gatwood, *Devi and the Spouse Goddess: Women, Sexuality and Marriage in India* (Delhi: Manohar Publications, 1985), 19.
53. Battacharyya, *History of Sakta Religion*; Gatwood, *Devi and the Spouse Goddess.*
54. Battacharyya, *History of Sakta Religion.*
55. In the Tamil Nadu village Kapadia studied, for instance, while the Brahmins give primacy to the Śiva-Shakti tradition, the non-Brahmins give primacy to

the Great Goddess Mariyammam, who is often unmarried, 'complete' (i.e. she possesses both wisdom and power), and is the Supreme Deity herself. Wadley, based on her fieldwork in Uttar Pradesh in notes, 'the Pantheon of the village of Karimpur is potentially enormous and without boundaries'. S. S. Wadley, *Shakti: Power in the Conceptual Structure of Karimpur Religion* (University of Chicago Studies in Anthropology), Department of Anthropology, University of Chicago. Also, as G.-D. Sontheimer observes in *Pastoral Deities in Western India* (New York: Oxford University Press, 1989), even a single deity can be infused with a range of co-existing and layered meanings, some old, others newly acquired. See also N. Sundar's thoughtful discussion in *Sabalterns and Sovereigns: An Anthropological History of Bastar, 1854–1996* (Delhi: Oxford University Press, 1997); and Hunter's description of varying religious beliefs and forms of Śiva worship among different communities in mid-nineteenth-century Bengal, in W. W. Hunter *The Annals of Rural Bengal* (Calcutta: R. K. Maitra, 11B Chowringhee Terrace, 1868, reprinted in 1965).

56. For an insightful discussion of how folk songs, folklore, proverbs, etc., can reveal and reinforce unequal gender ideology, with examples from the colonial period, see especially P. Chowdhry, *The Veiled Women: Shifting Gender Equations in Rural Haryana, 1880–1990* (Delhi: Oxford University Press, 1994).
57. Among other practices which impinged significantly on women's social situation are child marriage, the treatment of widows and female infanticide. See, for example, various essays in K. Sangari and S. Vaid (eds.), *Recasting Women: Essays in Colonial History* (Delhi: Kali for Women, 1989); these also illuminate how during the colonial period Indian women's position in the pre-colonial period (including ancient India) was glorified by some of the nationalists, and by some others. See also U. Chakravarti, 'Of Dasas and Karmakaras: Servile Labour in Ancient India', in U. Patnaik and M. Dingwaney (eds.), *Chains of Servitude: Bondage and Slavery in India* (Madras: Sangam Books, 1985), 35–75; U. Chakravarti, 'Wifehood, Widowhood, and Adultery: Female Sexuality, Surveillance and the State in 18th Century Maharashtra', *Contributions to Indian Sociology* 29 (1995), 3–22.
58. See among others, S. Saxena, R. Prasad and V. Joshi, 'Time Allocation and Fuel Usage in Three Villages of the Garhwal Himalaya, India', *Mountain Research and Development* 15 (1995), 57–67; S. Dasgupta and A. K. Maiti, *The Rural Energy Crisis, Poverty and Women's Roles in Five Indian Villages.* Technical Cooperation Report, International Labour Office, Geneva, 1986; L. Sen 'Class and Gender in Work Time Allocation', *Economic and Political Weekly* 23 (1988), 1702–6; A. H. Akram-Lodhi, 'You are Not Excused from Cooking: Peasants and the Gender Division of Labour in Pakistan', *Feminist Economics* (Summer, 1996), 87–105.
59. On women's work among various castes and tribes in southern India, see, for example, F. Buchanan, *A Journey from Madras through the Countries of Mysore, Canara, and Malabar,* Vol. II (London: Black, Parry and Kingsbury, 1807) and E. Thurston and K. Rangachari, *Castes and Tribes of Southern India* (Madras: Government Press, 1909). On Assam and other parts of the northeast, see Allen *et al.*, *Gazeteer of Bengal and North East India*; and Chowdhry, *The Veiled Women* on north-west India. See also V. Ramaswamy,

'Women and Farm Work in Tamil Folk Songs', *Social Scientist* 21 (1993), 113–29, for descriptions of peasant women's workloads in Tamil folksongs in the early Christian era.

60 Buchanan, 311.

61. B. C. Allen, E. A. Gait, C. G. H. Allen and H. F. Howard, *Gazetteer of Bengal and North East India* (reprinted in 1979) (Delhi: Mittal Publication, 1906).

62. Chowdhry, *The Veiled Woman.*

63. Shiva, *Staying Alive,* 220.

64. Agarwal, 'Bargaining and Gender Relations: Within and Beyond the Household', *Feminist Economics,* 3 (1997), 1–51; A. K. Sen, 'Gender and Cooperative Conflicts', in I. Tinker (ed.), *Persistent Inequalities: Women and World Development* (New York: Oxford University Press, 1990).

65. Agarwal, *A Field of One's Own.*

66. Ibid.

67. Ibid.

68. *Matrilineal*: ancestral property passes through the female line. *Bilateral*: ancestral property passes to and through both sons and daughters. *Patrilineal*: ancestral property passes through the male line.

69. See Agarwal, *A Field of One's Own*; P. Viegas and G. Menon, 'Forest Protection Committees of West Bengal: Role and Participation of Women', paper prepared for the ILO Workshop on 'Women and Wasteland Development', International Labour Organization, New Delhi, 9–11 January 1991; A. Baviskar, 'Tribal Politics and Discourses of Environmentalism', *Contributions to Indian Sociology* 31 (No. 2, 1997); and G. Kelkar and D. Nathan, *Gender and Tribe: Women, Land and Forests in Jharkhand* (London: Zed Books/New Delhi: Kali for Women, 1991).

70. Agarwal, *A Field of One's Own.*

71. Agarwal, *A Field of One's Own.*

72. E.g., Birkeland, 'Ecofeminism: Linking Theory and Practice'; Shiva, *Staying Alive.*

73. For a more detailed exposition of changes in women's property rights during the colonial and post-colonial period, see Agarwal, *A Field of One's Own.*

74. For details, see B. Agarwal, 'Gender, Resistance and Land: Interlinked Struggles Over Resources and Meanings in South Asia', *Journal of Peasant Studies* 22 (1994), 81–125.

75. Figures for India are indicative: in the judiciary, in 1985, women constituted only 3.6 per cent of advocates registered with the state bar councils, and 2.8 per cent of High Court and Supreme Court judges. In the administration, in 1987, only 7.4 per cent of the officers in the central government services taken together were women. And in the legislature in 1984, only 8.0 per cent of the elected candidates in the Lok Sabha were women. See Government of India, *Women in India: A Statistical Profile – 1988* (New Delhi: Ministry of Human Resource Development).

76. Merchant, *The Death of Nature,* xix.

77. Shiva, *Staying Alive,* 47

78. See Agarwal, *A Field of One's Own* for examples from across South Asia.

79. Many incorrectly conflate passivity and victimhood, and assume that the absence of passivity (equated with an assertion of agency) implies the presence of victimhood. For instance Eduards (1994) notes that it is possible

for all human beings 'to be an agent rather than a passive being, a victim'. But as O'Hanlon points out: 'the mere celebration of what look like autonomous defiances may do grave disservice to those who refuse to conform . . . , in underestimating the actual weight and harsh social cost entailed in contesting authority'. See M. L. Edwards, 'Women's Agency and Collective Action', Women's Studies International Forum 17 (1994), 181–6; R. O'Hanlon, in D. Haynes and G. Prakash (eds.), *Contesting Power: Resistance and Everyday Social Relations in India* (Delhi: Oxford University Press, 1991), 104.

80. In A. K. Sen, 'Well-Being, Agency and Freedom: The Dewey Lectures 1984', *The Journal of Philosophy* 82 (1985), 169–221, 203, 'agency freedom' is defined as that which 'the person is free to do and achieve in pursuit of whatever goals or values he or she regards as important'. There can, however, be restrictions on a person's 'agency freedom', including restrictions imposed by social norms and values. Equally, as Sen also points out ('Well-Being, Agency and Freedom' and 'Gender and Cooperative Conflicts'), the exercise of agency by women need not always enhance their well-being. They may choose to exercise agency to improve the well-being of the family or community, even if it reduces their own well-being. Also see U. Butalia, 'Community, State and Gender: On Women's Agency During Partition', *Economic and Political Weekly* 28 (1993), WS12–WS24., for examples which raise particularly complex questions in this regard.
81. Agarwal, *A Field of One's Own*, and Agarwal, 'Gender, Resistance and Land'.
82. Lalita *et al.*, *We Were Making History*.
83. Cited in Lalita *et al.*, *We Were Making History*, 73.
84. Lalita *et al.*, *We Were Making History*, 18.
85. Sharma *et al.*, 'Women in Struggle'; S. Jain, 'Women and People's Ecological Movement: A Case Study of Women's Role in the Chipko Movement in Uttar Pradesh', *Economic and Political Weekly* (1984), 1788–94.
86. Agarwal, 'Environmental Action, Gender Equity and Women's Participation'.
87. Agarwal, 'Environmental Action, Gender Equity and Women's Participation'; G. Raju, R. Vaghela and M. S. Raju, *Development of People's Institutions for Management of Forests* (Ahmedabad: VIKSAT, 1993).
88. S. B. Roy, R. Mukerjee and M. Chatterjee, 'Endogenous Development, Gender Role in Participatory Forest Management', Indian Institute of Bio-Social Research and Development, Calcutta, 1992.
89. U. Narain, 'Women's Involvement in Joint Forest Management: Analyzing the Issues', draft paper, Ford Foundation, New Delhi, 1994.
90. Sarin, 'Regenerating India's Forests'.
91. Sarin, 'Regenerating India's Forests'; Agarwal, 'Environmental Action, Gender Equity and Women's Participation'.
92. M. K. Shah and P. Shah, 'Gender, Environment and Livelihood Security: An Alternative Viewpoint from India', *IDS Bulletin* 26 (1995), 75–82.
93. N. Singh and K. Kumar, 'Community Initiatives to Protect and Manage Forests in Balangir and Sambalpur Districts', SIDA, New Delhi, 1993.
94. P. Guhathakurta and K. S. Bhatia, 'A Case Study on Gender and Forest Resources in West Bengal', World Bank, Delhi, 16 June 1992.
95. For India, see J. Mencher, 'Women's Work and Poverty: Women's Contribution to Household Maintenance in Two Regions of South India', in D. Dwyer and J. Bruce (eds.), *A Home Divided: Women and Income Control*

in the Third World (Stanford: Stanford University Press, 1989); and H. Noponen, 'The Dynamics of Work and Survival for the Urban Poor: A Gender Analysis of Panel Data from Madras', *Development and Change* (1995), 233–60. See also M. Roldan, 'Renegotiating the Marital Contract: Intrahousehold Patterns of Money Allocation and Women's Subordination Among Domestic Outworkers in Mexico City', in Dwyer and Bruce, *A Home Divided*, 229–47, for Mexico. For some other countries, see R. L. Blumberg, 'Income Under Female vs. Male Control: Hypotheses from a Theory of Gender Stratification and Data from the Third World', in R. L. Blumberg (ed.), *Gender, Family and Economy The Triple Overlap* (Newbury Park, C. A. Sage Publications, 1991), 97–127.

96. Sarin, 'Regenerating India's Forests', 90.
97. Sarin, 'Regenerating India's Forests'.
98. Agarwal, 'Environmental Action, Gender Equity and Women's Participation'.
99. O. Mansingh, 'Community Organization and Ecological Restoration: An Analysis of Strategic Options for NGOs in the Central Himalaya, with particular reference to the Community Forestry Programme of the NGO Chirag', MA thesis in Rural Development. AFRAS, University of Sussex, 1991; Britt, 'Out of the Wood'; personal observation.
100. M. Correa, 'Gender and Joint Forest Planning and Management: A Research Study in Uttara Kannada District, Karnataka', mimeo, India Development Service, Dharwad, Karnataka, 1995; Guhathakurta and Bhatia, 'A Case Study on Gender and Forest Resources'.
101. S. B. Roy, *et al.*, 'Profile of Forest Protection Committees at Sarugarh Range, North Bengal', IBRAD Working Paper No. 16, Indian Institute of Bio-Social Research and Development, Calcutta, 1993, 15–16.
102. For a detailed discussion on the types of social restrictions faced by rural women, in different regions and contexts see Agarwal, *A Field of One's Own.*
103. Britt, 'Out of the Wood?', 18.
104. Britt, 'Out of the Wood?'; Correa, 'Gender and Joint Forest Planning'.
105. Cited in Britt, 'Out of the Wood?', 146.
106. Roy *et al.*, 'Profile of Forest Protection Committees'.
107. Personal observation in Gujarat and the Uttar Pradesh hills. See also, A. Sharma and A. Sinha, 'A Study of the common Property Resources in the Project Area of the Central Himalaya Rural Action Group', mimeo, Indian Institute of Forest Management, Bhopal, Madhya Pradesh; and Viegas and Menon, 'Forest Protection Committees of West Bengal'.
108. ISO/Swedforest, 'Forests, People and Protection: Case Studies of Voluntary Forest Protection by Communities in Orissa', Swedish International Development Agency (SIDA), New Delhi, 1993, 46.
109. M. Sarin, and C. Sharma, 'Experiments in the Field: The Case of PEDO in Rajasthan', in A. Singh and N. Burra (eds.), *Women and Wasteland Development in India* (Delhi: Sage Publishers, 1993), 122.
110. For instance, a woman grassroots activist in the region noted an increasing incidence of suicides among young women, due to growing work burdens and family tensions associated with ecological degradation. Women's long hours spent in collecting water, fodder, and fuel for domestic use caused tensions with their mothers-in-law (in whose youth forests were plentiful), and soil erosion compounded the difficulty of producing enough grain for

subsistence in a region of high male outmigration. S. Bahuguna, 'Women's Non-violent Power in the Chipko Movement', *Manushi*, No. 6 (July-August, 1980), 34–36.

111. Agarwal, 'The Gender and Environment Debate'.
112. In specific terms, in my formulation of feminist environmentalism, I suggest that 'women's and men's relationship with nature needs to be understood as rooted in their material reality, in their specific forms of interaction with the environment. Hence insofar as there is a gender and class (/caste/race) division of labour and distribution of property and power, gender and class (/caste/race) structure people's interactions with nature, and so structure the effects of environmental change on people and their responses to it . . . Ideological constructions such as of gender, of nature, and of the relationship between the two, may be seen as (interactively) a part of this structuring, but not the whole of it', (Agarwal, 'The Gender and Environment Debate', 126–7). For elaboration, see the original article.
113. Gadgil and Guha, *This Fissured Land*, 173.
114. Ibid., 189. West Bengal also virtually ignored women's claims in its otherwise significant land reform initiative—Operation Barga—in the late 1970s, and basically strengthened male rights in land (Agarwal, *A Field of One's Own*; J. Gupta, 'Land, Dowry, Labour: Women in the Changing Economy of Midnapur', *Social Scientist* 21 (1993), 74–90).
115. They uncritically draw upon Marxism for equity. But as a vast body of feminist writings shows, Marxism alone cannot illuminate the complexity of social inequities, especially gender inequities (see M. Barrett, *Women's Oppression Today: Problems in Marxist Feminist Analysis* (London: Verso, 1980) for a useful overview of the debate).
116. Agarwal and Narain, *Towards Green Villages*, 89.
117. Ibid., 26, my emphasis.
118. Braidotti *et al.*, *Women, the Environment and Sustainable Development*, 94; Jackson, 'Women/Nature or Gender/History?', 398.
119. Braidotti *et al.*, *Women, the Environment and Sustainable Development*, 95.
120. WEDO, *Women's Congress for a Healthy Planet.*
121. Ibid., 25.
122. Mies and Shiva, *Ecofeminism*, 319.
123. Shiva, *Staying Alive*, 43.
124. Agarwal, 'Bargaining and Gender Relations', elaborates on the concept of 'bargaining' in relation to gender in all four arenas, and on the factors likely to affect women's bargaining power. The paper also critically reviews other relevant literature.
125. Although the non-unitary nature of communities is often recognized in terms of caste, class, or religious differences, these are *household-level* characteristics that take little account of possible intra-household gender-based conflicts of interests.
126. In Mies and Shiva, *Ecofeminism*, 220.
127. Agarwal, *A Field of One's Own.*
128. I use the term 'gender-progressive' organizations for those groups whose activities are centrally or partially aimed at reducing gender inequities. This could include organizations with mixed (male and female) membership but with a specific gender focus in their activities, as well as women's groups

promoting gender-specific programmes. 'Gender-retrogressive' implies the opposite.

129. These elements are in turn interconnected—a change in one would impact on the others. Political power, for instance, might derive from mass mobilization and collective action, but it is also linked to a person's or a group's command over property. Similarly, shifts in ideas (including ideas about the gender division of labor, or about the link between people and nature) are not independent of who commands authority and political power and is thus able to influence the institutions (educational, religious, the media) through which ideologies justifying or challenging unequal social relationships are constructed and sustained.
130. In Agarwal, *A Field of One's Own*, I have discussed at length how women's command over property might be strengthened.
131. Agarwal, 'Environmental Action, Gender Equity and Women's Participation'.
132. See, especially, case studies in A. Singh and N. Burra (eds.), *Women and Wasteland Development in India* (New Delhi: Sage Publications, 1993).
133. The Seventy-Third Constitutional Amendment reserves for women one-third of all seats in the Panchayati Raj institutions (the village, block and district level bodies). Many women's groups are now seeking a similar reservation in Parliament, in the face of substantial opposition from many male parliamentarians.
134. See Agarwal, *A Field of One's Own*; and 'Disinherited Peasants, Disadvantaged Workers', for examples.

30 Difference, Diversity, Differentiation

Avtar Brah *

Black Feminism, White Feminism?

During the 1970s there was little serious and sustained mainstream academic engagement with issues such as the gendered exploitation of post-colonial labour in the British metropolis, racism within state policies and cultural practices, the radicalization of black and white subjectivity in the specific context of a period following the loss of Empire, and the particularities of black women's oppression within feminist theory and practice. This played an important part in the formation of black feminist organizations as distinct from the 'white' Women's Liberation Movement. These organizations emerged against the background of a deepening economic and political crisis and an increasing entrenchment of racism. The 1970s was a period when the Powellism of the 1960s came to suffuse the social fabric, and was gradually consolidated and transmuted into the Thatcherism of the 1980s. Black communities were involved in a wide variety of political activities throughout the decade. There were major industrial strikes, several led by women. The Black Trade Union Solidarity Movement was formed to deal with racism in employment and trade unions. There were massive campaigns against immigration control, fascist violence, racist attacks on person and property, modes of policing that resulted in the harassment of black people, and against the criminalization of black communities. There were many self-help projects concerned with educational, welfare and cultural activities. Black women were involved in all these activities, but the formation of autonomous black women's groups in the late 1970s injected a new dimension into the political scene.

The specific priorities of local black women's organizations, a

* From Avtar Brah, 'Difference, Diversity, Differentiation' from *Cartographies of Diaspora* by Avtar Brah (Routledge, 1996), 95–127.

number of which combined to form a national body—the Organization of Women of Asian and African Descent (OWAAD)—varied to an extent according to the exigencies of the local context. But the overall aim was to challenge the specific forms of oppression faced by the different categories of black women. The commitment to forging unity between African, Caribbean and Asian women demanded sustained attempts to analyse, understand and work with commonalties as well as heterogeneity of experience. It called for an interrogation of the role of colonialism and imperialism and that of contemporary economic, political and ideological processes in sustaining particular social divisions within these groups. It required black women to be sensitive to one another's cultural specificities while constructing common political strategies to confront patriarchal practices, racism and class inequality. This was no easy task and it is a testimony to the political commitment and vision of the women involved that this project thrived for many years, and some of the local groups have survived the divisive impact of ethnicism and remain active today.[1]

The demise of OWAAD as a national organization in the early 1980s was precipitated by a number of factors. Many of these divisive tendencies have been paralleled in the women's movement as a whole. The organizations affiliated to OWAAD shared its broad aims, but there were political differences among women on various issues. There was general agreement that racism was crucial in structuring our oppression in Britain, but we differed in our analysis of racism and its links with class and other modes of inequality. For some women, racism was an autonomous structure of oppression and had to be tackled as such; for others it was inextricably connected with class and other axes of social division. There were also differences in perspectives between feminists and non-feminists in OWAAD. For the latter, an emphasis on sexism was a diversion from the struggle against racism. The devaluation of black cultures by the onslaughts of racism meant that for some women the priority was to 'reclaim' these cultural sites and to situate themselves 'as women' within them. While this was an important project, there was, at times, more than a hint of idealizing a lost past. Other women argued that, while affirmation of cultural identity was indeed crucial, it was equally important to address cultural practices in their oppressive forms. The problem of male violence against women and children, the unequal sexual division of labour in the household, questions of dowry and forced marriages, clitoridectomy, heterosexism and the suppression of lesbian sexualities: all these were issues demanding immediate attention. Although most women in

OWAAD recognized the importance of these issues, there were nonetheless major differences about priorities and political strategies to deal with them.

Alongside these tendencies there was an emerging emphasis within the women's movement as a whole on identity politics. Instead of embarking on the complex but necessary task of identifying the specificities of particular oppressions, understanding their interconnections with other oppressions, and building a politics of solidarity, some women were beginning to differentiate these specificities into hierarchies of oppression. The mere act of naming oneself as a member of an oppressed group was assumed to vest one with moral authority. Multiple oppressions came to be regarded not in terms of their patterns of articulation but rather as separate elements that could be added in a linear fashion, so that the more oppressions a woman could list the greater her claims to occupy a higher moral ground. Assertions about authenticity of personal experience could be presented as if they were an unproblematic guide to an understanding of processes of subordination and domination. Declarations concerning self-righteous political correctness sometimes came to substitute for careful political analysis.[2]

Despite the fragmentation of the women's movement, black women in Britain have continued to raise critical questions about feminist theory and practice. As a result of our location within diasporas formed by the history of slavery, colonialism and imperialism, black feminists have consistently argued against parochialism and stressed the need for a feminism sensitive to the international social relations of power.[3] Hazel Carby's article 'White women listen', for instance, presents a critique of such key feminist concepts as 'patriarchy', 'the family' and 'reproduction'. She criticizes feminist perspectives which use notions of 'feudal residues' and 'traditionalism' to create sliding scales of 'civilised liberties', with the 'Third World' seen at one end of the scale and the supposedly progressive 'First World' at the other. She provides several illustrations of how a certain type of Western feminism can serve to reproduce rather than challenge the categories through which 'the West' constructs and represents itself as superior to its 'others'.

These critiques generated some critical self-reflection on the part of white feminist writers. In an attempt to re-assess their earlier work, Barrett and McIntosh, for example, acknowledged the limitations of the concept of patriarchy as unambiguous and invariable male dominance undifferentiated by class or racism. They opted for the use of 'patriarchal' as signifying how 'particular social relations combine a public dimension of power, exploitation or status with a dimension of personal servility'.[4] But they failed to specify how and why the concept of 'patriarchal' should prove to have greater analytical edge over that of 'patriarchy' in studying the interconnections between gender, class and racism. The mere substitution of the concept of patriarchy by that of patriarchal relations cannot in itself address the charges of ahistoricism, universalism or essentialism that have been levelled at the former, although, as Walby[5] argues, it is possible to provide historicized accounts of patriarchy. As a response to such reconceptualizations of patriarchy, Joan Acker suggests that it might be more appropriate to shift 'the theoretical object from patriarchy to gender, which we can define briefly as structural, relational, and symbolic differentiations between women and men'.[6] She remains cautious about this shift, however, as 'gender', according to her, lacks the critical political sharpness of 'patriarchy' and could much more easily be coopted and neutralized within 'mainstream' theory. It is as well to remember that this whole debate was generally located within the parameters of the binary male/female and does not address the indeterminacy of 'sex' as a category.[7]

I prefer retaining the concept of 'patriarchal' without necessarily subscribing to the concept of 'patriarchy'—whether historicized or not. Patriarchal relations are a specific form of gender relation in which women inhabit a subordinated position. In theory, at least, it should be possible to envisage a social context in which gender relations are not associated with inequality. In addition, I hold serious reservations about the analytical or political utility of maintaining system boundaries between 'patriarchy' and the particular socio-economic and political formation (for example, capitalism or state socialism) in which it is embedded. It would be far more useful to understand how patriarchal relations articulate with other forms of social relation in a determinate historical context. Structures of class, racism, gender and sexuality cannot be treated as 'independent variables' because the oppression of each is inscribed within the other—is constituted by and is constitutive of the other.

Acknowledging the black feminist critique, Barrett and McIntosh[8] stress the need to analyse the ideological construction of white femininity through racism. This, in my view, is essential, since there is still a tendency to address questions of inequality through a focus on the victims of inequality. Discussions about feminism and racism often centre around the oppression of black women rather than exploring how both black and white women's gender is constructed through class and racism. This means that white women's 'privileged position' within racialized discourses (even when they may share a class position with black women) fails to be adequately theorized, and processes of domination remain invisible. The representation of white women as 'the moral guardians of a superior race', for instance, serves to homogenize white women's sexuality at the same time as it fractures it across class, in that the white working-class woman, although also presented as 'carrier of the race', is simultaneously constructed as prone to 'degeneracy' because of her class background. Here we see how class contradictions may be worked through and 'resolved' ideologically within the racialized structuration of gender.

Barrett and McIntosh's article generated considerable debate.[9] While acknowledging the importance of the reassessment of a part of their work by two prominent white feminists, the critics argued that their methods of re-examination failed to provide the possibility of radical transformation of previous analysis, thus leaving the ways in which 'race' features within social reproduction largely untheorized. This feminist exchange contributed to the wider debate as to whether the social divisions associated with ethnicity and racism should be seen as absolutely autonomous of social class, as reducible to social class, or as having historical origins but articulating now with the divisions of class in capitalist society.

I would argue that racism is neither reducible to social class or gender nor wholly autonomous. Racisms have variable historical origins but they articulate with patriarchal class structures in specific ways under given historical conditions. Racisms may have independent effectivity, but to suggest this is not the same as saying, as Caroline Ramazanoglu does,[10] that racism is an 'independent form of domination'. The concept of articulation suggests relations of linkages and effectivity whereby, as Hall says: 'things are related as much by their differences as through their similarities'.[11] In similar vein, Laclau and Mouffe[12] note that articulation is a practice and not the name of a given relational complex; that is, articulation is not a simple joining of two or more discrete entities. Rather, it is a transformative move of relational configurations. The search for grand theories specifying the interconnections between racism, gender and class has been less than productive. They are best construed as historically contingent and context-specific relationships. Hence, we can focus on a given context and differentiate between the demarcation of a category as an object of social discourse, as an analytical category, and as a subject of political mobilization, without making assumptions about their permanence or stability across time and space. This means that 'white' feminism or 'black' feminism in Britain are not essentialist categories but rather that they are fields of contestation inscribed within discursive and material processes and practices in a post-colonial terrain. They represent struggles over political frameworks for analysis; the meanings of theoretical concepts; the relationship between theory, practice and subjective experiences, and over political priorities and modes of mobilization. But they should not, in my view, be understood as constructing 'white' and 'black' women as 'essentially' fixed oppositional categories.

More recent contributions to the debate make somewhat different points, and their object of critique is also different in that they interrogate black and/or anti-racist feminism. One argument has been that, far from facilitating political mobilization, black/anti-racist feminist discourses of the late 1970s and 1980s actually impeded political activism. Knowles and Mercer, for example, contend that Carby's and Bourne's emphasis on the inscription of racism and gender inequality within processes of capitalism, colonialism and patriarchal social systems produced functionalist arguments—that sexism and racism were inherent within these systems and served the needs of these systems to perpetuate themselves. They believe that this approach demanded nothing short of an all-embracing struggle against these 'isms', and thereby undermined more localized, small-scale political responses. Yet, we know that the 1970s and the 1980s witnessed a wide variety of political activity at both local and national levels. Their own method of dealing with what they presume are the shortcomings of an emphasis on macroanalysis is to suggest that racism and sexism be 'viewed as a series of effects which do not have a single cause'.[13] I would accept the arguments that the level of abstraction at which categories such as 'capitalism' or 'patriarchal relations' are delineated does not provide straightforward guidelines for concrete strategy and action, and also that racism and sexism are not monocausal phenomena. Nonetheless, I am not sure how treating racism and sexism as a 'series of effects' provides any clearer guidelines for political response. The same 'effect' may be interpreted from a variety of political positions, and lead to quite different strategies for action. Taking up a specific political position means that one is making certain assumptions about the nature of the various processes that underline a social phenomenon, of which a particular event may be an effect. A focus only on 'effects' may render invisible the workings of such ideological and material processes, thereby hindering our understanding of the complex basis of inequalities. Although crucial in mobilizing specific constituencies, the single-issue struggles as ends in themselves may delimit wider-ranging challenges to social inequalities. The language of 'effects', in any case, does not get away from an implicit subtext of 'causes'.

I share Knowles and Mercer's (1992) reservation about analytical and political perspectives in which social inequality comes to be personified in the bodies of the dominant social groups—white people, men, or heterosexual individuals in relation to racism, sexism or heterosexism—but we cannot ignore the social relations of power that inscribe such differentiations. Members of dominant groups do occupy 'privileged' positions within political and material practices that attend these social divisions, although the precise interplay of this power in specific institutions or in interpersonal relations cannot be stipulated in advance, may be contradictory, and can be challenged.

A slightly different critique of black feminism challenges its validity as representing anything more than the interests of black women.[14] By implication, black feminism is cast as sectarian in comparison with radical or socialist feminism. This comparison is problematic, since it constructs black feminism as being outside radical or socialist feminism. In practice, the category 'black feminism' in Britain is only meaningful *vis-à-vis* the category 'white feminism'. If, as I have argued earlier, these two categories are contingent rather than essentialist, then one cannot ask the question, as Tang Main does, whether 'black feminism' is open to all women, without simultaneously asking the same question of 'white feminism'. Tang Main's characterization of radical or socialist feminism as 'open to all women' flies in the face of massive evidence which shows that, in Britain and the USA at least, these feminisms have failed to take adequate account of racism and the experience of racialized groups of women. The ideology of 'open to all' can in fact legitimize all kinds of *de facto* exclusion. Socialist feminism, for example, cannot really include women who are subjected to racism unless it is a non-racist socialist feminism, or lesbian women unless it is simultaneously non-heterosexist, or lower-caste women unless it is also non-casteist. But these issues cannot be realized in the abstract, nor can they be settled once and for all, but through ongoing political struggles.

For similar reasons, Floya Anthias and Nira Yuval-Davis's[15] critique of the category 'black' on the grounds that it failed to address diversity of ethnic exclusions and subordinations seems misplaced.

The boundaries of a political constituency formed around specific concerns are dependent upon the nature of the concerns and their salience and significance in the lives of the people so affected. Black feminism constructed a constituency in terms of the gendered experience of anti-black racism. White ethnic groups who were not subjected to this particular form of racism could not, therefore, be part of this constituency. This does not mean that their experiences of, say, anti-semitism are any the less important. Rather, anti-black racism and anti-semitism cannot be subsumed under each other. This becomes patently clear if we compare the experience of a white Jewish woman and a black Jewish woman. The black woman is simultaneously positioned within two racialized discourses. Anthias and Yuval-Davis make some incisive points about ethnicity as a category of social differentiation, but their contention that 'black feminism can be too wide or too narrow a category for specific feminist struggles'[16] remains problematic, since the emergence of the black women's movement as a historically specific response is a testament that organization around the category 'black women' is possible.

It bears repetition that black feminism was constituted in articulation with a number of political movements: the project of 'African-Asian Unity' around the sign 'black'; class politics; anti-colonial movements; global feminist movements; and gay and lesbian politics. This multi-locationality marked the formation of new diasporic subjectivities and identities; and it produced a powerful new political subject. Like most political subjects, this one, too, embodied its own contradiction—in/of multiplicity. As we saw earlier, its seeming coherence was disrupted by internal debate and contestation. But it was one of the most enabling and empowering political subjects of the period. Black feminism's figuration of 'black'—as was the case generally with the politics of 'black'—dislodged this signifier from possible essentialist connotations and subverted the very logic of its racial codings. At the same time, it undermined gender-neutral discourses of 'black' by asserting the specificities of black women's experiences. In so far as black women comprised a highly differentiated category in terms of class, ethnicity, and religion, and included women who had migrated from Africa, the Asian subcontinent and the Caribbean, as well as those born in Britain, the black in 'black feminism' inscribed a multiplicity of experience even as it articulated a particular feminist subject position. Moreover, by foregrounding a wide range of diasporic experiences in both their local and global specificity, black feminism represented black life in all its fullness, creativity and complexity.

Black feminism prised open discursive closures which asserted the primacy of, say, class or gender over all other axes of differentiation; and it interrogated the constructions of such privileged signifiers as unified autonomous cores. The point is that black feminism not only posed a very serious challenge to colour-centred racisms, but its significance goes far beyond this challenge. The political subject of black feminism decentres the unitary, masculinist subject of Eurocentric discourse, as well as masculinist rendering of 'black' as a political colour, while seriously disrupting any notion of 'woman' as a unitary category. That is to say that, while constituted around the problematic of 'race', black feminism performatively defies confines of the boundaries of its constitution.

Black feminism did not preclude coalitions across other boundaries, and black women have worked with white women and men, and other categories of people across a spectrum of political opinion on issues of common concern. I fully recognize that the category 'black' as a political colour no longer has the purchase it used to have. As a part of the Left project, it has suffered similar predicaments to the British Left as a whole. The New Right politics which reached their apotheosis during the Thatcher years, the demise of state socialism in Eastern Europe, formation of the European Union, economic restructuring, the rise of political religious movements, the resurgence of new forms of youth cultures, etc., have all made significant impact on all aspects of life. These changes call for new configurations of solidarity. The point, however, is that any alternatives to the political category 'black', such as 'women of colour' or some term as yet not in currency, cannot be willed in the abstract or decided in advance. They can only emerge through new modes of contestation within a changed economic and political climate.

My proposition that 'black' and 'white' feminisms be addressed as non-essentialist, historically contingent discursive practices implies that black and white women can work together towards the creation of non-racist feminist theory and practice. The key issue, then, is not about 'difference' *per se*, but concerns the question of who defines difference, how different categories of women are represented within the discourses of 'difference', and whether 'difference' differentiates laterally or hierarchically. We need greater conceptual clarity in analysing difference.

DIFFERENCE; WHAT DIFFERENCE?

It is axiomatic that the concept of 'difference' is associated with a variety of meanings in different discourses. But how are we to understand 'difference'? In the analytical framework that I am attempting to formulate here the issue is not about privileging the macro- or the micro-level of analysis, but rather, how articulating discourses and practices inscribe social relations, subject positions and subjectivities. The interesting issue then is how micro- and macro-levels inhere in the above inscriptions. How does difference designate the 'other'? Who defines difference? What are the presumed norms from which a group is marked as being different? What is the nature of attributions that are claimed as characterizing a group as different? How are boundaries of difference constituted, maintained or dissipated? How is difference interiorized in the landscapes of the psyche? How are various groups represented in different discourses of difference? Does difference differentiate laterally or hierarchically? Questions such as these raise a more general problematic about difference as an analytic category. I would suggest four ways in which difference may be conceptualized: difference as experience, difference as social relation, difference as subjectivity, and difference as identity.

Difference as Experience

Experience has been a key concept within feminism. Women's movements have aimed to give a collective voice to women's personal experiences of social and psychic forces that constitute the 'female' into the 'woman'. The everyday of the social relations of gender—ranging from housework and child care, low-paid employment and economic dependency to sexual violence and women's exclusion from key centres of political and cultural power—have all been given a new significance through feminism as they have been brought out of the realm of the 'taken for granted' to be interrogated and challenged. The personal, with its profoundly concrete yet elusive qualities, and its manifold contradiction, acquired new meanings in the slogan 'the personal is political', as consciousness-raising groups provided the forums for exploring individual experiences, personal feelings and women's own understandings of their daily lives. As Teresa de Lauretis noted, this original feminist insight proclaimed 'a relation, however complex it may be, between sociality and subjectivity, between language and consciousness, or between institutions and individuals . . .'[17]

That there are some considerable limitations to the consciousness-raising method as a strategy for collective action is not at issue. The point is that consciousness-raising foregrounded one of feminism's most powerful insights, which is that experience does not transparently reflect a pre-given reality, but rather is itself a cultural construction. Indeed, 'experience' is a process of signification which is the very condition for the constitution of that which we call 'reality'. Hence, the need to re-emphasize a notion of experience not as an unmediated guide to 'truth' but as a practice of making sense, both symbolically and narratively; as a struggle over material conditions and meaning.

Contrary to the idea of an already fully constituted 'experiencing subject' to whom 'experiences happen', experience is the site of subject formation. This notion is often missing from those discussions about differences between people where difference and experience are used primarily as a 'commonsensical term'.[18] Not surprisingly, such discussions flounder or result in 'talking at cross purposes' when dealing with the contradictions of subjectivity and identity. For instance, how are we to deal with the racism of a feminist, the homophobia of someone subjected to racism, or indeed the racism of one racialized group towards another racialized group, each presumably speaking from the vantage point of their experience, if all experience transparently reflected a given 'truth'? Indeed, how can a project such as feminism or anti-racism, or a class movement, mobilize itself as a political force for change if it did not start by interrogating the taken-for-granted values and norms which may legitimize dominance and inequality by naturalizing particular 'differences'? Attention to this point reveals experience as a site of contestation: a discursive space where different *and* differential subject positions and subjectivities are inscribed, reiterated, or repudiated. It is essential, then, to address the questions of which ideological matrices or fields of signification and representation are at play in the formation of differing subjects, and what are the economic, political and cultural processes that inscribe historically variable experiences. As Joan Scott argues, 'Experience is at once always already an interpretation *and* is in need of interpretation'.[19]

To think of experience and subject formation as processes is to reformulate the question of 'agency'. The 'I' and the 'we' who act do not disappear, but what does disappear is the notion that these categories are unified, fixed, already existing entities rather than modalities of multi-locationality continuously marked by everyday cultural and political practices.

It is useful to distinguish difference as a marker of the distinctiveness of our collective 'histories' from difference as personal experience inscribing individual biography. These sets of 'differences' constantly articulate, but they cannot be 'read off' from each other. The meaning attached to a given event varies enormously from one individual to another. When we speak of the constitution of individual into subject through multiple fields of signification we are invoking *inscription* and *ascription* as simultaneous processes whereby the subject *acquires* meaning in socio-economic and cultural relations at the same moment as she *ascribes* meaning by making sense of these relations in everyday life. In other words, how a person perceives *or* conceives an event would vary according to how 'she' is culturally constructed; the myriad of unpredictable ways in which such constructions may configure in the flux of her psyche; and, invariably, upon the political repertoire of cultural discourses available to her. Collective 'histories' are also, of course, culturally constructed in the process of assigning meaning to the everyday of social relations. But, while personal biographies and group histories are mutually immanent, they are relationally irreducible. The same context may produce several different collective 'histories', differentiating as well as linking biographies through *contingent specificities.* In turn, articulating cultural practices of the subjects so constituted mark contingent collective 'histories' with variable new meanings.

Difference as Social Relation

The concept of 'difference as social relation' refers to the ways in which difference is constituted and organized into *systematic* relations through economic, cultural and political discourses and institutional practices. That is to say that it highlights *systematicity across contingencies.* A group usually mobilizes the concept of difference in this sense when addressing the historical genealogies of its collective experience. Indeed, difference and commonality are relational signs, interweaving narratives of difference with those of a shared past and collective destinies. In other words the concept of 'difference as social relation' underscores the historically variable articulation of macro and micro regimes of power, within which modes of differentiation such as gender, class or racism are instituted in terms of *structured* formations.

The category 'working class', for instance, highlights positioning in structures of class relations. But to say this is not to point simply to the designation of a subordinate location within socio-economic and political structures of power, but also to underline systems of signification and representation which construct class as a cultural category.

Difference in the sense of social relation may be understood as the historical and contemporary trajectories of material circumstances and cultural practices which *produce the conditions* for the construction of group identities. The concept refers to the interweaving of shared collective narratives within feelings of community, whether or not this 'community' is constituted in face-to-face encounters or imagined, in the sense that Benedict Anderson suggests.[20] It is the echo of 'difference as social relation' which reverberates when legacies of slavery, colonialism or imperialism are invoked; or when attention is drawn to the 'new' international division of labour and the differential positioning of different groups within its continually evolving systems of production, exchange, and consumption which result in massive inequalities within and between various parts of the globe. But this does not mean that the concept of social relation operates at some 'higher level of abstraction' referencing the 'macro' as opposed to the 'micro' context. The effects of social relations are not confined to the seemingly distant operations of national or global economies, politics, or cultural institutions, but are also present in highly localized arenas of the workplace, the household (which, in some cases, as with homeworkers or highly paid executives 'working from home', becomes both a unit of labour—albeit differentially remunerated—and a place of work), as well as in the interstices of the mind where intersubjectivity is produced and contested. All these spheres have always been interlinked, but they articulate in quite unique ways in the present historical moment. As Donna Haraway argues:

> The home, workplace, market, public arena, the body itself—all can be dispersed and interfaced in nearly infinite, polymorphous ways, with large consequences for women and others—consequences that themselves are very different for different people and which make potent international movements difficult to imagine and essential for survival. . . . Communication technologies and biotechnologies are the crucial tools recrafting our bodies. These tools embody and enforce new social relations for women worldwide. . . . The boundary is permeable between tool and myth, instrument and concept, historical systems of social relations and historical anatomies of possible bodies, including objects of knowledge.[21]

Social relations, then, are constituted and perform in all sites of a social formation. This means that, in practice, experience as social relation and the everyday of lived experience do not inhabit mutually exclusive spaces. For example, if we speak of 'North African women in France', we are, on the one hand, referring to the social relations of gendered post-coloniality in France. On the other hand, we are also making a statement about the everyday experience of this post-coloniality on the part of such women, although we cannot specify, in advance, the particularity of individual women's lives or how they interpret and define this experience. In both instances, the question of how difference is defined remains paramount. Are perceptions of difference acting as a means of affirming diversity or a mechanism for exclusionary and discriminatory practices? Do discourses of difference legitimize progressive or oppressive state policies and practices? In what ways are different categories of women represented in such discourses? How do women themselves respond to these representations?

When understood in this way, the idea of difference as social relation hopefully sheds any claims of privileging 'structural' as the command centre of a social formation in favour of a perspective which foregrounds articulation of the different elements.

Difference as Subjectivity

Issues of difference have been central to the theoretical debate around subjectivity. Much of the contemporary debate is conducted in various critiques of the humanist conceptions of the subject: as a unified, unitary, rational, and rationalist 'point of origin'; as centred in consciousness; and, in terms of the idea of a universal 'Man' as the embodiment of an ahistorical essence. These critiques emerged from several different directions. In the post-World War II period the projects of post-structuralism, feminism, anti-colonialism, anti-imperialism, and anti-racism have all, in one form or another, taken serious issue with universalizing truth claims of grand narratives of history which place the European 'Man' at its centre. But although these projects have overlapped in some respects, the problematic they have addressed has not been identical. Nor have they always engaged one another. Indeed, a major source of contention amongst them has been the relative lack of attention or, in some cases, an almost complete amnesia by one project about issues central to the other. For example . . . few early canonical texts of post-structuralism address questions of colonialism or decolonization, or issues of racism in any systematic way, despite their regular invocation of the 'crisis' of the 'West'. Hence, the importance of powerful critiques of the discourse of European Man which emerged from anti-colonial struggles for independence as women, men, and children expressed defiance in Africa, Asia, the Caribbean and other parts of the world. Fanon instantiated one moment of this critique when he exhorted his readers to:

> Leave this Europe where they are never done talking of Man, yet murder men everywhere they find them, at the corner of every one of their own streets, in all the corners of the globe. . . . That same Europe where they are never done talking of Man, and where they never stopped proclaiming that they were only anxious for the welfare of Man: today we know with what suffering humanity has paid for every one of their triumphs of the mind.[22]

Similar critiques surfaced in more recent anti-racist resistance movements and within what is sometimes called 'colonial discourse' theory. These currents in politics and theory intersect with those within feminism, peace movements, environmental campaigns and other similar projects. Together they underscore the notion that the subject does not exist as an always already given, but is produced in discourse. Yet, enabling though this insight into the production of the subject has been, it could not by itself adequately account for non-logocentric operations of subjectivity. As Henriques *et al.* posed the problem, how does one avoid, on the one hand:

> a kind of discourse determinism which implies that people are mechanistically positioned in discourses, a view which leaves no room for explicating either the possibilities for change or individual's resistance to change, and which disregards the question of motivation altogether (and, on the other hand, the notion of) a *pre-given* subject which opts for particular subject positions?[23]

Such a predicament led feminists and others to re-visit psychoanalysis (especially its post-structuralist and object-relations variants), and to re-think its relationship to theories of 'deconstruction' and 'micro-politics of power'. There was growing acknowledgement that a person's innermost emotions, feelings, desires, and fantasies, with their multiple contradictions, could not be understood purely in terms of the imperatives of the social institutions. The new readings were essential to a more complex account of psychic life. Psychoanalysis disrupts notions of a unitary, centred and rational self by its emphasis on an inner world permeated by desire and fantasy. This inner world is addressed as the site of the unconscious with its unpredictable effects on thought and other aspects of subjectivity. At the same time, psychoanalysis facilitates understanding of the ways in which the subject-in-process is marked by a sense of coherence and continuity, a sense of a core that she or he calls the 'I'.

Jane Flax[24] argues that, despite the many shortcomings which have been the subject of considerable debate, there are many ambiguities in Freud's thought which have made it accessible to different readings. The ambiguities in the theories of the libido and the unconscious, for instance, have made it possible for the boundaries between ego, superego and id, or those between the psychic, the somatic and the cultural, to be understood as unfixed and permeable. The mind/body dualism is problematized when instinct or drive is conceptualized simultaneously as psychic, somatic and cultural, in that a need, a want or a desire is never purely a bodily sensation but is constituted and regulated within a cultural space. Freud's conceptualisations of the mind as non-unitary, conflictual, dynamic, embodied and constituted in ways that cannot be 'synthesised or organised into a permanent, hierarchical, organisation of functions or control'[25] undermines both rationalist and empiricist concepts of mind and knowledge.

In this type of post-structuralist/feminist appropriation of Freud, the mind's constitutive elements—ego, superego and id—emerge as *relational* concepts constituted in and through 'inner' and 'outer' experience. Hence, the subject is understood as decentred and heterogeneous in its qualities and dynamics. Subjectivity, then, is neither unified nor fixed but fragmented and constantly in process. For feminists, such accounts have proved especially attractive, for they problematize 'sexual difference': sexual difference is something to be explained rather than assumed. Some have turned to Lacan's re-reading of Freud for a non-reductive understanding of subjectivity. Others find a re-working of the object-relations strands of Freud's schema more useful for developing feminist projects. Compelling arguments have been made in favour of the importance of psychoanalysis for feminism against those critics who assume that the notion of a fragmented identity constantly in process is at odds with the feminist project of constructing oppositional consciousness through collective action. Nonetheless, some feminists remain sceptical about psychoanalysis altogether. The debate continues unabated.[26]

Such argumentation is essential and productive given the many difficulties and problems that continue to beset the meta-narrative of psychoanalysis which the protagonists in the debate seek to confront in their own ways. The psychic effects of racism, for instance, only rarely feature in these discussions when the 'race' discourse has been a central element in the constitution of the category 'West'. Fanon's work notwithstanding, engagement with the problematic of racialization of subjectivity is as yet limited. How would psychoanalytic narratives be disrupted by addressing racism? Hortense Spillers[27] interrogates psychoanalysis even as she uses it in her analysis. Her ambivalence is instructive when she says:

> I attempt this writing, in fact, as *the trial* of an interlocking interrogation that I am persuaded in by only 50 percent. Is the Freudian landscape an applicable text (to say nothing of appropriate) to social and historic situations that do not replicate moments of its own historic origins and movements? The prestigious Oedipal dis-ease/complex, which apparently subsumes the Electra myth, embeds in the 'heterosexual' nuclear family that disperses its fruits in vertical array. Not only 'one man, one woman' but these two—this law—in a specific locus of economic and cultural means. But how does this model, or does this model, suffice for occupied or captive persons and communities (of African slaves in the Americas) in which the rights and rites of gender functions have been exploded historically in to sexual neutralities.[28]

Her discourse underlines the point raised by Dalal[29] in relation to what he claims as the Jungian paradigm's complicity with racialized discourses. It highlights the importance and necessity of paying greater attention to how subjectivity is conceptualized in cultures other than Western and the transcultural traffic between ideas.

Over the years there have been attempts to combine different approaches to the study of subjectivity. Teresa de Lauretis, for example, suggests that semiotics and psychoanalysis might be jointly mobilized in furthering our understanding of subjectivity. She argues the case for 'locating subjectivity in the space contoured by the discourses of semiotics and psychoanalysis, neither in the former nor in the latter, but rather in their discursive intersection'.[30] The aim is to explore the relationship between personal change and social change without recourse to reductive explanations of simple determination.

In other words, we need conceptual frames which can address fully the point that processes of subjectivity formation are at once *social* and *subjective*; which can help us understand the psychic investments we make in assuming specific subject positions that are socially and culturally produced.

Difference as Identity

Our struggles over meaning are also our struggles over different modes of being and becoming: different identities.[31] Questions of identity are intimately connected with those of experience, subjectivity and social relations. Identities are inscribed through experiences culturally constructed in social relations. Subjectivity—the site of processes of making sense of our relation to the world—is the modality in which the precarious and contradictory nature of the subject-in-process is signified or *experienced* as identity. Identities are marked by the multiplicity of subject positions that constitute the subject. Hence, identity is neither fixed nor singular; rather it is a constantly changing relational multiplicity. But during the course of this flux identities do assume specific patterns, as in a kaleidoscope, against particular sets of personal, social and historical circumstances. Indeed, identity may be understood *as that very process by which the multiplicity, contradiction, and instability of subjectivity is signified as having coherence, continuity, stability; as having a core—a continually changing core but the sense of a core nonetheless—that at any given moment is enunciated as the 'I'*.

As we have already seen, the relationship between personal biography and collective history is complex and contradictory. While personal identities always articulate with the collective experience of a group, the specificity of a person's life experience etched in the daily minutiae of lived social relations produces trajectories that do not simply mirror group experience. Similarly, collective identities are irreducible to the sum of the experiences of individuals. Collective identity is the process of signification whereby commonalities of experience around a specific axis of differentiation, say class, caste, or religion, are invested with particular meanings. In this sense a given collective identity partially erases, but also carries traces of other identities. That is to say that a heightened awareness of one *construction* of identity in a given moment always entails a partial erasure of the *memory or subjective sense* of internal heterogeneity of a group. But this is not at all the same as saying that the power relations embedded in heterogeneity disappear. How and if patterns of social relations change would be contingent upon the power of the political challenges which specific discourses and practices are able to effect.

The partial suppression of a sense of one identity by the assertion of another does not mean, however, that different 'identities' cannot 'co-exist'. But if identity is a process, then it is problematic to speak of an existing identity as if this is always already constituted. It is more appropriate to speak of discourses, matrices of meanings, and historical memories which, once in circulation, can form the basis of *identification* in a given economic, cultural and political context. But the identity that is proclaimed is a *remaking*, a context-specific construction. The *proclamation* of a specific collective identity is a *political* process as distinct from identity as a process *in* and *of* subjectivity. The political process of *proclaiming* a specific collective identity entails the *creation* of a collective identity out of the myriad collage-like fragments of the mind. The process may well generate considerable psychic and emotional disjunction in the realm of subjectivity, even if it is empowering in terms of group politics.

In other words, political mobilization is centrally about attempts to re-inscribe subjectivity through appeals to collective experience. Paradoxically, the commonality that is evoked can be rendered meaningful only in articulation with a discourse of difference. The precise ways in which the discourse of commonality/difference is invoked, and with what effects for different segments of the constituency it seeks to mobilize, or indeed for those it constructs as outside this constituency, varies enormously. But essentially such discourses are renditions of some view—re-memory, re-collection, re-working, re-construction—of collective history and, as such, these discourses of identity (whether they invoke notions of 'culture', or are centred around ideas about 'shared economic or political circumstances') are articulations of subjectivity in what I have called 'difference as social relation'.

All discursive formations are a site of power, but there is no single and overarching locus of power where dominance, subordination, solidarity and affiliation based on egalitarian principles, or the conditions for affinity, conviviality and sociality are produced and secured once and for all. Rather, power is performatively constituted in and through economic, political, and cultural practices. Subjectivities of both the dominant and the dominated are produced in the interstices of these multiple, intersecting loci of power. The precise interplay of this power in specific institutions and interpersonal relations is difficult to predict in advance. But if *practice* is productive of power then *practice* is also the means of challenging the oppressive *practices* of power. This indeed is the implication of the Foucauldian insight that discourse is practice. Similarly, a visual image is also a practice. The visual image is also productive of power, hence the importance of understanding the movement of power in technologies of the eye—visual arts such as painting and sculpture, cinematic practice or dance, and the visual effects of communication technologies. The same holds for the aural register—music and other sounds are productive of power. Indeed, the whole body in all its *physicality, mentality and spirituality* is productive of power, and it is within this relational space that the mind/body dualism disappears. A particular 'identity' assumes shape in political practice out of the *fragmentic relationality* of subjectivity and dissolves to emerge as a trace in another identity-formation. As I have stressed all along, the subject may be the effect of discourses, institutions and practices, but at any given moment the subject-in-process experiences itself as the 'I', and both consciously and unconsciously replays and resignifies positions in which it is located and invested.

The concept of difference, then, refers to the variety of ways in which specific discourses of difference are constituted, contested, reproduced, or resignified. Some constructions of difference, such as racism, posit fixed and immutable boundaries between groups signified as inherently different. Other constructions may present difference as relational, contingent and variable. In other words, difference is not always a marker of hierarchy and oppression. Therefore, it is a contextually contingent question whether difference pans out as inequity, exploitation and oppression *or as* egalitarianism, diversity and democratic forms of political agency.

Stuart Hall regards ethnicity as one potential modality of difference—marking the specificity of collective historical, political and cultural experience—which could possibly interrogate and challenge essentialist constructions of group boundaries. He suggests that it should be possible to retrieve ethnicity from racialized nationalist discourses:

> The fact that this grounding of ethnicity in difference was deployed, in the discourse of racism, as a means of disavowing the realities of racism and repression does not mean that we can permit the term to be permanently colonised. That appropriation will have to be contested, the term disarticulated from its position in the discourse of 'multi-culturalism' and transcoded, just as we previously had to recuperate the term 'black' from its place in a system of negative equivalences.[32]

In practice, however, it is not always easy to disentangle these different moves of power. Nationalist discourses may serve both ends. For instance, ethnicities are liable to be appropriated as signifiers of permanently fixed boundaries. Hence, the 'Englishness' of a particular class can come to represent itself via racism as 'Britishness' against those ethnicities that it subordinates—such as those of the Irish, Scottish, Welsh, black British, or the ethnicities of the formerly colonized world (although, as we noted earlier, white/European ethnicities are subordinated differently from 'non-white', 'non-European' ethnicities). Moreover, ethnicities are always gendered and there is no guarantee that their non-essentialist recuperation will simultaneously challenge patriarchal practices unless this task is made a conscious objective. Indeed, it cannot be taken for granted that the process of recuperation will itself not inscribe essentialist differences. This can be especially problematic for women if the cultural values that the groups in question excavate, recast, and reconstruct are those that underscore women's subordination.

Although I have argued against essentialism, it is apparent that it is not easy to deal with this problem. In their need to create new political identities, dominated groups will often appeal to bonds of common cultural experience in order to mobilise their constituency. In so doing they may assert a seemingly essentialist difference. Spivak[33] and Fuss[34] have argued in favour of such a 'strategic essentialism'. They suggest that the 'risk' of essentialism may be worth taking if it is framed from the vantage point of a dominated subject position. This will remain problematic if a challenge to one form of oppression leads to the reinforcement of another. It seems imperative that we do not compartmentalize oppressions but instead formulate strategies for challenging all on the basis of an understanding of how they interconnect and articulate. I believe that the framework I have outlined here can help us to do this. It is a perspective that calls for continually interrogating essentialism in all its varieties.

Notes

1. Brixton Black Women's Group, 'Black women organising autonomously', *Feminist Review*, 17 (1984); B. Bryan, S. Dadie and S. Scafe, *Heart of the Race* (London: Virago, 1985); Southall Black Sisters, 'Against the Grain' (Southall, Middlesex: SBS).
2. S. Ardill and S. O'Sullivan, 'Upsetting an applecart: difference, desire and lesbian sadomasochism', *Feminist Review*, 23; M. L. Adams, 'Identity politics', *Feminist Review*, 31.
3. H. Carby, 'Schooling in Babylon' and 'White women listen! Black feminism and boundaries of sisterhood', in Centre for Contemporary Cultural Studies, *The Empire Strikes Back* (London: Hutchinson, 1982); P. Parmar, 'Gender, race and class: Asian women in resistance', in Centre for Contemporary Cultural Studies, *The Empire Strikes Back; Feminist Review* (1984); A. Brah and R. Minhas, 'Structural racism or cultural difference: schooling for Asian girls', in G. Weiner (ed.), *Just a Bunch of Girls* (Milton Keynes: Open University Press, 1985); A. Brah, 'Journey to Nairobi', in S. Grewal, J. Kay, L. Landor, G. Lewis and P. Parmar (eds.), *Charting the Journey: Writings by Black and Third World Women* (London: Sheba Press, 1987); A. Phoenix, 'Theories of gender and black families', in G. Weiner and M. Arnot (eds.), *Gender Under Scrutiny*

(Milton Keynes: Open University Press, 1987); Grewal *et al.*, *Charting the Journey*; A. Mama, 'Violence against black women: gender, race, and state responses', *Feminist Review*, 32 (1989); G. Lewis, 'Audre Lorde: vignettes and mental conversations', *Feminist Review*, 34 (1990).

4. M. Barrett and M. McIntosh, 'Ethnocentrism and socialist-feminist theory', *Feminist Review*, 20 (1985), 39.
5. S. Walby, *Theorizing Patriarchy* (Oxford: Basil Blackwell, 1990).
6. J. Acker, 'The problem with patriarchy', *Sociology*, 23/2 (1989).
7. J. Butler, *Gender Trouble: Feminism and the Subversion of Identity* (New York: Routledge, 1990).
8. Barrett and McIntosh, 'Ethnocentrism and socialist-feminist theory'.
9. See contributions by Ramazanoglu, Kazi, Lees and Safia-Mirza, *Feminist Review* (1986); K. K. Bhavnani and M. Coulson, 'Transforming socialist feminism: the challenge of racism', *Feminist Review*, 23 (1986).
10. C. Ramazanoglu, *Feminism and the Contradictions of Oppression* (London: Routledge, 1989).
11. S. Hall, 'Race, articulation and societies structured in dominance', in *Sociological Theories: Race and Colonialism* (Paris: UNESCO, 1980), 328.
12. E. Laclau and C. Mouffe, *Hegemony and Socialist Strategy: Towards a Radical Democratic Politics* (London: Verso, 1985).
13. C. Knowles and S. Mercer, 'Feminism and anti-racism', in J. Donald and A. Rattansi (eds.), '*Race*', *Culture and Difference* (London: Sage, 1992), 110.
14. G. Tang Main, 'Black women, sexism and racism: black or anti-racist?', *Feminist Review*, 37 (1990).
15. F. Anthias and N. Yuval-Davis, 'Contextualising feminism', *Feminist Review*, 15 (1982).
16. Ibid., 63.
17. T. de Lauretis (ed.), *Feminist Studies/Critical Studies* (Bloomington: Indiana University Press, 1986), 5.
18. M. Barrett, 'The concept of difference', *Feminist Review*, 26 (1987).
19. J. W. Scott, 'Experience', in J. Butler and J. W. Scott (eds.), *Feminists Theorize the Political* (New York: Routledge, 1992), 37.
20. B. Anderson, *Imagined Communities* (London: Verso, 1983).
21. D. Haraway, *Simians, Cyborgs, and Women: the Reinvention of Nature* (London: Free Association Books, 1991), 164–5.
22. F. Fanon, *The Wretched of the Earth* (London: Penguin, 1967), 251.
23. J. Henriques, W. Holloway, C. Urwin, C. Venn and V. Walkerdine, *Changing the Subject: Psychology, Social Regulation and Subjectivity* (London: Methuen, 1984), 204.
24. J. Flax, *Thinking Fragments: Psychoanalysis, Feminism and Post-modernism in the Contemporary West* (Berkeley: University of California Press, 1990).
25. Ibid., 60.
26. de Lauretis, *Feminist Studies*; Henriques *et al.*, *Changing the Subject*; J. Rose, *Sexuality in the Field of Vision* (London: Verso, 1986); C. Weedon, *Feminist Practice and Poststructuralist Theory* (Oxford: Basil Blackwell, 1987); C. Penley, *The Future of an Illusion: Film, Feminism and Psychoanalysis* (London: Routledge, 1989); Flax, *Thinking Fragments*; and R. Minsky, '"The Trouble is it's ahistorical": the problem of the unconscious in modern feminist theory', *Feminist Review*, 36 (1990).

27. H. J. Spillers, 'Mama's Baby, Papa's May Be: An American Grammar Book', *Diacritics* (Summer 1987); and 'The permanent obliquity of an in(pha)llibly straight: in the time of the daughters and fathers', in C. A. Wall (ed.), *Changing Our Own Words: Essays on Criticism, Theory, and Writing by Black Women* (Rutgers University Press, 1989).
28. Spillers, 'The permanent obliquity of an in(pha)llibly straight', 128–9, emphasis added.
29. F. Dalal, 'The racism of Jung', *Race and Class*, 24/3 (1988).
30. T. de Lauretis, *Alice Doesn't: Feminism, Semiotics, Cinema* (Bloomington: Indiana University Press, 1984), 168.
31. T. T. Minh-ha, *Women, Native, Other: Writing Post Coloniality and Feminism* (Indianapolis: Indiana University Press, 1989).
32. S. Hall, 'New Ethnicities', in Donald and Rattansi, '*Race*', *Culture and Difference*, 257.
33. G. C. Spivak, *In Other Worlds: Essays in Cultural Politics* (London: Methuen, 1987).
34. D. Fuss, *Essentially Speaking* (London: Routledge, 1989).

31 Crosscurrents, Crosstalk: Race, 'Post-coloniality' and the Politics of Location

Ruth Frankenberg and Lata Mani *

This chapter had its immediate point of origin in the invitation to contribute to a lecture series on 'Post-coloniality and California' in the spring of 1991. Commonplace as the term 'post-coloniality' has rapidly become in literature, anthropology and Cultural Studies in recent times, the title begged a number of questions, about the notion of 'post-coloniality' and its efficacy, either in relation to California in particular, or to the United States in general. If the concept of 'post-coloniality' is spreading like brushfire through the terrain of cultural theory, what we propose by way of remedy is a carefully strategized 'controlled burn' approach that begins by posing the following questions.

What does 'post-coloniality' mean, for whom does it resonate, and why? What are the risks and effects of too hastily globalizing the concept?[1] In what senses, for example, are India, Britain or the United States 'post-colonial' locations? What are the multiple implications of 'post-ness' in relation to 'colonialism', in context, for example, of the persistence and current escalation of racism? We will argue that rigorous attention to that which neo-Gramscians and Althusserians call 'conjuncture', and some feminists describe as a 'politics of location', is critical to specifying both the limits and value of the term 'post-colonial'. In this chapter we sketch the beginnings of what we call a 'feminist conjuncturalist' approach to the issue of which spaces and subjects might be conceived as 'post-colonial', and in what senses such a description might hold.[2]

* From Ruth Frankenberg and Lata Mani, 'Crosscurrents, Crosstalk: Race, "Postcoloniality" and the Politics of Location', from *Cultural Studies*, 7:2 (Taylor & Francis, 1993), 292–310, reprinted by permission of the publisher.

NOTES ON THE TERM 'POST-COLONIAL', OR WHAT WE THINK IT MEANS, ANYWAY

India

'Post-colonial' implies independence from Britain; birth of the nation-state; end of territorial colonialism; inauguration of a path of economic development characterized by the growth of indigenous capitalism; neo-colonial relationship to the capitalist word; aid from socialist countries and horizontal assistance from other Third World countries non-aligned to either the First or Second World.

Britain

'Post-colonial' signals loss of most, though not all, former colonies—bear in mind Hong Kong, Northern Ireland, the appearance on British landscapes of a significant number of people from the former colonies: 'We are here because you were there.' The transition from a society of predominantly white ethnic groups to one that is multi-racial. The 'Other' no longer geographically distanced, but within, and over time significantly shaping landscape and culture. Samosas at the National Theatre café. Race riots.

USA

Here, the term 'post-colonial' sticks in our throats. White settler colony, multiracial society. Colonization of Native Americans, Africans imported as slaves, Mexicans incorporated by a border moving south, Asians imported and migrating to labor, white Europeans migrating to labor. US imperialist foreign policy brings new immigrants who are 'here because the US was/is there', among them Central Americans, Koreans, Filipinos, Vietnamese and Cambodians. The particular relation of past territorial domination and current racial composition that is discernible in Britain, and which lends a particular meaning to the term 'post-colonial', does not, we feel, obtain here. Other characterizations, other periodizations, seem necessary in naming for this place the shifts expressed by the term 'post-colonial' in the British and Indian cases: the serious calling into question of white/Western dominance by the groundswell of movements of resistance, and the emergence of struggles for collective self-determination most frequently articulated in nationalist terms.

'Post-Civil Rights' is a possible candidate for signalling this double articulation in the United States context. Let us emphasize at the outset that we use the term 'post-Civil Rights' broadly, to refer to the impact of struggles by African-American, American-Indian, La Raza and Asian-American communities that stretched from the mid-1950s to the 1970s, movements which Michael Omi and Howard Winant have credited with collectively producing a '"great transformation" of racial awareness, racial meaning, racial subjectivity'.[3] However, the name, 'post-Civil Rights', would only grasp one strand of our description of the US. The term would have to be conjugated with another, one that would name the experience of recent immigrants/refugees borne here on the trails of US imperialist adventures, groups whose stories are unfolding in a tense, complicated relation—at time compatible, at times contradictory—with post-Civil Rights USA.

POST-*WHAT*?!

We are quite aware that the terms 'post-colonial' and 'post-Civil Rights' are, in important senses, incommensurable. First, 'colonial' refers to a system of domination while 'Civil Rights' designates collective struggle *against* a system or systems of domination. Strictly speaking, the analogous term to 'post-Civil Rights' would be 'post-decolonization struggle'. Conversely, the term analogous to 'post-colonial' at its most literal would be 'post-facist'. This in turn underscores the dangers of a literalist reading of the word 'post-colonial'. It seems to us that placing the terms 'post-colonial' and 'post-Civil Rights' alongside one other immediately serves to clarify some of the temporal and conceptual ambiguities of the 'post' in both cases. From the vantage point of the US today, it draws attention to the unfinished nature of the processes designated by both terms. It undermines, specifically, the sense of completion often implied by the 'post' in 'post-colonial', and which, if political conservatives could have their way, would settle upon the 'post' in 'post-Civil Rights'. In doing so it helps to clarify that the 'posts' in both cases do not signal an 'after' but rather mark spaces of ongoing contestation enabled by decolonization struggles both globally and locally. Finally, 'post-Civil Rights' has not, to our knowledge, been used to name or claim identity. Questions of subject formation have on the other hand been integral to a consideration of the 'post-colonial'.[4] Accordingly, in this chapter we move between considering 'post-colonial' as periodization and axis of subjectivity. By contrast, 'post-Civil Rights' is developed here as a form of periodization that we believe to be particularly helpful in coming to terms with the ideological and political landscape of the US today.[5]

POST-COLONIAL(ITY?): A STATE OF BEING?

Taking the word apart, with the help of the dictionary, we find that 'post', in the sense that it interests us here, means variously 'after in time', 'later', 'following', or 'after in space'. Without the benefit of the dictionary, we take it that 'colonization', and 'colonialism' indicate a system of domination, in particular one involving geographical and/or racial distanciation between the rulers and the ruled, and one which, like all systems of domination, has interlinked political, economic and discursive dimensions. The suffix, 'i-t-y', in English 'ity', in French 'ité', in Latin 'itas' is said to mean 'character', 'condition' or 'state', with 'state' defined as 'a set of circumstances or attributes characterizing a person or thing at a given time', a 'way or form of being'. This confirms the suffix, 'ity' in 'post-coloniality' as connoting a condition that is evenly developed rather than internally disparate, disarrayed or contradictory.

Dictionary explorations, of course, mean little, in the sense that there is no collective unconscious, nor even a common Spellcheck and Thesaurus in the hard-drive, by means of which cultural critics continually confirm their intended meanings by reference to Webster's. But it seems to us that this staged form of attention to both prefix and suffix dramatizes the crux of what is problematic in the concept of 'post-coloniality'. The first problem lies with the 'post'. 'Post' means 'after in time'. But what happened during that time—presumably in this instance a time between 'colonialism', or 'coloniality', and now? In what senses are we now situated 'after' 'coloniality' in the sense of 'coloniality' being 'over and done with'? What, about 'the colonial', is over, and for whom? This is not a rhetorical but a genuine question for it seems to us that, in relation to colonialism, some things are over, others transformed, and still others apparently unreconstructed. What, by the way happened to 'neo-colonialism' in all of this talk of the colonial and the post? In short, what do we too hasily elide when we involve the 'post-colonial', especially as an 'ity', as a condition, state, way or form of being spread evenly over an area without specified borders or unevenness or contradiction? [. . .]

SOMETHING 'POST-COLONIAL' IS HAPPENING—BUT WHAT, WHERE AND TO WHOM?

It is this notion of a political, economic and discursive shift, one that is decisive without being definitive, that we would like to argue regarding the term 'post-colonial'. For it enables us to concede the shift effected by decolonization without claiming either a complete rupture in social, economic and political relations and forms of knowledge (an end to racial inequality, economic self-sufficiency for new nations, 'the end of History') or its opposite, admittedly argued by few, that the present is nothing more than a mere repetition of the past.

The distinction between 'decisive' and 'definitive' seems to us important given the enabling status accorded to decolonization in discussions of the new ethnography, contemporary cultural theory, and the crisis in the Humanities. [. . .]

We would also urge a greater awareness than is sometimes evident in such debate that, despite the impact in certain quarters of the critique of specific textual practices and philosophical presumptions, elsewhere much remains the same—it's business as usual. The integrity of the Subject may have been exposed as a ruse of bourgeois ideology by philosophers and cultural critics, but law, to take one powerful institution, still operates as though this were not the case. To cite only one example, the legitimacy of land-rights claims of indigenous or Fourth World peoples turns on ahistorical conceptions of culture and essentialist notions of identity. An American anthropologist, having recently discovered Benedict Anderson,[6] can unwittingly create complications for Maori land claims in arguing that Maori traditions are 'invented'.[7] The point here is not so much that anti-essentialist conceptions of identity are reactionary, as that, so long as other conceptions of identity have effectivity in the world, we necessarily need to engage them.[8] A position of abstract theoreticism that adjudicates between positions solely on the basis of 'theoretical correctness' seems to us to aggrandize theory, while failing to grasp the complex and contradictory workings of power/knowledge.

Returning to our conception of the term 'post-colonial' then, we would like to accent the ambiguity of the 'post' in 'post-colonial' and underscore the *twin* processes that are evoked by it, namely colonization/decolonization. We would argue that 'post-colonial' marks a decisive, though not definitive shift that stages contemporary encounters between India and Britain and between white Britons and their non white Others, though not always in the same way or to the same degree.

Location is in many respects key in determining the importance of the 'post-colonial' as an axis staging cross-racial encounters. In Britain at least, it seems to us that the 'post-colonial' is an axis with effectivity. The memory and legacies of colonization/decolonization form one axis through which social relations and subjectivities are shaped. The operation of the 'postcolonial' axis—of the memories and legacies of colonization/decolonization —may be either explicit or implicit. When we argue that the axis of colonization/decolonization stages cross-racial encounters in Britain, we suggest that whether through negation, denial, affirmation, repression or evasion, the history condensed in the sentence 'We are here because you were there', is necessarily engaged. To say this is not to indicate anything about *how* this history of colonization/decolonization is engaged. One need only point to the positions taken on *Satanic Verses*[9] by Salman Rushdie himself, the Bradford fundamentalists, the irate white conservatives, the confused and then outraged white liberals, and the feminist group Women Against Fundamentalism, to note something of the range of possible ways of negotiating this history.[10] The example of *Satanic Verses* also serves to clarify another point. It is also not our claim that colonization/decolonization is the only axis with effectivity in the British context. For, obviously, positions on the Rushdie controversy were equally shaped by other axes, among them gender, race, religion, sexuality, political orientation.

The 'post-colonial' as an axis of subject formation is constructed not simply in dialogue with dominant white society, but is an effect of engagement between particular subjects, white society, region of origin and region of religious and/or political affiliation, what Paul Gilroy[11] describes as 'the dialectics of diasporic identification'. Thus, many African or South Asian Muslims in Britain, would include in this matrix the home of their religion, the Middle East. Similarly, the films of Isaac Julien and the Black film collective Sankofa, for instance, *Passion of Remembrance* and *Looking for Langston*, are transatlantic meditations on African-Caribbean political and sexual identity. The struggle of African-Americans in the USA becomes a political resource for forging imagined diasporic communities. The engagement of colonization/decolonization thus has transnational dimensions, its local expressions multiply inflected by regional and global affinities and considerations, in turn crosscut by class, race, gender, sexuality, etc.

Not all places in this transnational circuit are, however, similarly 'post-colonial'. The active, subjective, inescapable, everyday engagement with the legacies of colonization/decolonization that is part of the British matrix for reggae, bhangra rap, Hanif Kureshi's screenplays, or Homi Bhabha's conception of 'hybridity',[12] are not the terms of theoretical, artistic or political endeavors in India. As noted earlier and argued more fully elsewhere,[13] in India it is the nation state and its failure to represent anything other than narrow sectional interests that provides grist for the mill of politics and theory. We are not claiming here that India is not 'post-colonial', that would be an absurd proposition; rather that it is not 'post-colonial' *in the same way*. The hand of the past in the shape of the present is multiply refracted such that the term 'post-colonial' fails to grasp the ways in which people are driven to apprehend the world and their relation to it.

MEANWHILE BACK AT THE RANCH IN THE GOOD OLD USA

We suggested at the very beginning of this paper that 'post-Civil Rights' may be to the USA what 'post-colonial' is to Britain: a name for a decisive though hardly definitive shift that implicitly or explicitly structures, whether through affirmation, negation, denial, repression or evasion, relations between the races in this country. We use the term 'Civil Rights' here to signal a range of struggles including those against segregation, for voting rights and political representation, for institutional and economic equality, as well as the cultural renaissance and cultural nationalisms of the late 1960s and early 1970s. Like 'post-colonial', 'post-Civil Rights' retains the ambiguity, perhaps more immediately telling given this is our backyard, of the 'post' in relation to Civil Rights: the way it simultaneously signals both the fight against entrenched institutional and cultural racism, and the need for continued struggles for racial equality. Whether one is left or right on the political spectrum, for or against affirmative action, for or against an ethnic studies requirement, it seems to us that we all necessarily do battle on a discursive and political terrain that is distinctly 'post-Civil Rights'. This was abundantly evident in the debates surrounding the nomination of Clarence Thomas to the Supreme Court and the challenge to it presented by Anita Hill's allegations of sexual harassment. Indeed, the concerted effort over the last decade by the Reagan and Bush administrations to dismantle the gains of the Civil Rights movement is testimony to the shifts effected by it and to the power of the term to signify both the history of colonial and racist domination and collective resistance to it.

The history of 1950s and 1960s civil rights movements is, however, the narrative of the domination and resistance of established communities of color in the USA: the original Native Americans, African-Americans, Latino/Chicanos, Asian-Americans. To this we must add the tales of recent immigrants/refugees, who rather more like Asians and African-Caribbeans in Britain represent the return of the repressed on the borders of the imperialist center. They also negotiate a 'post-Civil Rights' US landscape. Their travel to the US has been occasioned by a history related to, but distinct from, that of people of color already here. Their historical experiences stretch existing categories—'Hispanic', 'Asian—inflecting them with new meanings. Relations between recent immigrants/refugees and those already here, whether whites or people of color, are constituted through discourses that draw heavily on colonial and racist rhetoric both in form and content. Such mutual ignorance and parochialism in the context of economic depression and state-supported nativism can be, and has been, explosive. Nothing but the most complex and historically specific conceptions of identity and subjectivity can sufficiently grasp the present situation and articulate a politics adequate to it.

MULTIPLE AXES, CONJUNCTURES, AND POLITICS OF LOCATION

Thus far, here, we have attempted to situate the term 'post-colonial' in time and space, pointing to differences in its effectivity in a range of contexts. In this final section we wish to take our argument a step further, suggesting that it is also necessary to view colonial/post-colonial relations as co-constructed with other axes of domination and resistance—that the 'post-colonial' is in effect a construct internally differentiated by its intersections with other unfolding relations. We propose here the value of what we will term a 'feminist conjuncturalist' approach, drawing tools and inspiration from both Marxist cultural criticism and US Third World feminism (for one definition of the latter see Sandoval).[14] We believe such a framework serves well our goal of benefiting from the analytical space opened up by the term 'post-colonial' while avoiding the dangers of failing to delimit it. It enables us to argue that at given moments and locations, the axis of colonization/decolonization might be *the* most salient one, at other times, not so.

In the past two decades, there has been underway in feminism, a process of decentering the white/Western subject (whether male *or* female) which has been at times similar to, enabling of, and indebted to, but most often separate from, the projects of poststructuralist and 'postcolonial' cultural criticism. Since the late 1960s, US women of color, frequently speaking simultaneously from 'within and against' *both* women's liberation *and* antiracist movements, have insisted upon the need to analyze and challenge systems of domination, and concomitant constructions of subjecthood, not singly, but multiply.[15] More recently and following their lead, US white feminists have made parallel arguments. [. . .]

What is significant to us here is the emphasis, within feminist theorizing, on the complexity of effective links between intersecting axes of domination, and the concomitant complexity of subjectivity and political agency. [. . .] Although not the direction or intent of all of the feminists involved in that process, it should be recognized that notions of 'multiplicity' have at times led critics down the very problematic path of what one might call 'neo-relativism', such that it is sometimes argued that 'we' are all decentered, multiple, 'minor' or 'mestiza' in exactly comparable ways. It becomes critical, then, to maintain a sharp analysis of the relationship between subjectivity and power, subjectivity and specific relations of domination and subordination. In this regard, some feminist theorists have argued for attention to the 'politics of location'. [. . .]

However, these problems *do* in a sense arise out of the current state of feminist theorization of subjectivity and systems of domination. For feminist theory—by no means a unified terrain—has vacillated over how to analyse the relationships between the multiple axes of oppression that it names. Thus, feminism seems to comprise at least four tendencies. First we can distinguish a white feminist 'rearguard' that continues to argue for the primacy of gender domination, as well as a second, so to speak, 'neo-rearguard' tendency, again especially by white feminists, to reabsorb notions of multiply determined subjectivity under the single 'mistress narrative' of gender domination.

Thirdly, other theorists and activists, frequently but not exclusively women of color, responding *both* to the prioritization of gender in 'hegemonic' feminism, and to the pervasive sexism and/or heterosexism and/or racism of other movements, insist on the 'simultaneity' of the workings of axes of domination.[16] This insistence on a non-hierarchical analysis of how oppression works was born of political practice and has been critical to coalition building. It is, in fact, articulated in response to prior elisions and erasures in analyses of subject and social formation, whether in feminism, La Raza, Black Power, the Marxist left, or elsewhere. There is finally a fourth tendency which is in fact an outgrowth of the third. This builds on and further complicates the ideas of 'simultaneity' and 'multiplicity' to examine how oppression may be experienced in specifiably complex and shifting relationships to different axes of domination.[17] Lest this four-part map be taken to describe a straightforward diachronic unfolding, it is important to point out that, in fact, the editors and contributors to *This Bridge Called My Back*, the 1981 anthology to which Alarcon's article refers, were already practitioners of the fourth tendency, that of complex, multiply engaged yet locally focused analyses.

Building complex analyses, avoiding erasure, specifying location: feminist analysts of this kind share a great deal, some consciously and others not, with 'postmodern conjuncturalism'. [. . .] We find postmodern conjuncturalism helpful to our current project for, like the feminist developments just noted, it firmly centers the analysis of subject formation and cultural practice within matrices of domination and subordination. Moreover, it does so in a way that neither conceives domination in single-axis terms nor falsely equalizes the effects of these relations on subjects:

> A conjunctural theory of power is not claiming [. . .] that all such relations of power are equal, equally determining, or equally liveable; these are questions that depend on the analysis of the specific, concrete conjuncture.[18]

Also key for our purposes, postmodern conjuncturalism asserts that there is an effective but not determining relationship between subjects and their histories, a relationship that is complex, shifting and yet not 'free'. The concept of articulation links subjects and structures dynamically, such that practices, meanings and identities 'are forged by people operating within the limits of their real conditions and the historically articulated "tendential lines of force"'[19]

This framework intersects with feminist appropriations of Althusser, such as de Lauretis's insistence on 'an identity that one *decides* to reclaim', (emphasis ours) and, stating even more succinctly the dialectic of agency and context, Alarcon's conceptualization of subjects 'driven to grasp' their subject positions across a shifting, though not *randomly* shifting, field.

> The concept of articulation within postmodern conjuncturalism foregrounds the production of contexts, the ongoing effort by which particular practices are removed from and inserted into different structures of relationships, the construction of one set of relationships out of another, the continuous struggle to reposition practices within a shifting field of forces.[20]

This brings us full circle to one of our arguments about the term 'post-colonial'. For we have noted the complex temporal and spatial repositioning and recombining of practices and signifiers from the histories of racism and colonization in the construction of contexts and identities in the USA and Britain. We have emphasized the ways practices may be given new meanings, and create 'new subjects', in different locations.

Finally, postmodern conjuncturalism's call for attention to the 'tendential lines of force', its insistence that the meanings and effectivity of particular practices and relations of power are dependent on historical moment and locale, underscores our other central argument about the term 'post-colonial'. For we have argued that the concept must be carefully specified, used to describe moments, social formations, subject positions and practices which arise out of an unfolding axis of colonization/decolonization, interwoven with the unfolding of other axes, in *uneven, unequal* relations with one another.

The affinities between US feminist developments we have described and a conjuncturalist approach to Cultural Studies are all the more interesting once one notes the context in which the latter came into being. For, in fact, the theoretical appropriations of Althusser and Gramsci we draw on here, like US Third World feminism, were not developed as part of an abstract 'race for theory'. [. . .]

British conjuncturalist analysis emerges from and speaks to a post-colonial Britain, just as US Third World feminism develops out of and addresses a post-Civil Rights USA.

What we have attempted here is to sketch in outline a feminist conjuncturalist reading of the term, 'post-colonial' in three locations—India, Britain and the USA. We wish to emphasize once again that we have not undertaken here a general reading of the 'post-colonial' that is applicable to all places at all times. Not only are we inadequately placed to undertake such a task, but we would argue against the idea that there is such a thing as '*the*' 'post-colonial' in any simple sense. This does not mean, however, that we are against theorizing the term, nor that it is without utility. Rather, as we have said, we would argue that the notion of the 'post-colonial' is best understood in context of a rigorous politics of location, of a rigorous conjuncturalism. There are, then, moments and spaces in which subjects are 'driven to grasp' their positioning and subjecthood as 'post-colonial'; yet there are other contexts in which, to use the term as the organizing principle of one's analysis, is precisely to 'fail to grasp the specificity' of the location or the moment.

Notes

We would like to thank Chetan Bhatt, Avtar Brah, Rosa Linda Fregoso, Lisa Lowe, Ted Swedenburg and Kamala Visweswaran for their comments on earlier incarnations of this Chapter.

1. In his analysis of artistic and literary production in Sub-Saharan Africa and the reception of the former in the US, Kwame Anthony Appiah makes a persuasive argument about the importance of circumscribing the post-colonial and specifying its relationship to postmodernism (Kwame Anthony Appiah, 'Is the post- in postmodernism the post- in postcolonial', *Critical Inquiry* 17, (Winter, 1991), 336–57).
2. We note with pleasure the publication of *Social Text* 31/32 on questions of the post-colonial, which appeared while our article was under review. Many of the concerns authors raise there intersect with our own. On questions about the efficacy of the term post-colonial, see especially, Anne McClintock, '"The Angel of Progress": Pitfalls of the term "Post-colonialism"', *Social Text* 31/32 (1992), 84–98; and Ella Shohat, 'Notes on the Postcolonial', *Social Text* 31/32 (1992), 99–113.
3. Michael Omi and Howard Winant, in *Racial Formation in the United States: From the 1960s to the 1980s* (New York: Routledge, 1986), 172, n. 2, state that the phrase 'great transformation' is taken from Karl Polyani, and is deployed by them to indicate the epochal nature of the transformation under consideration in their text.
4. See, for example, Edward Said, 'Intellectuals in the Post-colonial World', *Salmagundi* 70–1 (1986), 45–64; Homi Bhabha, 'Location, Intervention, Incommensurability: a Conversation with Homi Bhabha', *Emergencies* 1 (Fall, 1989), 63–88; Sarah Harasym (ed.), *The Post-Colonial Critic: Interviews, Strategies, Dialogues: Gayratri Chakravorty Spivak* (New York: Routledge, 1990).

5. The terms 'post-colonial' and 'post-Civil Rights' as we use them, are periodizations that name the *initiation* of particular struggles. These struggles were, of course, to develop in heterogeneous directions, for example, socialism and bourgeois nationalism in the case of India, cultural nationalism and revolutionary race–class struggle in the example of the USA.
6. Benedict Anderson, *Imagined Communities: Reflections on the Origin and Spread of Nationalism* (London: Verso, 1983).
7. Allan Hanson, 'Probably Not: A Reply to Jean Jackson's "Is There a Way to Talk about Making Culture Without Making Enemies?"', American Ethnological Society 113th Annual Spring Meeting, Charleston, SC, March 15, 1990.
8. James Clifford, 'Identity in Mashpee', in *The Predicament of Culture* (Cambridge: Harvard University Press, 1988), 277–346; Evelyn Legaré, 'Native Indian Identity: the Need to be Other', American Ethnological Society 113th Annual Spring Meeting, Charleston, SC, March 15, 1990.
9. Salman Rushdie, *Satanic Verses* (New York: Viking, 1989).
10. For a sense of the debate, see Lisa Appignanesi and Sara Maitland (eds.), *The Rushdie File* (London: ICA, 1989); Women Against Fundamentalism, Press Statement, 9 March 1989, *Feminist Review* 33 (Winter 1989), 110; Clara Connelly, 'Washing Our Linen: One Year of Women Against Fundamentalism', *Feminist Review* 37 (Spring 1991), 68–77; and for Rushdie's shifting position, Salman Rushdie, *Imaginary Homelands: Essays and Criticism 1982–1991* (London: Viking, 1991), 393–432.
11. Paul Gilroy, 'It Ain't Where You're From, It's Where You're At: the Dialectics of Diasporic Identification', *Third Text* 13 (Winter 1990–1), 3–16.
12. Homi Bhabha, 'Signs Taken for Wonders: Questions of Ambivalence and Authority under a Tree Outside Delhi, May 1817', *Critical Inquiry* 12 (1985), 1, 144–65.
13. Lata Mani, 'Multiple Meditations: Feminist Scholarship in the Age of Multinational Reception', *Feminist Review* 35 (Summer 1990), 24–41.
14. Chela Sandoval, 'U.S. Third World Feminism: the Theory and Method of Oppositional Consciousness in the Postmodern World', *Genders* 10 (May 1991), 18, n. 3.
15. Parallel debates have also gone on in Britain. See the journals *Spare Rib* and *Outwrite*, and also Valerie Amos *et al.* (eds.), *Many Voices, One Chant, Feminist Review* 17 (Summer 1984), Special issue.
16. Combahee River Collective, 'A Black Feminist Statement, April 1977', in Zillah R. Eisenstein (ed.), *Capitalist Patriarchy and the Case for Socialist Feminism* (New York: Monthly Review Press, 1979), 362–72; Patricia Zavella, 'The Problematic Relationship of Feminism and Chicana Studies', *Women's Studies* 17 (1988), 123–34.
17. Cherrie Moraga and Gloria Anzaldua (eds.), *This Bridge Called My Back: Writings by Radical Women of Color* (Watertown, MA: Persephone Press, 1981, republished by Kitchen Table Women of Color Press, 1984); Sandoval, 'U.S. Third World Feminism'.
18. Lawrence Grossberg, 'The Formation of Cultural Studies: an American in Birmingham', *Strategies* 2 (1989), 138.
19. Ibid., 136.
20. Ibid., 137.

Genealogies, Legacies, Movements

M. Jacqui Alexander and Chandra Talpade Mohanty *

FEMINIST GENEALOGIES

[. . .] We both came to feminist studies in the US academy through a series of geographical, political, and intellectual dislocations. Our journeys were marked by an educational process in which anticolonial struggle against the British (in Trinidad and Tobago and India) and the founding of the nation-state infused the fabric of everyday life. Our consciousnesses were thus shaped by the burden of persistent colonialisms and the euphoric promise of nationalism and self-determination. We both inherited the belief that education was a key strategy of decolonization, rather than merely a path toward mainstream credentials and upward mobility. In other words, for us, education was always linked to the political practice of service to community and to nation. However, nationalism at this stage had done little to transform the practices of colonial education, nor had it necessarily imagined us (in Jacqui's case, daughter now lesbian; in Chandra's, woman not mother) as the legitimate heirs of the new nation. Then, as now, nation and citizenship were largely premised within normative parameters of masculinity and heterosexuality.

We both moved to the United States of North America over fifteen years ago. None of the racial, religious, or class/caste fractures we had previously experienced could have prepared us for the painful racial terrain we encountered here. We were not born women of color, but became women of color here. From African-American and US women of color, we learned the peculiar brand of US North American racism and its constricted boundaries of race. Psychic residues of different

* From M. Jacqui Alexander and Chandra Talpade Mohanty, 'Introduction: Genealogies, Legacies, Movements' from *Feminist Genealogies, Colonial Legacies, Democratic Futures* (Routledge, 1997), xiii–xlii.

colonialisms made it necessary for us to grapple with the nuances of the interconnectedness of struggles for decolonization. Racism against African-American people was distinct, although connected to racism against Chicano, Native, or Asian peoples. The challenge of negotiating these politics of racial fragmentation has brought us to this moment. Through a politics of decolonization, we have learned that racial solidarity is necessary, even if that means grappling with the differences between oppositional and relational consciousness. Our own experiences of the multiple sites of racism in the US have also convinced us that we must understand the local as well as the global manifestations of power.

The institutionalization of a particular definition of Women's Studies in the US academy exposed another set of contradictions in our own lives as feminist activists, scholars, and teachers. By 'contradictions', we mean the sense of alienation, dislocation, and marginalization that often accompanies a racialized location within white institutions. As 'immigrant' women of color, we were neither the 'right' color, gender, or nationality in terms of the self-definition of the US academy, or by extension, of the Women's Studies establishment. In Women's Studies contexts, the color of our gender mattered. The citizenship machinery deployed by the state which positioned us as resident aliens ('deviant' non-citizen; 'legal' immigrants) operates similarly within Women's Studies: it codifies an outsider status which is different from the outsider status of women of color born in the United States.[1] For instance, our racialization as Caribbean and Indian women was assimilated into a US narrative of racialization, naturalized between African-Americans and Euro-Americans. Our experiences could be recognized and acknowledged only to the extent that they resembled those of African-American women.

However, the specificities of our national and cultural genealogies—being Black and Brown women—and our statuses as immigrants were constantly being used to position us as foreign, thus muting the legitimacy of our claims to the experiences of different racisms.[2] Working in solidarity with different women of color was at times insufficient to entirely subvert acts of racial fragmentation aimed at separating women of color from each other. We remained (differently) less threatening than African-American women to white women, who often preferred to deal with our 'foreignness' rather than our racialization in the US. This, in turn, sometimes created divisive relations between us and African-American feminists. On many occasions we experienced the contradictory ironies of invisibility and hypervisibility. In fact, the experience of these contradictions is partly responsible for our particular reading of injustice and our vision of social transformation. Out of a strong intellectual and political commitment to feminism, we remain committed to the creation of feminist communities, founded on different grounds than those we have experienced in many liberal academic circles.

The feminist genealogies that lie behind this project can be charted on various levels. Besides our own individual and collective genealogies, we want to consider (i) the contours of feminist intellectual and political practice as it is institutionalized within Women's Studies programs in US colleges and universities; (ii) the effects of postmodernist theory on the theorization of the experience, consciousness, and social identities of women of color, especially in terms of the formulation of international or global feminisms; and (iii) the significance of self-examination and reflection on the genealogies of feminist organizations. In the last case, we want to offer here a comparative, relational way of thinking about feminist praxis that is grounded in the concrete analysis and visionings of the authors/communities in this collection.

[. . .] One of the effects of globalization over the last two decades has been a new visibility of women's issues on the world stage. Witness the large numbers of international conferences on topics like violence against women, women's health, reproductive politics, and 'population control'. At the same time, feminism has been quantified for consumption within the global marketplace of ideas (we call this 'freemarket feminism'). We take issue with this freemarket feminism in crafting our vision of democratic futures. The experiences, histories, and self-reflections of feminists of color and Third-World feminists remain at the center of the anthology, but geopolitical shifts and the particular forms of globalization over the last decade necessitate an active, deliberate focus on questions of genealogies, legacies, and futures in comparative feminist praxis. We have, therefore, deliberately chosen to map these specific paths by which feminist communities, organizations, and movements call up and reflect upon moments in their own collective histories and struggles for autonomy. Thus, our use of words like 'genealogies' or 'legacies' is not meant to suggest a frozen or embodied inheritance of domination and resistance, but an interested, conscious thinking and rethinking of history and historicity, a rethinking which has women's autonomy and self-determination at its core.

After more than two decades of struggles around questions of racism and heterosexism, a particular characterization of gender—

naturalized through the history and experiences of middle class, urban, Euro-American women—continues to be propagated in Women's Studies and gender studies programs in the US academy. By not challenging the hegemony of whiteness (and of capitalism) within academic institutions, for instance, these Women's Studies programs often end up bolstering inherited regimes of race and Eurocentrism. Although in the 1970s, the formulation of the category of gender and its diffusion throughout a variety of disciplines was one of the most important goals of Women's Studies, in the 1990s new and radically different intellectual challenges emerged. Those challenges compelled Women's Studies to face head on some of the more crucial questions of class divisions, racialization, and heterosexualization operating within the US polity and within Women's Studies programs themselves. The recent diffusion of Eurocentric consumer culture in the wake of the further consolidation of multinational capital, for example, foregrounds the importance of theorizing the ways inequality structures values, desires, and needs for different groups and classes of women. Any understanding of women's experiences based on a narrow conception of gender would simply be incapable of fully addressing the homogenizing and hierarchizing effects of economic and cultural processes which are the result of this consumer culture.

This is why *Genealogies* aims to provide a comparative, relational, and historically based conception of feminism, one that differs markedly from the liberal-pluralist understanding of feminism, an inheritance of the predominantly liberal roots of American feminist praxis.[3] Clearly, one of the things being charted here is a convergence between the way gender emerged as a primary category of analysis and the social, demographic, and class composition of those who actually theorized gender in the US academy. In other words, we want to suggest a link between the positions of power held by white women in Women's Studies, the subject of their theorizing, and the kinds of analytic tools they deployed.

In addition, serious intellectual, analytic, and political engagement with the theorizations of women of color has not occurred. Instead, this work has been largely appropriated and often erased, and thus does not figure in the institutional memory or canonical formulations of Women's Studies knowledge. [. . .]

The liberal-pluralist multiculturalism that is often evident in women's studies syllabi, with a week or two on 'women of color' and 'sexuality', testifies to this appropriation of the work of women of color. Token inclusion of our texts without reconceptualizing the whole white, middle-class, gendered knowledge base effectively absorbs and silences us. This says, in effect, that our theories are plausible and carry explanatory weight only in relation to our *specific* experiences, but that they have no use value in relation to the rest of the world. Moreover, postmodernist theory, in its haste to dissociate itself from all forms of essentialism, has generated a series of epistemological confusions regarding the interconnections among location, identity, and the construction of knowledge. Thus, for instance, localized questions of experience, identity, culture, and history, which enable us to understand specific processes of domination and subordination, are often dismissed by postmodern theories as reiterations of cultural 'essence' or unified, stable identity.[4]

Postmodernist discourse attempts to move beyond essentialism by pluralizing and dissolving the stability and analytic utility of the categories of race, class, gender, and sexuality. This strategy often forecloses any valid recuperation of these categories or the social relations through which they are constituted. If we dissolve the category of race, for instance, it becomes difficult to claim the experience of racism. Certainly, racism and the processes of racialization are far more complicated now than they were when W. E. B. Du Bois predicted that the 'problem of the color line is the problem of the twentieth century'.[5] But the relations of domination and subordination that are named and articulated through the processes of racism and racialization still exist, and they still require analytic and political specification and engagement. Global realignments and fluidity of capital have simply led to further consolidation and exacerbation of capitalist relations of domination and exploitation—what we refer to as 'processes of recolonization'. Thus, while the current 'color line' may suggest more complicated forms of racialized identities, the hierarchical relationships among racial groups and geographies have not disappeared. Yet, race does not figure in most 'first world' considerations of postmodernism.[6] [. . .]

Understanding the various constructions of self and identity during late capitalism—when transnationalization confounds neo-colonial processes and women's relationship to them, and when fluid borders permit the mobility of 'free' market capital is a complicated enterprise that cannot be simply invoked by claiming fluid or fractured identities. What kind of racialized, gendered selves get produced at the conjuncture of the transnational and the neo-colonial? Are there selves which are formed outside of the hegemonic heterosexual contract that defy dominant (Western) understandings of identity construction?

Are they commensurate with the multiple self constructed under (American) postmodernism? What kinds of transformative practices are needed in order to develop nonhegemonic selves? Are these practices commensurate with feminist organizational struggles for decolonization? These are some of the urgent questions we seek to engage and which the authors in *Genealogies* take up. These questions force us to take seriously the authority and validity of consciousness and the experiences of domination and struggle in the formation of identities that are simultaneously social and political.

The rapid institutionalization of a particular brand of postmodernist theorizing in the US academy is significant for another reason. The knowledge base of a discipline has a profound effect on both pedagogic strategies and the kinds of knowledge that are developed within the classroom. This is one of the central questions that Leslie Roman examines when she argues that 'relativist postmodernism' (which rejects 'realist epistemologies' that would 'weigh a person's or group's subjective claims against and in relation to adequate structural analyses of their objective social locations') has led to a certain kind of racial relativism or white defensiveness in the classroom. By 'white defensiveness', Roman means 'the relativistic assertion that whites, like "people of color," are history's oppressed subjects of racism'. It is this sort of defensiveness that prevents teachers from taking critical antiracist pedagogical positions that would adjudicate between "the epistemic standpoints of fundamentally oppressed groups and those in more privileged positions'.[7] We cannot overestimate the need for conscious self-reflexivity about the complicity of intellectual frameworks in politics, in the fact that something is at stake in the very process of reauthorizing and mediating inequalities or regressive politics of different kinds.[8]

Another intellectual and political movement that draws upon earlier formulations of a global sisterhood took root in the academy in the 1990s through discussions about international feminism.[9] Beyond the fact that these claims about an international feminism almost always originate in the West, there are some common themes which unite them. Drawing from an often unspecified liberal episteme, they tend to invoke a difference-as-pluralism model in which women in the Third World bear the disproportionate burden of difference. 'International' feminism embraces an approach of the articulation of many voices to specify an inclusive feminism—calls for 'global sisterhood' are often premised on a center/periphery model where women of color or Third World women constitute the periphery. Race is invariably erased from any conception of the international based on nation, devoid of race, all the more so because of a strict separation between the international and the domestic, or an understanding of the ways in which they are mutually constituted. To a large extent, underlying the conception of the international is a notion of universal patriarchy operating in a transhistorical way to subordinate all women. The only plausible methodological strategy here, then, is to make visible and intelligible (to the West) the organizational practices and writings of Third-World women through a discrete case-study approach. 'International', moreover, has come to be collapsed into the culture and values of capitalism.

Missing from these definitions of 'international' (what we refer to as 'transnational' from now on) are at least three elements: (i) a way of thinking about women in similar contexts across the world, in *different* geographical spaces, rather than as *all* women across the world; (ii) an understanding of a set of unequal relationships among and between peoples, rather than a set of traits embodied in all non-US citizens (particularly because US citizenship continues to be premised within a white, Eurocentric, masculinist, heterosexist regime); and (iii) a consideration of the term 'international' in relation to an analysis of economic, political, and ideological processes which foreground the operations of race and capitalism (for instance, those that therefore require taking critical antiracist, anti-capitalist positions that would make feminist solidarity work possible).

To talk about feminist praxis in global contexts would involve shifting the unit of analysis from local, regional, and national culture to relations and processes across cultures. Grounding analyses in particular, local feminist praxis is necessary, but we also need to understand the local in relation to larger, cross-national processes. This would require a corresponding shift in the conception of political organizing and mobilization across borders. The practices of democracy, justice, and equality, for example, would not be subsumed within the white, masculinist definition of the US. Ideas about justice would apply across cultural and national borders. The ideologies of 'immigrants', 'refugees', 'guestworkers', and 'citizens' would need to be reconceived within new definitions of justice. Our very understanding of democracy and its practices would have to become cross-cultural. In place of relativism, this critical application of feminist praxis in global contexts would substitute responsibility, accountability, engagement, and solidarity. We foreground a paradigm of decolonization which stresses power, history, memory, relational analysis, justice (not just representation), and ethics as the issues central to our analysis of globalization.

Practices of globalization are crucial to the conceptual mapping of genealogies of organizing. [. . .] Our framework challenges the still firmly embedded notion of the originary status of Western feminism. It does not simply position Third-World feminism as a reaction to gaps in Western feminism; it does not summon Third-World feminism in the service of (white) Western feminism's intellectual and political projects. Instead, it provides a position from which to argue for a comparative, relational feminist praxis that is transnational in its response to and engagement with global processes of colonization.

Central to our theorization of feminism is a comparative analysis of feminist organizing, criticism, and self-reflection; also crucial is deep contextual knowledge about the nature and contours of the present political economic crisis. Individual analyses are grounded in the contemporary crisis of global capitalism, suggesting that these particular contexts are the ones which throw up very specific analytic and political challenges for organizations. Here, no false dichotomy exists between theory and practice. We literally have to think ourselves out of these crises through collective praxis and particular kinds of theorizing. Crises are what provoke the opportunity for change within organizations. [. . .]

COLONIAL LEGACIES: THE STATE, CAPITALISM, AND PROCESSES OF COLONIZATION

We use the formulation 'colonial legacies' to evoke the imagery of an inheritance and to map continuities and discontinuities between contemporary and inherited practices within state and capital formations. We wish to mark in particular the accelerated processes of recolonization typical of this contemporary moment. At the outset, then, we want to foreground an understanding of the historicity of state and capital in the organization and deployment of sexual politics. [. . .]

The historicity of the state enables an analysis of contemporary relations and hierarchies and positions the state as a focal point of analysis for feminists. We examine the form and operation of the American state in advanced capitalism (which is different from the advanced capitalist state) as a way to analyze the simultaneous processes that advanced capital has generated in relation to capitalism and to advanced colonialism. M. A. Jaimes Guerrero has argued that the US state manages a set of advanced capitalist relations at the same time that it mediates colonial relations both within its borders (Native peoples and communities of color in the US) as well as outside (in Puerto Rico, Hawai'i, and the Pacific where these operations are masked by an ideology of statehood and commonwealth status). We focus on the American state because of our own location in the US and because of its post–Cold War status as the new imperial power in, for example, the Caribbean and India. [. . .] We also mean by 'historicity' the use of specific inheritances around counterhegemonic histories that interrupt state and capitalist dominance. The different modes of feminist practice ... assume their particular trajectories from a complicated overlapping of historical matrices of left liberation struggles, contemporary nationalisms (in spite of feminism's contestatory relationship to nationalism), and the very presence and intervention of the state itself. There are no fixed prescriptions by which one might determine in advance the specific counterhegemonic histories which will be most useful. [. . .]

The importance of oppositional historical records cannot be underestimated. As Patricia J. Williams has argued, 'To be without documentation is too unsustaining, too spontaneously ahistorical, too dangerously malleable in the hands of those who would rewrite not merely the past but [my] future as well'.[10] Even memory is not an unmediated category here, for insinuated within counterhegemonic inheritances are the inheritances of violence and trauma, what Elizabeth Alexander has called 'traumatized memory'. Such memories must be scrutinized and sifted. For feminism, then, the structuring of new modes of consciousness through praxis is both politically and psychically necessary.

Because no variety of feminism—particularly feminism in the Third World—has escaped state intervention, control, discipline, and surveillance; and because the state (particularly the neo-colonial state) facilitates the transnational movement of capital within national borders and is, therefore, instrumental in the reconfiguring of global relationships; and because capitalism and these processes of recolonization structure the contemporary practices of neo-colonial and advanced capitalist/colonial states, the state figures centrally in any analytic attempt to grapple with colonial legacies. Thus, a focus on the state seems especially crucial at a time when many of the attempts to manage the global crisis in capitalism are enacted by the state apparatus. Structural Adjustment Policies (SAP), the most recent unequal realignments among multinational capital, the International Monetary Fund, and the World Bank, are a case in point. [. . .] Moreover, unlike other institutions, the state engages in an almost microscopic surveillance of women's bodies and continues to bring more and more areas of daily life under its jurisdiction, even when it lacks the capacity or authority to do so successfully.

We are not suggesting, however, that the imperatives of the neo-colonial state and those of advanced capitalist/colonial states are identical. Admittedly, they share these important characteristics: (i) they own the means of organized violence which most often get deployed in the service of 'national security'; (ii) they are both militarized—in other words, masculinized; (iii) they invent and solidify practices of racialization and sexualization of the population; and (iv) they discipline and mobilize the bodies of women—in particular Third-World women—in order to consolidate patriarchal and colonizing processes. Women's bodies are disciplined in different ways: within discourses of profit maximization, as global workers and sexual laborers; within religious fundamentalisms, as repositories of sin and transgression; within specifically nationalist discourses, as guardians of culture and respectability or criminalized as prostitutes and lesbians; and within state discourses of the originary nuclear family, as wives and mothers. Both neo-colonial and advanced capitalist/colonial states organize and reinforce a cathectic structure based in sexual difference (i.e., heterosexuality), which they enforce through a variety of means, including legislation. In almost all instances, however, these states conflate heterosexuality with citizenship and organize a 'citizenship machinery' in order to produce a class of loyal heterosexual citizens and a subordinated class of sexualized, nonprocreative, noncitizens, disloyal to the nation, and, therefore, suspect.[11]

Yet, there are important differences. In the global reconsolidation of capitalism, for instance, neo-colonial states are subordinated to advanced capitalist/colonial states, although both mediate capital accumulation. In neo-colonial contexts, state managers facilitate the entry and diffusion of international capital within national boundaries and help to produce an exploited feminized workforce in export-processing zones. The US state is similar to a neo-colonial state in its ideological approach toward the North American Free Trade Agreement (NAFTA) and the Caribbean Basin Initiative. Neo-colonialism utilizes the dictates of the US economy to set the terms by which capital functions across national boundaries. In advanced capitalist/colonial contexts, transnationalization provides the rationale for hypernationalist intervention into the economies of the Third World, undermining power and legitimacy in far more significant ways than in the US state, for example. This raises the charge that the neo-colonial state has forfeited its claim to sovereignty (the central nationalist promise) through complicity in its own recolonization. As early as 1972, Hamza Alavi had argued that the relative autonomy of the post-colonial state from indigenous and metropolitan class interests seemed to be almost entirely supplanted. Now in the contemporary period, the neo-colonial state operates more directly 'as an instrument of global ruling-class interests.'[12]

Larger processes of globalization make it both difficult and necessary to talk about the nation-state, to talk specifically about nationalism and, for our purposes, the problematical relationship of Third-World women to it. Anti-colonial nationalism has always mobilized women's labor in order to help consolidate popular nationalism, without which state nationalism would never have been able to solidify itself. It is not accidental, therefore, that feminism often emerged within anti-colonial movements. But the state mobilization of the feminine is contradictorily inflected. While, as Geraldine Heng has argued, 'women, the feminine, and figures of gender have traditionally anchored the nationalist imaginary', certain women such as sex workers and lesbians are now being disciplined and written out of the nation's script; they have been invested with the power to corrupt otherwise loyal heterosexual citizens, positioned as hostile to the procreative imperative of nation-building, and, therefore, invested with the ability and desire to destroy it. It is not only around questions of sexuality and gender that nation-states have structured their exclusions, however, but also in relationship to race and class hierarchies. [. . .]

The fact that religious fundamentalist movements now occupy center stage in a number of neo-colonial and advanced capitalist/colonial states is yet another indication of the contradictory effects of nationalist mobilizations of men and women. Gita Sahgal and Nira Yuval Davis link the global rise of religious fundamentalism to the failure of both capitalism and communism to provide for people's material, spiritual, and emotional needs.[13] They suggest that in neo-colonial societies, and among people of color in the West, religious fundamentalism is also linked to the failure of nationalist and socialist movements to bring about liberation from oppression. Fundamentalist movements are deeply heteropatriarchal in suggesting the control and regulation of women's sexuality as the panacea for all of these failures.

Analyzing the nexus of state, capitalist and patriarchal relations in the consolidation of religious fundamentalism in India, Amrita Chhachhi has shown that state-supported fundamentalism reinforces the shift of control over women from kinsmen to any man of the 'religious' community—the public is profoundly patriarchal. Within religious fundamentalist discourses and state practices, women's bodies and minds, as well as the domestic and public spaces they occupy, become the primary ground for the regulation of morality and inscriptions of patriarchal control. This is another crucial arena for mapping the gendered processes of recolonization at the end of the twentieth century.[14]

No understanding of these post-Cold War processes would be complete, however, without an analysis of the strategic function of militarized masculinity in the reproduction of colonization. An official designation of 'post-Cold War' does not automatically erase the effects of colonization. In addition to the dislocations and dispersals of Third-World women whose lives were previously tied to militarization, the concept of soldiering (which has historically been linked to masculinity) is also undergoing profound transformation. [. . .]

In neocolonial contexts, the crisis becomes evident in the legal (re)production of heterosexuality through state moves to contain desire between women. In '(de)militarized' contexts such as the United States, the figure of the hyper-masculinized soldier, previously embodied in the image of whiteness, is diffused globally as the agent of US might, the symbol of white manliness, and the naturalization of Third-World women's sexual labor organized primarily through prostitution. The work of Thanh-dam Truong and Kamala Kempadoo is most useful here in demystifying the extent to which prostitutes' labor contributes to the processes of private capital accumulation and the state's reliance on it as a way to continue the heterosexualization of defense, military productivity, and the like.[15] New kinds of racial and sexual reconfigurations occur in this era of demilitarization and Cold War politics, when white masculinity can no longer figure itself around particular definitions of soldiering. Because of shifts in the US economy, for instance, the job of state policing now draws disproportionately on the labor and bodies of people of color, both women and men. The state, no doubt, has to work harder ideologically to resituate white masculinity as its presence, at least in the lower echelons of the military, is being erased.

One of the most dramatic examples of the crisis in heteromasculinity was the recent state-generated discourse in the United States on 'gays' in the military. Ostensibly, the purpose of this debate was to determine whether 'effeminate' masculinity (practiced, but not spoken) could be relied upon to undertake one of the most important tasks of citizenship: that of loyalty to and defense of one's country. The central preoccupation was whether such feminized masculinity (which was deemed neither masculine nor citizen at all) would jeopardize manly masculinity (heteromasculinity) as it undertook its job: defense of the imperial nation. After months of contestation (including a predictable state lament over its own threatened identity in the context of a reduced military), heteromasculinity reasserted itself, rendered 'gay' sexuality present yet silent, and erased lesbian sexuality almost entirely. Further, this conclusion premised homosexuality in whiteness, making it possible for 'invisible' lesbian and gay soldiers to intervene in the Third World and within communities of color at home.

At this point, the central analytic formulation about the state and capital's activity in the processes of recolonization poses a fundamental challenge to the ways in which dominant liberal feminism has organized itself. There are many feminist critiques of the failures of liberalism and its epistemic claims around individual rights and liberties, freedom of individual choice, and the mythology of equal access.[16] In spite of these critiques and their very clear understanding of the operations of state power, however, the sanctity of individual right and choice protected by and bolstered through capitalism still constitute its core premises and practices. [. . .]

Our analyses have foregrounded questions of colonization, economic imperialism, and territorial sovereignty as central to feminism. In this regard, they part company with liberal formulations of a disinterested state, as well as with the state's representation of itself as national and democratic. We suggest that taking seriously state intervention within and across nations might, at the very least, make it possible to imagine and create solidarity struggles across the artificial borders which both state and capital construct.

DEMOCRATIC FUTURES: FEMINIST CONSCIOUSNESS, ORGANIZING VISIONS

Sistren help bring about the awareness of women in me definitely. For the first time even if me go out a street and hear people, whether man or woman, talk tings fi downgrade woman me wouldn't know how to address it. Now me find meself, if me hear anybody say anything to downgrade woman, me can address it. It give me courage to deal wid anybody, no care who you maybe.

Becky[17]

I start with bodies because political states always have an interest in them; because politics usually derive from such interests; and because, as we move increasingly toward new technologies that redefine female bodies, we must recognize these interests as utterly political. Feminists can insist on using our bodies to push out the boundaries of democratic theory.

Zillah Eisenstein[18]

Taken together, the statements of Becky, a member of the Jamaican feminist collective Sistren, and of Zillah Eisenstein, a US feminist political theorist, capture the contradictions and the challenges involved in thinking beyond the various colonizations of our minds and bodies. [. . .]

Given the limitations of Western, liberal conceptions of democracy, we want to conceptualize what might be called 'feminist democracy' in relation to the project of decolonization—in other words, to think through an anti-colonialist, anti-capitalist vision of feminist practice. Further, we want to craft a working definition of feminist democracy that is anchored in the analyses and visions provided by activist-scholars in *Genealogies*. Such a vision necessarily involves acknowledging the objectifying, dehumanizing effects of colonization (e.g., imitation of the colonizer, horizontal violence, self-deprecation due to internalized oppression, self-distrust, psychic and material dependency, desire to assimilate)—and building actively anti-colonialist relationships and cultures as a crucial part of the project of feminist democracy.[19]

What is our working definition of feminist democracy? First, sexual politics are central to the processes and practices of governance, which means not only the effects of governance on women or 'what happens to women' under state rule but also the way the entire apparatus of government treats women.

Secondly, feminist democracy suggests a different order of relationships among people. It suggests understanding socioeconomic, ideological, cultural, and psychic hierarchies of rule (like those of class, gender, race, sexuality, and nation), their interconnectedness, and their effects on disenfranchised peoples *within* the context of transformative collective or organizational practice. Thus, the transformation of relationships, selves, communities, and the practices of daily life leading to self-determination and autonomy for all peoples is crucial in crafting a different order of relationships. Thirdly, in formulations of feminist democracy, agency is theorized differently. Women do not imagine themselves as *victims* or *dependants* of governing structures but as agents of their own lives. Agency is understood here as the conscious and ongoing reproduction of the terms of one's existence while taking responsibility for this process. And agency is anchored in the practice of thinking of oneself as a part of feminist collectivities and organizations. This is not the liberal, pluralist individual self under capitalism. For precisely this reason, decolonization is central to the definition and vision of feminist democracy.

New modes of governance are not possible until the profound effects of hierarchies of colonization are taken into account. What is needed . . . is a *new political culture.* Decolonization involves thinking oneself out of the spaces of domination, but always *within* the context of a collective or communal process (the distinction between identification as a woman and gender consciousness—the former refers to a social designation, the latter to a critical awareness of the implications of this designation). This thinking 'out of' colonization happens only through action and reflection, through praxis. After all, social transformation cannot remain at the level of ideas, it must engage practice. It is the concrete analyses of collective and organizational practices within feminist communities that offer provisional strategies for dismantling the psychic and social constellations put in place by colonization. Some essays in *Genealogies* draw attention to the too-quick transition of Third-World countries from colonized nations, to anti-colonial struggles, to nationalist governing bodies which remain stubbornly patriarchal and heterosexist. In other words, these essays chart the failures of anti-colonial nationalism and decolonization movements to take seriously the psychic and pedagogical aspects of decolonization, especially in relation to sexual politics. Decolonization has a fundamentally pedagogical dimension—an imperative to understand, to reflect on, and to transform relations of objectification and dehumanization, and to pass this knowledge along to future generations. Our formulation of feminist democratic practice seeks to address the pedagogic failure of inherited nationalism.

Fourthly, our notion of feminist democracy draws on socialist principles to address hierarchies of rule and to craft an alternative vision for change. [. . .]

Finally, our definition of feminist democracy has specifically transnational dimensions. At this time, global processes clearly require global alliances. Decolonization, in fact, becomes an urgent project precisely because of the homogenization and cross-border domination effected by global capitalist processes. We suggest that feminist democracy needs to include some theorization of transborder participatory democracy which is outside the purview of the imperial. It is transnational feminism, not global sisterhood (defined as a 'center/periphery' or 'first-world/Third-World' model), that is our vision. And since questions of practice are central to this vision, another aspect of our version of feminist democracy involves reimaging the (often artificial) divide between feminist activism and scholarship. [. . .]

In what follows, we begin with a brief critique of freemarket/capitalist and procedural notions of democracy, move on to a discussion of some useful feminist theorizations of democracy, and finally arrive at our elaboration of the meaning of feminist democracy, based on the above sketch. In this analysis, we use 'Democracy' with a capital *d* (to suggest its congealed, commonsensical usage) when referring to institutionalized, hegemonic (often repressive), freemarket-based uses of the term, and 'democracy' (with a small *d*, suggesting collective structures and practices in process) to refer to the feminist rethinking of the idea and promise of this concept. While, on the one hand, a hegemonic rhetoric of Democracy (a disguise for Western, liberal capitalist processes) has been constitutive of the very processes of capitalist recolonization—many unjust imperialist practices have, after all, been sanctioned in the name of preserving Democracy—a different conception of democracy that guarantees liberation as a permanent condition for all peoples has also provided the material and ideological ground for feminist mobilization.

The term 'Democracy' has often been utilized in the service of repressive national and international state practices. However, the analytic and political importance of thinking about the egalitarian and emancipatory aspects of democracy at this time in history cannot be underestimated—after all, democracy does have to be made and remade by each generation.[20] If democracy is to be government by the people, or self-government requiring the people's participation, on the basis of merit not inherited status, then the question of how 'the people' is defined becomes fundamental. Thus, one of our major tasks is foregrounding the racialized, gendered, and heterosexualized relations of rule typified under hegemonic Democracy, and analyzing the myth of the 'universal citizen'. Another task is formulating a working definition of feminist democracy which is anti-capitalist and centered on the project of decolonization. In other words, our goal is to elaborate the ways a feminist democracy must interpret the hierarchies of governance, their interconnectedness and effects, while moving from an individual to a collective feminist practice.

We have argued that sexual politics are constitutive of all social relations and that colonizing processes are formulated and practiced through the disciplining of Third-World women's bodies. [. . .]

Conceptualizing 'the people' and citizenship within the framework of a specifically anti-colonialist, feminist understanding of democracy, in this instance, requires theorizing from the epistemological location and experiences of Third-World women. [. . .]

Hegemonic Democracy, Citizenship, and Capitalist Patriarchies

Our location in the United States, and the dominant position it occupies as *the* Democratic nation par excellence necessitate a clarification of the use of the rhetoric of Democracy by the US state. This section grapples with the hierarchies of rule that we have identified as a crucial aspect of the process of dismantling, decolonizing, and transforming capitalism in order to clear the ground for an anti-capitalist, anti-colonialist feminist democracy. Earlier discussions of colonialism, capitalism, and state practices suggest that colonial, imperial, sexist, and racist practices of rule by the US state are obfuscated by the rhetoric and ideology of Democracy. The ideology of freedom and Democracy works in such a way that the discourse of human rights is often invoked only when US economic and political interests are at stake. Thus, the US state appears to be Democratic while sanctioning imperialist invasions (e.g., Panama, Grenada, Nicaragua, etc.) in the name of preserving Democracy elsewhere in the world. This imperial aspect of the state is often ignored by US feminists involved in struggles for political change. Liberal feminist demands for equal rights, welfare, and social services, and equal pay for women, while crucial arenas for struggles against the state, address the state as if it were self-evidently Democratic.[21] This theorization of the American state as Democratic by US liberal feminists addressing sexism often obscures relationships of colonial domination and, thus, potentially precludes the formation of alliances between Third World women within colonizing nations or between women in colonizing and colonized/neo-colonial nations.

How do we understand the idea of universal citizenship (for us, citizenship which is defined through and across difference), and the way the state mobilizes a citizenship machinery which excludes and marginalizes particular constituencies on the basis of their 'difference'? Iris Marion Young argues that 'the ideal of universal citizenship carries at least two meanings in addition to the extension of citizenship to everyone: 1) universality defined as general in opposition to particular; what citizens have in common as opposed to how they differ; and 2) universality in the sense of laws and rules that say the same for all and apply to all the same way; laws and rules that are blind to individual and group differences.'[22] However, in the case of capitalist patriarchies which are also so-called Democracies, the construct of the universal citizen has very particular gender-, race-, class-, and sexually specific contours. Because, during moments of crises under capitalism, citizenship is defined through the figures of the (white) consumer and the taxpayer, and because this racialized, masculinized figure is the basis of a series of exclusions in relation to citizenship (exclusions of the very constituencies from whose locations we theorize), understanding the deployment of these categories is crucial to rethinking democracy. It is this deployment of exclusionary citizenship that leads us to argue for an explicitly anti-colonialist feminist democracy. [. . .]

From this position, a crucial question for feminists is whether the failure to fully address welfare rights on the US feminist agenda indicates a valorization of wage-labor in ways that prompt a convergence between state racism and racism within the feminist movement. The state machinery which positions women of color as dependants, and, therefore, morally inferior is a script that feminists in organized movements have yet to challenge. This, then, is one of the most significant ethical, intellectual, and political problems for liberal and socialist feminist movements. It is precisely in theorizing questions of privilege, dependency, and domination from the standpoint of, for instance, women of color as 'welfare recipients' or immigrant women as 'undocumented workers', that feminist struggles take on explicitly anti-colonial and anti-capitalist questions.

A number of critics have analyzed the convergence of capitalist values and liberal Democratic understandings of Democracy. Instead of rehearsing these arguments in detail, we draw on Paulo Freire's early work in *Pedagogy of the Oppressed* to sketch the ways in which the 'myths' utilized by the ruling class to preserve the capitalist status quo are simultaneously propositions about 'Democracy' within a liberal, capitalist culture. Together, these myths constitute a rhetoric of freedom and equality that consolidates the very oppressive practices and values of capitalist domination. Under these conditions freedom and equality function as guaranteed rights under capitalism, foregrounding questions of economic access and choice, of individual freedom, of economic and social mobility, of equality defined as access, opportunity, and choice, and of private property and ownership as constitutive of self-worth. And these myths beg the question of who is the presumed citizen entitled to these rights. They define freedom as access and the choice to work (rather than the material and psychic conditions that make such access and choices possible on an equitable basis), and equality as the same opportunities and rights under the law, without regard to the fact that the implied legitimate citizen is the white, ruling-class, heterosexual, male consumer and taxpayer. The myth of 'private property as fundamental to human development', wherein ownership of land is conflated with the personal value, prestige, and evolution of the owner—in contrast to communal ownership of land or world views which suggest that human beings don't own land but live in relation to it—all suggest a systematic world view whereby capitalist values infuse ideas about citizenship and liberal Democracy. In fact, it is almost as if democracy has been colonized under capitalism, thus making it impossible to raise the question of democracy in relation to socialist practice. Thus, the project of specifying feminist democracy at this point in history involves uncoupling the collapse of capitalism into Democracy and recasting the ethical and substantive understandings of democratic processes in anti-capitalist terms. [. . .]

The challenge for feminists, then, is to critique and move away from a formulation that usually leads to the erasure of the centrality of the experiences of colonization in the lives of Third World women and US women of color. This erasure also allows first world feminists to polarize 'survival' versus 'feminist' issues in Third and first world terms, thus colonizing the experiences of Third World women and making alliances on materialist terms impossible. [. . .]

Imagining Feminist Democracy: Anatomies of Selves, Communities, Organizing

The preceding discussion foregrounds the hierarchies of governance and rule that produce the liberal individual self under capitalist Democracy. The analysis of the limits of a procedural, free-market understanding of Democracy draws attention to the precise hierarchies against which feminist collectivities and organizations position themselves in crafting practices of decolonization and envisioning transformative feminist democracy. [. . .]

While we find the work of Elshtain, Pateman, Young, Mouffe, Fraser, Eisenstein and Williams useful in defining the limits of citizenship and democratic rights for women under capitalism, we want to refocus these concerns to democratic possibilities in the formulation of citizenship drawing on socialist principles. In what follows, we explore what it might mean to (a) address decolonization in relation to democracy, and (b) envision critical consciousness and agency outside free-market, procedural conceptions of individual agency. Thus, the question we ask is, how do women conceive of themselves and their communities in the context of this retheorization? The way to think ourselves out of the limitations of the Western liberal formulations of Democracy analyzed earlier is to imagine political mobilization as the practice of active decolonization. Transformation of consciousness and reconceptualizations of identity are, therefore, necessary aspects of democracy conceptualized as the practice of decolonization.

The centrality of collective practice in transformations of the self and re-envisioning organizational democracy anchors feminist thinking. In fact, feminist thinking, here, draws on and endorses socialist principles of collectivized relations of production and organization. It attempts to reenvision socialism as a part of feminist democracy with decolonization at its center. However, while feminist collectives struggle against hegemonic power structures at various levels, they are also marked by these very structures—it is these traces of the hegemonic which the practice of decolonization addresses. [. . .]

The conditions under which feminist movements emerge, the crafting of organizational practices and political agendas, the women who get drawn into the movements, and the visions of new modes of organizational practice are all fundamental issues in thinking about feminist democracy. This thinking includes the question of what it means to imagine oneself as an agent outside repressive state structures. As mentioned earlier, within the essays, feminists imagine themselves as agents (not victims or dependants) in relation to citizenship. This begs the question of what it would mean for Third World and poor women to envision and demand democratic space where their histories, agency, autonomy, and self-determination would be at the center.

Within the capitalist patriarchal understanding of Democracy, the acquisition of material property and the fulfilling of consumer needs become the marks of self-worth. Thinking differently about feminist democracy, thus, involves decolonization in these very specific anti-capitalist terms. In order for solidarity between Third World women in the geographical Third World and women of color in the first world to take place, imperialist domination and capitalist attitudes towards acquisition and advancement must become part of a feminist project of liberation. Feminist democratic practice in this context, then, cannot be about self-advancement, upward mobility, or maintenance of the first world status quo. It has to be premised on the decolonization of the self and on notions of citizenship defined not just within the boundaries of the nation-state but across national and regional borders. We would dare to suggest that in the context of feminist democracy defined in the ways we suggest above, capitalist feminism is a contradiction in terms. Conceptually, feminist democracy which is global in scope needs to be based on anticolonialist, socialist principles.

While the notion of transborder participatory democracy (one in which it is not the state but people themselves who emerge as the chief agents in defining the course of the global economic and political processes that structure their lives) has been low on the agenda of women's movements for democracy, perhaps this is an idea whose time has come.[23] Anti-colonialist feminist democracy involves thinking transnationally, and, in a world increasingly refigured by global economic and political processes, transnational democracy is as necessary as national democracy. [. . .] While it is difficult at this time to conceive of democratic practices of representation, responsibility, and accountability in relation to these institutions (media, tourism, SAP, organization of labor), the need to democratize cannot be ignored. Then, the World Bank, the IMF, and the GATT, organizations that make decisions that affect everyone's lives, can be made more accountable. In fact, decision-making processes in these institutions must be opened up for feminist participation and scrutiny. [. . .] Thus, the issues of feminist democracy—decolonization as central to self- and collective transformation; the fundamentally pedagogic character of feminist praxis; the profoundly anticapitalist, socialist imperative in imagining and enacting global feminist struggles—constitute the fabric of our action, reflection, and vision of the future.

Over the years of working against the grain in hegemonic, colonizing institutions, and in feminist and other grassroots communities, we have come to learn that the emotional terror produced by attempts to divest oneself of power and privilege and in the struggle for self-determination needs to be scrutinized very seriously. The challenge lies in an ethical commitment to work to transform terror into engagement based on empathy and a vision of justice for everyone. After all, this is at the heart of building solidarity across otherwise debilitating social, economic, and psychic boundaries. The most profound effects of our organizing and envisioning liberation as a permanent condition for all peoples may not be experienced for at least seven generations. As Frantz Fanon has argued, each generation has a responsibility to produce and transform the terms of struggle and liberation so that succeeding generations can assume the ongoing task in different but more advanced ways.[24]

Notes

1. David Evans, *Sexual Citizenship: The Material Construction of Sexualities* (New York and London: Routledge, 1993).
2. Stuart Hall, 'Cultural Studies and Its Theoretical Legacies', in Lawrence Grossberg *et al.* (ed.), *Cultural Studies* (New York and London: Routledge, 1992), 277–94.
3. Examples of this historically based analysis which offer an implicit and explicit critique of liberal feminism are Maria Mies, *Lace Makers of Narsapur: Indian Housewives Produce for the World Market* (London: Zed Press, 1983) and *Patriarchy and Accumulation on a World Scale* (London: Zed Press, 1986); and Vron Ware, *Beyond the Pale: White Women, Racism and History* (London: Verso, 1992).
4. Michael Warner, *Fear of a Queer Planet: Queer Politics and Social Theory* (Minneapolis and London: University of Minnesota Press, 1993); and Cathy Cohen, 'Punks, Bulldaggers and Welfare Queens: The Real Radical Potential of Queer Politics', paper presented at a conference entitled 'Identity, Space and Power', at the City University of New York, March 1995.
5. W. E. B. Du Bois, *The Souls of Black Folk* (New York: New American Library, 1969).
6. Inderpal Grewal and Caren Kaplan, *Scattered Hegemonies: Postmodernity and Transnational Feminist Practice* (Minneapolis: University of Minnesota Press, 1994); bell hooks, *Outlaw Culture: Resisting Representations* (New York: Routledge, 1994) and *Teaching to Transgress* (New York: Routledge, 1994); Barbara Christian, 'The Race for Theory,' in Abdul JanMohamed and David Lloyd (eds.), *The Nature and Context of Minority Discourse*, (New York: Oxford University Press, 1990), 37–49; and Wahneema Lubiano, 'Shuckin' Off the African American Native Other: What's "Po-Mo" Afro-America', *Cultural Critique* 18 (Spring 1991), 149–86.
7. Leslie Roman, 'White Is a Color! White Defensiveness, Postmodernism, and Anti-Racist Pedagogy', in Cameron McCarthy and Warren Crichlow (eds.), *Race, Identity and Representation in Education*, (New York: Routledge, 1993), 71–88.
8. R. Radhakrishnan, 'Feminist Historiography', in E. Meese and A. Parker

(eds.) *The Difference Within: Feminism and Critical Theory* (Amsterdam: J. Benjamins Publishing Co., 1989), 189–203.

9. Robin Morgan, *Sisterhood is Powerful: An Anthology of Writings from the International Women's Liberation Movement* (New York): Random House, 1970) and *Sisterhood is Global: The International Women's Movement Anthology* (Garden City, NY: Anchor Press/Doubleday, 1984); and Charlotte Bunch, *Passionate Politics: Feminist Theory in Action, Essays 1968–1986* (New York: St Martin's Press, 1987).
10. Patricia Williams, *The Alchemy of Race and Rights: Diary of a Law Professor* (Cambridge: Harvard University Press, 1991), 54.
11. Evans, *Sexual Citizenship*; Ruthann Robson, *Lesbian (Out)law: Survival under the Rule of Law* (Ithaca: Firebrand, 1992), 247–58; and Kendall Thomas, 'Bowers vs. Hardwick: Beyond the Privacy Principle', in Dan Danielsen and Karen Engle (eds.) *After Identity: a Reader in Law and Culture*, (New York: Routledge, 1995), 277–93.
12. Hamza Alavi, 'The State in Post Colonial Society: Pakistan and Bangladesh', *New Left Review*, No. 74 (1972), 59–81. A more contemporary elaboration of this point is made in Henrik Secher Marcussen and Jens Erik Torp, *The Internationalization of Capital: The Prospects for the Third World* (London: Zed Press, 1982).
13. Gita Sahgal and Nira Yuval-Davis, *Refusing Holy Orders: Women and Fundamentalism in Britain* (London: Virago Press, 1992).
14. Amrita Chhachhi, 'Forced Identities: The State, Communalism, Fundamentalism and Women in India', in Deniz Kandiyoti (ed.), *Women, Islam and the State* (Philadelphia: Temple University Press, 1991), 144–75. See also essays in Valentine M. Moghadam, (ed.), *Identity Politics and Women: Cultural Reassertions and Feminisms in International Perspective* (Boulder CO: Westview Press, 1994). Amrita Chhachhi and Renée Pittin, *Multiple Identities, Multiple Strategies: Confronting State, Capital and Patriarchy* (The Hague: Institute of Social Studies, 1991).
15. Thanh-dam Truong, 'Foreign Exchange: Prostitution and Tourism in Thailand', in *Sex, Money and Morality* (London: Zed Press, 1990); and Kamala Kempadoo, 'Regulating Sexuality: Prostitution in Curaçao', paper delivered at the Caribbean Studies Association Conference, Curaçao, May 1995.
16. Mary G. Dietz, 'Context Is All: Feminism and Theories of Citizenship', in Chantal Mouffe (ed.), *Dimensions of Radical Democracy: Pluralism, Citizenship, Community* (New York/London: Verso, 1992). 1–24.
17. Sistren with Honor Ford-Smith, *Lionheart Gal: Life Stories of Jamaican Women* (Toronto: Sister Vision Press, 1989).
18. Zillah Eisenstein, *The Color of Gender: Reimaging Democracy* (Berkeley: University of California Press, 1993), 171.
19. Frantz Fanon's *Black Skin White Masks* (New York: Grove Press, 1967) and *The Wretched of the Earth* (Harmondsworth: Penguin, 1967); Albert Memmi's *The Colonizer and the Colonized* (Boston: Beacon Press, 1969); and Paulo Freire's *Pedagogy of the Oppressed* (New York: Continuum, 1993) are most instructive here.
20. Cornel West, *Keeping Faith: Philosophy and Race in America* (New York: Routledge, 1993), 107–18; 236–47; *The American Evasion of Philosophy: A Genealogy of Pragmatism* (Madison: University of Wisconsin Press, 1989).

21. Ann Ferguson, *Sexual Democracy: Women, Oppression and Revolution* (Boulder: Westview Press, 1991); Nancy Fraser, *Unruly Practices: Power, Discourse and Gender in Contemporary Social Theory* (Minneapolis: University of Minnesota Press, 1989); and Williams, *The Alchemy of Race and Rights.*
22. Iris Marion Young, 'Polity and Group Difference: A Critique of the Ideal of Universal Citizenship', in Cass R. Sunstein (ed.), *Feminism and Political Theory* (Chicago: University of Chicago Press, 1990), 117. See also essays by Iris Young, *Throwing Like a Girl and Other Essays in Feminist Philosophy and Social Theory* (Bloomington: Indiana University Press, 1990).
23. Muto Ichiyo, 'For an Alliance of Hope', in J. Brecher, J. Brown, and J. Cutler (eds.), *Global Visions: Beyond the New World Order* (Boston: South End Press, 1993), 147–62.
24. Fanon, *The Wretched of the Earth, passim.*

33 Exploding the Canon

Jane L. Parpart and Marianne H. Marchand *

In the last few decades postmodernist critiques have increasingly dominated scholarship in the humanities and social sciences. Grand theories of the past have been called into question; particularities and difference(s) have triumphed as universal claims to knowledge have come under fire. Feminist scholars have reacted to postmodernist thought in a number of ways. Some reject it outright, while others call for a synthesis of feminist and postmodernist approaches. This is particularly true of scholars concerned with the marginalization of Third World women and women of color in the North.[1] However, many scholars and activists concerned with development issues in the South, especially poverty and economic development, dismiss this approach as a 'First World' preoccupation, if not indulgence, with little practical application for Third World women's development problems. Again other scholars have challenged this view, arguing for the relevance of postmodern feminist thought to development issues. [. . .]

POSTMODERNISM

Postmodernism is not easily encapsulated in one phrase or idea as it is actually an amalgam of often purposely ambiguous and fluid ideas. It represents the convergence of three distinct cultural trends. These include an attack on the austerity and functionalism of modern art; the philosophical attack on structuralism, spear-headed in the 1970s by poststructuralist scholars such as Jacques Derrida, Michel Foucault and Gilles Deleuze; and the economic theories of postindustrial

* From Jane L. Parpart and Marianne H. Marchand, 'Exploding the Canon' from *Feminism/Postmodernism/Development* by Marianne H. Marchand and Jane L. Parpart (Routledge, 1995), 1–22, reprinted by permission of the publisher.

society developed by sociologists such as Daniel Bell and Alain Touraine.[2] [. . .]

These insights have spawned an interest in the construction of identity and the concept of difference(s). The search to discover the way social meanings are constructed has highlighted the importance of difference and the tendency for people to define those they see as different ('other') in opposition to their own perceived strengths. European and North American scholarship, benefiting from its hegemonic position in world discourse, has of course dominated the construction of such definitions. For example, Western Orientalists have for the most part defined and represented the Orient as inherently irrational and unreliable. This construction has projected the dark side of the West on to the Oriental 'other', thus reinforcing the superiority of the supposedly rational, scientific West.[3] This focus on the hegemonic nature of colonial/neo-colonial discourse has shifted of late. Scholars such as Sara Suleri call for a more interactive approach, one that recognizes the interplay between those who 'control' discourse and those who 'resist' the dominant discourse. Colonial and neo-colonial discourses thus do not merely reflect the construction of a Third World 'other', they also are influenced by post-colonial voices/ discourses as well.[4]

In sum, postmodernist thinkers reject universal, simplified definitions of social phenomena, which, they argue, essentialize reality and fail to reveal the complexity of life as a lived experience. Drawing on this critique, postmodernists have rejected the search for broad generalizations. They emphasize the need for local, specific and historically informed analysis, carefully grounded in both spatial and cultural contexts. Above all, they call for the recognition and celebration of difference(s), the importance of encouraging the recovery of previously silenced voices and an acceptance of the partial nature of all knowledge claims and thus the limits of knowing.

POSTMODERNISM/FEMINISM

Feminists have responded to postmodern ideas in a number of ways. The strongest opposition has come from feminists working in the liberal (modern) or Marxist traditions, both of which are embedded in Enlightenment thinking. Liberal feminists, who have been preoccupied with policy formulation and the improvement of women's status within the structures of Western thought and society, generally write as if postmodern critiques have little or no applicability for their own work. This is particularly true of the many reports churned out on the status of women by established institutions, especially universities, government bureaucracies and international agencies such as the United Nations (UN), the World Bank (IBRD) and the International Labor Organization (ILO) reports on the status of women.[5] The possibility that 'modernization' and 'progress' may be unobtainable and undesirable goals in a postmodern world has rarely been considered by liberals working within these structures.[6]

Marxist feminists have also expressed considerable opposition to postmodern ideas. Sylvia Walby argues that 'postmodernism in social theory has led to the fragmentation of the concepts of sex, race and class and to the denial of the pertinence of overarching theories of patriarchy, racism and capitalism'. The postmodern critique of grand theory 'is a denial of significant structuring of power, and leads to mere empiricism'.[7] [. . .]

Some feminists believe feminist theory has always dealt with postmodern issues and indeed, has more to offer women than male-centric postmodern writers. Feminist anthropologists, Frances Mascia-Lees, Patricia Sharpe and Colleen Cohen,[8] attack postmodern anthropology for its profoundly sexist nature, noting that studies such as George Marcus and Michael Fischer's *Anthropology as Cultural Critique*, ignore feminist contributions to the discussion of the 'other' and long-standing feminist critiques of Western notions of 'truth'. These scholars see postmodernist anthropology as an attempt to stave off the loss of Western male power 'by questioning the basis of the truths that they are losing the privilege to define'.[9] They believe feminism, with its openly political stance and its grounding in actual differences between women, has more to offer anthropology and the search for sexual justice than postmodernist theory.[10]

Similar arguments have been launched by the standpoint feminists, such as Sandra Harding, Somer Brodribb and Dorothy Smith,[11] who focus on women's lived experiences as the basis of feminist knowledge. This 'feminine' knowledge, according to Smith, 'disrupts and disorganizes the discourse of modernity',[12] and thus contributes to the postmodern assault on modernity. However, standpoint feminists reject postmodernist attacks on the subject, as their critique of male hegemony is based on the authority of a female subjectivity grounded in women's daily lives. These scholars see no need, and indeed considerable danger, in adopting male-centric postmodernist thinking, particularly the attack on the subject. [. . .]

Feminists of various persuasions have expressed concern about the political implications of a postmodernist feminist perspective. Linda Hutcheon, for example, believes postmodernism threatens feminism's transformative agenda. She is particularly wary of postmodernist scepticism towards the subject. 'Postmodernism', she argues, 'has not theorized agency; it has no strategies of resistance that would correspond to the feminist ones'[13]. [. . .]

However, while agreeing that postmodernism, taken to its extreme and as practiced by its mostly white middle-class male proponents, appears to undermine feminists' search for a more egalitarian world, a growing number of feminists believe postmodernist thinking has much to offer feminist theorizing and action. Some see little conflict between postmodern thought and feminist politics.[14] Others are more sceptical about postmodernist ideas and call for 'an encounter, a strategic engagement between feminism and poststructuralism [postmodernism], that transforms both sides in significant ways'.[15]

One of the most appealing aspects of postmodernism to many feminists has been its focus on difference. The notion that women have been created and defined as 'other' by men has long been argued and explored by feminists in the North, most notably Simone de Beauvoir in her book *The Second Sex.*[16] She challenged male definitions of 'woman' and called on women to define themselves outside the male/female dyad. Women, she urged, must be the subject rather than the object (other) of analysis. [. . .]

However, the concern with women as 'other' emanated largely from the writings of middle-class white women from Europe and North America, whose generalizations were grounded for the most part in their own experiences. Feminist theory produced by these scholars generally 'explained' women as if their reality applied to women from all classes, races, cultures and regions of the world. Feminist concern with female 'otherness' ignored the possibility of differences among women themselves.[17]

Not surprisingly, the postmodern focus on difference coincided with a growing critique of this position and thus provided further ammunition to women who felt excluded by the writings and preoccupations of these scholars and activists. Black and Native women in North America became increasingly vocal about their unique problems, arguing that race, culture and class must be incorporated into feminist analysis. While minority feminists have been calling for some time for racially and ethnically specific feminisms,[18] postmodernism has provided a space which legitimizes the search for 'the voices of displaced, marginalized, exploited and oppressed black people'.[19] [. . .]

A number of feminists in the South have taken up this position as well. They have accused Northern scholars of creating a colonial/neo-colonial discourse which represents women in the South as an undifferentiated 'other', oppressed by both gender and Third World underdevelopment. [. . .]

The tendency to essentialize and distort the lives of Third World women does not just occur in the writings of women in the North. It is also pronounced in some of the work of Third World scholars trained in Northern institutions, particularly when writing for a Northern audience. As Rey Chow points out, Orientalists are not only white, they can also be non-Western students from privileged backgrounds 'who conform behaviorally in every respect with the elitism of their social origins . . . but who nonetheless proclaim dedication to "vindicating the subalterns"'.[20] [. . .]

These critiques have inspired considerable soul-searching among feminists in the North, and have encouraged an openness to difference and a reluctance to essentialize 'woman' that bodes well for global feminist understanding. The writings emerging in this vein draw heavily on postmodernist thinking, particularly the focus on language and the question of subjugated knowledge(s).[21] They reveal a sensitivity to historical, spatial and cultural specificity,[22] a recognition of the multiple oppressions of race, class and gender,[23] a focus on the body as a locus of social control [24] and a commitment to uncovering previously ignored voices and resistances.[25] The emphasis on the role of place and location in the construction of identities and difference(s), particularly the emphasis on marginality as a site of resistance, has aroused a new interest in the way spatial contexts influence women's lives.[26]

While few feminists argue for the wholesale adoption of postmodernist thought, and most continue to worry about its political implications, feminists of various persuasions are increasingly convinced that at least some aspects of postmodernist thinking are relevant to feminist theor(ies) and praxis. These syntheses have taken a number of forms. [. . .]

Much current feminist writing is concerned with the debate between philosophy and politics.[27] In *Materialist Feminism and the Politics of Discourse*, Rosemary Hennessy calls for a feminism that recognizes the importance of difference(s) and local complexities without abandoning attention to larger political and economic structures.

She believes feminists should adopt 'a way of thinking about the relationship between language and subjectivity that can explain their connection to other aspects of material life'.[28] Rey Chow advocates the 'careful rejection of postmodernist abandon' while remaining committed to the need for the carefully situated, historical analysis of difference.[29] Mary Poovey urges feminists to rethink 'deconstruction' in order to make it useful for feminist agendas.[30]

The issue of subjectivity, and the limitations that postmodern critiques of the subject pose for the female voice/subject, are of particular concern to many feminists otherwise sympathetic to postmodernist thinking. Loath to lose the authority of the female voice, yet wary of the unproblematized subject, some feminists are calling for a female subjectivity characterized by partial identities and mobile subjectivities.[31] They argue for a 'reconceptualization of the subject as shifting and multiply organized across variable axes of difference'.[32] These multiple, mobile subjectivities are embedded in the historical, spatial and institutional contexts of daily life and must be understood in that context.[33] This approach integrates the standpoint feminists' 'effort to interpret the subject women, and the postmodernist effort to examine how specific subjects came to be (or not) and what they have to say. . . . It looks for new forms and mobilities of subjectivity that can replace single-subject categories, inherited homes, without denying, nonrecognizing, the currently existing subject.'[34]

For these scholars, and many others, the encounter between feminism and postmodernism is clearly ongoing, indeterminate and fluid. It is contested terrain, which will no doubt continue to foster debate and dialogue. For many feminists, it provides an arena where differences and ambiguities can be celebrated without sacrificing the search for a 'broader, richer, more complex, and multilayered feminist solidarity, the sort of solidarity which is essential for overcoming the oppression of women in its "endless variety and monotonous similarity"'.[35]

RETHINKING DEVELOPMENT AND GENDER

Does this debate have anything to offer theorists and practitioners concerned with development, particularly women's development? We think it does. The critique of modernity and Western hegemony, the focus on difference and identity, the emphasis on the relationship between language and power, the attention to subjugated knowledge(s) and the deconstruction of colonial and post-colonial representations of the South as the dependent 'other' have much to say to those involved in the development business.

After all, the development enterprise, whether drawing on liberal or Marxist perspectives, has been largely rooted in Enlightenment thought. The liberal approach to development grew out of the postwar period in the 1940s, when economists and policy-makers believed development could be achieved by the simple adoption of Western political and economic systems. The Marxists, while critical of international capital and the class structure, never questioned the equation between modernization and development. Both saw development as a fairly straightforward, linear process, in which a nation or people moved from underdevelopment, which was equated with traditional institutions and values, to full development, i.e. modern/rational/industrialized societies based on the Northern model.[36] The rationale for this progression was provided by colonial (and later neo-colonial) discourses which compared 'backward, primitive' Third World peoples and cultures unfavourably with the 'progressive' North.[37] More recently, economic crises in the South and the demise of socialism have reinforced a predominantly American version of development, which draws on neoclassical economics, modernization theory and evolutionism to provide 'failsafe' prescriptions for Third World development (often known as structural adjustment programs (SAPs)).[38] However, development has continued to be seen largely as a logistical problem. Its goal, to make the world modern, i.e. Western, has rarely been in dispute.

This approach has not gone unchallenged. In the 1960s, continuing poverty in the South inspired a critique of mainstream development. Latin American scholars argued that international capitalism, far from developing the world, was perpetuating and benefiting from Third World underdevelopment.[39] They called for separation from the centers of international capital (the metropole) and for self-reliant development in the South (periphery). This attempt to turn modernization on its head soon ran into trouble. Critics questioned the linear, inevitable characterization of metropole/periphery relations, and the lack of attention to class forces in the Third World.[40] While debates within this perspective still continue,[41] a number of scholars on the left have responded to the current impasse in development theory by adopting a post-Marxist approach to development.[42] Acknowledging the limitations of classical Marxist analysis, particularly its economistic, linear character, these scholars emphasize instead the fluid, contingent nature of capitalist development, the importance of human agency and the complexity of social transformation.[43]

While this is an important and still developing critique, it has done little to undermine the equation between development, modernity and the West. In contrast, scholars drawing on postmodernist perspectives have challenged the very essence of mainstream and radical development discourse.[44] Above all, they question the universal pretentions of modernity, and the Eurocentric certainty of both liberal and Marxist development studies. They point out that much of the discourse and practice of development has exaggerated Western knowledge claims, dismissed and silenced knowledge from the South and perpetuated dependence on Northern 'expertise'. They call for a new approach to development, one that acknowledges difference(s), searches out previously silenced voices/knowledges and recognizes the need to welcome multiple interpretations and 'solutions' to developmental problems. While some scholars argue for a synthesis of post-Marxist and postmodern approaches,[45] all celebrate postmodernism's 'emphasis on iconoclastic questioning rather than predetermination, on openness rather than pre-empting closure, on plurality rather than essentialism'.[46]

The impasse within development theory has been exacerbated/aggravated by recent changes in the world's geopolitical outlook. The crumbling of the Soviet empire was interpreted by Francis Fukuyama[47] as a victory of (Western) liberalism and, by extension, of modernization theory. Given the ongoing processes of global political and economic restructuring which are also seriously affecting the 'former West', the issue is more complicated than Fukuyama believed. Within the field of development studies a serious rethinking of the embeddedness of modernization theory in Cold War (ideological) structures is necessary.[48] In addition to shedding its Cold War legacy, the field of development studies also needs to address the changing global realities, including the restructuring of the international political economy as well as, quite paradoxically, the emergence of regionalism. New categories of possible recipient countries and groups are emerging, including some people in the North. Clearly, this renaming/relabeling requires students of development to critically analyze the current restructuring of development practices.[49]

Are similar issues and critiques relevant for the development of women? We think they are. Certainly development specialists initially saw Third World women as an impediment to development, if they considered them at all. They readily adopted colonial representations of Third World women 'as exotic specimens, as oppressed victims, as sex objects or as the most ignorant and backward members of "backward" societies'.[50] This vision of Third World women as tradition-bound beings, either unable or unwilling to enter the modern world, fits neatly into Western and neo-colonial gender stereotypes, and provided a rationale for ignoring women during the first two development decades (1950s–60s).

By the mid-1960s some economists began to realize that development was not taking place as easily as they had hoped, particularly in regard to women. In 1970 Ester Boserup's landmark study, *Women's Role in Economic Development*, reported that many development projects, rather than improving the lives of Third World women, had deprived them of economic opportunities and status. Inspired by Boserup's work, a new subfield of development, Women in Development (WID) gradually emerged.[51] Steeped in the liberal tradition, this approach sought greater equity between women and men, but Western gender stereotypes went largely unchallenged. Women's development was seen as a logistical problem, rather than something requiring a fundamental reassessment of gender relations and ideology.[52]

In the 1970s, emerging critiques of development and patriarchy influenced some development practitioners concerned with women's issues. The dependency theorists' call for self-reliant development[53] and the radical feminists' assertion that women could only develop outside patriarchal power structures,[54] served as a backdrop for a new approach to the development of women, one that built on and celebrated women's culture, emphasized women only projects, and warned against close co-operation with male-dominated institutions. This approach, sometimes known as Women and Development (WAD), has been influential in the policy and programming of many non-governmental organizations (NGOs).[55]

WID proponents responded to these critiques by modifying mainstream development policy for women as well. Concern with equality between women and men fell by the wayside as planners emphasized basic human needs, particularly for health, education and training. WID specialists argued that this approach would increase women's effectiveness and efficiency at work, thus assisting both economic development and women's lives.[56]

In the 1980s, some scholars and activists in both the North and South began calling for a new approach to women's development.

Drawing on concerns about the growing poverity of women (and men) in the South, as well as radical feminist concern with global patriarchy, a socialist feminist position gradually emerged in various parts of the world. Feminists in the South contributed to this debate as they sought their own answers to developmental problems. The series of international conferences celebrating the UN Decade for Women (1976–85) highlighted the unique problems facing women in the South and encouraged the development of organizations to foster research and writing by Third World scholars.[57] The scholarship emerging from these organizations[58] has strengthened the voice(s) of Southern scholars and activists, and is providing the basis for feminist theorizing and action grounded in Southern realities (more recently called the 'empowerment' approach to women's development.[59] It has also inspired links with feminists in the North concerned with global and gender inequities. A commitment to understanding class, race and gender inequality in a global context thus provided an intellectual meeting-point for like-minded feminists from around the world.[60]

The resulting dialogue, increasingly known as Gender and Development (GAD), focuses on gender rather than women, particularly the social construction of gender roles and relations. 'Gender is seen as the process by which individuals who are born into biological categories of male or female become the social categories of men and women through the acquisition of locally-defined attributes of masculinity and femininity'.[61] The possibility of transforming gender roles is thus established, for the gendered division of labor and power is revealed as a constructed rather than natural part of life. While GAD proponents rarely challenge the goal of modernization/Westernization, some scholars believe the GAD perspective provides the possible (discursive) space to do so.[62]

This approach has had considerable influence on academic development discourse, but its willingness to consider fundamental social transformation does not sit well with most mainstream donor agencies. Most development agencies shy away from the language of transformation, particularly in such a sensitive area. Although some government agencies (most notably the Scandinavians, Dutch and Canadians) and some NGOs have officially adopted a more gender-oriented, transformative approach to their development programs, at least at the level of training, this perspective is rarely integrated into development planning.[63] Development discourse, whether mainstream or radical, for the most part continues to characterize women (and children) in the South as vulnerable, helpless victims.[64] Renewed interest in efficiency and increased donor support for women entrepreneurs[65] has done little to shake this image or to undermine most development specialists' belief in the modernization project.

In recent years various scholars have started to look at the intersection between gender, development and the environment. In the view of some authors, women's relation to nature is different (and more 'natural') than that of men. Moreover, they emphasize that there are parallels/similarities between patriarchy (i.e. man's dominance over woman) and man's attempt to dominate nature. Therefore the best starting-point for formulating sustainable development strategies is (to analyze) the relationship between women and nature.[66] While sympathetic to a woman-centered focus to environmental issues, scholars such as Bina Agarwal[67] reject the essentialist character of this argument and call for a more nuanced, materialist approach. Others draw on feminist and postmodern critiques of science and modernity to challenge the growth model of development and its implications for women and the environment.[68]

POSTMODERN FEMINISM, GENDER AND DEVELOPMENT

While these various perspectives have contributed important theoretical and practical insights to developmental issues facing women in the South (and many women in the North), they have for the most part ignored some of the more intractable impediments to women's development. They rarely challenge Northern hegemony, nor have they been able to provide the tools to dismantle patriarchal gender ideologies in the South (and North). [. . .]

The issue of colonial/neo-colonial discourse has thus far been the most immediate 'link' between postmodern feminism and gender and development. The critique of colonial constructions of the 'Third World woman' has revealed the hierarchical, dualistic nature of Western thought, and its tendency to reify and reinforce the North/South divide for women as well as men. While some scholars have acknowledged the interactive nature of colonial discourse, the emphasis has been on the discourse of the powerful and the hegemonic character of colonial/neo-colonial representation. [. . .]

The need to deconstruct development discourse is all the more crucial at the current conjuncture, when global restructuring and environmental degradation are challenging the traditional realm being 'covered' by gender and development theory (and practice). More and more there is talk about the Third World within the First World. Increased differentiation in the South (as well as the new 'South' in Eastern Europe and the former Soviet Union) is casting doubt on the myth of the North/South divide. Gender and development theory and practice has not been able adequately to incorporate/address these changes. It is still directed at the South, which partially serves to perpetuate the North's domination of the South. This position is increasingly untenable as emerging powers in the South, especially in Asia, and growing dislocations in the North, undermine old certainties and raise developmental issues for women in the North as well as the South. Clearly, new thinking about women/gender and development is required.[69] [. . .]

Postmodern feminist thinking, with its scepticism towards Western hegemony, particularly the assumption of a hierarchical North/South divide, provides new ways of thinking about women's development. It welcomes diversity, acknowledges previously subjugated voices and knowledge(s) and encourages dialogue between development practitioners and their 'clients'. [. . .]

This approach also brings the role of the development analyst/expert into question. It reminds us of the close connection between control over discourse/knowledge and assertions of power. Indeed, the authority of many Northern development 'experts' and like-minded analysts in the South has been maintained and reinforced (until recently) by their virtual monopoly over the discourse on 'Third World women'. While acknowledging the individual contributions of many thoughtful and committed development practitioners, this critique raises important issues about development practitioners' claims to 'know' the answers to women's developmental problems in the South (or North). It suggests the need for a more inclusive, open approach to women's development, one that rejects the tendency to undervalue women's knowledge unless it comes from Northern institutions or carries the seal of approval (i.e. certificates) from Northern experts.

The recovery of women's knowledge/voices, especially those of the poor, is not a simple matter however. The post-colonial literature, with its focus on the discourse of the powerful, offers important insights into the forces silencing women, but it has less to say about the way women actively construct their own identities within the material and discursive constraints of their lives. The postcolonial analysis of resistance, hybridity and mimicry, with its attention to the multiple forms of resistance against Western hegemony,[70] along with postmodern feminists' attention to difference, language and power, have much to offer discussion on this issue. [. . .] Above all, they emphasize the need to situate women's voices/experiences in the specific, historical, spatial and social contexts within which women live and work. However, they are wary of an unproblematic 'Third World woman', and acknowledge the need to adopt an approach that recognizes the multiple axes/identities which shape women's lives, particularly race, class, age and culture. [. . .]

The celebration of differences and multiple identities has provided a welcome plurality and richness to feminist analysis, but in its extreme form, it raises questions about the ability of women to speak for each other, to mobilize political action and to call for the defense of women's rights. If women's identities are constructed and fluid, and the world is full of uncertainty and confusion, how can women in both the South and North mobilize to defend their interests? Indeed, how can women even understand each other? And how can we deal with the recurrent theme of social/political/economic marginalization of most women? Postmodern feminists have drawn our attention to the dualistic, patriarchal tendencies in Western society and in much of the discourse on women's development. These deeply embedded structures of language and meaning interfere with communication. Dialogue across differences is not simply a matter of good will. It requires a recognition of the power of language, a conscious effort to situate one's own knowledge and a willingness to open oneself to different world views.[71]

An approach to development that accepts and understands difference and the power of discourse, and that fosters open, consultative dialogue can empower women in the South to articulate their own needs and agendas. Instead of simply seeing women as a disempowered 'vulnerable' group in need of salvation by Western expertise, Gender and Development experts can rethink their approach to development. Attention to women's lived realities and understandings, and genuine partnership between North and South can lead to development policies that foster self-reliance and self-esteem, rather than ignoring women's knowledge and creating policies and projects that increase patriarchal control over women's bodies and labor.[72] [. . .]

However, there are dangers in this approach which must be addressed. Postmodern feminism, taken to its extreme, can stymie collective action among women, both within nations and on a world scale. The emphasis on difference and indeed on the often deep divisions between women in the South, minority women in the North and more privileged (often white) women in the North (and some in the South as well) offers both insights and dangers. While reminding us of the need to guard against glib assumptions about global feminist solidarity, this focus on difference can exacerbate differences among women and undermine possibilities for collective action by women, thus reinforcing the power of patriarchy and reducing the chance that women can challenge the gender hierarchies and ideologies that construct and maintain their subordination. Indeed, Maria Nzomo and Mridula Udayagiri question the ability of postmodern analysis to address these questions. As Maria Nzomo points out, the rejection of universals can undermine women's struggles for democratic rights and greater participation in development and the state. Others believe political decisions and action can be mobilized around an empathetic understanding of people's daily lives, based on the carefully situated, partial knowledge of people's daily lives rather than on empty slogans about 'universal' principles.[73] The impenetrable jargon of much postmodern writings is an issue as well. Daunting even for the educated, postmodern language is often an insurmountable obstacle for people mired in widespread illiteracy and economic crisis.

[. . .] We do not want premature closure of this important debate. Rather we want to think through and contest the issues at hand, in the hope that this debate will encourage the development of a more politicized and accessible version of postmodern feminist thought—one which can address the problems and prospects facing women in an increasingly complex and interrelated world.

Notes

1. Throughout this chapter, the term Third World is adopted as a shorthand for Africa, Latin America and Asia, with the understanding that these areas, while exhibiting certain similarities, have many differences as well. The term is not to be seen as an assumption that Third World peoples, especially women, can be lumped in one undifferentiated category. Similarly, the term First World is a shorthand for the more industrialized countries, but it too suggests a uniform condition which is increasingly false, particularly for minorities. We have adopted the terms South and North to indicate our belief that global economic rivalries and status are no longer defined on an East-West axis, but rather increasingly around the less industrialized economics in the South and the more industrialized economies in both the North and South (particularly the NICs in Southeast Asia). The West refers specifically to Europe and North America.

2. A. Callinicos, *Against Postmodernism* (Oxford: Polity Press, 1989).
3. E. Said, *Orientalism* (New York: Pantheon, 1979, also New York: Vintage Books), 9–10.
4. S. Suleri, *The Rhetoric of English India* (Chicago: University of Chicago Press, 1992), 4–7. This book will use the terms colonial and neo-colonial discourse to refer to the writings/discourse of Western/Northern authors on the South. The term postcolonial refers to the writings of authors in the South, some of whom are based in the North. This terminology is fluid and a continuing matter for debate (see Bhabha 1994; McClintock 1992; Shohat 1992). The postcolonial critiques of Western discourse on the South have been particularly well developed among Indian historians (Guha and Spivak 1988; Prakash 1990).
5. See also K. Gillespie, 'The Key to Unlocking Sustainable Development', (Washington, DC: World Bank, mimeo, 1989); S. Joekes, *Women in the World Economy* (Oxford: Oxford University Press, 1987).
6. World Bank, *Recognizing the 'Invisible' Woman in Development* (Washington, DC: World Bank, 1979; *Kenya World Bank Country Study Report* (Washington, DC: World Bank, 1989); and 'Paradigm Postponed: Gender and Economic Adjustment in Sub-Saharan Africa'. Technical Note, Human Resources and Poverty Division, Technical Department, Africa Region (Washington, DC: World Bank, 1993).
7. S. Walby, 'A Critique of Postmodernist Accounts of Gender', paper presented at Canadian Sociological Association Meetings, Vancouver, British Columbia, 1990, 2.
8. F. Mascia-Lees, P. Sharpe and C. B. Cohen, 'The Postmodernist Turn in Anthropology: Cautions from a Feminist Perspective', *Signs* 15 (1989), 394–408.
9. Ibid., 401–2.
10. See also D. M. Tress, 'Comments on Flax's "Postmodernism and Gender Relations in Feminist Theory"', *Signs* 14 (1988), 196–200.
11. S. Harding (ed.), *Feminism and Methodology* (Bloomington: Indiana University Press, 1987); and 'Subjectivity, Experience and Knowledge', *Development and Change* 23 (1992), 175–94; S. Brodribb, *Nothing Mat(t)ers: A Feminist Critique of Postmodernism* (Toronto: James Lorimer and Co., 1992); and D. Smith, *The Conceptual Practices of Power* (Toronto: University of Toronto Press, 1990).
12. Smith, *The Conceptual Practices of Power*, 203.
13. L. Hutcheon, *The Politics of Postmodernism* (London: Routledge, 1989), 168.
14. J. Butler and J. W. Scott (eds.), *Feminists Theorize the Political* (New York and London: Routledge, 1992); J. Flax, 'Feminists Theorize the Political', in Butler and Scott, *Feminists Theorize the Political*; S. J. Hekman, *Gender and Knowledge* (Boston: Northeastern University Press, 1990).
15. K. Canning, 'Feminist History after the Linguistic Turn: Historicizing Discourse and Experience', *Signs* 19 (1994), 373; R. Chow, 'Postmodern Automatons', in Butler and Scott, *Feminists Theorize the Political*; N. Fraser and L. Nicholson, 'Social Criticism Without Philosophy: An Encounter between Feminism and Postmodernism', in L. Nicholson (ed.), *Feminism/Postmodernism* (New York: Routledge, Chapman and Hall, 1990); M. Lloyd, 'Feminist "Hyphenisation": Decentring the "Prototypical Woman"', paper

presented to the Women in a Changing Europe Conference, University of Aalborg, Denmark, 1991.

16. S. de Beauvoir, 'The Point of View of Historical Materialism', in her *The Second Sex* (London: Penguin Books, 1949).
17. C. Gilligan, *In a Different Voice* (Cambridge: Harvard University Press, 1982); E. Spelman, *Inessential Woman* (London: Women's Press, 1990).
18. F. Anthias and N. Yuval-Davis, 'Contextualising Feminism—Gender, Ethnic and Class Divisions', in T. Lovell (ed.), *British Feminist Thought: A Reader* (Oxford: Basil Blackwell, 1990); G. Anzaldua (ed.), *Making Face, Making Soul/ Haciendo Caras: Creative and Critical Perspective by Women of Color* (San Francisco: Aunt Lute Press, 1990); P. H. Collins, 'The Social Construction of Black Feminist Thought', *Signs* 14 (1989), 745–73; A. Lorde, 'The Master's Tools Will Never Dismantle the Master's House', in C. Moraga and G. Anzaldua (eds.), *This Bridge Called My Back: Writings by Women of Color* (Watertown, MA: Persephone Press, 1981, republished New York: Kitchen Table Women of Color Press, 1983); and *Sister Outsider* (New York: Crossing Press, 1984); Moraga and Anzaldua (eds.), *This Bridge Called My Back.*
19. b. hooks, *Feminist Theory: From Margin to Center* (Boston: South End Press, 1984), 25; and *Black Looks: Race and Representation* (Boston: South End Press, 1992).
20. R. Chow, *Writing Diaspora* (Bloomington: Indiana University Press, 1993), 14.
21. H. Eisenstein and A. Jardine (eds.), *The Future of Difference* (New Brunswick, NJ: Rutgers University Press, 1988); D. Riley, *Am I That Name? Feminism and the Category of 'Women' in History* (Minneapolis: University of Minnesota Press, 1988); Spelman, *Inessential Woman.*
22. J. Momsen, *Women and Development in the Third World* (London: Routledge, 1991); C. Weedon, *Feminist Practice and Poststructuralist Theory* (Oxford: Basil Blackwell, 1987).
23. b. hooks, *Yearning: Race, Gender and Cultural Politics* (Boston: South End Press, 1990); S. M. James and A. P. A. Busia, *Theorizing Black Feminism* (London: Routledge, 1993).
24. A. Jaggar and S. Bordo (eds.), *Gender/Body/Knowledge* (New Brunswick, NJ: Rutgers University Press, 1989).
25. M. di Leonardo (ed.), *Gender at the Crossroads of Knowledge* (Berkeley: University of California Press, 1991); M. Hirsch and E. Fox Keller (eds.), *Conflicts in Feminism* (New York: Routledge, 1990).
26. J. Momsen and V. Kinnaird (eds.), *Different Places, Different Voices* (London: Routledge, 1993); G. Pratt and S. Hanson, 'Geography and the Construction of Difference', *Gender, Place and Culture* 1 (1994), 5–30.
27. Some of the many feminists seeking a strategic encounter between feminism and postmodernism are Kathleen Canning, Kathy Ferguson, Moya Lloyd, Chris Weedon, Donna Haraway and Christine Sylvester.
28. R. Hennessy, *Materialist Feminism and the Politics of Discourse* (New York: Routledge, 1993), 37.
29. Chow, 'Postmodern Automatons', 114.
30. M. Poovey, 'Feminism and Deconstruction', *Feminist Studies* 14 (1988), 51, 60, 63.
31. K. E. Ferguson, *The Man Question: Visions of Subjectivity in Feminist Theory* (Berkeley: University of California Press, 1993), 158; see also A. M. Goetz,

'Feminism and the Limits of the Claim to Know: Contradictions in the Feminist Approach to Women in Development', *Millennium* 17 (1988), 477–96. Reprinted in R. Grant and K. Newland (eds.), *Gender and International Relations* (Bloomington: Indiana University Press, 1991).
32. T. de Lauretis, 'Eccentric Subjects: Feminist Theory and Historical Consciousness', *Feminst Studies* 16 (1990), 116.
33. Canning, 'Feminist History after the Linguistic Turn', 368–404.
34. C. Sylvester, *Feminist Theory and International Relations in a Postmodern Era* (Cambridge: Cambridge University Press, 1994), 59.
35. Fraser and Nicholson, 'Social Criticism Without Philosophy, 35.
36. D. Johnston, 'Constructing the Periphery in Modern Global Politics', in G. Murphy and R. Tooze (eds.), *The New International Political Economy* (Boulder: Lynne Reinner, 1991).
37. P. Curtin, *The Image of Africa* (Madison: Wisconsin University Press, 1974); Said, *Orientalism*; and *Culture and Imperialism* (New York: Alfred A. Knopf, 1993).
38. J. N. Pieterse, 'Dilemmas of Development Discourse: the Crisis of Developmentalism and the Comparative Method', *Development and Change* 22 (1991), 5–29.
39. A. G. Frank, *Dependent Accumulation and Under-development* (London: Macmillan, 1978).
40. F. Cooper, 'Africa and the World Economy', *African Studies Review* 24 (2/3, 1981), 1–86.
41. R. Munck, 'Political Programmes and Development: The Transformative Potential of Social Democracy', in F. J. Schuurman (ed.), *Beyond the Impasse* (London: Zed Books, 1993).
42. Schuurman blames the impasse in development theory on: the continuing gap between rich and poor; the lack of long-term planning in the 1980s; the realization that economic growth has had a catastrophic impact on the environment; the delegitimation of socialism as a viable alternative; the recognition that globalization undercuts the relevance of the nation-state; the growing differentiation within the Third World; and the advancement of postmodernism within the social sciences (F. J. Schuurman, 'Introduction: Development Theory in the 1990s', in Schuurman, *Beyond the Impasse.*
43. D. Booth, 'Marxism and Development Sociology: Interpreting the Impasse', *World Development* 13 (1985), 761–87; S. Corbridge, 'Post-Marxism and Development Studies: Beyond the Impasse', *World Development* 8 (1989), 623–40; Schuurman (ed.), *Beyond the Impasse*, especially the introduction; D. Slater, 'Theories of Development and Politics of the Post-modern', *Development and Change* 23 (1992), 283–319.
44. M. DuBois, 'The Governance of the Third World: A Foucauldian Perspective on Power Relations in Development', *Alternatives* 16 (1991), 1–30; A. Escobar, 'Discourse and Power in Development: Michel Foucault and the Relevance of His Work to the Third World', *Alternatives* 10 (1984–5), 377–400; and 'Imagining a Post-Development Era? Critical Thought, Development and Social Movements', *Social Text* 31/32 (1992), 20–56; Ferguson, *The Man Question*; Johnston, 'Constructing the Periphery'; D. Moore, 'The Dynamics of Development Discourse: Sustainability, Equity, and Participation in Africa'. Commissioned by International Development and Research Centre, Ottawa,

Canada, 1992; Pieterse, 'Dilemmas of Development Discourse'; D. Slater, 'The Political Meanings of Development', in Schuurman, *Beyond the Impasse.*
45. Schuurman, *Beyond the Impasse*; Slater, 'Theories of Development'.
46. Slater, 'Theories of Development', 311.
47. F. Fukuyama, 'The End of History', *The National Interest* 16 (Summer 1989), 3–18.
48. For example, Samuel Huntington, a soviet specialist, has begun contributing to development studies (S. Huntington, *The Politics of Postmodernism* (London: Routledge, 1993).
49. See *A World in Conflict* by the Dutch minister of development co-operation, Jan Pronk (The Hague: Government of the Netherlands, 1993), which assigns new labels to countries and regions.
50. J. de Groot, 'Conceptions and Misconceptions: the Historical and Cultural Context of Discussion on Women and Development', in H. Ashfar (ed.), *Women, Development and Survival in the Third World* (London: Longman, 1991), 115.
51. Most development agencies did not have full-time WID professionals until the mid-1980s (A. Mueller, 'Peasants and Professionals: The Production of Knowledge about Women in the Third World', paper presented at the Association for Women in Development meeting, Washington, DC, 15–17 April 1987.
52. E. M. Rathgeber, 'WID, WAD, GAD: Trends in Research and Practice', *Journal of Developing Areas* 24 (1990), 489–502; I. Tinker, 'The Making of a Field: Advocates, Practitioners and Scholars', in I. Tinker (ed.), *Persistent Inequalities: Women and World Development* (Oxford: Oxford University Press, 1990).
53. S. Amin, *Accumulation on a World Scale: A Critique of the Theory of Underdevelopment* (New York: Monthly Review Press, 1974); and *Imperialism and Unequal Development* (New York: Monthly Review Press, 1977).
54. M. Daly, *Gyn/Ecology: the Metaethics of Radical Feminism* (Boston: Beacon Press, 1978).
55. J. L. Parpart, *Women and Development in Africa* (Lanham, MD: University Press of America, 1989); Rathgeber, 'WID, WAD, GAD'. Although often relegated to small-scale, women-only projects, the WAD approach also influenced development practitioners working on international projects (see International Women's Tribune Center (IWTC) Newletters).
56. D. Kandiyoti, 'Women and Rural Development Policies: The Changing Agenda', *Development and Change* 21 (1990), 5–22; C. O. N. Moser, *Gender Planning and Development* (London: Routledge, 1993).
57. Some examples are Development Alternatives with Women for a New Era (DAWN), which covers the entire Third World; the Association of African Women for Research and Development (AAWORD); the Women and Development Unit of the University of the West Indies (WAND); and the Asian Women's Research and Action Network (AWRAN).
58. AAWORD 1986; G. Sen and C. Grown, *Development, Crises, and Alternative Visions: Third World Women's Perspectives* (New York: Monthly Review Press, 1987).
59. Moser, *Gender Planning and Development.*
60. Sussex University in England and the Institute for Social Studies at The Hague

provided important meeting-points in Europe for like-minded scholars from around the world.

61. N. Kabeer, 'Rethinking Development from a Gender Perspective: Some Insights from the Decade', paper presented at the Conference on Women and Gender in Southern Africa, University of Natal, Durban, 1991, 11.
62. M. H. Marchand and J. L. Parpart (eds.), *Feminism/Postmodernism/Development* (London and New York: Routledge, 1995), ch. 11.
63. Moser, *Gender Planning and Development.* The GAD approach has offered development planners a way to differentiate between practical (i.e. specific, daily) gender needs and strategic (or more long-term, empowerment) needs for women. This approach seems to be making some inroads into development thinking and planning, but primarily at the level of training (interview, Sherry Greaves, CIDA, WID Unit, Ottawa, 28 February 1992; see also R. Chow, 'CIDA's Women in Development Program: Evaluation Assessment Report'. (Ottawa: Canadian International Development Agency, 1991).
64. Commonwealth Expert Group on Women and Structural Adjustment, *Engendering Adjustment for the 1990s.* Report (London: Commonwealth Secretariat, 1989); G. A. Cornia, R. Jolly and F. Stewart (eds.), *Adjustment with a Human Face. Vol. I, Protecting the Vulnerable and Promoting Growth* (Oxford: Oxford University Press, 1987).
65. Moser, *Gender Planning and Development*, 56–7.
66. M. Mies and V. Shiva, *Ecofeminism* (Halifax: Fernwood Publications and London: Zed Books, 1993).
67. B. Agarwal, *Engendering the Environment Debate: Lessons from the Indian Subcontinent*, CASID Distinguished Speakers Series, No. 8 (East Lansing, MI: Center for Advanced Study of International Development, Michigan State University, 1991).
68. R. Braidotti, E. Charkiewicz, S. Häusler and S. Wieringa (eds.), *Women, Environment and Sustainable Development: Towards a Theoretical Synthesis* (London: Zed Books in association with International Research and Training Institute for the Advancement of Women (INSTRAW), 1994).
69. A first tentative attempt to capure these changes is the refocusing of Women in Development Europe (WIDE), a European network of development practitioners and scholars. WIDE is now starting to emphasize the need for gender and ethnic analysis of the position of women in Europe in order to better understand the impact of global restructuring on women in the North and South, as well as relations between them (WIDE Conference, Amsterdam, 28–9 May 1994).
70. H. K. Bhabha, *The Location of Culture* (London and New York: Routledge, 1994); G. C. Spivak (S. Harasym, ed.), *The Post-Colonial Critic: Interviews, Strategies, Dialogue* (London: Routledge, 1990).
71. P. Connelly, T. Li, M. MacDonald and J. Parpart, 'Restructured worlds/Restructured Debates: Globalization, Development and Gender', *Canadian Journal of Development Studies* (1995).
72. Ferguson, *The Man Question*; Johnston, 'Constructing the Periphery'.
73. See Goetz, 'Feminism and the Limits of the Claim to Know'.

Index